THE LAW AND PRACTICE OF RESTRUCTURING IN THE UK AND US

THE LAW AND PRACTICE OF RESTRUCTURING IN THE UK AND US

Edited by

Christopher Mallon and Shai Y. Waisman

OXFORD
UNIVERSITY PRESS

OXFORD
UNIVERSITY PRESS

Great Clarendon Street, Oxford OX2 6DP

Oxford University Press is a department of the University of Oxford.
It furthers the University's objective of excellence in research, scholarship,
and education by publishing worldwide in

Oxford New York

Auckland Cape Town Dar es Salaam Hong Kong Karachi
Kuala Lumpur Madrid Melbourne Mexico City Nairobi
New Delhi Shanghai Taipei Toronto

With offices in

Argentina Austria Brazil Chile Czech Republic France Greece
Guatemala Hungary Italy Japan Poland Portugal Singapore
South Korea Switzerland Thailand Turkey Ukraine Vietnam

Oxford is a registered trade mark of Oxford University Press
in the UK and in certain other countries

Published in the United States
by Oxford University Press Inc., New York

First published 2011

British Library Cataloguing in Publication Data
Data available

Library of Congress Cataloging in Publication Data
Data available

Typeset by Glyph International, Bangalore, India
Printed in Great Britain
on acid-free paper by
CPI Antony Rowe, Chippenham, Wiltshire

ISBN 978–0–19–958377–5

1 3 5 7 9 10 8 6 4 2

PREFACE

The world debt markets are dominated by two systems of law—the laws of England and the laws of the United States, particularly New York. For the vast majority of the time they co-exist happily but every so often, particularly where a company is faced with severe stress or distress, they run hard up against each other.

Any company of any size operating across borders will almost certainly have debt governed by English law and New York law. Where this is the case a troubled company will require expert practitioners from both disciplines to work quickly and effectively together to find common solutions (or an effective compromise) to the issues facing the company. What had become patently clear to Shai and me, as we have worked on cases together over recent years, was that there is no single text available to a practitioner which could help him identify the many issues facing a troubled company in this situation.

This book is an attempt to fill that gap. As far as we are aware, this is the first attempt to grapple with these issues from both an English law and a US/New York law perspective in a single volume. Both Shai and I are immensely grateful for the efforts of all our contributors in what has been a challenging and revealing process. The subjects addressed in the book cover different stages in the spectrum from dealing with the first signs of stress through to full blown insolvency. They also address seperately the discrete problems that will almost always arise for companies in areas such as governance, tax, pensions, and employment. It has not proved possible, in all cases, to examine the law relating to a particular subject in a given jurisdiction separately and then go on simply to compare and contrast the law in the other jurisdiction. In some areas (for example, in relation to pre-packs), the regulatory framework and the law and practice are so different that the real value of the book springs from the realization that an expression used in the context of one legal system has a totally different meaning in another or that there is no obvious parallel for a particular process in the other jurisdiction. This has resulted in a very different approach being taken to the analysis of a particular subject in one part of the book from the approach taken in another. We make no apologies for this and believe that the book is immeasurably stronger for recognizing and adapting to the different demands of these sometimes very different topics.

There are many people whom we need to thank for their help and support which have enabled our idea to become a reality. The partners and staff of both Skadden, Arps, Slate, Meagher & Flom LLP and Weil, Gotshal & Manges LLP have been a constant source of inspiration and this book would not have been possible without their immense dedication and commitment. We are also very grateful to our editors at OUP, particularly Rachel Mullaly, Jessica Huntley, and Benjamin Roberts. As we say above, our contributors deserve our undying gratitude and thanks, not least for reading and re-reading their texts and for patiently enduring and accepting our many vexing questions and comments. To the extent that any errors and omissions remain, they are of course ours.

We dedicate this book to our respective families.

CM
SW

CONTENTS

LIST OF CONTRIBUTORS

Editors

Christopher Mallon co-leads the corporate restructuring practice in Europe. Mr Mallon works closely with the London Finance, Corporate M & A, and Private Equity teams, and the US Corporate Restructuring Department, and has a major role in growing the Firm's restructuring practice in Europe. His restructuring and insolvency credentials span cross-border reorganizations involving a number of jurisdictions including England, the USA, Ireland, India, Russia, the Cayman Islands, Bermuda, Poland, Germany, Holland, Italy, and Luxembourg. His clients have included Enron, Global Crossing, WorldCom, Loral, Telewest, Parmalat, Eurotunnel, Gate Gourmet, Carlyle, and Calyon.

Shai Y. Waisman is a partner in the Business Finance & Restructuring department of Weil, Gotshal & Manges LLP. His practice incorporates crisis management, financial restructuring, and acquiring troubled companies. Mr Waisman also has developed an expertise in complex cross-border restructurings and representing purchasers and sellers of assets of distressed enterprises. Mr Waisman has significant experience in a wide array of industries, including airline, apparel, biotechnology, leisure, energy, finance, medical device manufacturing, multimedia news, retail, supermarket, and telecommunications. He has been recognized as one of the world's leading restructuring lawyers by numerous organizations including Law 360, Institutional Investor News, Turnarounds & Workouts, Investment Dealers Digest and Crain's New York.

Contributors

Adam Al-Attar BA (Oxon), BCL; practices at 3–4 South Square, Gray's Inn. Mr Al-Attar specializes in insolvency and company law, banking and financial law, and the law of trusts.

Daniel Bayfield is a barrister (practising from 3–4 South Square, Gray's Inn) specializing in corporate insolvency and restructuring. Mr Bayfield advises insolvency office holders, banks, and other creditors in relation to formal insolvency procedures and companies and creditors in relation to schemes of arrangements and informal restructuring procedures.

Ryan Chen is an associate in the Los Angeles office of Skadden, Arps, Slate, Meagher & Flom LLP. Mr Chen's practice concentrates primarily on mergers and acquisitions, recapitalizations, securities offerings, and corporate restructurings. Mr Chen has also represented creditors, investors and asset-purchasers in complex chapter 11 cases.

Nikolas K. Colbridge specializes in international corporate finance, focusing on offerings of equity and debt and liability management. Mr Colbridge principally represents public companies (or companies seeking a listing) from the emerging markets. Mr Colbridge was educated at Université de Paris I, Pantheon-Sorbonne and King's College, University of London and is Counsel at the London office of Skadden, Arps, Slate, Meagher & Flom.

Peter J. Coulton is a partner in Skadden, Arps, Slate, Meagher & Flom LLP's London office. He advises on a wide range of banking and finance matters, with a particular focus on leveraged finance and debt restructurings. Mr Coulton's clients include senior and mezzanine lenders and private equity sponsors, hedge funds, and corporate borrowers.

Alper Deniz is a partner in Chadbourne & Parke's London office. He specializes in finance and restructuring and has extensive experience of international financing transactions, structured finance, debt capital markets, debt restructuring, and derivatives transactions, in each case representing a variety of lenders, arrangers, issuers, sponsors, and borrowers.

Casey T. Fleck is a partner in the Los Angeles office of Skadden, Arps, Slate, Meagher & Flom LLP. Mr Fleck represents public and private companies, investment banks and private equity funds in a broad range of corporate transactions, including public and private securities offerings, mergers and acquisitions, corporate restructurings, recapitalizations, tender offers, and consent solicitations.

Jay M. Goffman, Global Co-Head of Skadden's Corporate Restructuring Department, is a recognized worldwide leader in restructuring and is widely regarded as a pioneer in the use of prepackaged restructurings, including the landmark 'one-day prepack' for Blue Bird Bus Corporation. Mr Goffman is regularly selected as one of the leading restructuring lawyers in the country and the world by various legal organizations including *Turnarounds & Workouts*, *Chambers USA*, *Chambers Global*, and *The Best Lawyers in America*. Recently named by *The National Law Journal* as 'One of the Most Influential Lawyers of The Decade', Mr Goffman's innovative and cost-efficient approach to business reorganizations both in and out of court has been honoured numerous times as 'Deal of the Year'. Recent award-winning representations include Metro-Goldwyn-Mayer Studios

Inc. in connection with its prepackaged plan of reorganization; Paul Allen, as principal shareholder of Charter Communications, Inc., in connection with Charter Communications, Inc.'s prearranged chapter 11 bankruptcy case; Leonard Blavatnik and Access Industries as the 100 per cent shareholders of LyondellBasell in connection with LyondellBasell's chapter 11 case; Centro Properties Group and Intrawest in their successful out-of-court cross-border restructurings and ION Media in its successful out-of-court recapitalization. Each of these deals has received numerous 'Deal of the Year' awards and other honours.

Stuart J. Goldring is a partner in the New York office of Weil, Gotshal & Manges LLP, and a recognized expert in US income tax matters involving troubled companies, including extensive experience advising debtors, creditors and potential acquirers. He is a co-author of a tax treatise on troubled corporations (published by CCH) and an Adjunct Professor at NYU Law School.

Max A. Goodman is a senior tax associate in Weil, Gotshal & Manges LLP's New York office, with significant restructuring experience. He is an active member of the New York State Bar Association's Tax Section, contributing to a number of its bar reports on troubled company issues, and received his JD *cum laude* from Harvard Law School.

Paula S. Greenman is a structured finance partner in the New York office of Skadden, Arps, Slate, Meagher & Flom LLP. She represents issuers, underwriters, and asset managers in a wide variety of structured finance transactions, specializing in structures involving credit derivatives.

Adrian Harris is a partner in the London office of Chadbourne & Parke LLP where he heads the firm's European insolvency and restructuring practice. He acts for a broad range of clients from buy-side funds and investment banks to international firms of accountants in all areas of corporate distress. He specializes in engagements with cross-border elements.

Philip Hertz has been a Partner in Clifford Chance LLP's London Office since 2002. His practice involves general insolvency and restructuring work, specializing in complex multi-jurisdictional restructurings and insolvencies. Mr Hertz is a member of the Insolvency Lawyers' Association Council as well as serving on its technical committee.

Nick Huffer is an Associate at Clarkslegal LLP and has over 10 years' experience in employment law, joining Clarkslegal in 2000. He has particular interest in collective dispute resolution, having advised in a number of industrial disputes. His major focus is organizational change, particularly restructuring, TUPE, outsourcing, procurement, and collective redundancy.

Eric Ivester is a partner in the corporate restructuring group in the New York office of Skadden, Arps, Slate, Meagher & Flom LLP. He has represented debtors, creditors, investors, and acquirors in complex corporate restructurings. He was recently named 'Dealmaker of the Week' by *The AmLaw Daily*, has been repeatedly selected for inclusion in *Chambers USA* and *The Best Lawyers in America*, and was also listed in the *Euromoney and Legal Media Group's 2009 Expert Guide to the World's Leading Insolvency and Restructuring Lawyers.*

Michael K. Kam received his JD from The National Law Center, George Washington University, and is the senior partner of the ERISA practice group at Weil, Gotshal & Manges LLP. He practices in the areas of employee benefits, executive compensation, fiduciary duties, prohibited transactions, and pension investments, and is knowledgeable in the context of mergers and acquisitions, financings, and business restructurings.

Daniel Kossoff has been a Partner in Clifford Chance LLP's London office since 1989. He specializes in corporate finance, general company, and commercial, insolvency, and corporate restructurings. He led the team advising British Energy on its restructuring in 2002–2005 and acted for KKR in purchasing Alliance Boots in 2007.

Matt Kriegel is an associate in the corporate restructuring group in the Chicago office of Skadden, Arps, Slate, Meagher & Flom LLP. His experience includes representations of debtors, creditors, investors, and lenders in out-of court workouts, chapter 11 reorganizations, and liquidations.

Ben Larkin heads up the Restructuring and Insolvency practice at Berwin Leighton Paisner LLP. He specializes in all aspects of corporate restructuring. Mr Larkin has particular expertise in relation to real estate related restructurings. He is recognized as a leading expert in the Legal 500 and Chambers and has featured in the Lawyer Top 100. He is a Fellow of the Association of Business Recovery Professionals, a member of the Editorial Board of International Corporate Rescue and sits on the City of London Law Society Insolvency Law Committee.

Duane McLaughlin is a New York-qualified partner based in Cleary Gottlieb Steen & Hamilton LLP's New York office. His practice focuses on the origination and restructuring of US and cross-border debt financing transactions. He regularly represents borrowers in amendment, refinancing, and restructuring transactions, with a particular focus on private equity portfolio companies and Latin America. He also represents banks and creditor committees in out of court restructurings. He recently represented the creditors' steering committee of Cemex in connection with its restructuring of approximately $15 billion of indebtedness and in subsequent amendment transactions.

Alastair Meeks is the head of the pensions group at Pinsent Masons LLP. He is a former chairman of the Association of Pension Lawyers and author of Tolley's Pensions Cases. His group advised the trustees of the Nortel Networks Pension Plan on the obtaining of financial support directions from the Pensions Regulator against companies in the Nortel Network group and the trustees of the Readers' Digest Pension Scheme, and the Singer & Friedlander Pension & Life Assurance Scheme on the problems thrown up by the insolvencies of their respective sponsoring employers. The group has also advised the employers in the Grampian Foods group and the Liberata group on the process of transferring the employers' pensions liabilities to the Pension Protection Fund.

Harvey R. Miller currently is a senior partner in the New York City based international law firm of Weil, Gotshal & Manges, LLP where he had been a member of the firm's management committee for over 25 years and created and developed the firm's Business Finance & Restructuring department specializing in reorganizing distressed business entities. Mr Miller is the lead partner in the bankruptcy cases of Lehman Bros. Holdings, Inc. and the former General Motors.

Gabriel Moss QC is a leading advocate, adviser, and author on insolvency law in England. He is a member of South Square Chambers and a bencher of Lincoln's Inn. An advocate and adviser in numerous international banking and insurance insolvencies, he is also authorized to sit as Deputy High Court Judge in the Chancery Division and has had several reported judgments on insolvency.

Hoyoon Nam is an associate at Weil, Gotshal & Manges LLP. Mr Nam routinely represents major financial institutions, private equity funds and corporate borrowers on a variety of financing and restructuring matters.

Philip Ridgway is a barrister practising from Temple Tax Chambers. One of his specializations is the taxation of insolvent companies and restructuring. He is a member of R3 having passed the JIEB examination and also Fellow of the Chartered Institute of Taxation. Mr Ridgway writes and lectures frequently for the tax and insolvency profession.

Seven Rivera received his JD from Harvard Law School and is a partner with Chadbourne & Parke LLP in New York. His practice involves all aspects of the bankruptcy and restructuring process while representing both secured and unsecured lenders, creditors, debtors, and creditor committees in complex and high-profile chapter 11 bankruptcy cases.

Gabrielle Ruiz is a senior lawyer at Clifford Chance LLP's London Office. She has over 13 years' experience specializing in all aspects of corporate restructuring and insolvency law. Ms Ruiz is also a member of the Insolvency Lawyers' Association technical committee.

Nick P. Saggese is a recently retired partner in the Los Angeles office of Skadden, Arps, Slate, Meagher & Flom LLP. Mr Saggese was co-head of the firm's Private Equity Practice and represented clients across the globe in connection with a variety of corporate transactions, including private equity, mergers and acquisitions, recapitalizations, securities offerings, and corporate restructurings. Recent representations include Metro-Goldwyn-Mayer Studios Inc. and CIT Group Inc. in connection with each of their prepackaged plans of reorganization; ION Media Networks, Inc. in a comprehensive recapitalization; and Paul Allen, as principal shareholder of Charter Communications, Inc., in connection with Charter Communications, Inc.'s prearranged chapter 11 bankruptcy case.

Howard Seife is a partner in Chadbourne & Parke LLP's New York office and chairs the firm's global bankruptcy and financial restructuring practice. He has built his reputation on representing financial institutions and creditors' committees in some of the largest and most complex chapter 11s and is a recognized leader in the area of cross-border insolvencies.

Andrew Shutter is an English-qualified partner based in Cleary Gottlieb Steen & Hamilton LLP's London office. Mr Shutter's practice focuses on the origination and restructuring of international debt and equity financing transactions and related derivatives. He regularly assists corporate debtors, creditors, investors, financial counterparties, and other interested parties in bankruptcy-related transactions and out-of-court workouts in the EMEA countries. Recent transactions include Alinta, Oerlikon, TI Automotive and Vita. Mr Shutter also works on sovereign debt matters and is the consultant editor of *A Practitioner's Guide to Syndicated Lending*.

Scott Simpson, Co-Head of Skadden's Global Transactions Practice, advises on European cross-border merger and acquisition transactions, including contested and hostile bids. Mr Simpson is recognized as one of the world's leading transactional lawyers and has been featured in publications including the *Financial Times*, the *Wall Street Journal*, and the *American Lawyer*.

Michael Sippitt is Managing Partner of Clarkslegal LLP head of the firm's employment practice. Mr Sippitt trained at Clarkslegal and became a partner in 1978. He has particular expertise in the employment aspects of restructurings, collective employment relations law, and strategy, industrial disputes, and crisis management, and is a member of the national Employment Panel of the Confederation of British Industry.

Joseph Smolinsky is a partner in the Business Finance and Restructuring Department of Weil, Gotshal & Manges LLP, resident in New York. His practice focuses on providing restructuring advice and strategy to borrowers, lenders, investors, and creditors. During a span of over twenty years, he has counseled clients in a wide variety of US and cross-border transactions.

Douglas R. Urquhart is a partner in Weil, Gotshal & Manges LLP's New York Office. Mr Urquhart specializes in bank debt financings (including leveraged cash-flow and asset-based loans, subordinated and second lien financings) and workouts (including DIP and exit facilities as well as out-of-court restructurings).

Glenn Walter is counsel at Skadden, Arps, Slate, Meagher & Flom LLP. Mr Walter's practice concentrates on corporate restructuring, insolvency, and bankruptcy issues. Mr Walter primarily represents financially troubled companies in out-of-court workouts and chapter 11 reorganizations. Mr Walter has also represented creditors, investors, and asset-purchasers in complex chapter 11 cases.

TABLES OF CASES

UK CASES

US CASES

TABLES OF LEGISLATION

TREATIES AND CONVENTIONS

Brussels Convention 7.02
EC Treaty 14.10
European Union Convention on
Insolvency Proceedings 14.83
Lugano Convention 7.02, 13.51

UK LEGISLATION

Statutes

Arbitration Act 1996
s 69 . . . . 7.122
s 82(1) 7.122
Companies Act 1985
s 135 . . . . 11.56
s 247 . . . . 7.26
s 735(1) 10.27
Companies Act 2006 . . . . 7.08
s 1 . . . . 10.27
s 170 . . . . 5.29, 5.37
s 170(1) 5.11
s 170(3) 5.29
s 170(5) 5.11
ss 171–177 . . . . 5.35
s 172 . . . . .5.07, 5.20, 5.30, 5.31
s 172(1) 2.61
s 172(3) 5.31
ss 173–175 . . . . 2.57
s 174 . . . . 5.30, 5.32, 5.36
s 175(1) 2.60
s 175(4) 2.60
s 175(5) 2.60
s 177 . . . . 2.57, 2.61
ss 190–195 . . . . 2.61
s 238 . . . . 5.55, 5.56
s 238(4) 5.55
ss 238–241 . . . . 5.53
s 239 . . . . 2.56, 2.60
s 250 . . . . 5.11
s 251 . . . . 2.87
s 251(1) 5.11
s 382 . . . . 7.26
s 549 . . . . 11.55
s 551 . . . . 11.55
ss 561–577 . . . . 11.54
s 641 . . . . 11.56
s 642 . . . . 11.56
s 656 . . . . 11.50
s 716 . . . . 9.67
s 717 . . . . 9.67
s 895 . . . . 14.23
s 895(1) 7.51
s 895(2) 7.60
ss 895–901 . . . . 11.39
s 896(1) 7.65
s 897 . . . . 7.67, 7.70
s 897(1) 7.66, 7.83
s 897(1)(a) 7.65
s 897(2) 7.83
s 897(3) 7.71
s 899(1) 7.72
s 899(3) 7.51
s 993 . . . . 5.43, 5.47
Company Directors
Disqualification Act
s 1 . . . . 5.62
s 2 . . . . 5.63
s 3 . . . . 5.63
s 6 . . . . 5.64
s 10 . . . . 5.47, 5.66
Corporation Tax Act 2009
s 9 . . . . 2.98
s 10 . . . . 2.98, 9.70
s 12 . . . . 2.98
s 39 . . . . 9.70
s 302 . . . . 9.78
s 303 . . . . 9.78, 9.79
s 304 . . . . 9.86

Statutory Instruments

EU LEGISLATION

Regulations

Directives

US LEGISLATION

1

INTRODUCTION

Two systems of law dominate the world debt markets: English law and New York law. Any company of any size, from pretty well anywhere in the world that is looking to raise finance will find itself heading either to London or New York and that the debt instruments that it then enters into will be governed by the laws of one or other of these jurisdictions.

The reasons for this are many and varied and could easily be the subject of a book in their own right. Most importantly, however, both systems of law are universally seen to be fair and consistent. Furthermore, they have both developed sophisticated systems for dealing with disputes and, as we will see, for enabling distressed companies to reorganize their finances with the approval of and to the benefit of the vast majority of their creditors. This enables bankers and their customers a fair degree of certainty when entering into commercial arrangements, which is essential to the smooth operation of the global debt markets.

When it comes to insolvency generally and to stressed and distressed companies in particular, it is instructive to look back on the history of bankruptcy and its evolution to the present day. What will become clear is that the US bankruptcy model, built as it is, on the foundations laid by English law has gone on to develop in a radically different way.

The earliest known laws regulating the relationship among debtors and creditors prescribed severe criminal punishment for those unable to pay their debts as they came due. In medieval Europe, a merchant who was unable to pay his bills was dealt with harshly: his creditors would come to the market and break his work-bench over his head. Accordingly, the broken bench—*banca rota* in Latin—is both the legal and linguistic root of modern bankruptcy. Of course, the result of the broken bench was often the debtor's inability to earn a livelihood bringing with it the attendant burdens upon society.

To early societies credit was an unfathomable concept, as merchants expected immediate payment for goods or services. The failure to pay for goods or services was considered a form of theft and was met with swift punishment.[1] The concept of enslaving debtors traces back to the Bible.[2] The Code of Hammurabi, circa 1750 BC, provided that a debtor unable to meet its obligations be sold into slavery.[3] In Hindu law, self-help permitted a creditor to seize the debtor, compel him to labour for him, or, in more extreme circumstances, kill or maim him in his home, or confine his wife, children or cattle.[4]

In 623 BC, Draco, ruler of Athens, instituted laws that likened indebtedness to murder and prescribed a punishment of death.[5] The Twelve Tables of Roman law, established circa 450 BC, presented a creditor with a choice of killing the debtor or selling him into foreign slavery.[6]

Other primitive societies provided a religious sanction as an alternative to slavery or execution. In ancient India, this practice was known as 'sitting d'harna', while in ancient Ireland a similar practice was known as 'fasting on'.[7] In each instance, the creditor would sit in the debtor's doorway until the debt was paid. This method proved effective, as a debtor feared a loss in society that would follow the starvation of a creditor in his doorway.[8] In Egypt, it was customary for a debtor to pledge the deceased body of a close relative. This pledge proved effective in light of the moral and spiritual consequences of the opening of a tomb and disturbance of the mummy.[9]

As commerce thrived and transactions crossed geographical boundaries and required the taking of calculated risks and the expenditure of time to consummate, societies began to understand the benefits that credit could provide for their economies. As a result, punishments associated with the failure to pay one's debts became less severe. Compensation began to replace retaliation or retribution as the consequence of default. Likewise, execution came to be directed against the property of the debtor, not his person.[10] For example, the Romans under Julius Caesar developed the law of *cession bonorum*, a progressive concept that permitted an insolvent debtor to forfeit all of his property to his creditors, rather than

1 See generally Louis E. Levinthal, 'The Early History of Bankruptcy Law', 66 U. Pa. L. Rev. 223 et seq. (1918).

2 See, eg, *2 Kings* 4:1 ('[A]nd the creditor is come to take to him my two sons to be slaves.'); *Isaiah* 50:1 ('Which of my creditors is it to whom I have sold you?'). See also *Exodus* 22:2; *St Matthew* 18:25.

3 Levinthal, above n. 5 at 230.

4 Ibid.

5 F. Regis Noel, *A History of the Bankruptcy Law* (William S. Hein & Co., 1919) 15.

6 Levinthal, above n. 5 at 231.

7 Ibid. at 229.

8 Ibid.

9 Ibid.

10 Ibid. at 232–3.

his life.[11] In feudal times, debtors and creditors would on occasion engage in an actual physical confrontation known as a 'wager of battel', wherein a debtor would either lose title to his land to the creditor or earn a discharge of the debt.[12]

American bankruptcy jurisprudence evolved out of English agrarian society going back approximately five centuries. Prior to the sixteenth century, there was no need for a specialized body of law governing relations among debtors and creditors, as the landed gentry (practically the only one's with any financial clout) required little more than the most rudimentary forms of credit.[13] English farmers were sceptical and fearful of extending credit and typically viewed merchants as 'cheats' or 'evil magicians' who manipulated intangible credit and property.[14]

The first bankruptcy statute, enacted by the English Parliament in 1543 amid an increase in domestic and international trade credit, provided criminal penalties for defrauding creditors. The law was more of a deterrent against fraud by foreign merchants than a provider of rights to an unfortunate debtor.[15] However, as England's colonial expansion continued throughout the sixteenth century, a modern system of mercantile credit, the Law Merchant, and a primitive system of courts developed, leading to the passage of England's first non-criminal bankruptcy statute in 1571.

> Where bankruptcy law had once stereotyped the merchant debtor as an elusive social deviant whom the law should criminally punish, it began to develop an opposite image of the merchant debtor as a noble and venerable statesman of society whom the laws should protect from the cruel contingencies of economic life.[16]

The 1571 Act codified a series of informal legal customs practised by prominent members of the merchant community. Pursuant to the Act, a bankruptcy proceeding could be commenced by a single creditor and subjected all of a debtor's property to the jurisdiction of the Court of Chancery, which had the power to stay individual creditor enforcement against the debtor until the bankruptcy proceeding was closed.[17]

---

[11] See Harvey R. Miller and Erica M. Ryland, 'The Role of Mega Cases in the Development of Bankruptcy Law' in the *Development of Bankruptcy & Reorganization Law in the Courts of the Second Circuit of the United States* (Bender, 1995) 189, 192.

[12] Noel, above n. 14, at 21.

[13] Miller and Ryland, above n. 20 at 192-3.

[14] See Robert Weisberg, 'Commercial Morality, the Merchant Character, and the History of the Voidable Preference' (1986) 39 Stan. L. Rev. 3, 13. See also above n. 2 and accompanying text.

[15] See Miller and Ryland, above n. 20, at 193.

[16] See Weisberg, above n. 23, at 6.

[17] See Miller and Ryland, above n. 20, at 195.

A major advance in bankruptcy law occurred in 1705 with the adoption of a right of discharge under the Statute of Anne.[18] By issuing a right of discharge to debtors who cooperated in the marshalling of their property for the benefit of creditors, Parliament conceded that a statute which provided penalties but no rewards was self-defeating.[19] However, the infamous 'Trader Rule' limited the application of these 'decriminalized' bankruptcy laws to large international or domestic traders. Based on the belief that the benefits of bankruptcy law should be limited to merchants and large traders whose losses were accidental or due to no fault of their own,[20] the Trader Rule continued to subject individual debtors and small traders to the harsh, punitive laws of insolvency.[21] The Trader Rule perpetuated a dualism whereby the *bankruptcy laws*, defined by their relative leniency, would protect merchants, while *insolvency laws* would be harshly applied to small businesses and individuals.[22]

Consistent with many of the views adopted by colonists fleeing English rule, the first American laws regulating the relationship among debtors and creditors assumed the principles of the progenitor English *bankruptcy laws*, giving merchants broad protections in recognition of the importance of credit and trade to the colonial economy. The early course for the nation's economic policy as to insolvency and commercial failure over the next several hundred years was thus established. Significantly, however, the American laws were more progressive in relaxing the nature of the oppressive English *insolvency laws* and their harsh treatment of individual and small business debtors.[23]

In yet another example of the framers' prophetic vision of the American political and economic system, the equitable treatment of creditors through the enactment of a uniform bankruptcy law was of manifest importance in the infant stages of American government. Article 1, section 8 of the US Constitution provided Congress with the power to 'establish.... uniform Laws on the subject of Bankruptcies throughout the United States'.[24] In Federalist No. 42, James Madison pronounced that '[t]he power of establishing uniform laws of bankruptcy is so intimately connected with the regulation of commerce, and will prevent so many frauds where the parties or their property may lie or be removed into

[18] See Weisberg, above n. 23, at 30-1.

[19] Ibid. at 30.

[20] 2 William Blackstone, *Commentaries* (4th edn, 1770) 473-4.

[21] See W. J. Jones, 'The Foundations of English Bankruptcy: Statutes and Commissions in the Early Modern Period' (1979) 69 Transactions of Am. Phil. Soc'y pt 3, at 24-5.

[22] Miller and Ryland, above n. 20, at 196.

[23] See Peter J. Coleman, *Debtors and Creditors in America: Insolvency, Imprisonment for Debt, and Bankruptcy, 1607-1900* (Beard Books, 1974) 11-15.

[24] US Const. art 1 s 8, cl 4.

different states, that the expediency of it seems not likely to be drawn into question'.[25]

From there US Bankruptcy law has gone on to develop in chapter 11 a system which recognizes that doing business involves risk, that companies will inevitably need protection while they restructure and (subject to supervision by their creditors and the court) that directors and management should be left to run the company as they see best. There is much to admire about chapter 11 and the way in which it has been used to restructure successfully so many companies. It is a testament to the influence it has worldwide that when new restructuring or insolvency laws are introduced pretty well anywhere in the world, they will be described as that particular jurisdictions' 'chapter 11'. The fact that for those with any knowledge or understanding of chapter 11 there seems little if any connection between the new legislation and chapter 11 is neither here nor there. It has been, and continues in many ways to be, the paradigm.

By way of contrast, English law has remained (despite recent efforts by successive governments to create and sustain a 'rescue culture') generally unrepentantly pro creditor. That said, largely as a result of the dominance of English law with debt markets worldwide, England and the English courts remain a vital part of the corporate restructuring process worldwide. Due to the flexibility of the common law system, the commercial and practical approach of the English courts and with the aid of legally sanctioned debt—compromise arrangement such as schemes of arrangements and company voluntary arrangements companies incorporated in many different parts of the world have been successfully restructured in England. This has been possible without the benefit of many of the protections provided for by the US Bankruptcy Code and relying often on the majority of creditors acting rationally in accordance with their economic interests.

The aim of this book has been to present side by side the approach taken by English law on the one hand, and US law on the other hand, to a number of the most important issues that may face a stressed or distressed company. Some of the issues explored, and the context in which they are explored, may seem somewhat ephemeral. The restructuring of structured finance vehicles and the issues around the purchase by a company of its outstanding debt, at a discount, in the secondary market, were the hot topics of 2008 and 2009. In 2011, they may no longer be centre stage. What is clear, however, is that having learnt how to use these new and different skills they are likely to continue to be important features of the restructuring landscape as we eventually work out the companies damaged by the recent financial downturn and as we prepare for the next.

[25] The Federalist No. 42, at 271 (James Madison) (Clinto Rossiter edn, 1961).

Sometimes the philosophy, the approach, and the language used when exploring a particular issue across the two jurisdictions is remarkably harmonious. At times it is jarringly different. We make no apologies for presenting them in this way. The aim is to expose as vividly as possible the differences between the two jurisdictions where they occur, enabling practitioners to understand graphically where issues will arise.

We hope this book proves to be both useful and enjoyable. Naturally, we extend our deep and heartfelt thanks to all our authors (and all those who assisted in the background) for their extremely hard work, professionalism and patience.

2

EMERGENCY SALES IN THE US AND THE UK[1]

2.1 Introduction

Troubled companies are often likened to 'melting ice cubes'—the value of the business recedes as customers and counterparties terminate relationships, key employees leave for competitors, and the goodwill and brand name of the business become tarnished. The potential for rapid decline of troubled companies was observable throughout the catastrophic global economic downturn that began in 2007. During this period, many famous and longstanding names of Wall Street **2.01**

[1] The authors would like to thank Brandon Duncomb of Skadden, Arps, Slate, Meagher & Flom LLP (in respect of the US portion), and Kevin King and Julie Bradshaw (in respect of the UK portion) and Alex Jupp (in respect of UK tax matters) each of Skadden, Arps, Slate, Meagher & Flom (UK) LLP, for their assistance in compiling this chapter.

and the City of London collapsed in dramatic fashion, not to mention the countless lesser-known businesses that suffered similar fates.

2.02 One lesson to come from the financial crisis is the need for troubled companies to respond quickly to dire financial circumstances before the value of the business melts away. In both the US and the UK, the best way to preserve value for a troubled companies' creditors often has been through an emergency sale of assets or shares. Yet, the best practices for conducting emergency sales differ starkly in the US and the UK. In particular, troubled companies in the US generally are best served by filing for protection under the US Bankruptcy Code[2] before consummating a sale. In contrast, troubled companies in the UK are well-advised to consider an emergency sale before initiating proceedings under the UK Insolvency Act 1986 (the 'IA 1986'), which may result in a fire-sale of the business by an administrator or liquidator. This chapter outlines the different strategic considerations taken into account by troubled companies in the US and the UK.

2.03 The first half of this chapter will examine the phenomenon of emergency sales in the US. It will (a) provide a brief overview of the fiduciary duties of directors and officers and detail how these duties change in a distressed sale environment, (b) outline the options available to financially troubled companies outside of bankruptcy, and (c) analyse the process of engaging in a distressed sale in the US through the chapter 11 bankruptcy process, touching on such subjects as the advantages of a sale through the bankruptcy process, the requirements of a sale under section 363 of the Bankruptcy Code, and recent developments affecting distressed sales in bankruptcy.

2.04 The second half will shift its focus to emergency sales of companies in the UK outside of formal insolvency proceedings. The topics covered by this section will include the (a) key features of an emergency sale in the UK, (b) the different manners of structuring a sale, (c) the duties of directors, (d) the reasons why certain transactions may be challenged, (e) the type of protective measures that can minimize the risk of directors' liability and of the transaction being set aside by a court, (f) the roles of the various stakeholders, and (g) the key differences of rescue sales that take place as part of an administration.

2.2 Emergency sales in the US

2.2.1 Distressed sales in the US

2.05 The recent global economic downturn has forced an unprecedented number of financially troubled companies in the US to maximize their value through some

[2] 11 USC ss 101-1330 (hereinafter referred to as the 'Bankruptcy Code').

form of distressed sale.[3] These sales have highlighted creditors' expanding influence over the restructuring of troubled companies in the US. The following sections of this chapter will discuss many of the options available to the officers and directors of financially troubled companies in the US, as well as some of the issues that may drive their decision-making process.

2.2.2 Distressed sales in the US outside bankruptcy

2.2.2.1 Fiduciary duties of officers and directors

(i) **Generally** Directors of a solvent Delaware corporation owe fiduciary duties exclusively to the corporation and, derivatively, to its shareholders.[4] There are three elements to directors' fiduciary duties: (a) a duty of care, (b) a duty of loyalty, and (c) a duty of good faith.[5] The duty of care requires that officers and directors make decisions with the care and diligence that an ordinarily prudent director can reasonably be expected to exercise in a like position under similar circumstances.[6] The duty of loyalty requires directors to act at all times in the best interests of the corporation, including an affirmative duty to refrain from conduct that would injure the corporation and its shareholders or that would be solely in the directors' or officers' own interests.[7] The duty of good faith is a subsidiary element of the duty of loyalty, and requires that directors act in a manner that they honestly believe to be in the best interests of the corporation.[8] **2.06**

The default standard by which courts review challenges to director actions is the business judgment rule, which is a presumption that 'in making a business decision the directors of a corporation acted on an informed basis, in good faith and in the honest belief that the action taken was in the best interests of the company'.[9] Directors and officers are not afforded the benefit of the business judgment rule, **2.07**

3 See aacer.com, 'U.S. business bankruptcies rise 38 pct in 2009' <http://www.aacer.com/us-business-bankruptcies-rise-38-pct-in-2009.html> (last visited 4 March 2010); aacer.com, 'Bankruptcy Filings Surged in '07' <http://www.aacer.com/bankruptcy-filings-surged-in-07.html> (last visited 4 March 2010) ('5,736 [US] businesses sought Chapter 11 protection to reorganize, an increase of nearly 24%.').

4 *Revlon Inc. v MacAndrews & Forbes Holdings, Inc.* 506 A2d 173, 179, 182 (Del. 1986).

5 *Smith v Van Gorkom* 488 A2d 858, 872-3 (Del. 1985).

6 *Re Walt Disney Co. Derivative Litig.* 907 A2d 693, 749 (Del. Ch. 2005), affd 906 A2d 27 (Del. 2006); Model Bus. Corp. Act s 8.30(b); *Briggs v Spaulding* 141 US 132, 152 (1891); *Van Gorkom* 488 A2d at 872-3. Many states, including Delaware, also have enacted exoneration statutes allowing corporations to eliminate or limit the liability of directors for breaches of their duty of care. See, eg, Del. Code Ann. 8 s 102(b)(7).

7 *Revlon* 506 A2d at 179-80.

8 *Disney* 907 A2d at 754.

9 *Gantler v Stephens* 965 A2d 695, 705-6 (Del. 2009) (quoting *Aronson v Lewis* 473 A2d 805, 812 (Del. 1984).

however, in suits for breaches of the duty of loyalty,[10] which requires that directors and officers place the corporation's interest ahead of their own.[11]

2.08 **(ii) Fiduciary duties of officers and directors in distressed sale situations** The tight timeframes often associated with emergency sales requires directors to be especially vigilant of their fiduciary duties. The seminal case setting out the fiduciary duties of officers and directors in a sale situation is *Revlon Inc. v MacAndrews & Forbes Holdings, Inc.*, in which the Delaware Supreme Court ruled that when a corporation is sold, directors have a duty to obtain the best price for shareholders.[12] Often referred to as '*Revlon* duties', the court held that once a board of directors recognizes that their company is for sale, the board has a duty to '[maximize] the company's value at a sale for the stockholders' benefit'.[13] Directors may face accusations that they acted too hastily and that the resulting fire-sale prices were detrimental to shareholders and other stakeholders. Close scrutiny will be placed on the sale process, particularly directors' valuation and marketing efforts. However, as noted by the Delaware Supreme Court, 'there is no single blueprint that a board must follow to fulfill its duties'.[14] In this regard, the Delaware court has held that directors are not required to conduct a public auction to ensure that the best possible price is achieved.[15] Instead, courts considering whether directors have satisfied their *Revlon* duties may take several factors into account in the absence of a public sale, such as: (a) directors' activity, sophistication, and general awareness of company value and market conditions; (b) whether any other potential purchasers had expressed an interest in a sale transaction or whether directors believed that other bidders would emerge; (c) whether directors

---

[10] See *Disney* 907 A2d at 747 (presumption of business judgment rule only applies when there is no evidence of fraud, bad faith, or self-dealing).

[11] See ibid. at 747 ('The duty of loyalty, in essence, "mandates that the best interest of the corporation and its shareholders take precedence over any interest possessed by a director, officer or controlling shareholder and not shared by the stockholders generally"' (quoting *Cede & Co. v Technicolor, Inc.* 634 A2d 345, 361 (Del.1993)). Courts also recognize, in certain circumstances, duties of disclosure and good faith. See *Stone ex rel. AmSouth Bancorporation v Ritter* 911 A2d 362, 370 (Del. 2006) (recognizing the duty of good faith as a 'subsidiary element' of the duty of loyalty); *Malone v Brincat* 722 A2d 5, 10-12 (Del. 1998) (recognizing duty of directors to make appropriate and fair disclosure of pertinent information within the board's control). For an in-depth analysis of the fiduciary duties of the officers and directors of distressed or insolvent companies, see generally D.J. (Jan) Baker, John Wm. (Jack) Butler, Jr., and Mark A. McDermott, 'Corporate Governance of Troubled Companies and the Role of Restructuring Counsel' (2008) 63 Bus. Law 855.

[12] *Revlon* 506 A2d at 182.

[13] Ibid. Maximizing value does not necessarily compel directors to accept the highest bid. Directors may also consider other factors, such as the feasibility of a bid: *Mills Acquisition Co. v Macmillan, Inc.* 559 A2d 1261, 1282 n. 29 (Del. 1988) (identifying several factors that may be considered by directors).

[14] *Barkan v Amsted Indus.* 567 A2d 1279, 1286 (Del. 1989).

[15] *Lyondell Chemical Co. v Ryan* 970 A2d 235, 242-4 (Del. 2009).

received a fairness opinion from an investment bank regarding the purchase price; and (d) whether directors attempted to negotiate a higher purchase price.[16]

2.2.2.2 Options available to financially troubled companies outside bankruptcy

(i) **Private sales** The sale of Bear Stearns ('Bear') to JPMorgan Chase ('JPMC') paints an all-too-graphic picture of the difficulties that a financially troubled company faces outside of bankruptcy.[17] As financial markets deteriorated over 2007 and 2008, due in large part to the decline of the US housing market, Bear continued to maintain a large position in mortgage-related securities based on its reluctance to sell these assets at market prices deemed to be significantly lower than their true value.[18] **2.09**

Between Monday, 10 March 2008, and Friday, 14 March 2008, Bear burned through the vast majority of its $18 bn in cash reserves.[19] On 14 March, Bear sought and was given relief from the Federal Reserve in the form of financing that would be provided 'as necessary'.[20] As a condition of the financing, however, the regulators required Bear to consummate a deal for the company within two days because they did not believe that the firm would survive the opening of the financial markets on Monday.[21] Bear was the proverbial 'melting ice cube' and needed to consummate a private sale of its assets to survive. Given the shortened timeframe, all potential bidders for the company dropped out with the exception of JPMC, which as clearing agent for the company, already had a firm grasp on the companies' assets. Bear was sold to JPMC on 16 March 2008, in a stock for stock transaction that valued Bear at approximately $2 per share, although that price was later increased to $10 per share following resistance by Bear's shareholders.[22] **2.10**

---

16 Ibid.

17 Bear's only other option was a chapter 7 liquidation, under which shareholders would have been wiped out and creditors would not have received 100 cents on the dollar, as they did in the JPMC deal. Bear could not have preserved its going concern value in bankruptcy because under s 109(d) of the Code securities and commodities brokers are ineligible to file under chapter 11. See Matt Miller and John Blakely, 'Bear Stearns: Ch. 11 Never an Option' *The Deal*, 17 March 2008, <http://pipeline.thedeal.com/tdd/ViewArticle.dl?id=1000597135>.

18 Kate Kelly, 'The Fall of Bear Stearns: Lost Opportunities Haunt Final Days of Bear Stearns' *Wall St. J.*, 27 May 2008, at A1.

19 Kate Kelly, 'The Fall of Bear Stearns: Fear, Rumors Touched Off Fatal Run on Bear Stearns' *Wall St. J.*, 28 May 2008, at A1.

20 Ibid.

21 Kate Kelly, 'The Fall of Bear Stearns: Bear Stearns Neared Collapse Twice in Frenzied Last Days' *Wall St. J.*, 29 May 2008, at A1.

22 A day after the sale of Bear to JPMC was finalized, a lawsuit was filed by Bear's shareholders claiming that the Bear misled investors about its finances. See Bloomberg.com, 'Bear Stearns Sued in New York by Investors, Employee' <http://www.bloomberg.com/apps/news?pid=newsarchive&sid=acq_gGTe8JR8&refer=home> (last visited 22 July 2010).

2.11 **(ii) State-law alternatives** A private sale is not the only alternative to a financially troubled company as a way to maximize the value of its assets. Several state-law alternatives to the federal bankruptcy process exist that allow distressed companies to satisfy debt using existing assets. Article 9 of the Uniform Commercial Code ('article 9') provides secured creditors a fast and inexpensive alternative to the bankruptcy process by providing for the satisfaction of debt obligations with collateral.[23] An article 9 foreclosure can be completed in as few as twenty days and may avoid the costs of a bankruptcy case. A foreclosure sale does not, however, release liens and other claims to the same extent possible in bankruptcy. In addition to article 9, several states allow assignments for the benefit of creditors. In these transactions, the distressed company transfers property to a third-party assignee, who reconciles creditors' claims against the company and liquidates assets for distribution to creditors in a manner similar to the Bankruptcy Code's absolute-priority rule. Finally, some states allow for the creation of a receivership, which is functionally similar to an assignment for the benefit of creditors except that a receivership is typically initiated by creditors.

2.2.3 Distressed sales in the US in bankruptcy

2.2.3.1 Advantages of a sale in bankruptcy

2.12 The chapter 11 bankruptcy process offers significant benefits both to troubled companies contemplating asset sales as well as prospective purchasers. Among the most prominent protections granted under the Bankruptcy Code is the automatic stay.[24] The automatic stay gives debtors breathing room to effectuate a restructuring plan and protects creditors' interests by preventing other predatory creditors from unfairly extracting a disproportionate recovery from the debtor.[25] The additional time afforded by the automatic stay can be particularly important to a seller in a distressed sale, especially to officers and directors in the exercise of their fiduciary duties. In some instances, a sale may only be possible in bankruptcy: many companies are prohibited by their charters from selling substantially all their assets without shareholder consent, but shareholder consent is not required for a sale in bankruptcy.

[23] In the absence of an objection by a junior secured creditor, outstanding debt may be satisfied by a secured creditor's acceptance of collateral: UCC s 9-620. If a party with a junior interest in the collateral objects, the collateral must be sold at a public auction: ibid. s 9-610.

[24] The automatic stay is provided for by s 362 of the Bankruptcy Code.

[25] H.R. Rep. No. 595, 95th Cong., 1st Sess. 340 (1977), as reprinted in 1978 USCCAN 5963, 6296–7.

Another important aspect of the automatic stay is that it consolidates all claims against the debtor into the bankruptcy-court proceedings. See *FDIC v Hirsch (In re Colonial Realty Co.)* 980 F2d 125, 133 (2nd Cir. 1992) (observing that the 'central purpose of the automatic stay [is] to have *all* creditors' claims resolved in a single court').

Bankruptcy also offers considerable benefits to purchasers. For example, bankruptcy can significantly limit a purchaser's liability after a sale as buyers in bankruptcy sales may purchase property free and clear of most claims, liens, and other encumbrances. Contrast this fact with sales outside of bankruptcy when obligations of the buyer can be passed along to the buyer under various doctrines of successor liability.[26] Another benefit to purchasers is the ability to selectively choose the assets and liabilities that they wish to buy. To this end, section 365 of the Bankruptcy Code also provides for the selective assumption and assignment of executory contracts and unexpired leases. Finally, under certain circumstances, the Bankruptcy Code also allows for the modification or termination of legacy obligations such as labour costs under collective bargaining agreements and pension and retiree liabilities.[27] **2.13**

The benefits of the chapter 11 bankruptcy process must, however, be weighed against bankruptcy's possible negative aspects. For example, bankruptcy may be expensive, time consuming, and generate negative publicity. It also may have a detrimental impact on other intangibles such as good will and employee morale. Moreover, nearly every decision of a debtor is scrutinized not only by the bankruptcy court, but by statutory committees, the US trustee, and the company's creditors. As a result, the decision to file a chapter 11 petition is not to be made without careful consideration. **2.14**

2.2.3.2 Fiduciary duties of officers and boards of directors in bankruptcy

As discussed above, officers and directors ordinarily owe fiduciary duties only to a corporation and, derivatively, to the corporation's shareholders; the obligations to creditors of a solvent corporation are defined solely by the terms of their contractual and business relationship with the corporation.[28] Once a corporation becomes insolvent, however, the corporation's creditors acquire standing to bring derivative actions against officers and directors for breach of their fiduciary duties to the **2.15**

---

[26] See, eg, *Phila. Elec. Co. v Hercules* 762 F2d 303, 310 (3rd Cir. 1985) (outlining the de facto merger doctrine); *Atlantic Richfield v Blosenski* 847 F Supp. 1261, 1284 (ED Pa. 1994) (explaining the substantial continuity doctrine); *United States v Atlas Mineral & Chems., Inc.* 824 F Supp 46 (ED Pa. 1993) (discussing the mere continuity doctrine).

[27] Sections 1113 and 1114 of the Bankruptcy Code set out the requirements for rejecting or modifying collective bargaining agreements and retiree benefit plans. Note that '[t]he majority of courts addressing the issue have found that a debtor in possession need not comply with the procedures and requirements of section 1114 if it has a right to unilaterally terminate retiree benefits under the retirement plan in question and applicable nonbankruptcy law': Alan N. Resnick and Henry J. Sommer (eds), 7 *Collier on Bankruptcy* (15th rev. edn) 1114.03[1]. But see *Re Farmland Indus.* 294 BR 903 (Bankr. WD Mo. 2003) ('[Section] 1114 prohibits a debtor from terminating or modifying any retiree benefits (as defined in that section) during a Chapter 11 case unless the debtor complies with the procedures and requirements of § 1114, regardless of whether the debtor has a right to unilaterally terminate the benefits.').

[28] *N. Am. Catholic Educ. Programming Found. v Gheewalla* 930 A2d 92, 101 (Del. 2007).

corporation.[29] Although the number of constituencies that may bring actions for breach of fiduciary duties expands when a corporation becomes insolvent, the nature of the fiduciary duties owed by officers and directors—care, loyalty, and good faith—and the requirements of the business judgment rule, remain the same[30] and continue to apply after a debtor files for federal bankruptcy protection.[31]

2.16 Foremost among directors' and officers' objectives in exercising their fiduciary duties in a chapter 11 case is maximizing the value of the estate for all constituencies.[32] Thus, the officers and directors of a chapter 11 debtor-in-possession are bound by similar obligations as those imposed by *Revlon* under Delaware law—the fundamental difference being that duties are owed by management to a company's creditors and other stakeholders, and not just the shareholders.[33] Directors of a chapter 11 debtor must, therefore, seek the best possible bid for assets sold from the bankruptcy estate.[34]

2.2.3.3 Sale process in bankruptcy

2.17 In bankruptcy, distressed sales may be implemented either pursuant to a plan of reorganization confirmed in accordance with section 1129 of the Bankruptcy Code (a 'Sale Pursuant to a Plan') or upon notice and a hearing before the bankruptcy court under section 363 of the Bankruptcy Code (a '363 Sale'). The Bankruptcy Code does not require public auctions or other formal bidding procedures for the sale of estate property. [35] Nevertheless, unless the circumstances

[29] *Gheewalla* 930 A2d at 101-2. See generally Baker, Butler, and McDermott, above n. 11.

[30] Ibid.; *Trenwick Am. Litig. Trust v Ernst & Young, L.L.P.* 906 A2d 168, 195 n. 75 (Del. Ch. 2006), affd mem. sub nom. *Trenwick America Litig. Trust v Billett* No. 495, 2006, 2007 WL 2317768 (Del. 14 August 2007); see also *Angelo, Gordon & Co. v Allied Riser Commc'ns Corp.* 805 A2d 221, 229 (Del. Ch. 2002).

[31] See, eg, *Fulton State Bank v Schipper (In re Schipper)* 933 F2d 513, 515 (7th Cir. 1991) (observing that the fiduciary duties owed by a debtor in bankruptcy are analogous to those owed under state law outside of bankruptcy).

[32] *Re Teleglobe Commc'ns Corp.* 493 F3d 345, 385 (3rd Cir. 2007) ('A fiduciary ordinarily has the obligation (protected by the business judgment rule) to manage the affairs of a corporation in such a way as to maximize its economic value.').

[33] See Dennis F. Dunne, 'The Revlon Duties and the Sale of Companies in Chapter 11' (1997) 52 Bus. Law 1333, 1339-48 (explaining the application of *Revlon* duties in chapter 11, but that '[t]he fiduciary duties of a solvent Delaware company are not coterminous with those of an insolvent company operating in Chapter 11' because the fiduciary duties owed to creditors are elevated above the duties owed to shareholders). Of course, *Revlon* also continues to apply to Delaware corporations in the sense that state-law fiduciary duties continue to apply to chapter 11 debtors. See above n. 31 and accompanying text.

[34] The best bid is not necessarily the highest bid. Directors are entitled to consider other factors, such as feasibility of the bid. See above n. 13.

[35] See Fed. R. Bankr. P. 6004(f)(1) ('All sales not in the ordinary course of business may be by private sale or by public auction.'); *Re President Casinos, Inc.* 314 BR 784, 786 (Bankr. ED Mo. 2004) ('Although there is a strong argument in support of prior court approval of bid procedures, and in

compel a quick sale (ie the melting ice cube situation), courts tend to prefer the market-based guidance of an auction over independent valuations to ensure that the estate receives the best possible price.[36]

Section 363 of the Bankruptcy Code authorizes debtors, with court approval after notice and a hearing, to sell any or all of its assets. A 363 Sale is generally the fastest way to capture value for distressed assets in bankruptcy because the sale is not imbedded within a plan of reorganization. Accordingly, parties to a 363 Sale are not required to address the treatment of all assets owned by a debtor or claims asserted against the debtor, nor are they required to comply with other creditor protections set out in section 1129 of the Bankruptcy Code. **2.18**

Creditors have long objected to 363 Sales of all or substantially all of a debtor's assets on the grounds that such sales constitute *sub rosa* plans of reorganization (ie, de facto plans designed to scheme around statutory protections afforded to creditors pursuant to section 1129 of the Bankruptcy Code).[37] Proponents of 363 Sales, on the other hand, have touted the relative efficiency of 363 Sales in comparison to the plan process.[38] In an effort to balance creditors' concerns with the need to maximize the value of a debtors' estate, courts attempted to find a middle ground that would authorize a debtor to sell all of its assets outside of the plan context in appropriate circumstances. Initially, the courts allowed 363 Sales of all or substantially all assets only to the extent there was a good business reason to do so.[39] Over time, courts became more comfortable with 363 Sales, regularly approving sales that liquidate most of a debtor's assets. **2.19**

The growing acceptance of 363 Sales as the principal transaction in a chapter 11 case was epitomized by the high-profile cases of Chrysler and General Motors. **2.20**

most circumstances such approval is appropriate, there is no section under the Bankruptcy Code that requires the Court to establish bid procedures under Section 363.'); *Re Trans World Airlines, Inc.* 2001 WL 1820326, at *4 (Bankr. D. Del. 2 April 2001) ('[I]t is worth noting that a § 363(b) sale transaction does not require an auction procedure. The auction procedure has developed over the years as an effective means for producing an arm's length fair value transaction.').

[36] See *Re Planned Sys., Inc.* 82 B.R. 919, 923-4 (Bankr. SD Ohio 1988) (rejecting private sale in favour of public auction because it was unclear that the private bid was in the best interests of the estate, stating that the court 'generally favors a public sale of property of the estate'); cf. *Re Lahijani* 325 BR 282, 287 (9th Cir. BAP 2005) ('Objections to sale that are based on inadequacy of price are often resolved by the court ordering an auction . . . .').

[37] See *PBGC v Braniff Airways, Inc. (Re Braniff Airways, Inc.)* 700 F2d 935, 939-40 (5th Cir. 1983). But see *Chrysler* 405 BR at 97 (holding that liquidating substantially all of a debtor's assets for later distribution under a plan does not constitute a *sub rosa* plan).

[38] See generally Doug G. Baird and Robert K. Rasmussen, 'The End of Bankruptcy' (2002) 55 Stan. L. Rev. 751; Doug G. Baird & Robert K. Rasmussen, 'Chapter 11 at Twilight' (2003) 56 Stan. L. Rev. 673.

[39] *Comm. Of Equity Sec. Holders v Lionel Corp. (R Lionel Corp.)* 722 F2d 1063 (2nd Cir. 1983) (finding that a sale of substantially all assets is permissible if the debtor can identify a clear business purpose).

In both of these cases, the debtors sold substantially all their assets through 363 Sales arranged before the companies' bankruptcy filings. In approving the sales, the courts noted the necessity of quickly consummating the transactions.[40] But recent cases, particularly *Chrysler* and *General Motors*, also have led some commentators to question whether courts have become too permissive in approving 363 Sales, effectively eviscerating the safeguards imposed by section 1129 of the Bankruptcy Code.[41]

2.21 363 Sales, while often faster and less burdensome than a Sale Pursuant to a Plan, also have limitations. Although creditor approval is not required for court approval of a 363 Sale, secured creditors often dictate whether a 363 Sale is viable. If secured creditors do not consent to a 363 Sale and the purchase price does not exceed the secured creditors' claims, it may not be possible to sell property free and clear of liens. [42] Additionally, the releases in a 363 Sale, particularly for successor and third-party liability, are arguably less robust than those obtainable under a plan of reorganization.[43]

---

[40] *Re Chrysler LLC* 405 BR 84, 96 (Bankr. SDNY 2009), affd 576 F3d 108 (2nd Cir. 2009); *Re General Motors Corp.* 407 BR 463, 493 (SDNY 2009).

[41] See AIFP Hearing, Cong. Oversight Panel, 23 July 2009 <http://cop.senate.gov/documents/testimony-072709-adler.pdf> (written statement of Barry E. Adler) ('When Judge Gonzalez approved the Chrysler sale, he stripped these [s 1129] protections from the secured creditors.'); *Ramifications of Auto Industry Bankruptcies, Part III: Hearing Before the Subcomm. on Commercial and Administrative Law of the H. Comm. on the Judiciary*, 111th Cong. 5 (2009) (statement of Douglas G. Baird) (arguing that the Chrysler sale amounted to a *sub rosa* plan); see also Ralph Brubaker, 'The *Chrysler* and *GM Sales*: § 363 Plans of Reorganization?' (Sept. 2009) 20 Bankr. L. Letter No. 9 (concluding that the *Chrysler* sale was not a *sub rosa* plan because the sale did not improperly dictate the distribution of sale proceeds but that the *GM* 363 Sale impermissibly allocated distributions among other classes without regard to the 'fair and equitable' requirements of the Bankruptcy Code). But see generally Stephen J. Lubben, 'No Big Deal: The GM and Chrysler Cases in Context' (2009) 83 Am. Bankr. L.J. 531 (arguing that the 363 Sales in GM and Chrysler complied with federal bankruptcy law and that academic criticisms of the sales have been largely irrelevant or conjectural). The courts in the Chrysler and General Motors cases addressed *sub rosa* arguments head-on, observing that a sale of substantially all assets does not constitute a *sub rosa* plan merely because the sale determines the value that creditors will ultimately receive under a plan of reorganization: see *Chrysler* 405 BR at 98; *Re General Motors Corp.* 407 BR 463, 495 (Bankr. SDNY 2009).

[42] Consent and purchase price are the only two options that are always theoretically available for a sale free and clear of liens under s 363(f) of the Bankruptcy Code. Most courts require that the purchase price exceed the aggregate value of all secured claims. See, eg, *Clear Channel* 391 BR at 41 (holding that '§ 363(f)(3) does not authorize the sale free and clear of a lienholder's interest if the price of the estate property is equal to or less than the aggregate amount of all claims held by creditors who hold a lien or security interest in the property beings sold'). Some courts, however, only require that the purchase price exceed the economic value of the underlying collateral. See, eg, *Re Beker Industries Corp.* 63 BR 474, 477 (Bankr. SDNY 1986) (holding that the 'value of all liens' means the actual economic value of the liens).

[43] Section 1141(c) provides that 'property dealt with by the plan is free and clear of all claims and interests of creditors, equity security holders, and of general partners in the debtor'. Plans may grant valuable releases against potential third-party claims targeting buyers and sellers, and often contain broad exculpation and limitations on liability for activities connected with the plan.

Sales Pursuant to a Plan[44] offer a number of benefits that are unavailable in a 363 Sale. A confirmed plan brings finality to a chapter 11 case, and offers broader releases and exculpation than ordinarily available in a 363 Sale. Additionally, certain tax benefits are available only in connection with a plan of reorganization.[45] But the plan process also can be time consuming and expensive, and opens the door for numerous objections that are inapplicable in a 363 Sale.[46] Additionally, at least one impaired class of creditors must vote in favour of the proposed plan, and to the extent a class rejects the plan, such plan must satisfy the requirements for 'cramdown'.[47] **2.22**

To reduce the time a debtor spends in bankruptcy and the associated costs, the terms of a 363 Sale or a plan may be negotiated before the debtor files for bankruptcy protection. In a prenegotiated 363 Sale, the debtor typically enters into an asset purchase agreement with a stalking-horse bidder before the bankruptcy and files a motion seeking approval of the agreement and corresponding bidding procedures.[48] Similarly, the terms of prepackaged and prenegotiated[49] plans of reorganization are negotiated with key creditors—usually holders of long-term debt—and filed with the bankruptcy court at the outset of the bankruptcy. Bankruptcy filings with a prepackaged or prenegotiated plan or a prenegotiated sale enhance the likelihood that the financially troubled companies' stay in bankruptcy will be greatly reduced, resulting in a corresponding reduction in fees and expenses, as well as less negative publicity. **2.23**

[44] 11 USC s 1123(a)(5)(D) (authorizing the 'sale of all or any part of the property of the estate' under a plan).

[45] The US Internal Revenue Code provides for both tax-free recapitalizations and reorganizations under a plan of reorganization: see 26 USC s 368(a)(1)(E), (G). Transaction structures have also developed that use a plan of reorganization as a platform to maximize tax efficiency: see generally, eg, Christopher Woll, 'Post Bruno's Bankruptcy Planning: An Analysis of Taxable Emergence Structures' (2005-6) 4 DePaul Bus. & Com. L.J. 277. In addition, a purchaser is also exempt from paying transfer taxes when a sale is under a plan of reorganization: 11 USC s 1146.

[46] For example, the plan process frequently produces litigation relating to disclosure, voting, allocation of plan distributions, cramdown, and feasibility of the plan, none of which are applicable in 363 Sales.

[47] 11 USC s 1129(b). See generally Kenneth N. Klee, 'All You Ever Wanted to Know About Cram Down Under the New Bankruptcy Code' (1979) 53 Am. Bankr. L.J. 133. To this end, a plan proposing a sale of secured creditors' collateral subject to the creditors' right to credit bid provides a basis to cram down a plan over the objection of secured creditors: ibid. s 1129(b)(2)(A)(ii).

[48] See generally William F. Gray, Jr. & Timothy B. Martin, 'Running On Empty: How the Lack of DIP Financing Is Reshaping the Bankruptcy Landscape' N.Y.L.J., 2 March 2009 (outlining the sale process for prenegotiated 363 Sales).

[49] The key difference between prepackaged and prenegotiated plans is the timing of solicitation: In prepackaged plans, solicitation is completed before the petition date; solicitation in a prenegotiated plan, solicitation continues after the petition date.

2.2.3.4 *Recent developments in distressed sales in bankruptcy*

2.24 While the mechanics of bankruptcy sales can take a number of different forms, a common characteristic to emerge among bankruptcy sales is the heightened degree of control exercised by secured creditors at the top of troubled companies' capital structures. In many instances, secured creditors hold considerable leverage over the direction of bankruptcy cases and often emerge as owners of the reorganized company. In fact, the extent to which secured creditors have usurped powers originally reserved for debtors has led some commentators to dub them 'creditors in possession'.[50] Nevertheless, the mounting influence of secured creditors has grown in recent years due, in part, to the absence of readily available debtor-in-possession financing. It is important for officers and directors to be aware of the options available to secured creditors when it comes to their collateral. This section discusses recent developments affecting secured creditors' control over the bankruptcy process.

2.25 (i) **Collective action in syndicated credit facilities** Secured lenders are often among a distressed company's largest and most influential creditors and, as a result, they play an important role in chapter 11 cases. Amid the frozen credit markets of the latest economic downturn, secured lenders have increasingly taken on the role of buyer in bankruptcy sales by credit bidding for collateral pursuant to section 363(k) of the Bankruptcy Code.[51] The proliferation of credit bidding has been assisted, in part, by recent court decisions clarifying the level of support required among secured lenders to pursue a credit-bidding strategy.

2.26 Until recently, the level of consensus among lenders in a syndicated credit facility needed to implement a credit-bidding strategy remained unclear. The debate largely turned on standard provisions of syndicated credit agreements with competing purposes. On one hand, enforcement rights upon an event of default are often given exclusively to the agent bank.[52] On the other, certain actions—such as the release of liens—traditionally require unanimous consent among lenders.[53] Moreover, several cases recognized the rights of individual lenders to part ways

---

[50] See generally Harvey R. Miller and Shai Y. Waisman, 'The Creditor in Possession: Creditor Control of Chapter 11 Reorganization Cases' (2003) 21 Bankr. Strategist 1 (identifying reasons for the ascendancy of creditor influence).

[51] In general terms, a 'credit bid' is an offer to cancel secured debt as consideration in a sale of collateral.

[52] See *Chase Manhattan Bank v Motorola, Inc.* 136 F Supp 2d 265, 271 (SDNY 2001) (observing that borrowers may desire to consolidate enforcement rights upon an event of default with the agent bank because '[t]he lead bank is often at the mercy of banks holding smaller positions, and precipitous actions of a minority can often dominate the majority will and induce disfavored action by the lead bank').

[53] For example, dissenting lenders in the *GWLS* and *Chrysler* bankruptcies invoked unanimous-consent provisions in their arguments against collective action: *Re GWLS Holdings, Inc.* No. 08-12430, 2009 WL 453110, at *2 (Bankr. D. Del. 23 February 2009); *Chrysler* 405 BR at 102.

with the majority and pursue their own remedies.[54] A number of recent rulings, however, have recognized the right of a majority of lenders to direct the agent bank to exercise remedies on behalf of all lenders under the credit facility.[55]

(ii) Blocking credit bids by offering secured creditors the 'indubitable equivalent' Traditionally, there have been two ways to challenge secured creditors' ability to credit bid at sales of their collateral: (a) attack the validity of the underlying secured claims or (b) assert that secured creditors should be prohibited from credit bidding for cause (eg collusion, inadequate consideration, or the absence of an escrowed funds in the event of a dispute over the priority of secured claims).[56] But recent decisions by the Third[57] and Fifth Circuit[58] Courts of Appeals recognized a third way to prevent secured creditors from credit bidding: providing secured lenders with the indubitable equivalent of their secured claims. **2.27**

In both *Philadelphia Newspapers* and *Pacific Lumber*, the debtors proposed to sell collateral under a plan of reorganization at a purchase price considerably less than the outstanding amount of secured debt, but at the same time prohibited the secured creditors from credit bidding. Instead, the plans proposed to make cash payments in the amount equal to the appraised value of the collateral in satisfaction of the secured claims. These payments were far below the face amount of the debt. Over the opposition of the secured lenders, the Third and Fifth Circuits held that section 1129(b)(2)(A)(iii) of the Bankruptcy Code permits the sale of secured lenders' collateral under a plan of reorganization free and clear of liens without requiring that secured creditors be allowed to credit bid, so long as the secured lenders receive the indubitable equivalent of their claims.[59] The extent to which other courts will reach the same result as the courts did in *Philadelphia Newspapers* and *Pacific Lumber* remains unclear. But secured creditors' influence over sales and **2.28**

[54] See *Bank One Texas, N.A. v A.J. Warehouse, Inc.* 968 F2d 94, 98 (1st Cir. 2002); *Commercial Bank of Kuwait v Rafidain Bank* 15 F3d 238, 242-3 (2nd Cir. 1994).

[55] *Chrysler* 405 BR at 102; *Re Metaldyne Corp.* 409 BR 671, 677-9 (Bankr. SDNY 2009); *GWLS* 2009 WL 453110, at *4-6 (Bankr. D. Del. 23 February 2009); *Beal Savings Bank v Sommer* 865 NE2d 1210, 1215 (NY 2007).

[56] Daniel P. Winikka and Debra K. Simpson, 'Will Bankruptcy Courts Limit the Right to Credit Bid?' (2008) 17 Norton J. Bankr. L. & Prac. 6, art 6.

[57] *Re Philadelphia Newspapers, Inc.* 599 F3d 278 (2010).

[58] *Bank of New York Trust Co. v Official Unsecured Creditors' Committee (Re Pacific Lumber Co.)* 584 F3d 229 (5th Cir. 2009).

[59] Unlike the Fifth Circuit, the Third Circuit did not reach a conclusion as to whether the debtors proposed plan would, in fact, provide secured lenders with the indubitable equivalent of their claims: *Philadelphia Newspapers* 599 F3d. at 312-3. As a result, the impact of the Third Circuit's ruling may be limited. Cases in which courts have found that secured creditors received the indubitable equivalent of their claims have typically involved circumstances where either: (a) secured creditors take possession of the collateral or (b) secured creditors receive a payment stream in the amount of their claim that is secured by different, but equally valuable, collateral. See Collier, above n. 27, at ¶ 1129.04[2][c]. Neither of these circumstances applied to the *Philadelphia Newspapers* plan.

the formation of a plan of reorganization is likely to be eroded in jurisdictions that adopt this approach.

2.3 Emergency sales in the UK

2.3.1 Introduction

2.29 Any business that relies on confidence in its financial position, its brand name or goodwill, talented (but mobile) employees or short-term contracts with customers or counterparties, will be particularly hard hit by suggestions that it is or may soon be experiencing financial distress. Businesses of this type have been likened to 'melting ice cubes'—once exposed to the heat of potential insolvency, value in the business melts away rapidly as customers and counterparties terminate relationships, key employees look to exit and the goodwill and brand name of the business become tarnished. The catastrophic and rapid collapse during 2008 of famous Wall Street and the City of London names illustrated this in dramatic fashion, but businesses of almost every type will suffer negative effects once financial difficulties become more widely known.

2.30 Directors of companies incorporated in the UK, or subject to the jurisdiction of the English courts as regards insolvency, may feel this problem more acutely than those of corporations in the US. There is no direct equivalent of the debtor-friendly chapter 11 procedure in the UK and despite efforts by the Department for Business, Innovation and Skills to foster a 'rescue culture',[60] the administration procedure provided for under the Insolvency Act 1986 (the 'IA 1986') is still the end of the road for many distressed companies, resulting at best in an insolvency fire-sale of the business. However, consistent with their duties under English law, directors may be able to minimize eventual losses to creditors by disposing of all or part of the business before administration, in an emergency sale.

2.31 Emergency sales may also be attractive in other stressed situations. Corporate groups approaching financial difficulties or facing a working capital shortfall may benefit, as well as financial institutions with urgent regulatory capital needs. Financial investors, including private equity houses, may consider disposals of portfolio businesses as one of a range of restructuring options where an operating business is relatively healthy, but maturing acquisition debt remains unlikely to be repaid or refinanced.

2.32 This section describes legal and practical issues arising on an emergency sale (outside insolvency proceedings) by companies incorporated in the UK, with

[60] See, for example, *A Review of Company Rescue and Business Reconstruction Mechanisms*, Interim Report (DTI, September 1999).

cross-border issues considered where relevant. It aims to deal with features peculiar to emergency share and asset sales in stressed situations, rather than share and asset sales generally. Certain tax, employment and pensions-related issues are described briefly, though relevant chapters of this book or other specialist works should be consulted. Sales of businesses by an administrator or a liquidator, which will be a further option for companies under stress, are not considered in detail. Some key differences between an emergency sale outside formal insolvency proceedings and a sale by an administrator are, however, set out in paragraph 2.69 below.

2.3.2 Key features

2.3.2.1 Planning a sale

Companies under financial stress and contemplating an emergency sale will need to focus on resolving potential impediments to completion in advance, since there may be limited scope for resolving these later on or extending deadlines. It may become necessary for the directors of the financially stressed company to place it into administration once it becomes apparent that there is no realistic prospect of completing a proposed sale or other rescue option. Identifying and putting in place advance strategies for dealing with potential impediments is important, as is agreeing on a clear timetable. A degree of brinkmanship, including by creditors of the seller and its group is, however, to be expected. **2.33**

Potential impediments to consider include: **2.34**

- no disposal covenants in financing documents and security over the shares or assets being sold;
- material employment law, pension scheme or environmental issues or liabilitie;
- valuation difficulties;
- regulatory consents or competition clearances;
- shareholder approvals.

2.3.3 Sale process

The auction process common to sales of non-stressed businesses may be difficult to implement in a stressed situation. There may be a limited number of potential purchasers with the resources (in cash) to complete the purchase on a shortened timetable. If any potential purchaser has regulatory or competition clearances to obtain or any offer is made subject to finance, this may rule that purchaser out. Sellers and their advisors should be proactive in diligence and evaluation of any potential purchaser's ability and intent to complete any proposed transaction in a timely manner. This may include seeking comfort from a potential purchaser's bankers or financial advisors. Sellers should be wary of allowing trade competitors to participate in a sale process indefinitely, where such competitors have an **2.35** interest either in prolonging negotiations while the value of the business deteriorates or in using the negotiating period to poach customers or to acquire a portion of the seller or the target's debt (at a low price) with a view to obtaining a role in any sale or restructuring or even itself acquiring control. As part of any confidentiality undertakings to be given by potential purchasers as part of becoming involved in the bid process, the seller may therefore also seek undertakings that a potential purchaser will not acquire any interest in the seller or the target company's bonds or other debt.

2.36 The best a stressed seller may be able to achieve is a limited or 'mini' auction process between at most two or three potential purchasers, conducted on a fast-track basis. In genuine emergency situations, where an immediate sale is the only option, it may be advantageous for the seller to invite all potential purchasers and their advisors to the offices of the seller's legal or financial advisors for emergency negotiations and an emergency auction process on the basis of draft sale documentation.

2.37 A seller might also seek to maintain a form of competitive tension with potential purchasers by managing a rescue sale process alongside other possible restructuring options, such as an initial public offering, other forms of capital raising or a debt restructuring. Running parallel processes has the advantage of providing a stressed company with a greater degree of control over its destiny and may improve its bargaining position. A parallel debt restructuring, scheme of arrangement or other method for compromising creditors' rights may also be necessary where the proceeds of the sale will not repay all the relevant debt, or where all lender consent is required to waive no disposal covenants or to release security over the assets subject for the sale. However, advisors will need to plan parallel processes very carefully, with close attention to key milestones and the timing of key decisions, together with coordination with any creditor committees.

2.38 Process letters or other instructions sent to potential purchasers should make it clear that disclosure of details of any bid to the sellers' lenders may be necessary in order for any bid to proceed (perhaps including disclosure to lenders of transaction documentation or a summary of the terms of the bid). A seller will seek to ensure that any confidentiality obligations imposed by a potential purchaser in respect of its bid do not prevent this disclosure.

2.3.4 Importance of valuation

2.39 Valuation and pricing of an emergency deal will take place against the backdrop of the common law and statutory duties of the directors of the seller, which require the directors to 'take every step to minimize potential losses to creditors' and which leave a 'transaction at an undervalue' potentially open to challenge. It is therefore common for directors of the seller to obtain formal, independent, third party valuations of the business being sold to minimize the risk of later challenge.

Accordingly, on any emergency disposal, seller directors will seek at the very least to achieve a higher price than would be realized in an administration or liquidation sale. Purchasers, on the other hand, will be anxious to take advantage of the seller's predicament and will be mindful of the lower value of contractual protection offered and the reduced scope for due diligence. **2.40**

The major creditors of the seller or the target company may also play an important role in determining price, depending on the value of their debts, their priority on a liquidation and their security position. **2.41**

2.3.5 Consideration

If the main purpose of any sale is to repay maturing debt in short order, the only form of consideration acceptable to a stressed seller is likely to be cash. For similar reasons, a stressed seller will be extremely keen to avoid any element of deferred consideration, earn-out or vendor finance. The position may differ where the disposal is made by a substantial seller group or if share consideration (in the form of a stake in the purchaser) offers the seller an ongoing strategic advantage or potential for upside in any future revival of the business. Consideration is often structured so that the purchaser pays a nominal purchase price in return for an assumption of debts or liabilities by the purchaser. **2.42**

2.3.6 Due diligence

There may be limited scope for a purchaser to carry out detailed due diligence. Advisors to a potential purchaser should obtain clear instructions on where to focus efforts and should clearly explain the limits of this work. Where concerns regarding the value of the assets exist, or potential mismanagement of the business is suspected, particular caution should be taken and use of industry or transaction specialist due diligence consultants may be advisable. **2.43**

2.3.7 Limited contractual protection

In contrast to a sale by an administrator within insolvency proceedings, stressed sellers can in theory provide contractual protection to the purchaser by way of warranties and indemnities. If the seller is a stressed group of companies taking remedial action by disposing of non-core assets, the purchaser may be willing to rely on a package of warranties and indemnities, particularly with a parental guarantee. If the seller is in a critical situation or will have no significant assets after the disposal, warranties and indemnities may be of limited value. A purchaser should either reflect this risk in the purchase price or look for other protections, such as **2.44** retention of a portion of the purchase price in a third party escrow account, bank guarantees or transaction insurance.

2.45 From a seller's perspective, retention of purchase price arrangements are generally undesirable since they may delay on-payment of the proceeds to creditors. Seller directors may, however, be able to justify the delay if delay under alternative processes (for example, an administration sale) would be greater and recovery lower. Where the purchaser is paying a reduced or nominal price, or is assuming or repaying debts of the seller, the retention amount is likely to be a proportion of the amount of debt to be repaid.

2.46 Purchasers should ensure that funds placed into escrow are expressed to remain as its property, with the seller's entitlement to transfer of ownership of the funds or rights to the escrow account balance conditional on satisfaction of all liabilities. Alternatively, the purchaser should obtain a charge over funds of the seller held in escrow. If instead the retention amount is expressed in the sale documentation to be an asset of the seller against which the purchaser has a right of set off, then on a subsequent insolvency of the seller such contractual rights of set off may cease to be fully effective where inconsistent with mandatory insolvency set off.[61]

2.47 A purchaser may be able to obtain transaction insurance from a specialist broker, covering, among other things, liability for breach of warranty or indemnity, employee transfer liabilities, the possibility of any sale being held to be a 'transaction at an undervalue' and defective title. Premiums on any such insurance may be high and subject to both an excess amount and a number of exclusions on claims. Specialist cover, such as cover for environmental liabilities, may incur greater premiums or not be obtainable, depending on the nature of the business being acquired. Insurers' legal advisers typically wish to review any due diligence reports and materials and may wish to perform their own diligence. If there is no time for insurers to carry out basic diligence, the increased risk may be reflected in the premium (though some insurers will sometimes agree to arrange cover post-closing).

2.48 If a seller enters administration or liquidation following closing of any share or asset sale, the purchaser and its advisors should promptly review any acquisition documentation for details of potential claims, to submit any claims to the administrator or liquidator (which are likely to rank as unsecured claims).

[61] See r 2.85 (companies in liquidation) and r 4.90 (companies in administration) of the Insolvency Rules 1986 (SI 1986/1925). See also William J. L. Knight, *The Acquisition of Private Companies and Business Assets* (7th edn, Sweet & Maxwell, 1997) 353.

2.3.8 Transitional services

Ordinarily, where a sale is completed very quickly, or structured as a disposal of selected assets only, transitional arrangements may be essential for the purchaser. If, however, the seller is likely to enter administration or liquidation subsequent to any sale, there may be limited value in these transitional service arrangements, post-closing. The purchaser should therefore be satisfied that the business to be acquired can continue to be run as a going concern, or used in its business, without any further assistance from the seller. If the seller is part of a wider group that is using the disposal to pay down debt, a purchaser may be willing to rely on transitional services arrangements with the seller. **2.49**

2.3.9 Sale structure

2.3.9.1 Share or asset sale

Whether an emergency sale is structured as a sale of business assets or shares in a subsidiary is likely to depend on, among other things, the nature and extent of the problem faced, the capital structure of the seller's group, the rights of creditors, tax, the preference of the purchaser, and timing. Employee and pension considerations may also have a significant impact on structure. **2.50**

2.3.10 Purchaser perspective

In most cases, the strong preference of a purchaser will be for an asset sale. Asset sales allow a purchaser a degree of cherry-picking of the most valuable assets, with most[62] types of liability left behind with the seller. The purchaser is then able to focus due diligence efforts on the assets it wishes to acquire. In contrast, on a share sale the purchaser will acquire all the (potentially significant) liabilities of the target company, whether disclosed by the seller or not. This leaves the purchaser heavily reliant on limited due diligence and contractual protection. From a UK tax perspective, the starting assumption of most purchasers in this scenario is likely to point to an asset sale. **2.51**

In certain circumstances, a purchaser may be amenable to structuring the transaction as a share sale, including where: **2.52**

- the business is more valuable if the transaction is structured as a share sale—for example where it holds valuable, but non-assignable licences, permits or contracts;

[62] For employment-related obligations, however, the TUPE 2006 (as defined below) means the position on an asset sale is likely to mirror the position on a share sale, with relevant employees automatically transferring. See para. 2.61 below.

- it is too expensive or time-consuming to transfer each of the assets (for example where the business is a regulated financial services business or has a large amount of real property);
- the relevant assets are situated overseas or subject to overseas security and the process for formal release is time-consuming;
- there are restrictions on direct foreign ownership of overseas assets;
- existing tax-related structuring would be adversely affected or existing tax assets in the target company or group would be of value to the purchaser or its group;
- the seller is likely to enter insolvency proceedings and accordingly, it is not attractive to a purchaser to leave assignments and transfers of assets being left until after closing (as is common in non-stressed asset sales) or to rely on 'wrong box' provisions of the acquisition agreement requiring the seller to transfer across any misallocated assets after closing;
- the seller is able to present an attractive, debt-free operating subsidiary to the purchaser, whether by virtue of where debt sits within its group or through a hive down;
- the purchaser is willing to acquire a debt-laden subsidiary of the seller in return for a much-reduced or nominal purchase price;
- a purchaser is comfortable that warranty and indemnity protection offered by the seller on a share sale will be of ongoing value—for example, where the proceeds of the sale will go a long way to resolving the seller's financial difficulties;
- tax considerations (eg a high transfer tax and/or VAT cost for the purchaser on an asset sale) tilt the balance in favour of a share sale.

2.3.11 Seller perspective

2.53 A seller will typically prefer to proceed by way of a sale of shares in a subsidiary. In this way, all the assets and liabilities of the subsidiary will be transferred to the purchaser. UK corporation tax payers may favour a share sale, particularly if any gains arising would be sheltered by the substantial shareholding exemption,[63] although an asset sale may not be unattractive if tax losses would be available to the seller to shelter potential tax charges arising on an asset sale such as chargeable gains or balancing charges in respect of capital allowances.

[63] Schedule 7AC of the Taxation of Chargeable Gains Act 1992.

2.3.12 Hive-downs

Hive-downs are a combination of an asset sale and a share sale. They involve a transfer of assets by the seller to a newly formed subsidiary, which subsidiary is then sold to the purchaser. Historically popular for tax reasons, hive-downs are now used mainly for commercial reasons since they allow a seller (or more often, its administrator) to package up assets for sale. There are three main methods under which a hive-down is typically implemented. The relevant assets are transferred to the new subsidiary in exchange for either shares in the new subsidiary, cash left outstanding as an intra-group loan, or future consideration to be determined by an expert valuer. Each method involves navigating a number of tax and valuation considerations, the detail of which is beyond the scope of this chapter. The upshot is that a hive-down will not always be a feasible option in a genuine emergency. **2.54**

2.3.13 Directors' duties

When a company begins to experience financial difficulties, directors' duties come to the fore and create a challenging framework within which director decision-making must take place. The near certainty of losses to creditors, whichever restructuring path is chosen, increases the likelihood that directors' actions and decisions will be subject to a later challenge by any administrator or liquidator, including in respect of emergency disposals. Issues relating to director's duties are more fully dealt with in chapter 5, but the paragraphs that follow deal briefly with their particular application to the decision by seller directors to pursue an emergency share or asset sale and to the conduct of any sale. **2.55**

2.3.13.1 Duties under the Companies Act 2006 and under common law

As a company nears insolvency, creditors are assumed to have the primary economic interest in the company's business and assets and directors are required under case law to have regard predominantly (though not exclusively) to the interests of creditors.[64] These are the interests of creditors generally, not the interests of a particular class of creditors—for example secured lenders. The precise timing of this shift in emphasis has not been established by the courts. Directors may find themselves in a 'zone of uncertainty' where both the interests of members and creditors are potentially relevant in a developing situation. Since the duty is then owed predominantly to creditors, the power of members under section 239 of CA 2006 to ratify any breaches of duty by the directors cannot be relied upon to **2.56**

---

[64] *West Marcia Safetywear Ltd v Dodd* [1988] 4 BCC 30. See Finch, *Corporate Insolvency Law* (CUP, 2002) 685–93.

prevent an administrator or liquidator of the company bringing a claim in future against the directors.[65]

2.57 Any decision to sell and the terms of any such sale will require directors to have regard to their usual duties, including the duties to:

- exercise reasonable care, skill and diligence;[66]
- avoid conflicts of interest[67] and declare interests in transactions;[68] and
- exercise independent judgment.[69]

2.58 In addition, section 214(3) of IA 1986 has the effect of imposing a further duty on directors of a company in financial difficulties to 'take all steps to minimise losses to creditors'.

2.59 In emergency situations, directors may be required to make time critical and often radical decisions based on limited information, but will still be expected to exercise reasonable, skill, care and diligence in any decision to undertake an emergency sale and in its conduct. Directors may need to be able to demonstrate that consideration was made of why a rescue sale was preferable to other restructuring options or to an administration sale, and why a particular purchaser was chosen above others.[70] A failure to consider an emergency sale where it would have been in the interests of the company to do so might also constitute a breach of this duty.

2.60 The duty to avoid conflicts of interest will require the directors and their advisors to consider very carefully any new situations that arise in which any of the directors 'has, or can have, a direct or indirect interest that conflicts, or may possibly conflict with the interests of the company'.[71] Any conflict situation that arises will need to be authorized (if possible under the articles of association) by non-conflicted directors or (if not possible) ratified by the members of the company.[72] Advisors should be alert to the need to update conflict authorizations when consideration of a potential emergency share or asset sale begins. The duty may be of particular relevance where directors are in discussions with the company, alone or backed by third party investors, to buy out a company's business. The duty to exercise independent judgment may also be relevant. A conflict may rise if a

65 *West Mercia Safetywear Ltd v Dodd*. See also Paul L. Davies, *Gower and Davies: The Principles of Modern Company Law* (8th edn, Sweet & Maxwell, 2008) para. 16-83.
66 CA 2006, s 174.
67 Ibid., s 175.
68 Ibid., s 177.
69 Ibid., s 173.
70 See *Re Welfab Engineers Ltd* [1990] BCLC 833 Ch D. The then Hoffmann J. was reluctant on the facts, however, to unpick the choices made by the directors.
71 CA 2006, s 175(1).
72 See ibid., ss 175(4), 175(5) and 239.

director of a stressed company is also a director of a corporate shareholder that is considering making a fresh equity investment, to preserve its interest in the business. Directors of multiple group companies may find that a rescue sale of the company's business may be more advantageous to creditors of one group company over another. Conflicts may also arise where directors also act as trustees of the company's pension scheme, in particular for an under-funded defined benefit scheme.

The duty to declare transactions in which the directors have an interest will clearly be applicable to any emergency sale to existing management.[73] Directors may also need to obtain the consent of members, since any sale to directors may fall within the scope of sections 190 to 195 of CA 2006 relating to 'substantial property transactions' with directors. **2.61**

The duty to exercise independent judgment may be relevant where a director was nominated by a shareholder or related private equity house and a restrictive shareholder or investment agreement is in place. Directors will remain subject to their overriding duties to the company and their actions may be open to challenge if, with a view to preserving shareholder participation in the business, they veto a rescue sale which might have proved beneficial to creditors. Ideally, a private equity house or other equity investors should not be represented in restructuring negotiations by their nominated director. Shadow directorship issues may also arise. **2.62**

Directors are also required to have regard to 'the interests of . . . employees' and 'the company's business relationships with suppliers, customers and others' as part of the duty 'to promote the success of the company in the interest of its members'.[74] A decision to pursue a rescue sale for the purpose of repaying creditors may not be inconsistent with this duty. The duty is expressed to be subject to any other duties under law to have regard to the interests of creditors. Although a rescue sale may result in a reduction in the number of employees or disruption to relationships with customers or suppliers, the situation for employees and others would often arguably be worse without the rescue sale. **2.63**

Directors might also take comfort from case law on the common law duty of directors to act for a proper purpose. It suggests that in a rescue sale scenario, when deciding on which of several purchasers' offers to accept, it will not be improper for directors to take into account which of the offers best preserves the business as a going concern, notwithstanding a lower price.[75] **2.64**

---

[73] Ibid., s 177 of CA 2006.
[74] Ibid., s 172(1) of CA 2006.
[75] *Re Welfab Engineers Ltd* [1990] BCC 600, per Hoffmann J.

2.3.14 Wrongful trading

2.65 The 'wrongful trading' provisions of section 214 of IA 1986 mean that it will almost always be appropriate for directors of a company in financial difficulties to consider whether an emergency sale is feasible and whether it will minimize potential losses to creditors when compared with other options, including an administration sale.

2.66 This stems from the potential liability of directors under section 214(1) which arises if 'the directors ought to have concluded that there was no reasonable prospect that the company would avoid going into insolvent liquidation', but did not place the company into administration or liquidation. The court may not however make a liability order if it is satisfied each director 'took every step with a view to minimising the potential loss to the company's creditors as... he ought to have taken'.[76]

2.67 A decision to place a company into administration or liquidation prematurely, when allowing the company to continue to trade could have further minimized losses to creditors is arguably also a breach of section 214.[77] Directors delaying formal insolvency when considering a possible rescue sale should only do so, however, for so long as this test can be met. The consequence of a breach of section 214 is that the relevant directors could be liable to personal contribution orders.

2.68 One area of difficulty may be where a potential purchaser is required to obtain regulatory or competition clearances before closing can take place under any rescue sale. Seller directors will need to consider very carefully whether the company can continue to trade while it awaits satisfaction of any conditions to closing.

2.3.15 Vulnerable transactions

2.3.15.1 Transactions at an undervalue

2.69 'Transactions at an undervalue' may be set aside or may be the subject of any other order that the court sees fit to make under section 238 of IA 1986. They include transactions or arrangements entered into by a company for consideration whose value 'in money or money's worth' is 'significantly lower than the value of the consideration provided by the company'.

---

[76] Section 214(3) of IA 1986.

[77] See Roy Goode, *Principles of Corporate Insolvency Law* (3rd edn, Sweet & Maxwell, 2005) para. 12–26.

These provisions are highly relevant to an emergency sale entered into in advance of insolvency proceedings at a depressed purchase price. The key issue for sellers, purchasers and their advisors is therefore valuation. Case law suggests that: **2.70**

- the court will look at the whole of the transaction (or a series of linked transactions);[78]
- valuation is determined from the selling company's point of view (not the purchaser's);[79]
- there is some limited scope for taking into account events which occur after the transaction in determining the value of the transaction;[80]
- the court will take into account consideration in the form of assumption of debts and liabilities;[81]
- there is no rule against a purchaser negotiating a good price on an arm's length basis.[82]

A defence is available under section 238(5) of IA 1986. The court may not make an order if it is satisfied 'that the company which entered into the transaction did so in good faith and for the purpose of carrying on its business' and 'that at the time it did so there were reasonable grounds for believing the transaction would benefit the company'. **2.71**

If the seller company does not enter administration or liquidation within two years of the transaction, section 238 will no longer apply to the sale. **2.72**

2.3.16 Preferences

Only transactions entered into by a company with one of its creditors, or with a surety or guarantor of the company's debts or other liabilities, are relevant for the purposes of section 239 of IA 1986 on 'preferences'. The possibility of an emergency share or asset sale being attacked as a preference by a court on the application of a future administrator or liquidator of a seller is only likely to arise if the purchaser is also a creditor or guarantor. The relevant transaction must have put the creditor in a better position than he would have been (were the company in insolvent liquidation),[83] and the company must have been 'influenced in deciding to give [the preference] by a desire' to put the creditor in that better position.[84] Case law[85] on the meaning of a 'desire' to prefer suggests that an emergency sale **2.73**

[78] See *Phillips v Brewin Dolphin Bell Lawrie Ltd* [2001] 1 All ER 673.
[79] *Re MC Bacon Ltd (No. 1)* [1990] BCLC 324.
[80] *Re Thoars (decd)* [2003] 1 BCLC 499.
[81] *Philips v Brewin Dolphin.*
[82] *Philips v Brewin Dolphin*, per Lord Scott at para. 30.
[83] Section 239(4)(b) of IA 1986.
[84] Ibid., s 239(5).
[85] *Re MC Bacon* [1991] Ch 127.

carried out with the main, overriding purpose of minimizing losses to creditors or to enable the company to survive is unlikely to fall foul of the preference rules. Although advisors should analyse any proposed transaction carefully, the circumstances in which an emergency sale may be set aside as a preference are likely to be limited.

2.3.17 Protective measures

2.74 The following protective measures might be taken by directors of a company considering an emergency share and asset sale to minimize the risk of later liability and of the transaction being set aside by a court:

- timely third party financial and legal advice;
- preparation of regularly updated management accounts;
- an independent third party valuation of the business;
- a paper trail demonstrating the reasoning and the decisions of directors, with board minutes appending details of third party valuations or reports and noting consideration of the views of key creditors;
- meetings with key stakeholders—obtaining their consent where necessary;
- a transparent auction, thoroughly testing the market.

2.75 Where an independent firm of accountants or financial advisors is instructed, it should be asked to provide advice on the impact of continued financial difficulties on the value of the business, together with the likely liquidation or fire-sale value of the business. Advice should be sought on specific offers made by potential purchasers, taking into account the company's situation and the lack of contractual protection available. Appropriate advice may diminish the likelihood that a rescue sale is set aside at a later date as a 'transaction at an undervalue' whether because the consideration received by the seller was within range of the consideration provided by the purchaser, or by providing the company with sufficient grounds to invoke the defence under section 238(5) of IA 1986, if necessary.[86] Well-advised purchasers are likely to insist on a valuation by the seller to help prevent later unpicking of the sale by an administrator or liquidator. In a genuine emergency, there may not be time to obtain a full third party valuation.

2.76 It has been noted as significant that in *Re Continental Assurance Co. of London plc*,[87] the directors who avoided liability for 'wrongful trading' had prepared management accounts and had been receiving advice from licensed insolvency practitioners at the relevant time.[88] Key groups of creditors may in any event insist that

[86] See paras 2.40–2.43 above.

[87] [2001] BPIR 733.

[88] Len Sealy and David Milman, *Sealy and Milman: Annotated Guide to the Insolvency Legislation 2009/2010* (12th edn, Sweet & Maxwell, 2009), notes to s 214 of IA 1986.

the company prepare business and/or restructuring plans in conjunction with outside advisors and may even have appointed their own investigating accountants to prepare a report on the company's business during an initial evaluation phase after the company's difficulties became known.

2.3.18 Role of stakeholders

2.3.18.1 Secured lenders

The process of conducting an emergency sale may be greatly complicated by the behind-the-scenes role of the seller's secured lenders and of its other creditors. **2.77**

The multifaceted nature of lending banks' exposure to a company in financial difficulties (as described below) and a general lack of transparency can leave both directors of stressed companies and potential purchasers with a negotiating headache. It is important therefore for the seller and the purchaser to seek to understand as much of the behind-the-scenes lender dynamics as possible to form effective negotiating strategies. **2.78**

Large lending banks employ specialists to deal with clients in default, who will contact an ailing company as soon as the onset of financial difficulties is obvious. Lender coordinating committees may also be formed and may need to be involved in negotiations. If sensitive information is to be disclosed to certain lenders, confidentiality and lock-up arrangements may be needed for lenders who come 'over the wall' to participate in discussions. **2.79**

Secured loan agreements frequently contain provisions that effectively prevent material disposals of a borrower company's assets or business, meaning that lender consent will be required for any emergency share or asset sale to take place. Carve-outs negotiated into these provisions may be helpful—though directors are highly unlikely to rely on, for example, common carve-outs for disposals made 'in the ordinary course of business'. **2.80**

While some borrowers may have close relationships with a small number of lenders, in many cases loan participations will have been 'syndicated' among a larger number of lenders, not all of whom will necessarily be banking institutions. The logistical difficulties of obtaining even majority or two-thirds (let alone unanimous) consent from a potentially disparate group of lenders may be prohibitive of a quick sale and restrictive or inflexible banking covenants in some circumstances may even be counterproductive to the interests of a majority of lenders.[89] Accordingly, companies considering rescue options, including any sale, will need to understand what contractual restrictions and security arrangements are in place **2.81**

[89] See Eilís Ferran, *Principles of Corporate Finance Law* (OUP, 2008) 330.

and the process and likely timetable for consent to be given and security released, particularly where complex financing arrangements exist, with multi-layered classes of debt (for example, 'senior', 'mezzanine' and 'high yield' debt) structurally or contractually subordinated to each other. Intercreditor arrangements are likely to determine which groups of creditors can block any disposal of assets, which creditors might be able to force a sale or an administration of the company, when secured lenders can enforce their security, and how the proceeds of any sale are to be applied. Lenders are likely to seek to impose additional fees for any consents sought.

2.82 Members of coordinating committees alone may not be able or willing to deliver the necessary consent for a transaction without an information process for, and a formal vote by, all lenders, even where members of the committees hold sufficient debt to approve the sale under the relevant finance documents. 'Over the wall' lenders may also push for full disclosure of everything learned during the sale process to the wider lender syndicate, to remove concerns over trading debt while in possession of non-public information (the inside information and market abuse regimes in the UK do not apply to loan participation trading, but may well apply to bonds).[90]

2.83 A disadvantage to lenders of a sale may be that losses on loans are likely to be realized and impairment charges or write-downs may need to be recognized immediately in the bank's loan book and accounts (if not already marked down). A secured lender may also have forms of insurance or have hedged their exposure to default by the company (perhaps through the credit default swaps market) and so it may sometimes stand to recover more under hedging insurance from an insolvency than from the proceeds of any rescue sale. Lending banks may also have equity investments in the company, as well as holding interests in several classes of debt. Lenders may be financial advisors to the company in some capacity or have facilitated hedging or other arrangements with the company. While some lenders may have held their participations since the loan was made, others may have purchased the participation at a discount to its face value in the secondary market. If the seller or the target is already in default, secured lenders may also be considering whether an enforcement sale will be cleaner than a rescue sale.

2.3.19 Shadow directorship issue

2.84 Liability for 'wrongful trading' under section 214 of IA 1986 attaches not only to directors but also to 'shadow directors' and to 'de facto' directors. A shadow

[90] See Part V of the Criminal Justice Act 1993 and s 118 of the Financial Services and Markets Act 2000. See also *Private and Inside Information in the Loan Market* (Loan Market Association, 2007).

director, under section 251 of IA 1986, is a person 'in accordance with whose directions or instructions the directors of the company are accustomed to act'. Under common law principles, a de facto director is a person who fulfils the functions of a director without having been formally appointed. Secured lenders and other key creditors will be anxious to avoid falling within either of these categories by virtue of their role in any rescue sale or other informal rescue and should clearly avoid providing directors with direct instructions to proceed to a rescue sale, particularly where unsecured and other creditors will not benefit from the sale. Case law has tended not to characterize the actions of lenders in restructuring situations as being those of shadow directors, even where lenders have imposed conditions on their continued support for the business. Nevertheless, caution is usually advised.

2.3.20 Bondholders

Much of what is said in relation to secured lenders above applies equally to bondholders, particularly where the bonds are secured or contain 'no disposal' covenants.[91] It may then be difficult for the company to obtain consent of all or the requisite majority of bondholders to carry out an emergency sale. In general, ownership of bonds is more widely dispersed and bonds are more frequently traded than participations in loans, and identification of and communication with the underlying holders may not be a simple process, though existence of a bond trustee may help.[92] A sale may not be attractive to bondholders if the value realized is not likely to be sufficient to repay prior ranking creditors in full, in which case bondholders may have nothing to lose by preventing it, if they can. **2.85**

2.3.21 Shareholders

Shareholders of a group of companies in financial difficulties may well be supportive of a sale of a division or a subsidiary if the proceeds will repay maturing indebtedness or provide urgently needed working capital and ensure the long-term survival of the group. In a genuine emergency, with value deteriorating rapidly, the supportiveness of shareholders of a stressed company is likely to depend on whether the sale proceeds will exceed the amount owed to creditors by the company. Many shareholders are likely to be interested in preserving their involvement and may not favour a wholesale disposal of the business unless administration or liquidation is the only alternative. This is likely to be particularly true of **2.86**

[91] Bonds typically contain less onerous covenants than secured loans: see Ferran, *Principles of Corporate Finance Law* 517.

[92] Bond trustees typically only agree to minor variations of the terms and conditions of the bonds without undertaking a full consent solicitation procedure.

family-run businesses. Financial investors, including private equity investors, who are shareholders may also be conscious of the possible adverse reputational effects of a fire-sale or an insolvency. They may well be balancing these concerns alongside consideration of whether to inject fresh funds into the company.

2.87 As noted above, liability for 'wrongful trading' or 'fraudulent trading' may attach to shareholders of a company in financial difficulties if they are held to have been acting as shadow directors or de facto directors. The definition of 'shadow director' under section 251 of IA 1986 does not carve out the parent of a subsidiary from its scope in the same way as the definition contained in section 251 of CA 2006.

2.3.22 Listed company shareholders

2.88 If either the purchaser or the seller has a premium listing on the London Stock Exchange and any rescue sale passes certain financial materiality tests (known as the 'class tests'), Listing Rule 10 will require the seller or the purchaser (as the case may be) to prepare an explanatory circular to its shareholders and obtain the consent of its shareholders in a general meeting before completing the sale.[93] This may be a significant impediment to completion of a successful sale, a fact that has been recognized by the UK Listing Authority (the 'UKLA'), at least in relation to a listed seller's obligations. Under Listing Rule 10.8, a listed seller may ask the UKLA to modify the shareholder consent requirements, provided that certain strict criteria are met and provided that the application is brought to the UKLA's attention at the earliest available opportunity and at least five clear business days before the terms of the disposal are agreed. The seller must demonstrate to the UKLA that it is in 'severe financial difficulties' and that it could not reasonably have entered into negotiations earlier to enable shareholder approval to have been sought. It must also provide a series of confirmatory documents, including a statement that the directors believe that the disposal is in the best interests of the company and shareholders as a whole and a statement that if the disposal is not completed the company will be unable to meet its financial commitments as they fall due and consequently will be unable to continue to trade resulting in the appointment of receivers, liquidators or administrators. Confirmation must be provided by the persons providing finance to the seller stating that further finance or facilities will not be made available and that, unless the disposal is effected immediately, current facilities will be withdrawn. A detailed notification must also be made to the market containing the information set out in Listing

---

[93] Shareholder consent is only required for 'Class 1' transactions. Notification to the markets in a prescribed form is required for transactions meeting lower class thresholds – see LR 10.2 and LR 10 Annex 1 (The Class Tests).

Rule 10.8.4. Recent examples of circumstances where a waiver has been granted include where lenders to an insolvent business would not permit the company to continue to trade for the period needed to obtain shareholder consent[94] and where lender standstill arrangements had expired and no further finance was available to the company.[95]

Listed companies in financial difficulties remain subject to the requirements of the Disclosure and Transparency Rules and, in particular, DTR 2 on the prompt disclosure of 'inside information' (see in particular DTR 2.5.4). Relevant inside information relating to a listed company's financial difficulties (including any agreement, or failure to agree, on a rescue sale) will likely be disclosable to the market in the usual way. These obligations will continue to apply while application is being made to the UKLA for a modification to the shareholder consent requirements.[96] Listed sellers may be able to delay disclosure of information relating to rescue sale negotiations for a limited period if these negotiations would be prejudiced by public disclosure. In particular, delay may be justified if such negotiations are designed to ensure the long-term financial recovery of the listed entity (which may not always be the case) and confidentiality can be maintained (see DTR 2.5.1 and DTR 2.5.3). The UKLA should be consulted if these provisions of the DTR are to be relied upon. If a purchaser is listed, similar considerations may apply. Creditors of the seller who become involved in the sale process and related discussions may need to enter into appropriate confidentiality obligations and consider their own position carefully. **2.89**

2.3.23 Employees

On a share sale, the employees of the target company remain as employees. Under an asset sale which amounts to the transfer of a business as a going concern, employees of the acquired business will also typically be transferred across to the purchaser automatically on identical terms and conditions of employment by virtue of the Transfer of Undertakings (Protection of Employees) Regulations 2006 ('TUPE 2006').[97] Regulation 13(1) of TUPE 2006 may also require that employees or their representatives are informed and consulted 'in good time' before any relevant transfer that will occur under TUPE 2006. Practically, this may not be possible in a genuine emergency, and although an exemption is **2.90**

---

94 Jessops PLC (September 2009) <http://www.jessops.com/corporate/SolventRestructuring.asp>.

95 JJB Sports PLC (March 2009) <http://www.jjbcorporate.co.uk/pdf/26%20March%202009.pdf>.

96 LR 10.8.7G. See DTR 2.2.6 for example. See also the comments of the UK Listing Authority in para. 2.2 of 'List! 20 – January 2009'.

97 Regulation 4.

available to the requirements for 'special circumstances',[98] case law suggests that insolvency in itself may not be a sufficient ground for the exemption to be invoked.[99] Failure to comply with the information and consultation requirements can lead to a liability to employees of up to 13 weeks' uncapped pay per employee. Liability for a failure to inform and consult will be borne jointly and severally by the seller and the purchaser.[100] In practice, where the seller is insolvent, the purchaser may bear the whole of this potentially significant cost and accordingly should seek to quantify it and factor it into the purchase price.

2.3.24 Pensions

2.91 Pensions-related issues may have an impact on the structure of an emergency sale, in particular where the seller or the target has an under-funded defined benefit occupational pension scheme. Trustees of such schemes have been encouraged to behave realistically in stressed situations,[101] but an informal rescue sale pre-insolvency may not attract their support if the sale proceeds will not be used to satisfy, at least in part, any unfunded liabilities. Trustees will have particular influence in decision-making if they have previously obtained from the Pensions Regulator a Financial Support Direction that involved the granting of a charge over some or all the intending seller's assets (or shares). If a stressed company has a defined benefit scheme that is eligible (under the strict criteria) for admission to the Pension Protection Fund,[102] it may be advantageous for any rescue sale to be effected through an administration sale of its assets.

2.92 General pensions issues arising on an emergency share or asset sale will likely be similar to those arising on a non-stressed share sale or asset sale, respectively, though the issues may be more acute. Clearance from the Pensions Regulator is advisable for any share sale of, or significant asset sale by,[103] a company with a defined benefit occupational pension scheme. In the absence of clearance, the Pensions Regulator may impose statutory contribution notices on the target company and its associates (including the purchaser) in respect of any unfunded liabilities. Although the procedure for obtaining clearance from the Pensions Regulator runs on a priority basis, there may not be sufficient time in an emergency situation to negotiate with the regulator and trustees to obtain formal clearance.

---

98 Regulation 13(9) of TUPE 2006.

99 *Clarks of Hove Ltd v Baker Union* [1979] 1 All ER 152 (CA).

100 Regulation 15(9) of TUPE 2006.

101 Paragraph 2.3 of Pensions Regulator Statement (September 2008), 'How the Pensions Regulator will regulate the funding of defined benefits'.

102 Under Part 2 of the Pensions Act 2004 and related subordinate legislation.

103 Paragraph 56 of the Clearance Guidance issued by the Pensions Regulator in June 2009.

TUPE 2006-related pension issues will apply in the usual way to any 'relevant transfer' under an emergency asset sale. In general, neither historic unfunded pension liabilities on an under-funded defined benefit scheme nor rights to pension provision under contracts of employment, transfer automatically with the transferring employees on an asset sale.[104] However, a purchaser may be required to provide equivalent benefits if the pension scheme provides benefits (such as redundancy benefits) not related to 'old age, invalidity or survivors'.[105] In addition, if the transferred employees had access, before the sale, to an occupational scheme to which the seller contributed, the purchaser must provide participating, transferring employees with access to a scheme to which the purchaser contributes[106] (in the case of a defined benefit scheme, an obligation to make matching contributions up to a maximum of 6 per cent of the employee's salary).[107] A purchaser should factor this potential liability so far as possible into the purchase price. **2.93**

See chapter 13 for further information on pension issues in insolvency generally. **2.94**

2.3.25 Regulators and competition authorities

A fuller discussion is set out in chapter 3 of the role of governmental authorities in restructuring processes. It is worth noting here that an emergency sale may be more difficult if the business is regulated. The field of potential purchasers may be smaller, and change of control authorizations or other regulatory consents may be required.[108] **2.95**

In the UK, the Office of Fair Trading may exercise its discretion not to refer an otherwise qualifying transaction to the Competition Commission if the 'failing firm' defence applies. Guidance published by the Office of Fair Trading suggests that this defence will only be available if the exit of the target company from the market is inevitable absent the rescue sale and if materially less anti-competitive alternatives are unavailable,[109] taking into account prevailing market conditions. The Office of Fair Trading is typically willing to give informal advice to struggling businesses. **2.96**

---

104 Regulation 10 of TUPE 2006.

105 Following the decisions in *Beckmann v Dynamoc Whicheloe Macfarlane Ltd* [2002] IRLR 578 and *Martin v South Bank University* [2004] IRLR 74.

106 Sections 257 and 258 of the Pensions Act 2004.

107 Regulation 3(1) of the Transfer of Employment (Pension Protection) Regulations 2005 (SI 2005/649).

108 For example, the FSA's control over authorized persons regime—see Part XII of the Financial Services and Markets Act 2000 and the FSA Handbook, SUP 11 and SUP 16.

109 See 'Restatement of OFT's position regarding acquisitions of "failing firms"' December 2008 (OFT 1047).

2.97 Where EU competition clearances are required for any sale under the EC Merger Regulation,[110] there is no way to waive the rules simply because the transaction is an emergency sale and the business is in serious distress and may otherwise go into insolvency proceedings. Procedurally, the parties may request a derogation of the otherwise applicable bar on closing before clearance is obtained. The EU Commission must be satisfied that there are no significant issues and that the effects of the bar on closing would be exceptionally adverse both to the parties and/or third parties. In terms of the substantive decision, it may be easier to obtain EU Commission consent to a transaction if it is demonstrated that the target firm is no longer a competitive force. There may also be a formal 'failing company defence' available where a transaction raises significant competitive concerns. However, this defence is rarely used because the conditions for invoking it are very strict. Not only do the parties need to show that absent the merger the firm would go into bankruptcy, but they also need to show that absent the merger the assets of the target firm would exit the market, and that no other bidders that do not pose competition concerns are available.[111]

2.3.26 Sales within insolvency proceedings

2.98 It is worth noting briefly for illustrative purposes some of the key differences between a rescue sale pre-administration and an administration or liquidation sale:

- An administration sale will almost invariably be structured as an asset sale (or occasionally as a share sale following a hive-down of assets).
- Warranty and indemnity protection on an administration sale will likely be extremely limited and the acquisition agreement will be very one-sided.
- The administrator is likely to require indemnities for, among other things, any employment law or pension law liabilities that arise as a result of the sale.
- Less onerous TUPE 2006 requirements may apply to the purchaser on an asset sale by an administrator (in relation to dismissals by the administrator in advance of the relevant transfer), though the uncertainty surrounding the applicability of these provisions and whether they may be relief upon may outweigh the benefits.[112]
- The cleansing effect of an administration will in general remove claw-back risk under the 'transactions at an undervalue' and other provisions of IA 1986 described above.[113] This is a major advantage of a pre-pack administration over an informal rescue sale.

110 Council Regulation (EC) No. 139/2004.

111 See, for example, *BASF/Pantochim/Eurodiol* (Case IV/M.2314).

112 See Finch, *Corporate Insolvency* 762–5.

113 See section 5 'Vulnerable transactions' above.

- Corporation tax arising on the seller's profits arising before entry into a formal insolvency regime generally ranks as an unsecured claim in a future insolvency of the seller whereas, on an administration or liquidation sale, it would generally be payable as a pre-preferential expense of the administration.[114] Creditors (other than HMRC) may therefore have access to a greater pool of assets as a result of a pre-insolvency sale.[115]
- A new tax period will commence for UK corporation tax purposes upon entering (and exiting) administration and upon commencement of the seller's winding up,[116] one consequence of which is that trading losses arising in earlier periods would no longer be available to set off against chargeable gains arising on a disposal in the new period.
- A seller in liquidation will no longer be treated as holding the beneficial ownership in its assets for UK tax purposes, which is likely to have a negative impact on the availability of any relief to mitigate UK direct and, potentially, indirect tax consequences of a liquidation sale.
- There may be some advantages to an administration sale if the seller has an unfunded liability in respect of a defined benefit pension scheme liability which scheme qualifies for the Pension Protection Fund.

As companies near insolvency, it is critical that they act swiftly to preserve maximum value for the companies' creditors and shareholders. Although the method for engaging in emergency sales varies significantly between US and UK companies, such sales can present an effective means of preserving value in either country. **2.99**

114 Rule 2.67(1)(j) and r 4.218 of the Insolvency Rules 1986; *Kahn v Inland Revenue Commissioners* [2002] 1 UKHL 6.

115 Section 12(72A) of the Income and Corporation Taxes 1988.

116 Sections 9, 10 and 12 of the Corporation Tax Act 2009.

3

US AND UK TENDER OFFERS, EXCHANGE OFFERS, AND OTHER OUT-OF-COURT RESTRUCTURINGS

3.1 Introduction

This chapter examines several options available to financially troubled companies in connection with out-of-court restructurings in the US and the UK, and provides practical guidance for each option. Specifically, we discuss tender offers, exchange offers and amendments of outstanding debt securities, including the use of exit consents, and their use in conjunction with prepackaged or prearranged bankruptcies in the US. We also discuss the principal legal framework surrounding bond repurchases, issues relating to such repurchases, and the liability management strategy of combining the consensual nature of the tender offer with an exit consent in the UK. **3.01**

3.2 US restructurings

3.2.1 General issues and considerations

3.02 US companies in financial trouble have several restructuring options available to them. A financially troubled company may be able to take advantage of numerous out-of-court restructuring options to reduce its expenses or modify its capital structure, including consent solicitations, private exchange offers, exchange offers under section 3(a)(9) of the Securities Act of 1933 (as amended, the 'Securities Act'), and a combination of the foregoing through exit consents. These options can also be paired with prearranged or prepackaged bankruptcies to help the company further restructure or undertake feats it could not otherwise accomplish outside of bankruptcy.

3.03 This chapter will discuss some of the restructuring options available to a financially troubled company and the multitude of accompanying issues. Some of these issues may dictate whether a financially troubled company's best course of action will be an out-of-court restructuring, an in-court restructuring, or a series of transactions that incorporates both out-of-court and in-court restructuring components. Ultimately, the path a company takes will depend on the company's unique situation, after consideration of limits set forth in corporate laws, securities laws, bankruptcy laws, and other laws relating to creditor rights.

3.2.1.1 Timing

3.04 Numerous timing issues arise when a company is in financial trouble. Passage of time without taking action is almost always detrimental for a troubled company—suppliers that are not timely paid may tighten or refuse to extend credit, customers may move their business to competitors that are more financially stable, employees may leave the company for more secure opportunities, and creditors may begin to scrutinize the company's operations. Practitioners should consider restructuring options as soon as it is apparent that the company is in financial difficulty.

3.2.1.2 Holdouts

3.05 Companies undertaking an exchange offer often encounter the problem of security holders that do not tender their shares in an offer ('holdouts'). In an exchange offer, the consideration paid may be less valuable than the holdout value of the security being surrendered if a significant portion of the outstanding securities is surrendered.[1] Holdouts may hope to negotiate a better deal or may believe that, if

[1] For example, if a company has $200 m of outstanding notes due in one year, and both the company and the market do not believe that the company has adequate funds to pay for the

restructuring efforts are successful, they will have a greater realization on their securities than they would if they had participated in the tender or exchange offer.[2]

Companies may employ a variety of incentives to encourage tender of the target securities and disincentives to discourage holdouts. In both tender offers and exchange offers, a company can condition consummation of the offer upon the tender of a high percentage of the target securities (typically 85–95 per cent). In an exchange offer, issuers may make the new securities more attractive to security holders by providing for higher dividend or interest rates, shorter maturities, structural seniority or lien priority to the target securities. As a disincentive to holdouts, an issuer may couple a tender or exchange offer with a consent solicitation, whereby tendering holders agree to amend documents governing the target securities to remove protective covenants and certain events of default (generally referred to as 'exit consents'). Finally, an issuer may couple an exchange offer with either a prearranged or prepackaged plan of reorganization that will bind all holdouts. **3.06**

3.2.1.3 Fiduciary duties

In the US, it has been well established by both statutory and case law that directors owe fiduciary duties to a corporation and its shareholders. Generally, directors owe the duties of care and loyalty.[3] The duty of care requires directors to 'discharge their duties in good faith and act as ordinarily prudent persons would under similar circumstances in like positions'.[4] In connection with the duty of care, US courts have adopted the 'business judgment rule', which is a 'presumption that in making a business decision, the directors of a corporation acted on an informed basis, in good faith and in the honest belief that the action taken was in the best interests of the company'.[5] Plaintiffs must therefore rebut the presumption that **3.07**

outstanding notes, the company may decide to commence an exchange offer for new notes due in five years. However, if holders of only $190 m of outstanding notes tender their notes, the remaining holders of $10 m in outstanding notes that hold out are likely to be paid in one year because, while the company may not have the ability to pay the $200 m in outstanding notes, it may have the ability to pay $10 m in outstanding notes.

[2] Security holders that have entered into credit default swaps may have increased incentive to hold out. In a credit default swap, the security holder buys protection against the issuer defaulting (a 'credit event') on a debt instrument. Generally, an out-of-court restructuring is not a credit event and therefore the security holder may prefer that the issuer enter into bankruptcy proceedings, which generally is a credit event under credit default swaps.

[3] Delaware case law on fiduciary duties is well developed and often cited, but case law relating to fiduciary duties may vary from state to state. Bankruptcy courts may also apply non-Delaware case law when reviewing directors' actions.

[4] *Francis v United Jersey Bank* 432 A2d 814, 821 (NJ 1981).

[5] *Aronson v Lewis* 473 A2d 805, 812 (Del. 1984).

the directors were informed in making their business judgment.[6] US courts are loathe to second-guess informed decisions by a board of directors, and therefore emphasis is placed on the *process* employed, rather than the decision reached.[7] The duty of loyalty requires directors to act in good faith in the best interests of the corporation and its shareholders, and to place the interests of the corporation above their own personal gain. More specifically, directors must refrain from self-dealing and usurpation of corporate opportunities.[8]

3.08 Aside from the corporation and its shareholders, directors typically do not owe fiduciary duties to any other parties (such as debtholders and creditors), whose rights are governed by contract, the implied covenants of good faith and fair dealing, and other laws protecting creditors.[9] Whether a corporation is solvent, nearing insolvency, or is insolvent, directors' fiduciary duties do not shift to creditors. As clarified by a recent leading Delaware case, '[w]hen a solvent corporation is navigating in the zone of insolvency. . . directors must continue to discharge their fiduciary duties to the corporation and its shareholders by exercising their business judgment in the best interests of the corporation for the benefit of its shareholder owners'.[10] However, creditors of an insolvent corporation often have the largest stake in the outcome of the restructuring process and will be the group most harmed by any breach of fiduciary duties to the corporation. As such, Delaware courts have recognized that, upon a corporation's insolvency, creditors gain standing to maintain a derivative claim against directors for breach of their fiduciary duties to the corporation.[11] Directors of corporations in financial trouble should therefore develop a record of performing their duties in a way that is intended to benefit the corporation as a whole. A detailed discussion of fiduciary duties is contained in a separate chapter herein.

[6] See ibid. See also *Smith v Van Gorkom* 488 A2d 858 (Del 1985) (discussing the duty of care and setting gross negligence as the standard for determining whether a business judgment reached by a board was an informed one).

[7] See *Re Caremark International Inc Derivative Litigation* 698 A2d 959 (Del 1996).

[8] See *Guth v Loft, Inc* 5 A2d 503 (Del 1939); *Thorpe by Castleman v CERBCO* 676 A2d 436 (Del 1996).

[9] See *Katz v Oak Industries, Inc* 508 A2d 873, 879 (Del Ch 1986); *North American Catholic Educational Programming Foundation, Inc v Gheewalla* 930 A2d 92 (Del 2007).

[10] *North American Catholic Educational Programming Foundation, Inc v Gheewalla* 930 A2d at 101. See also *Trenwick America Litigation Trust v Ernst & Young, LLP* 906 A2d 168 (Del Ch 2006).

[11] See *North American Catholic Educational Programming Foundation, Inc v Gheewalla*, above n. 10 at 101–2.

3.2.1.4 Laws and regulations

A vast array of US laws and regulations may apply to a company undertaking restructuring efforts, including: 3.09

- the Securities Act;
- the General Rules and Regulations Under the Securities Act of 1933 (the 'Securities Act Rules');
- the Securities Exchange Act of 1934, as amended (the 'Exchange Act');
- the General Rules and Regulations Under the Securities Exchange Act of 1934 (the 'Exchange Act Rules')
- the Trust Indenture Act of 1939, as amended (the 'Trust Indenture Act'), which applies to certain debt securities;[12]
- statutory and case law governing fiduciary duties;
- state securities laws;
- applicable securities exchange rules;
- tax laws, including legislation regarding cancellation of indebtedness income and original issue discount; and
- bankruptcy laws.

The application of these laws to each restructuring option will vary depending on the identity of the company, its security holders, and the company's specific situation.

3.2.1.5 Restructuring of bank loans

A significant amount of debt issued in the US is in the form of bank loans, which are generally not viewed as 'securities' covered by US securities laws.[13] Bank loans may be restructured through several methods, including refinancings, debt-for-equity swaps, forbearances, waivers, standstills and amendments. However, because bank loans are often 'syndicated,' or offered by a group of lenders, the consent of a minimum number of lenders (typically a majority) is often required to undertake some of these restructuring options. As a result, the problem of holdouts is also present in the context of restructuring of syndicated loans. A detailed discussion of restructuring options for bank loans is contained in a separate chapter herein. 3.10

3.2.2 Cash repurchases of outstanding securities and tender offers

3.2.2.1 Offers that constitute a 'tender offer'

A company may undertake a cash repurchase of its outstanding securities to take advantage of the low market value of their securities or to reduce their interest and 3.11

[12] See Trust Indenture Act, ss 303–305.

[13] See *SEC v Texas Int'l Co* 498 F Supp 1231 (ND Ill 1980); *Banco Espanol de Credito v Security Pacific National Bank* 973 F2d 51, 55–6 (2nd Cir 1992).

dividend expense. Under certain circumstances, a cash repurchase of outstanding securities may constitute a 'tender offer' and may have to comply with sections 13(d), 13(e), 14(d), 14(e), or 14(f) of the Exchange Act.

3.12 The Exchange Act does not define what constitutes a 'tender offer'. Whether an offer to purchase is a tender offer is a question of fact. The oft-cited case on whether an offer constitutes a 'tender offer' is *Wellman v Dickinson*,[14] which sets out eight factors that characterize a tender offer (with no single factor being dispositive):

(1) active and widespread solicitation of holders;
(2) solicitation for a substantial percentage of outstanding shares;
(3) payment of a premium over market price for the shares;
(4) terms of the offer are firm rather than negotiable;
(5) the offer is contingent on the tender of a minimum number of shares;
(6) the offer is open for a limited time;
(7) there is pressure on holders to sell their shares; and
(8) public announcements accompany the offer.[15]

3.13 If an offer to purchase is determined to be a tender offer, it may have to comply with additional rules and regulations, the more notable of which include section 14(e), regulation 14E, and rules 13e-3 and 13e-4.

3.2.2.2 Section 14(e) and regulation 14E

3.14 Section 14(e) of the Exchange Act and regulation 14E (adopted under the Exchange Act) are applicable to all tender offers. Section 14(e) is a general anti-fraud provision that provides:

> It shall be unlawful for any person to make any untrue statement of a material fact or omit to state any material fact necessary in order to make the statements made, in the light of the circumstances under which they are made, not misleading, or to engage in any fraudulent, deceptive, or manipulative acts or practices, in connection with any tender offer or request or invitation for tenders, or any solicitation of security holders in opposition to or in favor of any such offer, request, or invitation. The Commission shall, for the purposes of this subsection, by rules and regulations define, and prescribe means reasonably designed to prevent, such acts and practices as are fraudulent, deceptive, or manipulative.

---

14 475 F Supp 783 (SDNY 1979).

15 *Wellman v Dickinson* 475 F Supp 783 at 823-4. See also Commission Guidance on Mini-Tender Offers and Limited Partnership Tender Offers, Release No. 34-43069 (24 July 2000) (recognizing courts' use of the *Wellman* eight-factor test in determining whether a particular acquisition programme constitutes a tender offer).

Regulation 14E sets out specific requirements. Pursuant to rule 14e-1 of regulation 14E: 3.15

(a) Tender offers must be held open for at least 20 business days from the commencement date.[16]
(b) If the offeror changes the percentage of the class of securities being sought, the consideration offered, or the dealer's soliciting fee, the offeror must hold the tender offer open for at least 10 business days from the date of notice of such change.[17]
(c) The offeror must promptly pay the consideration offered or return the securities deposited upon termination or withdrawal of the tender offer.
(d) If the offeror extends the length of the tender offer, the offeror must issue a notice by press release or other public announcement.

Rule 14e-1(b) is typically triggered when an offeror commences an exit consent 3.16 solicitation in connection with a tender or exchange offer and, in connection therewith, offers a fixed premium (a 'consent payment') above the tender offer consideration to security holders that tender their consent before a specified date (the 'consent date'). Even if an offeror does not seek consents, it may decide to offer a premium (an 'early tender premium') to security holders who tender before a specified date (the 'early tender date') to incentivize security holders to tender early and so that the offeror may gain greater visibility on the success of the tender offer. Because the total consideration offered is decreased upon the expiration of the consent date or early tender date, as applicable, under rule 14e-1(b) the offeror is required hold the tender offer open for at least 10 business days after the consent date or early tender date, as applicable. However, in limited circumstances the SEC has allowed tender offers to be held open for less than 10 days after the expiration of the consent date.[18]

---

[16] Issuers and holders should take into consideration that the time periods set out in r 14e-1 impose certain risks on both parties due to fluctuations in market interest rates. In limited circumstances involving investment grade securities, the US Securities and Exchange Commission (the 'SEC') has relaxed their enforcement of ss (a) and (b) of r 14e-1 in order to provide some relief from market fluctuations. See Salomon Brothers Inc, SEC No-Action Letter (12 March 1986). See also Merrill Lynch, Pierce, Fenner & Smith Inc, SEC No-Action Letter (16 July1993); Goldman, Sachs & Co, SEC No-Action Letter (3 December 1993). However, these exceptions are generally unavailable in a restructuring context.

[17] The SEC has also indicated that a tender offer should remain open for at least five business days after other material amendments to the terms of the tender offer. See Interpretative Release Relating to Tender Offer Rules, 34-24296 Release No. 24,296 (3 April 1987).

[18] See Playtex, Inc, SEC No-Action Letter (22 November 1988) (no-action recommendation where Playtex's tender offer for its non-convertible debt securities would expire less than 10 business days after expiration of the consent date). At the very least, the expiration of the consent date is a material amendment to the terms of the tender offer and therefore the tender offer must remain open for at least five business days after the expiration of the consent date.

3.17 The SEC has also taken no-action positions in several situations where the consideration paid in a tender offer is based upon a fixed formula, without requiring the tender offer to be held open for 10 business days after the last change in the dollar amount of consideration. Typical formula prices have been based on a spread to benchmark securities;[19] a share-for-share formula;[20] and, more recently, formulas based on share price for exchange offers for convertible bonds.[21]

3.18 Offerors may also conduct a single offering to retire more than one class of securities, which will likely lead to a less expensive and more efficient process than separate tender offers. When proceeding with a tender for multiple classes of securities, but not any and all of those securities, offerors may utilize a waterfall structure to prioritize the classes of securities that the offeror wishes to purchase or exchange. In a waterfall structure, the offeror will accept first priority securities before accepting lower priority securities, and will accept the lowest priority securities on a pro rata basis, if necessary.[22]

3.19 Finally, in contrast to rule 13e-4 (discussed below), practitioners should note that regulation 14E does not require the offeror to provide withdrawal rights to security holders.[23]

3.2.2.3 Rule 13e-4: Tender offers by issuers

3.20 Exchange Act Rule 13e-4 applies to tender offers by an issuer (or such issuer's affiliate) for any class of such issuer's equity securities. By its terms, rule 13e-4 only applies to an issuer who (a) has a class of equity security registered pursuant to

[19] See Salomon Brothers Inc, SEC No-Action Letter (1 October 1990) (no-action recommendation where the issuer will purchase its debt securities from holders 'at a price determined on each day during the tender period by reference to a fixed spread over the then current yield on a specified benchmark U.S. Treasury security'); Embassy Suites, Inc, SEC No-Action Letter (15 April 1992); The Times Mirror Company, SEC No-Action Letter (15 November 1994) (granting no-action relief for fixed-spread tender offer where the nominal price would be determined one day before the expiration of the tender offer).

[20] See Lazard Freres & Co., SEC No-Action Letter (11 August 1995) (no-action recommendation where exchange ratio would be based upon average trading prices over a specified period, provided that the equity securities to be received in the exchange offer are listed on a US securities exchange); TXU Corp, SEC No-Action Letter (13 September, 2004) (no-action recommendation where the consideration paid would be determined by reference to the volume weighted average trading price for TXU common stock over a period).

[21] See Citizens Republic Bancorp, Inc, SEC No-Action Letter (21 August 2009) (no-action position with respect to Citizens Republic Bancorp, Inc's issuance of common shares in exchange for its outstanding non-convertible subordinated notes and trust preferred securities, where the number of common shares to be exchanged for each target security would be determined on the expiration date in accordance with a formula that was fixed through the duration of the exchange offer).

[22] See, eg, Citizens Republic Bancorp, Inc, above n. 21.

[23] SEC Division of Corporation Finance, *Manual of Publicly Available Telephone Interpretations*, Tender Offer Rules and Schedules, s 13, <http://www.sec.gov/interps/telephone/cftelinterps_tender.pdf> (last visited 1 July 2010).

section 12 of the Exchange Act, (b) is required to file periodic reports pursuant to section 15(d) of the Exchange Act, or (c) is a closed-end investment company registered under the Investment Company Act 1940.[24] Rule 13e-4 contains the requirements set out in rule 14e-1(a)-(e), as well as several additional requirements:

(a) Tendered securities may be withdrawn at any time before expiration of the offer period.
(b) Tendered securities may withdrawn after 40 business days from the commencement of the offer if not yet accepted for payment.
(c) If the tender offer is for less than all the outstanding securities of a class and a greater number of securities were tendered than will be accepted, the issuer must generally accept the tendered shares on a pro rata basis.
(d) If the consideration offered is increased during the tender offer, all security holders (whether tendering before or after the increase) must be paid the amount of the increased consideration.
(e) The tender offer must be open to all security holders of the subject class of securities.
(f) For 10 business days after expiration of the tender offer, the issuer and its affiliates may not purchase any target or offered security, any security of the same class or series as the target or offered securities, or the right to purchase such securities.
(g) In contrast to tender offers that are subject to only regulation 14E, tender offers subject to rule 13e-4 must also comply with certain disclosure and filing requirements, as set out in rule 13e-4.[25]

Practitioners should be aware of rule 13e-3, which applies to 'going private' transactions. A going private transaction is generally a transaction (or series of transactions) that has either a reasonable likelihood or a purpose of, directly or indirectly, causing (a) the registration of the target securities to be terminated, along with the reporting obligations with respect to such class or (b) any class of equity securities to be delisted from a national securities exchange.[26] Generally, registration of the target securities may be terminated pursuant to rule 13e-3 if the security holders of record fall below 300 persons (or 500 persons if the entity's assets were not greater than $10 m on the last day of each of the most recent three fiscal years).[27] If by taking any of the actions in this chapter the issuer is deemed to be undertaking a going private transaction, the issuer will have to comply with the additional requirements listed in rule 13e-3. **3.21**

[24] Exchange Act r 13e-4.
[25] Ibid., r 13e-4.
[26] Ibid., r 13e-3(ii).
[27] Ibid., rr 13e-3, 12g-4, and 12h-6.

3.2.3 Registered, section 3(a)(9), and section 4(2) exchange offers

3.2.3.1 General

3.22 A company that is undertaking restructuring efforts may not have the cash necessary to purchase securities pursuant to a tender offer. An alternative is for the company to offer new debt or equity securities in exchange for its outstanding debt or equity securities. Under the Securities Act, an exchange of new securities for old securities is an 'offer' and 'sale' of securities.[28] Therefore, the exchange offer must either comply with the registration requirements of section 5 of the Securities Act or fall within an exemption to such requirements. Some commonly used exemptions are those listed under section 3(a)(9) and section 4(2) of the Securities Act, each discussed below.

3.2.3.2 Registered exchange offers

3.23 Registering new securities for an exchange offer can be time consuming and costly. Generally, an offering may not be commenced until a registration statement for the new securities is declared effective by the SEC. Under this standard commencement process, once an issuer files a registration statement covering the new securities, it typically must wait four to six weeks for the SEC to provide comments. If the comments are substantial, the offering may be further delayed as the issuer responds. After the registration statement is cleared by the SEC, the registered exchange offer may be launched and then must comply with the 20 business day offering period requirement. However, under limited circumstances, the SEC now allows issuers to launch an exchange offer concurrently with SEC review of the registration statement.[29] Under the early commencement process, an issuer may commence the exchange offer with a preliminary prospectus when the registration statement is filed, and the offering period will run during the SEC's period of review.[30] If an issuer chooses the early commencement option however, it must (a) provide withdrawal rights to the extent required under rule 13e-4 or regulation 14D and (b) should a material change occur in the information published, sent or given to security holders, the issuer must (i) disseminate information of such change to security holders and (ii) after such notice, must hold the offering period open with withdrawal rights for the applicable minimum period, as required by

[28] See *United States v Riedel* 126 F2d 81, 83 (7th Cir 1942) (a 'sale' also includes an exchange of securities); *United States v Wernes* 157 F2d 797, 799 (7th Cir 1946).

[29] Pursuant to Securities Act r 162, early commencement is not available for going-private transactions (as defined by Exchange Act r 13e-3) and roll-up transactions (as described by item 901 of reg S-K).

[30] Securities Act r 162. See also Commission Guidance and Revisions to the Cross Border Tender Offer, Exchange Offer, Rights Offerings, and Business Combination Rules and Beneficial Ownership Reporting Rules for Certain Foreign Institutions, Release No. 34-58597 (19 September 2008).

rule 13e-4(e)(3) or rules 14d-4(b) and (d).[31] Consummation of the offering may occur only following SEC approval of the registration statement and the satisfaction of applicable time period requirements.[32]

Although registration can be time consuming and costly, registering the new securities leads to several advantages. If the target securities are widely distributed, the issuer may need to engage professionals to solicit the exchange, which is prohibited if the issuer utilizes the section 3(a)(9) exemption. Registration may also be necessary to conduct a successful exchange offer if the securities are widely held by holders who are not qualified to purchase the securities under a section 4(2) private exchange. **3.24**

3.2.3.3 Section 3(a)(9) exchange offers

Section 3(a)(9) exempts from registration 'any security exchanged by the issuer with its existing security holders exclusively where no commission or other remuneration is paid or given directly or indirectly for soliciting such exchange' (except with respect to a security exchanged in a chapter 11 bankruptcy case).[33] Generally, section 3(a)(9) contains three requirements: **3.25**

(1) The issuer must be exchanging new securities for its own securities (the 'same issuer requirement').
(2) Except for the exchanged securities, the exchanging security holder must not provide any additional consideration in the exchange (the 'exclusively by exchange requirement').
(3) The issuer may not pay any consideration for solicitation of such exchange (the 'solicitation restriction').

No registration is required for section 3(a)(9) exchange offers, and therefore section 3(a)(9) exchange offers can be completed in a shorter time frame than registered exchange offers. The costs associated with section 3(a)(9) exchange offers are also relatively low, because no registration is required and issuers will not be offering cash consideration. However, one disadvantage is that the new securities may be subject to transfer restrictions that would not otherwise result from a registered exchange offer—generally, securities issued pursuant to a section 3(a)(9) exchange offer takes on the same character of the securities being exchanged.[34] **3.26**

[31] Securities Act, r 162.

[32] Registration of securities is also subject to each individual state's securities laws (known as 'blue sky laws').

[33] Securities Act, s 3(a)(9).

[34] See Clevepak Corp, SEC No-Action Letter (23 March 1984); SEC Division of Corporation Finance, *Manual of Publicly Available Telephone Interpretations*, Securities Act Sections, s 35, <http://www.sec.gov/interps/telephone/cftelinterps_securitesactsections.pdf> (last visited 1 July 2010).

3.27 **3.2.3.3.1 The same issuer requirement** Through a progression of no-action letters, the SEC has provided limited flexibility in terms of the same issuer requirement.[35] The SEC has allowed the identity of the new issuer to be different from that of the original issuer in limited circumstances, such as where the identities of the issuers differ due to a merger or acquisition,[36] dissolution of an entity,[37] or where the new issuer assumed joint and several liability for the obligations of the original issuer.[38]

3.28 In the context of restructurings, the principal flexibility that the SEC has afforded relates to guaranteed securities, where the SEC has allowed the issuance of securities by a parent issuer that has fully and unconditionally guaranteed all of its wholly-owned subsidiary's obligations with respect to the old securities issued by such subsidiary.[39] A guarantee is itself a security and the issuer would therefore be exchanging securities issued by one issuer for securities issued by multiple issuers. However, the economic reality is that investors view the exchange as an exchange of the parent guarantees for the new parent securities, and the SEC has declined enforcement in such situations.[40]

3.29 More recently, the SEC also allowed 'the issuance of a security (without any guarantee) in exchange for an outstanding security that is fully and unconditionally guaranteed by one or more of the issuer's 100 per cent-owned subsidiaries'.[41] The reasoning presented to the SEC was that investors view the parent issuer and the

---

[35] From a plain reading, the same issuer requirement appears to require the issuer offering new securities to be the same entity that offered the old securities.

[36] See, eg, Perpetual Sav Bank, Perpetual Fin Corp, SEC No-Action Letter (29 February 1988); Time Warner, Inc, SEC No-Action Letter (15 November 2000); BP Amoco plc, SEC No-Action Letter (27 March 2001).

[37] See, eg, Pan American World Airways, Inc, SEC No-Action Letter (30 June 1975).

[38] See, eg, Heritage Bancorp, SEC No-Action Letter (14 February 1973); Pan American World Airways, above n. 37; Pacwest Bancorp, SEC No-Action Letter (13 November 1979); Financial Corp of Santa Barbara, SEC No-Action Letter (22 June 1987); McKesson Corp, SEC No-Action Letter (10 August 1987); Perpetual Sav Bank, Perpetual Fin Corp, above n. 36; Exxon Mobil Corp, SEC No-Action Letter (28 June 2002). See also SEC Division of Corporation Finance, *Compliance and Disclosure Interpretations:* Securities Act Sections, Question 125.02 <http://www.sec.gov/divisions/corpfin/guidance/sasinterp.htm> (last visited 1 July 2010).

[39] See American Motors Corp, SEC No-Action Letter (8 July 1982); Daisy Systems Corp, SEC No-Action Letter (10 April 1989) (no-action position where parent holding company guaranteed obligations on securities of acquired company and exchanged parent-issued securities for acquired company's securities); FHC-CompCare, Inc, SEC No-Action Letter (12 October 1989); Echo Bay Mines Ltd, SEC No-Action Letter (18 May 1998) (no-action position where the parent company proposed to exchange its securities for outstanding securities of its wholly-owned subsidiary, whose outstanding securities were guaranteed by the parent); The Warnaco Group, Inc, SEC No-Action Letter (7 August 1998).

[40] See Echo Bay Mines Ltd, above n. 39; The Warnaco Group, Inc, above n. 39.

[41] See Section 3(a)(9) Upstream Guarantees, SEC No-Action Letter (13 January 2010). As defined in r 3-10 of reg S-X, a subsidiary is 100 per cent-owned if either all of the subsidiary's outstanding voting shares or the sum of all of the subsidiary's interests is owned, either directly or indirectly, by its parent company.

100 per cent-owned subsidiary as a single, indivisible business and the 'upstream guarantee' of the old securities simply served as a structural subordination device (similar to an exchange of senior notes for subordinated notes).[42]

3.2.3.3.2 The exclusively by exchange requirement The exclusively by exchange requirement requires an issuer to offer new securities in exchange for only the old securities, without any additional consideration from security holders. However, there are several situations, described in Securities Act Rules 149 and 150 and in no-action letters, where some flexibility has been added to the exclusively by exchange requirement. **3.30**

In a section 3(a)(9) exchange offer, it may be necessary for security holders to surrender additional rights in addition to the securities. For example, it is commonplace for the security holders to waive any accrued interest and dividends (effectively, a payment to the issues).[43] Rule 149 allows security holders to make such payments without loss of the section 3(a)(9) exemption.[44] In several no-action letters, the SEC has also allowed holders of securities to waive claims and causes of actions against the issuer of securities[45] and allowed the issuer to obtain the consent of holders of the securities to amend terms of the old securities.[46] **3.31**

The exclusively by exchange requirement does not prohibit payments *by the issuer* to the security holders. Securities Act Rule 150 confirms that an issuer may make payments 'directly or indirectly, to its security holders in connection with an exchange of securities for outstanding securities, when such payments are part of the terms of the offer of exchange'. Rule 150 permits issuers to make payments to security holders for, among other things, accrued dividends,[47] fractional shares,[48] and indirect payments through reduction of the conversion price on a convertible **3.32**

---

[42] Ibid.

[43] See, eg, Diversa-Graphics, Inc, SEC No-Action Letter (20 July 1972); Canrad Precision Industries, Inc, SEC No-Action Letter (27 September 1973); Four-Phase Systems, Inc, SEC No-Action Letter (10 December 1973); Geoscience Technology Services Corp, SEC No-Action Letter (8 February 1976); NJB Prime Investors, SEC No-Action Letter (4 July 1976); Shop Rite Foods, Inc, SEC No-Action Letter (14 October 1981); ECL Industries, Inc & Norlin Corp, SEC No-Action Letter (16 December 1985); The Royale Group Ltd, SEC No-Action Letter (4 November 1988); Seaman Furniture Co, Inc, SEC No-Action Letter (10 October 1989).

[44] Securities Act r 149 permits 'such payment in cash by the security holder as may be necessary to effect an equitable adjustment, in respect of dividends or interest paid or payable on the securities involved in the exchange, as between such security holder and other security holders of the same class accepting the offer of exchange'.

[45] See, eg, First Pennsylvania Mortgage Trust, SEC No-Action Letter (4 March 1977); Metagraphic Sys, SEC No-Action Letter (1 May 1975); Seaman Furniture Co, Inc, above n. 43.

[46] See, eg, Bayswater Realty & Capital Corp, SEC No-Action Letter (30 April 1982); Shop Rite Foods, above n. 43; Four-Phase Sys, above n. 43; Daitch Crystal Dairies, SEC No-Action Letter (13 November 1972). As discussed in section 3.2.1.2, above, consent solicitations may be used to deal the problem of holdouts in tender offers and exchange offers.

[47] See Steiner Am Corp, SEC No-Action Letter (4 May 1973).

[48] See WestMarc Communications, SEC No-Action Letter (20 November 1989).

security.[49] In contrast to rule 149, rule 150 does not limit the consideration that issuers may pay to security holders.[50]

3.33 3.2.3.3.3 **The solicitation restriction** The solicitation restriction prohibits an issuer from enlisting the services of a professional or other third party to specifically solicit exchanges. The solicitation restriction also extends to paying any of the issuer's employees specifically to solicit the exchange—generally, employees soliciting the exchange should have had significant duties before the date of the offer and should continue to perform their pre-existing duties throughout the exchange.[51]

3.34 Despite the foregoing prohibition, the SEC has recognized that an issuer undertaking an exchange offer may require assistance from certain professionals, including financial advisors, investment banks, and other third parties.[52] The SEC has allowed third parties to assist the issuer with two types of activities. First, the issuer's third-party professionals may assist the issuer with respect to the terms and mechanics of an exchange.[53] In such capacity, permissible activities have included financial analysis, participating in meetings and discussions between the issuer and banks, and setting out and discussing the issuer's proposals and counterproposals during such meetings.[54] Second, the issuer's third-party professionals may perform other administrative tasks for the issuer in connection with obtaining tenders (such as disseminating materials, acting as a financial intermediary, and maintaining records).[55] When performing administrative tasks and communicating with security holders, such professionals (a) may not make recommendations to security holders regarding the exchange offer,[56] (b) may answer substantive questions regarding the transaction by directing security holders to the appropriate portions of the offering materials,[57] and (c) may not engage in any activities with respect to security holders other than providing administrative assistance in obtaining tenders.[58]

---

[49] See *Browning Debenture Holders Committee v DASA Corp* 1975 US Dist LEXIS 12838 (SDNY 1975).

[50] See, eg, Systemedics, Inc, SEC No-Action Letter (19 February 1976); Rapid-Am Corp, SEC No-Action Letter (30 October 1981).

[51] See URS Corp, SEC No-Action Letter (8 May 1975); Chris-Craft Industries, Inc, SEC No-Action Letter (9 October 1972).

[52] See Seaman Furniture Co, Inc, above n. 43.

[53] See ibid.

[54] See ibid.

[55] See, eg, Dominion Mortgage & Realty Trust, SEC No-Action Letter (29 October 1975); Barnett Winston Investment Trust, SEC No-Action Letter (9 February 1978); Mortgage Investors of Washington, SEC No-Action Letter (8 October 1980).

[56] See Stokely-Van Camp, Inc, SEC No-Action Letter (29 April 1983).

[57] See Trans-Sterling, Inc, SEC No-Action Letter (16 June 1983).

[58] See Western Pacific Industries, SEC No-Action Letter (11 October 1976); Grolier Inc, SEC No-Action Letter (2 December 1977); Mortgage Investors of Washington, above n. 55; Stokely-Van Camp, Inc, above n. 56; Trans-Sterling, Inc, above n. 57.

To prevent any appearance of solicitation, if the issuer's financial advisor has rendered (or may render) a fairness opinion in connection with the exchange offer, that financial advisor should not have any contact with security holders or their representatives.[59] Also, to disincentivize any behaviour that could be construed as solicitation, advisory fees should be structured as fixed fees earned on the commencement date of the exchange offer, plus reasonable expenses.[60] **3.35**

3.2.3.4 Section 4(2) private exchanges

Another exemption to registration that an issuer can take advantage of is the private offering exemption under section 4(2) of the Securities Act. As with the section 3(a)(9) exemption, a section 4(2) private exchange potentially saves the issuer from the significant time and expense burdens that accompany the registration process. Section 4(2) exempts 'transactions by an issuer not involving any public offering'. Whether an offering qualifies for the section 4(2) exemption is a question of fact and ultimately depends on purchasers' need for the protections offered by registration.[61] In order to qualify for the exemption, the SEC has stated that: **3.36**

- purchasers must 'have enough knowledge and experience in finance and business matters to evaluate the risks and merits of the investment (the "sophisticated investor"), or be able to bear the investment's economic risk';
- purchasers must 'have access to the type of information normally provided in a prospectus';
- purchasers must 'agree not to resell or distribute the securities to the public'; and
- offerors 'may not use any form of public solicitation or general advertising in connection with the offering'.[62]

Securities Act Rule 506 provides a 'safe harbour' for section 4(2) private exchanges. Under rule 506, securities may be purchased by an unlimited number of accredited investors and up to 35 non-accredited purchasers; issuers have affirmative disclosure obligations if the securities may be purchased by non-accredited investors; and resale of the offered securities is restricted. **3.37**

[59] See Hamilton Bros Petroleum Corp, SEC No-Action Letter (14 August 1978); American Can Corp, SEC No-Action Letter (12 May 1980); National City Lines, SEC No-Action Letter (11 April 1985).

[60] Several no-action letters granting relief have specifically noted that the advisors' fees were not contingent upon the success of the s 3(a)(9) exchange offers. See Varco International, SEC No-Action Letter (24 March 1986); Calton, Inc and Subsidiaries, SEC No-Action Letter (30 September 1991).

[61] See *SEC v Ralston Purina Co* 346 US 119 (1953).

[62] SEC, *Q&A: Small Business and the SEC*, s VI.B, <http://www.sec.gov/info/smallbus/qasbsec.htm> (last visited 1 July 2010).

3.38 **3.2.3.4.1 Purchasers** Typically, section 4(2) private exchanges are limited to accredited investors (who are deemed sophisticated),[63] qualified institutional buyers (who are considered super-sophisticated investors),[64] and non-US persons under regulation S.[65] Whether any other purchaser is sophisticated is subject to a fact-based test that introduces undesirable elements of uncertainty, and therefore issuers often limit offers to accredited investors, qualified institutional buyers, and non-US persons under regulation S. Prior to the exchange offer, issuers may send each offeree an investor questionnaire to determine whether they fall into one of the three aforementioned groups.

3.39 **3.2.3.4.2 Solicitation** Offerors in section 4(2) private exchanges 'may not use any form of public solicitation or general advertising in connection with the offering'.[66] Even if all purchasers are sophisticated investors, general solicitations are still prohibited by section 4(2). General solicitations include mass mailings[67] and even mailings to certain targeted persons.[68] However, in contrast to the absolute prohibition on solicitation in section 3(a)(9) exchange offers, solicitation may be allowed in section 4(2) private exchanges where there is a pre-existing relationship between the issuer (or broker-dealer) and the offeree, which the SEC has indicated is an important factor weighing against a general solicitation.[69]

63 Under Securities Act r 501, 'accredited investors' generally includes banks, savings and loans associations, brokers and dealers, insurance companies, investment companies, the issuer's directors and executive officers, any person with net worth exceeding $1 m, any person with an individual income in excess of $200,000 in each of the two most recent years, any entity in which all of the equity owners are accredited investors, and certain other entities with a certain amount of assets.

64 Under Securities Act r 144A(a), qualified institutional buyers generally include 'entities, acting for its own account or the accounts of other qualified institutional buyers, that in the aggregate owns and invests on a discretionary basis at least $100 m in securities of issuers that are not affiliated with the entity'; banks, and savings and loan associations that, in addition to the foregoing requirement, have an audited net worth of $25 m; and registered dealers that 'in the aggregate owns and invests on a discretionary basis at least $10 million of securities of issuers that are not affiliated with the dealer'.

65 Reg S, promulgated under the Securities Act, is a 'safe harbour' from registration requirements for securities that will come to rest outside of the US. A discussion of reg S is outside the scope of this chapter, but practitioners should be aware of its potential availability.

66 SEC, *Q&A: Small Business and the SEC*, above n. 62.

67 See *Johnston v Bumba* 764 F Supp 1263 (ND Ill 1991) (mass mailing of 2,500 copies of offering memoranda is a general solicitation); In the Matter of Priority Access, Inc, Release No. 33-7904 (3 October 2001) (mass email sent in search of investors is a general solicitation); Use of Electronic Media for Delivery Purposes, Release No. 33-7233 (6 October 1995) (placing of offering materials on the internet is a general solicitation). However, posting information on a password-protected webpage that will only be available to prequalified investors is not deemed a general solicitation. See IPOnet, SEC No-Action Letter (26 July 1996); Angel Capital Electronic Network, SEC No-Action Letter (25 October 1996).

68 See, eg, *Re Kenman Corp, SEC* [1984-1985 Transfer Binder] Fed Sec L Rep (CCH) ¶83,767 (19 April 1985) (general solicitation where broker–dealer sent materials to persons who had participated in prior offerings, certain executive officers, physicians, managerial engineers, and presidents of certain companies).

69 See Mineral Lands Research & Marketing Corp, SEC No-Action letter (4 December 1985).

The pre-existing relationship requirement may be satisfied through the use of an investor questionnaire (which may also used to determine sophistication), sent before the commencement of the section 4(2) private exchange. Once a potential investor's questionnaire has been returned with satisfactory answers, the issuer (or broker–dealer) may solicit such investor upon commencement of the section 4(2) private exchange.[70]

3.2.3.4.3 **Restrictions on resale** Registered securities are not bound by the section 3(a)(9) and section 4(2) restrictions on resale. Securities issued pursuant to the section 3(a)(9) exemption take on the same character as the exchanged security.[71] In contrast, securities issued pursuant to a section 4(2) private exchange are restricted securities that cannot be sold to the public absent registration.[72] As such, issuers should be concerned about resales of such securities, which may retroactively void the original exemption.[73] Purchasers must not purchase the securities with the intent of reselling them to the public, which would defeat the purpose underlying the section 4(2) exemption. Issuers often take three actions to protect themselves against resale. First, issuers should obtain signed statements of investment intent from purchasers, which state that the purchasers are purchasing the securities for investment, and not resale, purposes. Second, restricted securities should contain a conspicuous legend stating that the securities are restricted. Finally, issuers should issue stop-transfer instructions to the transfer agent so that they will not process any transfers without the issuer's prior consent.[74] **3.40**

3.2.3.4.4 **Additional considerations** In contrast to section 3(a)(9) exchange offers, potential issues arise when section 4(2) private exchanges are used in connection with prepackaged bankruptcies. The section 4(2) exemption permits solicitation of only 'sophisticated investors' and prohibits public solicitation, while rule 3018(b) of the U.S Federal Rules of Bankruptcy Procedure (the 'Bankruptcy Rules') requires solicitation of 'substantially all' creditors and equity holders of the same class (regardless of their sophistication).[75] Because of these **3.41**

[70] See EF Hutton, SEC No-Action Letter (3 December 1985); Bateman Eichler, Hill Richards, Inc, SEC No-Action Letter (3 December 1985); Royce Exchange Fund (Quest Advisory Corp), SEC No-Action Letter (28 August 1996).

[71] SEC Division of Corporation Finance, *Manual of Publicly Available Telephone Interpretations*, Securities Act Section, s 35, above n. 34.

[72] See Investment Company Act 1940 Release No. 5847 (21 October 1969).

[73] See, eg, *United States v Hill* 298 F Supp 1221 (D Conn 1969).

[74] Securities Act r 144 provides a safe harbour for the public resale of restricted securities and control securities, and allows such resale if certain requirements are met. One requirement is that the securities must be held for a specified length of time before resale is permissible. Recent amendments to this rule have shortened the holding period, as well as codified SEC staff positions, which have permitted tacking of the holding period if the securities sold were acquired from the issuer solely in exchange for other securities of the same issuer. Under certain circumstances, the securities may longer be restricted after a private placement exchange offer.

[75] See Fed R Banker P 3018(b); section 3.2.2.3, below.

competing concerns, it may be difficult to use a section 4(2) private exchange in connection with a prepackaged bankruptcy, except in limited circumstances (for example, if all security holders and creditors were accredited investors).

3.2.3.5 Integration with other issuances

3.42 Issuers should consider whether their section 3(a)(9) or section 4(2) offerings are at risk of integration with another exempt offering by the issuer. An integration of offerings can cause exemptions to be unavailable if the integrated offering does not comply with the requirements of each exemption being used. Generally, two or more exempt offerings are likely to be integrated if:

- the offerings are part of a single plan of financing;
- the offerings were made for the same general purpose;
- the same class of securities was offered;
- the offerings were conducted at or about the same time; and
- the same type of consideration was offered.[76]

3.2.4 **Amendments of outstanding debt securities**

3.43 A company with outstanding debt securities may wish to amend the terms of those securities in order to remove restrictive covenants, which may currently prohibit incurrence of debt, sales of assets or other restructuring transactions. A company's ability to amend its debt securities will be governed mainly by the terms of the securities (typically, a majority or two-thirds vote is required to amend restrictive covenants) and possibly the Trust Indenture Act (which prohibits the amendment of provisions governing payment of principal and interest, maturity dates, and a security holder's ability to institute suit for enforcement of the foregoing, without the consent of each security holder affected).[77]

3.44 As previously discussed, a company can solicit exit consents from security holders in an exchange offer, including one that is also a tender offer, to amend the terms

[76] See Securities Act, rr 147 and 502(a); Securities Act Release Nos 4552 and 4434. Different rules may apply to the integration of a public offering with an exempt offering. See, eg, SEC Division of Corporation Finance, *Compliance and Disclosure Interpretations:* Securities Act Sections, Question 139.25 <http://www.sec.gov/divisions/corpfin/guidance/sasinterp.htm> (last visited 1 July 2010).

[77] See Trust Indenture Act, s 316(b). Companies may also wish to amend their preferred stock, if any. Generally, the ability to amend preferred stock and the duties owed to preferred stockholders are contractual in nature. See *Jedwab v MGM Grand Hotels, Inc* 509 A2d 584 (Del Ch 1986). However, directors may owe fiduciary duties to preferred stockholders where the right at issue 'is not to a preference as against the common stock but rather a right shared equally with the common'. *Jedwab v MGM Grand Hotels, Inc* 509 A2d at 594. See also *Re Trados Inc S'holder Litig* 2009 Del Ch LEXIS 128 (Del Ch 24 July 2009). Thus, in amending the terms of preferred stock, directors may need to take into consideration their fiduciary duties to the preferred stockholders.

of the target securities.[78] Exit consents may serve as a disincentive to holdouts because the target securities may be stripped of protective covenants once the requisite amount of exit consents have been received. However, an offer and consent solicitation usually requires a high percentage (85–95 per cent) of holders to tender their securities, which may not be obtainable. A viable alternative or second step may be a prearranged or prepackaged plan of reorganization, which requires the consent of only one-half of creditors actually voting holding at least two-thirds the amount of claims in order for a class of creditors to accept the plan.[79]

3.2.5 Prepackaged plans of reorganization

3.2.5.1 General

The US Bankruptcy Code (the 'Bankruptcy Code')[80] does not define 'prepackaged' or 'prepack' bankruptcies. Rather, these are terms of art used to describe a plan of reorganization that will be confirmed by a bankruptcy court as part of a bankruptcy case, but where the negotiation and solicitation of votes to accept the plan are conducted in anticipation of, but before, the commencement of the chapter 11 case. If the prepetition solicitation results in sufficient acceptances to confirm the plan, then the company will commence a chapter 11 bankruptcy case and seek prompt confirmation of the plan. Unlike an exchange offer or other out-of-court restructuring, a confirmed plan binds all holders of claims and interests. Additionally, the Bankruptcy Code provides certain procedural and substantive advantages, such as the protection of the automatic stay, the ability to reject burdensome leases and contracts (and in some cases to cap the liability associated with rejection), and a single forum to address disputes. In sum, a prepackaged bankruptcy allows a company to implement a more comprehensive restructuring of its capital structure and operations than an out-of-court restructuring. **3.45**

3.2.5.2 Best candidate for a prepackaged plan

Although a prepack can be a highly effective means of restructuring a company, not all distressed companies are viable candidates for a prepack. A prepack is most likely to succeed where there is a need to deleverage the capital structure but where **3.46**

---

78 See section 3.2.1.2, above. Issuers should be careful not to take any actions that would effectively violate provisions of the Trust Indenture Act. See *Federated Strategic Income Fund v Mechala Group Jam Ltd* 1999 US Dist LEXIS 16996 (SDNY 1 November 1999) (finding a violation of the Trust Indenture Act where the elimination of guarantors and simultaneous disposition of asset materially impaired a holder's right to sue). Additionally, an amendment of key terms of a security may be deemed an offer and sale of new securities requiring compliance with securities laws pertaining to new issuances.

79 See section 3.2.6.2.5, below, for a more detailed discussion.

80 11 USC ss 101–1532.

the underlying business is relatively solid. In other words, a prepack is a better tool to implement a balance sheet restructuring than it is to implement an operational restructuring. The reason for this is that securities laws and the solicitation requirements of the Bankruptcy Code make it legally and practically very difficult to solicit the votes of trade creditors or holders of contingent, unliquidated or disputed claims before the commencement of a bankruptcy case. To avoid the need to solicit the votes of the holders of such claims, prepacks typically leave such claims unimpaired. Therefore, if the company's problems are more complex than a balance sheet deleveraging or require a substantial operational restructuring, a prepack may not be a practical alternative.

3.2.6 Bankruptcy Code provisions and rules relating to prepackaged chapter 11 plans

3.2.6.1 General

3.47 The Bankruptcy Code expressly permits the prepetition solicitation of votes to accept a plan.[81] In order for the bankruptcy court to confirm the plan, however, the solicitation must have been in compliance with any applicable non-bankruptcy law, including securities law, the Bankruptcy Code, and the Bankruptcy Rules, and the plan must satisfy the requirements for confirmation set out in the Bankruptcy Code. In addition to the Bankruptcy Code and the Bankruptcy Rules, the debtor must comply with any local rules of the bankruptcy court with jurisdiction over its case. Of particular note in this regard, the US Bankruptcy Court for the Southern District of New York has adopted specific guidelines for prepackaged bankruptcy cases.[82] The SDNY Prepack Guidelines are intended to provide 'bankruptcy practitioners with help in dealing with practical matters which either are not addressed at all by statute or rules or are addressed indirectly in a piecemeal fashion by statutes, general rules, and/or local rules' that did not contemplate prepacks.[83] Notably, the SDNY Prepack Guidelines are 'advisory only', and the court retains the power to depart from them.[84] Given the strong influence of the US Bankruptcy Court for the Southern District of New York, the SDNY Prepack Guidelines are persuasive authority for courts throughout the

[81] 11 USC s 1126(b).

[82] Amended Procedural Guidelines for Prepackaged Chapter 11 Cases in the United States Bankruptcy Court for the Southern District of New York, General Order No. M-387 s II (Bankr SDNY 24 November 2009) (hereinafter 'SDNY Prepack Guidelines') (amending Procedural Guidelines for Prepackaged Chapter 11 Cases in the United States Bankruptcy Court for the Southern District of New York, General Order No. M-203 (Bankr SDNY 24 February 1999)).

[83] Ibid., s I.

[84] Ibid.

country, and a practitioner would be advised to be versed in the Guidelines even if the bankruptcy case is going to be filed in a different jurisdiction.[85]

3.2.6.2 Prepetition disclosure and solicitation

3.2.6.2.1 Section 1126(b)(1)—Application of non-bankruptcy law disclosure standards Section 1126(b)(1) of the Bankruptcy Code authorizes the prepetition solicitation of votes to accept a plan. Section 1126(b) provides that plan acceptances received prepetition are valid if the solicitation was in compliance with any applicable non-bankruptcy law, rule or regulation governing the adequacy of disclosure (eg, federal and state securities laws). Therefore, if the plan provides for the issuance of new securities, the securities offered must be registered with the SEC, unless an exemption applies. As a practical matter, if securities are going to be issued under the plan, the delay and costs associated with registration often preclude the use of a prepack, which is usually only pursued if a securities law exemption is available. The most common registration exemption that is relied upon is section 3(a)(9) of the Securities Act, but, in a fewer instances, debtors have also relied on the exemption provided by section 4(2) of the Securities Act.[86] **3.48**

Compliance with section 1126(b) is a condition to confirmation, but it does not automatically validate a prepetition solicitation conducted in accordance with applicable non-bankruptcy law. Section 1126 does not eliminate the need to distribute the plan to substantially all similarly situated creditors entitled to vote on the plan or to provide such parties with a reasonable amount of time to vote, even if the company was otherwise in compliance with applicable non-bankruptcy law.[87] Section 1126 also does not eliminate the requirement that the company solicit votes from the beneficial, as opposed to the record, holders.[88] **3.49**

Furthermore, reliance solely on the disclosure required under applicable non-bankruptcy law is problematic because of the uncertainty inherent in subsequent bankruptcy court review.[89] Even with respect to solicitations commenced in **3.50**

[85] The United States Bankruptcy Court for the Southern District of Indiana adopted procedures broadly similar to the predecessor version of the SDNY Prepack Guidelines, while some other courts have adopted one or more prepack-specific provisions in their local rules. See, eg, Procedures for Prepackaged Chapter 11 Cases, General Order No. 03-11 (Bankr SD Ind 18 September 2003).

[86] See, eg Disclosure Statement for the Debtors' Prepackaged Joint Plan of Reorganization Pursuant to Chapter 11 of the Bankruptcy Code, dated 25 April 2009 at 69-70, *Re Source Interlink Companies, Inc et al* No. 09-11424 (Bankr D Del 27 April 2009) (discussing debtor's reliance on s 4(2) of the Securities Act for prepetition solicitation).

[87] Fed R Bankr P 3018(b).

[88] See *Re Southland Corp* 124 BR 211, 223–5 (Bankr ND Tex 1991); See also *Re Pioneer Fin Corp* 246 BR 626, 633 (Bankr D Nev 2000).

[89] See *Re Southland Corp* 124 BR at 225–6 (discussing uncertainty regarding the determination of the adequacy of disclosure under applicable non-bankruptcy law).

compliance with federal securities law, the SEC does not approve the adequacy of the disclosure set out in the solicitation documents.[90] Therefore, there remains an opportunity for a party in interest to object to the adequacy of the disclosure statement. Accordingly, a practitioner should draft the disclosure statement so that it complies with the standards that would be applied in a traditional chapter 11 case, in addition to what is required under applicable non-bankruptcy law.

3.51 **3.2.6.2.2 Section 1126(b)(2)—Application of Bankruptcy Code's 'adequate information' standard** If there is not controlling applicable non-bankruptcy law, section 1126(b)(2) permits prepetition votes to be used in seeking confirmation if 'adequate information' was disclosed before solicitation. Bankruptcy Code section 1125(a)(1) defines 'adequate information' as:

> information of a kind, and in sufficient detail, as far as is reasonably practicable in light of the nature and history of the debtor and the condition of the debtor's books and records, including a discussion of the potential material Federal tax consequences of the plan to the debtor, any successor to the debtor, and a hypothetical investor typical of the holders of claims or interests in the case, that would enable such a hypothetical investor of the relevant class to make an informed judgment about the plan, but adequate information need not include such information about any other possible or proposed plan and in determining whether a disclosure statement provides adequate information, the court shall consider the complexity of the case, the benefit of additional information to creditors and other parties in interest, and the cost of providing additional information. . . .[91]

3.52 The adequate information standard is 'flexible' and determined on a 'case-by-case' basis.[92] Although a disclosure statement is analogous to a prospectus or a proxy statement, strict compliance with the security law disclosure rules is not required. The results-oriented nature of the 'adequate information' standard has also led courts, in appropriate cases, to require a disclosure statement to include information not customarily included in a prospectus. Generally, a disclosure statement describes the following: (a) the events leading to the bankruptcy filing; (b) the

[90] See Securities Act r 408; Exchange Act, r 12b-20; *TSC Indus, Inc v Northway, Inc* 426 US 438, 444 (1976) (material information must be disclosed in proxy statement); *Kronfeld v Trans World Airlines, Inc* 832 F2d 726, 732 (2nd Cir 1987) (material information must be disclosed in prospectus).

[91] 11 USC s 1125(a)(1). While the 'adequate information' standard does not explicitly require truthfulness, truthfulness is an aspect of the adequacy of the disclosures: Marvin E. Jacob and Sharon Youdelman (eds) *Reorganizing Failing Businesses: A Comprehensive Review and Analysis of Financial Restructuring and Business Reorganization* (American Bar Association, 2006) 12-30, n. 97.

[92] *Re Ionosphere Clubs, Inc* 179 BR 24, 29 (SDNY 1995) (whether disclosure statement contains adequate information is determined on a case-by-case basis). see also HR Rep No. 95-595, at 226–27 (1977), reprinted in 1978 USCCAN 6179–80. The Bankruptcy Abuse Prevention and Consumer Protection Act of 2005, Pub L No. 109-8, 119 Stat 23 (codified as amended in scattered sections of 11 USC) amended s 1125(a)(1) to require a court determining the adequacy of a disclosure statement to consider the complexity of the case, the benefit of additional information and the cost of providing such additional information.

debtor's available assets and their value; (c) the debtor's present condition and major events in its chapter 11 case; (d) a liquidation analysis of what creditors would receive if the debtor were liquidated under chapter 7; (e) the debtor's future management, including the compensation of any insider of the debtor; (f) a summary of the proposed plan; (g) the debtor's administrative expenses in chapter 11; (h) the claims against the debtor's estate; (i) financial information and projections relevant to creditors' decision to accept or reject the plan; and (j) the accounting and valuation methods used to produce the financial information in the disclosure statement.[93]

This list is a guideline only. In some cases, one or more of these factors may not be relevant to providing 'adequate information'. Similarly, in some cases, additional disclosure may be required. Notably, Bankruptcy Code section 1125(a)(1) explicitly provides that 'adequate information need not include. . . information about any other possible. . . plan'.[94] In other words, a debtor does not need to disclose the existence of potential alternatives to the plan being proposed by the debtor. **3.53**

3.2.6.2.3 **Bankruptcy Rule 3018(b)** Bankruptcy Rule 3018(b) implements Bankruptcy Code section 1126(b). Bankruptcy Rule 3018(b) provides that prepetition votes will not be counted if (a) the plan was not transmitted to substantially all creditors and equity security holders of the same class, (b) an unreasonably short time was allowed for the acceptance or rejection of the plan, or (c) the solicitation did not comply with Bankruptcy Code section 1126(b). Bankruptcy Rule 3018(b) does not just create additional requirements, but, in some cases, can create a tension with the securities laws that must be carefully analysed on a case-by-case basis. For example, as set out above, to qualify for a section 4(2) exemption, the exchange must be limited to 'sophisticated investors'.[95] On the other hand, to satisfy Bankruptcy Rule 3018(b), the plan must be transmitted to 'substantially all' creditors and equity holders of the same class regardless of their investment prowess or financial wherewithal. Therefore, use of the section 4(2) exemption **3.54**

---

[93] See, eg, *Re Scioto Valley Mortgage Co* 88 BR 168, 170–71 (Bankr SD Ohio 1988) (citing cases); *Re Metrocraft Publ'g Servs, Inc* 39 BR 567, 568 (Bankr ND Ga 1984) (same).

[94] See, eg, *Re Aspen Limousine Serv, Inc* 193 BR 325, 334 (D Colo 1996) ('The purpose of a disclosure statement is . . . to assist the creditors in evaluating the plan on its face, rather than to promote a comparison among various proposed plans.') (citations omitted); *Kirk v Texaco, Inc* 82 BR 678, 684 (SDNY 1988) (debtor's equityholders could not successfully challenge adequacy of disclosure statement 'successfully merely by citing its failure to discuss some other possible plan') (citation omitted); *Re Brandon Mill Farms, Ltd* 37 BR 190, 192 (Bankr ND Ga 1984) ('disclosure statement is intended to assist the creditors in evaluating the plan on its face rather than to promote a comparison among various proposed plans'). Notably, the 'adequate information' standard does not require 'speculat[ion] as to future uncertainties, such as the consequences of the various possible outcomes of pending litigation'. *Re CDECO Maritime Constr Inc* 101 BR 499, 501 (Bankr ND Ohio 1989) (citation omitted).

[95] SEC, *Q&A: Small Business and the SEC*, above n. 62.

could be foreclosed in a prepack for failure to satisfy Rule 3018(b) if the security was held by enough non-sophisticated investors such that the plan could not be transmitted for 'substantially all' creditors of the same class, even if the amount of securities held by sophisticated investors would be sufficient for a successful out-of-court exchange.

3.55 **3.2.6.2.4 Length of the solicitation period** Other than Bankruptcy Rule 3018(b)'s prohibition against providing an 'unreasonably short' period to vote on a plan, the Bankruptcy Code and the Bankruptcy Rules do not establish a specific minimum period for soliciting votes on a plan. It is common for a debtor to provide a 25-day voting period,[96] but several cases have successfully confirmed plans utilizing much shorter solicitation periods.[97] The SDNY Prepack Guidelines provides that '[u]nder ordinary circumstances' a voting period (measured from the commencement of mailing) of: (a) 14 days for securities not traded on an exchange, (b) 21 days for securities traded on an exchange, and (c) 21 days for other claims and interests.[98] Ultimately reasonableness is judged on a case-by-case basis. The practitioner should analyse the facts of the case in setting the solicitation period. A complex solicitation that requires that solicitation materials work their way through several levels of intermediaries, or of securities that are widely held by foreign investors, may dictate a longer period. Conversely, a short solicitation period may be acceptable if the debtor is only soliciting from a small number of easily identified parties and there are business exigencies that dictate a short solicitation period.

3.56 **3.2.6.2.5 Counting votes** Bankruptcy Code section 1126(c) provides that a class of claims accepts a plan if 'creditors... that hold at least two-thirds in amount and more than one-half in number of the allowed claims' actually voting in such class vote to accept the plan.[99] This bankruptcy voting requirement differs from typical exchange offers (or debt instrument waivers or amendments) in several important ways. First, unlike typical corporate voting that requires that a

---

[96] The practice of providing a 25-day voting period can be traced to some practitioners' view that Fed R Bankr P 2002(b)(2), which set out a 25-day period to object to confirmation of the plan, implicitly prescribed a minimum voting period. Fed R Bankr P 2002(b)(2) was recently amended to provide a 28-day period to object to plan confirmation.

[97] See, eg, Interim Order Approving Disclosure Statement and Confirming Chapter 11 Plan of Reorganization, *Re Blue Bird Body Co* No. 06-50026 (Bankr D Nev 27 January 2006) (approving two-day solicitation period); Order Pursuant to 11 USC § 1125, 1126(b), 1129(a) and (b) and Fed R Bank P 3016, 3017, 3018 and 3020 Approving Disclosure Statement and Confirming Chapter 11 Plan, *Re Davis Petroleum Corp* No. 06-20152 (Bankr SD Tex 10 March 2006) (approving four-day solicitation period); Order Approving Debtors' Disclosure Statement and Solicitation Procedures, *Re Harvest Foods, Inc* No. 94-1198 (Bankr D Del 29 Deember 1994) (approving 13-day solicitation period).

[98] SDNY Prepack Guidelines, above n. 82, s VII.A.

[99] 11 USC s 1126(c).

threshold be satisfied based on the outstanding amount of the debt, plan acceptance is determined by considering only votes actually cast. Second, section 1126(c) contains a numerosity requirement (more than one-half in number) unique to bankruptcy. In determining if the numerosity requirement has been met, beneficial holders, not record holders, are the metric.[100] Furthermore, the numerosity requirement is tied to claims not creditors. There is case law holding that a creditor who has acquired multiple claims may vote each such claim, and each claim is counted separately for purposes of determining if the numerosity threshold has been met.[101] However, these cases deal with claims arising from unrelated transactions and not multiple bonds or participation in bank debt.

3.2.6.3 Case commencement and first day motions

In addition to the types of first day motions filed in a traditional chapter 11 case, a debtor may also seek relief that is unique to prepacks. Among the procedural relief that would be sought are orders to (a) set a joint confirmation and disclosure statement hearing; (b) waive certain reporting requirements of the debtor, such as the need to file schedules of assets and liabilities and statements of financial affairs; and (c) direct the US Trustee not to convene a meeting of creditors. It is also common for a debtor in a prepack case to seek authority to pay all unimpaired creditors in the ordinary course of business.[102] The foregoing types of relief are contemplated by the SDNY Prepack Guidelines, and routinely granted in prepackaged bankruptcy cases. **3.57**

3.2.6.4 Official committees in prepackaged cases

Bankruptcy Code section 1102(a) provides that, unless the bankruptcy court orders otherwise, the US Trustee shall appoint a committee of unsecured creditors to represent the interest of unsecured creditors. Prepacks typically seek to solicit holders of bank or bond debt and leave general unsecured creditors unimpaired.[103] Therefore, unsecured creditors do not need special protection as their claims are either unimpaired or their class of claims has already been solicited and the debtor has obtained sufficient votes to confirm the plan. Therefore, as the SDNY Prepack **3.58**

[100] Eg, *Re Pioneer Fin Corp* 246 BR at 635 (holding that 'beneficial holders of bonds, not merely the record holders, must receive the disclosure statement, plan and ballot' for solicitation to be proper); *Re Southland Corp* 124 BR at 227 (denying plan confirmation where only record holders were solicited).

[101] See, eg, *Re Concord Square Apartments of Wood County, Ltd* 174 BR 71, 74 (Bankr SD Ohio 1994).

[102] See, eg, Order Under USC §§ 105, 363, 1107, and 1108 and Fed R Bankr P 6003 Authorizing Payment of General Unsecured Claims in the Ordinary Course of Business, *Re Mrs Fields' Original Cookies, Inc* No. 08-11953 (Bankr D Del 26 August 2008). See also SDNY Prepack Guidelines, above n. 82, s VI.C.16 (discussing typical first day motions in a prepack).

[103] See SDNY Prepack Guidelines, above n. 82, s VIII.C.

Guidelines recognize, an unsecured creditors' committee will typically not be appointed in prepackaged cases.[104]

3.2.6.5 Special issues in prepacks

3.59 **3.2.6.5.1 Solicitation fees in connection with exchange offers** Prepacks (particularly for large companies) often involve the restructuring of publicly held debt. To solicit acceptances of a plan, the debtor must necessarily communicate with its debtholders and encourage them to vote in favour of the plan. Although the securities laws permit issuers to pay certain solicitation fees to securities brokers and dealers in certain out-of-court transactions,[105] no similar authority permits the payment of solicitation fees in connection with a plan of reorganization. Indeed, a strong concern with respect to conflict of loyalty between securities brokers and dealers and their customers exists, even if the brokers and dealers simply encourage holders to vote—without advocating which way those votes are cast.[106] Accordingly, debtors should be cautious in the payment of any fees that may be viewed as impermissible solicitation fees.[107]

3.60 To address this problem, debtors have been guided by the 'no paid solicitation' requirement of section 3(a)(9) of the Securities Act. Specifically, the section 3(a)(9) exemption to registration requires, among other things, that 'no commission or other remuneration is paid or given directly or indirectly for soliciting such exchange'.[108] Despite this broad prohibition, the SEC has recognized the benefit of advisors to assist with an exchange solicitation[109] and there exists a body of no action letters that provides guidance on appropriate fee arrangements and the parameters of acceptable and impermissible activities.[110] It is, therefore, common for a debtor to retain financial advisors under customary section 3(a)(9) fee arrangements to assist in the prepetition solicitation of votes to accept a plan, but

104 See ibid.

105 *Steadman v SEC* 603 F2d 1126, 1136 (5th Cir 1979), affd, 450 US 91 (1981) ('In accordance with the custom in the industry, the offerors paid tender solicitation fees to brokers who successfully solicited their clients to tender').

106 See *Re Southland Corp* 124 BR at 220-1 (holding solicitation fees are improper).

107 Ibid.

108 15 USC s 77c(a)(9).

109 See, eg, Chris-Craft Industries, Inc, above n. 51 (payment for ministerial assistance is not 'for soliciting the exchange but merely to facilitate the publication of the Exchange Offer to [security holders] to whom it is addressed and to make sure that they will not through inadvertence lose the opportunity to accept').

110 See, eg, Stokely-Van Camp, Inc, above n. 56 (financial advisor may not convey management's views or recommendations on s 3(a)(9) exchange offer, even if those views or recommendations are contained in exchange materials); National City Lines, above n. 59 (when issuer's financial advisor has rendered or may render fairness opinion in connection with s 3(a)(9) exchange offer, that financial advisor should not have any contact with any holder of target securities or any advisor to or other representative of any such holder); American Can Corp, above n. 59 (same).

not to otherwise pay fees or commissions to any other broker, dealer or other party.[111]

3.2.6.5.2 **Independence of voting decision; integrity of voting process** When an exchange offer and a prepack are solicited together, the typical goal is to restructure through the exchange offer and only file the prepack if the exchange offer fails to receive enough votes. In some early prepacks, the securities holders tendering in to the exchange were presumed to accept the prepack as well.[112] Although the court confirmed the prepackaged plan in several such instances, the better practice is to separate the two decisions: (a) whether to tender into the exchange offer and (b) whether to accept/reject the prepack. **3.61**

3.2.6.5.3 **Section 1145 exemption** Plans of reorganization often include the issuance of new securities in consideration of the obligations being discharged under the plan. Generally, section 5 of the Securities Act requires that any security offered or sold be registered with the SEC, unless an exemption applies.[113] Bankruptcy Code section 1145 provides an exemption from the registration requirements of the Securities Act for the offer or sale by a debtor (including certain of its affiliates and successors) of its securities under a plan in exchange for a claim or equity interest or principally in such an exchange and partly for cash or property. In a traditional bankruptcy, where the solicitation occurs after the commencement of the bankruptcy case, Bankruptcy Code section 1145(a) clearly provides a registration exemption because both the offer and sale are under a plan and relate to securities of the debtor. The SEC, however, has taken the position that section 1145 does not provide an exemption for prepetition solicitation.[114] The SEC's argument is that the company is not a debtor at the time that the securities are offered, so technically the securities offered are not 'securities of the debtor' at the time of the offer, even though they will be 'securities of the debtor' by the time they are issued.[115] Although the SEC's position on this issue seems overly technical, a plan that offers securities should only be pursued as a prepack if another securities law exemption is available. **3.62**

3.2.6.5.4 **Section 1125(e) safe harbour** Bankruptcy Code section 1125(e) creates a limited safe harbour from federal and state liability for the good faith solicitation of acceptance or rejection of a plan or participation in any offer, issuance, **3.63**

[111] See, eg, Notice of Filing of Amended Offering Memorandum, Disclosure Statement and Solicitation of Acceptances of a Prepackaged Plan of Reorganization, dated 16 October 2009 (as supplemented) at 163, *Re CIT Group Inc* No. 09-16565 (Bankr SDNY 2 November 2009).

[112] See, eg, *Re Republic Health Corp* No. 389-38127 (Bankr ND Tex 17 April 1990).

[113] 15 USC s 77e.

[114] Jonathan P. Friedland, *Strategic Alternatives for Distressed Businesses* (West 2010) § 5.23.

[115] Even if the s 1145 exemption applied to the offer and sale of the securities under a prepack, an exchange offer accompanying the prepack would need to be registered unless an exemption was available.

sale or purchase of securities.[116] As with section 1145, however, it is not clear whether the safe harbour is available to prepetition solicitations of votes on prepackaged chapter 11 plans. Given this uncertainty, a prudent course is to include reference to section 1125(e) in the confirmation order and to specifically extend the safe harbour provision to every person involved in the good faith solicitation of votes and the offer, issuance, sale, and purchase of securities under the prepackaged plan. Plans extending the section 1125(e) protection to parties who engaged in pre-filing solicitation have been confirmed by courts,[117] but the issue of the application of section 1125(e) to pre-filing solicitation has not been contested.

3.64 3.2.6.5.5 **Impairment of claims** Under section 1126(f), a class of claims or interests that is not impaired under a plan is conclusively deemed to accept the plan and solicitation of votes on the plan is not required.[118] The ability to designate a class as unimpaired, therefore, has great strategic significance, especially in the prepack context. Under section 1124, a class is 'unimpaired' if the plan 'leaves unaltered the legal, equitable, and contractual rights to which such claim or interest entitles the holder of such claim or interest' or if the plan 'reinstates' the claim by curing any default and compensating the holders of any damages.[119] Traditionally, understanding the nuances of impairment was primarily important to avoid inadvertently creating an impaired class which could delay confirmation by requiring solicitation of such class. Recently, however, unimpairment has been used to 'reinstate' prepetition debt facilities upon emergence to maintain a favourable interest rate.[120]

3.65 3.2.6.5.6 **Deemed rejection and 'cramdown'** Under Bankruptcy Code section 1126(g), a class of claims or interests that does not receive or retain property under a plan is 'deemed' to have rejected the plan and is not entitled to vote. A plan rejected by one or more impaired classes may be confirmed as a 'cramdown' if (a) all other confirmation requirements under section 1129(a) are satisfied (including the acceptance by at least one impaired class, without reference to votes cast by

---

[116] The benefit of the s 1125(e) safe harbor is limited to actions taken in good faith; the legislative history states that this safe harbor 'does not affect civil or criminal liability for defects and inadequacies that are beyond the limits of the exoneration that good faith provides'. S Rep No. 95-989, at 122 (1978), reprinted in 1978 USCCAN 5787, 5908.

[117] See, eg, *Re Bally Total Fitness of Greater NY, Inc* No. 07-12395, 2007 Bankr LEXIS 4729, at *26 (Bankr SDNY 17 September 2007).

[118] Conversely, classes of claims or interests that will not receive anything under the plan are deemed to automatically reject the plan. 11 USC s 1126(g).

[119] 11 USC s 1124.

[120] See *JPMorgan Chase Bank, NA v Charter Commc'ns Operating LLC (Re Charter Commc'ns)* 419 BR 221, 244–9 (Bankr SDNY 2009) (holding senior lenders were not impaired under plan and permitting reinstatement of senior credit agreement with favorable interest rate); Order Confirming Joint Plan of Reorganization of Spectrum Jungle Labs Corporation, et al, Debtors, *Re Spectrum Brands Inc* No. 09-50455 (Bankr WD Tex 15 July 2009) (reinstatement issue settled on eve of trial on terms favorable to debtor).

insiders); (b) the plan does not 'discriminate unfairly' against the rejecting impaired classes; and (c) the plan is 'fair and equitable' to the rejecting impaired classes by following the absolute priority rule.[121] If the debtor's value is insufficient to provide a recovery for equity or junior creditors, a debtor may pursue a prepack providing no recovery for these classes and only solicit prepetition votes from the impaired classes receiving recoveries under the plan.

Even if a class of claims or interests will not receive distributions under a plan, such class still has some rights with respect to the confirmation progress. Accordingly, such class should be provide, at a minimum, notice of (a) the confirmation hearing date, (b) the confirmation objection deadline, (c) its lack of recovery under the plan, (d) the distributions to other classes, and (e) who to contact to receive a copy of the plan and disclosure statement at the debtor's expense.[122] Unless a court order is obtained approving limited notice, the prudent course is for debtors to also send a copy of the disclosure statement to classes subject to cramdown. In pursuing a prepack cramdown, the primary assumption is that there is no value for the junior classes. Holders of claims or interest in junior classes will have an opportunity to object to their treatment if they can demonstrate that sufficient value was available to provide them with any recovery. If such an objection was successful, the plan would have to be amended to provide a recovery to such class, and such class would then be entitled to vote on the plan and cause a delay in confirmation. **3.66**

3.2.6.5.7 **Prearranged bankruptcy** In a 'prearranged' bankruptcy, the debtor commences a chapter 11 bankruptcy case after having negotiated the terms of the plan with its major stakeholders. On or shortly after commencing the bankruptcy case, the debtor will file the previously negotiated plan and move toward confirmation of the plan. A prearranged bankruptcy differs from a prepack because the solicitation occurs after the commencement of the case. Because solicitation occurs post-petition, the solicitation is governed by section 1125 of the Bankruptcy Code, which requires, among other things, bankruptcy court approval of a disclosure statement before soliciting acceptances of the plan.[123] Therefore, a prearranged bankruptcy case is typically longer than a prepack. **3.67**

[121] The absolute priority rule requires that (a) rejecting, impaired secured classes receive the 'indubitable equivalent' of their secured claims and (b) rejecting, impaired unsecured creditors receive property of a value, as of the effective date of the plan, equal to the allowed amount of the claim with no junior classes of claims or interests receiving any property under the plan on account of such claims or interests. See 11 USC s 1129(b).

[122] Fed R Bankr P 3017 explicitly permits such limited disclosures to unimpaired classes, but does not specifically address creditors or stockholders that will not receive distributions under the plan.

[123] 11 USC s 1125(b).

3.68 **3.2.6.5.8 Plan support (lock-up) agreements** To ensure that a debtor has sufficient votes to confirm a prepackaged or prearranged plan, a debtor will often enter into 'plan support' or 'lock-up' agreements with major stakeholders. Under such agreements, the parties agree to support confirmation of a plan that embodies an agreed upon restructuring proposal. The issue raised by lock-up agreements is whether they violate section 1125(b) of the Bankruptcy Code, which prohibits post-petition solicitation after a case is commenced until a disclosure statement is approved by the bankruptcy court.[124]

3.69 In a prepack, because the solicitation is completed before the commencement of the bankruptcy case, the debtor must comply with any applicable securities laws, but is not at risk of violating section 1125(b) by entering into a prepetition lock-up agreement. In the prearranged plan context, there were several decisions that held that prepetition lock-up agreements could violate section 1125(b) if there was even minor post-petition actions related to the lock-up agreement.[125] In 2005, however, a safe harbour was added to the Bankruptcy Code. Specifically, new section 1125(g) of the Bankruptcy Code provides that:

> Notwithstanding [section 1125(b)] an acceptance or rejection of the plan may be solicited from a holder of a claim or interest if such solicitation complies with applicable non-bankruptcy law and if such holder was solicited before the commencement of the case in a manner complying with applicable non-bankruptcy law.[126]

Therefore, assuming that a prepetition lock-up agreement constitutes a solicitation, section 1125(g) permits the debtor to pursue confirmation without concern of whether there will be a technical violation of section 1125(b) related to post-petition activities. Section 1125(g) also remedied the dilemma caused by the commencement of an involuntary bankruptcy case after prepetition solicitation of a prepack had commenced.

3.3 UK bond repurchases and amendments

3.3.1 General issues and considerations

3.70 Companies in the UK that are in financially distressed situations are subject to similar dynamics in their relations with stakeholders as companies in the

[124] 11 USC s 1125(b). The seminal case on post-petition lock-up agreements is *Re Texaco, Inc Trans World Airlines, Inc v Texaco Inc (Re Texaco Inc)* 81 BR 813 (Bankr SDNY 1988) (upholding lock-up agreement that provided that parties would use best efforts to obtain plan confirmation).

[125] See *NII Holdings Inc* No. 02-10882 (Bankr D Del 30 September 2002) (holding that lock-up agreement violated s 1125(b) when lock-up agreement was negotiated prepetition but some creditors did not execute until a few days after the bankruptcy case was commenced).

[126] 11 USC s 1125(g).

US discussed in the previous sections. In such precarious financial situations, such companies are not only seeking to effectively manage burdensome debt portfolios and covenant packages, but also to capitalize opportunistically on discounted trading of the companies' liabilities by retiring debt at a price that is, taking into account the present value of future scheduled debt service costs, lower than the redemption amount due at maturity. But this is in most respects a consensual process and, in very much the same way as in the US, companies in the UK will, to a certain extent, rely on the cooperation of interested parties whose interests and accompanying strategies vary widely from holdouts to loan-to-own lenders to parties who want nothing more than a fast exit at any price. A publicly quoted company, or a company whose liabilities take the form of publicly listed debt, has the added dynamic of reassuring stakeholders of the continued viability of the business through careful and considered disclosure of the management of this process all in accordance with the applicable legal disclosure regime.

Whilst the following sections will discuss some of the liability management strategies that are used by distressed companies in tackling publicly listed debt in the UK, these tools are equally available to companies that are not in a distressed financial situation. **3.71**

In the first part, we will discuss the principal legal framework surrounding bond repurchases either as *ad hoc* trades in the open market or as part of an organized tender offer. Unlike the US where repurchases are subject to rigorous formalities prescribed by the Exchange Act, there are few formalities specific to bond repurchases in the UK. The UK financial regulator, the Financial Services Authority, and the legislature have instead chosen to allow such transactions to be regulated by the general rules relating to market abuse, insider dealing and transparency of the market. This culminated in the deletion of the UK Listing Rule ('Listing Rule')[127] relating to bond repurchases, which had given some certainty to the requirement to announce such trades. Consequently the following sections focus on the potential abusive nature of repurchases and the requirement, if any, to announce such trades. **3.72**

In the second part, we will discuss the liability management strategy of combining the consensual nature of the tender offer with the coercive nature of an exit consent to cram down minority holders. Whilst again this tool, employed in potentially forcing a non-consensual retirement of debt, is not subject to a prescriptive legal regime in the UK, there are legal concerns relating to equality of treatment of holders of the debt that will prescribe the manner in which the strategy is employed. Consequently the following sections will discuss the various **3.73**

[127] The UK Listing Rules (available at http://fsahandbook.info/FSA/html/handbook/LR), inter alia, govern issuers of debt securities listed on the Official List of the Financial Services Authority .

combinations available to cram down dissentient holders and the potentially abusive nature of such actions.

3.74 The following sections only discuss repurchases of debt that is governed by English law and is listed on a UK market regulated for the purposes of the Markets in Financial Instruments Directive.[128] The following sections do not cover equity-linked debt (such as convertible and exchangeable debt) which, inter alia, is subject to separate disclosure rules.[129]

3.3.2 Repurchase of publicly listed debt

3.75 A company in a distressed financial situation is acutely aware of the extent to which the management of its restructuring process, and the communication of this to its stakeholders and the public, will impact the trading prices of its securities and consequently the cost at which it may be able to retire its debt. Companies are therefore naturally inclined to resist any disclosure of its intention to repurchase debt unless legally required to do so. Whether or not the company is so legally required is governed by several laws including:

- the Market Abuse Directive[130] as implemented through the Financial Services and Markets Act 2000;
- the Criminal Justice Act 1993; and

[128] Directive 2004/39/EC of the European Parliament and of the Council of 21 April 2004 on markets in financial instruments amending Council Directives 85/611/EEC and 93/6/EEC and Directive 2000/12/EC of the European Parliament and of the Council and repealing Council Directive 93/22/EEC.

[129] There are specific Listing Rules relating to tender offers and repurchases applicable to debt convertible into equity shares with a UK premium listing – see Listing Rule 12.5.1 which requires that, except where the purchases consist of individual transactions made in accordance with the terms of the relevant securities, where a listed company intends to purchase any of its securities convertible into its equity shares with a premium listing it must: (1) ensure that no dealings in the relevant securities are carried out by or on behalf of the company or any member of its group until the proposal has either been notified to a RIS or abandoned; and (2) notify a Regulated Information Service of its decision to purchase. Any purchases, early redemptions or cancellations of a company's own listed equity securities convertible into equity shares with a premium listing by or on behalf of the company or any other member of its group must be notified to a RIS when an aggregate of 10 per cent of the initial amount of the relevant class of securities has been purchased, redeemed or cancelled, and for each 5 per cent in aggregate of the initial amount of that class acquired thereafter (Listing Rule 12.5.2). The notification must be made as soon as possible and in any event no later than 7:30 am on the business day following the calendar day on which the relevant threshold is reached or exceeded (Listing Rule 12.5.3).

[130] Directive 2003/6/EC of the European Parliament and of the Council of 28 January 2003 on insider dealing and market manipulation (market abuse).

- the Transparency Directive[131] as implemented through the Disclosure Rules and Transparency Rules ('DTR') (in particular DTR2).[132]

The repurchase of publicly listed debt can occur on the open market, usually through financial intermediaries, or through publicly announced tender offers. This section principally discusses those trades executed through financial intermediaries, or by the issuer directly, where there is no announced offer. Announcement of the repurchase is not in itself a safe harbour from market abuse and insider dealing concerns—even in an announced offer a company must take into account whether or not, for example, it is in breach of insider dealing rules if it agrees the terms of a repurchase at a time when it possesses inside information. This section focuses on the act itself of repurchasing debt and assumes that the company is not otherwise committing market abuse. **3.76**

3.3.2.1 The market abuse regime

The current market abuse regime in the UK was implemented on 1 December 2001 through section 118 et seq. of the Financial Services and Markets Act 2000 ('FSMA'). The Market Abuse Directive was implemented in the UK on 1 July 2005 and resulted in certain amendments to the then existing regime. One such amendment was the deletion of the Listing Rule requirement to publicly disclose purchases of a company's own listed debt securities by or on behalf of the company or any other member of the group of which the company forms part on reaching certain thresholds. Those thresholds—10 per cent of the initial issue size and, thereafter, 5 per cent of the initial issue size—allowed a company some certainty in determining its public disclosure requirements upon making open-market purchases of its debt. Consistent with the deletion of this Listing Rule, the safe harbours introduced by the Market Abuse Directive for share buybacks were not replicated for debt securities. Without the benefit of any such safe harbours, a company must consider on a case-by-case basis whether a proposed trade may be in breach of the market abuse regime. **3.77**

Securities that fall within the market abuse regime must be 'qualifying investments' and admitted to trading on a 'prescribed market'. Qualifying investments includes debt securities and prescribed market includes the regulated market of the London Stock Exchange plc. **3.78**

---

[131] Directive 2004/109/EC of the European Parliament and of the Council of 15 December 2004 on the harmonization of transparency requirements in relation to information about issuers whose securities are admitted to trading on a regulated market and amending Directive 2001/34/EC.

[132] The Disclosure Rules and Transparency Rules (available at <http://fsahandbook.info/FSA/html/handbook/DTR>), inter alia, set out certain disclosure and information requirements imposed on issuers of debt securities listed on the Official List of the UK Financial Services Authority.

3.79 3.3.2.1.1 **Market abuse under section 118(2) of FSMA—Dealing or attempting to deal on the basis of inside information** In a bond repurchase context, market abuse may be committed if the company has inside information at the time of the repurchase. Section 118(2) of FSMA prohibits an insider dealing in qualifying investments on the basis of inside information. For the purposes of section 118(2) of FSMA, 'inside information' is defined in section 118C(2) as information that is of a precise nature and that is (a) not generally available, (b) relates, directly or indirectly, to the company or the securities and (c) would, if generally available, be likely to have a significant effect on the price of the securities or of related investments. Section 118C(6) clarifies that information would be likely to have a significant effect on the price if a reasonable investor would be likely to use the information as part of his or her investment decision.

3.80 Care must be had in assessing whether the company is in possession of inside information, such as information relating to the wider restructuring process that may impact negatively the credit rating of the company. In a restructuring scenario it is possible that the company has information relating to the process in respect of which the disclosure is being legitimately delayed pursuant to applicable disclosure rules (see DTR2.5.1). Notwithstanding this ability to delay disclosure, if the information is inside information for the purposes of section 118(2) of FSMA, the company may be committing market abuse if it repurchases debt at such time and consequently the repurchase should precipitate an end to any delaying strategy under DTR2.5.1. Conversely, while bonds are trading at a discount, any positive information relating to the company will make this determination equally important. The company will additionally expose itself to a risk of allegations of market abuse if it trades during a period during which the company typically is in possession of price-sensitive information—the so-called 'closed periods'—occurring before trading updates and the announcement of results, which apply to all companies with premium share listings on UK regulated markets. A solution to this, of course, would be for the company to disseminate a 'cleansing' announcement that purges the company of the previously undisclosed inside information and/or wait until the end of the closed period.

3.81 Assuming that the company has made a cleansing announcement, or has otherwise assured itself that it is not in possession of inside information, the company must determine whether its own liability management strategy is information that by its very nature is inside information and that therefore must be disclosed before dealing. The company is naturally not predisposed to making any such announcement that would risk alerting holders to the possible distressed scenario in which the company is prepared to buy its own debt and thereby risk increasing the trading price of that debt. It is useful here to distinguish between the situation before and after the initial repurchases are made.

An intention to repurchase where no repurchases have yet been made Prior to the company having carried out any market purchases it is unlikely that the company would have to disclose to the market its intention to undertake open market purchases. The Code of Market Conduct[133] ('MAR') states at MAR 1.3.6 that the carrying out of a person's intention to deal is not in itself market abuse. In this situation, absent inside information which relates to matters other than the intention to repurchase (in respect of which we have assumed there is none), it is reasonably safe to assume that there is no possession of information by the company of which a reasonable investor should be aware before making any such trade. Other than the intention to deal, all market participants are appraised of the same information. The same cannot be said for an intention to trade once repurchases have already been made. **3.82**

An intention to repurchase where repurchases have already been made After repurchases have been made, only the company, and perhaps the trustee of the debt instruments repurchased, are aware that the liquidity of the debt has been reduced. The tightness of the market between supply and demand is likely therefore to be a factor unknown to the investor and a factor which, depending on the significance of the reduction in liquidity, a reasonable investor should be aware before agreeing a trade. If significant, the company must not deal further in the debt before announcing its intention to do so. **3.83**

If the company has established a repurchase programme with a financial intermediary, the parameters of that programme should be considered carefully. If the upper limit on that programme would impact the liquidity of the debt such that a reasonable investor would be entitled to take this into account before dealing, it is advisable that the programme be the subject of an announcement upon being established with subsequent announcements being made when pre-established thresholds are reached. Listing Rule 15 of the pre-July 2005 Listing Rules assisted in this analysis by requiring announcements to be made at fixed thresholds. The 10 per cent threshold, and subsequent 5 per cent thresholds, are still adopted by some practitioners as 'rule of thumb' but this is not a safe harbour under section 118(2) of FSMA. The particular characteristics of the class of the debt, and in particular its historic trading activity, or lack of it, need to be considered to determine whether in fact a lower threshold is more appropriate on a case-by-case basis. **3.84**

3.3.2.1.2 Market abuse under section 118(5) of FSMA—manipulating transactions It is an offence under section 118(5) of FSMA to deal in debt securities **3.85**

[133] Published by the Financial Services Authority pursuant to s 119 of FSMA.

in a manner (otherwise than for legitimate reasons and in conformity with accepted market practices on the relevant market), which:

(a) give, or are likely to give a false or misleading impression as to the supply of, or demand for, or as to the price of such debt securities; or
(b) secure the price of one or more such debt securities at an abnormal or artificial level.

3.86 In a bond repurchase context, market abuse may be committed if the company repurchases its debt in a manner that distorts the actual supply, demand or pricing of the debt. The company and its advisors should consider whether it is a distortion of supply and demand for the company to give the impression that there is demand for a security in respect of which, on the contrary, the company is about to reduce the liquidity. Is the company, by concealing its identity and its liability management strategy, securing the price of the security at a level that is artificially lower than that which it would have obtained if such matters were disclosed to the seller?

3.87 Similar to our analysis with respect to section 118(2), this section assumes that the company is not otherwise committing market abuse and is not motivated in its repurchase strategy by an intention which, aside from the repurchase strategy, would constitute market abuse.

3.88 *Legitimate reasons and accepted market practices* Where the company's intention to repurchase is founded on bona fide commercial purposes (such as retiring debt to avoid a breach, taking advantage of discounted trading in the debt and simply reducing debt levels of the company), it would be difficult to argue that the trade is not made for legitimate reasons. MAR assists in interpreting 'legitimate reasons' by providing at MAR 1.6.7 that:

> it is unlikely that the behaviour of market users when trading at times and in sizes most beneficial to them (whether for the purpose of long term investment objectives, risk management or short term speculation) and seeking the maximum profit from their dealings will of itself amount to distortion. Such behaviour, generally speaking, improves the liquidity and efficiency of the market.

3.89 To benefit from the 'legitimate reasons' exception, the company must also comply with 'accepted market practices'. 'Accepted market practice' is defined in section 130A(3) of FSMA as practices that are reasonably expected in the financial market or markets in question and are accepted by the UK Financial Services Authority. There is no interpretation of this in MAR and consequently care should be taken in relying on this provision without further determining the substance of the transaction on a case-by-case basis.

3.90 *Identity of the purchaser* Without there being another, illegitimate, reason to trade, the repurchase at a price lower than that which the market participant would have otherwise insisted on had it been aware of the identity of the seller should not amount to market abuse. The market is fully aware, and is not misled, that participants in the demand and, to a lesser extent, supply of Eurobond debt include the issuer of that debt. It is a standard term of the terms and conditions of Eurobond debt that the issuer is entitled to buy its debt in the market at any price (although less common that the issuer may resell such debt). A more conservative analysis of this should be undertaken in the unusual circumstance where the terms and conditions of the debt securities do not provide for the ability of the issuer to repurchase debt in the market or otherwise.

Liquidity of the market Is the market misled as to liquidity? This will depend on how significant the trade is. The abuse articulated by section 118(5) of FSMA relates to the distortion of the market of the debt securities, the emphasis being on the effect on the particular market in those securities. Consequently, the effect on supply and demand should be considered on a case-by-case basis and the company should not be tempted to rely solely on the historic 10/5 per cent thresholds without consideration of the particular circumstances. If the company determines with its advisors that a trade, or series of trades, will result in a reduction in liquidity that would, all other things being equal, affect the pricing of the securities, then the company should not deal without first announcing its intention. **3.91**

3.3.2.2 Criminal Justice Act 1993 ('CJA')

In addition to the civil offence under section 118(2) of FSMA, insider dealing is also a criminal offence under the CJA. It is an offence under the CJA for a person with inside information to deal in 'price-affected securities' (which includes debt securities listed on any market of the London Stock Exchange plc) or for such a person to encourage another to deal in such securities. 'Inside information' for the purposes of the CJA means information which (a) relates to particular securities or to a particular issuer of securities or to particular issuers of securities and not to securities generally or to issuers of securities generally; (b) is specific or precise; (c) has not been made public; and (d) if it were made public would be likely to have a significant effect on the price of any securities.[134] Securities are 'price-affected' in relation to inside information if and only if the information would, if made public, be likely to have a significant effect on the price of the securities.[135] **3.92**

Only an individual can commit an offence under the CJA and can thereby be liable to unlimited fines and/or imprisonment. If an individual arranges for a company to repurchase its debt securities on the basis of inside information, that **3.93**

[134] Section 56(1) of CJA.
[135] Section 56(2) of CJA.

individual may commit the offence of encouraging the company to deal and the company itself could be guilty of conspiracy under the CJA.

3.94 There are similarities between the definition of inside information for FSMA and CJA purposes and consequently the analysis referred to above with respect to section 118(2) of FSMA should be sufficient in determining whether the company is in possession of inside information for CJA purposes.

3.3.2.3 Practical steps for the company

3.95 The legal framework discussed above imposes a practical burden on the company in assessing whether or not it can safely trade. If the company repurchases its debt securities, then it should review before any repurchase transactions whether it is in possession of inside information (including with respect to the liquidity of the securities) and, if it is, it must refrain from purchases until this information has been adequately published. As discussed above, the company should be particularly sensitive to insider dealing considerations during pre-earnings announcement blackout periods. This may make it necessary to limit dealing to dealing windows following publication of results or one-off market notifications.

3.96 The company may establish a trading programme to be implemented on a discretionary basis by a buying agent operating independent of the company, consistent with the UK Model Code trading procedures. The UK Model Code governs dealings in securities of a company with a premium share listing and does not apply to dealings in debt securities by a company that does not have such a listing. Compliance with the UK Model Code is not a safe harbour from section 118 of FSMA or the CJA but by adopting this high standard of governance in implementing a trading plan a company can (a) address the practicalities of insider dealing that may arise on a day-to-day basis; and (b) put the company in a strong position to respond to any criticism from stakeholders.

3.3.3 Cramming down using debt tender offers and covenant strips

3.3.3.1 Introduction to debt tender offers and bondholder meetings

3.97 A tender offer is a consensual process in which bondholders are invited to tender some or all their bonds at a price (which may be fixed or within a range) either for cash (a 'cash tender offer') or for new bonds (an 'exchange offer').[136] The terms and conditions of debt securities at times specify that a tender offer with respect to such securities be addressed to all bondholders. If the company oportunistically dips into the market, it must carefully navigate between clearly recognisable open

[136] This chapter does not discuss exchange offers which raises offering-related issues under the Prospectus Directive.

market purchases and repurchases that may be recharacterized as a tender offer not only for US reasons (as discussed above) but also to comply with any such terms and conditions.

There are a variety of methods used to structure debt tender offers, including (a) a 'fixed tender' where the purchaser offers to purchase a specified amount of bonds at a fixed price, (b) an 'open tender' where the purchaser launches an offer for an unspecified amount of a particular series of bonds at a fixed price, and is prepared to buy back the full amount of the bonds at the announced price and (c) a 'Dutch auction' where the purchaser invites bondholders to tender their bonds within a specified price range following which bonds are accepted, beginning with those for which the lowest price has been specified, until the issuer has purchased the desired number of bonds, with the result that bonds are purchased at multiple prices.[137] **3.98**

In addition to taking into account the price at which bonds are trading at the time of the offer, in determining a price which will be sufficiently attractive to investors, the tender will often be structured with a tender fee. To further incentivize investors to tender early in the process, the fee is often only payable, or payable at a higher rate, if investors tender before a specific deadline some time before expiry of the tender period. This is often referred to as an 'early bird fee'. **3.99**

The company launching a tender offer still needs to consider the insider dealing and market abuse issues referred to above, but issues relating to liquidity and identity of the repurchasing entity are clearly mitigated by the transparent process involved. **3.100**

The company may also consider convening a meeting of the holders of the debt securities, all in accordance with the bondholder meeting provisions set out in the bond documentation, to propose a resolution to remove many of the restrictive covenants and events of default in conjunction with a cash tender offer or an exchange offer (often referred to as an 'exit consent'). In this case the exit consent is often structured such that acceptances of the tender offer by bondholders will constitute a vote in favour of the proposed resolution at the bondholder meeting.[138] If sufficient acceptances are received to pass the resolution, holders who do not tender into the offer will continue to hold their old securities but with fewer covenant protections (often referred to as a 'covenant strip'). The company will **3.101**

---

[137] In a 'modified Dutch auction' the bond purchase price is determined based on the lowest price that allows the bidder to buy the number of bonds sought in the offer and the bidder pays that price to all bondholders that tendered at or below that price on a pro rata basis.

[138] Bonds held by, or on behalf of, or for the benefit of, the issuer, a subsidiary of the issuer, a holding company of the issuer or a subsidiary of a holding company are usually not entitled to be voted.

often, at a minimum, condition the tender offer on receiving sufficient acceptances to pass the relevant resolutions so that, if insufficient tenders/votes are received, the company may withdraw the tender offer. It is important to bear in mind that there are two processes being undertaken in the combined offer and consent—the offer is made on, theoretically, whatever terms the company has decided to launch the tender, whereas the consent strictly follows pre-agreed formalities. Consequently, the company will be advised to reserve itself a wide discretion in its ability to withdraw the offer, a discretion to which the company is not entitled with respect to the meeting.[139] In this situation the bondholder meeting will typically have to proceed even though the offer has been withdrawn—if the resolutions are passed, the company would still have the option to not execute the amendment documentation.[140]

3.102 Use of the tender offer and exit consent can be very effective in coercing or incentivizing holders to tender their securities in order that the company may maximize, if indeed this is the objective, its opportunity to retire the whole class of debt the subject of the tender. The bondholder meeting could be convened to consider a combination of alternatives to achieve this, such as the insertion of an issuer call option, an amendment to the maturity date of the debt securities or a covenant strip. Whilst the latter is not in itself effective to retire the debt, the risk of a holder being left with a debt security without covenants will arguably be a persuasive element of the offer.[141]

3.103 The requisite quorum and majorities required should be carefully analysed to determine the likelihood of each scenario. Insertion of an issuer call option, or advancing the maturity date, would typically require an increased quorum or majority and consequently may affect whether this option is chosen by the company.

3.3.3.2 Disclosure requirements for the tender offer memorandum

3.104 The tender offer memorandum will set out the terms of the offer and will be circulated to the debt security holders by the tender agent but not otherwise made public. Notwithstanding the limited circulation of the document, which, by limiting circulation to creditors of the company, should exempt the document from

[139] Bondholder meeting provisions typically do not allow for the cancellation of meetings that have been convened.

[140] The various alternative outcomes should all be clearly set out in the tender offer memorandum.

[141] The financial intermediary assisting in the offer, the dealer manager, will advise on whether this strategy, in light of the investor base holding the securities, is too aggressive and would potentially be viewed negatively.

financial promotion requirements under FSMA,[142] the memorandum will most likely contain representations made to the debt security holders that are aimed at inducing the holder to make an investment decision based on the memorandum. Consequently the company will be liable for the contents of the memorandum under general UK anti-fraud laws, both statutory (such as section 397 of FSMA (misleading statements and practices) and section 2(1) of the Misrepresentation Act 1967) and in common law (such as negligent misstatement). Provided that the memorandum is solely soliciting tenders for cash, whether or not combined with an exit consent, the memorandum will not constitute an offer of securities for the purposes of the Prospectus Directive 2003/71/EC and consequently will not need to comply with the disclosure obligations set out therein and in its implementing legislation. In customary bond documentation there are no disclosure requirements with respect to tender offers relating to the bonds.

If the tender offer is being combined with an exit consent, the memorandum will have appended to it[143] the terms of the bondholder resolution(s). The resolutions must comply with the formalities set out in the bondholder meeting provisions and will be reviewed and commented upon by the trustee or fiscal agent of the debt securities who will be involved in the meeting process. There are additional Listing Rule disclosure items for circulars relating to amendments to trust deeds (where, for example, exit consents are contemplated) and early redemptions (where, for example, the exit consent includes the inclusion of an issuer call option). Listing Rule 17.3.10 requires, inter alia, that the memorandum, or circular, as it is referred to in the Listing Rules, contain an explanation of the proposed amendments to the related trust deed. Listing Rule 17.3.12 requires, inter alia, that the memorandum sets out, in addition to an explanation of the reasons for the early redemption, the market values of the debt securities on the first dealing day in each of the six months before the date of the memorandum and on the latest practicable date before the date of the memorandum and a statement of any interests of any director in the debt securities.[144] **3.105**

3.3.3.3 Excluding jurisdictions from the tender offer

As noted above, the tender offer may be made on whatever terms the company decides. This is a consensual process which, subject to the following paragraph, the company may choose to offer to a category of debt security holders that does **3.106**

---

[142] Article 43 of Financial Services and Markets Act 2000 (Financial Promotion) Order 2005.

[143] In customary bondholder documentation there are no requirements that the bondholder meeting notification be appended to the memorandum, but this is typically done in order that a security holder can consider a single package of documents.

[144] The entire text of Listing Rule 17 should be referred to for the full requirements.

not comprise the entire investor base.[145] Companies often exclude the US to avoid compliance with the Exchange Act (notably the requirement to maintain the offer open for at least 20 business days). Exchange Act, or other local requirements in other jurisdictions, will affect the speed and manner of execution, which may be critical to the process. This is of course considered taking into account the principal amount of securities held by persons residing or otherwise subject to the laws of that jurisdiction and the possible need to include them in the target investor base for the offer. The bondholder meeting notification, however, must be addressed to all holders of the debt securities in accordance with the terms of their meeting provisions.

3.107 Excluding jurisdictions can give rise to other issues, however, including equality of treatment. Take for example the following situation where the company is on the brink of a bond default that will trigger cross-defaults into all its other debt. The company would like to retire all the bond debt but believes that it may not be able to do so consensually and, moreover, that it would not be able to achieve the acceptance threshold required at a bondholder meeting to bring forward maturity. The company is aware, through testing European investor sentiment or otherwise, and always mindful of its obligations under the Disclosure Rules, that it can successfully complete the offer and pass the covenant strip resolutions by offering a fee of 1 per cent without having to approach investors in the US. The company has checked the terms of the debt securities to ensure that there is no provision restricting tender offers to those addressed to all holders only. The company proposes the following:

- a tender offer at par open for 21 days[146] beginning on launch (T) where tenders also constitute a vote in favour of the resolutions;
- an early bird fee of 1 per cent available to all persons to whom the tender offer is addressed and whose tenders are accepted by the company on or before T+10;
- a bondholder meeting notified on T to be convened on T+23[147] to consider and, if thought fit, pass a resolution to strip covenants; and
- US-based investors excluded from the tender (but not vote).

3.108 Under the Transparency Rules of the Financial Services Authority, DTR6.1.3[148] requires that an issuer of debt securities must ensure that all holders of debt

---

[145] This assumes that there are no contractual restrictions in the terms and conditions of the debt securities requiring tenders to be made to all holders.

[146] Tender offer closes shortly prior to the bondholder meeting.

[147] Bondholder meeting notification period is typically 21 clear calendar days.

[148] There are exceptions to the applicability of this rule, in particular where the issuer is incorporated outside the European Economic Area provided the relevant state of incorporation lays down similar investor protection rules.

securities ranking *pari passu* are given equal treatment in respect of all the rights attaching to those debt securities. Considering the example above, from an economic perspective, the result of a successful offer would be as follows:

- a tendering holder receives 101 per cent of the debt tendered;
- a non-tendering holder, having exercised its right not to tender, receives zero and holds amended debt securities; and
- a holder in the US is excluded from the tender, receives zero and holds amended debt securities.

The result is not defensible by the company with respect to the US holder and can result in allegations of fraud on the minority against the company and, possibly, the majority holders. An alternative action against the company in such a situation would be breach of DTR6.1.3[149] but note that this action is brought by the Financial Services Authority and results in a fine payable to the Financial Services Authority. **3.109**

In order to avoid any such allegations or contraventions of DTR6.1.3, consider the following revised proposal: **3.110**

- a tender offer at par open for 21 days beginning on launch (T) where tenders also constitute a vote in favour of the resolutions;
- an early bird fee of 1 per cent available to all persons to whom the tender offer is addressed and whose tenders are accepted by the company on or before T+10;
- a bondholder meeting notified on T to be convened on T+23 to consider and, if thought fit, pass two resolutions:
  - first resolution: strip covenants;
  - second resolution: insert a bondholder put option exercisable by holders excluded from the tender offer for a limited period of time following completion of the tender offer;
- holders excluded from the tender are eligible for a voter fee of 1 per cent of those bonds which are voted in favour; and
- US-based investors excluded from the tender (but not vote).

The economic result of this is as follows: **3.111**

- A tendering holder—who has voted bonds in favour and tendered—receives 101 per cent of debt which it has voted/tendered.

[149] Section 91(1B) of FSMA imposes a fine on a company which contravenes, or a director of the company who was knowingly concerned in the contravention of, the Transparency Rules in an amount considered appropriate by the Financial Services Authority.

- An excluded holder—who has voted bonds in favour—receives a fee of 1 per cent based on the bonds which it has voted plus 100 per cent of the debt 'tendered' to the company under the put.

3.112 The combined offer and consent has therefore been structured to achieve economic equivalence for the excluded holders even though the methodology is different. The company has managed to avoid compliance with the Exchange Act, but it has nevertheless offered the same economic deal to all holders.

3.4 Conclusion

3.113 A financially-troubled company that is restructuring in the US or the UK may take advantage of one or more of the restructuring options briefly discussed in this chapter. Each of these options present different advantages, but also different obstacles and restrictions. The path to restructuring that a company chooses will ultimately depend on the speed with which it needs to restructure, the regulations it is bound by, and other factors unique to the company.

4

LOAN BUYBACKS

4.1 Introduction

In the years preceding the global financial crisis that started in late 2007, the primary and secondary loan markets prospered. Fuelled by the entry of new participants (such as hedge funds, collateralized loan obligations and other institutional investors), liquidity in the loan markets soared. This high degree of liquidity, coupled with declining margins on newly issued loans, ensured that fully performing leveraged loans to borrowers typically traded in the secondary market at, or even above, their face value. However, after the start of the global financial crisis, forced selling in the secondary market imposed downward pressure on the prices of leveraged loans, notwithstanding that in many cases the underlying credit quality was not impaired.[1] This created an opportunity for borrowers (or their affiliates) to restructure their balance sheets by purchasing the loans at a discount to par.[2] These forms of loan purchases are commonly referred to as loan buybacks.[3] **4.01**

[1] Between September 2008 and August 2009, fully performing leveraged loans were typically trading between 15 per cent and 35 per cent below par.

[2] The opportunity to acquire loans at a deep discount to par proved to be short lived where the underlying credit quality of the loans was not impaired, as the price of such loans increased as market conditions improved.

[3] This chapter discusses only the buyback of bank loans. See chapter 3 for discussion on the bond repurchases. Unless context requires otherwise, the term 'debt' in this chapter refers to bank loans.

4.02 Set out below are some of the drivers for loan buyback transactions.

(a) *Reduced leverage and interest expense*: if outstanding loans are purchased at a discount to par by the borrower or an affiliate within the borrower's credit group[4] and the loans are extinguished by operation of law or retired, the borrower's credit group will have reduced its total debt (and therefore its interest expense) at a cost that is lower than the cost of prepaying the loans at par.[5]
(b) *Increased profits and recognition of EBITDA gain*: where the loan documentation (taking into account the applicable accounting rules) allows it, the difference between the face value of the loans purchased by a member of the borrower's credit group and the market value (ie the purchase price) of such loans may be included in the consolidated EBITDA[6] of the borrower's credit group for the purpose of financial covenant calculations. The opportunity may also exist for loans to be purchased at a discount and subsequently sold for a profit.
(c) *Strategic advantages*: depending on the terms of the underlying loan documentation and the amount of debt acquired, the purchaser of the loans may be able to use the voting rights attached to the acquired loans to block actions being taken against the borrower by other lenders or to protect the borrower against non-consensual debt restructurings.[7]

4.03 This chapter outlines the key legal issues under English law and New York law (and relevant US federal law) arising in connection with the purchase of syndicated loans by a borrower or its affiliates.[8] The legal analysis of loan buybacks is complex and turns on the specific facts and terms of the underlying loan documentation. This chapter discusses the key themes in general terms by reference to the most common loan buyback structures. Needless to say, the specific terms of the relevant loan documents, any local law issues and the tax, accounting and

[4] As used in this chapter, the 'borrower's credit group' refers to the group of entities that are restricted by the terms of the loan documents including the borrower, guarantors and restricted subsidiaries.

[5] Depending on the terms of the relevant loan documentation, it may also be possible to reduce the net debt of the borrower's credit group for the purpose of financial covenant calculations without retiring the purchased loans. See section 4.2.2.10.1.

[6] As used in this chapter, 'EBITDA' means earnings before interest, tax, depreciation and amortization. EBITDA is the most common measure of the cash-generating capacity of the borrower's credit group under both European Loan Market Association ('LMA') and US loan documentation (although the precise definition of EBITDA varies from deal to deal).

[7] Whilst such voting rights are a useful tool (especially for stressed or distressed borrowers), the retention of such voting rights in the US is rare because buybacks under US loan documentation usually require the consent of the lenders. See section 4.2.3.4.2. In the UK, the voting rights are typically not retained by the purchaser of loans where the underlying credit is not impaired. See sections 4.2.3.4.1 and 4.2.7.1.

[8] This chapter addresses the restructuring of non-convertible debt. The buyback of convertible debt may raise additional legal issues which are outside the scope of this chapter.

regulatory consequences of the proposed buyback transaction need to be considered carefully before a buyback can be sanctioned in any particular case.

4.2 UK and US perspectives on buyback

4.2.1 Common buyback structures

Loan buybacks usually fall into one of the three broad categories set out below. **4.04**

(a) *A purchase of loans by the borrower.* To date, this structure has rarely been used for buybacks under European LMA loan documentation[9] for the reasons set out in section 4.2.2.1.1 below. However, recent changes to the LMA Standard Form which expressly contemplate the buyback of loans by borrowers may see this structure used more frequently in the UK market going forward.[10] When used in the US, this structure often takes the form of a discounted voluntary prepayment (which, strictly speaking, is not a buyback but achieves a similar effect) for reasons set out in section 4.2.5.1 below.

(b) *A purchase of loans by a sponsor or an affiliate of the sponsor.* The main benefit of this structure is that the purchaser of the loans sits outside the borrower's credit group and, as such, is unlikely to be regulated by the restrictions in the loan documents. The main disadvantage of this structure is that a deleveraging effect of the buyback can generally only be achieved if the purchased loans are forgiven[11] by the purchaser or contributed to the borrower as equity[12] or if the terms of the underlying loan documentation permit shareholder or

[9] The Loan Market Association (the 'LMA') is the trade association for the European loan market. While every loan agreement is different and there is no 'standard' UK or European loan agreement, the LMA has developed standard forms of loan agreement for use in both the investment grade and leveraged finance markets. Such LMA standard forms have gained wide acceptance in the UK and European loan markets, and are often used as the starting point for negotiations between lenders and borrowers. References in this chapter to 'European LMA loan documentation' and the 'LMA Standard Form' are references to the LMA's standard form facility agreement for leveraged finance transactions, draft dated February 2008.

[10] See section 4.2.7.1.

[11] Under European LMA loan documentation, the forgiveness of the loans by the affiliate would cause problems. The LMA Standard Form provides that 'an amendment or waiver that has the effect of changing or which relates to a reduction in the amount of any payment of principal' requires the consent of all of the lenders. Whilst it seems counter-intuitive that a lender should need permission from other lenders if it wishes to forgive its own claims (and an argument could be made that the clause was not intended to prevent a lender from doing so), there is a risk that an English court would view the forgiveness of loans by the sponsor or sponsor affiliate as falling within the categories of amendments and waivers that requires the consent of all of the lenders.

[12] Under European LMA loan documentation, the contribution of the loans by the affiliate to the borrower is likely to require the consent of the majority lenders (typically lenders whose commitments represent at least $66^2/_3$ per cent of the total commitments), whereas typical US loan documentation would permit the sponsor to contribute the purchased loans to the borrower, which will then be deemed extinguished.

investor debt to be excluded from the calculation of total debt for the purpose of the financial covenants.[13]

(c) *A purchase of loans by another member of the borrower's credit group*. A purchase of loans by a member of the borrower's credit group (other than the borrower itself) has the advantage of deleveraging the group for the purpose of financial covenant calculations without the need for the purchased loans to be extinguished.[14] This structure also allows the buyback to be funded by cash flow generated by the borrower's credit group (subject to any restrictions on the use of such cash flow in the loan documents).

4.05 There are, of course, numerous variants of the structures mentioned above. The application of loan buyback schemes in stressed and distressed situations, in particular, have been the most innovative. A couple of examples are described below.

(a) The amounts injected by a sponsor into the borrower's credit group by way of an equity cure[15] have been used to implement loan buybacks. Consequently, not only is the borrower's cash flow (and, depending on the terms of the loan documents, EBITDA) increased by the amount of the equity injection, but the borrower's net debt is also reduced by the face value of the loans purchased.

(b) Under US loan documentation,[16] a borrower may be permitted to create an unrestricted subsidiary to effect the loan buyback, relying on an exception under the investments covenant in the loan agreement. Such unrestricted subsidiary is not part of the borrower's credit group and, thus, is unlikely to be restricted by the covenants in the loan documents that might prevent a buyback by a restricted subsidiary.[17]

---

[13] See section 4.2.2.10.1.

[14] See section 4.2.2.10.

[15] 'Equity cure' rights allow a breach of financial covenants to be remedied through the injection of new equity or subordinated debt into the borrower's credit group (which equity or subordinated debt is included in the calculation of cash flow (and sometimes EBITDA) and/or applied in reduction of total debt). Such rights are sometimes found in European LMA and US loan documentation (but are more prevalent in transactions involving private equity sponsors).

[16] There is no such document as a 'standard' form of US loan documentation. Most major financial institutions in the US loan market maintain their own forms of loan documentation. As used in this chapter, 'US loan documentation' refers to loan documentation including terms commonly seen in the US leveraged loan market and governed by the laws of the State of New York.

[17] The distinction between restricted and unrestricted subsidiaries is less common in European LMA loan documentation. However, the establishment of a special purpose subsidiary of the borrower may be useful to circumvent restrictions on transfers and assignments under European LMA documentation. See section 4.2.2.1.1.

4.2.2 Documentation issues

Prior to the collapse of the secondary loan market in late 2007, most syndicated loan documentation contemplated that the only way for a borrower to retire its loans was to repay or prepay them in order of seniority, at par and pro rata among the lenders. Such syndicated loan documents simply did not contemplate the purchase of loans by the borrower or its affiliates. This contrasts markedly with the position in typical bond documentation, where the repurchase of bonds by the issuer is usually not restricted. Unlike bond repurchase programmes, which have enjoyed a history of success and market acceptance, the purchase by a borrower of its own syndicated loans is a relatively recent and controversial[18] phenomenon in the syndicated loan market both in Europe and in the US. **4.06**

Until recently, European LMA loan documentation typically did not expressly prohibit loan buybacks.[19] Consequently, loan buybacks in the European market have been effected without the consent of lenders. However, European LMA loan documentation generally does operate to restrict the manner in which a buyback could be effected. **4.07**

By contrast, US loan documentation often contains restrictions on the assignment of loans to the borrower or an affiliate. Consequently, loan buybacks in the US market almost always require the consent of the lenders. The level of consent required depends on the precise terms of the underlying loan documents.[20] **4.08**

Whether the buyback transaction is effected under European LMA or US loan documentation, it needs to be structured in a manner that complies with the restrictions contained in the underlying loan documents.[21] Set out below are some of the key documentary considerations that are common to many buybacks. The analysis below assumes that the buyback will be effected by way of a transfer of the loan pursuant to the transfer provisions of the relevant loan agreement, and not by way of a sub-participation, total return swap or other derivative transaction (each **4.09**

[18] Such purchase is controversial insofar as buybacks can be construed as a prepayment which does not comply with the rules for prepayment set out in the loan documentation, especially where the debt that is being bought is junior or subordinated debt. See sections 4.2.2.2 and 4.2.2.9.

[19] The LMA Standard Form, which has been widely adopted in the European market, was amended in September 2008 in response to the wave of loan buyback transactions which followed the collapse of the secondary loan market. See section 4.2.7.1 for a summary of the loan buyback provisions of the revised LMA Standard Form.

[20] The percentage of votes required may be all lenders, all affected lenders or the requisite majority lenders (under US loan documentation, usually 50.1 per cent of the total commitment amount).

[21] This is particularly important for buybacks effected under European LMA loan documentation. Because such buybacks often do not involve an amendment to the loan documents (as is usually the case in the US), the terms of the loan documents need to be reviewed carefully in order to avoid any unintended consequence of effecting a buyback.

of which would involve the relevant 'purchaser' taking some degree of third party counterparty risk).[22]

4.2.2.1 Restrictions on transfers and assignments

4.10 4.2.2.1.1 UK A common restriction in European LMA loan documentation is that the transferee of any loan must be (a) a bank or financial institution or (b) a trust, fund or other entity which is regularly engaged in or established for the purpose of making, purchasing or investing in loans, securities or other financial assets. Most borrowers are unlikely to satisfy either of these criteria,[23] but a special purpose vehicle ('**SPV**') incorporated by a member of the borrower's credit group or by the sponsor specifically for the purpose of making, purchasing and investing in loans, securities or other financial assets (and whose constitutional documents reflect such corporate purpose) would.[24] For this reason, and for the reasons set out in section 4.2.2.2 below, loan buybacks under European LMA loan documents are usually effected by an SPV that is an affiliate of the borrower or the sponsor.[25]

4.11 4.2.2.1.2 US Under many US loan agreements, the transferee of any loan must be an 'eligible assignee'. A typical definition of 'eligible assignee' would include (a) existing lenders and their affiliates and (b) commercial banks and other types of financial institutions that meet certain criteria (eg total asset threshold and engagement in the business of making loans). Because corporate borrowers usually do not meet the requirements for an eligible assignee (and the definition sometimes expressly excludes the borrower, the sponsor and their respective affiliates), the restrictions on transfers and assignments are often the first hurdle that a borrower looking to buy back loans under the US loan documents must overcome.[26]

[22] See section 4.2.5 for such alternative structures.

[23] There may be exceptions. For example, it could be argued that an entity that acts as a treasury conduit for its group is an entity that is 'regularly engaged in the making of loans'.

[24] This assumes that the incorporation of a special purpose vehicle ('SPV') by a member of the borrower's credit group is permitted under the terms of the relevant loan documentation (which is usually the case).

[25] The use of an SPV established for the purpose of purchasing or investing in loans should also address concerns that the provisions of the LMA Standard Form regarding transfers and assignments should be construed as prohibiting transfers to a borrower. For example, the transfer provisions in the LMA Standard Form contemplate the borrower and any transferee assuming rights and obligations towards one another that differ from the obligations existing between the borrower and the transferor only insofar as the borrower or the transferee have assumed and/or acquired the same in place of the borrower or the transferor. It has been argued that this is impossible to achieve if the underlying obligation or right has been extinguished (as is arguably the case if the borrower purchases loans made to it).

[26] If the buyback transaction is structured as a voluntary prepayment (as is often the case under US loan documentation), any restrictions relating to the eligible assignee definition do not come into effect. See section 4.2.5.1.

An amendment of the eligible assignee definition, however, usually only requires consent from the majority of lenders.

4.2.2.2 Restrictions on prepayment

Under both English law[27] and New York law[28], if the borrower acquires loans made to it, such loans are generally thought to be extinguished by operation of law. This has led some to argue that the acquisition by a borrower of loans made to it constitutes a prepayment (rather than a transfer) of loans, and that the buyback must therefore comply with the restrictions on prepayments set out in the loan documentation. **4.12**

Both European LMA and US loan documentation almost always require any prepayment of the loans to be made at par.[29] To the extent that a loan buyback constitutes or could be recharacterized as a loan prepayment, such buyback transaction (which contemplates the acquisition of loans at a discount to par) would almost certainly breach such restrictions. **4.13**

In addition, both European LMA and US loan documentation typically contains provisions requiring amounts received by any lender in satisfaction of the borrower's payment obligation under the loan agreement to be shared pro rata among all lenders.[30] If such pro rata sharing provisions were to apply to loan buybacks, they would defeat the purpose of the lender selling the loans.[31] However, if the buyback transaction were not a prepayment, it is unlikely that the pro rata sharing provisions would apply, as the payment made by the borrower (as purchaser of the loan) is not in satisfaction of the borrower's payment obligation under the loan agreement, but rather is consideration for the transfer of the loan under the relevant transfer document.[32] **4.14**

---

[27] There is a long line of English case law establishing that a party cannot contract with itself. There are exceptions to that general rule, but the transfer or assignment of a loan to the borrower of such loan does not appear to fall within any of the exceptions.

[28] For example, in *Persky v Bank of Am. Natl. Assn.* 261 NY 212, 185 NE 77, New York Court of Appeals indicated that: '[t]here must always be two parties to a contract and a promise to pay … ceases to be a contract when the promisor becomes the owner of his own promise'.

[29] Other restrictions may include (a) a prohibition on the prepayment of junior debt without the consent of the senior lenders (see section 4.2.2.9), (b) a minimum prepayment amount and (c) a notice requirement.

[30] For example, the LMA Standard Form provides that if a lender receives an amount from the borrower other than through the normal payment procedures and applies this amount towards a payment due under the loan agreement, that lender must pay the receipt to the agent so that it can be shared with the other lenders.

[31] The reason is that the transferor would be required to share the consideration received for the transfer of the loan with the other lenders.

[32] While some pro rata sharing provisions specifically exclude amounts received in connection with an assignment, others may be broadly drafted. The precise language of such provisions must be carefully reviewed.

4.15 The issues arising from restrictions on prepayment and pro rata sharing can usually be avoided by ensuring that the purchase of the loans is made by an affiliate of the borrower or the sponsor, rather than by the borrower itself.[33]

4.2.2.3 Restrictions on acquisitions and holding company restrictions

4.16 Both European LMA and US loan documentation sometimes include restrictions on acquisitions by members of the borrower's credit group, which may apply to the acquisition of loans. These restrictions generally do not apply to the purchase of loans by entities sitting outside the borrower's credit group (such as the sponsor or a sponsor affiliate).

4.17 Similarly, both European LMA and US loan documentation sometimes restrict the activities of the borrower to those of a holding company.[34] These restrictions may prohibit the buyback of loans by the holding company in the borrower's credit group.

4.2.2.4 Restrictions on extensions of credit

4.18 As mentioned above, the prevailing view under both English law and New York law is that if a borrower acquires loans made to it, such loans are extinguished by operation of law. Therefore, any restrictions in the loan documents on making loans would not apply to a loan buyback effected by the borrower. Similarly, a loan purchase made by another member of the borrower's credit group is also likely to be permitted under most European LMA and US loan agreements as such loan agreements usually permit loans made between members of the borrower's credit group.[35]

4.2.2.5 Limitations on incurring indebtedness

4.19 Both European LMA and US loan documents typically limit the incurrence of further indebtedness by the borrower's credit group. Such limitations may restrict the ability of the borrower (or any other member of the borrower's credit group) to finance the loan buyback from new borrowings. Additionally, loans purchased through a buyback should continue to constitute permitted indebtedness under

---

[33] The reason is that under both English law and New York law, a loan buyback structured as a purchase by an affiliate of the borrower or by the sponsor or a sponsor affiliate would not result in the loan being extinguished by operation of law.

[34] For example, the LMA Standard Form prohibits the borrower from trading, carrying on any business, owning any assets or incurring liabilities except for the provision of administrative services, intra-group activities and incurring the professional fees of advisers.

[35] However, under both European LMA and US loan documentation, a loan from a member of the borrower credit group to another member would sometimes be required to be unsecured or subordinated. The precise terms of any restriction on the extension of loans or credit should be checked carefully.

both European LMA and US loan documentation because indebtedness incurred under the loan documents is generally permitted.[36]

4.2.2.6 Negative pledge (or limitations on liens)

Under both European LMA and US loan documentation, the security for the acquired loans would typically constitute permitted security (on the basis that the security granted under the relevant loan documents is permitted). However, the precise language of the negative pledge (or lien covenant) and any intercreditor arrangements should be checked carefully to ensure this is the case.[37] Restrictions on liens (or negative pledges) may also operate to prevent the incurrence of secured debt to finance the buyback. **4.20**

4.2.2.7 Restriction on guarantees

Under both European LMA and US loan documentation, the guarantees for the acquired loans would typically continue to be permitted guarantees (on the basis that guarantees granted under the relevant loan documents are permitted).[38] However, the precise language of the restriction on guarantees and any intercreditor arrangements should be checked carefully. **4.21**

4.2.2.8 Restrictions on disposals and mandatory prepayment from disposal proceeds

Under both European LMA and US loan documentation, where the acquired loans are intended to be warehoused by the purchaser pending a subsequent sale of such loans, the provisions of the loan documents that restrict disposals and require mandatory prepayment of the loans from disposal proceeds should be carefully considered. A sale by a member of the borrower's credit group may be prohibited by the restriction on disposals and, even if it is not, it is likely that **4.22**

[36] Under European LMA loan documentation, the purchase of loans by a sponsor or a sponsor affiliate can lead to a curious result in the context of leveraged finance transactions. On the one hand, any senior debt that is purchased by a sponsor or sponsor affiliate may continue to fall within the definition of senior debt (because it is debt incurred under the senior finance documents). On the other hand, if the debt is purchased by a sponsor or sponsor affiliate, it is also likely to constitute shareholder debt (which, under the terms of most leveraged loan documentation, is usually required to be subordinated to the senior debt). In some cases, the terms of the loan documentation (and any existing intercreditor agreements) may need to be amended to clarify that the acquired loans constitute 'subordinated debt' and not 'senior debt'. In other cases, a separate subordination agreement may be necessary.

[37] The analysis as to whether any security for the acquired loans is permitted is usually more complicated if the intercreditor arrangements purport to subordinate intra-group debt or shareholder/investor debt. See section 4.2.2.9.

[38] The analysis as to whether any guarantees for the acquired debt are permitted is usually more complicated if the intercreditor arrangements purport to subordinate intra-group debt or shareholder/investor debt. See section 4.2.2.9.

the terms of the loan documentation will require the proceeds of any subsequent sale of the loans to be applied in mandatory prepayment of the loans.

4.2.2.9 Intercreditor issues

4.23 Where there are multiple tranches of debt with different rankings and priority within the capital structure, this adds another layer of complexity to the analysis. The intercreditor arrangements under both European LMA and US loan documentation typically restrict payments in respect of the junior debt for so long as the senior debt remains outstanding. Whilst such restriction does not necessarily operate to prohibit a buyback of the junior debt (provided that the acquired debt is not extinguished or forgiven and the buyback could not otherwise be construed as a prepayment of the acquired debt), a buyback of junior debt without the consent of the requisite majority of senior lenders is likely to be controversial.

4.24 In addition, loan buybacks under European LMA loan documentation need to be structured carefully to ensure that they do not inadvertently breach other provisions of the intercreditor agreement.[39] For example:

(a) Loans purchased by the borrower or a member of the borrower's credit group are likely to fall within the definition of intra-group debt. Intercreditor arrangements in leveraged finance transactions in the UK market sometimes prohibit members of the borrower's credit group from giving guarantees or security for intra-group debt, and the pre-existing security and guarantees for the purchased loans may breach this covenant. Accordingly, the purchaser of the loans may need to disclaim any guarantees or security for the acquired loans from which it might otherwise benefit.

(b) Similarly, loans purchased by a sponsor or sponsor affiliate are likely to fall within the definition of shareholder or investor debt. Intercreditor agreements for leveraged finance transactions in the UK market often prohibit members of the borrower's credit group from giving guarantees or security for shareholder and investor debt, and the pre-existing security and guarantees for the purchased loans may breach this covenant. Accordingly, the sponsor or sponsor affiliate who purchases the loans may need to disclaim any guarantees or security for the acquired loans from which it might otherwise benefit.

(c) Intercreditor agreements for leveraged finance transactions in the UK market typically prohibit payments of principal or interest in respect of shareholder and investor debt. More restrictive intercreditor agreements may also

[39] While such provisions are not as common under US loan documentation, some US loan documents also require that intra-group or shareholder debt be unsecured or subordinated in right of payment to the loans under the loan agreement.

prohibit payments in respect of intra-group debt (some before the occurrence of an event of default and many after the occurrence of an event of default or acceleration). Any payment or repayment (of interest or principal) in respect of the purchased loans are likely to breach such restrictions.

4.2.2.10 Financial covenants

As mentioned above, one of the main advantages of loan buybacks is that they generally have a deleveraging effect on the borrower's credit group. Loan buybacks may also affect the calculation of cashflow (and, in turn, excess cashflow), EBITDA and finance charges. Structuring a buyback transaction in a way that results in the most favourable impact on financial covenant calculations is particularly relevant for borrowers in stressed or distressed situations. Set out below is a summary of the potential issues relating to financial covenant calculations.[40] **4.25**

4.2.2.10.1 Total debt Whether or not a loan buyback transaction will result in a reduction in total debt[41] depends on whether the buyback is effected by the borrower itself, by another member of the borrower's credit group, or by the sponsor or a sponsor affiliate.[42] Each alternative is considered below. **4.26**

(a) If the loans are purchased by the borrower itself and extinguished by operation of law, this will generally reduce total debt by an amount equal to the face value of the purchased loans.
(b) If the loan documentation excludes intra-group debt from the calculation of total debt, then loans purchased by another member of the borrower's credit group may reduce total debt by the face value of the purchased loans.[43]
(c) However, if total debt is calculated net of any cash balances within the borrower's credit group, any reduction in the amount of total debt that results from the loans being extinguished (if they are purchased by the borrower) or excluded from the calculation of total debt (if they are purchased by another member of the borrower's credit group) will be partially offset by the reduction in the amount of cash within the borrower's credit group. Therefore, in such case, the net reduction in total debt will be equal to the difference between the face value of the loans and the purchase price of the loans.

---

[40] This section considers some of the common issues under both European LMA and US documentation. However, the actual terms of the financial covenants are likely to be very specific to the particular transaction and should be considered carefully.

[41] The term 'total debt' as used herein is loosely defined to mean the amount of the borrower credit group's total debt calculated on a consolidated basis.

[42] The extent to which leverage is reduced depends on the structure of the buyback and on the precise terms of the financial covenants in the loan documents.

[43] Under typical European LMA loan documentation, the definition of total debt explicitly excludes intra-group debt from the financial covenant calculations.

(d) A purchase of loans by the sponsor or an affiliate that is not a member of the borrower's credit group may result in a reduction in total debt if the terms of the loan documents provide for shareholder loans to be deducted from total debt or if the purchased loans are forgiven by the sponsor or affiliate (or if the terms of the loan documents permit such loans to be contributed to the borrower as equity). European LMA loan documentation usually permits such shareholder loans to be deducted from total debt, provided that the loans are subordinated to the claims of the other lenders under the facility.[44]

4.27 4.2.2.10.2 **Finance charges** Where the loans are purchased by the borrower itself and extinguished by operation of law, this should result in a reduction in the amount of the borrower credit group's finance charges.[45] In addition, some loan documents (particularly European LMA loan documentation) may permit interest owing to other members of the borrower's credit group to be excluded in the calculation of finance charges. Therefore, where the loans are purchased by a member of the borrower's credit group, any interest, fees and other finance charges in respect of the purchased loans accruing from the date on which such loans are purchased may be excluded from the calculation of finance charges.

4.28 4.2.2.10.3 **EBITDA** There have been several high profile loan buyback transactions in the European market in which the borrower sought to include the gain arising from the extinguishment, forgiveness or resale of purchased loans in the calculation of EBITDA. However, whether the gain represented by the 'discounted' element of the purchased loans can be included in the calculation of EBITDA depends on the precise terms of the relevant loan documents and the accounting treatment of such gain. For example, under both European LMA and US loan documentation, the calculation of EBITDA typically excludes any exceptional, one-time, non-recurring or extraordinary items and any material gains or losses of an unusual or non-recurring nature. To the extent the purchase price paid for a loan buyback, or any gain resulting from an extinguishment, forgiveness or resale of the loans constitutes such an exceptional or extraordinary item under the terms of the loan documents and the applicable accounting rules, it would generally not be included in the calculation of EBITDA.

[44] Under European LMA loan documentation, the subordination of the acquired debt is usually a straightforward documentary process: the sponsor or sponsor affiliate simply accedes to the intercreditor agreement as a subordinated creditor.

[45] The term 'finance charges' as used herein is loosely defined to mean the amount of the borrower credit group's finance charges (including interest, fees and other finance charges) calculated on a consolidated basis.

4.2.2.10.4 Excess cashflow Both European LMA and US loan documentation often requires excess cashflow[46] of the borrower's credit group to be applied toward prepayment of the outstanding loans. In calculating excess cashflow, European LMA and US loan documentation typically permits the amount of any cash payment in respect of any exceptional or extraordinary items to be deducted. The effect of such deduction is that the amount of cash that has been used to fund the loan buyback is typically not included in the calculation of excess cashflow. However, if the buyback is funded from the proceeds of an equity contribution or subordinated shareholder debt, the effect on the calculation of excess cashflow is likely to be neutral (because the amount of any cash receipts in respect of any exceptional or extraordinary items is usually added to excess cashflow). **4.29**

4.2.3 Other legal and practical considerations

4.2.3.1 Cooperation of the facility agent

4.2.3.1.1 UK As a practical matter, it should be possible to effect a loan buyback under European LMA loan documentation without the cooperation of the facility agent. Under the LMA Standard Form, the validity of a transfer or assignment is stated to be conditional upon, among other things, the counter-signature of a transfer certificate by the facility agent. Provided that the certificate appears on its face to be in order and the conditions to the transfer or assignment appear to have been satisfied, the facility agent's role is a perfunctory one limited to performing 'know your customer' checks. That said, to avoid any suggestion that the transfer certificate does not on its face appear to be in order (for example, on the basis that a borrower does not qualify as a permitted transferee, or that a transfer to the borrower amounts to a prepayment), loan buybacks under European LMA documentation are typically effected by a special purpose vehicle incorporated with the express purpose of purchasing or investing in loans.[47] **4.30**

4.2.3.1.2 US Under most US loan documentation, an assignment of the loan to an eligible assignee that is not already an existing lender requires the consent of the facility agent. However, often the facility agent is required not to withhold or delay such consent unreasonably. As most buybacks under US loan documentation are effected through an amendment, the facility agent's consenting right to an assignment typically does not come into play. **4.31**

[46] The term 'excess cashflow' as used herein is loosely defined to mean the amount of the borrower credit group's excess cash flow calculated on a consolidated basis.

[47] See section 4.2.2.1.

4.2.3.2 Securities law concerns

4.32 4.2.3.2.1 UK Absent unusual circumstances, commitments in syndicated loans are not 'securities' for the purposes of the provisions of the Criminal Justice Act 1993 (UK) regarding insider dealing or 'qualifying investments' for the purposes of the provisions of Financial Services and Markets Act 2000 (UK) relating to market abuse. Accordingly, the provisions of the UK statutory regime relating to insider dealing and market abuse are unlikely to apply to the purchase of syndicated loans.

4.33 4.2.3.2.2 US Pursuant to rule 10b-5 under the Securities Exchange Act of 1934, it is unlawful to trade in securities while in possession of material non-public information relating to such securities. The borrower or an affiliate effecting a buyback may possess such material non-public information and be prevented from acting on that information, unless it discloses such information to the seller of the loans.

4.34 Legal practitioners in the US, however, have historically taken the position that loans are not 'securities' for US securities law purposes and, hence, not subject to such laws. Nonetheless, many market participants do give consideration to securities laws when dealing with loans as a matter of good practice and for reputational reasons.

4.35 New York courts have, however, held that a duty to disclose material non-public information may be modified by contract, and sometimes parties try to circumvent such duty by entering into a so-called 'big boy' letter where a buyer of loans acknowledges asymmetry of information and waives any claims arising out of such asymmetry. In the presence of such a 'big boy' letter negotiated on an arm's length basis between sophisticated parties, New York courts are likely to reject a fraud claim based on the non-disclosing party's failure to disclose material facts regarding the transaction.

4.2.3.3 Other regulatory considerations

4.36 Regulatory considerations (including market or exchange-specific disclosure requirements) may be relevant in the jurisdiction in which the purchaser of the loan is incorporated, has listed securities or carries on business, or in other jurisdictions in which the loan is traded.[48] Additionally, if the loans are purchased by a sponsor or sponsor affiliate, such sponsor or sponsor affiliate will need to ensure that it complies with its own regulatory requirements.[49]

---

[48] For example, if the purchaser effecting a buyback is a reporting company for US securities law purposes, the purchaser may be required to disclose publicly its plans for a buyback as such information may be material information.

[49] See section 4.2.3.6.

4.2.3.4 Voting rights and information privileges

4.2.3.4.1 UK The purchaser of loans will normally be entitled to all the rights of a lender, including voting and information rights. There is no reason under English law why such a lender should not be entitled to vote in its own (or its credit group's) self-interest. The acquisition of over one-third of the loans under the facility would give the purchaser under European LMA loan documentation a blocking stake in respect of matters requiring the consent of lenders holding at least two-thirds of the commitments. However, while such rights are of real strategic benefit to stressed or distressed borrowers, given lender sensitivities on the matter, such voting and information rights have been seen by some borrowers as an incidental benefit of a buyback and something that they are prepared to concede. **4.37**

4.2.3.4.2 US Loan buybacks effected under US loan documentation typically do not involve the borrower or an affiliate retaining voting or information rights, access to lender meetings or other privileges that would disrupt the syndicate group's ability to enforce its remedies. Because most loan buybacks under US loan documentation require lender consent, the lenders voting on any amendment effecting the buyback would likely be opposed to the borrower or an affiliate gaining such privileges as a member of the syndicate group. In order to minimize the effect of the misalignment of interests, lenders may make their consent to the buyback conditional upon certain protections being granted. For example, lenders may require:[50] **4.38**

(a) voting privileges to be stripped out entirely from the loans being acquired by the borrower or its affiliate, or agreement from them to vote with the majority of or in proportion to the unaffiliated lenders;[51] or
(b) a limitation on the percentage of loans (typically set at 25 per cent or less) to be acquired by the borrower or its affiliate, so that the borrower cannot block any action requiring majority lender approval, or use its vote to block approval of a plan of reorganization supported by the other lenders.[52]

---

[50] Many sponsors would, however, insist that such restrictions not apply to the affiliates of a sponsor that regularly invest in and trade loans (such as the trading arm of the sponsor financial institution).

[51] Whether any waiver of voting rights by the borrower or an affiliate will be enforced by a bankruptcy court may still be a question in the US. Case law on this point arises in the context of voting rights pursuant to a subordination or intercreditor agreement. A leading case is *Aerosol Packaging, LLC v Wachovia Bank, N.A.*, where the court held that subordination agreements are enforceable in bankruptcy to the extent enforceable under non-bankruptcy law.

[52] Section 1126(c) of the US Bankruptcy Code (Title 11, US Code entitled 'Bankruptcy') says that '[a] class of claims has accepted a plan if such plan has been accepted by creditors ... that hold at least two-thirds in amount and more than one-half in number of the allowed claims of such class held by creditors ... that have accepted or rejected such plan'.

4.2.3.5 Ratings considerations

4.39 If the borrower or the loan has a credit rating, careful consideration should be given to the ratings criteria of the relevant ratings agency to determine whether the buyback is likely to constitute a default under such ratings criteria (and therefore have a detrimental impact on the rating). For example, a ratings agency may consider a loan buyback as a distressed exchange if the purpose of the buyback was to avoid a breach of the financial covenants or other events of default under the loan documents.

4.2.3.6 Limitations under sponsor fund documents

4.40 Where the buyback is effected by a sponsor or sponsor affiliate, it will need to comply with the investment criteria set out in the constitutional documents of the sponsor (such as the partnership agreement in the case of a limited partnership). Such criteria may relate to the investment type (eg, debt versus equity), investment amount, industry concentration or investment period (which in turn may restrict the fund's ability to effect a buyback).

4.2.3.7 Tax issues

4.41 A buyback transaction under both European LMA and US loan documentation is likely to give rise to a number of tax issues. The tax impact should be considered carefully before undertaking a buyback. See chapter 9 for further details.

4.2.4 Buyback methods

4.2.4.1 Privately negotiated

4.42 To the extent that the loan documents permit it, the borrower or an affiliate may privately negotiate a transfer of loans (as any financial institution seeking to acquire loans in the secondary market would) usually with a sophisticated, institutional seller.[53]

4.2.4.2 Open market purchase (through investment bank intermediary)

4.43 The borrower or an affiliate looking to buy back loans may purchase them from individual lenders in the open market through an investment bank intermediary.

4.44 Open market purchases offer the purchaser an ability to effect buybacks discretely without affecting the market price. It may not be an effective way to purchase a large amount of loans, but the transaction costs may be minimal and the loans can usually be purchased at the prevailing market price.

[53] The disadvantage of this method is that an unsuccessful attempt to buy back loans through a privately negotiated transfer (ie not through an intermediary) may affect the market price for the loans (due to information leaks).

4.2.4.3 Tender offer

The borrower or an affiliate looking to buy back loans may send an open invitation to all lenders to tender their loans during a specified period to be sold at a fixed price (usually subject to the tendering of a minimum amount). It normally requires a premium to the prevailing market price. This can be an effective way to purchase a large percentage of the outstanding loans. **4.45**

4.2.4.4 Modified Dutch auction

Under a modified Dutch auction, the borrower or an affiliate looking to buy back loans would specify the aggregate principal amount (or a range of such amounts) of loans it wishes to purchase and a price range within which it is willing to purchase such loans. Lenders would tender their loans at a price they are willing to accept. The tenders are compiled, and the lowest price that enables the purchaser to purchase the required amount of loans is determined to be the clearing price. The purchaser would purchase the loans at the same clearing price from the lenders who made tenders at or below the clearing price. To the extent that the total tendered amount exceeds the required purchase amount at the clearing price, a predetermined allocation mechanism comes into effect. Whereas a tender offer provides the potential sellers with one fixed price, a Dutch auction creates the possibility of multiple tenders at different prices, thereby achieving a higher probability of success. In addition, like tender offers, Dutch auctions instil a sense of fair play by offering the opportunity to all lenders.[54] **4.46**

4.2.5 Alternatives to buybacks

4.2.5.1 Voluntary prepayments at a discount

Many, if not most, buybacks effected under US loan documentation have taken the form of a non-pro rata voluntary prepayment at a discount to par for various reasons. First, because the loan buyback is a relatively recent phenomenon, an assignment of loans to the borrower is not a concept readily embraced by lenders under typical US loan documents. On the other hand, the concept of a voluntary prepayment is well understood by lenders and already provided for in the loan documents. An amendment seeking revisions to the voluntary prepayment provision of the loan documentation that allows for a non-pro rata prepayment at a discount is therefore thought to have a better chance of success than an amendment **4.47**

[54] In most buybacks effected under US documents, transparency minimizes the risk of the buyback being challenged by disgruntled lenders. However, transparency is less of an issue for buybacks effected under European LMA documentation (because buybacks under European LMA documentation often do not require the consent of the lenders).

of the assignment provision.[55] Second, as discussed above, while the prevailing view is that the loans purchased by the borrower are extinguished by operation of law, there is lingering doubt that they may still be outstanding, which may implicate various provisions under the loan documents. This uncertainty can be avoided if the buyback is effected by way of voluntary prepayment.

4.2.5.2 Funded sub-participation

4.48 Another alternative to a loan buyback might be for a bank or other financial institution to front the purchase and enter into a funded sub-participation with the borrower or a member of the borrower's credit group (referred to in the United States as a participation). Whereas a transfer or assignment of the loans would entitle the purchaser to become the legal and beneficial owner of the loans with all the rights and obligations of a lender under the loan documents, a sub-participation entails the 'participant' obtaining an economic interest in the loans. A sub-participation is a contractual undertaking between the lender and the participant only; the participant does not have any rights of a lender or any recourse to the borrower under the loan documents. Because a participant entering into a sub-participation does not become the lender of record, any restrictions on assignment contained in the loan documents do not apply to the participant (and the loan documentation often does not contain any restriction as to who is eligible to be a participant).[56] A funded sub-participation would need to be structured so that the obligations of the members of the borrower's credit group under the participation arrangements do not breach the restrictions on guarantees and indemnities under the loan documents. The terms of the relevant loan documents should also be checked carefully to ensure that any initial and subsequent payments to the fronting lenders are permitted.

4.2.5.3 Total return swap

4.49 A total return swap is a derivative instrument that allows one party to obtain the economic benefit of owning an asset without becoming the beneficial owner in exchange for paying a counterparty (ie the lender) a periodic cash flow. As in a sub-participation, a party to a total return swap involving a loan does not assume any obligations or obtain any rights of a lender under the loan documents. It is a contractual arrangement between the lender who owns the loans and a counterparty

[55] Under US loan documentation, amendments to both the voluntary prepayment provision and the assignment provision typically require a majority lender vote.

[56] However, to the extent such sub-participation is entered into by a member of the borrower's credit group, it is important to ensure that such transaction is permitted under the other provisions of the loan documents. For example, such sub-participation may be deemed an 'investment' which may be restricted under the loan documents.

(ie the borrower or an affiliate) looking to reap the economic benefits of owning the loans. A total return swap may achieve the same (or similar) economic result as a loan buyback, but without breaching any restrictions on transfers and assignments under the loan documentation.

4.2.6 Market trends

The depressed pricing of fully performing loans in the past few years may have been something of an historic anomaly. With the recovery in the secondary loan market, the window of opportunities for borrowers looking to buy back loans at a deep discount to par may now be closed. However, the opportunity to effect loan buybacks may continue to exist for distressed borrowers, so loan buybacks may remain a useful restructuring tool. **4.50**

4.2.7 Industry group developments

4.2.7.1 UK

The LMA Standard Form, which has been widely adopted in the UK and European market, was amended in September 2008 in response to the wave of loan buyback transactions that followed the collapse of the secondary loan market. Whereas previous versions of the LMA Standard Form contained no specific provisions dealing with the purchase of loans by the borrower (or another member of the borrower's credit group) or any sponsor or sponsor affiliate, the revised LMA Standard Form includes two drafting alternatives dealing with the purchase of loans by the borrower or another member of the borrower credit group and by sponsors or sponsor affiliates. **4.51**

Option 1 is an absolute prohibition on the parent, and any other member of the borrower's credit group from entering into any debt purchase transaction. Option 2 permits debt purchase transactions, subject to strict criteria. In each case, 'debt purchase transaction' is drafted widely to cover the various methods by which a member of the borrower's credit group might acquire the loans or an interest in the loans, including: **4.52**

(a) purchases by way of assignment or transfer;
(b) sub-participations; and
(c) any other agreement or arrangement having an economic effect substantially similar to a sub-participation.

A summary of the key features of each option is set out below. **4.53**

(a) *Option 1—Restriction on debt purchase transactions* The first option in the LMA Standard Form is an absolute prohibition on the parent or any other member of the borrower credit group entering into any debt purchase transaction. Option 1 also contains optional wording that restricts any member of the borrower's credit group from beneficially owning all or any part of the share capital of a company that is a lender or a party to a debt purchase transaction. Option 1 will be appropriate where it is commercially agreed that no member of the borrower credit group will enter into debt purchase transactions.

(b) *Option 2—Limited purchase rights* The second drafting option in the LMA Standard Form permits debt purchase transactions by borrowers subject to the following criteria:
   (i) the purchase is at a price less than the par value, made by way of assignment and only in respect of term loans (ie the acquisition of revolving credit facility loans is not permitted);
   (ii) no default is continuing at the time of the purchase;
   (iii) the consideration for the purchase is funded from excess cash flow (that is not required to be prepaid) or new shareholder injections (ie funds from additional equity or subordinated debt investment by the sponsor); and
   (iv) the purchase is pursuant to a solicitation[57] or open offer[58] method.

4.54 Option 2 provides that loans that are the subject of a debt purchase transaction are extinguished and that any provisions of the loan documentation that may otherwise have been breached[59] do not apply to the debt purchase transaction.

4.55 Purchases of loans by sponsor affiliates[60] are separately dealt with and are not restricted per se but are subject to various disenfranchisement provisions that strip the voting rights and certain information rights from any loans held by a sponsor affiliate.

4.56 Clearly the LMA's standard provisions are only a starting point for discussion, but it is likely that going forward new transactions will contain some form of

---

[57] The solicitation method involves lenders making offers to the borrower as to the price and amount of their participation they are prepared to assign. The borrower is free to choose which lenders to take an assignment from subject to a requirement to accept the lowest offers first and to accept pro rata in relation to any identical offers as to the price.

[58] The open offer method involves the borrower making an offer to the lenders to purchase a given portion of loans at a certain price. The borrower is required to accept any offers from lenders pro rata (ie it cannot choose to purchase from just one lender if additional lenders accept).

[59] See section 4.2.2.

[60] As used in this paragraph, a 'sponsor affiliate' is widely defined to cover the management company of the relevant private equity fund, together with its affiliates and related trusts, partnerships and other trusts, funds and entities managed or under the control of the sponsor or its affiliates (excluding any CDOs of the sponsor which are managed independently of the sponsor).

restrictions based on the aforementioned concepts. Much of that discussion may focus on the issues set out below.

(a) Borrowers faced with Option 1 should consider carefully the optional wording that restricts members of the borrower's credit group from having any beneficial interest in a company that is a lender or party to sub-participation or similar arrangements. This is very wide-ranging and would appear to prevent a member of the borrower credit group from owning shares in a financial institution that might at some point participate in the facilities.
(b) Option 2 applies to borrowers only and does not permit any member of the borrower credit group which is not a borrower to enter into a debt purchase transaction. In particular, because this option is limited to purchases by the borrower (with the loans thereby being extinguished), it effectively prevents borrowers (or other members of the borrower's credit group) from purchasing and holding their own loans with the intention of realizing further value (for example, as a result of the value of the loans increasing in the secondary market).
(c) Debt purchase transactions are only permitted at a discount to the par value of the loans. Borrowers may not wish to limit themselves to purchasing at a discount. For example, the purchase of loans carrying call protection or prepayment premium at par may present an opportunity for borrowers to realize value and may be welcomed by lenders seeking liquidity.

4.2.7.2 US

Whilst the LMA's standard loan documentation enjoys immense success in the European loan market, there is no comparable standard form documentation that has been widely adopted in the US (with certain exceptions, including loan assignment provisions that are becoming standardized). Whilst the Loan Syndications and Trading Association (the 'LSTA') in the US has published certain model credit agreement provisions, many major financial institutions insist upon using their own standard form. The LMA in Europe has played a crucial role in making loan buybacks an acceptable practice by proposing standard terms, but there has not yet been similar progress in the US. The LSTA was known to be in the preliminary stage of considering model terms for loan buybacks, but their progress is as yet unknown, perhaps because of the lukewarm reactions to buybacks in the marketplace in general. **4.57**

4.2.8 Recent cases

At the date of publication, there have been no reported English cases relating to loan buybacks. Similarly, there have been few cases in the US providing guidance on loan buybacks in general. Set out below is a notable recent case in the US that may have an implication on loan buybacks. **4.58**

4.2.8.1 Concord Real Estate CDO 2006-1, Ltd et al. v Bank of America, N.A. (Del. Ch., 14 May 2010)

4.59 The issue in this case revolved around whether the holders of junior tranche debt of a collateral debt obligation may surrender their debt with a view to having it extinguished in an effort to avoid the failure of the over-collateralization ratio test. The court concluded that barring a specific restriction in the underlying indenture, the holders had the right to surrender the debt for cancellation. The court, interpreting an indenture governed by New York law, indicated that under New York law 'where an obligee delivers up the obligations which he holds against another party, with the intent and for the purpose of discharging the debt ... such surrender operates in law as a release and discharge of the liability thereon; nor is any consideration required to support such a transaction when it has been fully executed'.

5

DUTIES OF DIRECTORS AND MANAGEMENT OF DISTRESSED COMPANIES

5.1 Introduction

5.01 When slightly modified, the oft-quoted statement from *Hamlet*, 'This above all: to thine own [Corporation] be true . . .'[1] made by Polonius to his son, Laertes, before his departure to Paris and liberation from his father's watchful eye and morality speeches,[2] succinctly states the normative principle underlying the laws of the UK and the US as to the fiduciary duties of company directors. That is to say the interests of the company come first, 'above all' else, in business transactions.

5.02 This simple statement does not change when a company either enters the ubiquitous 'zone' or 'twilight' of insolvency or, indeed, if it becomes insolvent. Rather, the laws of each nation recognize that when a company is solvent, it is the shareholders who are the primary stakeholders and beneficiaries of the fiduciary duties

[1] William Shakespeare, *Hamlet*, Act 1, scene 3, 78–82.

[2] In contrast, the law definitively does not require that directors take Polonius' other most famous advice to his son: 'Neither a borrower nor a lender be . . . ' *Hamlet*, Act 1, scene 3, 75–7.

imposed on directors. As insolvency intrudes, the interests of the entity rise to the forefront. In that context, directors' actions that benefit the entity will enhance the interests of the economic stakeholders whether they are creditors or shareholders. Dependent on the entity's solvency, either shareholders or creditors (or their representative), as appropriate, will have the power to pursue remedies for the benefit of the company when a director has breached his or her fiduciary duties.

5.03 US law strives to act as Polonius to Laertes and provide its company directors with bright line rules of conduct that still encourage reasonable risk aimed at maximizing returns to stockholders and economic stakeholders. However, residual owners' remedies for breach of such duties are more limited. As discussed in detail later in the chapter, under US law, when a company becomes insolvent, it is the creditors, rather than stockholders, who may pursue the company's rights of action against its directors for breach of the fiduciary duties of care, loyalty, or disclosure and who can recover any damages resulting from any breach. Indeed, certain US jurisdictions allow creditors to recover additional damages for the 'deepening insolvency' (ie exacerbation of already existing financial distress) of the company if such damages are found to flow from the breach of the director's fiduciary duty. A minority of US jurisdictions also provide creditors with an independent tort claim against directors for 'deepening insolvency'. Irrespective of solvency, however, courts will support a director's business judgment where it was reasonable and made in accordance with a sound rationale. In the absence of a breach of fiduciary duty to the company, creditors' remedies against directors are fairly limited. This limitation reflects, in part, an underlying policy that liability for directorial service should be limited so as not to discourage knowledgeable and experienced candidates from serving as directors of companies and that, once in service, their actions, even if somewhat risky, should be protected as long as they are reasonable in the context of their business judgment and executed in accordance with their fiduciary obligations.

5.04 Similarly, the laws of the UK provide certain bright line rules with respect to directorial conduct, including requiring directors, to promote and protect the best interests of the company at all times, irrespective of its financial condition. However, when a company enters the 'twilight period', ie is on the brink of insolvency or preparing for an insolvency proceeding—it is appropriate for UK directors explicitly to consider the interests of creditors over those of shareholders. Indeed, failure to do so may result in personal liability. Thus, when a company is in liquidation, UK law empowers the company or its liquidator (rather than individual creditors) to exercise certain remedies against directors found to have breached their duties to the company.[3] One such remedy is an action for 'wrongful

[3] As discussed within this chapter, UK statutory law also empowers a liquidator with specific remedies against a director alleged to have committed actual fraud and/or breached his/her fiduciary duty as a result of misfeasance. Such actions are outside the scope of this introduction.

trading', which essentially attaches personal liability to a director of a failed corporation where such director knew, or should have known, that the company had no reasonable prospect of avoiding insolvent liquidation and the director did not then take every step to minimize losses to a company's creditors.

As a result, when a company is in the 'twilight period', UK law protects directors relying upon advice of professionals and acting in accordance with established procedures. Personal liability may attach if a duty is breached. The director may be ordered to contribute to the liquidation costs and thus increase the assets available to satisfy creditors. Thus, when a company is found to be insolvent, UK law also enables the disqualification of a director who has breached his or her duties. In certain circumstances, a disqualification order may bar that person from serving as a director of a company for, in some cases, up to 15 years. UK law may establish a more demanding standard for performance and a spectrum of penalties for a defaulting director of an insolvent company than under US law. As a result, there can be a greater incentive for directors of UK financially distressed companies actively to follow creditor interests, even if the proposed action might obviate the need for formal insolvency proceedings. **5.05**

This chapter provides an overview of the similarities and some of the differences between the applicable governance laws of the US and the UK. With the increasing susceptibility of directors of public companies to the rules of different and diverse jurisdictions, this chapter presents a succinct statement of material issues that may be confronted by those faced with financial distress. The financial crisis that erupted in the fall of 2008 has further intensified the study of governance rules and principles and it is likely that they will be subject to ever more comprehensive analyses in both the public and private sector. This is likely to result in the strengthening of the rules governing the conduct of directors in an effort to avoid a repetition of the crisis of confidence that emerged in September 2008 and that revealed significant weaknesses in the governance of major commercial companies. **5.06**

5.2 Fiduciary duties of corporate directors within the context of insolvency in the UK

The duties of directors of English companies arise under the common law and by statute. At common law, a director is subject to fiduciary duties and a duty of skill and care and, in more recent times, certain of the common law duties have been codified under the Companies Act 2006. Directors' duties are owed to the company for the benefit of its members as a whole,[4] subject to any enactment or rule **5.07**

[4] Companies Act 2006, s 172.

of law requiring directors, to consider the interests of creditors.[5] The obligation to have regard to the interests of creditors applies generally when the company, whether technically insolvent or not, is in financial difficulty such that its creditors' money is at risk.[6]

5.08 In recent years, but particularly since the global financial crisis, corporate governance issues and directors' duties have become an issue of increasing prominence. The British Government's stimulus package, including the public bailout of some of its largest banks, means there is now a greater public interest in how directors consider and control corporate risk. In response to this, in early 2009, the former Prime Minister Gordon Brown commissioned Mr David Walker to examine corporate governance procedures in the UK's banking industry. Mr Walker's final recommendations were published in November 2009 in 'The Walker Report'.

5.09 The Walker Report contains recommendations regarding corporate governance matters including (but not limited to) the size, composition and qualification of boards of directors and their members, the functions of the board and governance of risk. The Walker Report was commissioned to analyse the corporate governance of financial institutions but many of its findings and recommendations are transferable to corporate entities outside of the financial sector. The Financial Reporting Council has announced that it 'proposes to adopt the recommendations in the Walker Report that it considers appropriate for all companies'.

5.10 The uncertain financial climate in which corporate entities now operate has created heightened concern among boards of directors about adequate corporate governance and compliance with their duties as directors. The focus of this chapter will be on those duties that a director owes to the company when that company's solvency position is uncertain.

5.2.1 Who owes the general duties?

5.2.1.1 Who is a 'director'?

5.11 The general duties specified in sections 171-177 Companies Act 2006 are owed by a director to the company.[7] A 'director' includes any person occupying the

---

[5] *Ferguson v Wilson* [1866] 2 Ch App 77, CA.

[6] *Re MDA Investment Management Ltd, Whalley v Doney* [2004] 1 BCLC 217, para. [70] (Park J.). See also *West Mercia Safetywear Ltd v Dodd* [1988] BCLC 250, CA (approving *Kinsela v Russell Kinsela Pty Ltd (in liquidation)*, CA (Street C.J.). See *Facia Footwear Ltd (in administration) v Hinchcliffe* [1998] 1 BCLC 218; *Yukong Lines Ltd of Korea v Rendsburg Investments Corpn of Liberia, The Rialto (No. 2)* [1998] 1 WLR 294; *Re Pantone 485 Ltd, Miller v Bain* [2002] 1 BCLC 266; *Colin Gwyer & Associates Ltd v London Wharf (Limehouse) Ltd, Eaton Bray Ltd v Palmer* [2003] 2 BCLC 153 [74] (Leslie Kosmin QC). See also *Official Receiver v Stern* [2000] 1 WLR 2230, CA, paras [31]–[32] (Morritt V.-C.).

[7] Companies Act 2006, s 170(1).

position of director, *by whatever name called.*[8] The general duties of directors also apply to 'shadow directors'.[9] These are persons with whose directions or instructions the directors of the company are accustomed to act.[10] A shadow director must be shown to have the ability to have real influence over a significant area of a company's central managerial activity. A shadow director should be distinguished from a person acting as a de facto director (who owes the standard fiduciary duties nonetheless).[11]

In *Gemma Ltd v Davies*[12] Jonathan Gaunt QC held that the tests to be applied in deciding whether a person was a shadow or de facto director were (a) whether he undertook functions in relation to the company that could properly be discharged only by a director, (b) whether he participated in directing the affairs of the company on an equal footing with the director and not in a subordinate role, and (c) whether he was shown to have assumed the status and functions of a company director and to have exercised real influence in the corporate governance of the company. On the facts, the defendant (who was held out by her husband to be a director) was considered not to be a de facto director on the basis that she had no real influence over managerial matters; she did not discharge directorial functions; and she had never described herself as a director.[13] **5.12**

5.2.2 Determining when duties may be owed to creditors

We will learn later that a director must make decisions and take appropriate actions to promote and protect the best interests of the company at all times. Where a company is solvent, the company's interests are represented by the interests of its shareholders, so it follows that directors must act in such a way as to promote the best interests, and maximize value, for the company's shareholders.[14] However, when a company's solvency is in doubt, there is a gradual shift in whose interests represent that of 'the company', away from the interests of shareholders in favour of the interests of the company's creditors. The directors of a company **5.13**

8 Ibid., s 250 Companies Act 2006.

9 Ibid., s 170(5).

10 Ibid., s 251(1).

11 See the analysis of Etherton J. in *Shepherd Investments v Walters* [2007] EWCA Civ 292, CA. Also see the analysis of Millet J. in *Re Hydrodan (Corby) Ltd* [1994] BCC 161, 163; however, note that it was later held in *Secretary of State for Trade and Industry v Deverell and another* [2001] Ch 304 applied in *Re Mea Corpn Ltd* [2007] 1 BCLC 618 that it was not an essential ingredient to the recognition of a shadow director that he should 'lurk in the shadows'.

12 [2008] 2 BCLC 281.

13 Also see *Re Paycheck Services 3 Ltd (HMRC v Holland)* [2009] WLR (D) 228, CA, which concerned the affairs of a complex structure of composite companies. The Court of Appeal stressed that a director of a corporate director of another company will not automatically be regarded as a director of that second company. The directors in question were held not to be de facto directors

14 *Re Smith and Fawcett* [1942] Ch 304, CA.

approaching insolvency must try to decide at which point the interests of creditors override the interests of shareholders. The timing of this decision is crucial and, therefore, directors must be able to identify when there is a risk of insolvency occurring.

5.14 When considering a company's insolvency position, whether it be under the cash-flow or balance sheet tests, it must be remembered that English law does not recognize the concept of 'group companies'—each company must be considered on a 'case-by-case' basis. 'Insolvency' for the purposes of English law is determined by reference to a company's 'inability to pay its debts'.[15] The cashflow test and balance sheet test can both be used to determine a company's inability to pay debts.

5.2.2.1 Cashflow test

5.15 The cashflow test looks at the question of whether the company is able to pay its debts as they fall due.[16] This is a question of fact to be determined on the balance of probabilities. It is clear from the case law that when determining solvency based on the cashflow test the courts look at the financial position of a company in its entirety. In *Re Cheyne Finance PLC (in receivership)*[17] Briggs J. made clear that there is some element of futurity in applying the cashflow test and therefore the cashflow position of a company should not be determined by focussing solely on debts due as at a relevant date.[18]

5.2.2.2 Balance sheet test

5.16 A company will be insolvent according to the balance sheet test if the value of its assets is less than the amount of its liabilities. Unlike the cashflow test, the balance sheet test expressly requires that the court take into account the company's

[15] For the purposes of the Insolvency Act, a company is deemed to be unable to pay its debts if:
(a) the company, having been served with a written demand (in the prescribed form) by a creditor to whom it is indebted in a sum exceeding £750, fails for three weeks to pay that sum or secure or compound for it to the reasonable satisfaction of the creditor (s 123(1)(a) Insolvency Act 1986), or
(b) in England and Wales, execution or other process issued on a judgment, decree or order of any Court in favour of a creditor of the company is returned unsatisfied in whole or in part (s 123(1)(b) Insolvency Act 1986) (with similar provisions for Scotland and Northern Ireland), or
(c) it is proved to the satisfaction of the Court that it is unable to pay its debts as they fall due (known as the 'cashflow test') (Insolvency Act 1986, s 123(1)(e)), or
(d) it is proved to the satisfaction of the Court that the value of the company's assets is less than the amount of its liabilities, taking into account contingent and prospective liabilities (known as the 'balance sheet test') (Insolvency Act 1986, s 123(2)).

[16] Insolvency Act 1986, s 123(1)(e).

[17] [2008] 2 All ER 987.

[18] *Re Cheyne Finance PLC (in receivership)* [2008] 2 All ER 987 [51].

contingent and prospective liabilities.[19] In *Re a Company*[20] Nourse J. stated: 'That cannot mean that I must simply add them up and strike a balance against assets. In regard to prospective liabilities I must principally consider whether, and if so when, they are likely to become present liabilities.' Commentators have suggested that the same approach should be taken in relation to contingent liabilities. Professor Goode, for example, states that 'the question to be asked is whether there is a real prospect that the contingency will occur'.[21] Thus there is a futurity aspect to the balance sheet test as with the cashflow test.

In addition to the concept of insolvency, market practice often refers to what is known as the 'twilight period'. The 'twilight period' is not a term of art—it is simply the period of time leading up to formal insolvency proceedings. This is not necessarily a time where the company may be considered technically insolvent on a cashflow or balance sheet basis but, during this time, transactions entered into by a company are still vulnerable to attack and may give rise to personal liability on the part of the directors. In light of the somewhat broad tests of insolvency under English law and the risk of liability during the twilight period, it is crucial that directors keep the financial position of the company under constant review. **5.17**

5.2.3 Directors' duties at common law

Under English common law, a director owes two types of duty to the company: (a) a fiduciary duty, and (b) a duty of skill and care. **5.18**

5.2.3.1 Fiduciary duties

Directors of a company owe a fiduciary duty to act bona fide in what they consider to be the best interests of the company.[22] This includes the duty to act in good faith, to exercise powers for a proper purpose,[23] not to act in conflict of interest[24] and not to make a secret profit.[25] **5.19**

A director's duties are owed to the company for the benefit of its members as a whole[26]—these duties are not owed to individual shareholders. This has effect **5.20**

---

19 Insolvency Act 1986, s 123(2).

20 [1986] BCLC 261, 263.

21 R. Goode, *Principles of Corporate Insolvency Law* (3rd edn, Sweet & Maxwell, 2005) 118

22 *Re Smith and Fawcett* [1942] Ch 304, CA.

23 For example, directors may not approve transfers in order to compromise proceedings against themselves: *Bennett's Case* (1854) 5 De GM & G 284; a director may not summon a company meeting at such a date as to prevent shareholders voting: *Canon v Trask* (1875) LR 20 Eq 669.

24 *Aberdeen Ry Co v Blaikie* (1854) 1 Mac 461, 471–2, applied in *Bhullar v Bhullar*[2003] 2 BCLC 241, CA.

25 *A-G for Hong Kong v Reid* [1994] 1 AC 324 PC, applied in *Dubai Aluminium Co Ltd v Al Alawi* (year) 5 ITELR 376, CA.

26 Section 172 Companies Act 2006.

subject to any enactment or rule of law requiring directors, in certain circumstances, to consider or act in the interests of creditors of the company.[27] That is, when a company, whether technically insolvent or not,[28] is in financial difficulty to the extent that its creditors are at risk, the courts have observed that the directors' duties extend to the interests of the company's creditors as a whole, as well as those of the shareholders.[29] The greater the risk of insolvency, the greater the weight that must be afforded to the interests of creditors. The rationale behind this is that on an insolvent liquidation of the company, the equity value is certainly nil and, therefore, it is only the creditors who will have an interest in, and receive a return on, the assets of the company.

5.21 For the reasons described above under English law, the mere fact that the company's shareholders have approved certain actions by the directors during a time of financial uncertainty will not of itself absolve the directors from liability for a breach of fiduciary duty. This point was best explained by Street C.J. of the New South Wales Supreme Court in *Kinsela v Russell Kinsela Pty*[30] where he stated:

> It is, to my mind, legally and logically acceptable to recognize that, where directors are involved in a breach of their duty to the company affecting the interests of shareholders, then shareholders can either authorize that breach in prospect or ratify it in retrospect. Where, however, the interests at risk are those of creditors I see no reason in law or logic to recognize that the shareholders can authorize the breach. Once it is accepted, as in my view it must be, that the directors' duty to the company as a whole extends in an insolvency context to not prejudicing the interests of creditors. . .the shareholders do not have the power or authority to absolve the directors from that breach. [31]

5.22 A director must always consider the interests of the individual company in which he or she is a director and not sacrifice the interests of that company for the greater good of the corporate group. Directors of one group company can however (to a limited extent) take into account group interests, provided the transaction involves an indirect benefit to the relevant company. Pennycuick J. in *Charterbridge Corporation*[32] stated (obiter):

> Each company in the group is a separate legal entity and the directors of a particular company are not entitled to sacrifice the interest of that company. This becomes

[27] *Ferguson v Wilson* (1866) 2 Ch App 77.
[28] Please see Chapter 12.
[29] See Park J. in *Re MDA Investment Management* [2004] 1 BCLC 217, CA.
[30] (1986) 4 NSWLR 722.
[31] The case was cited with approval by the Court of Appeal in *West Mercia Safietywear Ltd (in liq) v Dodd* [1988] BCLC 250, CA and has been considered extensively in the English courts, including by the House of Lords in *Moore Stephens (a firm) v Stone Rolls Ltd (in liquidation)* [2002] All ER (D) 343 and by the Court of Appeal in *RBG Resources plc v Rastogi and others* [2005] 2 BCLC 592 and *Official Receiver v Stern and another* [2002] 1 BCLC 119, CA.
[32] *Charterbridge Corporation v Lloyds Bank Limited* [1970] Ch 62, 74.

apparent when one considers the case where the particular company has separate creditors. The proper test, I think, in the absence of actual separate consideration, must be whether an intelligent and honest man in the position of a director of the company concerned, could, in the whole of the existing circumstances, have reasonably believed that the transaction was for the benefit of the company.

The Cork Committee has emphasized that the present law, however difficult it may be to implement in practice, is that the directors of each group company owe duties to that separate company and must consider that individual company's interests.[33] **5.23**

5.2.3.2 *Consequences of a breach of fiduciary duty*

A breach of a director's duty may give rise to a claim against that director by the company or on behalf of the company (for example by a liquidator) only. If the company has been dissolved, the liability of that company's directors is extinguished, unless the dissolution is set aside by the court. A third party creditor cannot initiate a claim for a breach of directors' duties.[34] **5.24**

A director who has breached his duties may be liable to reimburse the company for any loss suffered by that company and in a liquidation, any amount recovered by a liquidator will be held on trust for the benefit of the company's creditors as a whole. **5.25**

5.2.3.3 *Common law duty of skill and care*

When a director is acting in the best interests of the company, the law also expects that director to exercise whatever skill he possesses and to exercise reasonable care. The test for the common law duty of skill and care was best articulated by Hoffmann J. in *Re D'Jan of London Ltd; Copp v D'Jan*[35] where he said 'in [his] view the duty of care owed by a director at common law is accurately stated in section 214(4) Insolvency Act 1986'. This is the conduct of a 'reasonably diligent person having both (a) the general knowledge, skill and experience that may reasonably be expected of a person carrying out the same functions as are carried out by that director in relation to the company, and (b) the general knowledge, skill and experience that director has'. **5.26**

Re D'Jan of London Ltd; Copp v D'Jan[36] makes clear that the test is both objective and subjective. The law will therefore expect a highly qualified director with a **5.27**

33 Cmnd 8558, para. 1924.
34 *Western Finance Co Ltd v Tasker Enterprises Ltd* (1979) 106 DLR (3d) 81, Man CA; cf. s 12 Insolvency Act 1986.
35 [1994] 1 BCLC 561, 563.
36 [1994] 1 BCLC 561.

specialist set of skills to exercise a higher standard of care and skill than a director who is not so qualified. A director in *Re Continental Assurance Co of London plc*[37] was not actually aware that his company was engaging in illegal transactions but, because of his background as a corporate financier, he should have appreciated what was involved in the company's dealings. Two non-executive directors in *Dorchester Finance Co Ltd v Stebbing* signed blank cheques and left them for a third director to fill in as he pleased. The court took into account the fact that, of the three directors in question, two were chartered accountants and the third had considerable experience in accounting. The court in *Re Queens Moat Houses plc (No. 2); Secretary of State for Trade and Industry v Bairstow and others (No. 2)*[38] took into account the fact that Mr Bairstow had had many years' experience as a director of Queens Moat and therefore should have been aware of the company's business and the nature of the company's income and profits.

5.28 The remedy available to the company for a breach by a director of his duty of care and skill is damages in negligence.

5.2.4 Directors' statutory duties under the Companies Act 2006

5.29 The Companies Act 2006 codifies certain of the duties owed by directors at common law and in equity. For this reason, the statutory duties must be interpreted in accordance with the common law and equitable principles on which they are founded.[39] As will become evident later in this chapter, the 'new' statutory duties are not exactly the same as the corresponding duties at common law and therefore it is reasonable to expect that a new body of case law will follow. The newly codified duties do not attempt to replace the duties owed by directors at common law and, therefore, directors must be mindful both of their obligation to adhere to their duties at common law and under statute whether codified or not. It is often the case that more than one of the general statutory duties and/or one of the common law duties will apply at the same time.[40]

5.30 The Companies Act 2006 sets out various general duties owed by directors to the company. This chapter will focus on the 'duty to promote the success of the company'[41] and the 'duty to exercise reasonable care, skill and diligence'[42] as these sections most closely mirror the common law position.

---

[37] [1997] 1 BCLC 48.
[38] [2005] 1 BCLC 136.
[39] Companies Act 2006, s 170(3) and (4).
[40] Ibid., s 179.
[41] Ibid., s 172.
[42] Ibid., s 174.

5.2.4.1 Duty to promote the success of the company

Pursuant to section 172 Companies Act 2006, a director must act in a way that he considers, in good faith, would be most likely to promote the success of the company for the benefit of its members[43] as a whole. Section 172(3) expressly states that the duty imposed by this section is subject to any rule or enactment that requires directors to consider and/or act in the interests of creditors of the company.[44] Therefore, as regards companies that are insolvent or likely to become insolvent, the common law duty to act in the best interests of the company (described above) continues to be the law. **5.31**

5.2.4.2 Duty to exercise reasonable care, skill, and diligence

A director of a company must exercise reasonable care, skill, and diligence.[45] In assessing what is 'reasonable' for this purpose, the test is both an objective and subjective one: it means the care, skill and diligence that would be exercised by a reasonably diligent person with (a) the general knowledge, skill and experience that may reasonably be expected of a person carrying out the functions carried out by the director in relation to the company; and (b) the general knowledge, skill and experience that the director has.[46] In light of this, directors should exercise caution before accepting a position on a board of directors. A director who does not possess the requisite qualifications or skills to properly perform his role on the board cannot avoid liability on this basis—there is still an element of objectivity or 'reasonableness'. **5.32**

In *Re Continental Assurance Co of London plc (In Liquidation (No. 1)*[47] a senior banking executive who also held a non-executive director role at the company and its subsidiary, argued that he should not be disqualified as director because he did not understand the purpose of certain upstream loans. The court held that in light of the director's experience in the banking sector and his ability to understand the accounts of the holding company, his lack of knowledge was not a defence to his actions but rather evidence that he lacked the appropriate degree of competence to perform his role as director of that company. **5.33**

The subjective element of the test in section 174 Companies Act 2006 raises the question whether any distinction should be made between the role of non-executive and executive directors. After all, it is fair to say that non-executive directors do not typically possess the same amount of knowledge as regards a **5.34**

---

[43] Ibid., s 22 for definition of 'member'.

[44] See also *Ferguson v Wilson* (1866) 2 Ch App 77, CA.

[45] Companies Act 2006, s 174.

[46] Ibid., s 174(2). This is the same test that is applied for wrongful trading at common law and under s 214 Insolvency Act 1986.

[47] [1997] 1 BCLC 48.

company's operational needs as an executive director. However, in the eyes of the law, there is no distinction between the role of non-executive director and executive director and, therefore, both roles attract the same legal duties and responsibilities. The Walker Report strongly emphasizes the need for non-executive directors to be 'ready, able and encouraged to challenge and test proposals on strategy put forward by the executive', which inevitably recognizes a need for non-executive directors to possess greater knowledge of a company's operations. One of the recommendations expected to be implemented by the Financial Reporting Council is an increased time commitment from non-executive directors.[48]

5.2.4.3 Consequences of a breach of statutory duty

5.35 The consequences of a breach of sections 171–177 Companies Act 2006 are the same as those that apply where the corresponding common law rule or equitable principle applies.[49] This includes (but is not limited to) damages, compensation or a requirement that the director account for any profit made as a result of the breach of his duties.

5.36 The general duties (with the exception of section 174 Companies Act 2006) are enforceable in the same way as any other fiduciary duty owed to a company by its directors.[50] As these duties are owed to the company, it is only the company who can commence an action for a breach of duty against its director(s). In certain limited circumstances, the shareholders of the company may bring a derivative claim on the company's behalf.[51]

5.2.4.4 Relief from liability

5.37 Full or partial relief from liability under section 170 Companies Act 2006 can be obtained if it can be established that the director in question acted (a) honestly, (b) reasonably and (c) ought fairly to be excused.[52] All three tests must be satisfied.[53] The breadth of this test is such that it is unlikely that a director falling within the ambit of the test would be in breach of his duties in the first place. Such was the case in *Re Ortega Associates Ltd*[54] where the court (having concluded there had not been a breach of duty) stated that if there had been a breach, relief would have been available to the director.[55]

---

48 See *Singer v Beckett* [2001] BPIR 733; *Re Bradcrown Ltd* [2001] 1 BCLC 547 and *Equitable Life Assurance Society v Bowley and Others* [2004] 1 BCLC 180.
49 Companies Act 2006, s 178(1).
50 Ibid., s 178(2).
51 Ibid., Part 11 Chapter 1.
52 Ibid., s 1157.
53 *Re Oxford Pharmaceuticals Ltd* [2009] 2 BCLC 485.
54 [2008] BCC 256.
55 Also see *Queensway Systems v Walker* [2007] 2 BCLC 577.

5.2.5 Directors' statutory duties under the Insolvency Act 1986

5.2.5.1 Wrongful trading

In a situation where a director[56] knows, or ought to conclude, that the company has no reasonable prospect of avoiding insolvent liquidation,[57] the directors of that company may face personal liability *unless* they take every step with a view to minimizing losses to the company's creditors. This is the concept of 'wrongful trading' and is set out in section 214 Insolvency Act 1986. Liability for wrongful trading only applies where a company goes into liquidation. In that situation, a liquidator (and only a liquidator)[58] is entitled to apply to the court, on behalf of the company, for an order against the director(s) requiring that they contribute to the company's assets.[59] **5.38**

To establish wrongful trading, the liquidator must prove on the balance of probabilities that: **5.39**

(a) the company has gone into insolvent liquidation (that is, the company's assets are insufficient to pay its debts and other liabilities, including contingent liabilities and expenses of the winding-up)[60];
(b) the person knew or ought to have concluded that there was no reasonable prospect of the company avoiding an insolvent liquidation. A director's knowledge, both actual and deemed, is tested both objectively and subjectively;[61] and
(c) the person was a director, or shadow director, of the company at the relevant time.[62]

It is a defence to an action for wrongful trading if the director can satisfy the court that he (knowing there was no reasonable prospect of the company avoiding an insolvent liquidation) took every step with a view to minimizing loss to the company's creditors as he ought to have taken.[63] The phrase 'every step' in this context is important and should be interpreted strictly. **5.40**

---

56 Wrongful trading liability may also be applied to shadow directors.

57 See *Singla v Hedman* [2010] EWHC 902 (Ch) for a recent example of a summary judgment application failing for want of establishing this aspect of liability.

58 See *Re International Championship Management Ltd* [2007] BCC 95.

59 An issue that is currently under review is whether a liquidator may be able to access floating charge funds in order to finance a s 214 Insolvency Act 1986 claim. *Leyland Daf* [2004] UKHL was recently reversed to this effect by the Court of Appeal.

60 Insolvency Act 1986, s 214(6).

61 See section 3 and also s 214(4) Insolvency Act 1986.

62 Insolvency Act 1986, s 214(7).

63 Ibid., s 214(3).

5.41 The assessment of liability for wrongful trading should not be judged with hindsight.[64] The correct time to cease trading will, of course, vary according to the particular circumstances of the case—a director must neither act too late nor too early in making the decision to place the company into liquidation. In *Re Continental Assurance*,[65] the balance between these competing interests was considered by Park J. who explained that putting the company into liquidation precipitously may expose the directors to criticism as liquidations are expensive and an early closure of the business would almost certainly mean the liquidation is an insolvent one, causing a greater loss to creditors. On the other hand, if the director delays taking action for too long he may expose himself to personal liability for wrongful trading.

5.42 For this reason and to protect against potential liability for wrongful trading, it is important (particularly during the period approaching insolvency) that appropriate procedures are implemented, and accurate records are kept relating to the conduct and decisions of the boards of directors, including, but not limited to, the following:

- *seek professional advice early:* it is of utmost importance that the board should seek appropriate legal and financial advice as early as possible. An individual director can seek his own advice if he is not happy with what the board as a whole is doing;
- *establish defined roles for each of the directors:* ensure there are no ambiguities as to the roles assigned to the directors on the board;
- *convene regular board meetings:* directors can only demonstrate that they have formed the view that there is a reasonable prospect of avoiding insolvent liquidation if they have taken steps to inform themselves about the financial situation of the company. Contemporaneous evidence of such steps should be kept. In particular, the minuting of board meetings will help to evidence that directors have complied with their duties. These actions are critical during this period;
- *review intra-group arrangements:* directors should review the existing financing arrangements between companies in the corporate group (notably in relation to intra-group funding), so that a clear picture exists as to how dependent particular companies are on other members of the group. As previously stated, the solvency position of a company is not determined on a 'group' basis and therefore directors must have a clear understanding of the financial position of each individual company;

64 See *Re Hawkes Hill Publishing* [2007] BCC 937 where the wrongful trading claim failed.
65 [2007] 2 BCLC 287 at 281.

- *review the financial accounts:* a review of the financial accounts will help to assess whether the legal solvency analysis differs from the accounting test. This may, for example, allow assets listed in the accounts at historical values to be revalued;
- *review material documentation*: it is important for directors to identify the key contracts and other agreements entered into by the company and to be familiar with their provisions. In particular, the directors should be aware of the provisions dealing with financial covenants, material adverse change, disclosure and termination in the event of the company's insolvency;
- *conduct of shareholders:* in general, shareholders should be aware of the risk of becoming shadow directors if they become involved in the management of the company or in the decisions of its directors (except to the extent that this is a natural consequence of their position as shareholders);
- *decision whether to stop trading:* this must be kept under review at all times. If the point arrives at which there is no hope of a successful restructuring, trading must stop immediately to avoid the company incurring liabilities that cannot be met. However, a premature decision to stop trading may be equally dangerous. For example, losses to creditors may be minimized by completing work in progress;
- *to resign or not to resign:* resignation is normally not advisable because it can be seen as an abdication, rather than a discharge, of the director's duties; further, wrongful trading applies to directors and former directors. By definition, a director who has resigned cannot assist the company in minimizing its losses to creditors. However, if a director finds himself in a position of irreconcilable conflict, he may have to resign;
- *counterparty strategies:* the attitudes and interests of stakeholders and counterparties should be considered. For example, a secured creditor may have the right to enforce security (and the lead banks may come under pressure from syndicate members to do so). However, those close to the situation may recognize that this will only devalue the security.

The liability which attaches to a director for a breach of section 214 Insolvency **5.43**
Act 1986 is civil, and not criminal.[66] A director found liable for wrongful trading may be ordered to contribute to the company's assets for the benefit of creditors. The aim is compensatory rather than penal. The required contribution from the relevant director(s) is left entirely to the court's discretion however it is likely that the contribution will be the amount of incremental loss suffered by the company from the time the director knew, or ought to have concluded, that there was no

[66] Cf. Companies Act 2006, s 993 regarding fraudulent trading.

real prospect that the company would avoid insolvent liquidation. Liability for a breach of section 214 Insolvency Act 1986 is several and therefore different directors may be held liable for different amounts depending on their individual actions, knowledge, skill and experience.[67]

5.2.5.2 Fraudulent trading

5.44 Fraudulent trading is the carrying on of any business of the company with an intention to defraud creditors of the company, or creditors of any other person, or for any fraudulent effect.[68] Any person who is knowingly a party to the carrying on of business in this manner may be held liable to make such contributions to the company's assets as the court thinks fit.[69] Like the wrongful trading provisions, applications under section 213 Insolvency Act 1986 may only be brought by a liquidator on the winding up of a company.[70] The standard of proof for fraudulent trading is the criminal standard, 'beyond reasonable doubt' and, therefore, far more onerous than the wrongful trading provisions. For this reason, applications under section 213 Insolvency Act 1986 are rare.

5.45 To establish liability under section 213 Insolvency Act 1986 a liquidator must prove that:

(a) the company is in the course of being wound up and the applicant is the liquidator of the company; and
(b) the business of the company was carried out with an intention to defraud creditors.

5.46 The leading authority on whether the business of the company was carried out with an *intention to defraud creditors* is the case of *Re Patrick and Lyon Ltd*[71] where Maugham J. stated that to prove intention to defraud there must be 'actual dishonesty, involving, according to current notions of fair trading between commercial men, real moral blame'.[72] The court has made it clear that it will apply strict criteria in determining whether or not a case of fraudulent trading has been made out.[73] Maugham J. held in *Re William Leich Bros* that 'if a company continues to carry on business and to incur debts at a time when there is, to the knowledge of the directors, no reasonable prospect of the creditors ever receiving payment of

[67] See *Valentine v Bangla TV* [2010] BCC 143.
[68] Insolvency Act 1981, s 213.
[69] Insolvency Act 1986, s 213(2).
[70] See *Re Overnight* Ltd [2009] Bus LR 1141 in relation to the limitation period for an action in fraudulent trading.
[71] [1933] Ch 78.
[72] *Re Patrick and Lyon Ltd* [1933] Ch 786.
[73] Also see *Mophitis v Bernascom & Co* [2003] Ch. 552, CA.

those debts, it is, in general, a proper inference that the company is carrying on business with intent to defraud'.[74]

As stated above in relation to wrongful trading, a person found to have engaged in fraudulent trading may be held liable by the court to make such contributions (if any) to the company's assets as the court thinks proper. Any recovery by the liquidator under this section must be held for the benefit of the company's creditors as a whole. In addition, but discussed in further detail below, a director may be subject to a disqualification order pursuant to section 10 of the Company Directors Disqualification Act 1986. Fraudulent trading is also a criminal offence pursuant to section 993 Companies Act 2006. **5.47**

5.2.5.3 Misfeasance or breach of fiduciary duty

Section 212 Insolvency Act 1986 applies if, in the course of the winding up of a company, it appears that a person who: **5.48**

(a) is or has been an officer of the company;
(b) has acted as liquidator or administrative receiver of the company; or
(c) not being a person falling within paragraph (a) or (b), is or has been concerned, or has taken part in the promotion, formation or management of the company,

has misapplied or retained, or become accountable for, any money or other property of the company or been guilty of any misfeasance or breach of any fiduciary duty in relation to the company.[75] This section applies to shadow directors[76] and de facto directors.[77]

An application to the court under section 212 Insolvency Act 1986 may be made by the official receiver, liquidator or by any creditor of the company or any assignee of such creditor.[78] If the court finds a director guilty of any misfeasance or breach of fiduciary duty under this section, it has a very wide discretion to make an order compelling that director to: **5.49**

(a) repay, restore or account for the money or property of the company, or any part of it, with interest at such rate as the court thinks just; or
(b) contribute such sum to the company's assets by way of compensation in respect of the misfeasance or breach of fiduciary or other duty as the court thinks just.[79]

---

74 [1932] 2 Ch 71, 77.
75 Insolvency Act 1986, s 212(1).
76 *Gemma Ltd v Davies* [2008] 2 BCLC 281.
77 *Re Paycheck Services 3 Ltd* [2009] WLR (D) 228, CA.
78 See *Mullarkey v Broad* [2008] 1 BCLC 638; *Re Southill Finance* Ltd [2009] EWCA Civ 2.
79 Insolvency Act 1986, s 212(3).

5.50 In *Transocean Equipment Manufacturing & Trading Ltd*[80] payments were made out of the company's account, notwithstanding that it had earlier been dissolved. Some of these payments had been authorized by the director in question and some of the payments were made by other persons in management. The director was aware that the company had, at that stage, been dissolved but took no steps to protect the assets of the company. Rather, he participated and acquiesced in the distribution of those assets for purposes that were plainly not for the benefit of the company. It was held that whether or not the director was the authorizing party as regards the payments, he was liable and responsible for all the payments because he acquiesced in the making of the payments. The company obtained an order for recovery of the funds misappropriated and misapplied, plus interest.[81]

5.2.6 Antecedent transactions

5.51 As outlined above, as a company's financial position becomes less certain, the stakeholders to whom the directors owe their primary duties shift from the shareholders of the company to its creditors. The actions and considerations of directors fulfilling their duties in these circumstances will therefore differ to those where the solvency of the company is more certain. Directors must be very careful in relation to the transactions payments it makes during the period leading up to insolvency as director's decision to enter into such transaction and/or make such payment may be reviewed at a later date.[82]

5.52 The term 'antecedent transactions' refers to transactions which have occurred in the past that are reviewable because they prejudice the interests of one or more of the company's creditors in some way—for example, the sale of an asset at an undervalue (depriving the company of consideration that it might otherwise have received to satisfy its creditors) or the payment to one creditor in preference to another (depriving the creditor in the event the company's funds are extinguished before its debts are repaid). Under English law, there are five main types of antecedent transactions:

(a) transactions at an undervalue;
(b) preferences;
(c) transactions defrauding creditors;

---

[80] [2006] BPIR 594.

[81] Also see *Re Ortega Associates Ltd* [2008] BCC 256 and *Re Continental Assurance* [2001] BPIR 733.

[82] *Re Oxford Pharmaceuticals Limited, Wilson and another v Masters International Limited and another* [2009] 2 BCLC 485 illustrates how antecedent transactions relate to the possibility of a breach of director's duty. See also *Giles v Rhind* [2008] 3 WLR 1233, CA which shows that the overlap is not absolute; the right to relief under s 423 Insolvency Act 1986 does not depend on showing the victim was a person to whom some duty was owed.

(d) extortionate credit transactions; and
(e) avoidance of floating charges.

Under sections 238–241 of the Insolvency Act 1986, where a company goes into administration or liquidation, the administrator or liquidator may apply to the court to set aside a transaction if: **5.53**

(a) the transaction was either:
    (i) at an undervalue (ie where there was a gift or the value of the consideration received by the company was 'significantly less' than the value of the consideration provided by it); or
    (ii) a preference in favour of an existing creditor (or a surety or guarantor for any of the company's debt or other liabilities) in certain circumstances,

    and was, in either case, entered into within two years (or, in the case of (ii) above six months but only if the parties are not 'connected') before the company enters into administration or the commencement of the winding up; and
(b) the company is at the time of the transaction, or becomes in consequence of it, unable to pay its debts within the meaning of the Insolvency Act 1986 (which inability is rebuttably presumed if the parties are 'connected' and the transaction in question is a transaction at an undervalue).

5.2.6.1 Transactions at an undervalue

A transaction is at an undervalue if the transaction constitutes a gift or if the value of the consideration obtained by the relevant entity is significantly less than the value of the consideration which it provides. **5.54**

In considering whether each transaction is a transaction at an undervalue recent case law suggests that it is appropriate to look at the transactions as a whole. In *Philips v Brewin Dolphin Bell Lawrie Ltd*[83] the court refused to consider two agreements separately for the purposes of section 238 Insolvency Act 1986. *Re M.C. Bacon Ltd*[84] is authority for the principle that section 238(4) Insolvency Act 1986 requires a comparison to be made between the value obtained by the company for the transaction and the value provided by the company. Both values must be measurable in money or money's worth and both must be considered from the company's point of view. For a transaction to constitute a transaction at an undervalue it must result in a depletion of the company's assets. **5.55**

Pursuant to section 238 Insolvency Act 1986, the court may make such order as it thinks fit for restoring the parties to the position which would otherwise have **5.56**

---

83 [2001] UKHL 2.
84 [1990] BCC 78.

existed but for the transaction. However, no order will be made under this section if the court is satisfied that the company entered into the transaction in good faith and for the purpose of carrying on its business and there were reasonable grounds for believing that the transaction would benefit the company (the 'good faith test').

5.2.6.2 Preferences

5.57 A company gives a preference to a person if that person is one of the company's creditors or a surety or guarantor of the company's debts or other liabilities and the company does anything or suffers anything to be done which has the effect of putting that person in a position that, if the company went into insolvent liquidation, would be better that the position he would have been in if the thing had not been done. The relevant 'claw-back' period for giving a preference is two years if the preference is given to a person who is connected with the company or, if there is no connection, six months. To be a preferential transaction within the Insolvency Act 1986 the company must also be or become (in consequence of the transaction or preference) unable at the time to pay its debts for the purposes of section 123 of the Insolvency Act 1986. This is presumed even if the parties are connected.

5.58 The court will not make an order under section 239 Insolvency Act 1986 unless the company which gave the preference was influenced by a desire to put the company to which the payment was made in a better position than it would be in on an insolvent winding up. It is not sufficient that the payer desired to make the payment and a necessary consequence of that was that the payee was put in a better position—'a man is not to be taken as desiring all the necessary consequences of his actions'.[85]

5.2.6.3 Transactions defrauding creditors

5.59 The court may also set aside transactions at an undervalue which were entered into for the purpose of putting assets out of reach of creditors pursuant to section 423 Insolvency Act 1986.

5.60 The definition of what constitutes a transaction at an undervalue arising on applications made under section 423 Insolvency Act 1986 is the same as previously described under section 238 Insolvency Act 1986.

5.61 Section 423(3) makes clear that the transaction must be intended to have some 'prejudicial effect' on the interests of creditors.[86] Unlike section 238 Insolvency Act 1986 there is no time limit for bringing an application under section 423

---

85 See Millett J. in *Re M.C. Bacon Ltd* [1990] BBC 78, 87.

86 *The Law Society v Southall* [2002] BPIR 336, CA.

Insolvency Act 1986; however the courts are very reluctant to review transactions entered into many years before. Applications under section 423 Insolvency Act 1986 may be brought by a wider category of persons than those permitted under section 238 Insolvency Act 1986.[87] An application made by any of these persons is treated as made on behalf of every victim of the transaction at an undervalue.[88]

5.2.7 Disqualification of directors

A director found to be in breach of his duties, may also be subject to a disqualification order[89] pursuant to the Company Directors Disqualification Act 1986 (the 'CDDA').[90] A disqualification order can be made against a director, whether the company in which he is a director is insolvent or not.[91] The effect of a disqualification order on a director is that it prohibits him from acting or being a director of a company, a receiver of a company's property or being concerned or taking part in the promotion, formation or management of a company (whether directly or indirectly) for a certain period of time without the leave of the court.[92] A disqualification order may be made by the court, notwithstanding that the director in question is criminally liable in respect of the same matter.[93] The maximum period of time in which a disqualification order can apply to a director will depend on the type of conduct engaged in by that director.[94] **5.62**

In relation to directors found guilty of misconduct (described in sections 2 and 3 of CDDA),[95] the court may in some circumstances impose a disqualification order of up to 15 years. In *R v Creggy*[96] the director was disqualified for seven years for using a company to shelter criminal property as these actions were considered to have a relevant factual connection with the 'management of the company'. **5.63**

[87] Insolvency Act 1986, s 424(1).

[88] Insolvency Act 1986, s 424(2).

[89] Disqualification proceedings can also be launched against both de facto and shadow directors: *Re Mea Corporation* [2007] 1 BCLC 618.

[90] For recent authority on evidential issues, see *Official Receiver v Key* [2009] BCC 11 and *Aaron v SoS for BERR* [2009] Bus LR 809, CA. For further procedural matters see *Re Blackspur Group (No. 4) (Eastaway v SoSTI)* [2008] 1 BCLC 153, CA; *SoS for BERR v Smith* [2009] BCC 497; *Re Hawkes Hill Publishing Co Ltd* [2007] BPIR 1305.

[91] *SoSTI v Arnold* provides authority for the position that the court has jurisdiction to entertain disqualification proceedings under the Company Directors Disqualification Act where a company has been dissolved.

[92] Section 1(1)(a) Company Directors Disqualification Act 1986.

[93] Company Directors Disqualification Act 1986, s 1(4).

[94] Ibid., s 1(2).

[95] Ibid., s 3, governs persistent breaches of companies legislations. 'Companies legislation' includes the provisions in the Companies Act governing, misfeasance, fraudulent trading, wrongful trading and antecedent transactions).

[96] [2008] BCC 323, CA.

5.64 Pursuant to section 6 CDDA the court shall make a disqualification order against a director (or shadow director) if it is satisfied that:

(a) he is or has been a director of a company which has at any time become insolvent (whether while he was a director or subsequently);[97] and
(b) his conduct as a director of that company (or taken together with his conduct as a director of any other company) makes him unfit to be concerned in the management of a company.[98]

5.65 If the court determines that the director in question is unfit to be concerned in the management of the company, the imposition of a disqualification order on that director is mandatory and the court will have no discretion to refuse the making of such an order.[99] The application for a disqualification order of this type must be made within two years of the company becoming insolvent, except if leave of the court is obtained.[100] The minimum period for disqualification is two years and the maximum period is 15 years.[101]

5.66 If a court has made a declaration against a director under section 213 Insolvency Act 1986 (regarding fraudulent trading) or section 214 Insolvency Act 1986 (wrongful trading), the court has a discretion to make a disqualification order against that director. The maximum period of disqualification is 15 years.[102]

5.3 Fiduciary duties of directors in management of distressed corporations in the US[103]

5.67 The emergence of financial distress of a business corporation should act as a catalyst for the corporations' directors to reassess their duties. Financial distress, generally, turns a bright light on the governance of a corporation and the actions

[97] A company is considered insolvent for this purpose if, at the time it goes into liquidation, its assets are insufficient for payment of its debts and other liabilities and expenses of the winding up, the company enters administration or an administrative receiver of the company is appointed (s 6(2) CDDA). Application may be brought under s 4 CDDA if its is solvent.

[98] See *Re AG (Manchester) Ltd, OR v Watson* [2008] 1 BCLC 321 which sets out guidance on the interpretation of unfitness for the purpose of this section.

[99] Company Director Disqualification Act 1986, s 9. In determining 'unfitness', the court may look to the matters set out in Part 1 (in all cases) and Part II (in the event the company is insolvent) of Sch 1, Company Director Disqualification Act 1986 which, includes any breach by the director of ss 238–240 Insolvency Act 1986.

[100] Ibid., s 7(2).

[101] Ibid., s 6(4) and s 7(2). See *Kappler v SoSTI* [2008] 1 BCLC 120; *Re Vintage Hallmalk plc* [2007] 1 BCLC 788; *Re City Truck Group (No. 2) (SoSTI v Gee)* [2007] 2 BCLC 649 for examples of recent disqualification orders.

[102] See Company Director Disqualification Act 1986, s 10.

[103] Harvey R. Miller, Senior Partner, Weil, Gotshal & Manges LLP. The author gratefully acknowledges the significant contributions of his associates Mark Bernstein and Zaw Win.

taken by its board of directors. Since the failure of a distressed corporation leads to a zero sum scenario, one or more groups of stakeholders will be 'out of the money'. Such out-of-the-money stakeholders may look to find a deep pocket to ease or otherwise recover their losses. Directors of a failed corporation often represent likely targets for disgruntled stakeholders. As a consequence, such directors need to be cognizant of their rights, protections and obligations when a corporation approaches insolvency or becomes insolvent and unable to satisfy its creditors in full and equity interests are wiped out. For many years, the raging debate has been the scope and extent of the fiduciary duties of the directors of a distressed corporation. Financial distress and the possibility of insolvency will affect the governance of a corporation. In such circumstances, diligent efforts should be made to ensure the effective and efficient administration of the business. Accounting and corporate governance policies should be reviewed and scrupulously observed. Where appropriate, strategic alternatives should be explored. The issue addressed in this chapter, however, is whether or to what extent the downward trend in a corporation's financial condition creates additional fiduciary duties flowing from directors to the creditors of the distressed corporation who may be the ultimate holders of the residual interests in the corporation.

The scope of the fiduciary duties that a board of directors owes to stockholders of **5.68**
a solvent corporation is well established. These generally consist of the twin duties of care and loyalty and are owed to the corporation and its shareholders. The gravity with which US law regards a director's duties to shareholders is a result of 'the fact that directors have control and guidance of corporate business affairs and property and hence of the property interests of the stockholders. Equity recognizes that stockholders are the proprietors of the corporate interest and are ultimately the only beneficiaries thereof.'[104] Courts, therefore, generally require complete loyalty, honesty and good faith from directors in their dealings with a corporation and its shareholders. Conversely, there is generally no fiduciary duty owed to a solvent corporation's creditors.[105] Instead, duties to creditors are limited and based upon the contractual instrument or other arrangement that created the debtor–creditor relationship and otherwise applicable laws enacted to protect the rights of creditors.

---

[104] *Ashman v Miller* 101 F2d 85, 91 (6th Cir. 1939).

[105] *See Simons v Cogan* 549 A2d 300 (Del. 1988) (holding that no fiduciary duties are owed to the holders of a corporation's convertible debentures); see also *Webb v Cash*, 250 P 1, 8 (Wyo. 1926) ('[I]t is difficult to perceive upon what principle a director of a corporation can be considered a trustee to its creditors. He is selected by the shareholders, not by creditors; he has no contractual relation with the latter; he represents a distinct entity, the corporation; and his relations to its creditors is exactly the same as the agent of an individual bears to creditors of such individual; and it is not pretended that in the latter case the agent would be the trustee of the creditors or his principal.'

5.69 In the US, the laws of the State of Delaware, as interpreted by the Delaware Court of Chancery and Delaware Supreme Court, are the primary source of legal principles governing corporate law and fiduciary duties of directors. Companies and lawyers around the world prefer the logical approach and certainty provided by Delaware laws, as evidenced by the fact that in the 1,020 merger agreements filed with the Securities Exchange Commission from 2004 to 2008, 66 per cent of such agreements opt for Delaware law and 60 per cent opt for Delaware courts as the relevant jurisdiction, while 62 per cent of the targets and 55 per cent of the acquirers were incorporated in Delaware.[106] Due largely to the predominance of Delaware law in the area of corporate law and fiduciary duties, this chapter will primarily focus on Delaware laws and standards, but may, in certain circumstances, note divergence by other states.

5.3.1 Duty of loyalty

5.70 The duty of loyalty requires that directors discharge their obligations to a corporation in good faith[107] and abstain from any actions that could be detrimental to the corporation and its shareholders or that are intended to benefit the director's own interests or the interests of a third party.[108] This prohibition includes both self-dealing and usurping corporate opportunities[109] and is not susceptible to being excused by a finding that the director was acting in good faith.[110] As the Delaware Supreme Court stated in its landmark decision *Guth v Loft, Inc.*:

> Corporate officers and directors are not permitted to use their position of trust and confidence to further their own private interest. . . . A public policy, existing through the years, and derived from a profound knowledge of human characteristics and motives, has established a rule that demands of a corporate officer or director, peremptorily and inexorably, the most scrupulous observance of his duty. . . . The rule that requires an undivided and unselfish loyalty to the corporation demands that there shall be no conflict between duty and self interest.[111]

5.71 The inviolability of the duty of loyalty is such that, under Delaware law, a corporation cannot indemnify directors for violations thereof, for acts or omissions not made in good faith, or that involve intentional misconduct or a knowing violation

---

106 See 'All Too Common' *The Deal*, 9 October 2009.

107 See *Stone ex rel. AmSouth Bancorporation v Ritter* 911 A2d 362, 370 (Del 2006).

108 See *Revlon, Inc. v MacAndrews & Forbes Holdings, Inc.* 506 A2d 173, 182 (Del 1986); *Ivanhoe Partners v Newmont Mining Corp.* 535 A2d 1334, 1345 (Del 1987).

109 See, eg. *Norlin Corp. v Rooney, Pace Inc.* 744 F.2d 255, 264 (2d Cir 1984).

110 See, eg, *AC Acquisition Corp. v Anderson, Clayton & Co.* 519 A2d 103, 115 (Del Ch 1986) ('Where director action is not protected by the business judgment rule, mere good faith will not preclude a finding of breach of the duty of loyalty. Rather, in most such instances (which happen to be self-dealing transactions), the transaction can only be sustained if it is objectively or intrinsically fair.').

111 5 A2d 503, 510 (Del 1939).

of law, or for any transaction from which the director derived a personal benefit.[112]

5.3.2 Duty of care

Directors are generally required to exercise 'that degree of care which a person of ordinary prudence would exercise under the same or similar circumstances'.[113] This duty incorporates an obligation for directors to, among other things, inform themselves 'before making a business decision, of all material information reasonably available to them', including a responsibility to consider alternatives and obtain professional advice where appropriate.[114] **5.72**

Delaware law permits a corporation to exculpate directors from personal liability for unintentional breaches of the duty of care,[115] to support the policy of encouraging 'capable persons to serve as directors of corporations by providing them with the freedom to make risky, good faith business decisions without fear of personal liability'.[116] A majority of US jurisdictions have followed Delaware's lead and have enacted similar statutes.[117] **5.73**

5.3.3 Duty of disclosure

Derivative of both the duty of care and the duty of loyalty is a duty of disclosure.[118] In Delaware, directors 'are required to disclose fully and fairly all material information within the board's control when it seeks shareholder action. . . [i]n the absence of a request for stockholder action'.[119] With respect to materiality, Delaware follows the US Supreme Court: 'An omitted fact is material if there is a substantial likelihood that a reasonable shareholder would consider it important **5.74**

---

[112] See Del Code Ann tit. 8 § 102(b)(7).

[113] *Meyers v Moody* 693 F2d 1196, 1209 (5th Cir 1982); see also *Graham v Allis-Chalmers Mfg. Co.* 188 A2d 125, 130 (Del. 1963) ('[D]irectors of a corporation in managing the corporate affairs are bound to use that amount of care which ordinarily careful and prudent men would use in similar circumstances.')

[114] *See Aronson v Lewis* 473 A2d 805, 812 (Del. 1984); see also Dennis J. Block et al., *The Business Judgment Rule: Fiduciary Duties of Corporate Directors 3* (3rd edn, Asper, 1989) (hereinafter Block).

[115] See Del Code Ann tit. 8 § 102(b)(7).

[116] *Production Resources Group, L.L.C. v NCT Group, Inc.* 863 A2d 772, 793 (Del. Ch. 2004).

[117] The following states have enacted statutes similar to Del Code Ann tit. 8 § 102(b)(7): Alaska, Arizona, Arkansas; California, Georgia, Colorado, Hawaii, Idaho, Iowa, Kansas, Kentucky, Louisiana, Maryland, Massachusetts, Michigan, Minnesota, Montana, Nevada, New Hampshire, New Jersey, New York, Oklahoma, Oregon, Pennsylvania, Rhode Island, South Dakota, Tennessee, Texas, Utah, Washington and Wyoming.

[118] See *Malone v Brincat* 722 A2d 5, 11 (Del. 1998) ('The duty of directors to observe proper disclosure requirements derives from the combination of the fiduciary duties of care, loyalty, and good faith.'); see also *Malpiede v Townson* 780 A2d 1075, 1086 (Del. 2001).

[119] Ibid. at 11-12.

in deciding how to vote.'[120] The duty of disclosure is complementary to, not pre-empted by, the disclosure requirements contained in federal securities law.[121]

5.75 Accordingly, a company contemplating bankruptcy is not required to disclose its contingency plans. In *Beleson v Schwartz*,[122] the court held that public policy dictates that it is necessary to allow a 'company operating near insolvency to make careful deliberations about its future free from any obligation to disclose a potential bankruptcy'.[123] Any rule requiring companies to disclose contingent bankruptcy planning would lead to a 'self-fulfilling prophecy, ensuring that all companies that begin contingent preparations for bankruptcy would inevitably go bankrupt' as investors and market participants would lose confidence in such company.[124] In addition, as was the case with Loral Space & Communications Ltd., before a bankruptcy, disclosure of prior financial statements and other corporate actions provide adequate notice to investors that a company is distressed.

5.3.4 Alternate entities

5.76 The discussion of directors' fiduciary duties in this chapter is generally limited to the directors of corporations and related fiduciary duties under the relevant corporate law. However, limited liability companies ('LLC') are growing in popularity, and it is now possible to decipher certain general principles in case law surrounding the governance of such entities. In Delaware, generally, managers and members of LLCs owe the same fiduciary duties as officers and directors of corporations and LLC statutes permit exculpation of members and managers in a similar, albeit at times more flexible, manner.[125] In defining such fiduciary duties in the distressed context, Delaware courts have cited the relevant corporate law cases as authority.[126] As such, the portions of this chapter that describe the duties of directors to various stakeholders when a company is distressed are instructive for members and managers of LLCs as well.[127]

---

[120] *Rosenblatt v Getty Oil Co.* 493 A2d 929, 944 (Del 1985) (quoting *TSC Indus., Inc. v Northway, Inc.* 426 US 438, 449 (1976).

[121] *Malone* 722 A2d at 13.

[122] See *Beleson v Schwartz* 599 F Supp 2d 519 (SDNY 2009) (holding Schwartz not liable for omitting to disclose bankruptcy planning).

[123] Ibid. at 527 (citing *Re Tower Auto. Secs. Litigation* 483 F Supp 2d 327 (SDNY 2007)).

[124] Ibid.

[125] See *Metro Communic'n Corp. BVI v Advanced Mobilecomm Techs* 854 A2d 121, 253 (Del. Ch. 2004): 'In addition to any contractual duties owed by [the LLC] and its managers, the managers owe a fiduciary duty of loyalty and care to [the LLC]'; see also *Flight Options Int'l. Inc. v Flight Options*, LLC, 2005 WL 2335353 *7 (Del Ch 2005); §18-1102 of the Delaware Limited Liability Company Act.

[126] *See U.S. Bank Nat'l Ass'n v U.S. Timberlands Klamath Falls, L.L.C.* 864 A2d 930, 934 (Del Ch 2004); *Blackmore Partners, L.P. v Link Energy LLC,* 2005 WL 2709639 *6 (Del Ch 2005).

[127] This general observation is subject to certain important exceptions. The Delaware Limited Liability Company Act, which provides the default governance and administration framework for limited liability companies organized in that state, may lead to a result completely different from

5.3.5 The business judgment rule

5.77 In evaluating whether a director has adequately discharged his or her responsibilities as to the duty of care, courts refer to the business judgment rule.[128] Courts, generally, avoid responsibility for making business decisions for a corporation and will be deferential to the business judgments of directors. The business judgment rule allows courts to focus on the process that directors undertake with respect to a particular decision, not its substantive merits. As the Delaware Court of Chancery noted in *Re Caremark Int'l Inc. Derivative Litig.*, the evaluation of a director's discharge of her fiduciary duties can never appropriately be judicially determined by reference to the *content of the board decision* that leads to a corporate loss, apart from consideration of the good faith *or* rationality of the process employed. That is, whether a judge or jury considering the matter after the fact believes a decision substantively wrong, or degrees of wrong extending through 'stupid' to 'egregious' or 'irrational', provides no ground for director liability, so long as the court determination that the process employed was either rational or employed in *a good faith* effort to advance corporate interests. Thus the business judgment rule is process oriented and informed by a deep respect for all good faith board decisions.[129]

5.78 The business judgment rule operates as a presumption that, before making a business decision, a director informed him or herself of relevant available information, acted in good faith, and with the honest belief that the actions taken were necessary and in the corporation's best interests.[130] The burden is on the party challenging the decision to establish facts rebutting the presumption.[131]

5.79 Reliance on the business judgment rule is reflective of the recognition by courts that *first*, they do not possess the analytical faculties, information, and business skills, to overturn considered business decisions, and, *second*, that business

what would be required under the Delaware General Corporation Law. For example, in a recent decision creditors of a limited liability company were denied standing to bring derivative actions on behalf of the limited liability company irrespective of issues of solvency. See CML V, *LLC v Bax* 6 A3d 238 (Del Ch 2010). This is in contrast to the Delaware General Corporation Law, which allows creditors to bring derivative actions when a corporation is insolvent. See eg, *North American Catholic Educational Programming Foundation, Inc. v Gheewalla* 930 A2d 92, 102 (Del 2007).

[128] One formulation of the business judgment rule provides that a director of officer, engaged in a business decision, fulfills his or her fiduciary duty if he or she (a) is not interested in the subject of the business judgment; (b) is informed with respect to the subject of the business judgment to the extent the director reasonably believes to be appropriate under the circumstances; and (c) rationally believes the business judgment is in the best interest of the corporation: *Principals of Corporate Governance* (American Law Institute, 1994).

[129] 698 A2d 959, 967-8 (Del Ch 1996) (emphasis in original).

[130] See eg. *Levine v Smith* 591 A2d 194, 207 (Del 1991); *Spiegel v Buntrock*, 571 A2d 767, 774 (Del 1990); *Grobow v Perot* 539 A2d 180, 187 (Del 1988); *Aronson* 473 A2d at 812; see also Block, above n. 14 at 29 ('The business judgment rule shields directors from liability when its five elements – a business decision, disinterestedness, due care, good faith and no abuse of discretion – are present and creates a presumption in favor of the directors that each of these elements has been satisfied.')

[131] *Aronson* 473 A2d at 812.

decisions inherently encompass risk that often cannot be judged by the ultimate result of the decision.

5.80 In that context, the general rule in Delaware is that directors owe fiduciary duties to the corporation and its shareholders, but not to creditors.[132] While shareholders rely on directors acting as fiduciaries to protect their interests, creditors are afforded protection through contractual agreements, fraud and fraudulent conveyance law, implied covenants of good faith and fair dealing, bankruptcy law, general commercial law and other sources of creditors' rights.[133]

5.3.6 Fiduciary duties in the zone of insolvency

5.81 It generally is well settled that the principles stated above govern when a corporation is solvent. However, controversy and uncertainty developed recently under Delaware law whether directors owe fiduciary duties to creditors as a corporation enters the 'zone of insolvency' ie may be approaching insolvency. The uncertainty in the law whether directors had direct fiduciary duties to creditors while in the zone of insolvency created potential conflicts for directors in determining how and whose interests they were to serve. This puzzle affected the decision-making process and exposed corporations to the probability of increased litigation. In addition, directors may have become unduly risk averse in the face of potential second guessing by courts and creditors if it was later determined that the corporation had been in an amorphous 'zone of insolvency'. Fortunately for directors, the Delaware Supreme Court clarified the fiduciary duties and potential liability of directors of Delaware corporations in the zone of insolvency.[134]

5.82 In *North American Catholic Educational Programming Foundation, Inc. v Gheewalla*, the court endeavoured to resolve any uncertainty as to the state of the law and provide directors with 'clear signal beacons and brightly lined channel markers' for any of their actions and business decisions if the corporation is navigating in the zone of insolvency.[135] Following *Gheewalla*, creditors do not have the right to assert a direct claim for breach of fiduciary duties against a director of a corporation even if it is in the zone of insolvency. The court stated 'when a corporation is navigating in the zone of insolvency, the focus for Delaware directors does not change: directors must continue to discharge their fiduciary duties to the corporation and its shareholders by exercising their business judgment in the best interests of the corporation for the benefit of its shareholder owners'.[136] The Delaware

132 *See Guth v Loft* 5 A2d 503, 510 (Del 1939).

133 See, eg. *Production Resources* at 790; Del Code Ann tit. 6, §§ 9-101-709; Del Code Ann tit. 8, §§ 160, 173, 174; Del Code Ann tit. 6, §§ 1301–1311; 11 USC §§547, 548.

134 *North American Catholic Educational Programming Foundation, Inc. v Gheewalla* 930 A2d 92, 101 (Del. 2007).

135 Ibid. at 101.

136 Ibid.

Supreme Court reasoned that a corporation operating in the zone of insolvency is in desperate need of effective and proactive leadership, as well as the ability to negotiate in good faith with its creditors, goals which would likely be significantly undermined by the prospect of individual liability arising from the pursuit of direct claims of creditors.[137] In addition, the creation of a direct right of action vesting in creditors for alleged breaches of fiduciary duties would create a conflict for directors as to their duties to maximize the value of the corporation for shareholders and an undefined duty to creditors.

The *Gheewalla* decision, in effect, overruled and clarified the erroneous interpretations of a growing line of cases holding that when a corporation is operating in the zone of insolvency the fiduciary duties of directors expanded to include creditors. This line of cases, and much of the confusion about whether fiduciary duties of directors expanded in the zone of insolvency to include creditors, resulted from the decision of the Delaware Court of Chancery in *Credit Lyonnais Bank Nederland, N. V. v Pathe Communications Corp.*[138] In *Credit Lyonnais*, the court held that when a corporation is operating in the 'vicinity of insolvency a board of directors is not merely the agent of the residue risk bearers, but owes its duty to the corporate enterprise'.[139] In an explanatory and oft-cited footnote, the chancery court provided that a board of directors should consider the 'community of interests' in the corporation when making a business judgment.[140] Subsequently, creditors argued, successfully in some cases, that *Credit Lyonnais* stood for the proposition that when a corporation is operating in the zone of insolvency, directors have fiduciary duties to creditors, and creditors are entitled to bring actions based on the breach of such fiduciary duties.[141] **5.83**

Accordingly, confusion reigned as to the true import of *Credit Lyonnais*. As a result, the Delaware Court of Chancery addressed the issues once again in *Production Resources*. In *Production Resources*, the Court of Chancery stated that *Credit Lyonnais* had been misinterpreted and was not intended to expand director's fiduciary duties to creditors, but merely to protect directors who considered the interests of creditors in the context of a potential insolvency.[142] Accordingly, when a company is in the zone of insolvency, under *Production Resources*, the directors' fiduciary duties run to the corporation and, indirectly, to its stakeholders. *Production Resources* makes clear that directors are protected from any **5.84**

137 See ibid. at 100.
138 1991 WL 277613 (Del Ch 30 December 1991).
139 Ibid. at *34.
140 See above n. 55.
141 See, eg. *Re Buckhead Am. Corp.* 178 BR 956 (D Del 1994) (denying defendant's motion to dismiss claim for breach of fiduciary duty where plaintiff amended complaint alleged with sufficient specificity that corporation was insolvent or operating in the vicinity of insolvency at the time directors engaged in certain transactions).
142 Ibid.

risks taken for the benefit of the equity holders notwithstanding that the corporation is in the zone of insolvency, so long as they comply with their fiduciary duties to the firm.[143]

5.85 Delaware courts have emphasized that the fiduciary duties of directors always run to the corporation. This is a simple yet important point. When a company is in distress and near insolvency, shareholders' interests and creditors' interests will begin to diverge. Creditors will have an incentive to seek to maximize the value of the corporation only to the extent necessary to repay their claims in full. Shareholders, conversely, have an incentive to support high risk strategies aimed at providing a return on their equity investments. By clarifying that the directors' fiduciary duties run to the corporation, *Credit Lyonnais* and *Production Resources* noted that the directors' fiduciary duties might require them to pursue a strategy that neither the stockholders nor the creditors prefer.[144]

5.86 *Gheewalla* and *Production Resources* clearly establish that there is a bright line rule when a corporation is solvent, creditors do not have a right to bring a lawsuit against directors (either directly or derivatively) for breach of fiduciary duties. It is irrelevant whether a company is in the zone of insolvency. This rule provides directors the comfort to make decisions that are most likely to bring a solvent company back from the brink of insolvency and maximize the value of a distressed company without fear of direct action by creditors.

5.87 *Gheewalla* and *Production Resources* carve out a safe harbour in which directors may consider interests other than those of the corporation and shareholders without violating their fiduciary duties. Concerned with the myopic view that the single-minded pursuit of profit may engender, many states have enacted statutes that provide similar safe harbours that allow, but do not require, directors to consider a broader range of interests in evaluating a particular business decision. For example, §717 of the NY Business Corporations Law provides:

> (b) In taking action, including, without limitation, action which may involve or relate to a change or potential change in the control of the corporation, a director shall be entitled to consider, without limitation, (1) both the long-term and the short-term interests of the corporation and its shareholders and (2) the effects that the corporation's actions may have in the short-term or in the long-term upon any of the following:
> (i) the prospects for potential growth, development, productivity and profitability of the corporation;
> (ii) the corporation's current employees;

---

143 Ibid. at 790.

144 *Credit Lyonnais* *34 n. 55; *Production Resources* at n. 57.

(iii) the corporation's retired employees and other beneficiaries receiving or entitled to receive retirement, welfare or similar benefits from or pursuant to any plan sponsored, or agreement entered into, by the corporation;
(iv) the corporation's customers and creditors; and
(v) the ability of the corporation to provide, as a going concern, goods, services, employment opportunities and employment benefits and otherwise to contribute to the communities in which it does business.

Nothing in this paragraph shall create any duties owed by any director to any person or entity to consider or afford any particular weight to any of the foregoing or abrogate any duty of the directors, either statutory or recognized by common law or court decisions.

Consistent with the previously described policies of Delaware law, even when a corporation becomes insolvent, a director's fiduciary duties are still owed to the corporation itself.[145] If the corporation is insolvent, however, creditors become the residual interest holders and principal constituency that would be injured by any breaches of the fiduciary duties to the corporation that diminish the firm's value.[146] In that context, creditors obtain the rights of the residual interest holders in the corporation and, as such, are permitted to bring derivative actions against directors for a breach of fiduciary duties.[147] **5.88**

5.3.6.1 Sale transactions

If the directors of a corporation experiencing financial difficulties decide to seek a strategic merger partner or to sell the company to a more stable entity and cash-out the stakeholders, the directors need to consider their fiduciary duties. In addition to the typical duties that directors have when entering into a sale transaction set as forth in *Revlon, Inc. v MacAndrews & Forbes Holdings, Inc.*[148] and its progeny, when a distressed company enters into a sale transaction, directors must consider whether the transaction will yield the best price taking into account the community of interests in the corporation inclusive of the shareholders. Since directors duties are to the entity and its shareholders, courts have held that when directors approve a sale transaction of substantially all of a company's assets and all the proceeds are distributed to the creditors, there is a reasonable inference of a breach of the directors' fiduciary duty of loyalty to shareholders.[149] The court in *Blackmore Partners* reasoned that 'it would appear that no transaction could have been worse for the unit holders and it is reasonable to infer... that a properly motivated board of directors would not have agreed to a proposal to wipe out the value of the **5.89**

[145] *Geyer v Ingersoll Publications Co* 621 A2d 784, 787 (Del Ch 1992).
[146] *Production Resources* at 792 n. 67.
[147] See *Gheewalla* at 101.
[148] 506 A2d 173 (Del 1986).
[149] *Blackmore Partners L.P. v Link Energy LLC* 864 A2d 80, 85-6 (Del Ch 2004).

common equity and surrendered all of that value to the company's creditors'.[150] Similarly, directors should be wary about sale transactions where the proceeds are used to pay dividends to preferred shareholders while the common shareholders' interests are wiped out. Under normal circumstances, 'directors owe fiduciary duties to preferred stockholders as well as common stockholders',[151] but 'where the interests of the common stockholders diverge from those of the preferred stockholders, it is *possible* that that a director could breach her [fiduciary] duty by improperly favoring the interests of the preferred stockholders over those of the common stockholders'.[152] Despite the above-noted presumptions, a director may not necessarily breach her fiduciary duty of loyalty by authorizing a sale transaction that results in a total loss for stockholders. However, the process must be fulsome and deliberate. If a corporation has declining revenues and no viable prospects for the future of the business, it may be that it is in the best interests of the corporation to effect the transaction. Directors should be cognizant of the inference that may be drawn by the transaction and establish a record that there will never be a better alternative for shareholders.

5.3.6.2 Defining the zone of insolvency and insolvency

5.90 Insolvency 'is a most important and material fact and the mere fact of its existence may change radically and materially [a corporation's] rights and obligations'.[153] Despite the plethora of legal decisions and articles written about the zone of insolvency, there is no universally recognized definition. In *Production Resources*, the court stated that:

> Defining the 'zone' for these purposes would also not be a simple exercise and talented creditors' lawyers would no doubt press for an expansive view. As our prior case law points out, as discussed above, it is not always easy to determine whether a company even meets the test for solvency.[154]

5.91 Defining 'insolvency' turns out to be equally amorphous, as there are differing statutory and common law definitions.

(a) *The Bankruptcy Code:* 'insolvent' means with reference to an entity other than a partnership and a municipality, financial condition such that the sum of such entity's debts is greater than all of such entity's property, at fair valuation, exclusive of –(i) property transferred, concealed, or removed with intent to

[150] Ibid. at 86.

[151] *Re Trados Incorporated Shareholder Litigation* 2009 WL 2225958 *7 (Del Ch 2009) (quoting *Jedwab v MGM Grand Hotels, Inc.* 509 A2d 584, 594 (Del Ch 1986)).

[152] Ibid. (quoting *Equity-Linked Investors, L.P. v Adams* 705 A2d 1040, 1042 (Del Ch 1997).

[153] *Commodity Futures Trading Comm'n v Weintraub* 471 US 343, 357 (1985) (quoting *McDonald v Williams* 174 US 397, 404 (1899)).

[154] *Production Resources*, at 790, n. 56.

hinder, delay, or defraud such entity's creditors; and (ii) property that may be exempted from property of the estate under section 522 of the Bankruptcy Code.[155]

(b) *The Uniform Fraudulent Transfer Act*- A debtor is insolvent 'if the sum of the debtor's debts is greater than all of the debtor's assets at fair valuation', and there is a presumption that a debtor 'who is generally not paying his [or her] debts as they become due' is insolvent.[156]

(c) *Definitions in common law*

(i) *Cash flow test:* an entity is insolvent if it is unable to pay its debts as they fall due in the usual course of business.[157]

(i) *Balance sheet test*: a company is insolvent when the value of a companies assets is greater than the value of its liabilities.[158]

(ii) *Unreasonably small capital test*—'relates to whether a company has enough capital to finance its planned future operations' and provides that '[i]f a company's capital is inadequate under the "unreasonably small capital test", then it is insolvent unless it can (1) successfully issue new equity or (2) restructure existing debt'.[159]

5.3.6.3 Deepening insolvency

Another issue that is likely to be of interest to directors of a struggling corporation is the tort of deepening insolvency, which has been described as the 'fraudulent prolongation of a corporation's life beyond insolvency, resulting in damage to the corporation caused by increased debt'.[160] US law generally does not impose an 'absolute obligation on the board of an insolvent company to cease operations and liquidate'.[161] Instead, 'directors of an insolvent company may pursue strategies to maximize the value of the company, including continuing to operate in hopes of turning things around'.[162] A rationale is that '[c]hapter 11 of the Bankruptcy Code expresses a societal recognition that an insolvent corporation's creditors (and society as a whole) may benefit if the corporation continues to conduct operations in the hope of turning things around'. **5.92**

155 11 USC 101(32).
156 Uniform Fraudulent Transfer Act § 2(a), (b).
157 *Thomas P. Geyer v Ingersoll Publications Co* 621 A2d 784 (Del Ch 1992).
158 Ibid.
159 Ibid.
160 *Re Global Service Group, LLC* 316 BR 451, 456 (Bankr SDNY 2004) (quoting *Schacht v Brown*, 711 F2d 1343, 1350 (7th Cir. 1983)).
161 *The Official Committee of Unsecured Creditors of Radnor Holdings Corp. v Tennenbaum Capital Partners, LLC (Re Radnor Holdings Corp.)* 353 BR 820 (Bankr D Del 2006) (citing *Trenwick Am. Litig. Trust v Ernst & Young, L.L.P. et al.* 906 A2d 168, 204 (Del Ch 2006)).
162 Ibid.

5.93 However, as the Third Circuit, applying Pennsylvania law, explained:

> [t]o the extent that bankruptcy is not already a certainty, the incurrence of debt can force an insolvent corporation into bankruptcy, thus inflicting legal and administrative costs on the corporation. . . . Aside from causing actual bankruptcy, deepening insolvency can undermine a corporation's relationships with its customers, suppliers, and employees. . . . In addition, prolonging an insolvent corporation's life through bad debt may simply cause the dissipation of corporate assets. These harms can be averted, and the value within an insolvent corporation salvaged, if the corporation is dissolved in a timely manner, rather than kept afloat with spurious debt.[163]

5.94 Courts have recognized several different theories of deepening insolvency including as a cause of action in tort against directors and insiders,[164] a cause of action in tort against outside lenders and professionals,[165] and as a measure of damages.[166]

5.95 Recognition of deepening insolvency as a cause of action against directors produces anomalous results. Even though, as discussed above, most states follow Delaware's lead in rejecting the existence of fiduciary duties running from directors to creditors where a corporation is in the zone of insolvency, by allowing creditors to bring an action based on deepening insolvency, courts are permitting creditors to pursue an end run around *Gheewalla* and thus creating pseudo-fiduciary duties running to creditors. Under the specter of the deepening insolvency doctrine, directors of distressed corporations will naturally become cognizant of the interests of creditors where it is clear that the directors might become liable to creditors for actions that may prolong the existence of a distressed corporation with a resulting increase in liability or diminution in the value of assets when the corporation fails.

5.96 The more recent court decisions appear to recognize the limitations of deepening insolvency as a cause of action against directors. The Delaware Chancery Court recently announced that Delaware does not recognize deepening insolvency as a tort. The Chancery Court in *Trenwick Am. Litig. Trust v Ernst & Young, L.L.P. et al.*,[167] held that:

> If the board of an insolvent corporation, acting with due diligence and good faith, pursues a business strategy that it believes will increase the corporation's value, but that also involves the incurrence of additional debt, it does not become a guarantor of that strategy's success. That the strategy results in continued insolvency and an

---

163 *Official Committee of Unsecured Creditors v R.F. Lafferty & Co., Inc.* 267 F3d 340, 349-50 (3rd Cir 2001).

164 See *Schacht v Brown* 711 F.2d 1343 (7th Cir 1983). Deepening insolvency as a measure of damages is more widely recognized and will be discussed at greater detail below.

165 See *Re Exide Techs., Inc.* 299 BR 732 (Bankr D Del 2003).

166 See eg, *Allard v Arthur Anderson & Co* 924 F. Supp. 488, 494 (Bankr SDNY 1996).

167 906 A2d 168, 204-5 (Del Ch 2006).

even more insolvent entity does not in itself give rise to a cause of action. Rather, in such a scenario the directors are protected by the business judgment rule.

The Chancery Court informed plaintiffs that if they cannot establish that the directors have breached their fiduciary duties of loyalty and care in the implementation of a business strategy, such parties may not seek a remedy merely because business strategy failed. **5.97**

New York courts and other courts applying New York law have also limited the doctrine of deepening insolvency. Chief Bankruptcy Judge Bernstein, of the US Bankruptcy Court for the Southern District of New York, surveyed New York state court decisions discussing deepening insolvency and determined that '[n]o reported New York case. . . has ruled that "deepening insolvency" is an independent tort'. 'Instead, one seeking to recover for 'deepening insolvency' must show that the defendant prolonged the company's life in breach of a separate duty, or committed an actionable tort that contributed to the continued operation of a corporation and its increased debt.'[168] **5.98**

Despite the ruling in *Trenwick* directors are not impervious to allegations of deepening insolvency. Under the guise of fiduciary duty claims, creditors have continued to pursue actions against directors for actions and decisions that result in deepening insolvency. Such creditors are careful in their pleadings not to use the term 'deepening insolvency' but the essential nature of actions is the same. Actions have been brought by statutory committees of unsecured creditors for breach of director's fiduciary duties based on (a) the incurrence of additional indebtedness,[169] and (b) the failure to direct a company to enter into asset sales or deal with rapidly escalating debts.[170] However, 'simply calling a discredited deepening insolvency cause of action by some other name does not make it a claim that passes muster'.[171] Unfortunately, the bright line rule under Delaware law that deepening insolvency **5.99**

[168] Ibid. Indeed, many jurisdiction require fraud as an element of deepening insolvency. See, eg. *Re Total Containment, Inc.* 335 BR 589 (Bankr ED Pa 2005) (holding that, under Pennsylvania law, the tort of deepening insolvency requires a showing of fraudulent conduct); but see *Smith v Arthur Andersen LLP* 421 F3d 989 (9th Cir. 2005) (recognizing deepening insolvency in the absence of intentional misrepresentations). For jurisdictions that require fraud as necessary element in the tort of deepening insolvency, it is not clear why a separate cause of action for deepening insolvency is necessary since the same the culpable conduct may be addressed through a cause of action for common law fraud. One commentator has argued that that the real source of the popularity of tort claims for deepening insolvency is that such claims avoid insurance carve-outs, which typically exclude fraudulent conduct from coverage. David C. Thompson, Note, 'A Critique of 'Deepening Insolvency' A New Bankruptcy Tort Theory' (2007) 12 Stan.J.L.Bus.& Fin. 536, 544.

[169] *Re Radnor Holdings Corporation* 353 BR 820, 842 (Bankr. Del. 2006)

[170] See *Official Committee of Unsecured Creditors of Magna Entertainment Corp. v MI Developments, Inc., et al.* (Amended Complaint) Adv. Proc. No. 09-51523, 19 August 2009 [Docket No. 17] (This action settled prior to resolution so it remains possible that a court might have found a breach of fiduciary duty under such circumstances.)

[171] *Re Radnor* 353 BR at 842.

is not a colourable cause of action has already begun to blur. In a recent case, *Re The Brown Schools*,[172] the court seemed to let deepening insolvency claims back in the door, by permitting a claim for the breach of fiduciary duty of loyalty on the grounds that the director 'prolonged the existence of the Debtors so that [it] could profit at the expense of the Debtors and their creditors, in violation of its duties of good faith, honest governance and loyalty'.[173] The court in *The Brown Schools* was careful to distinguish this case from *Trenwick* and *Re Radnor*, and noted that it was only allowing the claim because the plaintiff had plead a sustainable breach of fiduciary duty of loyalty claim, and such a breach based on self-dealing, in that case, did not constitute a claim for deepening insolvency claim in disguise.[174] Furthermore, in *The Brown Schools*, the Delaware Bankruptcy Court held that causing a deepening insolvency is a valid theory of *damages* (not a tort), because as a result of the breach of the fiduciary duty of loyalty by the directors, the debtors insolvency increased by more than $22 m.[175] Thus, Delaware appears to have changed course and may be following other jurisdictions by permitting the use of the deepening insolvency doctrine as a measure of damages.[176]

5.100 Recent rulings on deepening insolvency could result in difficult decisions for directors. In *In re Trados Incorporated Shareholder Litigation*, for example, the Delaware Chancery Court found that directors could be found to have breached their fiduciary duty to common shareholders where they approved a transaction whereby their struggling software company was sold to a third party for a price that that resulted in near complete recovery for preferred shareholders to the exclusion of any recovery for common shareholders.[177]

5.101 Trados Incorporated ('*Trados*') was a software development company that had issued several classes of preferred shares to various third parties.[178] The holders of these preferred shares designated four of Trados's seven board members.[179] Based on Trados' poor financial performance, its board decided to seek a merger and eventually entered into a transaction with a third party for a merger price of $60 m (the 'Merger').[180] Of that amount, approximately $52 m was distributed to

---

172 *Re The Brown Schools* 386, BR 37 (Bankr Del 2008).

173 Ibid. at 45.

174 Ibid. at 47.

175 Ibid. at 48.

176 *Alberts v Tuft (Re Greater Southeast Cmty Hosp. Corp. I)* 353 BR 324, 333 (Bankr DC 2006) (the trustee alleged that the defendant directors breached their fiduciary duties of care and loyalty by allowing the company and its subsidiaries to take on additional debt in a fiscally irresponsible manner and by misusing corporate assets).

177 *Re Trados Incorporated Shareholder Litigation* 2009 WL 2225958 (Del Ch 2009) (unpublished).

178 Ibid. at *1.

179 Ibid.

180 Ibid. at *2-4.

preferred stockholders in partial satisfaction of a $57.9 m liquidation preference and approximately $7.4 m was distributed to the executive officers as part of a bonus plan.[181] Common shareholders received nothing.[182]

The plaintiff, a former shareholder of Trados, brought a claim for breach of (among other things) fiduciary duties.[183] The breach of fiduciary duties claim was based on an alleged breach of the duty of loyalty arising out of the directors' alleged failure to give sufficient consideration to the interests of the common stockholders in the director's negotiation of the Merger.[184] **5.102**

The court began its analysis by outlining the general fiduciary duty analysis. Accordingly, '[d]irectors of a Delaware corporation are protected in their decision making by the business judgment rule'.[185] A plaintiff can survive a motion to dismiss, however, by establishing that 'a majority of the board was interested or lacked independence with respect to the relevant decision'.[186] 'A director is interested in a transaction if 'he or she will receive a personal financial benefit from a transaction that is not equally shared by the stockholders' or if 'a corporate decision will have a materially detrimental impact on a director, but not on the corporation and the stockholders'.[187] The benefit must be 'of a sufficient material importance, in the context of the director's economic circumstances, as to have made it improbable that the director could perform her fiduciary duties. . . without being influenced by her overriding personal interest. . .'.[188] At the summary judgment stage of a proceeding, lack of independence can be shown by pleading facts that support a reasonable inference that a director is beholden to a controlling person.[189] **5.103**

The court acknowledged that it had previously held that 'directors owe fiduciary duties to preferred stockholders as well as common stockholders' but only 'where the right claimed by the preferred 'is not to a preference as against the common stock but rather a right shared equally with the common'.[190] In situations where the interest of common and preferred shareholders are not aligned, however, 'generally it will be the duty of the board, where discretionary judgment is to be exercised, to prefer the interests of common stock—as the good faith judgment of **5.104**

[181] Ibid. at *4.
[182] Ibid.
[183] Ibid. at *1.
[184] Ibid. at *6.
[185] Ibid. (quoting *Aronson v Lewis* 473 A2d 805, 812 (Del 1984)).
[186] Ibid.
[187] Ibid.
[188] Ibid. (quoting *Re Gen. Motors Class H S'holders Litig.* 734 A2d 611, 617 (Del Ch 1999)).
[189] See *Rales v Blasband* 634 A2d 927, 936 (Del. 1993).
[190] Ibid. (quoting *Jedwab v MGM Grand Hotels, Inc.* 509 A2d 584, 594 (Del Ch 1986)).

the board sees them to be—to the interests created by the special rights, preferences, etc., of preferred stock, where there is a conflict'.[191]

5.105 Ultimately, the court found that the plaintiff had provided sufficient evidence that certain of the directors were interested to deny the defendant's motion for summary judgment with respect to the breach of fiduciary duty claim.[192]

5.106 Arguably, *Trados* supports the position that if a corporation can restructure or continue operating in hopes of returning to profitability, directors should not sell the corporation (or substantially all of its assets) at a price that provides for no recovery for stockholders. Juxtaposing *Trados* and *The Brown Schools,* in determining the likelihood that a restructuring or continued operations of a distressed corporation would result in an increased return for stockholders, directors should consider that the damages for any breach of a fiduciary duty of care of loyalty in connection which such determination may be measured in comparison to distributions had the corporation (or substantially all of its assets) been sold in a prior opportunity. If deepening insolvency as a tort were to reappear, directors would have a dilemma determining whether to sell a corporation wiping out the stockholders or to continue operations as they would risk litigation should the chosen strategy falter.

5.3.6.4 SubMicron and lender liability

5.107 Directors should also be concerned, particularly those appointed by a corporation's lenders, that the lenders' claims could be equitably subordinated if a court finds that the appointed directors acted inequitably, and violated their fiduciary duties to the corporation.[193] While courts have not, however, flushed out exactly what limitations, obligations and additional duties exist for directors appointed to the board of a corporation by the corporation's lenders, beyond basic fiduciary duties, *Re SubMicron Systems Corp.* gives an indication of how a court in Delaware

[191] Ibid. (quoting *Equity-Linked Investors, L.P. v Adams* 705 A2d 1040, 1042 (Del Ch 1997)).

[192] Ibid. at *9.

[193] Equitable subordination involves a determination of 'whether a legitimate creditor engaged in inequitable conduct, in which case the remedy is subordination of the creditor's claim 'to that of another only to the extent necessary to offset injury or damage suffered by the creditor in whose favor the equitable doctrine may be effective.' *Cohen v KB Mezzanine Fund II, L.P. (Re SubMicron Systems Corp.)* 291 BR 314, 323 (D Del 2003) affd 432 F3d 448 (3d Cir 2006) (quoting *Re W.T. Grant Co.* 4 BR 53, 74 (Bankr SDNY 1980) In order to establish equitable subordination, a movant must typically establish that (i) the claimant engaged in some type of inequitable conduct, (ii) the inequitable conduct caused injury or conferred an unfair advantage on claimant, and (iii) the subordination of the claim is consistent with the Bankruptcy Code. Note that in Delaware at least, this element may not be required. See *Cohen v KB Mezzanine Fund II, L.P. (Re SubMicron Systems Corp.)* 432 F3d 448, 462 (3rd Cir 2006).

might analyse the issue.[194] SubMicron Systems Corporation ('SubMicron'), a manufacturing company enfeebled by a weak market for semiconductors,[195] entered into a series of loan agreements with a group of investment funds (the 'Lenders').[196] Pursuant to these loan agreements, the Lenders acquired the right to appoint half of SubMicron's directors and, as a result of resignations, eventually controlled a majority of the board. As SubMicron's condition continued to deteriorate, the board authorized management to pursue an exit strategy.[197] SubMicron eventually entered into a transaction with Sunrise Capital Partners, L.P. ('Sunrise') pursuant to which Sunrise would create and partially fund an acquisition subsidiary, SubMicron would file for bankruptcy under chapter 11, and the Lenders would assign their claims to Sunrise to allow Sunrise to credit bid in an eventual sale of substantially all of SubMicron's assets under section 363 of the Bankruptcy Code.[198] In exchange for their claims and other consideration, the Lenders received equity in the acquisition subsidiary.[199]

The bankruptcy court, noting that there were no other bidders for SubMicron's assets and that SubMicron would be forced to close its doors without a sale transaction, approved the sale.[200] **5.108**

In a complaint challenging the sale, SubMicron's administrator alleged equitable subordination and breach of fiduciary duty along with several other claims.[201] The administrator asserted that the Lenders, through their designees on SubMicron's board, were insiders of SubMicron and, as such 'owed fiduciary duties to unsecured creditors while the company was in the zone of insolvency and as director[s] of the debtor in possession' and that they breached those fiduciary duties by '(1) allowing the use of an improper credit bid; (2) misrepresenting the cash component of the transaction; (3) allowing the "double bidding" of $5.5 million; (4) failing to give reasonable notice of how they were obtaining an equity interest in [the acquisition subsidiary]; (5) artificially inflating the bid to chill interest from other potential bidders; and (6) misrepresenting the transaction to the court at the asset sale hearing.'[202] **5.109**

The bankruptcy court found that the administrator failed to establish that any of the defendants breached their fiduciary duties or that unsecured creditors were **5.110**

---

[194] Ibid.
[195] Ibid. at 316-8.
[196] Ibid. at 318-20.
[197] Ibid. at 319.
[198] Ibid. at 319-20.
[199] Ibid. at 320-1.
[200] Ibid. at 320-1.
[201] Ibid.
[202] Ibid. at 328.

harmed by defendant's actions.[203] Thus the bankruptcy court's decision provides some guidance to nominee directors.[204]

5.4 Conclusion

5.111 The business judgment rule, perhaps the most useful innovation in modern corporate law, provides directors with comfort that, in spite of the financial state of their corporation, their decisions will not be second-guessed by the courts to the extent they are not interested in the subject of the business judgment, are informed with respect to the subject of the business judgment to the extent the director reasonably believes to be appropriate under the circumstances and rationally believes the business judgment is in the best interest of the corporation.

5.112 Delaware courts have sought, and succeeded, in setting clear rules that directors' fiduciary duties do not change when a company becomes distressed, and such duties always run to the entity. Directors, however, should take note that in certain circumstances, such as insolvency or imminent sale transactions, the constituency that makes up the residual interest holders in the enterprise may shift from shareholders to creditors and adjust their decision-making accordingly.

---

203 Ibid. at 328-9.

204 Unfortunately, on appeal however the Third Circuit dodged the issue of whether the directors' conduct violated fiduciary duties. Since the bankruptcy court found that the administrator had failed to establish injury, an adequate independent basis for rejecting the administrator's claims, there was no reason for the Third Circuit to decide the issue of breach of fiduciary duties.

6

WAIVERS, AMENDMENTS, AND STANDSTILLS

6.1 Introduction

In the context of a book on the law and practice of restructuring, waivers, amendments, and standstills are generally the paths of least resistance and, if no further paths need to be pursued to reach the desired resolution, should be the preferred route to a successful consensual restructuring. They are the key-hole surgery alternatives to the more radical procedures discussed elsewhere in this work. For some companies they will be all that is required to enable a return to full heath. For others, amendments, waivers, and standstills will be just a triage technique; a method of putting off or stabilizing the patient before the deep cuts needed can be made. **6.01**

6.1.1 Waivers—temporary fixes

For companies in financial distress the most likely waivers will be of breaches of maintenance financial covenants. A sudden unexpected drop in EBITDA or asset values that are required by the terms of a financing to be maintained can be dealt with by a one-off waiver. A waiver may be required if the breach was not anticipated and may be appropriate if the breach is expected to be just a one-off **6.02** aberration and the following testing of the financial covenants is expected to pass without a breach. These 'temporary' problems will usually be met with equal relief by both the borrower and the lenders. They are however rare.

6.03 Waivers are frequently used even though the problem is not a temporary one. If so, the main purpose would be to buy time for negotiations and, in the meantime, remove the issues of leaving unwaived an event of default that could have adverse effects on the position of the directors, the company vis-à-vis its other creditors as a result of triggering cross-default provisions and on other aspects of the defaulting company's business (eg, withdrawal of credit insurance and loss of competitiveness relative to competitors in better financial health).

6.04 In some financing agreements, although undesirable, there may be need to seek a wavier of an event of default even where the default has been remedied in order for the resulting event of default to cease to be 'continuing' and for the consequential threat of acceleration to be removed.

6.1.2 Amendments—short- or long-term fixes

6.05 There is little that can be achieved by a waiver that cannot also be achieved by an amendment (although an analysis of cross-default provisions may indicate a waiver of past defaults is desirable as well as amending provisions that if left unamended would have resulted in a breach and it is usually better to deal directly with the issue than indulge in the metaphysical debate of whether a subsequent amendment cures a default that occurred before the amendment).

6.06 Unlike waivers that are usually not forward looking, an amendment is a logical way to deal with expected financial covenant breaches that will not be one-off but will not be so severe as to require a full balance sheet restructuring. These prospective amendments to financial covenants, intended to reduce the risk for the borrower of events of default during a period of underperformance and for the lender the risk of having to mark down the value of the loan on its books, are called 'covenant resets'. If done properly for a company that has the ability to forecast with some degree of accuracy and in an economy that broadly follows the assumptions underlying the company's forecasts, covenant resets are all the restructuring a company may need. Too often, however, they are a 'band aid' or 'sticking plaster' (depending on the side of the Atlantic you are on) with the result that the covenant reset leads on to a further breach, a payment default and/or a full restructuring at a time when the opportunities to take operational or strategic actions to halt the financial decline may have been missed.

6.07 Other amendments that may assist a company in financial distress would be amendments that permit disposals that would enable the company to delever or permit debt to be incurred to refinance existing debt.

6.08 As well as amendments that prevent covenant events of default, amendments (although not waivers) can be used to extend the dates for repayments. Amendments extending the date on which installments or all outstanding principal have to be paid are usually the most difficult to achieve as they have the highest voting threshold but, even when 100 per cent of creditors are required, they are frequently achieved in the case of syndicated loans. Again, if a deferral of principal payments till an operational restructuring or a rebound in the economy is sufficient, an amendment to do so may be all a company needs. An amendment that just defers the pain that all stakeholders will inevitably be required to suffer may result in a worse outcome for many stakeholders, and may fall into the category of amendments referred to as an 'extend and pretend'.

6.1.3 Standstills—contractual or mandatory eg chapter 11/administration

6.09 Standstills are contractual or mandatory. The mandatory standstills, a side effect of the commencement of a debtor-protection procedure, such as chapter 11 in the US or administration in the UK, are effected through statute and covered elsewhere in this work. A contractual standstill is often combined with waivers and/or amendments and involves lenders agreeing that for certain prescribed events of default, the lenders will not exercise their rights to accelerate. Where not in conjunction with a waiver or amendment the standstill may be all that can be achieved if there are insufficient lenders positively to grant a waiver or amendment. In either case the intention is to give the company a breathing space in which to negotiate a set of permanent amendments or a full balance sheet restructuring.

6.1.4 Legal considerations

6.10 Although the contractual provisions commonly found in financing agreements are considered in detail in the following paragraphs, it is important to remember that the contractual voting provisions may be inconsistent with or overridden by mandatory rules that apply as a result of the governing law of the financing arrangement or the insolvency procedures of the borrower's jurisdiction of incorporation.

6.11 In the UK and the US, it is well established that parties can contractually agree that the minority can be bound by the will of the majority, although there are some safeguards against an abuse of the minority.[1]

---

[1] See *Redwood Master Fund Ltd v TD Bank Europe Ltd* [2002] EWHC 2703 (Ch) (the majority of the lenders in a syndicate could vary the terms of the original syndication agreement, thus binding the minority, provided that this power was exercised in good faith and for the purpose for which it was conferred); *British America Nickel Corp Ltd v M J O'Brien Ltd* [1927] AC 369 at 371 (Viscount Haldane) (when exercising an authority conferred on the majority of classes enabling them to bind

6.12 Some jurisdictions however have statutory provisions that require voting by certain creditors under certain types of financing to be carried out in a predetermined way. Examples include the rules for bondholder voting in Belgium[2] and the mandatory 'all holder' matters that an indenture required to be subject to the Trust Indenture Act are required to include and preserve for the individual holder with no possibility for the majority to bind the minority.[3]

6.13 As covered elsewhere in this work the voting provisions of the financing agreements themselves may be overridden by legal proceedings, such as the scheme of arrangement under English law, which only requires a vote of more than 75 per cent in value and 50 per cent in number of each relevant class of creditors, or insolvency proceedings, such as chapter 11, which only requires a vote of more than two-thirds of each relevant class of creditors.

6.2 Voting requirements

6.2.1 Unanimous/super majority matters

6.14 Where the amendments required fall into a certain category of importance, such as additional time for debtor in distress to repay interest or principal, or the amount of interest to be repaid, a unanimous or a super-majority consent may well be needed. The following are the matters that require all lender consent, as set out in the Loan Market Association ('LMA') form of syndicated loan agreement for leveraged borrowers:

(a) changes to the definition of 'majority lenders';
(b) extension of the payment date of any amount, excluding extensions in relation to a mandatory prepayment provision;
(c) reduction in the margin or the amount of any payment of principal, interest, fees or commission payable;
(d) changes to the currency of payments;
(e) increases in or extension of any commitment or the total commitments;
(f) changes to the borrowers or the guarantors, other than in accordance with provisions governing changes to the obligors;
(g) changes to any provision that expressly requires all-lender consent;

minorities, this 'must be exercised for the purpose of benefiting the class as a whole, and not merely individual members only'); and *Chalmers v Nederlandsch Amerikaansche Stoomvaart Maatschappij* 36 NYS 2d 717, 726 (N.Y. App. Div. 1942) (where an agreement clearly provides that a majority vote will be binding on all bondholders, bond obligations may be changed by such a vote).

[2] Chapter IV of the Belgian Company Code, arts 568–580.

[3] See Trust Indenture Act of 1939 15 USC s 77ppp(b) (2010).

(h) changes to finance parties' rights and obligations, changes to the lenders, or changes to the list of matters that require all-lender consent;
(i) changes to the nature or scope of the guarantee and indemnity, the charged property, or the distribution of the proceeds generated by enforcing the transaction security, other than as expressly permitted by any finance document;
(j) release of any guarantee and indemnity or of any transaction security, other than as expressly permitted by any finance document;
(k) changes to the order of priority or subordination in the intercreditor agreement.[4]

Releases of guarantees or security commonly, if not all-lender matters, require the consent of holders of loans outstanding under the syndicated loan agreement which in aggregate represent at least 85 per cent or 90 per cent of the loans outstanding. **6.15**

The following matters are required by the Trust Indenture Act to be reserved to all holders of bonds which are subject to the terms of the Trust Indenture Act: **6.16**

(a) effecting amendments that affect the right of any holder to receive payment or interest on the date it is due; and
(b) bringing suit for the enforcement of payment.[5]

High yield bonds not required to be subject to the Trust Indenture Act (for example, if sold outside the US) usually follow the Trust Indenture Act, but sometimes set the voting requirement at 90 or 95 per cent rather than 100 per cent. **6.17**

Investment grade English law governed bonds are the exception among typical types of financing in recognizing that there may be overall a benefit to holders to allow even matters typically reserved to all lenders or holders to be determined by a majority so that a restructuring that is the best course of action for an issuer and its creditors is not derailed by the inability to obtain consent of all holders (this is particularly important in a market which has its origins in bearer bonds, rather than registered bonds which was the norm in the US, where locating all holders is virtually impossible, let alone getting them to agree on a unanimous basis). **6.18**

Relatively recently even in the case of New York law bonds, where the issuer is a sovereign, 'majority action' clauses have been introduced (and allowed for **6.19**

---

[4] Loan Market Association, Senior Multicurrency Term and Revolving Facilities Agreement for Leveraged Acquisition Finance Transactions, cl 41 (3)(a)(i)-(xi).

[5] The 'reserved matter' in (a) is subject to the proviso that a postponement of an interest payment can be approved by holders representing at least 75 per cent of the principal amount of the debt and in relation to (b) an indenture can contain provisions limiting or denying the right to bring suit when, if brought, such suit would result in the surrender, impairment, waiver or loss of the lien upon any property subject to such lien.

registered issues where Trust Indenture Act compliance would usually be required but for the issuer being a sovereign).[6]

6.2.2 Majority lender/holder matters

6.20 Apart from the all-lender consent matters, the typical voting requirement seen in syndicated loan agreements for waivers or amendments of covenant defaults and enforcement action is two-thirds in English law governed loan agreements and over 50 per cent in loan agreements governed by New York law. Enforcement action includes declaring all or part of the loans outstanding to be 'on demand' or immediately due and payable. Why the practice for English loans is different to the practice for NY law governed loans (even when originated for borrowers outside the US) is something of a mystery. On the one hand, stronger borrowers would prefer to have a 50 per cent voting requirement to make the approval of waivers and amendments easier, but, on the other hand, the two-thirds voting requirement makes blocking enforcement action possible with only a third of the lenders. The worst of both worlds, a two-thirds voting requirement for approval of waivers and amendments and a 50 per cent voting requirement for taking enforcement action, is rarely seen.

6.21 Although hedging counterparties often share in the security granted to secure loans made available under a syndicated loan, the exposures of hedging counterparties are not usually included for the purposes of waivers, amendments or enforcement action under the loan agreement (however, the amounts owed to hedging counterparties, on a mark-to-market basis, may be included in the majorities required to instruct the security agent or trustee to take enforcement action).

6.22 The approach to including or excluding unfunded commitments in the voting requirements can vary according to the situation. Lenders who are committed to provide revolving credit facilities to a borrower under a loan agreement that also has funded term debt may have good reason to be concerned if their unfunded commitments are not included as they may not be able to block a waiver of a covenant breach that would otherwise have been a 'draw stop' that would have entitled the lenders to refuse to fund their unfunded commitments (whereas the term lenders would usually want to allow the drawing to be made to provide liquidity that could be critical to preserving the value of the funded commitments).

[6] See Lee C. Buchheit and G. Mitu Gulati, 'Sovereign Bonds and the Collective Will' (2002) 51 Emory L. J. 1317 at 1329.

In the case of bonds, again there is a difference between practice in Eurobonds, which are usually investment grade when issued and governed by English law, and New York law governed bonds, which can be investment grade or sub-investment grade (also known as 'high yield'). High yield bond issuers do not have a monopoly on getting into financial difficulty and needing restructuring, but as investment grade bonds typically have very few covenants, waivers and amendments of investment grade bonds are less frequent than they are for high yield bonds. It would be relatively unusual for both investment grade and high yield bonds to have maintenance financial covenants capable of being breached as a result of the issuer's performance, so one of the most frequent causes for waivers and amendments under syndicated loan agreements is rarely a feature of bonds. Also, unlike syndicated loan agreements, the voting requirement for waivers and amendments is not usually the same. **6.23**

In New York governed bonds, a simple majority (ie 50 per cent) of all outstanding bonds is required to make amendments that are not reserved to all bondholders. In English law governed bonds, the voting requirement is often a simple majority (ie 50 per cent) for lesser matters and 75 per cent for matters that would, in a loan agreement or New York law governed bond, be reserved to all holders. Most importantly, the voting requirement for English law governed bonds applies not to all outstanding bonds, but to the bonds held by bondholders attending a bondholders' meeting. Usually there is a quorum requirement for the first meeting but, if the quorum requirement is not met, the subsequent meeting of bondholders will be quorate if at least two bondholders attend. **6.24**

6.2.3 Negative control

If a waiver or amendment cannot be obtained because insufficient debt holders can be persuaded to vote for it, the position is sub-optimal for a borrower as events of default that have not been waived or avoided by an amendment will put the borrower at risk of cross-defaults under other financing arrangements. However, there is often a position for the borrower to fall back to, which is to obtain the agreement of sufficient lenders or noteheolders to refuse to join in the majority needed to accelerate or enforce (either of which would usually be a rapidly followed by a free-fall insolvency, which is usually an unfortunate outcome for all stakeholders). **6.25**

This fall-back position is only available if there is a minimum threshold required for acceleration or enforcement. Some bonds allow each lender to accelerate the notes it holds and then take action to recover the accelerated debt. Bonds with trustees usually require holders of a minimum amount of the bonds outstanding to ask the trustee to accelerate, and often only the trustee can bring enforcement proceedings on behalf of the noteheolders. However, in the case of bonds, the **6.26** threshold for acceleration is usually low, such as 10 per cent in English law governed bonds or 25 per cent in New York law governed bonds. It is in the context of syndicated loans that the possibility of a blocking position is most likely to be useful, either because some lenders are not actively participating so a blocking group of 45 per cent may effectively prevent acceleration or because the voting requirement for acceleration is two-thirds and holders of a third of the debt can be persuaded to forbear from joining a group of lenders trying to form the majority required to accelerate.

6.2.4 Disenfranchisement of certain debt holders

6.27 The arguments surrounding disenfranchisement arise in the context of borrowers (or their affiliates) buying back their own loans at prices below their nominal value. These opportunities arose following the collapse of the secondary market for bank loans as a result of the credit crunch.

6.28 English law governed bonds and New York law governed bonds typically have always disenfranchised the votes of holders who are affiliated with the issuer (although the drafting for this is difficult to find in many English law bond documents, as the disenfranchisement occurs as a result of the way 'outstanding' is defined to exclude bonds held by or on behalf of the issuer or its affiliates).

6.29 The possibility of borrowers buying back their own loans understandably gives rise to a concern on the part of existing lenders that the borrower (or its affiliate) may then use its voting rights to the prejudice of the other lenders, for example by blocking enforcement action proposed by the other lenders or by forcing through amendments or waivers.

6.30 Despite the traditional silence of European facility agreements as to whether the borrower (or an affiliate) can buy back its own debt on the secondary market, recent market practice suggests that European market participants accept buy-backs as permissible unless prohibited by the facility agreement.

6.31 The LMA has published optional debt buy-back provisions for its form of syndicated loan agreement for leveraged borrowers. The parties may agree to either prohibit debt buybacks entirely or permit them subject to various conditions including the extinguishment of the loans upon completion of the buyback. With regard to disenfranchisement, both LMA options acknowledge that it is possible for 'sponsor affiliates' to enter into buy-back transactions but only subject to the automatic loss of voting rights.

6.32 The formal position as to disenfranchisement remains unsettled as it is not yet clear which of the LMA options the market will adopt. For the time being, it is likely that lenders who are willing to permit debt buybacks will insist on purchaser disenfranchisement to avoid a potential conflict of interest between members of the syndicate.

6.3 Dealing with hold outs

6.3.1 Snooze and lose

Syndicated loans have become more widely distributed as more players have entered the secondary loan market over the last decade. Obtaining the required level of consents from lenders in these larger and more diverse syndicates can be a time-consuming and challenging process for a borrower, in part because the voting mechanism used by syndicated loan agreements treats a lender's failure to respond as a negative response. **6.33**

'Snooze and lose' provisions aid borrowers by altering this voting mechanism. Just as a bondholder's vote may not be counted if it does not attend the bondholder's meeting or lodge a proxy (provided the requisite quorum is present to transact business at the meeting), a lender in a syndicated facility who fails to respond to a request from the facility agent within a specified period of time after receipt will have its participation excluded from the total amount of loans or commitments used to determine whether the required level of lender consent has been reached. **6.34**

The relevant time period is usually between 5 and 15 days, although this period may be a subject of negotiation. Similarly, the question whether this provision should apply to matters requiring all lender or special majority consent may also be negotiated. Here a borrower may argue that snooze and lose provisions may be most significant, for example if all-lender consent is needed to avoid insolvency, and that in matters of such importance lenders should engage with the borrower. **6.35**

6.3.2 Yank the bank

For matters requiring all lender consent, each lender has, in effect, a veto right over a proposed amendment or waiver. 'Yank the bank' clauses can remedy this holdout problem. The yank the bank clause in the LMA form of syndicated loan agreement for leveraged borrowers applies where an amendment or waiver that requires all-lender consent has been requested, and consent has been obtained from lenders whose aggregate commitments equal a specified percentage of the total commitments. Usually this percentage will be two-thirds or more of the total. **6.36**

Where these conditions have been met, the borrower can require any holdout lender to transfer its rights and obligations under the facility agreement to a **6.37** replacement lender of the borrower's choice, for a purchase price equal to the outstanding principal amount of the holdout lender's participation plus accrued interest and break costs. Typically this replacement lender must also be reasonably acceptable to the facility agent.

6.38 The use of yank the bank clauses is rare in a restructuring as, where debt is trading at less than par, there will be reluctance from other lenders to allow one lender to 'get out whole'. So if the clause is used it will be in small amounts and in a low-key way, as a matter of expediency to get a restructuring agreed.

6.3.3 Forward starts

6.39 If the amendment sought is to extend the maturity of the facility, some or all lenders in the syndicate may enter into a 'forward start' facility with the borrower. The forward start is a facility that refinances, in whole or in part, an existing facility on its maturity, but which is entered into well before that maturity. The forward start operates like an amendment to extend, but on a piecemeal, lender-by-lender basis, which avoids the all-lender consent necessary to extend the maturity of the loan under a syndicated loan agreement. Borrowers reduce their risk by having funds committed to refinancing upon agreed terms, while the lenders who participate receive fees from the date that the forward start begins, rather than the later date of the actual refinancing.

6.4 Process—How to obtain waivers and amendments

6.4.1 Syndicated loans UK/US

6.40 Following a borrower's request for an amendment or waiver, the facility agent (also known as the 'administrative agent' in a syndicated loan agreement under New York law) will seek responses from the lenders and act as an intermediary between the borrower and the lenders during the negotiation process. Several factors may influence the direction of negotiations, including the nature of the proposed amendment or waiver, the relationship between the borrower and the various lenders, and market conditions at the time. Once agreement on the amendment or waiver is reached, the requisite lenders will either sign the amendment agreement or waiver letter themselves or, more usually, will instruct the facility agent to sign on their behalf.

6.41 The consent of the lenders may be subject to conditions, such as consent fees, an increased margin, amendments to covenants, additional guarantors or security, and changes to the borrower's capital structure such as new equity injections or agreements to deleverage. As regards increased margin and amendments to covenants, lenders will generally aim to align the facility with current market conditions.

In a difficult market, even amendments that do not affect payments to lenders may be hard to obtain, as lenders will use their negotiating power to adjust other terms to secure sufficient compensation for their consent.

In a particularly diverse syndicate, a borrower may need to take an active role in managing the consent process. Relationship banks are generally accommodating if the proposal is fair and workable, but investors that are not relationship banks may push for further concessions, particularly fees and increased margin. Short-term investors in particular may take an aggressive approach. A lender intending to impose further requirements may request the facility agent to canvass other lenders with the aim of rallying support before submitting the proposal to the borrower. To prevent an undesirable proposal from swaying the majority, the strong borrower will stay in communication with its relationship banks and request regular updates from the facility agent. **6.42**

If a lender assigns or transfers its participation in the facility between giving consent and executing the amendment or waiver, it may be difficult to determine whether the requisite level of consent has been achieved. To avoid this difficulty, the assignment or transfer document will commonly include a confirmation of the consent by the assignee or transferee. Where it does not, borrowers that have consent rights on transfers can also avoid this issue arising by instructing the facility agent to declare a freeze on trading in the loans during the intervening period. **6.43**

Lastly, borrowers should be aware of the relationship between the flexibility that lenders have in assigning or transferring their participations and the ease of obtaining their consents to amendments or waivers. Borrowers who have a consent right in assignments or transfers will retain control of the syndicate's membership, and will therefore be better placed to manage the amendment or waiver process. However, in recent years there has been a shift toward lenders strongly resisting any restriction on their right to assign or transfer, and borrowers have for the most part agreed to give up the right of consent for the lesser right to be consulted or notified. **6.44**

6.4.2 Bonds

6.4.2.1 Eurobond meetings

Terms and conditions of bonds governed by English law typically create quorum requirements for bondholders' meetings, which require the presence of bondholders whose aggregate commitments equal a specified percentage of the total amount outstanding. The quorum percentage may range from 10–50 per cent, depending on the agreement and on the nature of the action to be taken at the bondholders' meeting. With a quorum present, bondholders representing some larger percentage of the total amount outstanding (generally two-thirds or three-quarters) must then approve any amendment or waiver. If a bondholder does not **6.45** attend a meeting of bondholders that has been properly convened, and does not lodge a proxy, its amounts outstanding may not be counted in the total used in calculating the relevant percentages.

6.4.2.2 Consent solicitations and exchange offers

6.46 The amendment provisions of a New York law bond indenture allow an issuer to make amendments with the consent of some percentage of bondholders, typically a majority or more. Bondholders may also be given an incentive to consent in the form of consent payments. Consent solicitations for all-lender matters are very rare, as it is typically impossible to achieve 100 per cent of consents.

6.47 An exchange offer can be the bond equivalent of a 'forward start'. New bonds are issued with the extended maturity or other desired amended terms in exchange for the existing bonds, which are 'tendered' by consenting holders. If an exchange offer includes an 'exit consent' the holders tendering their bonds in exchange for new bonds can validly amend the terms of the bonds they are 'exiting'. If, for example, tendering bondholders representing the required percentage of the total amount outstanding, typically a majority or more, consent to strip the existing bonds of all covenants, leaving only a bare promise by the issuer to pay the bondholder, this can be a compelling tool to ensure a high take up of the exchange offer. The risk of being 'left behind' holding bonds without covenants is a strong incentive to holders of the existing bonds to tender into the exchange offer. There are reputational issues for a bond issuer to consider before using exit consents to increase the likelihood of success, but for a company in a restructuring the imperative to make the exchange offer succeed usually outweighs sensitivities about being viewed as coercing investors. The exchange offer process will usually be required, by law or the terms of the New York law governed bonds indenture, to follow the process set out in the Exchange Act 1940.

6.4.3 Fees

6.48 There is nothing like cash to get the attention of lenders. Fees are, accordingly, a common feature of waivers and amendments (less so perhaps standstills, as the situation resulting in a standstill often means the borrower has rapidly diminishing liquidity, which is better used to continue operations than to pay lenders).

6.49 A financial covenant waiver or amendment will typically be considered a matter for which lenders expect to be remunerated with a fee, usually as a percentage, such as 0.25 or 0.50 per cent of the amount of the loans outstanding. If markets have moved since the loans were first granted the lenders may take the opportunity of the amendment request to bring the margin paid on the loans in line with the prevailing market position.

In the context of a bond consent solicitation the fees will be an important inducement to getting to the required threshold of all bonds outstanding and 'early bird' fees set at a higher level than fees for holders who consent later are a common feature. **6.50**

In each case there may be an incentive to pay a higher fee to a creditor who is being particularly difficult. This will be tempting but needs to be considered carefully as, in the case of listed securities, it can result in a breach of 'equal treatment' rules of the relevant securities exchange. In the case of loans there may be a 'most favoured nation' provision that will require all lenders to be paid the same fee if a particular lender is given a fee. Even if the payment of fees is not regulated by the exchange or the documentation, there will be franchise and reputation issues for the borrower if lenders subsequently learn of special deals being cut for certain lenders only. There may not be much the lenders can do about it as a legal matter but the resulting bad feeling will, without doubt, make the next request for a waiver or amendment that much more of a struggle to get approved. **6.51**

7

GIVING EFFECT TO DEBT COMPROMISE ARRANGEMENTS—BINDING THE MINORITY OR OUT OF THE MONEY CLASSES OF CREDITORS[1]

7.1 Introduction

7.01 When it comes to remedies at a pre-insolvency proceeding stage, it can be said that England and US are two countries separated by a common law.[2] In particular, the hardening of common law and equitable rules into clear statements that could be set out in a text book in the nineteenth century in England does not appear to have been replicated to the same extent in the US. England has a strict system of precedent and very clear notions of equitable doctrines and statutory interpretation, whereas the US has a looser approach.

7.02 Central to this chapter is the notion of a statutory compromise capable of binding a dissenting minority. This notion did not exist at common law, but has a long statutory history. On the international scale, the concept is mentioned in the

[1] The authors would like to thank Charlotte Cooke for her help in preparing this chapter for publication.

[2] George Bernard Shaw has had attributed to him the quip: 'England and America, two countries separated by common language.'

Brussels and Lugano Conventions, the Jurisdiction and Judgments Regulation 44/2001, and in Article 25 of the EC Insolvency Regulation 1346/2000. In England and in European systems such statutory compromises can occur before and instead of insolvency proceedings as well as being capable of being used as an exit route from them. By contrast, unless there is a contractual regime in place which provides for such a binding effect, in the US the minority can only be bound through the mechanism of a Chapter 11 plan.

7.03 There has been some limited borrowing between the English and US approaches. The ideas of pre-packaged insolvency proceedings and lock-up agreements have in recent years been found attractive in England. In the other direction, the appeal of schemes of arrangement for insurance companies in run-off has had some limited attraction in the US, where insurance insolvency is a matter of State law.

7.04 The different approaches of the two systems have to be understood in the light of the very different culture which still pertains when comparing the US to England. The US is still very much a pro-debtor country. The debtor is treated with respect in the bankruptcy court and often assisted by the bankruptcy judge to a degree which seems very surprising to an English visitor. England by contrast remains essentially a pro-creditor jurisdiction in which being over-indebted is a disgrace and remedies have to be viewed in the light of the best interests of the creditors, with little interest in the welfare of shareholders or management.

7.05 In an ideal world we would have wanted to set out the English and American aspects side-by-side for comparative purposes, but as can be seen from the text in relation to the two jurisdictions, the systems and law are so different that it is impossible to place exact equivalents side-by-side and it is more the results that sometimes approximate rather than the legal rules or procedures. The result is in effect that the reader is presented with two mazes, and, it is hoped, a helpful guide through each of them, leading to similar goals at the end.

7.2 English law

7.06 Debt compromises or arrangements are of two kinds. The first, and in practice more common, is a compromise or arrangement which is entered into consensually and without a formal insolvency or court process. The second, in an arrangement which modifies or extinguishes the rights of minority creditors without their consent by recourse to some statutory right which overrides them.

7.07 The focus of this chapter is on compromises and arrangements of the second kind in which apathetic or dissenting minority creditors are bound, sometimes in the face of their active opposition. In these cases it is relevant to ascertain whether the minority is in, or out of, the money. In the absence of a real (as opposed to merely theoretical) economic interest in the company to be restructured, such creditors' rights are to be ignored because they are of no value and their existence should not be allowed to frustrate what would otherwise be a fair restructuring in the interests of those with an economic interest in the company.

Such arrangements cannot however be understood without some regard to arrangements of the first kind, not least because it is often against the background of a failed consensual restructuring that a company voluntary arrangement or scheme of arrangements falls to be considered. The discussion below sets out some basic principles relevant to contractual compromises and arrangements alongside the principal methods of statutory compromise available under English law, namely a company voluntary arrangement under the Insolvency Act 1986 and a scheme of arrangement under the Companies Act 2006. **7.08**

7.2.1 Contractual compromise

7.2.1.1 Novation of existing documents

The contractual principles underpinning an informal workout, for example of a syndicated loan agreement, are straightforward. A party to a contract cannot assign the burden of his obligations, and a contract cannot be compromised by mere forbearance and requires sufficient consideration.[3] It follows that all lenders party to the syndicated loan agreement must agree to vary or surrender their respective rights against the debtor company and one another in exchange for a new set of rights or, in cases involving a true novation, in exchange for new rights against the new company incorporated to receive the business and assets of the debtor company but with the burden of its renegotiated liabilities only. The mutual release of rights by the lenders and the debtor company is sufficient consideration for both the compromise and the new rights created. **7.09**

Such an arrangement can, by definition, achieve any lawful end to which the parties are prepared to agree but, without the support of a pre-existing contractual framework, it cannot be initiated by the debtor company or by a lender except informally and will, where events of default have occurred or might imminently occur, require the agreement of some form of standstill if there is to be any chance of a successful negotiation. Without some pre-existing restriction under, for example, an inter-creditor agreement or by virtue of a standstill agreement (which **7.10**

[3] The effect of an estoppel by representation or promissory estoppel is generally to suspend a party's rights and only in very rare circumstances (if at all) will it extinguish them: see eg *Hughes v Metropolitan Rly* (1877) 2 App Cas 439, HL, 447, 452 and *Brikom Investment v Carr* [1979] QB 467, CA, 484–5 per Lord Denning MR.

may itself require careful negotiation) there is nothing to stop a single creditor enforcing against the debtor company for its own benefit and potentially to the detriment of other creditors.

7.2.1.2 Variation under existing documents

7.11 To anticipate some of the problems inherent in an informal workout, it is usual for loan documents to incorporate or to be subject to some form of inter-creditor agreement. For example, an inter-creditor agreement will ordinarily set out the priority which each lender enjoys and, corresponding to that priority, an agreed order of enforcement rights in which senior lenders will have first option to enforce with a corresponding right to stay (for a time at least) the rights of mezzanine and junior lenders.

7.12 An inter-creditor agreement, if not the loan documents themselves, may also incorporate rights of the majority[4] lenders to vary the terms of the lending arrangements to which the debtor company is subject. Ancillary to such a clause there may also be options which entitle the majority or any one of them to buy out a dissenting minority lender by reference to an agreed mechanism.

7.13 A question is the extent to which (if at all) the majority lenders must have regard to the interests of the minority lenders in exercising their contractual right to vary the terms of the loan document or to waive any default. Company cases raise a similar question, namely whether a proposed variation of a company's articles of association is bona fide in the best interests of the company[5] even in contexts in which the company as a commercial entity distinct from its members is indifferent to the variation at hand.[6] It is meaningless to ask what is bona fide in the best interests of the company as a whole because, given that the true contest is between two or more divided classes of the company's members, it is inevitable that one class must lose. There is no hypothetical class of the company's members whose standpoint the court can adopt to assess the fairness of the proposed variation. A hypothetical class would not in any way correspond to a class whose rights and interests were in issue without an implicit choice to favour one class over another.[7]

[4] A related clause is a unanimous consent clause. Such a clause adds nothing to the ability of creditors to achieve a compromise (merely affirming what is already within their gift) but the obligation not to vary rights without unanimous consent may impact on the entitlement of the majority to achieve, by participation in a company voluntary arrangement or scheme of arrangement, that which cannot do by contract.

[5] *Allen v Gold Reefs of West Africa Ltd* [1900] 1 Ch 656, CA.

[6] See eg *Peters' American Delicacy Co Ltd v Heath* (1939) 61 CLR 457, Aus HC; and *Greenhalgh v Arderne Cinemas Ltd* [1951] Ch 286, CA.

[7] Ibid., 511–3.

In *Redwood Master Fund Ltd v TD Bank Europe Ltd & Others*,[8] Rimer J. (as he then was) recognized just these difficulties in assessing the fairness of a default waiver letter issued by the majority lenders which, by the terms of the syndicated loan documentation, was binding on all lenders. The appropriate question was whether the proposed variation was imposed in bad faith or was in some other way improper, for example by virtue of it being a capricious or irrational exercise of a power, a fraud on a power or the exercise of a power for a collateral or improper purpose.[9] The examples of bad faith have been carefully defined in the company law context (by reference to analogous concepts in the law of trusts and estates) and provide a useful bedrock from which to assess the actions of the majority lenders. **7.14**

Applying the company case law by analogy, Rimer J. rejected the submission that a default waiver letter issued by the majority lenders and binding by the syndicated loan agreement on all lenders was invalid. Similarly, he indicated that the majority lenders would be entitled to relax the financial covenants if necessary to enable the debtor company to draw down funds to continue trading.[10] In each case, the power had been conferred by a freely agreed contract and was properly exercised. **7.15**

7.2.2 Voluntary arrangements

A company voluntary arrangement ('CVA') is an arrangement under which the rights of unsecured creditors are compromised,[11] or the affairs of the debtor company otherwise arranged by, for example, a moratorium,[12] and which may be imposed by a three-quarter majority of creditors by value voting at the creditors' meeting. Its commercial uses are as an alternative to liquidation, either following or in anticipation of a winding up or as an exit from administration or, alternatively, as a method of debt reduction which enables a company to continue to trade. The so-called 'trading out' CVA is typically one in which the debtor company compromises with its creditors on the basis that it will maintain a series of regular contributions to the supervisor of the arrangement to discharge the debts admitted for less than their nominal value. Such arrangements are regularly effected as a way of reducing unsecured debt (including that resulting from a shortfall in security) in advance of an injection of equity. **7.16**

8 [2006] 1 BCLC 149.
9 Ibid. at [87]–[105].
10 Ibid. at [98].
11 *Commissioners of Inland Revenue v Adam & Partners Ltd* [2000] 1 BCLC 222, CA, at [39].
12 Ibid. at [40], applying *Re NFU Development Trust Ltd* [1972] 1 WLR 1548.

7.17 The detailed procedure for proposing a CVA is set out in sections 1–7B of the Insolvency Act 1986 and rules 1.1–1.29 of the Insolvency Rules 1986. A summary is set out below, but the focus is on four key issues: the nature of the statutory compromise; creditors bound by the CVA and the rights of those who are not; the assets subject to the arrangement; and the methods of challenge available to the dissenting minority.

7.2.2.1 A hypothetical contract binding by statute

7.18 Whereas an informal workout is a process ordinarily initiated by creditors, a CVA is a process initiated by those in control of the debtor company, being its directors or administrator or liquidator as appropriate.[13]

7.19 It follows that the right to propose a CVA is conditioned by the duties binding on directors and officeholders. If the debtor company is in serious financial difficulty[14] it is incumbent on directors to consider whether or not a CVA would benefit the debtor company and its creditors, whose interests would be aligned in such a case. Similarly, a CVA might be used to impose an effective claims resolution and or distribution mechanism through which to exit from administration or through which a liquidator might achieve a better return for creditors than through the mechanism which would otherwise apply in a winding up.[15]

7.20 Notwithstanding that a debtor company is not entitled to propose a CVA, a CVA is analysed as a hypothetical contract between the debtor company and its unsecured creditors that is given effect by statute.[16] Section 5(2) of the 1986 Act provides:

> (1) The voluntary arrangement-
> (a) takes effect as if made by the company at the creditors' meeting, and
> (b) binds every person who in accordance with the rules-
> (i) was entitled to vote at that meeting (whether or not he was present or represented at it), or
> (ii) would have been so entitled if he had had notice of it,
>
> as if he were a party to the voluntary arrangement.

---

[13] IA 1986, s 1(1). The powers of directors are displaced in administration and terminate on liquidation: *Conway v Petronius Clothing Co Ltd* [1978] 1 WLR 72; IA 1986, Sch B1 para 64. IA 1986, s 1(3) extends to an administrator or liquidator the right to put a proposal for a CVA to the company and its creditors.

[14] *Facia Footwear Ltd (in administration) v Hinchliffe* [1998] 1 BCLC 218, 227–8.

[15] It may be that the money available for distribution is so limited, or the number of creditors so large, that the funds which would otherwise be available for distribution would be so eroded by the office holder inviting creditors to prove their claims in accordance with the Insolvency Rules 1986 as to make it necessary to impose a rough and ready claims valuation and/or determination process through a CVA. In certain circumstances, it is appropriate for accuracy to give way to expedience.

[16] *Prudential Assurance v PRG Powerhouse* [2008] 1 BCLC 289 at [45]–[47]; *Johnson v Davies* [1999] Ch 117, CA, 129–30.

A CVA is useful precisely because it is binding on every person entitled to vote at the members' and creditors' meetings if the requisite statutory majority is attained. A proposal is approved if either it is approved at a meeting of the company's members and at a creditors' meeting, or by the creditors' meeting,[17] subject to the right of a member to apply to the court for an order giving effect to the decision at the company meeting.[18] **7.21**

If the proposal is approved, it is the debtor company and its creditors in their capacity as such (and not any third party) that are entitled to enforce the terms of a CVA.[19] A hypothetical agreement entails privity between the parties to it just as an actual agreement does.[20] **7.22**

A CVA cannot operate directly[21] to release the liability of a third party, although it may have that effect by releasing a primary liability of the debtor company upon which a secondary liability of a third party is contingent, or it may require a creditor not to sue a third party / to treat such a liability as released.[22] For example, a parent company guarantee of a debtor company's debt may be released by a compromise of the primary liability, or a principal creditor may be bound as a creditor not to sue the guarantor.[23] **7.23**

A CVA is binding only to the extent of its terms, which include any terms that may be implied. The basis for implying a term into a CVA is that the proposal approved at the meeting (with any proposed modification) must be construed, like any other document, to give effect to its intended meaning, and the boundary between implication and construction is thin, the former merely spelling out what is implicit in the document read as a whole.[24] There is no need to justify the implication of terms by assimilation of the hypothetical statutory contract with an actual contract.[25] The key issue, on which there is no direct authority, is whether it is **7.24**

---

[17] IA 1986, ss 4(1), 4A(2) and IR 1986, r 1.19.

[18] IA 1986, ss 4A(2)(b), (3), (4) and (5).

[19] *Prudential Assurance v PRG Powerhouse* [2008] 1 BCLC 289 at [47], [51]–[55]; *RA Securities Ltd v Mercantile Co Ltd* [1994] BCC 598.

[20] Creditors not bound by a CVA are considered below.

[21] *Johnson v Davies* [1999] Ch 117, CA, 130. However, despite the view taken in the Court of Appeal it is very arguable in the higher courts that the legislative history shows that guarantee liabilities are not regarded as being released by statutory compromises such as a CVA.

[22] Ibid. at [60]–[61], [69].

[23] It is invariably necessary to ensure that the guarantor is released or treated as released because otherwise he would have a right of indemnity against the debtor company exercisable upon payment of the principal creditor in full and the debtor's affairs would not, usefully, have been rearranged at all. See *Re Lehman Brothers International Europe (in administration)* [2009] EWCA Civ 1161 at [62]–[65].

[24] *A-G (Belize) v Belize Telecom Limited* [2009] UKPC 10 at [16]–[18].

[25] Cf. *Re Hellard and Goldfarb (The Joint Supervisors of Pinson Wholesale Ltd)* [2007] BPIR 1322 at [22].

more difficult to imply a term into a CVA than into a contract by virtue of the statutory framework. There are certain contracts such as articles of association into which a term cannot be implied by virtue of extrinsic circumstances (as opposed to so-called constructional implication from the language itself) because the fact of their public registration requires a meaning that could be deduced by a third party.[26] The statutory filing requirements in relation to a CVA suggest that a similar approach should be adopted,[27] especially as a CVA is binding on creditors who would have been entitled to vote at the creditors' meeting if they had had notice of it.[28]

7.25 The terms of a CVA determine the extent of the compromise or arrangement and the way in which a distribution is to be made to creditors. If, by those terms, a debtor company should default, the primary recourse by creditors will be as set out by those terms. The usual consequence of a failure, for example a failure to maintain the level of contributions under a so-called 'trading out' CVA, is the termination of the arrangement and a revival of creditors' rights, to the extent that they have not been discharged, which may then be asserted in the liquidation or such other insolvency proceeding as the supervisor may be required to apply for.

7.2.2.2 Procedure

7.26 A CVA is initiated by the proposal of the debtor company's directors or its administrator or liquidator. The proposal must be formulated with care and, where the company is not already in a formal insolvency procedure, will usually involve an authorized insolvency practitioner from the outset, who, if he agrees to act, will be the nominee required to submit a report to the court.[29] Provision for a moratorium to come into force as a first step has been made by the legislature in respect of certain types of company,[30] but the scope of those provisions in terms of eligibility is so restrictive[31] that these provisions are of little or no use.

7.27 In the case of a proposal made by the directors to facilitate the submission of the nominee's report, the directors must submit a proposal to the nominee alongside a statement of the debtor company's affairs and the further information prescribed.[32] The proposal must provide a short explanation of why, in the

26 *Bratton Seymour Service Co Ltd v Oxborough* [1992] BCLC 693, CA.
27 IA 1986, ss 2(2) and 4(6); IR 1986, r 1.24.
28 Ibid., s 5(2)(b)(ii).
29 Ibid., s 2(2).
30 Ibid., s 1A; IR 1986, rr 1.35–1.42.
31 Two of: (a) turnover of less than £6.5 m; (b) balance sheet of less than £3.26 m; and (c) fewer than 50 employees: IA 1986, Sch A1 paras 2, 3 and CA 1985, s 247 repealed and replaced by CA 2006, s 382.
32 IA 1986, s 2(3); IR 1986, rr 1.5 and 1.6.

directors' opinion, a CVA is desirable and why creditors might be expected to concur with the arrangement.[33]

In order that creditors might give it proper consideration, the proposal must set out the matters prescribed in rule 1.3(2) of the Insolvency Rules 1986. These matters are extensive, but, as is readily apparent from the discussion of material irregularity below, a CVA is looked on as something akin to a contract of *uberrima fides* and positive disclosure of material matters is required.[34] The rigour of this requirement is only tempered by a saving that entitles the directors not to include information the disclosure of which could seriously prejudice the commercial interests of the debtor company.[35] **7.28**

If the nominee reports to the court that in his opinion a company meeting and creditors' meeting should be summoned, he is to proceed to summon those meetings by sending to every creditor of whose claim and address he is aware a copy of the proposal, a copy the statement of affairs and his comments on the proposal.[36] **7.29**

At the creditors' meeting, a three-quarter majority by value of those present and voting (including voting by proxy) is required to pass a resolution approving the proposal and a majority for any other resolution.[37] For this purpose, votes in respect of claims that have not been notified, or that are secured and the secured creditor refuses to estimate the unsecured component, are to be left out of account.[38] A resolution is invalid if those voting against it include more than half in value of the creditors to whom notice was sent, whose votes are not left out of account and who are not, to the best of the chairman's belief, persons connected with the debtor company.[39] **7.30**

At the company meeting, a majority by value is required to pass a resolution approving the proposal. For this purpose value is determined by the number of votes conferred by the debtor company's articles of association.[40] **7.31**

A proposal is approved if either it is approved at both a meeting of the company's members and a creditors' meeting, or by the creditors' meeting,[41] subject to the **7.32**

33 IR 1986, r 1.3(1).
34 *Somji v Cadbury Schweppes plc* [2001] BPIR 172, CA, at [24] and [40]–[44].
35 IR 1986, r 1.3(4).
36 IA 1986, s 3(1); IR 1986, r 1.9(3).
37 IR 1986, rr 1.19(1) and (2).
38 Ibid., r 1.19(3).
39 Ibid., r 1.19(4).
40 Ibid., r 1.20(1).
41 IA 1986, ss 4(1), 4A(2) and IR 1986, r 1.19.

right of a member to apply within 28 days to the court for an order giving effect to the decision at the company meeting.[42]

7.2.2.3 Creditors

7.33 A CVA cannot bind secured creditors without their consent.[43] Secured creditors may rationally seek to participate in a CVA to the extent of any shortfall in the amount of their security, or for some other reason that may involve a release of their security, in the hope of realizing a better return through the arrangement as a whole.

7.34 Similarly, a CVA cannot reorder the priority of preferential creditors, or provide for a differential treatment of preferential creditors, without the consent of the preferential creditors concerned.[44] There is however nothing to prevent the introduction of third party funds on terms that unsecured creditors receive a greater dividend than preferential creditors.[45]

7.35 But for these special cases, a CVA can bind creditors generally but special care is required to bind contingent and disputed creditors who, once their debts accrue or are established, would otherwise be able to enforce their rights outside the arrangement. To this end, a contingent or disputed debt is valued at £1 for voting purposes subject to the discretion of the chairman of the creditors' meeting to put a higher value on it,[46] or to reject the claim.[47]

7.2.2.4 Creditors not bound

7.36 A CVA is only binding on creditors who, in accordance with the rules, were entitled to vote at the creditors' meeting, or would have been entitled had they had notice of it. Dissenting creditors and creditors whose votes are required to be left out of account are therefore bound by a resolution of the requisite majority.

7.37 A CVA did not always have this effect. As enacted, the relevant provisions bound only those creditors who had notice of the creditors' meeting,[48] which tended to force certain arrangements otherwise suitable for compromise within a CVA into the arguably more cumbersome procedure of a scheme of arrangement. For this reason, the primary legislation was extended to bind creditors who would have been entitled to vote had they had notice of the creditors' meeting,[49] although the

42 Ibid., s 4A(2)(b), (3), (4) and (5).
43 Ibid., s 4(3).
44 Ibid., s 4(4).
45 *IRC v Wimbledon Football Club Ltd* [2005] 1 BCLC 66.
46 IR 1986, r 1.17(3).
47 Ibid., r 1.17A.
48 Cf. *Re a Debtor (No. 64 of 1992)* [1994] BCC 55.
49 IA 1986, s 5(2).

secondary legislation that confers that entitlement continues to define the entitlement to vote by reference to notice.[50] A creditor who would have been entitled, in accordance with the rules, to vote at the creditors' meeting if he had had notice of it has 28 days, beginning with the day on which he became aware that the meeting had taken place, in which to apply to challenge the approval of a CVA.[51] In practice, if a substantial period of time has elapsed, a challenge is likely to be unattractive in many cases because what has been done (for example, a realization and distribution) is likely to be difficult to reverse even if there are grounds for revoking the arrangement.

A creditor not bound by a CVA (for example a creditor whose claim has been rejected in total and who was therefore not entitled to vote) is not subject to its terms and is entitled to enforce any rights he may have irrespective of the arrangement in place between the debtor company and its other creditors. **7.38**

7.2.2.5 Assets

A question that has arisen, and that is crucial to the destination of assets subject to a CVA following its failure or the liquidation of the debtor company, is how assets are held within a CVA. In *Re NT Gallagher & Sons Ltd*,[52] the Court of Appeal laid down the following guidelines at paragraph 54 of its judgment: **7.39**

(1) Where a CVA provides for moneys or other assets to be paid to or transferred or held for the benefit of CVA creditors, this will create a trust of those moneys or assets for those creditors.
(2) The effect of the subsequent liquidation of the debtor company on a trust created by the CVA will depend on the provisions of the CVA.
(3) If the CVA provides what is to happen on liquidation (or failure of the CVA), effect must be given to those provisions.
(4) If the CVA does not so provide, the trust will continue notwithstanding the liquidation or failure and must take effect according to its terms.
(5) The CVA creditors can prove in the liquidation for so much of their debt as remains after payment of what has been or will be recovered under the trust.

In stating these guidelines, the Court of Appeal placed emphasis on the general law, under which trust assets are unaffected by a trustee company's liquidation,[53] and on the fact that the legislature had intended CVAs to be a viable alternative to winding-up or administration proceedings.[54] If a default rule were to apply to the effect that trust assets under the CVA that happened not to have been distributed before the liquidation would become available to meet the claims of post-CVA **7.40**

[50] Ibid., r 1.17(1).
[51] Ibid., s 6(2)(a) and (3)(b).
[52] [2002] BCLC 133.
[53] Ibid. at [49].
[54] Ibid. at [50].

creditors as well as CVA creditors, that would be a disincentive to creditors to agree to a CVA and to keep it in operation.

7.41 Applying these guidelines, if the assets of the debtor company are transferred to the supervisor on trust, those assets are not available to satisfy the claim of any creditor not bound by the arrangement. A more ambitious approach, and one left open on the authorities, is one in which a trust might exist also in respect of assets not transferred but to be transferred at some future point. In *Oakley-Smith v Greenberg*,[55] Chadwick L.J. observed that:

> [I]t could well be said, on one view at least, that the effect of the agreement by the company, acting by the administrators, that all its assets shall be realized by the administrators and (subject to the specified exceptions) paid by the administrators to the supervisors for the purposes of the voluntary arrangement is that, subject to control by the court in the administration, the company's assets are subject to a trust to give effect to the terms of the voluntary arrangement.

7.42 The practical impetus for such a trust in *Greenberg* was the fact that the arrangement was a so-called 'winding-up' CVA that arose out of the collapse of London Trust Bank plc as an alternative to voluntary or compulsory liquidation. As such, whatever the soundness of such an approach as a matter of the law of trusts,[56] such a construction would not be viable in respect of a 'trading-out' CVA in which the debtor company must retain freedom to deal with its assets unless and until transferred to the supervisor of the arrangement.

7.2.2.6 Challenging a voluntary arrangement

7.43 7.2.2.6.1 **Unfair prejudice:** A dissenting creditor may challenge a CVA on the ground that its terms[57] unfairly prejudice his interests and, if the challenge is successful, the court may revoke or suspend any decision approving the voluntary arrangement with any supplementary directions it thinks fit.[58]

7.44 The leading case is *Prudential Assurance v PRG Powerhouse*,[59] in which Etherton J. (as he then was) outlined two useful comparators for considering the issue of unfair prejudice, which is to be judged at the time that the proposal was approved[60]

---

[55] [2005] 2 BCLC 74, CA.

[56] A specifically enforceable contract can create an enforceable trust in exceptional circumstances, but in *Greenberg* the terms of the arrangement appear to have been to realize assets and to transfer the proceeds of realization.

[57] *IRC v Wimbledon Football Club Ltd* [2005] 1 BCLC 66 at [18]

[58] IA 1986, s 6(1), (4) and (6).

[59] [2008] 1 BCLC 289. See also *SISU Capital Fund Ltd v Tucker* [2006] BPIR 154, in which Warren L.J. gave detailed consideration to the same issue.

[60] Ibid. at [71].

and in respect of anything that leaves the creditors in a less advantageous position than before the CVA:[61]

(1) The vertical approach (winding up).[62]
   (a) On the assumption that a particular distribution would be achieved on a winding up and within an acceptable timescale, a CVA should be held to unfairly prejudice the interests of a creditor if it provides less than he would expect to receive upon such a distribution.
   (b) The fact that a CVA provides a better outcome than would be available in a winding up does not however close out unfairness in cases of differential treatment as between creditors.[63]
   (c) Differential treatment per se is not sufficient to render an arrangement unfair.[64]
   (d) What is required is a disproportionate prejudice to one class of creditor[65] which cannot be justified, for example as necessary for the continuation of the debtor company's business.[66]

(2) The horizontal approach (other classes of creditor).[67] Comparison with the position if there had been a scheme of arrangement may be helpful on the issue of unfair prejudice, although care must be taken because, as set out below, creditors under a scheme of arrangement consult in discrete classes defined in terms of their ability to consult together in their common interest, whereas a creditors' meeting for the purposes of a CVA comprises a single class. For example, the fact that a dissenting class of creditor might have frustrated a scheme of arrangement may be an indication of unfairness but does not automatically lead to the conclusion that a CVA is unfair.

Such comparators are however only a supplement to, and not a substitute for, a **7.45** proper assessment of all the circumstances, including, in particular, the alternatives available and the practical consequences of a decision to confirm or reject the arrangement.[68] An arrangement that prejudices a creditor's interests is not unfair however merely because it is not the best arrangement the debtor could have put forward.[69] In considering the terms of any CVA, the court proceeds on the basis that in commercial matters creditors who are fully informed of material facts and have had a sufficient opportunity to consider the proposal are usually much better

---

[61] Ibid. at [72]. Unfair prejudice, in this respect, corresponds to the same concept as used in relation to minority shareholders under CA 2006, ss 994–996. The focus is on the wider concept of interests and not only rights.

[62] Ibid. at [77]–[90].

[63] *Re a Debtor (No. 101 of 1999)* [2001] 1 BCLC 54.

[64] Ibid., 63.

[65] *Doorbar v Alltime Securities Ltd (No. 2)* [1996] BPIR 128, 132.

[66] *SISU Capital Fund Ltd v Tucker* [2006] BPIR 154 at [69].

[67] Ibid. at [91]–[96] applying *SISU Capital Fund Ltd v Tucker* [2006] BPIR 154 at [74]–[78] and *Re T&N Ltd* [2005] 2 BCLC 44 at [81]

[68] Ibid. at [74].

[69] *SISU Capital Fund Ltd v Tucker* [2006] BPIR 154 at [72]–[73].

judges of their own interests than the courts and will be slow to differ from the views expressed by creditors at the meeting.[70]

7.46 7.2.2.6.2 **Material irregularity:** An irregularity is a breach of some requirement at or in relation to the company meeting or the creditors' meeting.[71]

7.47 An irregularity is material if it would be likely to have made a material difference to the way in which the members or creditors would have considered and assessed the terms of the proposed arrangement.[72]

7.48 Asking whether an irregularity is material is not the same as asking whether a new vote would produce a different result.[73] Although, in practice, an application should not normally be made where the requisite majority continue to support the proposal and would carry the vote. An application might exceptionally be made if creditors entitled to vote abstained from voting and a different result might be obtained if a further meeting were convened.

7.49 If the creditors' meeting rejects the proposal, any creditor entitled to vote at the creditors' meeting may apply to have the proposal deemed approved, or for a direction that another creditors' meeting be convened to consider that proposal or a modified proposal.[74] Such an application is likely only[75] if the chairman has allowed an alleged creditor to vote but marked his claim as '*objected to*'. A claim so marked is not admitted but the alleged creditor is allowed to vote against the CVA,[76] and the court is entitled to look at the matter afresh with regard to all the evidence that could then have been available to the chairman.[77] If a material irregularity is made out, the issue for the court is whether calling a further meeting would be '*useful*' having regard to all the circumstances (including the costs of doing so).[78]

7.50 If the creditors' meeting approves the proposal, a creditor entitled to vote at the creditors' meeting[79] may apply to revoke that approval.[80]

---

70 Ibid. at [78].

71 *Re a Debtor (No. 222 of 1990)* [1992] BCLC 137, 145b.

72 *Cadbury Schweppes plc v Somji* [2001] BPIR 172, CA, 182 at [25] approving *Re Tack* [2000] BPIR 164.

73 *Monecor (London) Ltd v Ahmed* [2008] BPIR 458, 465–6, at [17]–[21].

74 IA 1986, s 6(2); IR 1986, rr 1.17A and 1.19. The debtor company has no right to appeal unlike a debtor in bankruptcy.

75 The factual basis for the application would have to be a complaint against a creditor and it is difficult to think of a practical example other than an inflated claim.

76 *Power Builders (Surrey) Ltd v Petrus Estates Ltd* [2009] BCLC 250, 255–6 at [12].

77 Ibid. at [14]–[18].

78 *Re a Debtor (No. 222 of 1990)* [1992] BCLC 137, 146; *Power Builders (Surrey) Ltd v Petrus Estates Ltd* [2009] BCLC 250, 257–9 at [21]–[26].

79 IA 1986, s 6(2).

80 IA 1986, s 6(4)-(6).

7.2.3 Schemes of arrangement

7.2.3.1 Introduction

A scheme of arrangement may be used to effect a compromise or arrangement between a company and either its creditors or any class of them or its members or any class of them.[81] If sanctioned by the court, a scheme of arrangement is binding on the company and all the relevant members or creditors.[82] **7.51**

A principal use of a scheme of arrangement is to effect a compromise with creditors involving the dissenting minority being bound by the decision of the majority. **7.52**

7.2.3.1.1 Nature A scheme of arrangement is a statutory compromise or arrangement with one or more classes of members or creditors that enables the absence of consent of a minority of members or creditors to be overcome provided that a majority in number and 75 per cent in value agree and the court sanctions the scheme.[83] **7.53**

A scheme ordinarily comes into effect when the order of the court sanctioning the scheme is delivered to the Registrar of Companies. It cannot become effective sooner than that, although it can have retrospective effect. Once a scheme has become effective, the court may not subsequently vary it.[84] To do so would be to substitute a scheme different from that proposed and approved at the meetings by the creditors or members as the case may be. **7.54**

A compromise or arrangement under a scheme has effect by operation of law. A release of rights in exchange for the scheme consideration is not an accord and satisfaction under the general law. A scheme that releases a creditor's claim does not preclude the creditor from claiming against a surety of the company's debt because the release of the principal debtor is effected by operation of law and not by the voluntary act of the creditor (even if he votes for the scheme).[85] Similarly, the release of the company from a debt owed on a joint and several basis is not an accord and satisfaction that discharges its co-debtors.[86] **7.55**

---

[81] CA 2006, s 895(1).

[82] CA 2006, s 899(3).

[83] *Sea Assets Limited v Perusahaan Perseroan (Persero) PT Perusahaan Penerbangan Garuda Indonesia* [2001] EWCA Civ 1696 at [2].

[84] *Kempe v Ambassador Insurance Co (in liquidation)* [1998] 1 BCLC 234, PC, 234. Cf. *Caratti v Hillman* [1974] WAR 92, 95.

[85] *Re London Chartered Bank of Australia* [1893] 3 Ch 540, 546–7. A scheme might incorporate a binding promise not to sue the surety or some equivalent right of restraint.

[86] *Re Garner Motors Ltd* [1937] Ch 594, 598–9.

7.56 It also follows from the compromise or arrangement having effect by operation of law that a scheme is not restricted to what the company and its creditors might achieve by consent.[87] For example, a compromise under a scheme is effective whether or not liability for the claim compromised could have been excluded or restricted under the Unfair Contract Terms Act 1977.[88]

7.57 A scheme is however only a compromise or arrangement between the company and its members or creditors *in their capacity as such*. A scheme cannot compromise or arrange rights as between a company as trustee and its creditors as beneficiaries.[89] Similarly, if sanctioned, a scheme cannot bind a third party to the scheme either by destroying or creating a relationship between him and the company or a creditor or a member.[90] It follows that if a scheme is contingent on the release of some right by a third party, or on that third party doing something, its sanction will turn on the court being satisfied of the execution of some contract or deed binding that third party outside the terms of the scheme.

7.58 7.2.3.1.2 **Scope** 'Compromise' and 'arrangement' have no precise legal meaning but each is distinct:

(1) A '*compromise*' implies some element of accommodation on each side,[91] presupposing some dispute about the rights compromised, or some difficulty in enforcing them if there is no dispute.[92]
(2) An '*arrangement*' is not limited to something that is analogous to a 'compromise' for example, it may be beneficial to the company and all its members[93] or it may not even alter the rights between the company and its creditors,[94] although it must involve some element of give and take, which would exclude a scheme of arrangement that would only expropriate the interests of

[87] *Re Cape plc* [2007] 2 BCLC 546 at [79].

[88] *Re Cape plc* [2007] 2 BCLC 546 at [81]–[90] following *Tudor Grange Holdings Ltd v Citibank NA* [1992] Ch 53, which held that the 1977 Act did not apply to a deed of release.

[89] *Re Lehman Brothers International Europe (in administration)* [2009] EWCA Civ 1161 at [33], [58]–[65]. Secured debts are different and can be varied or released by a scheme. See *Re Empire Mining Company* (1890) 44 Ch D 402 and *Re Alabama, New Orleans, Texas and Pacific Junction Railway Co* [1891] 1 Ch 213. It is the debt secured that may be subject to a compromise or arrangement, which, if sanctioned, would have a consequential impact on any security. If the debt is discharged the security ought to be defeated. The logic of this distinction is clear from the registration of charges cases which distinguish between a trust (which is not registrable) and an equitable charge (which is registrable and should be registered) on the basis that a trust, unlike a charge, is not tied to a debt and defeasible by its discharge.

[90] *Re Glendale Land Development Ltd* [1982] 1 ACLC 540; *Re Glendale Land Development Ltd (No. 2)* [1982] 1 ACLC 562; *City of Swan v Lehman Brothers Australia Ltd* (2009) FCAFC 130 at [99]–[104].

[91] *NFU Developments Trust Ltd* [1972] 1 WLR 1548, 1555.

[92] *Re Guardian Assurance Co Ltd* [1917] 1 Ch 431, 442–3.

[93] *Re General Motor Cab Co Ltd* [1913] 1 Ch 377, 384; *Re Guardian Assurance Co Ltd* [1917] 1 Ch 431, CA, 448–50.

[94] *Re T & N Ltd (No. 3)* [2007] 1 BCLC 563 at [53].

a member or creditor.[95] An 'arrangement' is partially defined as including a reorganization of a company's share capital by consolidating different classes of shares or dividing shares into different classes,[96] but the court has not found it necessary or desirable to sharpen its meaning and will exceptionally[97] even consider sanctioning a scheme that contained provision for future amendment.[98]

7.2.3.1.3 **Procedure** The scheme of arrangement process can be divided into three stages: **7.59**

(1) the application to the court to convene the members' or creditors' meetings to approve the scheme;
(2) the holding of meetings convened to vote on the proposed scheme; and
(3) the application to the court to sanction the scheme so approved.

7.2.3.1.4 **International jurisdiction** Any company that is liable to be wound up under the Insolvency Act 1986 is entitled to put a scheme of arrangement to its members or creditors or any class of them.[99] Both companies incorporated in England and Wales and foreign companies that have a sufficient connection with England and Wales may be wound up under the Insolvency Act 1986. **7.60**

There are three conditions that must be satisfied for the making of a winding-up order in relation to a foreign company: (1) a sufficient connection with England and Wales (to which the presence of assets is not essential); (2) a reasonable possibility of benefit to the petitioner if a winding-up order is made; and (3) the existence of one or more persons interested in the distribution of assets of the company over whom the court can exercise jurisdiction.[100] The second and third conditions however are not essential for the court to have jurisdiction to sanction a scheme of arrangement.[101] A sufficient connection with England and Wales is all that is required. **7.61**

The better view is that the international jurisdiction of the court is unaffected by Council Regulation 1346/2000 on insolvency proceedings (the 'Insolvency Regulation') or Council Regulation 44/2001 on the recognition and enforcement **7.62**

95 *Re NFU Developments Trust Ltd* [1972] 1 WLR 1548, 1555; *Re Savoy Hotel Ltd* [1981] Ch 351, 359.
96 CA 2006, s 895(2).
97 The absence of clarity and certainty as to the terms of the arrangement and how they will affect creditors, and the obvious possibility that creditors may be content with the arrangement in its original form but not as it is subsequently amended, would be strong grounds for not sanctioning a scheme which contains amendment provisions unless such provisions are restricted to non-material and technical matters.
98 *Re Cape plc* [2007] 2 BCLC 546 at [72]–[73].
99 CA 2006, s 895(2).
100 *Stocznia Gdanska SA v Latreefers Inc (No. 2)* [2001] 2 BCLC 116 at [20], [30]–[31].
101 *Re Drax Holdings Ltd* [2004] 1 WLR 1049 at [28]–[36].

of judgments in civil and commercial matters (the 'Judgments Regulation'). The jurisdiction to sanction a scheme of arrangement turns on whether a company is *liable* to be wound up (not on whether the conditions to make a winding-up order are satisfied at any given moment) and so transient characteristics such as the location of a company's centre of main interests (COMI) for the purpose of the Insolvency Regulation or its solvency do not affect the court's jurisdiction to sanction a scheme.[102]

7.63 7.2.3.1.5 **Convening hearing** *Procedure* The application to the court to convene the meetings may be made by:

(1) the company;
(2) any member or creditor of the company; or
(3) if the company is being wound up or is in administration, by the liquidator or administrator.[103]

7.64 The application for an order to convene meetings is made by the issue of a claim form under CPR Part 8[104] out of the Companies Court or a Chancery District Registry.[105] The application must be supported by written evidence and set out the prescribed statutory information and the terms of the proposed compromise or arrangement.[106]

7.65 At the convening hearing, the court is emphatically not concerned with the fairness of the scheme.[107] If the court is satisfied it has jurisdiction, it may order a meeting of the members or creditors, or any class of them, on such terms as it thinks fit.[108]

7.66 Following the direction to convene the relevant meetings, the notices convening those meetings must be sent out with the explanatory statement[109] and forms of proxy. The court will usually also direct the advertisement of the proposed scheme

[102] *Re DAP Holding NV* [2006] BCC 48 at [11]. With regard to solvent schemes by non-UK member state companies, the Jenard Report to the Brussels Convention was not cited to Lewison J. It is arguable that, having regard to the terms of that pre legislative text, a solvent scheme of arrangement would not be outside the Judgments Regulation because of the exception to its scope in relation to *'judicial arrangements'*, although there remains some doubt as to whether a scheme is a *lis* capable of being subject to the jurisdictional provisions of that regulation. With regard to insolvent schemes by non-UK member state companies, the need to show jurisdiction to wind up under the Insolvency Regulation was left open in *Sovereign Marine & General Insurance Co Ltd* [2007] 1 BCLC 228.

[103] CA 2006, s 896(2).

[104] CPR PD 49, para 5(1).

[105] Ibid., para 5(2).

[106] Ibid., para 15(1) and (3).

[107] *Re Telewest Communications plc (No. 1)* [2005] 1 BCLC 752 at [14].

[108] CA 2006, s 896(1).

[109] CA 2006, s 897(1)(a).

of arrangement in one or more national newspapers, in which case a copy of the explanatory statement must be provided free of charge upon request.[110]

A breach of the obligation to send out a notice with the explanatory statement or other failure to comply with the above is an offence for which the company and any officer in default is liable.[111] **7.67**

The explanatory statement and other documents sent to members or creditors with whom the scheme is to be made should together[112] set out the scheme and its purpose adequately and accurately so that the persons who are entitled to vote on it may do so in a properly informed manner.[113] If a member or creditor called to vote is to be able to exercise reasonable judgment on whether the scheme is in his interest or not, an explanation of the effect of the scheme requires an explanation of how the scheme will affect him commercially.[114] For example, in the case of an insolvent scheme, if the alternative is liquidation, a creditor needs to be given such up-to-date information as can reasonably be provided on what he can expect if the company goes into liquidation and what he can expect under the scheme.[115] **7.68**

In the context of a creditors' scheme in relation to an insolvent company, a useful guide as to what sort of information is required for such a comparison is the prescribed information required in the context of a CVA[116] as supplemented by the general requirement to make disclosure of any material matter.[117] A statement of affairs and anticipated outcome in liquidation or administration and under the scheme expressed in terms of p/£ would be expected. **7.69**

The explanatory statement must also state any material interests of the directors (whether as directors or as members or as creditors of the company or otherwise)[118] and the effect of the scheme on those interests in so far as it differs from the effect on the interests of other persons.[119] The precise extent of directors' interests must **7.70**

---

110 CA 2006, s 897(1)(b) and (4). The court is unlikely to require notice of the meeting(s) to be given by advertisement if satisfied, on the evidence, that each and every scheme creditor will have the scheme and the composition of the classes of scheme creditors brought to their attention by notices being sent to them, whether by post or otherwise. The use of electronic notification, including by Intralinks, is common in the case of schemes proposed to a company's lenders.

111 CA 2006, s 897(5)-(8).

112 *Re Moorgate Mercantile Holdings Ltd* [1980] 1 WLR 227, 242.

113 *Re Dorman Long & Co* [1934] Ch 635, 657–8.

114 *Re Heron International NV* [1994] 1 BCLC 667, 672.

115 Ibid.

116 IR 1986, r 1.3(2).

117 *Somji v Cadbury Schweppes plc* [2001] BPIR 172, CA, at [24] and [40]–[44].

118 For example as trustees other than for independent beneficiaries: *Second Scottish Investment Trust Co Ltd, Petitioners* (1962) SLT (Notes) 78, Ct of Sess.

119 CA 2006, s 897(2).

be disclosed, being akin to the strict duty of disclosure imposed on a director as a fiduciary.[120]

7.71 The same requirements apply in relation to a trustee of any deed securing debentures issued by the company.[121]

7.72 At each of the meetings convened, there are two requirements for the necessary majority:

(1) a majority in number of those present and voting;
(2) representing three-quarters in value of their aggregate shareholdings or debt (as the case may be).[122]

7.73 Members of the class who do not vote, even if present at the meeting, do not count.[123]

7.74 As regards the tallying of votes, each share is given its nominal value whereas the value of a creditor's vote depends on the value of his debt.

7.75 A member or creditor who is properly a member of two or more classes is entitled to vote at each meeting, but the court will not sanction a scheme if the required majority comprises persons acting in bad faith or not in the interests of the class to which they belong.[124]

7.76 A challenge to the approval at the meetings (and not only the fairness of that approval) is a challenge to the jurisdiction of the court to sanction the scheme and is confined to perversity, dishonesty or irrationality.[125] If the outcome of a meeting is to be challenged, the application must be supported by cogent evidence that there has been a failure to comply with the statutory requirements or the directions of the court.[126] An allegation of collateral interest is serious and proper evidence is required before the court will consider disenfranchizing a member of a class who is otherwise entitled to vote.[127]

7.77 *Class issues (generally)* The jurisdiction of the court to sanction a scheme of arrangement is confined to sanctioning a scheme approved by a class. If a meeting convened to consider a scheme in fact comprises two or more classes, the court is

120 *Coltness Iron Co Ltd, Petitioners* (1951) SC 476, 480, Ct of Sess.
121 CA 2006, s 897(3).
122 Ibid., s 899(1).
123 *Re Bessemer Steel and Ordance Co* (1875) 1 Ch D 251, 253.
124 *Re Wedgwood Coal and Iron Co* (1877) 6 Ch D 627, 635–6.
125 *Re The Scottish Lion Insurance Co Ltd* [2009] CSOH 127 at [35]–[41] applying *Re Sovereign Marine & General Insurance Company Ltd* [2007] EWHC 1331 (Ch) at [54]–[61].
126 *Re Linton Park* (2008) BCC 17 at [12].
127 Ibid.

without jurisdiction regardless of whether or not the meeting voted unanimously in favour of the scheme.[128]

A class[129] is not positively defined, for example as preferred or ordinary shareholders or unsecured creditors. A class does not require the set of its members to have objectively recognizable common characteristics and is instead negatively defined as a set of persons whose rights (and not interests)[130] are not so dissimilar as to make it impossible for them to consult together with a view to their common interest.[131] It is not practical to look to interests or motives (as opposed to rights) because interests and motives are disparate and idiosyncratic. The court is to protect against collateral interests or improper motives in considering whether to sanction the scheme.[132] **7.78**

Accordingly, a company is free to select the class(es) to which it proposes a scheme of arrangement and who will be bound if the scheme is approved and sanctioned.[133] **7.79**

In applying the above test to determine whether a given class was properly identified, the court is required to look at: **7.80**

(1) the rights released/varied, and
(2) the new rights (if any) conferred by the scheme.[134]

Pre 2001 the court would make no enquiry as to the accuracy of the classes at the convening hearing. This aspect of the procedure was wasteful because it meant that the company was at risk of making an error that would only be picked up at the sanction hearing, the meetings having been held and the costs of the exercise having been incurred. **7.81**

The procedure was reformed in 2002 by the issue of a Practice Statement which requires the company to draw to the attention of the court any potential problems ('creditor issues') at the convening hearing, including as to the constitution of the meetings of creditors or matters which otherwise affect the conduct of those meetings. **7.82**

---

128 *Re Hawk Insurance Company Limited* [2001] 2 BCLC 480, CA.

129 A meeting of members or creditors must consist of more than one person unless the class is a class of one: *Re Altitude Scaffolding Ltd* [2007] 1 BCLC 199 at [18]–[21].

130 *Re Cape plc* [2007] 2 BCLC 546 at [33]; *Re BTR plc* [2000] 1 BCLC 740, CA.

131 *Sovereign Life Assurance Co v Dodd* [1892] 2 QB 573, CA, 583; *Re Hawk Insurance Company Limited* [2001] 2 BCLC 480, CA, 516; *Sea Assets Limited v Perusahaan Perseroan (Persero) PT Perusahaan Penerbangan Garuda Indonesia* [2001] EWCA Civ 1696 at [22]–[25], [32]–[46].

132 *Re BTR plc* [2000] 1 BCLC 740, CA.

133 *Sea Assets Limited v Perusahaan Perseroan (Persero) PT Perusahaan Penerbangan Garuda Indonesia* [2001] EWCA Civ 1696 at [51].

134 *Re Hawk Insurance Co Ltd* [2001] 2 BCLC 480 at [30].

7.83 For the purpose of drawing to the attention of the court at the convening hearing such creditor issues, the company should take all steps reasonably open to it to notify any person affected by the scheme that it is being promoted, the purpose that the scheme is designed to achieve, the meetings of creditors that the applicant considers will be required and their composition, unless there are good reasons for not doing so.[135]

7.84 The key advantage for the company following from the Practice Statement is that, although it continues to be subject to the burden correctly to identify the relevant classes, the court will ordinarily proceed, without requiring detailed reconsideration of the classes issue, on the basis that jurisdiction has already been established to its satisfaction, unless persuaded to the contrary by a dissenting creditor.[136] If objections only arise at the sanction hearing the court will expect the objectors to show good reason the issue was not raised earlier. Where no good explanation is given, the court is likely to be somewhat reluctant to find that it has no jurisdiction to sanction the scheme and there may be adverse cost consequences for the objector.

7.85 In determining whether the rights of creditors are so dissimilar that it would be impossible for them to consult together it must be borne in mind that it is necessary to ensure not only that those whose rights are really so dissimilar that they cannot consult together with a view to a common interest should be treated as parties to distinct arrangements, but also that those whose rights are sufficiently similar to the rights of others that they can properly consult together should be required to do so. The test should not be applied in such a way that it becomes an instrument of oppression by a minority.[137]

7.86 Scheme creditors can have rights that are materially different, but that are not so different that it is 'impossible' for them to consult together. A broad approach is taken and differences may be material, or at least certainly more than de minimis, without leading to separate classes.[138] For example, under a solvent scheme 'late joiners' who were likely to have substantially stronger mis-selling claims were properly put in the same class as other claimants;[139] similarly, under an insolvent scheme contingent policyholder claims given a 'crude or rough and ready' valuation rather than a 'proper' determination in a liquidation were within the same class as creditors with pre-existing rights.[140]

---

135 CA 2006, s 897(1) and (2); *Practice Statement* [2002] 1 WLR 1345 at [4].
136 *Re Hawk Insurance Company Limited* [2001] 2 BCLC 480, CA at [21].
137 Ibid. at [33].
138 *Re Telewest Communications plc (No. 1)* [2004] BCC 342 at [37].
139 *Re Equitable Life Assurance Society* [2002] BCC 319.
140 *Re Hawk Insurance Company Limited* [2001] 2 BCLC 480, CA.

7.2.3.1.6 Sanction hearing *Procedure: Sanction (generally)* A scheme of arrangement must be proposed between the company and its members or creditors. It follows that the court cannot sanction a scheme of arrangement: 7.87

(1) that is ultra vires the company;[141]
(2) that does not have the approval of the company either through the board or a resolution of the members; and
(3) unless the resolutions have been passed by the correct majorities at a meeting or meetings duly convened and held in accordance with its directions.

The court will not sanction a scheme of arrangement if no explanatory statement was sent out, or that statement was defective. The notice and explanatory statement must be clear and together provide a reasonable sufficiency of information. What is needed is an explanation of how the scheme affects the members or creditors commercially. For example, in the case of an insolvent scheme where the alternative is liquidation, a creditor needs to be given such up-to-date information as can reasonably be provided on what he can expect if the company goes into liquidation and what he can expect under the scheme.[142] 7.88

The court otherwise has a wide discretion whether to sanction a scheme of arrangement. In exercising that discretion the court will not simply register the decision of the meeting, but it will recognize that the best assessment of whether a scheme is in the interests of those to be bound by it is the vote of those present and voting at the meetings.[143] The court must therefore be satisfied that the vote is representative. If the court is not satisfied that the meeting is representative, or is satisfied that those voting at the meeting have done so with a special interest to promote that differs from the interest of the ordinary independent and objective member or creditor, then the vote in favour of the resolution is not to be given effect by the sanction of the court.[144] Accordingly, at the sanction hearing an objector may make a wider attack on the integrity of the process on the ground of unfairness than an attack focused solely on impugning the vote itself.[145] For example, a creditor who has an equity interest in the company has a special interest that another creditor without such an interest does not have and may be motivated to vote in favour of a scheme to reduce the company's debt burden to realize the benefit of his equity interest. 7.89

---

[141] If such a scheme is sanctioned, the company cannot dispute any consequent liability on the ground that the scheme was ultra vires.

[142] *Re Heron International NV* [1994] 1 BCLC 667, 672

[143] *Re English, Scottish, and Australian Chartered Bank* [1893] 3 Ch 385, 408–9

[144] *Re BTR plc* [2000] 1 BCLC 740, 747, CA.

[145] *Re The Scottish Lion Insurance Co Ltd* [2009] CSOH 127 at [37]; *Re UDL Holdings Limited* [2002] 1 HKC 172, 185.

7.90 The question for the court is whether the scheme of arrangement is reasonable in all the circumstances. If the scheme is one that an intelligent and honest man who is a member of the class to whom the scheme is put would consider fair and reasonable, the court should sanction the scheme.[146]

7.91 The key issue is whether the scheme is fair as between the various interests involved and so could reasonably be approved by the meetings, but the court may also look to the effect on third parties and to any irregularity at the meetings convened.

7.92 If sanctioned, the order of the court has no effect until a copy has been delivered to the Registrar of Companies.

7.93 7.2.3.1.7 **Costs** The court has until fairly recently applied a relatively benign costs regime in relation to schemes of arrangement in which the company would pay the objectors' costs and no order would be made that one member or creditor should pay the costs of another.[147]

7.94 The more modern approach is for the court to look at all the relevant circumstances in each case and decide, against that background, the appropriate costs order.[148]

7.95 There is now no general rule to the effect that an objector is entitled to his costs unless there is a counterbalancing factor that indicates that no costs order should be made;[149] but the court will not make a costs order against an objector if his objections are not frivolous and have been of assistance to the court,[150] unless the objector is not directly affected by the scheme of arrangement in which case the court is to decide what the justice of the case demands in relation to costs.[151]

7.2.3.2 Creditors' schemes of arrangement

7.96 A creditors' scheme of arrangement is a statutory compromise or arrangement with one or more classes of creditors that enables the absence of consent of a minority of creditors to be overcome provided that enough of the relevant creditors agree and the court gives approval.[152]

7.97 A company is free to select the creditors to whom a scheme of arrangement should be put provided that the rights of the creditors and the effects of the scheme on

---

146 *Re Alabama, New Orleans, Texas and Pacific Junction Railway Co* [1891] 1 Ch 213, 247.
147 *Re Esal (Commodities) Ltd* [1985] BCLC 450.
148 *Royal & Sun Alliance v British Engine* [2006] EWHC 2947 (Ch) at [31].
149 Ibid. at [30]–[31].
150 *Re Peninsular and Oriental Steam Navigation Co* [2006] EWHC 3279 (Ch) at [38].
151 Ibid. at [46]–[47]; *Royal & Sun Alliance v British Engine* [2006] EWHC 2947 (Ch) at [28].
152 *Sea Assets Limited v Perusahaan Perseroan (Persero) PT Perusahaan Penerbangan Garuda Indonesia* [2001] EWCA Civ 1696 at [2].

those rights are not so dissimilar as to make it impossible for those creditors to consult together with a view to acting in their common interest.[153]

A company need not include in a scheme any class of creditors whose rights are not altered by the terms of the scheme.[154] **7.98**

A creditors' scheme of arrangement can be used to as a means of avoiding an insolvent liquidation or as an alternative to the normal rules for the distribution of assets in an insolvency proceeding.[155] A scheme of arrangement, and not a series of individual compromise arrangements under section 167 of the Insolvency Act 1986, is the proper way to distribute assets of the company other than strictly in accordance with creditors' rights in a winding up.[156] **7.99**

Typical uses of a scheme of arrangement are to alter the rights of creditors or the nature of their debentures; to effect a debt for equity swap in the form of a release and issue of fully paid-up shares; to compel creditors to accept an assignment of their debts to another company; to require secured creditors to cede priority to a subsequently created charge; and to provide a limitation on future, uncertain claims against the company to enable it to raise finance. **7.100**

The focus in recent cases has been on asset transfer schemes in which a scheme of arrangement is used in conjunction with a pre-agreed administration sale (a so-called 'pre pack') to enable the senior lenders to enjoy the entire benefit of the restructured company or group of companies.[157] **7.101**

In such a case, a scheme of arrangement is necessary only if there is disagreement, or an inability to reach agreement, between the senior lenders. The function of the scheme is to bind dissentient and apathetic[158] senior lenders, and there is no need to put the scheme to junior lenders, whether or not the junior lenders have a real economic interest in the company or group of companies. **7.102**

The corollary is the case in which the senior lenders are able to enforce or appoint an administrator (with or without the co-operation of the company's board of **7.103**

[153] Ibid. at [45], [51] and [66].

[154] *Re British & Commonwealth Holdings plc* [1992] 1 WLR 672, 680b-c, 682d-e.

[155] *Re London Chartered Bank of Australia* [1893] 3 Ch 540, 546. The necessary link between liquidation and a scheme of arrangement was severed by the Companies Act 1907, which extended the power to promote a scheme to all companies and not only those in liquidation.

[156] *Re Trix Ltd Re Ewart Holdings Ltd* [1970] 1 WLR 1421, 1423–4. The liquidator in *Trix* had asked the court to sanction a series of conditional compromises thereby depriving the creditors of the chance to consent or object prior to approval individually or at a meeting.

[157] A scheme of arrangement is often implemented without an administration proceeding. If there is no asset transfer, for example only a debt for equity swap, there is no need for an administration proceeding.

[158] For example, if a senior lender is insolvent it may be difficult to obtain consent in a workable timeframe.

directors) to execute a pre-agreed administration sale. If so, there is no need for a scheme of arrangement between any set of creditors. *Re Hellas Telecommunications (Luxembourg) II SCA*[159] is currently the leading example of a case of this kind.[160] The company's directors applied to appoint administrators who would, if appointed, effect a sale of the company's business and assets to a new company controlled by the senior lenders, leaving the junior creditors with worthless claims against a company without assets. The key issue was whether it was proper to appoint the administrators in those circumstances. Lewison J. considered that such cases are likely to fall into one of three categories:

(1) Category 1 in which the evidence indicates that a pre-agreed sale is the only reasonable option—in which case the appointment of administrators would be coupled with an order granting them liberty to execute the sale but without prejudice to the right of creditors to initiate a subsequent challenge (for example, on the basis that the sale was at an undervalue).
(2) Category 2 in which the evidence does not so clearly demonstrate the merits and fairness of the pre-agreed sale—in which the case appointment of the administrators (if it is right to appoint administrators) would be made without the court giving them liberty to enter into the pre-agreed sale but without enjoining the administrators from so doing.
(3) Category 3 in which the evidence gives rise to serious concerns as to the merits and fairness of the pre-agreed sale—in which case the proposed administrators might not be appointed at all.[161] The court might dismiss the application, appoint alternative insolvency practitioners or appoint the proposed administrators but direct them not to enter into the pre-agreed sale.

7.104 *Hellas* was held to be a case within Category 1, the company having attracted only one bid to which the senior lenders would consent.[162]

7.105 If a case is within Category 2, the only real recourse available to junior lenders is to challenge the propriety of the sale as unfairly prejudicing their interest as creditors, or, exceptionally, if a cross-undertaking can be funded or relieved, to seek an order enjoining the proposed sale and/or the removal of the administrators.[163] The starting point for such a challenge is proper scrutiny of the sale process and Statement of Insolvency Practice 16 (SIP 16), which sets out guidelines for

[159] [2009] EWHC 3199 (Ch).
[160] The case is of particular interest because the company has effected a shift in its centre of main interests (COMI) for the purpose of Council Regulation 1346/2000 on insolvency proceedings to enable it to take advantage of English insolvency law and procedure.
[161] Ibid. at [8]
[162] Ibid. at [9].
[163] *Clydesdale Financial Services Ltd v Smailes* [2009] EWHC 1745 (Ch).

disclosure and independence, is likely to play a key role in assessing whether the sale process was in some way defective.

The use of an asset transfer scheme coupled with an administration sale[164] is, as such, only necessary if the senior lenders cannot unanimously agree as to the appropriate course of action to the requisite majority under the security documentation. In such a case, it should be unnecessary to put the scheme to the juniors lenders who should, logically, also have no standing to challenge the sanction of the scheme that does not purport to, and that cannot, affect their rights and that is independent of the subsequent asset transfer that may affect the enjoyment of their rights if at an undervalue. A challenge to the sanction of such a scheme by the junior lenders should be looked on as a challenge by an outsider and not be subject to the benign costs regime applied to dissentient members of the class(es) to which the scheme is put. **7.106**

7.2.3.2.1 **Creditors** Any person having a pecuniary claim against the company capable of estimate is a creditor. Such claims may be due, prospective or contingent, liquidated or unliquidated, provided that they are capable of estimation.[165] **7.107**

Whether the debt is secured or unsecured is irrelevant to the issue of whether it can be compromised or arranged, although it may give rise to class issues. It is the underlying debt that is compromised or arranged and not the security interest.[166] **7.108**

The governing law of the debt is also irrelevant to the issue of whether it can be compromised or arranged. Any compromise or arrangement would be effective in relation to any foreign law debt in relation to assets within the jurisdiction of the court and in relation to any English law debt wherever in the world the company's assets are, or the debt is, situated.[167] **7.109**

If there is any practical limitation in relation to a foreign law debt, it is the potential class issue that might arise by treating foreign law creditors and English law creditors as members of the same class. If the company has material assets outside the jurisdiction, the foreign law creditor might be in a relatively better position than English law creditors, having an incentive to vote for the compromise or **7.110**

[164] There is no need for the appointment of an administrator to effect the sale. The board of directors has such a power, but, from the point of view of the court, it is useful for the sale to be subject to the scrutiny of an independent officeholder.

[165] *Re Albert Life Assurance Co* (1871) 6 LR Ch App 381, CA, 386; *Re Midland Coal, Coke & Iron Co* [1895] 1 Ch 267, CA, 277; *Re T&N Ltd* [2006] 2 BCLC 374 at [32]–[40].

[166] *Re Empire Mining Co* (1890) 44 Ch D 402, 409.

[167] *New Zealand and Mercantile Agency Co v Morrison* [1898] AC 349, PC, 359. Under English law, the discharge of a debt is determined by its applicable law: *Gibbs v Metaux* (1890) 25 QBD 399, CA, 405–7, 409–10; *Wight v Ekhardt Marine* [2004] 1 AC 147 at [16]–[25].

arrangement to eliminate competition in enforcing against those assets.[168] However if the debt is not governed by English law an English scheme of arrangement relating to an English law debt would be expected to be recognized by a foreign court. To assist recognition, the court may confirm that the scheme administrator is an authorized representative.[169] In the case of English law debts, the class issue is theoretical and should not impact on the jurisdiction of the court.[170]

7.111 Contingent and unliquidated claims however create practical problems that must be accommodated in the procedure leading to the sanction hearing and within the terms of the scheme.

7.112 *Notification* As set out above, the company is required to take all steps reasonably open to it, before the convening hearing, to notify any creditor affected by the scheme unless there are good reasons for not doing so.[171] If the class of creditor is extensive and certain of its members unknown, and the proposed scheme raises issues that are legally uncertain, it may be appropriate to notify only a representative set of such creditors to resolve those issues at the convening hearing (or, perhaps, at a prior hearing).[172]

7.113 To enable the company to discharge the obligation to take all reasonable steps to give notice in a case in which the class is extensive and unknown, the court will usually direct the company to place one or more advertisements targeted to the class in question.[173] If such advertisement is reasonably likely to achieve that end, the court would be unlikely to order a more extensive creditor-identification process if the cost of doing so would be disproportionate to the likely benefit.[174]

7.114 A particular problem, in relation to which there is little reported authority, is the notification of underlying financial creditors such as notheolders or bondholders whose interests are overlain by a complex financial structure. The approach in recent cases has been to give notification through the clearing system and various intermediaries as part of the process of enfranchising underlying financial

---

168 *Re Sovereign Marine and General Insurance Co Ltd* [2007] 1 BCLC 228 at [186]–[187]. The scheme could, if this poses a serious problem, allow all creditors to attach assets abroad if they are threatened by an individual creditor.

169 *Re Telewest Communications plc (No. 1)* [2005] 1 BCLC 752 at [60]–[61].

170 Ibid. Cf. the German Court of Appeal decision which refused to recognize a long-sanctioned scheme in relation to Equitable Life under either the Judgments Regulation or the Insolvency Regulation, requiring recourse to be had solely to local rules of recognition in a case where the relevant consumer insurance policies were governed by German law.

171 *Practice Statement* [2002] 1 WLR 1345 at [4].

172 *Re Cape plc* [2007] 2 BCLC 546 at [20]–[24]. The administrators had made a pre-convening application to notify only those involved with the claims of the extensive and unknown class to ensure representation at the convening hearing in relation to the uncertain issues.

173 Ibid. at [127]–[128]

174 *Re British Aviation Insurance Co Ltd* [2006] 1 BCLC 665 at [47]–[48], [78]–[81] (notification pre convening hearing) and [98] (notification pre sanction hearing).

creditors and not any nominee, trustee or depositary.[175] The premise for enfranchising such creditors is that, by the terms of the security documentation, they are likely to be contingent creditors of the company irrespective of the probability of the occurrence of the contingency and the extant rights of any nominee, trustee or depositary.[176]

Estimation (for voting purposes) Unliquidated and disputed claims are sources of potential irregularity at the creditors' meeting. If such claims are admitted for £1 or such other value as the chairman might determine, there is only a value issue in play but if, for example, a dispute claim is rejected for voting purposes there is both a numerosity and value issue which, if sustained, may impact on the integrity of the process. **7.115**

The general duty of the chairman of a company meeting is to conduct the meeting in such a way that the business is facilitated and the results of that business clearly defined.[177] In the context of a scheme of arrangement in which the meeting is convened by a direction of the court, and the court lays down rules for assessing the validity and value of votes, the vote can be impugned if the chairman does not conduct the meeting substantially in accordance with the procedure laid down by the court on the convening hearing.[178] In particular, the chairman's decision to admit or reject a claim or to place a value upon it may be impugned if he did not act honestly or acted perversely or capriciously.[179] **7.116**

If unliquidated or disputed claims are particularly problematic, the company may make use of an independent vote assessor to assist the chairman. This is done regularly in the context of schemes promoted by solvent insurance or reinsurance companies that wish to bring an end to the run off of their long-tail business by **7.117**

---

175 *Re Gallery Capital SA*, unreported 21 April 2010; *Re Castle Holdco 4 Ltd* unreported 23 March 2009 per Norris J; *Re Glencore Nickel Pty Ltd* [2003] 44 ACSR 210. The alternative approach is to deal with the nominee, trustee or depositary directly as the holder of the legal right against the company: see *Re Dunderland Ltd* [1909] 1 Ch 446, 452–3 and 'Bondholder Schemes of Arrangement: Playing the Numbers Game' (2003) Insolvency Intelligence 73. In such a case, the trustee, if the trust deed permits, should split his vote at the creditors' meeting according to the direction of the underlying financial creditors. Cf. *Re Equitable Life Assurance Society* unreported 26 November 2001 per Lloyd J. applying *Re Polly Peck International plce* [1991] BCC 503 in relation to the vote of a policyholder trustee in the context of a creditors' scheme of arrangement.

176 Ibid. See also *Re T&N Ltd* [2006] 2 BCLC 374 at [46]–[61] applying *Winter v IRC* [1963] AC 235, HL, 249, 253–4, 263.

177 *National Dwelling Society v Skyes* [1894] 3 Ch 159.

178 *Re British Aviation Insurance Co Ltd* [2006] 1 BCLC 665 at [66]. Such procedural provisions are now common in English schemes but not necessarily in other jurisdictions which have schemes.

179 Ibid. at [65]. The risk of personal liability to the chairman is minimal and is likely to relate only to wasted costs. If the vote is impugned, the result of the meeting will be reversed and no prejudice will have been caused; conversely, if the vote is not impugned, the creditor in question will have suffered no loss because the valuation would have been for voting purposes only.

estimating the value of their contingent liabilities and paying those claims in full. An independent assessor would be expected by the relevant financial services regulations to be used and might deflect potential criticism of the process in cases in which the value of unliquidated claims is uncertain, the valuation technique controversial and any dealing with some but not all creditors in relation to such claims might give rise to the appearance of preferential treatment as between supporting and opposing creditors.[180] The same reasoning would equally apply to disputed claims.

7.118 *Estimation (for dividend purposes)* To achieve certainty and finality, it is proper to require claims to be submitted within a time limit to be agreed or, in the case of dispute, to be determined by an independent adjudicator.

7.119 The appropriate period for the submission of claims between the effective date and the bar date is to be determined having regard to all the circumstances:

(1) A very short period (one day) was appropriate in relation to ancillary claims of known financial creditors where there had been widespread publicity and notification coupled with an ample opportunity to submit claims beforehand.[181]
(2) A short period (two months) was appropriate where it was unlikely that creditors of significant value were unknown and would be unable to put in their claims.[182]
(3) A long period (one year) may be regarded as appropriate where the class of creditors is extensive and some of its members unknown and only likely to be notified of the scheme by advertisement.[183]

7.120 The determination of the independent adjudicator is binding only in so far as the law allows and must be expressed to be so qualified if it is not to infringe public policy[184] or the right to a hearing before an independent and impartial tribunal.[185]

7.121 The precise extent to which the determination is required to be qualified by the right of appeal to the court turns on the question the independent adjudicator is called on to determine:

(1) If the reference is confined to questions of fact and any incidental question of law, the determination of the adjudicator as an expert could exclude appeal to

---

[180] Ibid. at [66] and [101]–[110].
[181] *Re Telewest Communications plc (No. 1)* [2005] 1 BCLC 75 at [8] and [56].
[182] *Re Pan Atlantic Co Ltd* [2003] 2 BCLC 678 at [18]–[20]. The scheme was sanctioned in 2003. The company had been in run off from 1991 and in provisional liquidation from 1996 but there was a real possibility that some creditors were unknown.
[183] *Re British Aviation Insurance Co Ltd* [2006] 1 BCLC 665 at [22] and [127].
[184] *Re Hawk Insurance Co Ltd* [2001] 2 BCLC 480, 504i-505h per Arden J.
[185] *Pan Atlantic Co Ltd* [2003] 2 BCLC 678 at [21]–[22] and [30]–[32].

the court save in cases of fraud or bias or mistake in the sense of a departure from the scope of the reference.[186]

(2) If the reference extends to questions of law that are not only incidental to a questions of fact, the determination of the adjudication (even if labelled an expert determination) would be the determination of a private tribunal and subject to an appeal to the court in the case of an error of law.[187]

The right of appeal might be attempted to be circumscribed by subjecting the determination to the Arbitration Act 1996 under which the right to appeal may be excluded by clear agreement.[188] It is however doubtful whether a scheme can subject members or creditors to that regime because an arbitration agreement[189] is a bilateral contract between the parties to the main contract and upon the appointment of an arbitrator it becomes a trilateral contract.[190] By contrast, a scheme of arrangement is a statutory compromise that has effect by operation of law[191] and because of the application to the court, the meeting and sanction.[192] **7.122**

7.2.3.2.2 **Relevant comparator** In applying the test whether the class(es) are properly constituted for the purpose of considering the compromise or arrangement, it is essential to identify the relevant comparator.[193] **7.123**

The relevant comparator is a question of fact to be determined by reference to the likely alternative to the scheme of arrangement proposed.[194] For example: **7.124**

- If the company is solvent, the relevant comparator if the restructuring should fail is a continuation of business[195] or a solvent winding up.[196]

---

[186] *Re Hawk Insurance Co Ltd* [2001] 2 BCLC 480, 499f-500h and 504i-505h applying *Jones v Sherwood Computer Service plc* [1992] 1 WLR 277, 287.

[187] *Lee v Showmen's Guild of Great Britain* [1952] 2 QB 329, 341, 342–3 and 353–4.

[188] Arbitration Act 1996, ss 69 (right of appeal) and 82(1) (question of law); *Shell Egypt West Manzala GmbH v Dana Gas Egypt Ltd* (2009) 127 Con LR 27 at [4], [16], [30] and [36]–[48].

[189] Ibid., s 6(1) 'an agreement to submit to arbitration present or future disputes (whether they are contractual or not)'.

[190] *K/S Norjarl A/S v Hyundai Heavy Industries Co Ltd* [1991] 1 Lloyd's Law Rep 525, 531. The analysis must be correct as an arbitration clause can be vitiated and terminated as any other contract subject to the doctrine of severability.

[191] *Re London Chartered Bank of Australia* [1893] 3 Ch 540, 546–7.

[192] *Kempe v Ambassador Insurance Co (in liquidation)* [1998] 1 BCLC 234, PC. Cf. *Re Hawk Insurance Co Ltd* [2001] 2 BCLC 480, 504c-g in which Arden J. considered that a scheme of arrangement was not 'wholly compulsory'.

[193] *Re T & N (No. 3)* [2007] 1 BCLC 563 at [87].

[194] *Re Cape plc* [2007] 2 BCLC 546 at [35].

[195] The business may continue as a going concern open to new business or as a business in run off, transacting no new business but performing existing contracts.

[196] *Re British Aviation Insurance Co Ltd* [2006] 1 BCLC 665 at [88]–[97].

- If the company is insolvent and would cease to trade should the proposed restructuring fail, the relevant comparator is insolvent liquidation.[197]
- If more would be realized by an administration than an immediate winding up, the relevant comparator is administration, being the proper course having regard to the duties of the company's board of directors and the likely rational choice of any creditor. The issue then is how the administration is likely to be conducted.
- If the appointment of an administrator would be fruitless (because of the security structure in place) and no restructuring other than the scheme proposed is acceptable to the senior lenders, the relevant comparator is enforcement under the security documentation,[198] specifically a market sale that seeks to obtain the best price reasonably available in all the circumstances.[199]

7.125 There may be scope for a relevant comparator in terms of some *other* restructuring if it is unrealistic, on the evidence, that the senior lenders would act contrary to their interests by enforcing rather than renegotiating *and* for the company's board of directors to act contrary to the interests of the company's creditors as a whole by initiating an insolvency proceeding when some other restructuring might be put forward as an alternative to that proposed that would yield a better return to creditors.[200]

7.126 The principal attraction of such a comparator from the point of view of the junior lenders is that it enables a valuation of the company, and so an assessment of the rights in issue, over the longer term. The court would not be confined to a break-up value or a sale in the market now but might realistically look on the company as a cash-generative asset held by senior *and* junior lenders for themselves that is capable of generating a relatively higher return beyond the short to medium term.

7.127 The difficulties with such a comparator are, firstly, sustaining it in the face of security documentation that is likely to subordinate the rights of junior lenders to the rights of the senior lenders in all respects and, secondly, integrating it with the duties of the directors of a company in serious financial difficulty. The objection that must be overcome is why the court should look to some *other* restructuring unacceptable to the senior lenders in circumstances in which their bargained for rights entitle them to enforce *and* the duties of the company's directors are,

[197] *Re Hawk Insurance Co Ltd* [2001] 2 BCLC 480 at [6]; *Re Re Telewest Communications plc (No. 1)* [2005] 1 BCLC 752 at [28]–[29].

[198] *Re Bluebrook Limited* [2009] EWHC 2114 (Ch)

[199] *Silven Properties Ltd v RBS plc* [2004] 1 WLR 997, 1005, CA; *Palk v Mortgage Services Funding plc* [1993] Ch 330, 337–8.

[200] *Re MyTravel Group plc* [2005] 2 BCLC 123 at [58]–[60].

rationally,[201] owed only to the senior creditors and not others out of the money classes of creditor.

If, on applying the relevant comparator, a class of creditor has no economic interest in the company, it is not necessary for the company to consult that class.[202] **7.128**

This rule is not confined to cases in which it is conceded that there is no economic interest or in which the absence of such an interest can be established as a matter of absolute clarity by a simple mathematical calculation.[203] **7.129**

If the relevant possibility of a surplus is purely theoretical or merely fanciful, the court is not required to hold that it has not been established that the relevant class has no interest in the assets of the company. The court is required to consider the evidence before it on the balance of probabilities.[204] **7.130**

In doing so, the court is required to make a realistic assessment of the matter[205] and it must ignore the possibility that, as between themselves, the company's creditors might come to some different arrangement.[206] In other words, the fact that the creditors might be prepared to do a deal does not confer an economic interest in the company.[207] **7.131**

Similarly, the fact that some valuable return is offered to creditors without an interest in an insolvency situation as part of a proposed restructuring is not a recognition of any economic interest but a gift to those creditors by others.[208] **7.132**

7.2.3.2.3 **Sanction** In asking whether a creditors' scheme of arrangement should be sanctioned, the court will have regard to the relevant comparator to the scheme. An intelligent and honest scheme creditor would give a special consideration to a comparison between the likely, or even probable, future of the company should there be, on the one hand, no scheme and should there be, on the other hand, the scheme proposed.[209] **7.133**

---

201 Whether members have an economic interest in a company is determined on a balance sheet basis as at a given date. The same approach should apply as between creditors according to the priority each class of creditor enjoys because any priority is no less intense than the statutory priority enjoyed by creditors as against members' claims (in their character of a member) under IA 1986, s 74(2)(f) and is more intense in the case of contractual subordination by virtue of a deed to which the company is a party also.

202 *Re Tea Corp Ltd* [1904] 1 Ch 12, 23–4.

203 *Re MyTravel Group plc* [2005] 2 BCLC 123, 149–50 at [54]; *Re Bluebrook Limited* [2009] EWHC 2114 (Ch).

204 Ibid.

205 *Re Telewest Communications plc (No. 1)* [2005] 1 BCLC 752, 763 at [29]; *Re MyTravel Group plc* [2005] 2 BCLC 123, 149–50 at [56]–[59].

206 *Re MyTravel Group plc* [2005] 2 BCLC 123, 152 at [60].

207 Ibid.

208 *Re Tea Corp Ltd* [1904] 1 Ch 12, 24.

209 *Re Marconi plc* [2003] EWHC 1083 (Ch) at [13]–[14].

7.3 US law

7.3.1 Introduction

7.134 While the framework for binding minority or out of the money classes of creditors in the UK is rather formalized, the US framework in this area has largely developed outside of legislative or judicial arenas. The US law and practice in this area is essentially a hodgepodge of contractually created and popularly used constructs, with several legal mechanisms created in reaction. This section of the chapter will examine the development of contractual terms designed to address collective action problems and the legislative and judicial efforts to define, corral and guide those experiments.

7.3.1.1 Collective action

7.135 The *'collective action'* problem arises with great frequency when dealing with credit agreements, bond indentures and other situations where there are large groups of lenders or bond holders operating under a single agreement. Given that bond indentures, credit agreements and other similar contracts often include both individual and group rights, a natural tension sometimes occurs between the two interests. On the one hand, credit documents often contain provisions signalling an intent that the creditors be treated as a single group represented by an agent. Typical provisions authorize the agent to act on behalf of the group and allocate various powers and responsibilities to the agent to achieve that action. On the other hand, credit documents often contain provisions that require, in certain circumstances, the consent of each and every individual creditor before any action can be taken. For example, most credit agreements require unanimous approval of the lender group before the maturity of a loan can be extended. The 'collective action' problem arises where the agent under a credit document seeks to exercise, or abstain from exercising, remedies under a credit document and such action is supported by some but not all the lenders. In a distressed situation, the dissenting minority could potentially prevent an out-of-court workout or agreement between a debtor and its creditors. The solution to this type of deadlock often lies within the contract itself.

7.3.1.2 Contractual provisions

7.136 The ability of the majority to bind the minority through out-of-court contractual agreements is largely a matter of the governance provisions set out in the underlying credit agreement or bond indenture.[210] Some illustrative examples of typical credit agreement provisions relevant to collective action include the following.

---

[210] Bond indentures are subject to additional restrictions set out in the Trust Indenture Act. For a more in-depth examination of typical bond indentures *see* Marcel Kaha, 'Rethinking Corporate Bonds: The Trade-Off Between Individual and Collective Rights' (2002) 77 NYUL Rev. 1040.

7.3.1.3 *Amendment provisions*

A typical amendment provision will contain language stating that no modification, amendment or waiver of any provision of an agreement or its related documents shall be effective unless in writing and signed by a specified percentage of lenders. Furthermore, such an amendment provision will identify certain changes that cannot be made without the approval of each of the individual lenders affected by such change. The most common example of an amendment that requires the individual support of every impacted lender is a reduction in the principal amount of the loan or the rate of interest payable to the lender. **7.137**

7.3.1.4 *Agency provisions*

The creation of an agent or other authority that acts on behalf of a group of lenders is essential to the success of majority action. Generally, agency provisions provide that each lender to an agreement (a) appoints an agent to act on its behalf under the credit documents and (b) authorizes the agent to exercise the powers provided in the credit documents, as well any powers reasonably incidental thereto that are necessary to enforce the terms of the agreement. **7.138**

7.3.1.5 *Enforcement provisions*

The enforcement provisions give the credit documents teeth and provide a remedy to the lender group should the borrower breach any provisions in the credit documents. Enforcement provisions are usually activated when an event of default occurs. Events of default are defined in the relevant documents and most often include such items as failing to make payments or filing for bankruptcy. Enforcement provisions usually fall into two categories: acceleration provisions and collection provisions. An acceleration provision allows an agent to declare all principal and any accrued interest to become immediately due and payable upon the occurrence of an event of default. Collection provisions, often set out in security documents executed simultaneously with the main credit agreement, allow the agent to exercise all rights and remedies of a secured party under applicable law, including the right to foreclose, sell, or otherwise dispose of any collateral securing a loan. **7.139**

7.3.1.6 *Majority action provisions*

This type of provision provides that an agent or trustee may take or refrain to take certain actions at the request of a majority of the lenders or bondholders. The requisite majority is normally defined within the bond indenture or credit agreement itself and can be based on the percentage of debt held, number of lenders or a combination of the two. **7.140**

The interaction of these various provisions, some protecting the individual lender and others focused on the group as a whole, is where tensions most often arise as **7.141** a result of dissenting creditors. How courts have reconciled these provisions is what defines permissible collective action.

7.3.1.7 Judicial rulings on collective action

7.142 Perhaps in recognition of the ability of dissenting creditors to impede collective action and thereby hamper reorganization efforts, bankruptcy courts generally interpret contractual provisions broadly so that, in certain distressed situations, minority or dissenting creditors can be bound by the actions of the agent or larger group. This emphasis on a contractually imposed 'majority rules' system can be seen in the case of *Re Chrysler LLC*,[211] where the Second Circuit Court of Appeals was asked to rule on the validity of the bankruptcy court's order authorizing the sale of substantially all of debtor Chrysler LLC's auto-manufacturing assets to a newly created automobile manufacturer. This decision emerged from the highly-publicized chapter 11 bankruptcy of Chrysler LLC and its related companies. Pursuant to the debtors' prepackaged plan of reorganization, the debtors proposed a sale under 11 USC section 363 of substantially all of its operating assets, which would be transferred to the newly created entity 'New Chrysler' in exchange for New Chrysler's assumption of certain liabilities and payment of $2 bn in cash.[212] The bankruptcy court approved the sale, which was immediately challenged by various parties. One of those challenges came from a group of secured lenders, the 'Indiana Pensioners', who argued that the sale impermissibly subordinated their secured interest and allowed assets over which they had a lien to pass free of those liens to other parties. In ruling on this objection, the Second Circuit Court of Appeals first noted that section 363(f) of the Bankruptcy Code provides that assets sold under that section could be sold 'free and clear' of liens when, inter alia, the entity holding the lien consents to the sale. In this case, the Indiana Pensioners had entered into a variety of credit agreements, including a collateral trust agreement, whereby they ceded to a trustee the power to consent to such a sale. Therefore, while the Indiana Pensioners had not themselves consented to the release, the consent to the sale by the collateral trustee, who had the authority to act on behalf of all the first-lien credit holders by operation of the contractual agreement, had bound the Indiana Pensioners.[213] The Indiana Pensioners had argued that their written consent was required for the sale to be approved because of a sub-clause in one of the loan agreements that stated that the written consent of all lenders was required if an amendment to the loan documents would result in a release of all the collateral property. The Second Circuit Court of Appeals

[211] 576 F3d 108 (2d Cir. 2009), *remanded by* 130 S.Ct. 1015 (2010), *vacated as moot by* 592 F3d 370 (2d Cir. 2010).

[212] Ibid. at 112.

[213] Ibid. at 119–20.

rejected this argument and held that the proposed sale did not entail amending the loan documents. In fact, the court pointed out that the sale was to be effected by 'implementing the clear terms of the loan agreements' themselves. These specific terms included: the terms by which (a) the lenders assigned an agent to act on their behalf, (b) the agent was empowered, upon request from the majority lenders, to direct the trustee to act, and (c) the trustee was empowered, at the direction of the agent, to sell the collateral in the event of a bankruptcy.[214]

In coming to this conclusion, the Second Circuit Court of Appeals noted that 'the minority lenders could not object to the trustee's actions since they had given their authorization in the first place'.[215] By interpreting the contract in this manner, the Second Circuit Court of Appeals found that the dissenting creditors had bound themselves under the plain language of the credit agreements to which they had entered. **7.143**

Similarly, the Delaware Bankruptcy Court in *Re GWLS Holdings* was faced with an objection from a single lender to the credit bid[216] of an agent under a first lien credit agreement.[217] The objecting lender, which held $1 m of the $337 m total first lien debt, argued that the terms of the credit agreement required the consent of all the lenders in order for the credit bid to proceed. To support its argument, the objecting lender pointed to specific provisions in the credit agreement, which stated that 'no Credit Document nor any terms thereof may be amended, supplemented or modified. . .' and that 'no such amendment, supplement or modification [shall be made] without the written consent of all Lenders. . .'.[218] In response, the agent argued that the credit agreement and its concurrently executed collateral agreement had appointed the agent to act on behalf of all the lenders in certain circumstances, including the exercise of all rights and remedies with respect to the collateral securing the loan in the event of a default. Interpreting what it asserted was an unambiguous contract based on the plain meaning of the various provisions, the Delaware Bankruptcy Court ultimately held that the agent had the authority to enter the credit bid on behalf of all the lenders pursuant to the terms of the credit and collateral agreements and, as such, the credit bid did not require an amendment to the documents themselves. **7.144**

[214] Ibid. at 120.

[215] Ibid. at 120.

[216] Credit bidding refers to the provision in s 363(k) of the Bankruptcy Code which permits a secured lender in a s 363 sale to 'bid' up to the full amount of the outstanding debt owed under a credit agreement. 11 USC s 363(k).

[217] *Re GWLS Holdings* 2009 WL 453110 (Bankr. D. Del. 23 February 2009).

[218] Ibid. at 2.

7.145 Finally, in *Re Metaldyne Corporation*[219] the Bankruptcy Court for the Southern District of New York was asked to rule on a similar objection to a credit bid, where over 95 per cent of the holders of a prepetition debt had agreed to credit bid and only 5 per cent of the prepetition holders objected.[220] As the Second Circuit Court of Appeals and Delaware Bankruptcy courts before it, the court in this case held that the dissenting creditor had assigned to an agent the right to credit bid and dispose of the collateral.[221] While the loan documents prevented the agent from unilaterally altering or waiving any provisions in the agreement without the consent of the entire lender group, the court held that no such amendment was needed to credit bid and therefore the agent was within its authority to act despite the objection of the minority creditors.[222]

7.146 These cases demonstrate that US courts view credit agreements or indentures that contain agency or majority action clauses as effective mechanisms to bind the dissenting minority in distressed or remedial situations. Thus, in these situations, based on contractual interpretations, US courts will generally resolve the inherent tension that arises when individual rights conflict with the collective by overruling the objections of the minority, who in any case agreed to be bound when they made the decision to join the group in the first place.

7.3.2 Out of court agreements between borrower and creditor(s)

7.3.2.1 Forbearance agreements/standstill agreements/waiver agreements

7.147 There are many types of agreements that are designed to modify the relationship between a borrower and its creditors during times of stress. These include forbearance agreements (also called standstill agreements) and waiver agreements, each of which restricts the actions of a credit group with respect to the enforcement provisions in a contract. By entering into these agreements, the creditors agree to modify or waive their rights under the underlying credit documents with respect to certain collection provisions or enforcement rights. These agreements are often entered into to avoid, or sometimes actually in anticipation of, a borrower's bankruptcy filing and provide the borrower with breathing room to negotiate with its creditors or arrange for its bankruptcy case. At times, however, the validity of such forbearance or waiver agreements has been questioned by dissenting creditors attempting to exercise individual rights.

---

219 *Re Metaldyne* 409 BR 671 (Bankr. SDNY 2009).
220 Ibid. at 672.
221 Ibid. at 678–9.
222 Ibid. at 679.

This issue came up in the case of *Beal Savings Bank v Sommer*.[223] There the New York State Court of Appeals was asked to determine whether one lender in a syndicated loan arrangement had the individual capacity to sue for breach of contract, despite the agreement by the other 36 lenders in the syndicate to forbear from pursuing their remedies under the loan documents.[224] This case arose from a credit agreement and an accompanying keep-well agreement, whereby certain of the borrower's affiliates agreed to make equity contributions if certain financial conditions were not met. Eventually the borrower sought bankruptcy protection. The administrative agent under the credit agreement, at the request of lenders holding 95.5 per cent of the outstanding principal, entered into a settlement agreement whereby the administrative agent agreed to forbear for a defined period of time from enforcing certain obligations under the keep-well agreement.[225] A lender holding a 4.5 per cent interest in the bank debt, and who acquired that interest after the borrower's bankruptcy filing, filed a claim under the keep-well agreement. The New York Supreme Court dismissed the claim for lack of standing, which decision was upheld by the Court of Appeals. Examining the various credit documents, the New York Court of Appeals held that the enforcement provisions in the credit agreement provided the administrative agent with the discretion to refrain from exercising its enforcement remedies as directed by a majority of the lenders. Given that the requisite number of lenders had directed the agent not to pursue legal action, and that each lender had authorized the agent to act on its behalf, the Court of Appeals held that entering into the forbearance agreement was well within the authority of the agent and that the language of the credit documents 'contemplated unified action by the Administrative Agent'.[226] Additionally, the court held that the provisions of the various agreements revealed 'an unequivocal collective design' and that the voting provisions were designed 'to protect all Lenders in the consortium from a disaffected Lender seeking financial benefit perhaps at the expense of other debtholders'.[227] Given this overall interpretation of the contract, the court noted that the authority of the administrative agent to act on behalf of the entire consortium at the direction of the required number of lenders was not overridden by a single provision stating that the keep-well agreement is 'enforceable by the Administrative Agent and each Lender'.[228] Ultimately, the Court of Appeals upheld the lower court's determination that one dissenting creditor did not have the authority to pursue enforcement in the face of a collective decision to refrain from action and enter into a forbearance **7.148**

---

223 8 NY 3d 318 (NY 2007).
224 Ibid. at 321.
225 Ibid. at 322.
226 Ibid. at 328.
227 Ibid. at 332.
228 8 NY 3d. at 327–8.

agreement despite language in the agreement that appeared to grant individual lenders certain enforcement rights.

7.149 The *Beal* decision is also noteworthy because of a rigorous dissent, which well articulates the natural tension between collective action and the individual rights of lenders in such situations. Judge Smith's dissent emphasized the 'normal expectation of the parties to [the loan documents] that each lender may sue separately to recover its loan, if the agreement does not say otherwise'.[229] Because the credit documents at issue contained no explicit waiver of an individual creditor's rights to pursue individual action, the dissent argued that it was 'clear that nothing in these agreements deprives the lenders of their rights to sue separately'.[230] Again, there is some merit in this argument, which demonstrates the equitable issues that arise when a majority of creditors seek to bind the minority against their will. In *Beal*, at least one court decided to side with collective action, which is generally the trend in the US.

7.150 The decision by the Bankruptcy Court for the Southern District of New York in *Re Delta Air Lines, Inc.* is another example of the collective action issue as it relates to forbearance agreements.[231] This case arose from the bankruptcy filing of Delta Air Lines, Inc., which was a party to various lease agreements, including one with Kenton County Airport Board. The lease payments under the agreement were tied to amounts due under certain special facilities revenue bonds, which bonds were issued under a trust indenture that appointed a bond trustee. After its bankruptcy filing, Delta notified the bond trustee that it would be rejecting the lease pursuant to its rights under the Bankruptcy Code. In order to assist in settlement discussions regarding the potential lease rejection, Delta and the bond trustee entered into a forbearance agreement, which provided that Delta would make certain monthly payments and in return each of the parties under the bond indenture would agree to forbear from exercising certain rights or remedies available to them for Delta's failure to make normal lease payments.[232] Assisted in part by the breathing room afforded by the forbearance agreement, the parties eventually reached a settlement agreement, which was approved by a group of bondholders holding approximately 60 per cent of the outstanding principal amount of the bonds. The settlement was then incorporated into Delta's plan of reorganization and was voted on and approved by approximately 97.35 per cent of the bondholders in dollar amount and 89.19 per cent of the bondholders in number.[233] Delta and the bond trustee then sought court permission to implement the

229 Ibid. at 334.
230 Ibid.
231 370 BR 537 (Bankr. SDNY 2007)
232 Ibid. at 542.
233 Ibid. at 540.

settlement, but five bond holders holding approximately $51 m of the face amount of the bonds (approximately 12.3 per cent) objected to the settlement, asserting that the bond trustee lacked the authority to bind them to the settlement.[234] After noting that the bonds were in default due to Delta's bankruptcy filing, the court then turned to the argument that the bond trustee lacked the authority to bind the dissenting bond holders to the agreed upon settlement.[235] Looking to the plain language of the bond indenture itself, the court focused on the following provisions: (a) an enforcement provision, which provided that in the event of a default and subject to instruction by a majority in principal of the bondholders, the trustee may seek various remedies; (b) a majority action provision, which provided that a majority of the holders of the outstanding principal can direct the trustee to pursue remedial proceedings; and (c) a limiting provision, which expressly limited the right of any individual bond holder to institute any enforcement provisions unless certain circumstances were present.[236] After examining these provisions, the court determined that the bond trustee had the authority to act on behalf of the bond holders, limited only by the direction in writing of a majority of the bond holders.[237] After noting that the authority to settle was implicit in the authority to pursue remedies, the court ultimately determined that: in default situations where contractual rights are already impaired by exogenous events, non-impairment clauses are moot and the trustee's power to sue and settle subject to direction by a majority in amount or specified minimum percentage will be sustained over the objection of a minority or individual.[238]

Therefore, the court held that the bond trustee did have the authority to bind the dissenting bond holders and enter into the settlement. **7.151**

Thus, where agreements, including forbearance agreements, can be considered to have a 'collective design' that contemplates the 'unified action' of the entire group, courts in the US have generally upheld that intent even if challenged by a dissenting minority. **7.152**

7.3.2.2 Lockup agreements/plan support agreements

Borrowers and creditors will also sometimes enter into plan support or lockup agreements.[239] These agreements are commonly used in connection with **7.153**

---

[234] Ibid.
[235] Ibid. at 541.
[236] 370 BR at 547–8.
[237] Ibid. at 548.
[238] Ibid. at 549.
[239] Though the terms 'plan support agreement' and 'lock up agreement' are often used interchangeably, some courts make a distinction between improper 'lock-up agreements', which contain provisions for specific performance which are effectively votes or the transfer to the debtor of the power to force a particular vote outside of the disclosure requirements of the Bankruptcy Code.

prepackaged bankruptcies, which will be discussed in depth in the next section. Essentially, a plan support agreement 'locks' creditors into voting to support a borrower's plan of reorganization and memorializes the material terms of a prepetition restructuring proposal, which can be as simple as a term sheet. The effect of a plan support agreement is to bind creditors to vote in support of a debtor's plan of reorganization and commits the debtor to implementing a plan consistent with the terms of the proposal.

7.154 The signatories to a plan support agreement have, by virtue of entering into the agreement, committed to supporting the terms of the debtor's proposed plan of reorganization. Therefore, instead of focusing on internal, contractual enforcement provisions to bind dissenting creditors, plan support agreements specifically contemplate the use of the Bankruptcy Code as an enforcement mechanism. The Bankruptcy Code provisions that provide courts with the power to enforce a plan of reorganization against all a debtor's creditors will be discussed in the next section; however, it should be understood that those are the provisions that make plan support agreements successful in binding minority creditors when the agreed upon plan of reorganization is put into effect.

7.155 Like the other forms of agreements described in this section, courts have occasionally been called upon to rule on the validity of plan support agreements. In *Re Heritage Organization, LLC*,[240] the Bankruptcy Court for the Northern District of Texas was asked to rule on an objection to a debtor's proposed plan of reorganization, which plan was supported by certain judgment creditors who had entered into a plan support agreement with the debtor. However, another group of judgment creditors objected to the confirmation of the plan, claiming that the plan support agreement had violated the solicitation and disclosure rules contained in the Bankruptcy Code. The objecting creditors argued specifically, among other things, that, through its negotiations, the debtor had attempted to solicit votes on its plan of reorganization before court approval of a disclosure statement.[241] Though the objection was eventually mooted when the debtor simply filed an amended plan and clearly complied with all the solicitation and disclosure requirements in the Bankruptcy Code, the bankruptcy court still upheld the concept of plan support agreements. The court specifically noted that courts should foster free negotiations and held that the plan support agreement was not an improper solicitation but rather 'the written memorialization of the negotiations toward

See Kurt A Mayr, 'Unlocking the Lockup: The Revival of Plan Support Agreements under New s 1125(g) of the Bankruptcy Code' (2006) 15 J. Bankr. L. & Prac. 6.

[240] 376 BR 783 (Bankr. N.D. Tex. 2007).

[241] Ibid. at 790–1.

settlement of the legal disputes that have prevented confirmation [of a plan of reorganization] to date. . .'.[242]

7.3.3 Prepackaged bankruptcies

7.3.3.1 Nature and scope

In general terms, prepackaged bankruptcy refers to the situation where, before actually filing a bankruptcy petition, the soon-to-be debtor approaches its creditors and proposes a plan of reorganization in advance. Following a period of negotiation, the debtor then files for bankruptcy protection with the votes for a plan of reorganization having already been solicited by the debtor and agreed to by the requisite number of creditors before the filing of the bankruptcy petition. In this scenario, the debtor files a chapter 11 petition and its 'first day' motions simultaneously with the creditor-supported plan of reorganization and disclosure statement. This simultaneous filing permits the bankruptcy court immediately to set a hearing date to approve the disclosure statement and, thereafter, the plan. In general, a prepackaged plan can be confirmed in as little as 30 days from the commencement of the bankruptcy case.[243] **7.156**

The court in *Re Pioneer Fin. Corp.*[244] provides a good summary of the difference between a prepackaged bankruptcy case and a conventional bankruptcy case. As the court in *Pioneer Fin. Corp.* states: **7.157**

> In a conventional Chapter 11 case, a debtor files a bankruptcy petition, then negotiates a reorganization plan and solicits votes after a disclosure statement has been approved. With a 'prepackaged' plan, however,. . . a plan proponent has negotiated a plan and solicited votes before the filing of a Chapter 11 petition and before there is a hearing to determine the adequacy of the disclosure. With prepackaged plans, the adequacy of the disclosure is evaluated under 'applicable nonbankruptcy law, rule or regulation' or, if there is none, under the 'adequate information' standard set out in [section 1125 of the Bankruptcy Code].

As noted above, the success of prepackaged bankruptcies is attributable, in part, by the acquisition of prior support of a large group of a debtor's creditors and by the ability of the Bankruptcy Code and Rules to bind all parties to a plan's terms. One example of a successful prepackaged bankruptcy case is that of CIT Group, Inc., which filed its prepackaged bankruptcy case on 1 November 2009 and **7.158**

---

[242] Ibid. at 792.

[243] Some cases can achieve successful emergence from bankruptcy in even less time. For example, it took only a day for Blue Bird Body Co. to file its prepack and receive plan confirmation. *Re Blue Bird Body, Co.*, No. 06–50026 (Bankr. D. Nev.); see also, Rhett G. Campbell, 'Prepacks Reduce Time and Costs of Business Filings' (2007) The Nat'l L. J., 5 March, <http://www.tklaw.com/resources/documents/Rhett%20Campbell_National%20Law%20Journal_Prepacks%20Reduce%20Time%20and%20Costs%20of%20Business%20Fiilings.pdf>.

[244] 246 BR 626 (Bankr. D. Nev. 2000).

obtained approval of its plan of reorganization on 8 December 2009.[245] By taking advantage of the bankruptcy provisions providing for prepackaged plans of reorganization, CIT Group, Inc. was able to achieve a successful reorganization in a very short period of time.

7.159 Prepackaged bankruptcies have grown increasingly popular over the years. In fact, in 2009 the rate of prepackaged bankruptcy filings tripled from the number filed in 2008.[246] Given the benefits that a prepackaged bankruptcy filing can provide a debtor, including increased speed in emerging from bankruptcy and decreased costs, practitioners predict that prepackaged bankruptcies will continue to increase in frequency.[247]

7.3.3.2 Procedure

7.160 There are specific provisions in the Bankruptcy Code and Rules designed to govern and promote prepackaged bankruptcies. These provisions indicate the Congressional recognition that fostering negotiations between a debtor and its creditors outside of a bankruptcy court can actually assist in the ultimate goal of bankruptcies, which is to reconcile the interests of a debtor and its creditors in the most mutually satisfactory way. The following provisions are essential to the continued success of prepackaged bankruptcies:

- *11 USC section 1102(b)(1).* An official committee of unsecured creditors is usually selected by the US Trustee. The US Trustee programme is a branch of the US Department of Justice that is charged with monitoring bankruptcy cases, overseeing related administrative functions and acting to ensure compliance with applicable laws and procedures. However, section 1102(b)(1) permits the official committee to be comprised of members organized by the creditors themselves before the commencement of the case, provided that they are 'fairly chosen' and are 'representative of the different kinds of claims to be represented'. Accordingly, the creditors who were originally involved in the negotiations with the debtor before the commencement of the case can continue their involvement throughout the case, with the additional benefit of enjoying the powers granted to official committees by the Bankruptcy Code.[248]
- *11 USC section 1121(a).* This section provides that a debtor may file a plan of reorganization simultaneously with its petition for a voluntary bankruptcy case.

---

[245] *Re CIT Group Inc.* 2009 WL 4824498 (Bankr. SDNY 2009).

[246] Mike Spector, 'The Quickie Bankruptcy: More Companies Enter Court, and Exit, in a Flash' *Wall St. J.*, 5 January2010, at C1.

[247] Dennis J. Connolly, 'Current Issues Involving Prepackaged and Prenegotiated Plans' 2004 Ann. Surv. of Bankr. Law Part I s B (October 2004).

[248] Such powers and limitations will be discussed in the next chapter.

- *11 USC section 1126(b) and Bankruptcy Rule 3018(b).* These provisions govern the allowance of prepetition solicitation of votes for approval of a plan of reorganization, as long as certain criteria are met. The requirements include that (a) the prepetition solicitation was in compliance with applicable non-bankruptcy law, rule or regulation governing the adequacy of disclosure in connection with such solicitation (for example, federal securities laws governing the dissemination of solicitation materials),[249] or (b) if there is no such applicable non-bankruptcy law, that the solicitation conducted occurred after the disclosure of 'adequate information', as defined in Bankruptcy Code section 1125(a)(1).
- *11 USC section 1125(g).* This is a provision added by Congress in 2005. Generally, section 1125 of the Bankruptcy Code governs the postpetition disclosure and solicitation necessary for a debtor to obtain support for a plan of reorganization. Section 1125 explicitly prohibits a debtor from soliciting an acceptance or rejection of a plan of reorganization after the commencement of a bankruptcy case unless the debtor transmits a written summary of the plan and a written disclosure statement that has been approved by the bankruptcy court. Thus, before subsection (g) was added to section 1125, debtors who sought a prepackaged plan of reorganization before filing for bankruptcy, but failed to achieve the requisite number of votes, were at risk of violating the solicitation and disclosure rules unless they went through the formal process of obtaining court approval of a disclosure statement and then attempting to re-solicit their creditors. In other words, debtors who had negotiated with creditors prepetition but did not seek a vote until after their bankruptcy filing were at risk of violating this provision unless they went through the formal process of achieving court approval of a disclosure statement. Section 1125 therefore became a prospective obstacle to the quick resolution that prepackaged bankruptcies were designed to achieve. Recognizing this potential impediment, through the creation of section 1125(g) Congress provided a safe harbour for debtors who attempted a prepackaged bankruptcy but failed to obtain the necessary votes prepetition. Section 1125(g) provides that debtors can solicit plan approval post petition if such solicitation complies with applicable non-bankruptcy law and if the holder whose approval is solicited was approached before the commencement of the case in a manner complying with applicable non-bankruptcy law.[250]

7.3.3.3 Local rules

In addition to these provisions, certain individual jurisdictions in the US have developed local rules governing the procedures for filing prepackaged bankruptcies **7.161**

---

[249] See Securities Exchange Act of 1934.

[250] House Report No. 109–31, Pt. 1, 109th Cong., 1st Sess. 87 (2005).

in their district. For example, the Bankruptcy Court for the Southern District of New York created local rules and guidelines to govern the filing of prepackages bankruptcy cases in that district, including what motions need to be filed and what form and content of notice must be given to the court.[251]

7.162 Like other arrangements referenced in this chapter, prepackaged bankruptcies may be subject to disruption and challenge by minority creditors. In *Re NRG Energy, Inc.*[252] a debtor had begun negotiations with certain of its creditors in anticipation of an out-of-court restructuring or filing a prepackaged bankruptcy plan. Certain other of its creditors, who were not party to the negotiations, filed an involuntary bankruptcy petition against the debtor before a prepackaged plan could be filed.[253] In response, the debtor sought to have the bankruptcy court abstain from exercising its jurisdiction over the involuntary bankruptcy case or, in the alternative, to dismiss the involuntary bankruptcy petition to allow the debtor to proceed with its negotiations or file a prepackaged plan. When ruling, the court focused on the fact that the debtor had already entered into substantial negotiations with a majority of its creditors, with the result that the debtor 'had the benefit of a general forbearance by its major lenders, under which none of them have taken any action that would affect any other's rights or those of the Debtor'.[254] This armistice with the majority of its lenders had allowed the debtor to take substantial steps toward filing its own negotiated restructuring, though the debtor asserted that it was not yet ready to do so and simply needed more time.[255] Turning to the issue of whether it should abstain from hearing the involuntary case, the court noted that its decision should be guided by the best interests of the debtor and the entire creditor group, not a single dissenting minority. Ultimately, the bankruptcy court decided to abstain, noting that there was:

> a significant risk that forcing the maintenance of the bankruptcy jurisdiction over negotiations well-started under different assumptions and rules would unduly distort the process, reduce creditors' ultimate realizations and prejudice results. This debtor was injected into involuntary bankruptcy by a small group of creditors whose claims were a very small component of a huge debt structure... at this time, abstaining from exercising the bankruptcy jurisdiction over [the debtor] and its creditors is more in the general interest then the alternative. ...[256]

7.163 In this case, supporting the majority rule required the bankruptcy court to refrain from exercising its jurisdiction instead of using its power to enforce contractual

[251] See Bankr. SDNY Rule 3018–2; Bankr. SDNY General Order M-201, amended by General Order M-203.

[252] 294 BR 71 (Bankr. D. Minn. 2003).

[253] Ibid. at 74–5.

[254] Ibid. at 76–7.

[255] Ibid. at 78–9.

[256] Ibid. at 87–86.

provisions against a minority creditor. Either way the result is the same: bankruptcy courts will generally look to support the outcome that is in the best interests of a debtor and its entire group of creditors even if it sometimes comes at the expense of the individual rights of minority creditors.

Minority creditors challenging prepackaged plans are also free to use many of the same challenges that are often brought against conventional chapter 11 plans, for example challenging the adequacy of the disclosure statement, arguing that votes were not properly solicited, that certain creditors are not receiving the 'indubitable equivalent' of their claim, or trying to assert that the plan is not feasible or that it was not filed in good faith. Prepackaged plans do not receive special treatment with respect to these challenges. Instead, courts apply similar analyses as in the case of conventional chapter 11 plans, as was demonstrated in the case of *Re Zenith Elecs. Corp.*, where the Bankruptcy Court for the District of Delaware rejected an objection by an equity group to a disclosure statement for a prepackaged plan.[257] **7.164**

Prepackaged bankruptcy cases provide a cost-effective and expeditious way for a majority of creditors to bind the minority in the US. However, there are still hurdles and potential challenges that minority creditors may successfully interpose to assert their rights in a prepackaged bankruptcy case. **7.165**

7.3.4 Chapter 15, section 304 and schemes of arrangement

Another means through which minority creditors can be bound in the US is through the adoption of schemes of arrangement or other foreign proceedings conducted in other countries, including those referenced in other sections of this chapter. As did former section 304 of the Bankruptcy Code, current chapter 15 of the Bankruptcy Code provides for the recognition of foreign insolvency proceedings in the US. **7.166**

7.3.4.1 Recognition of a foreign proceeding under former section 304

Prior to 2005, the operative bankruptcy provision governing recognition of foreign proceedings in the US was section 304 of the Bankruptcy Code.[258] Section 304 authorized a 'foreign representative' to commence a 'case ancillary to a foreign **7.167**

[257] 241 BR 92 (Bankr. D. Del. 1999) (analysing whether a disclosure statement and plan should be rejected because of improper disclosure, based on lack of fair and equitable treatment and for lack of good faith).

[258] 11 USC s 304, repealed by Pub. L. No. 109–8, tit. VIII, s 802, 119 Stat. 23, 146 (2005). Former s 304 applied to all cases commenced under title 11 prior to 17 October 2005. See Pub. L. No. 109–8, tit. VIII, sec. 802, 119 Stat. 23, 216 (2005).

proceeding' by filing a petition in US bankruptcy court.[259] The case of *Re Bd. of Dirs. of Hopewell Int'l Ins. Ltd.* is a good example of an ancillary proceeding brought under former section 304. In that case, the Bankruptcy Court of the Southern District of New York recognized and enforced a scheme of arrangement between a company and its creditors in accordance with Bermuda law. The ruling provides an extensive discussion of the principals of recognition under former section 304.[260]

7.168 In connection with such ancillary cases, bankruptcy courts were granted broad authority to issue a wide range of relief, including the ability to bind minority creditors, as necessary.[261]

7.3.4.2 Recognition of a foreign proceeding under chapter 15

7.169 Incorporating the provisions of the Model Law on Cross-Border Insolvency, and replacing former section 304 of the Bankruptcy Code, chapter 15 was enacted in 2005 and was designed to 'provide effective mechanisms for dealing with cases of cross-border insolvency. . .'.[262] Generally, the provisions of chapter 15 are applicable where 'assistance is sought in the United States by a foreign court or a foreign representative in connection with a foreign proceeding'.[263]

7.170 In many ways similar to former section 304, relief under chapter 15 is available only after a foreign representative commences an ancillary proceeding for recognition of a foreign proceeding before a US bankruptcy court.[264] Recognition of a foreign proceeding will only occur so long as: (a) it is a foreign 'main' proceeding (a proceeding pending in a country where the debtor's main interests are located) or a foreign 'non-main' proceeding (a proceeding pending in a country where the

[259] 11 USC s 304, repealed by Pub. L. No. 109–8, tit. VIII, s 802, 119 Stat. 23, 146 (2005).

[260] 238 BR 25 (Bankr. SDNY 1990).

[261] Under former s 304, various schemes of arrangements were recognized. See, eg, *Re DAP Holding N.V.* 05-18816 (Bankr. SDNY 27 October 2005); *Re Mercantile & General Reinsurance Co. Ltd.* 05-14076 (Bankr. SDNY 7 September 2005); *Re Unione Italiana (UK) Reinsurance Co. Ltd.* 04-17989 (Bankr. SDNY 8 June 2005); *Re The Prudential Assurance Co. Ltd.* 4-14884 (Bankr. SDNY 9 September 2004); *Re Aviation & General Insurance Co. Ltd.* 04-13499 (Bankr. SDNY 5 August 2004); *Re Ludgate Insurance Co. Ltd.* 04-10590 (Bankr. SDNY 8 April 2004); *Re Arig Insurance Co., Ltd.* 03-17057 (Bankr. SDNY 9 December 2003); *Re Marlon Insurance Co. Ltd.* 03-42343 (Bankr. SDNY 6 November 2003); *Re Assurantiemaatschappij 'De Zeven Provincien'* NV 02-16430 (Bankr. SDNY 28 March 2003); *Re The Nichido Fire & Marine Insurance Co. Ltd.* 01-15987 (Bankr. SDNY 131 February 2002); *Re Ramus Insurance Ltd.* 01-12160 (Bankr. SDNY 7 June 2001); *Re Osiris Insurance Limited,* 98-45518 (Bankr. SDNY 16 November 1998); *Re Board of Directors of Hopewell Intern. Ins. Ltd.* 238 BR 25, 34 Bankr. Ct. Dec. (CRR) 1273 (Bankr. SDNY 1999), order affd, 275 BR 699, 48 Collier Bankr. Cas. 2d (MB) 362 (SDNY 2002).

[262] 11 USC s 1501.

[263] 11 USC s 1501(b)(1).

[264] 11 USC s 1504.

debtor has an establishment[265] but not its centre of main interests);[266] (b) the petition is brought by a 'foreign representative', or a person or body authorized in a foreign proceeding to administer the reorganization or the liquidation of the debtor's assets or affairs or to act as a representative of such proceeding;[267] and (c) the petition meets the requirements of section 1515, which include that the petition be accompanied by sufficient documentation evidencing the existence of the foreign proceeding and the appointment and authority of the foreign representative.[268] Failure to follow these guidelines will result in a US court's inability to exercise jurisdiction, as was the case in *US v J.A. Jones Constr. Group, LLC.* There a receiver to the property of a defendant in a law suit sought a stay of the litigation against the defendant because it was subject to Canadian insolvency proceedings. The District Court for the Eastern District of New York determined that it had no jurisdiction to hear the motion for stay because the receiver had failed to commence an ancillary proceeding before a US bankruptcy court to have the Canadian insolvency proceeding recognized.[269] The court held that, in the absence of recognition under chapter 15, it had no authority to consider the requested relief. However, recognizing that US courts should accord foreign bankruptcy proceedings comity, the court did temporarily stay the action to allow the receiver the opportunity to seek appropriate relief under chapter 15.

Once recognition has been achieved, chapter 15 provides a court broad authority to order any appropriate relief necessary to effectuate the 'purpose of this chapter and to protect the assets of the debtor and the interests of the creditors',[270] provided that such action is not 'manifestly contrary to the public policy of the United States'.[271] Judging by the case law under former section 304, and the developing law under capter 15, binding minority creditors to a restructuring or scheme of arrangement for the greater good of the majority is exactly the type of relief envisioned by capter 15.[272] **7.171**

7.3.4.3 Schemes of arrangement—Rhode Island

At least one US state has drafted a statute designed to implement a mechanism similar to the schemes of arrangement provided for under section 425 of the **7.172**

[265] An establishment is a place of operations where the debtor carries out a long term economic activity. 11 USC s 1502(2).

[266] 11 USC s 1502.

[267] 11 USC s 101(24).

[268] 11 USC ss 1515, 1517.

[269] 333 BR 637 (EDNY 2005).

[270] 11 USC s 1521.

[271] 11 USC s 1506.

[272] The legislative history of chapter 15 reveals that while it was contemplated that chapter 15 would repeal and replace former section 304, 'access to the jurisprudence which developed under section 304' was to be maintained. H.R. Rep. 107-3(I) at p. 90.

Companies Act 1985 of the UK.[273] In 2002, Rhode Island adopted a statute that permits solvent insurance companies to implement a scheme under state law. Under section 27-14.5 of the General Laws of Rhode Island, '[a]ny commercial run-off reinsurer may apply to the court for an order implementing a commutation plan'. Such a commutation plan will be approved if 50 per cent in number and 75 per cent in value of all creditors vote in favour of the plan.[274] Though relevant only in this state, this statute provides another potential mechanism for binding minority creditors.

7.4 Conclusion

7.173 While perhaps not as formally developed as the law supporting schemes of arrangement in the UK, the US legal system has developed contractual and legal measures that can bind minority or out of the money creditors in a borrower's restructuring efforts. However, as discussed in the following chapter, there are also more formal statutory mechanisms set out in the Bankruptcy Code and Rules that provide powerful tools to enforce majority action and prevent minority, dissenting creditors from derailing a company's reorganization efforts.

[273] Howard Seife and Francisco Vazquez, 'U.S. Courts Should Continue to Grant Recognition to Schemes of Arrangement of Solvent Insurance Companies' (2008) 17 Norton J. Bankr. L. & Prac. 571.

[274] R.I. Gen. Laws s 27-15.5-1-4 (2007).

8

RESTRUCTURING THROUGH US CHAPTER 11 AND UK PREPACK ADMINISTRATION

8.1 Introduction

The legal processes for addressing corporate insolvencies vary dramatically between the US and the UK. Chapter 11 of title 11 of the US Code (the 'Bankruptcy Code') governs most court-supervised reorganizations in the US. It offers a broad range of tools and protections to debtors that freeze creditor actions, facilitate financing, discharge debt, make certain prepetition liens and transactions avoidable, provide the ability to disavow most contracts and leases, and reorganize without the consent of all creditor constituencies. The tools provided under the Bankruptcy Code have been employed in a number of different contexts by a broad range of companies that have successfully emerged as deleveraged entities. While chapter 11 may carry some stigma, it is widely recognized as a **8.01** value-preserving and value-enhancing exercise. During the chapter 11 case, a debtor can operate its business largely unaffected by the filing.

8.02 One of the hallmarks of chapter 11 is its flexibility. Chapter 11 cases take a wide variety of paths, from very quick asset sales to multi-year reorganizations culminating in contentious valuation fights before a bankruptcy judge. Some chapter 11 cases are 'prepackaged' or 'prearranged' restructurings that have been negotiated, and, in some cases, even voted on by creditors out of court and, therefore, last for only a period of weeks. Others, however, are more traditional 'free falls,' in which a company files for chapter 11 to take advantage of the automatic stay imposed upon the filing or to access financing that is only available under the protective provisions of chapter 11. Only after stabilization of the business and development of a business plan after consultation with stakeholders is a plan for emergence developed, voted on by creditors, and approved by the court. Once approved by a bankruptcy court, the plan binds all prepetition creditors having notice of the proceedings, without exception. It is the ability of management to stay in control while prosecuting a reorganization that is one significant distinction which sets chapter 11 apart from insolvency schemes in other jurisdictions.

8.03 Insolvency law in the UK, on the other hand, is far less conducive to non-consensual balance sheet restructurings. An administrator (who must be a licensed insolvency practitioner) may be appointed by the court, or out of court by the company, its directors, or the holder of a qualifying floating charge. While a moratorium on certain creditor actions is imposed, contractual counterparties can exercise rights to terminate contracts. Unlike the Bankruptcy Code, UK insolvency law does not allow for the priming of preexisting security interests, making it impossible in many instances to attract new financing to allow the administrator to trade the business in administration. Perhaps most significantly, under administration, existing management is replaced by the administrator.

8.04 The debtor-friendly chapter 11 process in the US has been instrumental in preserving the going concern value not only of small family enterprises but also of companies whose survival is critical to the economy as a whole. Some of the nation's most high-profile companies, including General Motors, Chrysler, CIT Group, Enron, Charter Communications, WorldCom, Calpine Corporation, Pacific Gas and Electric Co., Kmart, and nearly every large US airline have emerged from chapter 11 in recent years under a wide variety of circumstances. These successes demonstrate the benefits of the flexibility offered by chapter 11. Some cases, such as those of automotive giants General Motors and Chrysler, involved very quick sales of the company's desirable assets, while the less desirable assets remained in chapter 11 to be liquidated under court supervision. Other cases, such as those of Calpine Corporation, Enron, WorldCom, Pacific Gas, Kmart and United Airlines, were lengthier cases during which negotiations—and at times contentious litigation—took place during the chapter 11 until a plan of reorganization was approved by the court. Still others, such as CIT Group and Charter Communications, had chapter 11 plans confirmed but all votes were solicited before the filing and the cases lasted only a few months.

But it is worth considering whether the UK's insolvency regime actually generates more out-of-court restructurings. The sheer difficulty of financing an administration and reaching a negotiated deal with all constituencies may cause a distressed company's principal stakeholders to agree to a consensual restructuring, out of a reluctance to test whether the company can survive the appointment of an administrator. In the US, on the other hand, while the threat of a chapter 11 is often a catalyst to an out-of-court workout, in most circumstances creditors and debtors alike have a higher degree of confidence that the company can survive in chapter 11. **8.05**

8.2 US chapter 11

8.2.1 Why use a formal insolvency process?

The Bankruptcy Code governs most court-supervised corporate reorganizations in the US. It offers a broad range of tools and protections to afford a debtor a breathing spell and provide an opportunity to rationalize its business with the assistance of restructuring professionals. **8.06**

Despite the considerable advantages afforded to chapter 11 debtors, it is often a last resort for American companies. There are significant disclosure requirements imposed on debtors so as to afford transparency to the court and creditors. These disclosure requirements can often exceed the scope of disclosure made even by large, publicly traded companies.[1] The chapter 11 process can also be expensive, as the debtor must not only pay its own professional restructuring advisors, but also must pay for the fees and expenses incurred by a committee of unsecured creditors appointed in the chapter 11 case.[2] Moreover, chapter 11 may put the company 'in play,' as the ability to purchase the company or certain assets free and clear of liens and interests often attracts distressed investors and there is a ready secondary market for investors to acquire a controlling interest in the company's debt. In addition, creditors or other parties in interest may, under certain circumstances, seek the appointment of a trustee to manage the debtor's business, or an examiner to investigate the debtor's affairs, both of which may serve as a threat to existing management.[3] Finally, customers and suppliers may be reluctant to **8.07**

[1] Fed. R. Bankr. P. 1007, 2015.
[2] 11 USC ss 328(a), 1103.
[3] 11 USC s 1104.

continue doing business, particularly in industries that rely on long-term contractual relationships, with a company mired in formal insolvency proceedings.

8.08 Nonetheless, for several reasons, a chapter 11 filing may be the only reasonable alternative for a company in severe financial distress. First, while 'financial' restructurings are commonly implemented outside chapter 11, it is often extremely difficult to effect an *operational* restructuring outside a court-supervised process. A company saddled with uncompetitive long-term contracts or leases will often find it extremely expensive, if not impossible, to consensually terminate those relationships outside chapter 11, particularly if there are hundreds or even thousands of counterparties. The Bankruptcy Code enables a debtor to reject executory contracts and leases, and the resulting damage claims asserted by contract counterparties are treated as prepetition, general unsecured claims against the estate.[4] Damages from the rejection of certain types of contracts, such as leases of nonresidential real property and employment agreements, are capped. The Bankruptcy Code also allows for contracts to be assigned to third parties (such as a purchaser of assets) over the objections of counterparties. In addition, a company may find it far easier to dispose of undesirable assets and the associated liabilities in chapter 11, which allows for the sale of assets 'free and clear' of liens, claims and encumbrances, than to do so under applicable nonbankruptcy law.[5]

8.09 Another feature of the Bankruptcy Code that makes chapter 11 an attractive or necessary alternative is the so-called 'automatic stay'.[6] Section 362 of the Bankruptcy Code provides that the filing of a chapter 11 petition serves to enjoin a broad range of creditor actions, including the commencement or continuation of any judicial, administrative, or other action or proceeding against the debtor that could have been commenced before the filing of the petition, or any action to recover on a claim that arose before the filing of the petition. This sweeping protection affords the debtor a 'breathing spell' upon the commencement of its chapter 11 case, allowing it time to focus on the stabilization and reorganization of its business, free from lawsuits and other actions relating to its prepetition affairs and indebtedness. Protection from prepetition lawsuits is of particular benefit to companies suffering under a deluge of 'mass tort' litigation. In these cases, the numerous, disruptive lawsuits are stayed, and the debtor is able to treat the underlying claims as prepetition liabilities subject to discharge in the reorganization. Chapter 11 even possesses provisions to estimate these types of claims, creating a fertile environment to settle these claims *en masse*.

[4] 11 USC s 365.
[5] 11 USC s 363(f).
[6] 11 USC s 362.

Chapter 11 may be the only available option for companies undertaking large, complex restructurings. While refinancing a single tranche of debt with a single bank group or a single lender may be possible outside a judicial forum, more complex restructurings involving multiple debt issuances, customer and supplier contracts needing modification, and labour unions may necessitate a chapter 11 filing. A formal process in a complex restructuring may be the only means to negotiate successfully for meaningful concessions from all parties within an acceptable time frame. Chapter 11 also lowers the threshold for approving a proposed restructuring plan. Typically, material changes to credit agreements or bond indentures require the approval of 100 per cent of participating lenders, making it difficult to overcome the problem of holdouts. In chapter 11, however, and as discussed in more detail below, a proposed chapter 11 plan only needs the approval of half in number and two-thirds in amount of those voting in a particular class.[7] This lower standard of approval often makes reorganization in chapter 11 far easier to effect than the same agreement would be outside chapter 11. **8.10**

One additional critical advantage of chapter 11 is that it offers a potential debtor liquidity sources that may not be otherwise available. Specifically, chapter 11 allows the debtor, under certain circumstances, to incur new, postpetition debt that ranks senior to all the company's preexisting debt.[8] The ability to offer senior liens and claims is often the only method by which an insolvent debtor whose assets are fully encumbered can obtain financing to fund the reorganization effort. While these so-called 'priming liens' are rare due to the litigation risks that would confront the debtor early on in the case, the mere threat of a priming lien is often enough impetus to get prepetition lenders to provide additional financing where they might otherwise not be inclined to do so. **8.11**

Each of these features of the Bankruptcy Code, as well as others, is discussed in more detail below. **8.12**

8.2.2 An overview of chapter 11

The filing of a chapter 11 petition immediately creates an estate, consisting of all the debtor's assets and interests. The debtor has a fiduciary obligation to manage the estate's affairs in the interests of its stakeholders. In doing so, the debtor is aided by a number of provisions of the Bankruptcy Code designed to protect the estate and preserve the going-concern value of the enterprise. **8.13**

[7] 11 USC s 1129.
[8] 11 USC s 364(d).

8.2.2.1 The automatic stay

8.14 One of the most basic and valuable debtor protections is the automatic stay which comes into effect immediately upon filing a petition for relief. The automatic stay, promulgated in section 362 of the Bankruptcy Code, bars, among other things,

- the commencement or continuation, including the issuance or employment of process, of a judicial, administrative, or other action or proceeding against the debtor that was or could have been commenced before the commencement of the case under this title, or to recover a claim against the debtor that arose before the commencement of the case;
- the enforcement, against the debtor or against property of the estate, of a judgment obtained before the commencement of the case;
- any act to obtain possession of property of the estate or of property from the estate or to exercise control over property of the estate; and
- any act to collect, assess, or recover a claim against the debtor that arose before the commencement of the case.[9]

8.15 The broad scope of the automatic stay is designed to afford the debtor a 'breathing spell' from its creditors, allowing the debtor to take the time necessary to negotiate a reorganization plan with creditors.[10] The automatic stay also bars creditors from a so-called 'race to the courthouse' in which unpaid creditors clamour to secure judgments and liens in the hope of securing a right to repayment ahead of other similarly situated creditors.

8.16 The automatic stay is subject to a number of exceptions, however, which are articulated in subsection (b) of section 362 of the Bankruptcy Code. Chief among them is the so-called 'governmental exception' to the automatic stay, which allows governmental units or agencies to commence or continue actions or proceedings against the debtor 'to enforce such governmental unit's or organization's police and regulatory power, including the enforcement of a judgment other than a money judgment . . .'.[11] The purpose of this exception is to allow governmental units or agencies to protect the public interests by preventing ongoing fraud, violations of consumer or environmental protection laws, or other police or regulatory laws.[12] Where the government's action is simply to protect its own pecuniary interest—that is, when the government is simply acting as another creditor—the action will be stayed.[13]

---

9 11 USC s 362(a)(1)–(3), (6).

10 See eg *Eastern Refractories Co. v Forty Eight Insulations* 157 F3d 169, 172 (2nd Cir. 1998).

11 11 USC s 362(b)(4).

12 *Re Nextwave Personal Communs., Inc.* 244 BR 253 (Bankr. SDNY 2000).

13 Ibid.

8.2.2.2 *Management of the debtor*

One of the core principles of chapter 11 is that unless a trustee is appointed by the court, the debtor's prepetition management will remain in place and will operate the debtor's affairs as a 'debtor in possession'. The debtor in possession has all the rights and powers that a trustee appointed to run the business would have, and operates with a fiduciary obligation to maximize the value of the estate for the benefit of creditors and interest holders.[14] This is in stark contrast to chapter 7 of the Bankruptcy Code, which governs liquidations, and under which the appointment of a trustee is automatic. **8.17**

The presumption in favour of existing management, rather than a trustee, to operate the business in chapter 11 is motivated by a belief that existing management is more familiar with the debtor's operations and therefore more able to reorganize the debtor and return it to solvency than a trustee unfamiliar with the debtor's business would be.[15] The practical effect is that a company's board of directors and senior management is far more likely to initiate a chapter 11 filing than if it were effectively removed as a consequence. **8.18**

Appointment of a chapter 11 trustee is an infrequent occurrence. Section 1104 of the Bankruptcy Code provides for the appointment of a trustee 'for cause, including fraud, dishonesty, incompetence, or gross mismanagement', or 'if such appointment is in the interests of creditors, any equity security holders, and other interests of the estate . . .'.[16] This provision, therefore, allows parties to ask the court to displace current management, provided that 'cause' is shown or the appointment of a trustee is otherwise demonstrated to be in the best interests of the estate. This standard is difficult to meet, as it will require a showing that a trustee, unfamiliar with the day-to-day operations of the business, will be able to better manage the estate's affairs than existing management. **8.19**

8.2.2.3 *Postpetition financing*

Section 364 of the Bankruptcy Code, entitled 'Obtaining Credit', governs a debtor's incurrence of postpetition debt. Section 364(a) of the Bankruptcy Code allows a debtor to continue to incur postpetition unsecured debt in the ordinary course of business, with the resulting claims against the estate afforded 'administrative expense' status, payable before all unsecured prepetition claims.[17] This provision allows a debtor to continue to operate its business on ordinary **8.20**

---

[14] 11 USC ss 1106, 1107.

[15] *Official Comm. of Unsecured Creditors of Cybergenics Corp. v Chinery (Re Cybergenics Corp.)* 330 F3d 548, 573 (3rd Cir. 2003).

[16] 11 USC s 1104.

[17] 11 USC s 364(a).

credit terms with customers and suppliers, without the necessity of seeking court approval.

8.21 Typically, however, a debtor needs more than trade credit to fund its operations and satisfy its restructuring expenses. It may need the ability to use the cash collateral of its existing lenders, or it may need additional third party financing. The Bankruptcy Code allows for both these options, with certain caveats. First, if a debtor seeks to use a lender's cash collateral in the operation of its business, it must either obtain the lender's consent, or it must demonstrate that the lender's interest in the cash collateral is 'adequately protected', which will often involve the granting of additional liens, claims, and security interests to compensate such creditor for a diminution in the value of its collateral, as discussed below. Adequate protection is critical for a secured creditor because, generally, a prepetition lien does not attach to assets that are generated postpetition.

8.22 A debtor seeking to obtain postpetition financing outside the ordinary course of business—commonly called 'debtor in possession financing' or 'DIP financing'—must seek court approval of the transaction. The Bankruptcy Code contemplates a number of different types of postpetition financing. For example, pursuant to section 364(b) of the Bankruptcy Code, with court approval, a debtor may incur unsecured credit outside the ordinary course of its business and grant the lender an administrative expense claim, payable as an expense of the estate, senior and prior in right to all prepetition claims against the debtor.[18] However, in many instances the lender will demand additional protections: that its claim not only be deemed to be an administrative expense of the estate, but that it be payable ahead of all other administrative expenses, that it be secured by a lien on previously unencumbered assets, and/or that it be secured by a junior lien on property of the estate that is subject to a lien.[19] Incurring these types of postpetition debt will not only require court authority, but will further require that the debtor demonstrate that it was unable to incur unsecured credit merely in exchange for an administrative expense.[20]

8.23 Not all postpetition financing must be junior to valid prepetition liens. The most powerful financing tool available to a chapter 11 debtor is the ability to prime preexisting liens on estate property. Section 364(d) of the Bankruptcy Code allows a debtor to incur senior or equal liens on property of the estate that is already subject to a lien, provided that the debtor demonstrate that (a) credit is not otherwise available, and (b) there is 'adequate protection' of the interest of the holder of the lien being primed.

---

[18] 11 USC s 364(b).
[19] 11 USC s 364(c)(1)–(3).
[20] 11 USC s 364(c).

The concept of 'adequate protection' arises both when a debtor seeks to use an existing lender's collateral, as well as when the debtor seeks to prime the liens of a preexisting lender by incurring senior debt. Adequate protection, as its name suggests, is designed to protect a lender against the diminution in value of its interest in collateral. Section 361 of the Bankruptcy Code provides some examples of what constitutes adequate protection of a lender's interest, but does not constitute an exhaustive list.[21] Adequate protection may take the form of periodic cash payments (often made as current interest payments on the secured debt), additional or replacement liens on estate property, payment of the professional fees and expenses incurred by the postpetition lender, and/or a waiver of the automatic stay in the event the debtor defaults on the agreed terms of the use of the cash collateral or loan proceeds. No prepetition secured creditor wants to have senior debt put on its collateral, or worse, be forced to take an alternative lien in inferior or less liquid collateral. As determining what constitutes adequate protection of one's prepetition lien is not a precise science, the risk that a new lender could prime the liens of a prepetition lender creates a significant incentive for prepetition lenders to provide debtor in possession financing. **8.24**

8.2.2.4 Avoidance actions and related bankruptcy litigation

The Bankruptcy Code makes available a number of statutory and equitable remedies to enable a debtor to avoid certain prepetition liens and payments, subordinate certain claims to other general unsecured claims, and to recharacterize certain obligations that superficially appear to be 'debt' into equity. These tools can be important to achieve a more equitable distribution of value to all constituents in the chapter 11 case. **8.25**

8.2.2.4.1 Preferences Section 547 of the Bankruptcy Code allows a debtor to recover certain transfers made before the commencement of the chapter 11 case. To be recoverable under this section, a transfer must (a) be to or for the benefit of a creditor; (b) be for or on account of an antecedent debt; (c) be made while the debtor was insolvent; (d) be made (i) on or within 90 days before the filing of the petition, or (ii) between 90 days and one year before the filing of the petition, if the creditor was an insider at the time of the transfer; and (e) enable such creditor to receive more than the creditor would receive if the case were a liquidation case under chapter 7 of the Bankruptcy Code, the transfer had not been made, and the creditor received payment on account of such debt to the extent provided in the Bankruptcy Code.[22] **8.26**

---

[21] 11 USC s 361.
[22] 11 USC s 547.

8.27 There are a number of defences to preference actions set out in the text of the statute that limit the reach of section 547. The most commonly employed defences exempt from preference exposure (a) contemporaneous exchanges for new value; and (b) payments made in the ordinary course of business on account of debts that were incurred in the ordinary course of business. These defences, and others, are intended to limit the scope of preference actions to causes of action in which one creditor was preferred over other similarly situated creditors. Upon a finding that a preferential transfer took place, the transferee must return the property or its value to the estate and the transferee will receive a general unsecured claim equal to the value of the transfer.

8.28 8.2.2.4.2 **Fraudulent transfers** Section 548 of the Bankruptcy Code enables a debtor in possession to avoid prepetition transactions that were made within two years of the petition date if (a) the transaction was consummated with 'actual intent' to hinder, delay, or defraud creditors, or (b) the transaction provided less than 'reasonably equivalent value' to the debtor, and (i) the debtor was insolvent at the time or was rendered insolvent by the transaction, (ii) the debtor was engaged in business or was about to engage in business with unreasonably small capital, (iii) the debtor intended to incur or believed it would incur debts that were beyond its ability to pay as the debts matured, or (iv) the transaction was with an insider under an employment contract and not in the ordinary course of business.[23] This provision allows the debtor (and its creditors) to look at the preceding two years of the debtor's business to consider whether any of the debtor's transactions in that period should be attacked as fraudulent transfers and unwound for the benefit of the estate.[24]

8.29 Section 544(b) of the Bankruptcy Code allows the debtor to avoid any transfer or obligation that is voidable under applicable law by an unsecured creditor.[25] This provision of the Bankruptcy Code essentially allows a debtor to rely on state law fraudulent transfer actions, to the extent they are more favourable than those provided under section 547 and 548 of the Bankruptcy Code. This provision has the effect of stretching the look-back period for fraudulent conveyance purposes from two years to as much as six years.

8.30 8.2.2.4.3 **'Strong-arm' powers** Section 544 of the Bankruptcy Code grants the debtor the powers of a 'hypothetical lien creditor' under state law.[26] This section of

---

[23] 11 USC s 548.

[24] Note that s 548 of the Bankruptcy Code does not impair a debtor's right to bring a fraudulent transfer action under state law pursuant to s 544 of the Bankruptcy Code. State fraudulent transfer laws may have longer 'reachback' periods or otherwise have more favorable terms to a debtor seeking to unwind a prepetition transaction.

[25] 11 USC s 544(b).

[26] 11 USC s 544(a).

the Bankruptcy Code allows the debtor to step into the shoes of a creditor who obtained a judgment lien on all the debtor's property as of the commencement of the case. This provision allows the debtor to avoid liens that were unperfected as of the commencement of the case, since the lien of the hypothetical lien creditor would be senior to that of an unperfected lien creditor.

Similarly, section 544(a)(3) affords a debtor the rights and powers of a bona fide purchaser of the debtor's assets. Typically, under state law, such a purchaser's rights would prevail over those of a holder of an unrecorded mortgage or deed of trust. Section 544(a)(3) provides that the debtor will be entitled to avoid the interests of a holder of an unrecorded mortgage or deed of trust to the extent a bona fide purchaser of real property would be able to do so under state law. **8.31**

8.2.2.4.4 **Equitable subordination and recharacterization** Section 510(c) of the Bankruptcy Code allows a debtor to subordinate an allowed claim to all or part of other allowed claims 'under principles of equitable subordination'.[27] The most commonly employed test for whether a claim or interest should be equitably subordinated requires that (a) the defendant creditor engaged in some form of inequitable conduct; (b) the misconduct resulted in injury to other creditors or conferred an unfavourable advantage on the defendant; and (c) equitable subordination is consistent with the provisions of the Bankruptcy Code.[28] While satisfaction of these factors is left to the discretion of the bankruptcy court, and equitable subordination is far more often threatened than granted, a bankruptcy court will subordinate a claim where the creditor is found to have engaged in misconduct for its own benefit to the detriment of other creditors. **8.32**

Recharacterization is another litigation tool in a debtor's arsenal that allows a bankruptcy court upon request to treat a transaction based on its economic nature and not necessarily on the title of the transaction documents or a self-serving statement of intent in the transaction documents. The most common form of recharacterization is when a debtor argues that a debt instrument has enough characteristics of an equity investment that it should be treated as such.[29] Unlike equitable subordination, there is no provision in the Bankruptcy Code explicitly authorizing a bankruptcy court to recharacterize a claim or transaction. For this reason, a few courts have found that bankruptcy courts do not have the authority to recharacterize claims as equity interests.[30] Most courts, however, have found to the contrary, and will recharacterize claims as equity interests where various factors, such as the presence or absence of a fixed maturity date and schedule of **8.33**

---

[27] 11 USC s 510(c)(1).

[28] *Benjamin v Diamond (Re Mobile Steel)* 563 F2d 692, 699 (5th Cir. 1977).

[29] Other types of recharacterization include efforts to treat a lease as a secured financing.

[30] *Re Pacific Express, Inc.* 69 BR 112 (BAP 9th Cir. 1986).

payments, the likelihood of repayment, the arm's length nature of the transaction, and the presence or absence of a fixed rate of interest, indicate that the claim was, in fact, a disguised equity interest.[31] Recharacterization could have a substantial impact on the treatment of an asserted claim under a plan of reorganization.

8.2.2.5 Assumption and rejection of executory contracts

8.34 Section 365 of the Bankruptcy Code provides a debtor with an election to assume or reject leases and other contracts. This is one of the most significant benefits of chapter 11 to a debtor; enabling it to cherry-pick the estate's beneficial contracts, while shedding burdensome contracts and leases, either in the expectation of entering into similar contracts and leases on more favourable terms, or in connection with the abandonment of a business location or product line.

8.35 Executory contracts can be assumed by the debtor, with court authorization, only upon the 'cure' of existing defaults and a demonstration that the debtor is able to fully perform in the future.[32] This will require the debtor to make the contractual counterparty whole, including through the satisfaction, in full, of any outstanding prepetition claim. Defaults based on the debtor's insolvency, the bankruptcy filing or a change in control under a plan of reorganization are ignored.[33] Once assumed, all obligations owing under the contract are administrative expenses of the estate, which must be satisfied before the payment of any prepetition claims. The standard for the assumption or rejection of an executory contract is simply whether the decision satisfies the relatively low threshold of a proper exercise of business judgment.[34]

8.36 Rejection of an executory contract is also subject to court approval. Upon the rejection of an executory contract, the debtor is no longer bound by its provisions, and the counterparty's claim for damages are treated as prepetition, unsecured claims, which will have the same priority as other prepetition general unsecured claims against the estate. The counterparty to a rejected contract who has provided goods or services during the chapter 11 case before the rejection, however, will be entitled to an administrative expense claim to the extent its performance under the contract during the chapter 11 case benefited the estate.[35] Certain

---

[31] *Re Outboard Marine Corp.* 2003 US Dist. LEXIS 12564 (Bankr. ND Ill. 21 July 2003).

[32] 11 USC s 365(b)(1)(A).

[33] Contracts that are non-delegable under applicable non-bankruptcy law, such as personal service contracts and certain intellectual property licenses, may fall within an exception to this general rule.

[34] *COR Route 5 Co., LLC v Penn Traffic Co. (Re Penn Traffic Co.)* 524 F3d 373, 383 (2nd Cir. 2008); *Orion Pictures Corp. v Showtime Networks (Re Orion Pictures Corp.)* 4 F3d 1095, 1099 (2nd Cir. 1993).

[35] 11 USC s 503(b); *Mason v Official Comm. Of Unsecured Creditors (Re FBI Distribution Corp.)* 330 F3d 36, 43 (1st Cir. 2003).

rejection damage claims are limited by statute, including those arising from the rejection of employment agreements and leases of non-residential real property.

8.2.2.6 Asset sales

A debtor is not restrained from selling assets in the ordinary course of business during the pendency of the chapter 11 case. Section 363(b) of the Bankruptcy Code, however, requires bankruptcy court approval before the sale of assets outside the ordinary course of business.[36] This provision allows a debtor to dispose of assets that are not essential to the reorganization in an effort to raise cash, shed related liabilities, and focus on the debtor's core businesses upon emergence. It also permits a debtor to sell substantially all its assets outside a plan of reorganization, but only upon a demonstration by the debtor that the assets are perishable and a sale outside a plan of reorganization is necessary to preserve the value of the assets. **8.37**

One of the most attractive features of an asset sale in chapter 11 to both debtors and purchasers is the ability to sell assets 'free and clear' of liens, claims, and other encumbrances pursuant to section 363(f) of the Bankruptcy Code. That provision of the Bankruptcy Code allows for an asset to be transferred free and clear of a lien, claim, or other encumbrance provided that one of the following five conditions is met: **8.38**

(1) applicable non-bankruptcy law permits the sale of such property free and clear of such interest;
(2) the holder of such interest consents;
(3) the interest is a lien and the price at which the property is to be sold is greater than the aggregate value of all liens on the property;
(4) the interest is in bona fide dispute; or
(5) the holder of the interest could be compelled, in a legal or equitable proceeding, to accept a money satisfaction of such interest.[37]

At least one of these five criteria need be present. The ability to transfer assets free and clear is instrumental to sparking interest from bidders who, outside chapter 11, would not be interested in taking on any of the subject assets due to a risk of successor liability. In these instances, chapter 11 becomes an attractive forum for the purchase and sale of distressed assets. **8.39**

[36] 11 USC s 363(b)(2).
[37] 11 USC s 363(f).

8.2.3 The plan confirmation process

8.2.3.1 Distribution of a disclosure statement

8.40 The goal of every chapter 11 case is to confirm a plan of reorganization. A debtor is given an exclusive period of 120 days to file a plan, and 180 days to solicit acceptances to the plan. These periods can be extended by the bankruptcy court upon a showing of cause, but not beyond 18 and 20 months, respectively. After the exclusive periods are terminated, any party in interest may propose a plan or multiple parties can propose competing plans.

8.41 Confirmation of a chapter 11 plan can only be achieved upon the completion of a vote by similarly situated groups of creditors and equity interest holders (referred to as 'classes') whose rights are impaired by the proposed plan. Votes are solicited from impaired constituents, but not until a disclosure statement has been approved by the bankruptcy court to accompany the plan of reorganization.[38] A diagram of the conventional chapter 11 process is below:

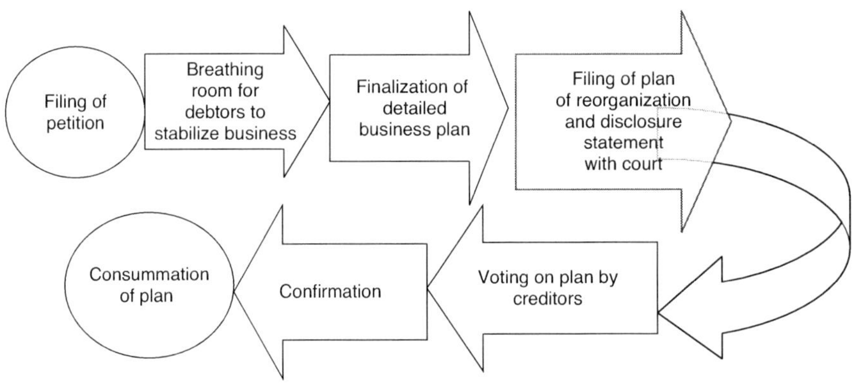

8.42 Section 1125(a) of the Bankruptcy Code requires that the disclosure statement accompanying a plan contain 'adequate information' designed to allow a 'hypothetical investor typical of the holders of claims or interests' to make an 'informed judgment about the plan'.[39] The only specific requirement in the statute is that the disclosure statement include a 'discussion of the potential material Federal tax consequences of the plan. . .'.[40] While the specific types of information included in a disclosure statement vary from case to case, a disclosure statement generally includes most or all the following categories of information: (a) a description of the debtor's business, (b) background information about the events leading up to the filing of the chapter 11 case, (c) the debtor's historic financial information,

[38] 11 USC s 1126.
[39] 11 USC s 1125(a)(1).
[40] Ibid.

(d) a description of the proposed plan of reorganization and means of implementation, (e) a liquidation analysis comparing recoveries under the plan to recoveries that would be received in a hypothetical chapter 7 liquidation, (f) management compensation details, (g) details regarding any pending litigation against the debtor, (h) financial projections for, and the enterprise valuation of, the reorganized debtor, and (i) details regarding transactions with insiders.[41] Ultimately, in determining whether the 'adequate information' standard has been satisfied, the Bankruptcy Code requires that courts consider the complexity of the case, the benefit of additional information, and costs associated with providing additional information.[42]

8.2.3.2 Classification of claims and interests

Solicitation of votes on a proposed plan of reorganization is done through various 'classes' of creditors and interest holders. Each member of a class must receive substantially the same treatment under the plan, and at least one impaired class must vote to accept the plan.[43] The Bankruptcy Code does not require that similar claims be placed in the same class; it does, however, require that claims in the same class be 'substantially similar."[44] This affords the plan sponsor flexibility in constructing a proposed plan. Nonetheless, a plan sponsor must be careful not to be perceived as structuring the classification scheme for the sole purpose of creating an impaired accepting class, a requirement for confirmation. Though courts are not always in agreement regarding the precise contours of impermissible gerrymandering, classifications based on that motivation alone are universally condemned.[45] **8.43**

8.2.3.3 Confirmation requirements

Section 1129 of the Bankruptcy Code sets out a number of requirements that must be met to have a confirmable plan. For instance, a plan must (among other things): **8.44**

- comply with the applicable provisions of the Bankruptcy Code (including provisions regarding classification, solicitation, and the treatment of claims);
- be proposed in good faith and not by means forbidden by law;

---

[41] *Re Scioto Valley Mortgage Co.* 88 BR 168 (Bankr. SD Ohio 1988).

[42] 11 USC s 1125(a).

[43] 11 USC s 1123(a)(4).

[44] 11 USC s 1122(a).

[45] *Zentek GBV Fund IV, LLC v Vesper* 19 Fed. Appx. 238, 249 (6th Cir. 2001) (noting that a debtor's flexibility in classifying claims must have limits to prevent gerrymandering); *Re Greystone III Joint Venture* 995 F2d 1274, 1279 (5th Cir. 1991) ('thou shalt not classify similar claims differently in order to gerrymander an affirmative vote on a reorganization plan ').

- provide for court approval of payments for services and expenses to be made by the proponent, the debtor, or by a person issuing securities or acquiring property under the plan;
- disclose the identity and affiliations of any individual proposed to serve as a director or officer of the reorganized debtor;
- disclose the identity and compensation for any insider to be retained by the reorganized debtor;
- provide for the cash payment in full of administrative expense claims on the effective date of the plan;
- provide for cash payment, on certain terms specified in the Bankruptcy Code, of certain priority claims;
- provide each dissenting holder of an impaired claim or interest with property of a value, as of the effective date of the plan, that is not less than the value such holder would recover if the debtor were liquidated under chapter 7 of the Bankruptcy Code (commonly referred to as the 'best interests' test); and
- be found to be 'feasible,' meaning 'there is a reasonable assurance of success' of the plan.[46]

8.45 A class votes to accept the plan only if approved by class members who (a) hold at least two-thirds of the amount of claims in that class, and (b) represent more than one-half in number of claims that voted on the plan.[47]

8.46 The plan proponent cannot always obtain the requisite votes from each class of claims or interests. A chapter 11 plan may nonetheless be confirmed over the dissenting vote of one or more impaired classes of claims or interests, provided that at least one impaired class (other than a class of insiders) has voted to accept the plan and the plan otherwise satisfies the requirements for 'cramming down' all classes that do not vote to accept the plan.[48] For a plan proponent to 'cram down' a plan over the objection of a dissenting class, the proponent must demonstrate that the plan (i) does not 'discriminate unfairly' against a rejecting class, and (ii) is 'fair and equitable' with respect to each rejecting class.

8.47 Though courts have struggled to define the exact contours of the 'unfair discrimination' test,[49] courts generally apply the test to allow for *some* discrimination among classes of claims of equal priority, for example, to permit classes of equal priority to receive different consideration, provided that the plan does not afford one class a materially lower recovery or materially greater allocation of risk.[50]

46 11 USC s 1129(a).
47 11 USC s 1126.
48 11 USC s 1129(b).
49 15 *Collier on Bankruptcy* ¶ 1129.03.
50 *Re Dow Corning, Inc.* 244 BR 705, 710–11 (Bankr. ED Mich. 1999).

The 'fair and equitable' test is more frequently litigated. This test is given specific meaning in the Bankruptcy Code. Section 1129(b)(2) provides that a plan is fair and equitable with respect to a class of secured claims if (a) it allows the holders of such liens to retain their liens and provides the holders with deferred cash payments totaling the allowed amount of the holder's secured claim; (b) it provides for the sale of the collateral, with the liens attaching to the proceeds of the sale and treated in accordance with section 1129(b)(2); or (c) the holders of secured claims are provided with the 'indubitable equivalent' of their secured claims.[51] With respect to a class of unsecured claims or equity interests, the fair and equitable test is defined to require that (a) the plan provide each holder of a claim in the impaired class with property of a value equal to the allowed amount of such claim or interest; or (b) the holder of any junior claim or interest not receive any property on account of such claims or interests. This is often referred to as the 'absolute priority' rule. **8.48**

8.2.4 Prepackaged, prenegotiated, and free-fall chapter 11 cases

While the foregoing provisions of the Bankruptcy Code will generally apply to all chapter 11 cases, one should not assume that all chapter 11 cases take the same path. The traditional chapter 11 case, often referred to as a 'free fall,' is one in which the debtor files for chapter 11 once all else has failed, and only to avoid an impending liquidity crisis, judgment, or other adverse event that could threaten the survival of the business. The debtor will have to determine how to finance its operations while in chapter 11, stabilize its business, and work with creditors and other parties in interest during the chapter 11 case to develop a business plan and negotiate a viable plan of reorganization around that business plan. Once the plan has been formulated —which could take years, in some complex cases —a disclosure statement will be presented for court approval, votes will be solicited, and the plan will be presented to the court for confirmation. A 'free fall' is the most typical chapter 11 case, but it is also the most tenuous. The company enters chapter 11 without having announced an exit strategy, generating concern within the creditor community whether the debtor can effectively reorganize. Under these circumstances, a well-developed publicity programme is essential to maintaining the confidence of vendors, customers, employees, and other constituencies. **8.49**

The type of filing with the most certain outcome is a 'prepackaged' chapter 11 case, not to be confused with the UK 'prepackaged' sale of the same name. In a 'prepackaged' chapter 11 case, the company will have negotiated a plan with impaired stakeholders *before* entering chapter 11, and will have drafted and distributed a disclosure statement and solicited votes as well. Upon the filing of the **8.50**

[51] 11 USC s 1129(b)(2)(A).

chapter 11 petition, the company will schedule a joint hearing to consider the adequacy of both the disclosure statement and the plan. If properly prepared, the company's stay in chapter 11 may be only four to six weeks, and even shorter in some instances. The Bankruptcy Code specifically contemplates prepackaged cases, ie section 1126(g) provides that acceptance of a plan may be solicited even if a disclosure statement has not been approved by the court, provided that the solicitation takes place *before* the commencement of the chapter 11 case, and complies with applicable non-bankruptcy law.[52] Prepackaged cases are typically implemented as an alternative to an out-of-court workout to utilize the lower approval standards in the Bankruptcy Code (half in number, and two-thirds in amount) for restructuring a debt obligation than are commonly found in credit agreements and indentures (which often require 100 per cent lender approval for modifications). Prepackaged plans are typically utilized when a restructuring involves a simple balance sheet restructuring and there is no need to impair ordinary trade claims.

8.51 In between a short, organized 'prepackaged' case and a sometimes chaotic 'free fall' lies the 'prearranged' or 'prenegotiated' chapter 11 case. In a prenegotiated chapter 11 case, the debtor will have negotiated the terms of a chapter 11 plan with at least some of its principal constituencies before the commencement of the case. The debtor may have successfully negotiated with one constituency but still be negotiating with another, or it may have successfully completed negotiations with all parties in interest. What sets the prenegotiated case apart from a prepackaged case, however, is that in a prenegotiated case, the debtor has *not* solicited votes before the commencement of the case, but has achieved significant consensus to announce publicly immediately upon the chapter 11 filing that an agreement in principle has been reached with certain of the debtor's primary creditors and that a plan and disclosure statement supported by such constituencies has been filed or will be filed immediately. The debtor would seek court approval of its disclosure statement after filing the chapter 11 case, and only after such approval has been received will the debtor be able to solicit votes on its proposed plan. A prenegotiated case will typically be far shorter in duration than a traditional free fall, and will generate positive momentum that can greatly ease creditor concern.

8.3 UK prepack administration

8.52 The primary objective of administration is meant to be to save the corporate entity. While company voluntary arrangements can be used effectively to achieve

[52] 11 USC s 1126(g).

this objective, they are few and far between. Despite the wording of the legislation, in reality the market focuses on saving the business, not the corporate entity, and this has moulded the way the legislative regime has been used to allow this result to be achieved.

The pre pack, as a concept, does not feature in or result from the legislative framework currently operating in England. It is, however, a feature of the way the current market has developed. The legislation envisages that an administrator will be appointed and, if appropriate, trade the business until a buyer is found. However, while the legislation allows the administrator to raise finance and grant security to fund a period of trading, the reality is that most companies' assets are already fully charged. Therefore, unless the company's existing lender is willing to advance further funds to the administrator or allow him to use floating charge realizations, he will be unable to raise the working capital necessary to trade the business. In contrast to the US, there is no concept of debtor in possession ('DIP') financing. **8.53**

The key stakeholders in an English insolvency are generally the senior secured lenders and the management/equity. They are generally also the primary beneficiaries of a pre pack. A pre pack preserves the underlying business. It also provides speed and certainty to the stakeholders and significantly reduces the period during which the administrator has control of the business. It is hardly surprising therefore that those in control of the strategy will push toward a pre pack. **8.54**

In contrast, in the US, chapter 11 proceedings do not carry the same negative perceptions which are often associated with a company in administration. Chapter 11 proceedings do not automatically end the involvement of the management team. Creditors are generally involved at a much earlier stage and are often willing to continue their relationship with the company. **8.55**

These key factors in each jurisdiction have led to very different uses of the formal insolvency regime to give effect to restructurings. **8.56**

8.3.1 What is a prepackaged insolvency sale or 'pre pack'?

A prepackaged insolvency sale ('pre pack') is the sale of an insolvent company's business and assets to a third party immediately following the placing of the company into a formal insolvency process. This term would equally apply to the sale of the shares of a subsidiary company as it would to the immediate sale of an actual business. The key factor differentiating a pre pack from any other sale by an office holder is that its terms are negotiated and agreed before the commencement of the formal insolvency process. **8.57**

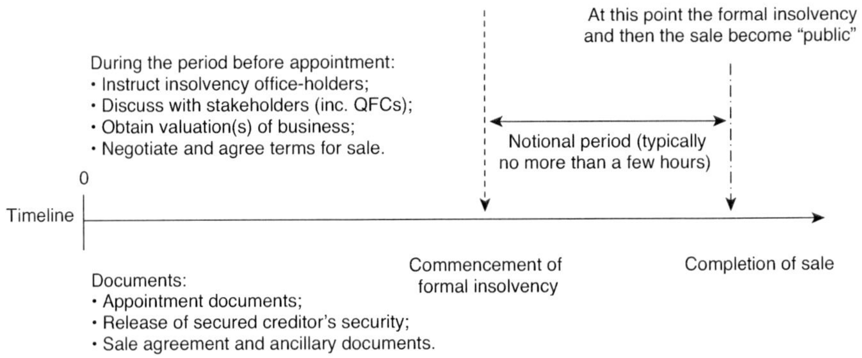

8.58 Following the pre pack, the insolvent company will invariably be left as a shell retaining only its liabilities and the proceeds from the sale.

8.59 The third party buyer can be either an independent party or connected to the insolvent company, for example a new company incorporated by the insolvent company's management team. The latter scenario is often referred to as a 'phoenix' and has legal and reputational consequences that would not apply to a genuine third party buyer.

8.3.2 Who drives the strategy in a restructuring?

8.60 Secured creditors play a key role in any restructuring and/or prepack process. Unlike almost any other jurisdiction, a qualifying floating charge holder ('QFCH') has a unique legal power to control the assets subject to the charge throughout the insolvency procedure. They must be involved at the pre-appointment negotiation stage for two reasons: (a) their consent to the appointment of an office holder will most likely be required and (b) they will need to provide a release in respect of the assets being sold (subject to an office holder joining in a senior secured creditor for the purpose of overreaching a junior creditor's charge or an administrator seeking leave of the court).

8.61 Where a company has one secured creditor the position is relatively straightforward. However, where a company has multiple lenders the position is more complex. In a restructuring with multiple lenders consideration must of course be given to the terms of any intercreditor agreements as these will invariably cover what steps may or may not be taken by the various lenders in respect of enforcement.

8.62 In practical terms, valuation, and in particular where the 'value breaks', is central to the issue of who will drive the strategy. For example, the valuation may indicate that on a sale, there will only be sufficient proceeds to repay the senior lender in full, with the junior lender likely to be repaid only part of its debt and the equity receiving nothing. In these circumstances, the junior lender is likely to want to take a much more active role in determining and implementing strategy, to maximize value and hence its recoveries. In practice, if the senior lender's position is fully covered, the senior lender may be content to leave the junior lender to do so, and to merely monitor the situation to ensure its interests are not being prejudiced. Intercreditor documentation regulating the relationship between the senior and junior lender is however likely to leave decision making with the senior lender until it is repaid in full. In the event of a conflict between the senior and junior lender, the junior lender may consider buying out the senior debt to obtain control (and intercreditor documentation typically gives them the right to do so, at par). Assuming that the equity are 'out of the money' their ability to determine strategy is usually almost non existent. Given the key importance of the valuation of the business, it is common for stakeholders to take professional advice on the suitability and adequacy of any valuation to confirm their economic interest (if any), and stakeholders are being increasingly assertive where there is any ambiguity in the valuation evidence.

8.3.3 Formal insolvency process

A pre pack is not specific to one particular formal insolvency regime. The nature and statutory formalities of liquidation, fixed charge receivership and company voluntary arrangements mean that, in most circumstances, they are not suitable insolvency procedures to combine with a pre pack. Practically speaking, the use of pre packs has been confined to administrative receivership and administration. **8.63**

8.3.3.1 Administrative receivership

Subject to certain exceptions, an administrative receiver can only be appointed by a secured creditor holding the appropriate security that was created before 15 September 2003.[53] This, together with the introduction of the out-of-court route for appointing administrators,[54] means that the use of pre packs is most prevalent within administration. As a result, the number of administrative receiverships has been in decline. **8.64**

8.3.3.2 Administration

The simplification of the entry route into administration by virtue of the Enterprise Act 2002 reforms to the Insolvency Act 1986 ('IA 1986') has reduced the complexity, formality and cost of a company entering into administration. **8.65**

An administrator can be appointed in court[55] or out of court by the company or its directors[56] or a QFCH.[57] Assuming that any QFCHs have consented to the appointment, it can be made by filing the necessary papers at court. The administrator's **8.66**

[53] IA 1986, ss 72A and 72B–72GA.
[54] Ibid., Sch B1, paras 14 and 22.
[55] Ibid., Sch B1, para 12.
[56] Ibid., Sch B1, para 22.
[57] Ibid., Sch B1, para 14.

appointment takes effect from the time the papers are filed. The speed at which an out-of-court appointment can be made fits well with the prepack process.

8.67 If the insolvent company proposes administration as the process by which to effect the pre pack, what considerations are there for the insolvency office holder appointed as administrator?

8.68 Administration is a collective insolvency procedure. As well as being an officer of the court,[58] an administrator must perform his functions in the interests of the company's creditors as a whole.[59] The administrator will need to bear in mind the statement that he is required to make on the Form 2.2B: 'I am of the opinion that the purpose of the administration is reasonably likely to be achieved.'

8.69 The primary objective of administration is 'rescuing the company as a going concern'. The inclusion of the word company in the context is key—where the office holder knows that immediately following his appointment, he will complete a prepack sale of the business and assets of the company, how can there be any prospect of the company, as a corporate entity, surviving? The company will be left as an insolvent shell with no meaningful assets other than the proceeds of sale. Therefore, when the office holder signs the statement on the Form 2.2B, what he must have in mind is that it is not the primary purpose for the administration that is reasonably likely to be achieved but rather the secondary objective of 'achieving a better result for the company's creditors as a whole than would be likely if the company were wound up (without first being in administration)', or the objective of last resort, being 'at realizing property to make a distribution to one or more secured or preferential creditors'.

8.70 Thus when an office holder proposes to accept an appointment as administrator with a prepack agenda, he will be well advised to prepare a report at the time of his appointment demonstrating why he believes that a prepack sale of the business and assets will be reasonably likely to achieve a better result for creditors than an immediate liquidation, or would be able to realize property for the benefit of secured and preferential creditors. In the event of later inquiry as to the basis for his decision, the office holder will then be well prepared to demonstrate the rationale behind it. Such a report could also form the basis of a defence to any action brought by a creditor seeking the court's interference with the earlier sale.

8.71 Where the office holder believes that the objective that is capable of achievement is the 'better realization' objective, he must perform his functions 'in the interests of the company's creditors as a whole'. This means that in considering the appropriateness of giving the statement on the form 2.2B that office holder must be

[58] Ibid., Sch B1, para 5.
[59] Ibid., Sch B1, para 3(2).

satisfied that the pre pack is in the creditors' interests. 'What if there is a class of creditors who would be unfairly prejudiced by the pre pack? Does this mean that the secondary objective is also incapable of fulfilment?' Absent any guidance on the intended meaning of 'interests of the company's creditors as a whole', it might be prudent for the office holder, where there is a risk of prejudice to a particular class, to seek to justify the pre pack on the basis that it is reasonably likely to satisfy the objective of last resort ie realize property to distribute to secured and preferential creditors. Cases where the only creditors to be paid a return on their debt are the secured and preferential creditors are, unfortunately for the majority of creditors, not uncommon. It is likely that many pre packs will only satisfy this third objective, the objective of last resort.

8.3.4 Considerations for the office holder

Certain considerations for the officer holder who is to effect the sale will remain key, whether as receiver or administrator. These include: **8.72**

- obtaining independent valuations of the assets before the sale. Given that there will be no opportunity post appointment to market the business and assets for sale, the office holder will need to be satisfied that the price to be paid by the prepack buyer is an appropriate price for the assets. If the price is too low, there is a risk of subsequent challenge to the sale by a liquidator/creditor, the company or a mortgagee;
- satisfying himself that the price achievable for the business and assets will be greater on a pre pack than on a delayed insolvency sale;
- ensuring that the terms on which the sale is concluded are similar to those in any usual receivership or administration sale. Again this is even more important where the buyer is connected, as the office holder will want to avoid any suggestion of giving the connected buyer special treatment and accepting lighter indemnities in favour of the seller and the receivers or administrators. Where the sale is by administrators rather than receivers, the office holder may have a better bargaining position in achieving the inclusion of protections for the seller company by relying on his status as an officer of the court with a duty to all creditors of the company as compared with the duties that a receiver has to the appointor;
- satisfying himself that no creditor approval is required. A receiver will need consent from his appointor as to the price and terms of the sale, subject to his power to apply to the court for an order for the sale of the charged property.[60] An administrator does not need the approval of the creditors of the company

[60] Ibid., s 43.

generally[61] but will need consent from lenders having fixed charge security over the assets to be sold, unless he proposes to seek an order authorizing the sale of such assets.[62] In the context of a pre pack however, it is likely that any secured lender will have been kept fully in the picture during the planning of the sale, so that consent to sell immediately post appointment can be assured.

8.3.5 Particular considerations for secured lenders

8.73 Unless the seller company granted floating charge security on or after 15 September 2003, the floating charge realizations following the sale of the business and assets by receivers or administrators will not be subject to top slicing, ie the receivers or administrators will not be under any obligations to ring fence a prescribed part of the floating charge realizations for distribution to unsecured creditors. The provisions of section 176A of the IA 1986 only apply to floating charges created on or after 15 September 2003.[63] Where either a receivership or administration commences on or after 15 September 2003 and a security granted by the seller company to its lender predates 15 September 2003, the lender stands to get a double benefit as the floating charge realizations arising from the disbursement of the business and assets by the office holder will not be subject to either payment of Crown preferential debts or top slicing.

8.3.6 Why do stakeholders use pre packs?

8.74 For these purposes it is important to distinguish between an operational pre pack and a pre pack that effectively disenfranchises a financial creditor.

8.75 Whilst being an acknowledged 'term of art' in the insolvency market place, a pre pack can cover a significant variety of situations including effecting a balance sheet restructuring.

8.3.6.1 Operational pre pack

8.76 An operational pre pack allows a fundamentally good business to survive with the valuable assets being transferred to a new company, leaving the undesirable assets and liabilities with the insolvent company.

---

[61] *Re T & D Industries* [2000] 1 All ER 333.

[62] IA 1986, Sch B1, para 71.

[63] Ibid., Sch B1, para 176A(9) and Insolvency Act 1986 (Prescribed Part) Order 2003 (SI 2003/2097).

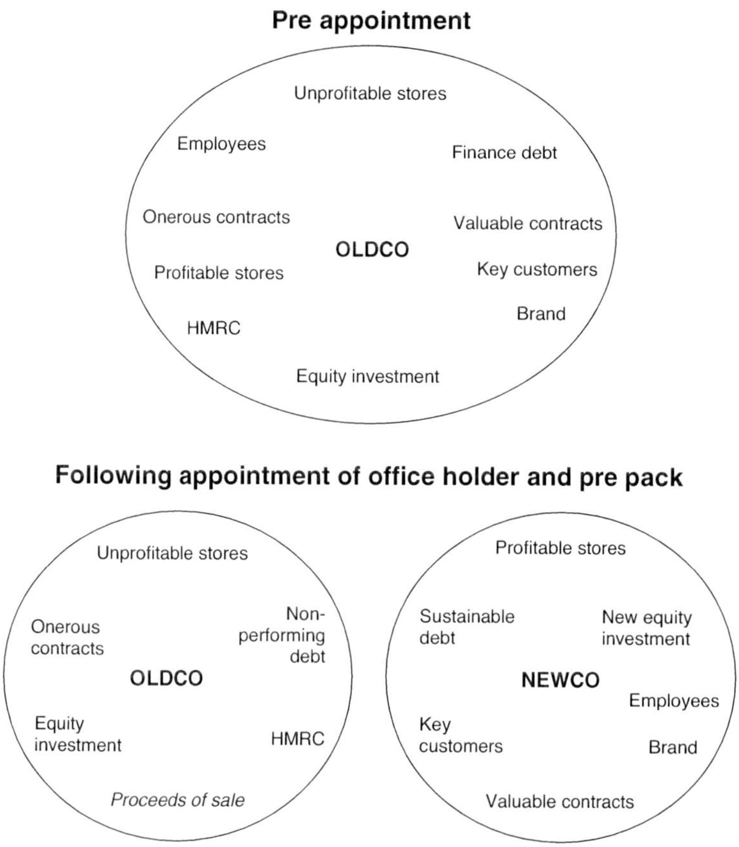

8.3.6.2 Financial stakeholder restructuring

A pre pack may be used within a financial stakeholder restructuring where a company is overindebted and the junior creditor, whether for legitimate or 'green mail' reasons will not agree to a consensual restructuring. In this scenario the prepack **8.77**

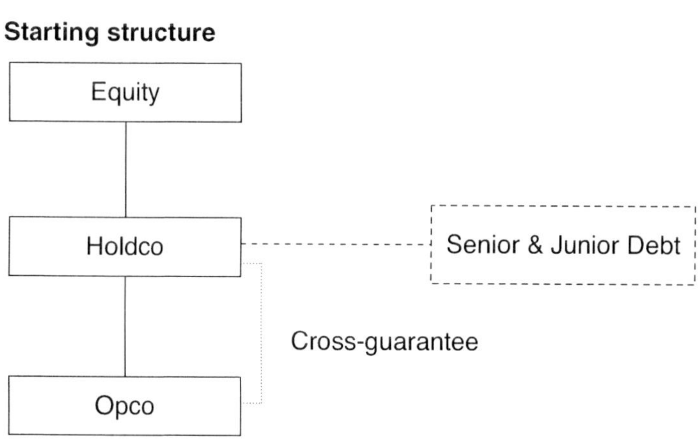

Appointment of office holder and pre pack sale

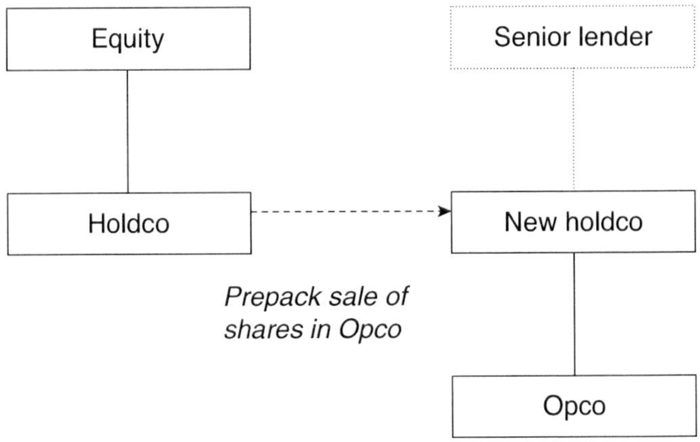

mechanism can be used to remove the junior creditor and 'out of the money' equity and bring the company's balance sheet back to a level where it can service its debt and give equity and management appropriate incentives.

8.78 Holdco is in financial difficulty and has both senior and junior debt. A valuation indicates that the 'value breaks' within the senior debt (ie on a sale insufficient proceeds would be realized to discharge the senior debt in full). Opco has a fundamentally good business but the group's balance sheet position is not sustainable.

8.79 In accordance with its rights under the intercreditor agreement, the senior lender instructs the agent to call an event of default under the facility documentation and to instruct the security trustee to take enforcement action and appoint an office holder in respect of Holdco. The office holder then sells Holdco's shares in Opco to New Holdco (owned by the senior lender) by way of a pre pack. The consideration would usually be a credit bid or release of indebtedness. Stamp duty would, however, be payable on the full value of the debt released. A more tax-efficient mechanism would be for the shares in Opco to be sold for a nominal value but subject to some of the group's existing debt. In well-drafted intercreditor agreements, the senior lender will typically have the ability to instruct the security trustee post-enforcement to release the Opco from its liabilities owed in respect of the junior debt, so that the junior debt can be left behind.

8.80 A significant amount of debt may well be left with the old group to ensure that the senior lender retains control. In addition to retaining control, leaving a slice of non-performing debt in the old group evidences that the value break occurred at senior level and the sale of the subsidiary was not a transaction at an undervalue in favour of the senior lender. Following the sale to New Holdco, a debt for equity swap could be used to reduce Opco's debt level to ensure that its balance sheet is sustainable going forward.

8.3.7 What is the purpose of a pre pack?

The speed and secrecy of the process is designed to maximize the consideration obtained for the insolvent company's business and assets and therefore maximize the possible return to creditors. It is generally accepted that entering formal insolvency has a negative impact on a company's business. Below is a non-exhaustive list of reasons why this might occur. **8.81**

8.3.7.1 Loss of key employees

Key employees may well have concerns over the security of their positions once a company enters formal insolvency. This could result in them actively seeking alternative employment and/or receiving approaches from competitors seeking to take advantage of the situation. This is of particular concern in businesses such as professional services, where key employees are critically linked to the value of the business. **8.82**

8.3.7.2 Maintaining essential supplies

Although suppliers may already be aware that the insolvent company is in financial difficulty, formal insolvency will crystallize the position. Once a company is in formal insolvency, suppliers will no doubt require assurances from the office holder regarding payment for ongoing supplies. In certain circumstances, they may even attempt to extract payment of arrears as a condition to agreeing to provide ongoing supplies. Certain suppliers may be easily replaced. However, where an alternative supplier cannot easily be arranged, the loss of that supplier may damage the insolvent company's business. **8.83**

8.3.7.3 Key customers

There are two aspects to the insolvent company's relationship with its customers—legal and practical. It is common for contracts to include formal insolvency as an event of default giving rise to a right to terminate the contract. This will be an issue even in a prepack situation as the insolvent company will still enter formal insolvency. However, at a practical level formal insolvency will cause some degree of disruption to the day-to-day running of the business. Any disruption or concerns regarding disruption may lead to customers taking their business elsewhere. A pre pack assists as the sale takes place often almost instantaneously with the **8.84** commencement of the administration, there is no disruption caused to the contract and it therefore promotes continuity of business.

8.3.7.4 Funding of the formal insolvency process

8.85 In order to trade a business in formal insolvency the office holder will need access to funding. In the absence of sufficient funding to trade the business, the office holder will have to dismiss the employees and cease trading. This will obviously result in a significant reduction in the value of the insolvent company's business.

8.86 The nature of the financing provided to UK corporates together with the fact that most lenders hold qualifying floating charges means that, in the majority of situations, all the company's assets upon an insolvency procedure are subject to a charge in favour of a secured creditor. If that secured creditor then refuses to provide additional funding to the office holder and the insolvent company has insufficient uncharged assets, the office holder may have little choice but to proceed by way of a pre pack, as the alternative of trading the business in formal insolvency while trying to find a buyer is simply not possible. In the author's view the legal impediment in the UK to debtor in possession ('DIP') financing is one of the main reasons why trading administrations are relatively rare.

8.3.7.5 Maximizing the realization of book debts

8.87 It is common for the buyer of the business through a pre pack to collect the book debts as agent of the insolvent company. Not only is this less likely to damage goodwill, but it should maximize collections where the debtor is dealing with a solvent company continuing the business rather than by a receiver or administrator who is unable to complete work in progress or deal with defects.

8.3.8 What are the disadvantages of a pre pack?

8.88 In general terms an officer holder is under a duty to maximize the value of the insolvent company's assets for the benefit of its creditors. As the sale of the insolvent company's business and assets takes place immediately following the appointment of an office holder, it will happen before any third party (other than any secured creditors) has been given notice of the formal insolvency. This lack of transparency leaves the pre pack, and indeed the office holder, vulnerable to criticism and possibly even to challenge by the insolvent company's creditors if the strategy to proceed by way of pre pack cannot be justified.

8.89 If the creditor profile of the insolvent company is such that only the secured creditor has an economic interest in the pre pack (ie there is no prospect of a dividend to unsecured creditors) then any subsequent challenge would appear unlikely. The involvement of a secured creditor may therefore provide a level of comfort for the office holder.

Although the speed and secrecy of the prepack process can on the one hand protect the value of the insolvent company's business, creditors often raise concerns over the absence of formal marketing and the general lack of transparency. There is a risk of a pre pack being challenged by a creditor after the event, as there may not have been time for a full marketing process by the administrators and the lack of marketing may, in the view of a creditor or creditors, have prevented the insolvent company from achieving the best price for the business or assets sold. **8.90**

8.3.9 Issues arising in the retail sector

Many retailers have been struggling with falling sales, crushed margins and rising costs. Retail collapses soared in the first quarter of 2009. Familiar UK high street names such as Woolworths, MFI and Zavvi fell victim to the recession. There were also a number of high profile pre packs, such as Whittards of Chelsea, Mosaic group (parent company to Karen Millen, Coast and Oasis among others) and Officers Club. It can be argued that these deals enabled brands to continue trading without interruption and devaluation, jobs to be saved, and more assets to be realized than would be possible on a liquidation. However, pre packs have been heavily criticized for leaving creditors such as suppliers and landlords out of pocket while the business continues to trade. **8.91**

Pre packs have been heavily criticized by landlords in particular. Frequently, prepack sale agreements permit the buyer to occupy a property under licence, pending the assignment of the lease. Where the insolvent company operates from a number of different sites it is unusual for the landlords to be consulted in advance of the pre pack. The licence to occupy granted to the buyer will invariably be granted without the landlord's consent, in breach of the terms of the lease. Where there are multiple sites, a buyer will cherry pick and only take on the most profitable outlets. Where the insolvent company is in administration, landlords are unable to use their usual remedies, without the permission of the administrator or the court, due to the statutory moratorium on creditor action. Once in occupation, the buyer will seek to negotiate either a licence to assign the existing lease or a new lease. The importance of the properties and the likelihood of assignments being achieved can impact on the consideration that the buyer is willing to pay. Where the sites are key to the business it is not unusual to see deferred consideration that only becomes payable as and when the buyer obtains the necessary assignments. **8.92**

8.93 In circumstances where the grant of a prohibited licence is temporary, it is necessary for the purpose of the administration and it is on terms such that the licence fee will be handed over to the landlord, the courts are likely to view applications by landlords for immediate restoration of their proprietary rights with some degree of caution. There is some comfort for landlords, however, as the courts have held[64] that if administrators cause the company to 'use' the premises for the benefit of the creditors, then rent is payable as an expense of the administration. The term 'use' would almost certainly include allowing the buyer of the company's business and assets into occupation under a licence.

8.94 It remains to be seen how the courts will apply the balancing exercise in different situations, for example where there is a serious issue about the covenant strength of a proposed assignee. In such a situation, the landlord may have a significant case that the value of its reversion is being damaged by reason of the unlawful occupation, which the courts will have to balance against the interests of the company's creditors in allowing the unlawful occupation to continue pending assignment or surrender.

8.3.10 Tax and pre packs

8.95 From a tax perspective, a pre pack is technically no different from a conventional business sale via administration, and a prudent office holder conducting prepack negotiations will take advice from a tax specialist as to how to structure the transaction to minimize potential tax charges.

8.96 It is worth noting that the appointment of an administrator will have a markedly different impact from a tax perspective to the appointment of an administrative receiver. Where the secured lender is able to appoint an administrative receiver, strategic tax advice should be taken pre-appointment to determine which route would be most beneficial.

8.3.11 Employee issues

8.3.11.1 Transfer of an insolvent business provisions in TUPE

8.97 The Transfer of Undertakings Regulations 2006 ('TUPE') contain provisions to deal specifically with insolvency situations and the transfer of an insolvent business. In particular, where the seller is subject to 'relevant insolvency proceedings', which are opened 'not with a view to the liquidation of the assets of the transferor', TUPE relaxes the general provisions relating to the automatic transfer of employment and employment debts and the restriction on changing terms of employment (regulation 8(6) TUPE). 'Relevant insolvency proceedings' are often referred to in commentary as 'non-terminal' insolvency procedures.

---

64 *Goldacre (Offices) Ltd v Nortel Networks UK Ltd (in administration)* [2009].

The provisions are complex but essentially provide that, in certain circumstances, the National Insurance Fund will pay certain amounts due to staff. More usefully, perhaps, the provisions allow a buyer (and even the administrators in certain circumstances) to change terms and conditions of employment but only if certain procedures are followed first. **8.98**

TUPE also contains provisions to deal with transfers made by a seller in an insolvency process that is 'opened with a view to the liquidation of the assets of the transferor' (regulation 8(7) TUPE). Transfers that fall within this 'terminal' insolvency proceedings exception attract even broader exemptions from TUPE employment protection principles and so may be more attractive for buyers. **8.99**

8.3.11.2 Pensions and pre packs

The pension scheme is often a significant unsecured creditor of the insolvent company, and where there is a defined benefit pension scheme the situation can become complex. The pension scheme may be the sole or main reason a company is in financial difficulties, and the company may face certain insolvency if it remains liable for the scheme. It is difficult to balance the interests of pensioners and other creditors. Most arrangements that result in the pension scheme being stripped away from the ongoing business will require consent by the trustees of the pension scheme and the Pensions Regulator. However, gaining this consent may take time, and must be balanced against the need for confidentiality and/or speed in negotiating the prepackaged sale. **8.100**

Under section 7 of the Pensions Act 1995, the Pensions Regulator is able to appoint independent trustees to defined benefit pension schemes with power to act to the exclusion of the existing trustees. Any such action is usually preceded by a warning notice, allowing affected parties to make representations before the appointment is finalized. **8.101**

However, the Pensions Regulator also has power to use a 'special procedure' under section 97 of the Pensions Act 2004, which enables it to act quickly and appoint a trustee without first warning the company, where it considers that the provision of a warning notice would present an immediate risk to the interests of scheme members or the scheme assets. In February 2009, the Regulator used this 'special procedure' to make an emergency appointment of an independent trustee to the defined benefit scheme of Graphex Limited ('Graphex'), in view of an imminent prepackaged administration sale. In this case, the Regulator was concerned that the proposed pre pack would mean that assets were stripped out of Graphex, and bought back by a Newco that would not assume the pension liability. It appeared that the directors of Graphex would also be the directors of Newco, and that some of those directors were also trustees of the scheme. **8.102**

It is clear that any party involved in the negotiation of a prepack sale where a relevant pension scheme is involved must give very careful consideration to the **8.103** interests of the pension scheme members. This can be a difficult balancing exercise for the proposed administrators.

8.3.12 Regulation of pre packs

8.104 As stated above the secrecy and speed of the prepack process has caused a level of concern among creditors. There has been significant recent media coverage questioning the potential scope for abuse. This has prompted the introduction of SIP16 (see below) and the ongoing monitoring of pre packs by the Insolvency Service.

8.105 Office holders are subject to two levels of regulation—statutory duties (see above) and professional guidance. All office holders must be qualified insolvency office holders. Insolvency office holders obtain their authorization from their relevant recognized professional body ('RPB').[65] The RPBs issue various joint guidance to insolvency office holders. The RPBs have issued the Insolvency Code of Ethics[66] to their members that contains general principles of conduct. There are five fundamental principles that should be adhered to—integrity, objectivity, professional competence and due care, confidentiality, and professional behaviour. The Code also specifically acknowledges that the objectivity of an insolvency office holder can be called into question in the context of a pre pack and provides some guidance to office holders.

8.106 The Code specifically recognizes that a pre pack could lead to an 'actual or perceived threat to objectivity' and states that the 'threats to objectivity may be eliminated or reduced to an acceptable level by safeguards such as obtaining an independent valuation of the assets or business being sold, or the consideration of other potential buyers'. Failure to observe the Code 'may not, of itself, constitute professional misconduct, but will be taken into account in assessing the conduct of an insolvency office holder'.

8.107 In addition, the RPBs issue Statements of Insolvency Practice ('SIPs'). SIP 16, which came into effect on 1 January 2009, specially deal with pre packs. The purpose of SIP 16 is to require administrators to provide better information to creditors regarding the sale of a company's business. The administrator must provide a detailed explanation and justification of why a pre pack was undertaken, so that creditors can be satisfied that he acted with due regard for their interests. In particular the administrator should disclose:

- the source of the administrator's initial introduction;
- the extent of the administrator's involvement before appointment;
- any marketing activities conducted by the company and/or the administrator;

[65] The RPBs covering England and Wales are the Association of Certified Chartered Accountants, the Insolvency Office holders Association, the Institute of Chartered Accountants in England and Wales and the Solicitors Regulation Authority.

[66] Revised 1 January 2009.

- any valuations obtained of the business or the underlying assets;
- the alternative courses of action that were considered by the administrator, with an explanation of possible financial outcomes;
- why it was not appropriate to trade the business, and offer it for sale as a going concern, during the administration;
- details of requests made to potential funders to fund working capital requirements;
- whether efforts were made to consult with major creditors;
- the date of the transaction;
- details of the assets involved and the nature of the transaction;
- the consideration for the transaction, terms of payment, and any condition of the contract that could materially affect the consideration;
- if the sale was part of a wider transaction, a description of the other aspects of the transaction;
- the identity of the buyer;
- any connection between the buyer and the directors, shareholders or secured creditors of the company;
- the names of any directors, or former directors, of the company who are involved in the management or ownership of the buyer, or of any other entity into which any of the assets were transferred;
- whether any directors had given guarantees for amounts due from the company to a prior financier, and whether that financier is financing the new business; and
- any options, buy back arrangements or similar conditions attached to the contract of sale.

In exceptional cases the information required by SIP 16 can be withheld; however the reasons for this must be given. In particular, if the sale is to a connected party it is unlikely that considerations of commercial confidentiality should outweigh the need for creditors to be provided with this information. **8.108**

The information should be provided with the first notification to creditors (unless it is impracticable to do so) and the administrator should hold the initial creditors' meeting as soon as possible after his appointment. If no initial creditors' meeting is to be held and it was impracticable to send the information with the first notification to creditors then it should be provided with the administrator's proposals, which should be sent out as soon as practicable following his appointment. **8.109**

Although, SIP 16 is guidance on the best practice for administrators involved in a prepack sale, it is not legally binding. However, the Insolvency Service has made it clear that it intends to ensure that SIP 16 is working in practice and that administrators are complying with both the letter and spirit. **8.110**

8.3.13 SIP 16 consultation and reporting

In March 2010, the Insolvency Service published a report on the operation of SIP 16 from July to December 2009. A key principle of SIP 16 is that creditors should **8.111** be given a detailed and clear explanation of why a prepackaged sale was necessary, so that they can be sure that the administrator acted in their best interests. Although the report comments that the quality and timeliness of information provided to creditors had significantly improved since their last report up to July 2009, it also found that the main areas of concern remained issues connected to timing, valuations, marketing, and asset details.

8.112 For example, there are concerns that information required by SIP 16 is not being sent to creditors within an appropriate timescale. Information should be sent to creditors within a few days of appointment or completion of the sale. SIP 16 information sent to creditors more than 14 days after appointment or completion of the sale without any explanation is deemed to be non-compliant. In addition, there are still cases where the amounts attributed to various assets, and the basis of those valuations are not made sufficiently clear to creditors.

8.113 Further guidance to insolvency practitioners was issued in October 2009, and the Insolvency Service has commented that it should now be clear to insolvency practitioners exactly what information is required to be given to creditors, and when. However, following the publication of its report in March 2010, the Insolvency Service launched a new consultation on whether increased measures are needed to strengthen transparency and confidence. This consultation ended in June 2010, and suggests various proposals, including giving SIP 16 statutory force, with penalties for non-compliance. At the time of writing, the results of this consultation had not yet been published.

8.4 Conclusion

8.114 Formal insolvency schemes in the US and the UK take very different approaches to preserving and maximizing going concern value of a debtor's enterprise. While the UK process supplants management with an administrator, does not incentivize new sources of liquidity and does not facilitate the assignment of leases and contracts, it affords through the prepack procedure almost unfettered discretion for the administrator to transfer businesses and assets as a going concern, with virtually no notice to the company's stakeholders other than its secured creditors.

8.115 Chapter 11 promotes a more orderly process that minimizes the disruption caused by the initiation of formal insolvency proceedings yet requires a debtor to comply with a gauntlet of processes and procedures before a restructuring or sale of the business can be effected. There can be little doubt that the US chapter 11 process is designed to preserve going concern value while protecting the interests of junior creditors.

9

TAX ISSUES IN RESTRUCTURING

9.1 Introduction

A company engaged in the modification or restructuring of its debt, or simply the buying back of its debt, should carefully consider the tax implications. In some cases, even what seems like an innocuous action (as in the case of the US tax rules relating to modifications of debt) may have significant tax implications. In other cases, advance planning may yield more efficient structures, or otherwise ensure that taxes are properly factored into the decision-making process. Depending on the situation, the tax cost can take the form of current or deferred tax payments, the reduction or elimination of the company's valuable tax benefits (such as net operating losses or tax basis), or other limitations on the company's use of such tax benefits. **9.01**

The first part of this chapter discusses the principal US federal income tax consequences for US debtor companies, and the second part of this chapter discusses the principal UK corporation tax consequences for UK debtor corporations, associated with certain types of debt restructuring or debt-reduction transactions. In particular, these are: **9.02**

- debt-for-debt exchanges (and modifications of debt);
- debt repurchases for cash, and related-party acquisitions; and
- exchanges of debt for equity.

9.03 The US discussion, after providing an overview of the principal US federal income tax consequences of these types of transactions, further explores some of the US tax rules applicable to debtors with respect to such transactions, including (a) the potential for income from the reduction of debt—or, as it is more commonly referred to in the US, the 'cancellation of debt' or COD—with a primary focus on corporate debtors; (b) the limitations that can be imposed upon a corporation's beneficial tax attributes following certain changes in its shareholder ownership; and (c) certain other special considerations.[1]

9.04 The UK discussion follows a slightly different format in that it begins with a general exploration of the UK tax rules applicable to the restructuring of a corporation's debt before examining the specific types of transactions described above, and then briefly considers the impact of a change of ownership on the carry forward and utilization of the debtor's tax losses.

9.05 A number of points regarding the scope of this chapter should be noted at the outset. As an initial planning matter, we observe that, under certain circumstances, it may be more advantageous from a tax perspective for the creditors to 'acquire the assets' of a corporate debtor—and, thus, obtain a fresh tax cost in its assets—rather than engaging in a recapitalization of the debtor. Such transactions are not discussed here. Second, the tax consequences of certain transactions that may be employed by a debtor to raise funds to repurchase debt, such as an equity issuance or a disposition of one of the company's businesses, are beyond the scope of this chapter. Third, a discussion of the potential tax consequences to the creditors and, particularly, equity holders is beyond the scope of this volume, except in very brief measure to provide some sensitivity for such consequences. Also, we want to remind the reader to consider state and local tax consequences. In the US, some states 'piggyback' on the federal tax rules, while others pick and choose, and still others impose a capital-based or gross receipts tax rather than an income tax.

9.06 In contrasting the US and UK tax consequences, it is important to note two particular respects in which the scope of the US and UK discussions differ. First, the US discussion describes the general tax consequences of an in-court debt restructuring, as well as an out-of-court restructuring. In contrast, the UK discussion only focuses on restructurings outside a formal insolvency process, as to which many of the beneficial tax reliefs allowed debtors in a formal process do not apply.[2]

---

[1] For a more detailed discussion of the US federal income tax consequences of corporate restructurings (including from a creditor and shareholder perspective), see Henderson and Goldring, *Tax Planning for Troubled Corporations: Bankruptcy and Non-Bankruptcy Restructurings* (CCH, 2011).

[2] In recent years, the UK has seen the rise of the 'prepack administration' in which the distressed company's assets are transferred to a new company immediately after the company is placed into administration, a formal insolvency process, allowing the company's business to continue shorn of many of its debts. As such transactions are entered into in connection with a formal insolvency process, they are not addressed in the UK discussion.

Second, given the greater popularity of entities taxable as partnerships in the US, the US discussion generally applies to US debbr partnerships as well as US corporate debtors, whereas the UK discussion applies only to UK corporations—ie, a limited company ('Ltd') or a public limited company ('PLC')—the principal form of business entity in the UK.

9.2 US tax[3]

9.2.1 Debt-for-debt exchanges, and significant modifications of debt

The most common form of restructuring might not look like a restructuring at all, **9.07** but rather may take the form of a modification (or amendment) of an outstanding debt. When it comes to modifications of debt, or the actual exchange of a new debt obligation for an old debt obligation, the substance and not the form of the transaction governs for US federal income tax purposes. If the terms of the new or modified debt obligation significantly differ from the terms of the old debt obligation (as discussed below), then an 'exchange' of old debt for new debt will be treated as having occurred for US tax purposes.[4]

Numerous tax consequences may then ensue, including the following. First, the **9.08** debtor may recognize COD (ordinary) income if the 'new' debt is considered to be issued at a discount to the amount previously owing, unless an exception—such as the insolvency or bankruptcy exception—applies.[5] Second, the new debt generally will be tested anew under any governing provisions, such as under the imputed interest rules of the US tax code (including to determine whether the

[3] All references herein to the 'IRC' are to 26 United States Code s 1 et seq. (commonly known as the 'Internal Revenue Code of 1986, as amended'), and all references herein to 'Treas. Reg.' are to the US Treasury Regulations promulgated thereunder. In addition, all references to a 'corporation' or 'partnership' refer to entities treated as a corporation or a partnership, respectively, for US federal income tax purposes (other than an S corporation, which is a special type of closely-held corporation for which an election has been made under IRC, s 1361). Certain entities, such as limited liability companies (LLCs), have the ability to elect their tax classification under the so-called 'check-the-box' regime of Treas. Reg., s 301.7701-3.

[4] Treas. Reg., s 1.1001-3(a).

[5] At the time of this writing, US corporations generally are subject to a maximum marginal US federal income tax rate of 35 per cent, regardless of whether their income is ordinary or capital. IRC, s 11. Individual US taxpayers generally are subject to a maximum marginal US federal income tax rate of 35 per cent with respect to ordinary income and 15 per cent with respect to most capital gain, although these rates are scheduled to increase pursuant to 'sunset' provisions in 2013. IRC, s 1. Corporations may offset capital losses only against capital gains, while other US taxpayers may offset capital losses only against capital gains and up to $3,000 of ordinary income annually. IRC, s 1211. Any COD income incurred by a partnership or other pass-through entity for US federal income tax purposes would be allocated and taxable to its partners, (IRC, s 701) subject to potential US withholding tax issues in the case of a US partnership with foreign partners.

new debt will be considered issued with original issue discount ('OID')),[6] or under general tax principles to determine if the new obligation is more properly characterized as equity (rather than debt) for US federal income tax purposes (though recent Treasury regulations limit the circumstances calling for such characterization).[7] Third, a creditor may recognize gain or loss, depending on its tax basis in the debt and the nature of the exchange.[8] The US tax treatment of the creditor does not necessarily mirror the tax treatment of the corporate debtor. Thus, the debtor may have COD income even though the creditor might not recognize a loss; or the debtor may have an available exception to COD income even though the creditor may have a taxable exchange.

9.2.1.1 Significant modifications

9.09 Whether the terms of a new or modified debt obligation are significantly different from those of the original obligation is a two-prong analysis under governing regulations. First, there are certain types of changes—generally, but not always, those that occur pursuant to the original terms of the instrument—that are not regarded as 'modifications' for this purpose.[9] Thus, it first must be determined which changes constitute modifications. Second, it must be determined if the modifications (sometimes alone, and sometimes collectively) are 'significant'.

9.10 In testing whether a particular modification is significant, certain specific rules apply. For example, a change in the yield of a non-contingent debt instrument is significant if the yield of the debt changes by more than the greater of (a) 25 basis points or (b) 5 per cent of the original yield (a low threshold).[10] Changes in interest rate obviously affect the yield of the debt, but other, less obvious modifications may cause a change in yield, including (a) consent fees or other amounts paid to creditors in respect of a modification,[11] (b) reducing the principal amount of the debt,[12] or (c) changing the timing of payments on debt (particularly where the debt was issued at a discount). Other specific rules apply to changes in timing of

[6] Any OID generally is required to be amortized over time, based on a constant rate of return, with the debtor generally entitled to an interest deduction for such amount, and the creditor generally is required to include such amount as interest income. See below 9.2.1.3. However, certain limitations on the deductibility of interest may apply.

[7] See Treas. Reg., s 1.1001-3(f)(7).

[8] The amount of such gain or loss would equal the difference between the issue price of the new debt and the creditor's adjusted basis in its old debt. Treas. Reg., s 1.1001-1(g). The determination of 'issue price' for US tax purposes is discussed below in 9.2.1.2. However, recognition of any such gain or loss may be limited in respect of corporate debt if the debt constitutes a 'security' for this purpose (a term of art which has nothing to do with how such term is defined under the US securities laws). IRC, ss 354(a), 368(a)(1)(E).

[9] Treas. Reg., s 1.1001-3(c)(1).

[10] Ibid., s 1.1001-3(e)(2).

[11] Ibid., s 1.1001-3(e)(2)(iii)(A).

[12] Ibid., s 1.1001-3(g), Ex. 3.

payments,[13] changes in obligor, changes in security or credit enhancement, changes in priority, changes in the recourse or non-recourse nature of a debt, and changes that result in instruments that are not debt for US federal income tax purposes.[14] Changes to, or additions or deletions of, 'customary' accounting or financial covenants are never significant.[15]

All modifications that are not covered by one of the specific rules must be aggregated and tested under the general rule for determining significance, which asks whether, based on all facts and circumstances, such changes are 'economically significant'.[16] In testing for significance under either the specific rules or the general rule, all prior modifications are taken into account on a cumulative basis (except for changes in yield occurring over five years ago).[17] As indicated above, if a debt is significantly modified, the original debt will be treated for US federal income tax purposes as exchanged for the modified debt. **9.11**

9.2.1.2 Determining cancellation of debt income

The principal concern of a distressed debtor that engages in a debt-for-debt exchange generally is the recognition of COD income (and the potential recharacterization of the new debt as equity for US federal income tax purposes).[18] A debtor may recognize COD income upon a debt-for-debt exchange even though the principal amount of the new debt is the same as that of the old debt. This is a common risk where the debt-for-debt exchange results from significant changes to the terms of a debt over its life, since the issue price of debt for US tax purposes may differ from its stated principal amount. As discussed below in 9.2.4, there are certain potential exceptions to the recognition of COD income; the most likely exceptions to apply to a distressed company are the insolvency and bankruptcy exceptions. Although such exceptions would preclude the debtor from being taxed on COD income, they generally involve the elimination or reduction of a debtor's favourable tax attributes (eg net operating losses ('NOLs') or tax basis). **9.12**

[13] A deferral of payments that results in a change in the accrual of interest, even if not considered to be significant such as to result in a deemed issuance of a new debt obligation, will require a reapplication of the OID rules to ensure the annual accrual of interest income by the holder. Treas. Reg., s 1.1275-2(j).

[14] Treas. Reg., s 1.1001-3(e)(3)–(5).

[15] Ibid., s 1.1001-3(e)(6).

[16] Ibid., s 1.1001-3(e)(1).

[17] Ibid., s 1.1001-3(f)(3).

[18] Recent Treasury regulations provide that a deterioration in the financial condition of the debtor should not be taken into account in determining whether the new debt is recharacterized as equity for US federal income tax purposes unless there is a change in obligor. Treas. Reg., s 1.1001-3(f)(7).

9.13 The amount of a debtor's COD income from a debt-for-debt exchange generally equals the excess, if any, of the 'adjusted issue price' of the original debt over the 'issue price' of the new debt.[19] The adjusted issue price of the original debt generally equals the original offering price of such debt, plus any accreted yield in the case of a debt instrument issued with OID, including any capitalized interest in the case of a pay-in-kind ('PIK') debt instrument.[20]

9.14 The determination of the issue price of the new debt can be quite involved and subject to substantial uncertainty. When new debt is exchanged for old debt, it must be determined whether the new debt is or the old debt was 'traded on an established market' (as specially defined for US federal income tax purposes) at any time during the 30-day period following or preceding the exchange. An established market need not be a formal market, and in some situations, may simply be the ready availability of quotes from brokers, dealers, or traders.[21] If there is an established market, the issue price of the new debt generally will equal the fair market value ('FMV') of the traded debt at the time of the exchange.[22] If not, the issue price generally will equal the new debt's stated principal amount (assuming it bears at least the 'applicable federal rate' of interest for debts of that maturity, as published monthly by the US Internal Revenue Service ('IRS')).[23]

9.15 Stated simply, if the principal amount of the old debt and new debt are the same, and either is traded on an established market, then the debtor is likely to realize COD income (subject to applicable exceptions) upon the exchange, given that debt of distressed companies often trades at a discount. Of course, if the principal balance of the debt is being reduced in the debt-for-debt exchange, COD income is likely to result regardless of whether the old debt or the new debt trades on an established market, though the amount of COD income may differ if the debt is traded.

---

[19] IRC, s 108(e)(10); Treas. Reg., s 1.61-12(c)(2)(ii).

[20] Treas. Reg., s 1.1275-1(b) sets out a more precise computation of a debt instrument's adjusted issue price.

[21] Ibid., s 1.1273-2(f).

[22] Ibid., s 1.1273-2(b)(1), (c)(1). Note that debt automatically will be treated as traded on an established market if a temporary restriction on trading is imposed with a purpose of avoiding such characterization, regardless of whether the restriction is imposed by the debtor or a third party. Treas. Reg., s 1.1273-2(f)(6). Also, if the old debt (but not the new debt) is the traded debt, and the creditor also is receiving other property (such as warrants or stock), the FMV of the old debt must be allocated between the new debt and the other property for purposes of determining the issue price of the new debt. IRC, s 1273(c)(2).

[23] Treas. Reg., ss 1.1273-2(d)(1), 1.1274-2(b).

9.2.1.3 Creation and amortization of original issue discount

Where the outstanding principal amount remains unchanged, the issuance of new debt at a discount (due to its lower issue price) means that the COD income realized by the debtor on the exchange frequently is matched by an equal amount of OID on the new debt. Even if the principal amount of the new debt is less than the outstanding principal of the old debt, the new debt may be issued with the same amount of OID. As a result of the OID, the debtor generally will be entitled to additional interest deductions over time as the OID is amortized (subject to any special limitations, such as the deferral or disallowance of interest deductions on certain high-yield debt obligations). **9.16**

OID is the amount by which the stated redemption price at maturity of a debt obligation exceeds its issue price, subject to a de minimis exception.[24] In practical terms, this means that OID generally is the discount at which a new debt obligation is issued. As indicated in the preceding discussion of COD income, the issue price will be based on FMV if the old or new debt is traded on an established market, and otherwise will be at or near the principal amount of the debt (subject to the existence of an adequate rate of interest). In addition to any discount to face, a debt may be considered to be issued with OID to the extent that the stated rate of interest on the debt is not consistently payable in cash at least annually.[25] Thus, the OID rules also ensure that an issuer cannot front-load its interest deductions and that a holder (even a cash basis holder) must accrue and include such interest in income over time. **9.17**

OID generally is amortized and accrued on a constant yield basis over the term of the debt, resulting over time in increased interest deductions to the issuer and increased interest income to the holder.[26] Various US tax rules may operate to defer or deny a debtor's deductions for accrued OID. One such rule defers the deductibility of OID until it is actually paid when debt is held by certain related foreign creditors.[27] Another rule operates to defer until paid, and possibly permanently disallow, OID deductions on certain debt with a term of more than five years where the yield is at least five percentage points above the 'applicable federal rate' and a significant amount of OID would remain unpaid after five years (assuming payments are made at the latest permitted dates). These rules can be particularly relevant to debt with a PIK or PIK toggle feature (which allows the issuer to elect to pay cash interest currently or PIK the interest). The application **9.18**

[24] IRC, s 1273(a).

[25] Such portion of the interest is considered part of the 'stated redemption price at maturity' of the debt, even if payable at some time prior to maturity. See Treas. Reg., s 1.1273-1(b), (c).

[26] IRC, ss 163(e) (for issuer), 1272(a) (for holder).

[27] Ibid., s 163(e)(3).

of this rule has been suspended with respect to certain debt issued in debt-for-debt exchanges in 2009 or 2010.[28]

9.2.2 Debt repurchases and related party acquisitions of debt

9.19 A simple repurchase or the satisfaction of a debt instrument at a discount for cash or other property, whether in-court or out-of-court, generally results in the debtor incurring COD income (subject to any applicable exceptions) in an amount equal to the excess of the adjusted issue price of the debt over the amount of cash paid or the FMV of other consideration.[29]

9.20 It is not uncommon for an affiliate of a distressed company (such as a controlling equity holder) to purchase the company's debt at a discount before or in connection with a restructuring of the company's debt, as this puts the debt in the hands of a friendly party who may be less likely to put the debtor into default and/or more likely to acquiesce in the restructuring of the debt. It is therefore important to understand that, when debt is purchased at a discount by a person *related to* the debtor (as specially defined for US federal income tax purposes) from a person unrelated to the debtor, the debtor generally will recognize COD income to the same extent as if the debtor directly acquired the debt for the same consideration.[30]

9.21 A similar related party rule can apply when the purchaser of the debt is not related to the debtor at the time it acquired the debt, but becomes related within six months thereafter, or otherwise acquired the debt in anticipation of becoming related to the debtor (an 'indirect' acquisition).[31] If the purchaser becomes related to the debtor within six months of the acquisition, the debtor generally would be treated, as of the time the relationship is established, as acquiring the debt for the purchaser's adjusted basis (ie the amount originally paid by the purchaser). If the indirect acquisition rule applies but the purchaser becomes related to the debtor more than six months following the acquisition, the debtor generally would be treated as acquiring the debt at its then FMV.[32]

9.22 Additionally, if the debtor realizes COD income due to a related party acquisition (even if the COD income is excludable under an applicable exception), the debt is treated as reissued at an issue price equal to the purchaser's adjusted basis or the

---

[28] Ibid., s 163(e)(5), (i); Notice 2010-11, 2010-4 I.R.B. 326.

[29] Treas. Reg., s 1.61-12(c)(2)(ii). The concept of adjusted issue price is discussed in 9.2.1.2 above. Also, as discussed below in 9.2.4 the cancellation of *non-recourse* debt can present additional considerations.

[30] IRC, s 108(e)(4); Treas. Reg., s 1.108-2 (termed a 'direct' acquisition).

[31] Treas. Reg., s 1.108-2(c).

[32] Ibid., s 1.108-2(f).

FMV of the debt on such date, as applicable, which means that the debtor will enjoy OID deductions going forward (subject to any applicable limitations, such as in respect of high-yield debt obligations) whereas the related holder will be required to include the OID in income over time (regardless of any deduction limitations on the debtor).[33] The related holder will not recognize gain or loss upon the deemed reissuance, unless the holder and the debtor are members of a consolidated group.[34]

A 'related' person for this purpose generally requires (a) ownership (actual or constructive) by the purchaser of more than 50 per cent of the corporate debtor or the profits or capital interests of the partnership debtor *or* (b) 50 per cent common ownership of stock (in the case of a corporation) or profits or capital interests (in the case of a partnership).[35] Special rules can apply, however, in the case of partnership debt. **9.23**

9.2.3 Debt-for-equity exchanges

A debt restructuring involving the issuance of equity implicates additional tax considerations, such as the change in ownership rules in the case of corporate debtors and additional valuation considerations in the case of debtors that are partnerships. **9.24**

A corporation's or partnership's use of its own equity to satisfy its outstanding debt obligation generally is treated for COD purposes just like the use of any other property to repurchase debt. Thus, it generally will incur COD income (subject to any applicable exceptions) in an amount equal to the excess, if any, of the adjusted issue price of the debt over the FMV of the equity.[36] There are at least two significant differences, however, in how the COD rules apply to partnerships. **9.25**

First, in the case of a partnership, the COD exceptions that generally apply in distressed situations—namely, the insolvency and bankruptcy exceptions discussed in the next section—apply only at the partner level. As a result, a partner of a distressed partnership is more likely to have taxable ordinary income from the cancellation of the partnership's debt.[37] **9.26**

---

[33] Ibid., s 1.108-2(g)(1).

[34] Ibid., ss 1.108-2(g)(2), 1.1502-13(g)(5), (6). For purposes of this discussion, a 'consolidated group' refers to a consolidated group for US federal income tax purposes, not the financial accounting concept.

[35] IRC, ss 267(b), 414(b), (c), 707(b)(1). Constructive ownership includes upward attribution from an entity to its owners and, in certain cases, attribution among partners.

[36] IRC, s 108(e)(8).

[37] Although the partner may have tax basis in its partnership interest as a result of such allocation of income, any loss from the write-off of such tax basis or the partner's subsequent disposition of its partnership interest may be a capital loss and, thus, not available to offset the partner's share of COD

9.27 Second, but from a more helpful perspective, recently proposed Treasury regulations would allow a partnership to use the liquidation value[38] (rather than the FMV) of the partnership interest to compute its COD income if certain conditions are met, although these regulations are not effective until they are published in final form.[39] The use of liquidation value in such a situation may avoid other adverse consequences to the partners (including the former creditors) under the partnership tax rules, a discussion of which is beyond the scope of this chapter.[40] Under these proposed regulations, the creditors would not recognize gain or loss on the debt-for-equity exchange unless the partnership interest is issued in satisfaction for unpaid interest, accrued OID, rent, or royalties.[41]

9.28 Although the COD rules can themselves be troublesome, it is still possible that a corporate debtor may have significant favourable tax attributes remaining. These debtors must also carefully consider the impact of the limitations that can result from a change in the corporation's stock ownership, as discussed below in 9.2.5. These limitations, particularly in the case of out-of-court restructurings, can be severe. Undertaking the restructuring in the context of a bankruptcy or similar case can provide some relaxation of these limitations, depending on the corporation's new capital structure and/or the nature of the debt exchanged for equity and the extent to which the debt has been trading and accumulated.

9.29 Regardless of the debtor's treatment, a creditor that receives a corporate debtor's own equity in repurchase or satisfaction of a debt obligation generally will recognize gain or loss upon the exchange (depending on the creditor's tax basis in the debt), except where the debt obligation constitutes a 'security' for US federal income tax purposes.[42] In the latter situation, the creditor generally would recognize no gain or loss, except possibly in respect of any accrued but unpaid interest and, in the case of gain, to the extent of any other consideration received (ie non-stock or securities).[43]

---

income (in the event the partner does not qualify for the insolvency or bankruptcy exception). IRC, s 741; Rev. Rul. 93-80, 1993-2 C.B. 239.

[38] Liquidation value is defined as the amount of cash that the partner would receive if, immediately after the issuance of the partnership interest, the partnership sold all of its assets for cash equal to their FMV and then liquidated.

[39] Prop. Treas. Reg., s 1.108-8.

[40] For a more detailed discussion of these partnership-related tax complications, see New York State Bar Association, Tax Section, Report on Proposed Regulations Under Sections 108(e)(8) and 721 on Partnership Debt-for-Equity Exchanges (26 June 2009), reprinted at 2009 Tax Notes Today 122-75.

[41] Prop. Treas. Reg., s 1.721-1(d).

[42] IRC, ss 354(a), 368(a)(1)(E).

[43] Ibid., ss 354(a), 356.

9.2.4 Cancellation of debt income exceptions

There are several statutory and common law exceptions under the US tax laws to the recognition of COD income. These include, among others: the exclusion of COD income where the payment of the debt would have resulted in a deduction;[44] statutory and common law purchase price adjustment exceptions with respect to purchase-money debt;[45] the cancellation or reduction of debt that did not increase the debtor's gross assets (often applied to the cancellation of guaranty claims);[46] shareholder contributions of corporate debt to capital (to the extent of the shareholder's tax basis in the debt);[47] statutory exceptions for the reduction of qualified real property business indebtedness and qualified farm indebtedness (with a corresponding reduction in the tax basis of applicable property);[48] a deferral election for COD income realized during 2009 or 2010;[49] and the statutory insolvency and bankruptcy exceptions discussed below. **9.30**

The cancellation or reduction of *non-recourse* debt in connection with the sale or other disposition of the underlying property does not generate COD income. Instead, the non-recourse debt will be taken into account as an additional amount realized in respect of the disposition of the property. As such, it would increase any gain or reduce any loss that would otherwise be realized, and any additional gain would not qualify for any of the exceptions to COD income.[50] **9.31**

9.2.4.1 Insolvency and bankruptcy exceptions, and attribute reduction

The two exceptions to COD income most prevalent in debt restructurings in the case of *corporate* debtors are the 'bankruptcy' and 'insolvency' exceptions. The bankruptcy exception applies when debt is discharged in a US bankruptcy case, the debtor is under the jurisdiction of the bankruptcy court, and the discharge is either granted by the court or is pursuant to a plan approved by the court, regardless of whether the debtor is insolvent at the time of the discharge.[51] The insolvency exception applies when the debtor is insolvent immediately before the discharge (and the bankruptcy exception is not available, such as in an out-of-court restructuring), but only applies to the extent of the debtor's insolvency at such time.[52] **9.32**

44 Ibid., s 108(e)(2).
45 Ibid., s 108(e)(5); Rev. Rul. 92-99, 1992-2 C.B. 35.
46 See, eg, *Bradford v Commissioner* 233 F2d 935 (6th Cir. 1956).
47 IRC, s 108(e)(6).
48 Ibid., s 108(a)(1)(C), (D).
49 Ibid., s 108(i).
50 Treas. Reg., s 1.1001-2; *Commissioner v Tufts* 103 S Ct 1826 (1983).
51 IRC, s 108(a)(1)(A), (a)(2)(A), (d)(2).
52 Ibid., s 108(a)(1)(B), (a)(3), (d)(3).

9.33 Insolvency is defined for this purpose as the excess (if any) of the amount of the debtor's liabilities over the FMV of its assets, as determined immediately before the COD event.[53] All assets, including off balance sheet assets (such as goodwill in many cases), should be taken into account as assets. The application of the insolvency exception, however, can often prove troublesome. For example, the proper valuation of the debtor's assets may be uncertain and the subject of heated debate by the various parties affected by the restructuring, and the IRS is not bound by the debtor's determination. In addition, although contingent liabilities may affect the everyday market value of a company, the US Tax Court has held that contingent liabilities can be taken into account *only if* it is more probable than not that the debtor will be called upon to satisfy such liabilities.[54] Given the factual difficulties and legal uncertainties in determining the extent of a debtor's insolvency (if any), a debtor seeking to ensure the applicability of an exclusion from COD income should consider restructuring its debt through a US bankruptcy proceeding. A debtor's time in bankruptcy can be relatively short if the debtor is able to 'prepackage' or 'prenegotiate' its plan of reorganization (as discussed in chapter 8).

9.34 There is a price that a debtor must incur for the benefit of these COD income exclusions, however. The debtor generally must reduce its tax attributes by the amount of the excluded COD income.[55] Thus, rather than being a permanent forgiveness, the exclusion is more in the nature of a deferral, since the debtor generally will have reduced deductions, and hence the prospect of increased income, in the future at a time when it has (hopefully) returned to profitability.

9.35 A corporate debtor's tax attributes are reduced in the following order, subject to the elective ability to reduce depreciable property first: NOLs, general business credits, alternative minimum tax ('AMT') credits, net capital losses, tax basis (within limits), passive activity losses, and, lastly, foreign tax credits.[56] If the amount of excluded COD income exceeds the amount of tax attributes available for reduction, the 'unabsorbed' balance of the excluded COD income—often referred to as 'black hole' COD—is generally forgiven without further tax cost.[57] Significantly, the reduction of the debtor's tax attributes generally occurs only

53 Ibid., s 108(d)(3).

54 *Merkel v Commissioner* 109 TC 463 (1997), affd, 192 F3d 844 (9th Cir. 1999).

55 IRC, s 108(b)(1).

56 Ibid., s 108(b)(2). With respect to NOLs and capital losses, current year losses are reduced first, followed by loss carryovers in the order in which they arose. IRC, s 108(b)(4)(B). Excluded COD income reduces losses on a dollar-for-dollar basis, whereas $33^1/_3$ cents of a tax credit are reduced for each dollar of excluded COD income. IRC, s 108(b)(3).

57 Treas. Reg., s 1.108-7(a)(2). The exceptions arise when the debtor corporation is a member of a consolidated group. See 9.2.4.1.2, below.

after the tax for the taxable year of the COD event has been determined.[58] Thus, the debtor's NOLs, tax basis, and other attributes remain available for the remainder of the taxable year (subject to any intervening limitations under the change in ownership rules discussed below in 9.2.5), assuming the restructuring does not occur on the last day of the year or otherwise terminate the taxable year. This can allow for significant planning opportunities.

Several special rules apply with respect to the reduction of tax basis. First, there is a 'liability floor,' such that the total amount of basis that is subject to reduction within the normal ordering rules is limited to the excess, if any, of the aggregate basis of the property held by the debtor *immediately after* the COD event over the amount of the debtor's liabilities at such time.[59] Conceptually, therefore, a debtor is not forced into a situation where an immediate sale of the debtor's assets to pay its remaining liabilities would result in a net gain and, thus, a tax liability. Second, the basis reduction is generally applied to properties in the following order: real property that secured the discharged debt; personal property that secured the discharged debt; property that did not secure the discharged debt; and, lastly, inventory, accounts receivable, and notes receivable (including those that would otherwise be described in the preceding items).[60] Third, any reductions in tax basis are treated as 'recapturable' items in the same manner as depreciation deductions (even if the property is not otherwise depreciable).[61] This generally results in the treatment of any gain recognized upon the disposition of such property as ordinary income.[62] **9.36**

A debtor may elect to have some or all its excluded COD income first reduce the basis of its *depreciable* property held as of the beginning of the next taxable year.[63] When this election is made, basis reduction is not limited by the liability floor.[64] Complex modelling sometimes is necessary to determine whether this election is advantageous. **9.37**

9.2.4.1.1 Special rules governing partnerships. In the case of a partnership, the insolvency and bankruptcy exceptions to COD income apply at the partner level, rather than at the entity level.[65] Thus, the fact that the partnership restructures **9.38**

[58] IRC, s 108(b)(4)(A). This includes any reduction in tax basis, but only for assets that the debtor continues to own as of the beginning of the next taxable year. IRC, s 1017(a).

[59] Ibid., s 1017(b)(2).

[60] Treas. Reg., s 1.1017-1(a).

[61] IRC, s 1017(d).

[62] See IRC, ss 1245, 1250. The recapture rules apply notwithstanding any other provision of the IRC (subject to certain exceptions). As such, it can require the recognition of the 'recapturable' portion of any gain even within an otherwise nontaxable transaction.

[63] IRC, s 108(b)(5).

[64] Ibid., s 1017(b)(2).

[65] Ibid., s 108(d)(6).

its debt pursuant to a bankruptcy proceeding or is insolvent is insufficient, by itself, to qualify its COD income for the bankruptcy or insolvency exception. As such, a partnership is more apt to recognize COD income in the first instance that is then allocated to its partners and, subject to any applicable exceptions at the partner level, includible in the partners' gross income. The allocation of COD income (although a form of non-cash or 'phantom' income) can create significant US withholding tax obligations in the case of a US partnership with foreign partners, despite the insolvency or bankruptcy of the partnership.

9.39 When a partner, applying the insolvency or bankruptcy exception, reduces the tax basis in its assets as a result of an allocation of COD income from a partnership, the partnership interest generally is the first asset subject to basis reduction.[66] In any case where a partner reduces the 'outside' basis in its partnership interest, the basis reduction should not trickle down and impact the partnership's 'inside' basis in its assets, unless the partner has made the election to first reduce its basis in its depreciable property. In such a case, the partnership interest can be treated as depreciable property to the extent of the partner's proportionate share of the partnership's inside basis in depreciable property, but only if the partner requests (or is required to request) and the partnership consents (or is required to consent) to a corresponding reduction in the partnership's inside basis in depreciable property with respect to such partner.[67]

9.40 9.2.4.1.2 **Special rules within consolidated groups.** When a debtor corporation is a member of a consolidated group for US federal income tax purposes and qualifies for the insolvency or bankruptcy exception to COD income, the attribute reduction rules are modified in part. The attribute reduction initially applies on a separate company basis to the debtor member.[68] If, however, the debtor member reduces its tax basis in the stock of a subsidiary group member, the subsidiary is similarly required to reduce its tax attributes by the amount of such reduction (with such reduction tiering down in succession to the extent that the stock basis in other subsidiary members is reduced).[69] After such reductions, any black-hole COD (ie any excluded COD income that would simply be forgiven in a non-consolidated context) reduces the tax attributes of *other* group members, other than asset basis or any other 'separate company' tax attributes.[70]

---

66 Treas. Reg., s 1.1017-1(g)(1).

67 Ibid., s 1.1017-1(g)(2).

68 Ibid., s 1.1502-28(a)(2)(i). For purposes of the election to reduce the tax basis of depreciable property first, a further election can be made to treat a debtor member's tax basis in the stock of a subsidiary member as depreciable property to the extent the subsidiary consents to a corresponding reduction in the tax basis of its depreciable property. IRC, s 1017(b)(3)(D).

69 Treas. Reg., s 1.1502-28(a)(3).

70 Ibid., s 1.1502-28(a)(4).

In what is often a trap for the unwary, the cancellation or discharge of a subsidiary member's debt can result in income to the consolidated group if the parent of the debtor member has a *negative* tax basis (also known as an 'excess loss account') in the stock of the debtor member *and* the debtor member has black-hole COD even after reducing the tax attributes of other group members. In such instance, the parent of the debtor member is required to include the excess loss account in income to the extent of the remaining black-hole COD.[71] **9.41**

9.2.4.2 Deferral election

As indicated above, a special deferral election is available for COD income realized during 2009 or 2010. The election may be made with respect to the cancellation of debt issued by a corporation or any other person (including a partnership) in connection with the conduct of a trade or business.[72] The debtor—whether solvent, insolvent, or in bankruptcy—may elect to defer all or any portion of the resulting COD income for five or four taxable years (depending on whether the COD was incurred in 2009 or 2010, respectively) and then include such deferred COD income in its gross income ratably over the succeeding five taxable years (generally 2014 to 2018). The insolvency and bankruptcy exceptions to COD income do not apply to any COD income electively deferred. If a partnership elects to defer less than all of its COD income, it may allocate the deferred portion and the non-deferred portion of its COD income among its partners however it likes. **9.42**

If the deferral election is made for COD incurred in a debt-for-debt exchange, in a related party acquisition, or in a repurchase by the debtor using proceeds from a new debt issuance, any OID deductions that accrue on the new debt issued (or deemed issued) during the deferral period (up to the amount of the deferred COD income) are also deferred during such period and taken into account ratably over five taxable years. **9.43**

The inclusion of any deferred COD income and OID deductions may be accelerated if, among other things, the debtor liquidates, sells substantially all of its assets, or ceases to do business. Additional acceleration rules apply to partnerships and other pass-through entities. **9.44**

Careful tax planning may be necessary to determine whether, and to what extent, a debtor should make a deferral election. **9.45**

[71] Ibid., ss 1.1502-19(b)(1)(ii), (c)(1)(iii)(B), -32(b)(3)(ii)(C).
[72] IRC, s 108(i); Rev. Proc. 2009-37, 2009-36 I.R.B. 309.

9.2.5 Change in ownership limitations on tax attributes

9.46 When a distressed corporation issues stock in exchange for its outstanding debt or new capital, either in court or out of court, the utilization of its tax attributes may become limited under certain change in ownership rules (in addition to possible reduction under the COD rules discussed above), in particular those under section 382 of the IRC. Section 382 generally imposes an annual limitation on the amount of a loss corporation's taxable income that may be offset by pre-change losses and credits (including certain 'built-in' losses and deferred deductions) following an ownership change of the loss corporation.[73] Although simple in its initial statement, section 382 involves detailed and complex rules, both as to what constitutes the generally feared 'ownership change' and with respect to the resulting annual limitation and its exceptions.

9.47 Section 382 is intended to provide an objective set of provisions to prevent the so-called trafficking in tax losses. A different statutory provision provides a more general, and subjective, anti-abuse rule. Under that provision, if a person (or group of persons) directly or indirectly acquires at least 50 per cent of a corporation's stock (by vote or value) and the principal purpose of such acquisition is the avoidance of US federal income tax by securing a tax benefit that the acquirer or corporation would not otherwise enjoy, the IRS may disallow such benefit.[74]

9.2.5.1 What constitutes an ownership change

9.48 An 'ownership change' of a loss corporation generally occurs when the percentage of stock owned by one or more 5 per cent shareholders has increased over its lowest point by more than 50 percentage points over a three-year period (or, if shorter, since the most recent ownership change).[75] A shareholder's percentage ownership is determined based on the relative value of stock owned actually and after applying various attribution rules,[76] and takes into account all stock other than so-called 'pure' preferred stock—namely, non-voting, non-participating, non-convertible

[73] IRC, ss 382(a), 383. These rules do not apply to partnerships, nor is such application necessary to fulfill the purposes of s 382. As a pass-through entity, the previously-incurred losses of a partnership are personal to the partner. Although there historically have been opportunities to transfer the ownership of a partnership that has a net built-in loss in its assets (ie the partnership's aggregate tax basis in its assets exceeds their total value), these opportunities have been limited—although not completely eliminated—by recent legislation. See, eg, IRC, s 743.

[74] IRC, s 269(a) (also applies to the acquisition of a corporation's assets by another corporation in certain carryover basis transactions).

[75] IRC, s 382(g)(1), (i).

[76] IRC, s 382(l)(3); Treas. Reg., s 1.382-2(a)(3)(i), -2T(h) (upward attribution from an entity to its owners and family attribution), -3(a) (aggregating certain groups of persons who have an understanding among themselves to make a coordinated stock acquisition), -4 (option attribution).

preferred stock that does not have an unreasonable liquidation or redemption premium.[77]

Significantly, although an ownership change requires more than a 50 per cent change in a corporation's stock ownership, such change can occur gradually over time and, due to certain tracking or 'grouping' rules, can occur by reason of stock issuances or redemptions by the loss corporation or market sales of stock by existing 5 per cent shareholders.[78] Thus, the determination of whether an ownership change occurs is not always obvious, and can require detailed and time-consuming computations. As such, a corporation with significant tax losses or credits (including a net 'built-in' loss in its existing assets) should carefully monitor the changes in its stock ownership and maintain an ongoing ownership change analysis. Due to the recent economic crisis and the US government's need to make significant equity investments in several major institutions with significant tax losses, special exceptions were created for the US government's ownership.[79] As of the date of writing, no comparable exceptions apply for ownership by other governments. **9.49**

Additionally, an ownership change can occur where a controlling shareholder (a shareholder that has held 50 per cent of the loss corporation's stock at any time in the last three years) claims a worthlessness deduction with respect to its stock for a taxable year and continues to hold the stock at the close of the taxable year.[80] In such instance, the stock is treated as newly acquired and, thus, in the case of a current 50 per cent shareholder, would automatically cause an ownership change. **9.50**

9.2.5.2 Bankruptcy court orders restricting stock trading

When a corporation enters bankruptcy with a significant amount of tax losses or credits that would be adversely affected by an ownership change, it is common for the corporation to seek an order from the bankruptcy court limiting acquisitions of stock, options and other equity interests by 5 per cent shareholders or by persons who would become 5 per cent shareholders upon such acquisition, and sometimes dispositions by 5 per cent shareholders as well.[81] Due to the speculation in a corporation's stock that often occurs immediately after its bankruptcy filing, such orders are frequently sought as part of the motions filed by the debtor **9.51**

[77] IRC, s 382(k)(6)(A); Treas. Reg., s 1.382-2(a)(3), -2T(f)(18) (including an anti-abuse rule, treating certain non-stock interests as stock, and vice versa).

[78] IRC, s 382(g)(4)(A); Treas. Reg., s 1.382-2T(g), (j).

[79] See Notice 2010-2, 2010-2 I.R.B. 251.

[80] IRC, s 382(g)(4)(D).

[81] See, eg, *Re Northwest Airlines Corp.* Ch. 11 Case No. 05-17930 (ALG) (Bankr. SDNY 2005); *Re Metrocall, Inc.* Ch. 11 Case No. 02-11579 (Bankr. D. Del. 2002); *Re Phar-Mor, Inc.* 152 BR 924 (Bankr. N.D. Ohio 1993). But consider *Re UAL Corporation* 412 F3d 775 (7th Cir. 2005) (in dicta, criticized restricting a 5 per cent shareholder's disposition).

at the start of the bankruptcy case. The purpose of the order is to preserve (a) the availability of the tax losses or credits for use during the bankruptcy case against any income from operations or gains from the sale of assets, and (b) in the case of a reorganizing corporation, the corporation's ability to benefit from the more liberal limitations that apply when the ownership change occurs pursuant to a plan of reorganization confirmed by the bankruptcy court (discussed below in 9.2.5.4).

9.52 The authority for bankruptcy courts to grant equity trading orders stems from the automatic stay imposed by the Bankruptcy Code, which stays, among other things, 'any act to . . . exercise control over property of the [bankruptcy] estate'.[82] In the seminal *Prudential Lines* case,[83] the Second Circuit Court of Appeals held that a parent corporation was precluded by the automatic stay from claiming a worthless stock loss with respect to its bankrupt subsidiary, because doing so would effectively eliminate the benefit of the subsidiary's NOLs.

9.2.5.3 Annual limitation, generally

9.53 The annual limitation imposed on the use of a corporation's pre-change losses and credits following an ownership change generally equals the product of (a) the FMV of the corporation's stock (including any preferred stock) *immediately before* the ownership change multiplied by (b) the 'long-term tax exempt rate' for the month during which the ownership change occurs (which is a rate calculated monthly by the IRS).[84] For example, the long-term tax exempt rate for ownership changes during January 2011 is 4.10 per cent. Any unused limitation can be carried forward to the next year.[85] Thus, if the loss corporation's current stock value is very low, the annual amount of useable NOLs similarly would be very small. As discussed below, a modified annual limitation applies if the ownership change occurs pursuant to a confirmed bankruptcy plan of reorganization or court order. Regardless, the annual limitation will be automatically set at zero if the loss corporation fails to satisfy a two-year continuity of business test,[86] effectively eliminating the corporation's use of its pre-change losses and credits (subject to the adjustment for net built-in gains and any alternative bankruptcy relief).

---

[82] 11 USC s 362(a)(3).

[83] *Official Committee of Unsecured Creditors v PSS Steamship Co. (Re Prudential Lines)* 928 F2d 565 (2nd Cir. 1991).

[84] IRC, s 382(b)(1), (e)(1), (f). The loss corporation's value for purposes of computing the annual limitation is reduced where a redemption or other corporate contraction occurs in connection with an ownership change, certain capital contributions are received by the corporation, or the corporation holds substantial non-business assets immediately after an ownership change, and is increased for the value of any options or similar rights. See, eg, IRC, s 382(e)(2), (l)(4); Notice 2008-78, 2008-41 I.R.B. 851; PLR 200442011 (23 October 2003).

[85] IRC, s 382(b)(2).

[86] IRC, s 382(c); Treas. Reg., s 1.368-1(d)(1).

9.54 A corporation's annual limitation generally can be enhanced if at the time of the ownership change it has a net built-in gain in its assets,[87] generally meaning that, were the company to sell all its assets for their respective FMVs, it would recognize a net gain. In such event, any built-in gain or income items recognized (or deemed recognized) by the corporation during the five-year period following the ownership change increases the annual limitation for the taxable year in which it is recognized, subject to an overall cap of the original net amount of built-in gain.

9.55 If a corporation has a net built-in loss in its assets (rather than a net built-in gain), any built-in loss or deduction recognized by the corporation during the five-year period following the ownership change will be subject to the annual limitation (in the same manner as other pre-change losses and credits), subject to an overall cap of the original net amount of built-in loss.[88] Any disallowed loss or deduction is carried forward in the same manner as an NOL or capital loss carryforward, as applicable, and remains subject to the annual limitation in the years to which it is carried.[89]

9.56 Complicating things somewhat further, a special adjustment applies for purposes of the AMT—ostensibly, a parallel tax regime that makes certain adjustments to a corporation's regular tax computations to eliminate, among other things, certain preferential deductions. If a corporation has a net built-in loss that is subject to the annual limitation for regular US federal income tax purposes, its tax basis in its assets must be stepped down to FMV for certain AMT purposes.[90] This is a permanent adjustment, in contrast to the limitation for regular tax purposes that only applies to built-in losses recognized within five years.

9.2.5.4 Special bankruptcy limitations

9.57 A corporation in a bankruptcy or similar case that undergoes an ownership change pursuant to a confirmed plan of reorganization or court order generally receives better treatment in that it is subject to one of two alternative limitations, either (a) an upfront adjustment to the amount of its loss and tax credit carryforwards or (b) a modified annual limitation.

9.58 The first special rule—referred to commonly by its code section, section 382(l)(5)—generally applies if shareholders and/or qualified creditors of the loss

[87] IRC, s 382(h); Notice 2003-65, 2003-2 C.B. 747. This adjustment only applies if the net built-in gain exceeds an administrative threshold, equal to the lesser of $10 m or 15 per cent of the FMV of the corporation's assets (other than cash and certain cash equivalents). IRC, s 382(h)(3)(B).

[88] IRC, s 382(h); Notice 2003-65. As in the case of net built-in gains, this limitation only applies if the net built-in loss exceeds the administrative threshold (see the preceding footnote).

[89] IRC, s 382(h)(4). The legislative history indicates that such disallowed losses or deductions cannot be carried back. H.R. Conf. Rep. No. 841, 99th Cong., 2d Sess. at II-191 (1986).

[90] IRC, s 56(g)(4)(G); Treas. Reg., s 1.56(g)-1(k).

corporation own immediately after the ownership change at least 50 per cent (by voting power and value) of the stock of the reorganized corporation (or of a controlling corporation if also in bankruptcy) as a result of their prior stock or debt holdings.[91] The benefit of this rule is that the annual limitation does *not* apply.[92] Rather, the amount of any NOLs or tax credits carried forward to a year ending after the ownership change must be redetermined to exclude the impact of any interest deductions claimed in respect of any debt exchanged for stock during the bankruptcy case, but only for deductions claimed for the taxable year of the ownership change and the three preceding years.[93] The reduction may be significant in the case of long-held high-yield debt, but may be non-existent in the case of any trade debt exchanged for equity.

9.59 Subject to certain exceptions, a creditor is 'qualified' only to the extent the debt for which it received stock either (a) was continuously held by the creditor since at least 18 months before the bankruptcy, (b) arose in the ordinary course of the corporation's business and has always been held by the creditor, or (c) was outstanding for at least 18 months before the bankruptcy or arose in the ordinary course of the corporation's business *and* the creditor (although not continuously holding the debt) does not become a 5 per cent shareholder in the reorganized corporation.[94] Thus, the effective intent of the provision is to give the creditors who are most likely to have funded the debtor's losses the chance to benefit from the corporation's losses. To guard against the creditors taking unfair advantage of the relief accorded by this provision, by quickly selling the company off to one or more substantial holders, the statute provides that, if a second ownership change occurs within two years of the ownership change under the bankruptcy plan, the annual limitation that applies with respect to such later change will be zero (with *no* adjustment for net built-in gains),[95] effectively rendering the corporation's then pre-change losses valueless on a going forward basis.

9.60 Because the special relief of section 382(l)(5) is supposed to be helpful, if the debtor determines that applying the annual limitation (and avoiding the reduction in the overall amount of its losses and credits and/or the two-year ownership

[91] No regulations have been issued directly addressing the application of this rule within the consolidated group context, although the IRS has indicated informally that it should be applicable if all material loss corporations are in bankruptcy.

[92] Under an anti-abuse rule, a corporation availing itself of s 382(l)(5) in certain circumstances may nevertheless be denied the benefit of its pre-change losses and credits where the corporation does not carry on more than an insignificant amount of an active trade or business during and subsequent to its bankruptcy case. Treas. Reg., s 1.269-3(d).

[93] IRC, s 382(l)(5)(B).

[94] IRC, s 382(l)(5)(E); Treas. Reg., s 1.382-9(d)(3).

[95] IRC, s 382(l)(5)(D).

change penalty) is beneficial, it can elect out of section 382(l)(5) when it files its tax return for the taxable year that includes the ownership change.[96]

If section 382(l)(5) does not apply, by election out or because the debtor does not qualify, the debtor will still potentially benefit from a modified annual limitation. For an ownership change occurring pursuant to a confirmed bankruptcy plan or court order, the annual limitation is generally computed using the FMV of the *reorganized* corporation (rather than the stock value immediately *before* the ownership change), but in no event can the value be greater than the gross value of the corporation's assets immediately before the change (with certain adjustments).[97] In effect, this permits the creditors to obtain the value benefit of converting all their debt to equity but, unlike the section 382(l)(5) rule, there is no restriction against a further ownership change. **9.61**

9.2.5.5 Claims trading orders and charter restrictions

As discussed above, one of the primary purposes for obtaining a bankruptcy court order aimed at avoiding an ownership change during the bankruptcy case is so the debtor can avail itself of the special bankruptcy limitations discussed above for the often inevitable ownership change that will occur under a plan of reorganization. Because the ability to qualify for section 382(l)(5) relief depends, in significant part, either on 'old and cold' creditors or on creditors not becoming 5 per cent shareholders under the plan, a debtor also will frequently seek an order from the bankruptcy court restricting the purchase of claims during the bankruptcy case that would impede qualification for section 382(l)(5), if potentially advantageous. The more recent formulations of such trading orders generally allow creditors to acquire claims pending the filing of a plan that seeks the benefits of section 382(l)(5) on the condition that any claims acquired from the time of the motion or order must be resold before the effective date of the plan if the ownership of such claims otherwise might impede the debtor's qualification for section 382(l)(5).[98] **9.62**

Where a plan does seek to benefit from section 382(l)(5), it is important to protect against a subsequent ownership change, particularly within the two-year period after bankruptcy (as discussed above in 9.2.5.4). It is therefore common for corporations whose stock will be widely held to include, in the charter of the reorganized corporation under the plan, stock transfer restrictions that operate in a similar manner to the stock trading orders described above in 9.2.5.2. **9.63**

[96] IRC, s 382(l)(5)(H); Treas. Reg., s 1.382-9(i).
[97] IRC, s 382(l)(6); Treas. Reg., s 1.382-9(j).
[98] See, eg, *Re Delta Airlines, Inc.* Ch. 11 Case No. 05-17923 (PCB) (Bankr. SDNY 2005); *Re Northwest Airlines Corp.* Ch. 11 Case No. 05-17930 (ALG) (Bankr. SDNY 2005).

9.2.6 Additional planning considerations

9.2.6.1 Holding company considerations

9.64 When a holding company owns a distressed operating company and a debt-for-equity exchange is contemplated, the creditors usually are indifferent from a *non-tax* perspective whether they receive stock of the holding company or the operating company. There can, however, be differing tax implications to a debtor corporation, as well as its creditors. In particular, in the context of a consolidated group, the tax consequence of the creditor receiving the parent corporation's stock (and thus preserving the tax group) can be dramatically different than the creditor receiving stock of a subsidiary debtor corporation that would cause the consolidated group to terminate.[99] And, depending on the facts, the interests of certain creditors (generally depending on whether the creditor desires non-recognition treatment) may be at odds with those of the debtor.

9.65 Within the consolidated group context, a significant potential concern is that there either exists or will be created as a result of the restructuring transactions negative stock basis (an excess loss account) within the group. Another is the extent to which there have been prior intercompany transactions that have resulted in deferred gains within the group. Upon a termination of the group by the creditors receiving the stock of a subsidiary member of the group, all deferred intercompany gains involving such lower-tier members and all lower-tier excess loss accounts (and possibly all deferred gains and excess loss accounts if the remaining companies will be liquidating) have to be taken into account.[100] Careful structuring of the transaction may sometimes avoid or mitigate the adverse impact, if present. Conversely, there may sometimes be positive results from the termination of the group, such as the manner in which the COD rules otherwise operate within the consolidated group context.

9.2.6.2 State and local transfer taxes

9.66 In leaving the discussion of US taxes, and although a discussion of the state and local tax consequences of a debt restructuring is beyond the scope of this chapter, we do observe that the US Bankruptcy Code provides an exemption from any US state and local stamp and similar taxes (eg real estate transfer taxes) that could otherwise apply to transactions undertaken pursuant to a confirmed bankruptcy plan.[101] This exemption does not apply to transfers undertaken during a bankruptcy case before a confirmed plan.[102]

---

[99] See Treas. Reg., s 1.1502-75(d)(1).
[100] Ibid., s 1.1502-13(d), -19.
[101] 11 USC s 1146(a).
[102] *Florida Dept. of Revenue v Piccadilly Cafeterias, Inc.* 128 S Ct 2326 (2008).

9.3 UK tax

The principal business entity in the UK is the company, either in the form of the limited company ('Ltd') or the public limited company ('PLC'), and partnerships.[103] Limited partnerships[104] and limited liability partnerships[105] have historically been used by professional services firms,[106] although nowadays partnerships are also used by property investors and private equity funds (among others) as investment vehicles. The principal advantage of using a partnership for UK tax purposes is that they are treated as transparent and this prevents their profits being taxed twice, once at the corporate level and again at the individual investor level on any distributions of previously-taxed profit. However, with the increasing rates of individual income tax in the UK (and the prospective decrease in the rates of corporation tax)[107] there is a move to incorporate such entities. Another recent addition to the range of UK business entities is the real estate investment trust ('REIT'); again the advantage is that for UK tax purposes these are treated as transparent.[108] The tax consequences of restructuring any of these tax transparent entities are outside the scope of this current volume. 9.67

Although this chapter examines the restructuring of debt, a number of points made in the introduction to this chapter are worth reiterating with regard to restructuring generally: first, there are other possibilities open to a company's management to reorganize its affairs; for example, the company could raise new funds by way of share issue or dispose of its business or one of its businesses to raise funds to pay down the debt; secondly, the type of restructuring discussed here happens outside a formal insolvency process and many of the beneficial tax reliefs that would otherwise be available in such a process will not be available; thirdly, as in the US, it may ultimately be more advantageous for the creditors to acquire the assets of the debtor company; and finally, notwithstanding that any course of action may be advantageous from a tax perspective, in practice a company's options may be restricted by either legal or commercial constraints or both. 9.68

---

103 Governed by the Partnership Act 1890.

104 Governed by the Limited Partnerships Act 1907.

105 Governed by the Limited Liability Partnerships Act 2000.

106 Historically, any other type of business had to incorporate if its membership exceeded 20. SI 2002/3203 repealed ss 716 and 717 Companies Act 1985.

107 It was announced, in the Emergency Budget of 22 June 2010, that the rate of corporation tax which at the time of writing is 28 per cent will be reduced for the financial year commencing 1 April 2011 to 27 per cent and then reduced by 1 per cent a year each year until 2014 when the rate for the financial year commencing 2014 will be 24 per cent. Companies' chargeable gains are taxed at the same rate as other profits.

108 Dealt with in Part 12 (ss 518-609), Corporation Tax Act 2010 ('CTA 2010').

9.69 In recent years, the UK has seen the rise of the 'prepack administration' in which the distressed company's assets are transferred to a new company immediately after the company is placed into administration,[109] a formal insolvency process, allowing the company's business to continue shorn of many of its debts. Such transactions are entered into in connection with a formal insolvency process and are outside the scope of the UK discussion; however, for comparative purposes there follows a brief description of the tax consequences of a prepack administration. It should be noted that, in general, the consequences are detrimental to the debtor company; however, the commercial advantages of the administration procedure are such that they outweigh any tax disadvantages.

9.70 In a prepack administration, the marketing is done and the sale is all but agreed before administration. The sale of the company's business takes place when the company is in administration, usually immediately after the administration order is granted. For tax purposes, administration ends an accounting period.[110] Any trading losses incurred in the accounting period immediately before the administration, if not used in that period, can only be carried forward to be set against profits of the same trade after administration. As the trade is sold immediately, such losses are lost unless they can be used for a terminal loss claim;[111] however, the fact that the company has entered administration might imply that it has been making losses for some time and that a terminal loss claim is irrelevant. Capital assets sold with the business may give rise to a gain; capital losses can be set against the gain, including any capital losses carried forward from previous accounting periods, but only trading losses made in the same accounting period can be set against a gain. For the reasons mentioned above, there would not be any such losses.

9.71 A company entering administration should not affect any capital gains tax group of which the company is a member.[112] The question of whether a group relief group is affected remains an open point. HMRC consider that an administration can break a group relief group; the author's view is that it does not.

9.72 Tax in administration is an expense of the administration,[113] whereas tax before administration is an unsecured claim. The effect of the pre pack, where a sale of the business gives rise to significant tax liabilities, therefore will be to elevate the Revenue from the position of unsecured creditor to that of pre-preferential.

---

109 Administration is a formal insolvency procedure governed by Sch B1 to the Insolvency Act 1986.

110 CTA 2009, ss 10(1)(i) and (2) and 9(1)(b).

111 Ibid., s 39.

112 TCGA 1992, s 170.

113 Insolvency Rules 1986, r 2.67.

The rules relating to the taxation of debts are complex and what follows is only an outline of the general situation. 9.73

9.3.1 Debt restructuring—general

The two objectives for the UK tax adviser in any debt restructuring are: first, to ensure that the debtor does not become subject to an increased level of taxation or accelerate payments of an existing or prospective tax liability; and, secondly, to ensure that the creditor gets a deduction for any losses that might be suffered as a result of the restructuring. However, it might be the case that an additional tax liability needs to be assumed to facilitate the restructuring and such a liability might then be reduced by using existing tax losses available to the debtor. The role of the tax adviser is then to ensure that such losses are available (ie the losses are of a type that can be used against the prospective tax liability and are not likely to be lost as a result of the restructuring). 9.74

For the debtor, the tax effect of the exchange, modification or cancellation of debt will depend on two factors: first, the type of debt, ie whether or not the debt is a 'loan relationship'; and secondly, whether the debtor and creditor are 'connected'. If the debtor is a UK company and the debt arises from the lending of money (by or to) it, it will always be a loan relationship (and so too will certain other transactions and other relationships connected with the debt with the consequence that these too will be brought within the loan relationship provisions).[114] Whether the creditor is a party to a loan relationship will depend on whether it is a corporate, in which case it will be a party to a loan relationship, or some other entity, in which case it will not. It has been assumed for the purpose of the UK discussion that the creditor restructuring the debt is a corporate; in any event, it is generally the tax consequences of restructuring the debtor that are being addressed. 9.75

In concept, the taxation of restructuring is simple: the taxation follows the accounting treatment unless the parties are connected, in which case the accounting treatment is overridden by specific rules. However, in reality, the rules have been changed many times to deal with avoidance and simplicity has given way to undue complexity. 9.76

9.3.2 Loan relationships

Before looking at specific transactions, it is necessary to look briefly at how the loan relationship rules apply in principle. 9.77

[114] See below 9.80.

9.78 Broadly, a company (PLC or Ltd) has a loan relationship if it stands in the position of a creditor or debtor 'as respects of any money debt' (whether by reference to a security or otherwise)[115] and the debt arises from a transaction of lending money.[116] A money debt is one that falls to be settled (a) by the payment of money,[117] (b) by the transfer of a right to settlement under a debt which is itself a money debt,[118] or (c) by the issue or transfer of any share in a company.[119] A money debt is also one that has at any time fallen to be settled in one of those three ways[120] or may, at the option of the debtor or creditor, be settled in one of those three ways.[121] Furthermore, a money debt is a loan relationship, notwithstanding that it does not arise from a transaction of lending money, if an instrument is issued by any person for the purpose of representing either security for the debt[122] or the rights of a creditor in respect of that debt.[123] This definition will therefore encompass most types of corporate debt, whether it be bank debt or debts represented by bonds or other securities, and whether or not those debts actually arise from the lending of money.

9.79 Loan relationships do not include debts arising from the sale of capital assets (including property) or from the sale of goods or services. There is an express exclusion from the definition of loan relationship for debts that arise from rights conferred by shares, for example a debt arising from an unpaid dividend.[124]

9.80 Some other types of debt are also brought into the scope of the loan relationship provisions notwithstanding that they do not arise from the lending of money;[125] most importantly for restructuring purposes are certain 'relevant non-lending loan relationships',[126] including (a) debts on which interest is payable by or to the company,[127] (b) debts in relation to which an impairment loss (or credit in respect of the reversal of an impairment loss) or release debit arises to the company in respect of an unpaid (or previously unpaid) business payment,[128] and (c) debts in relation to which a relevant deduction has been allowed to the company and which is released.[129]

---

115 CTA 2009, s 302(1)(a).
116 Ibid., s 302(1)(b)9.
117 Ibid., s 303(1)(a)(i).
118 Ibid., s 303(1)(a)(ii).
119 Ibid., s 303(1)(a)(iii).
120 Ibid., s 303((1)(b).
121 Ibid., s 303(1)(c).
122 Ibid., s 303(3)(a).
123 Ibid., s 303(3)(b).
124 Ibid., s 303(4).
125 Ibid., s 479(1)(b).
126 Ibid., Part 6, Chapter 2.
127 Ibid., s 479(2)(a).
128 Ibid., s 479(2)(c).
129 Ibid., s 479(2)(d).

9.3.2.1 Connection

The loan relationship rules are modified where there is a 'connected companies relationship' between the debtor and another company that stands in the position of a creditor as respects the debt in question.[130] This includes both direct and indirect relationships.[131] The rules therefore cannot be circumvented by placing an unconnected party making back-to-back loans between the debtor and creditor. **9.81**

Generally, a connected companies relationship exists if one of the companies has control of the other or both are controlled by a third company.[132] For these purposes, control means the power of a person to secure that the affairs of the company are conducted in accordance with the person's wishes (a) by means of the holding of shares or the possession of voting power in or in relation to the company or any other company[133] or (b) as a result of the powers conferred by the articles of association or other document regulating the company or other company;[134] this will include, for example, a shareholders' agreement. Where shares are held as trading stock, for example by a financial institution, voting powers on the shares are ignored.[135] **9.82**

If the companies are connected at any time in an accounting period, they are connected for the whole of the accounting period.[136] **9.83**

9.3.2.2 Consequences of a connected companies relationship

There are three consequences of a loan relationship being a connected companies relationship: first, generally, both the debtor and creditor must bring any profits or losses on the loan relationship into account on an amortized cost basis;[137] second, the debits and credits on any related transactions (see 9.88 below) are limited to what they would have been had the transaction not taken place and no amount had accrued after the transaction had taken place;[138] and third, no impairment loss can be brought into account subject to an exception where there is a debt-for-equity swap and the parties become connected because of the debt-for-equity swap[139] (see 9.104 below). **9.84**

130 Ibid., s 348(2).
131 Ibid., s 348(3).
132 Ibid., s 466(2).
133 Ibid., s 472(2)(i).
134 Ibid., s 472(2)(ii).
135 Ibid., s 472(3).
136 Ibid., s 466(1).
137 Ibid., s 349.
138 Ibid., s 352.
139 Ibid., s 354(2)(a). There is also an exception where the creditor is insolvent (ibid., ss 354(2) and 357). This prevents the debtor having to bring interest into account on an accruals basis where there is no prospect of receiving it.

9.3.2.3 Accounting for loan relationships

9.85 The loan relationship rules were introduced in 1996[140] (although heavily amended since)[141] and were intended to align the taxation of debt (and certain other transactions) with its treatment in the company's accounts. Consequently, the starting point for determining the tax treatment of the profit and loss on a loan relationship is the profit or loss that is recognized in determining the company's profits and losses for the purposes of generally accepted accounting practice ('GAAP').[142] However, although GAAP is the starting point, the legislation introduces many modifications and now it is almost true to say that tax follows the accounts unless it does not.

9.86 The legislation provides that the general rule is that the amounts to be brought into account by a company may be determined on any basis of accounting that is in accordance with GAAP, but then specifies two particular methods: the amortized cost basis of accounting and fair value accounting.[143] The profits and losses to be brought into account include all profits and losses arising from the loan relationship and all related transactions[144] (see 9.88 below), all interest under those relationships,[145] and all expenses incurred by the company under or for the purposes of those relationships or transactions.[146]

9.87 The debtor will usually apply the amortized cost basis of accounting and will therefore get a deduction for interest on an accruals basis determined by the treatment in the statutory accounts. Consequently, the debtor will be entitled to a deduction regardless of whether the interest is paid or not.

9.88 The profits and losses that need to be brought into account include those on related transactions.[147] A related transaction includes situations where rights or liabilities under the loan relationship are transferred or extinguished by any sale, gift, exchange, surrender, redemption or release.[148] Consequently, the release of a debt owed to an unrelated party would be a related transaction and would give rise to an accounting profit for the debtor and therefore to a tax charge on the accounting profit recognized in the accounts.

9.89 Another consequence of the accounting treatment governing the tax treatment is that if, as the debtor company starts to suffer cashflow difficulties, it cannot service

---

140 FA 1996, ss 80-105 and Schs 8–15 rewritten to Part 5 CTA 2009.
141 Most recently in the Finance Act 2010.
142 Ibid., s 307(2).
143 Ibid., s 313(1).
144 CTA 2007, s 307(3)(a).
145 CTA 2009, s 307(3)(b).
146 Ibid., s 307(3)(c).
147 Ibid., s 307(3)(a).
148 Ibid., s 304(2).

the debt, it may still be able to take a deduction for the accruing interest for tax purposes. Relief in this situation is permitted unless it is paid in one of four specific situations that are disallowed by statute. These are: first, where there is a connection in the accrual period between the debtor and creditor;[149] second, where the debtor is a close company and the creditor is a participator, the associate of a participator or a company which is itself controlled by a participator;[150] third, the creditor is a company with a major interest in the debtor or vice versa;[151] or fourth, the creditor is a pension fund for the debtor's employees.[152] Before 1 April 2009, the first three of these exceptions applied where the creditor was not liable to corporation tax; however, this included companies resident for tax purposes in the EU and consequently infringed EU law and so, to comply with EU law, amendments were introduced by the Finance Act 2009 which mean that after 1 April 2009[153] the exceptions only apply to creditor companies resident for tax purposes in a non-qualifying territory[154] or effectively managed in a non-taxing non-qualifying territory.[155] For all practical purposes, this now means that there is no limit on the deductibility of interest on an accruals basis if the creditor is resident and taxed in a jurisdiction that has a tax treaty containing a non-discrimination clause.

9.3.2.4 Costs of restructuring debt

In order to get a deduction for the costs of restructuring debt under the loan relationship provisions the expense must both be recognized as such in the company's accounts under GAAP[156] and be incurred by the company under or for the purposes of the relationship and any related transaction.[157] Furthermore, the expense must be incurred directly for one of four purposes: first, in bringing the loan relationship into existence;[158] second, in entering into or giving effect to any related transaction;[159] third, in making payments under the loan relationship or as a result of a related transaction;[160] and fourth, in taking steps to ensure the receipt of payments under the loan relationship or in accordance with a related transaction.[161] Where the debtor is obliged under the terms of the restructuring to pay **9.90**

149 Ibid., ss 373and 374.
150 Ibid., ss 373 and 375.
151 Ibid., ss 373 and 377.
152 Ibid., ss 373 and 378.
153 Subject to transitional provisions.
154 Ibid., ss 374(1A)(a), 375(4A)(a) and 377(2)(a).
155 Ibid., ss 374(1A)(b), 375(4A)(b) and 377(2)(b).
156 Ibid., s 307(2).
157 Ibid., s 307(3)(c).
158 Ibid., s 307(4)(a).
159 Ibid., s 307(4(b).
160 Ibid., s 307(4)(c).
161 Ibid., s 307(4)(d).

the creditors' costs, these will normally be deductible under the principles outlined above.

9.3.3 Debt restructuring—specific cases

9.91 Having examined the rules as they apply generally to a company's debt relationships, there follows a discussion of specific transactions typically undertaken in a debt restructuring.

9.3.3.1 Debt-for-debt exchange

9.92 One way of restructuring a company's debt is for the existing debt to be repaid either in full or partially out of new debt raised by issuing new bonds or from new borrowings. Although this might be seen as one transaction, the exchange of old debt for new, for tax purposes it is two transactions: the repayment of the old debt and the issue of the new debt, *albeit* that the old debt is never repaid by the debtor nor the new debt advanced to the debtor. The tax treatment will therefore follow the accounting treatment for each. Where the amount of the new debt is equal to that of the old, there should be no significant tax charge; however, in these circumstances the terms of the debt will be altered and this may result in a tax cost where, for example, the rate of interest alters with the consequence that the debtor will accrue a different amount and take a different deduction for tax purposes. Similarly, where the old debt is repurchased at a premium, relief will be given for it and, where it is bought in at a discount, the amount of the discount will be taxable. In recent years a practice developed of buying in the old debt into a company that was a member of the same group as, and therefore connected with, the debtor. The purpose of this was to take advantage of the exemptions to the rules in section 361, Corporation Taxes Act ('CTA') 2009. This was seen by HMRC as avoidance and the rules were amended in the Finance Act ('FA') 2010; this is dealt with in 9.112 below. The costs of issuing the new debt should be deductible in accordance with the principles set out above.[162]

9.93 Where the lender is connected with the borrower,[163] the connected party rules will apply. In this case the debtor will not get relief for any premium nor be taxed on any discount.[164] Similarly, the creditor will not get relief for any impairment loss or for any loss arising on the release.[165]

---

162 See 9.90 and CTA 2009, ss 307(2) and 308(1).

163 See 9.81–9.83 above.

164 CTA 2009, s 358.

165 Ibid., s 354. A loss arising on a release is referred to as a 'release debit'. Ibid., s 476.

9.3.3.2 Modifications of debt

9.94 The tax treatment of modification of debt for the debtor will follow the accounting treatment. The modification of the debt will only have tax consequences if it has financial consequences in the company's accounts. This may be the case where, for example, debt repayments are rescheduled and as a consequence accrued interest becomes payable in a different period. Where the parties are connected, the connected party rules will apply.

9.3.3.3 Debt-for-equity swaps

9.95 A debt-for-equity swap will involve the creditor foregoing some or all the debt in exchange for equity. Mechanistically, this can be achieved in a number of ways; for example, the debt could be treated as repaid and then immediately used to subscribe for shares (or vice versa) or alternatively, the debt can be treated as waived or released in consideration for an issue of shares.[166] In this latter case the waiver or release by the debtor will give rise to an accounting profit[167] which is then used to issue the share capital. Given this divergence of treatment, on 26 November 2009 the International Financial Reporting Committee ('IFRIC') issued Interpretation 19 'Extinguishing Financial Liabilities with Equity Instruments'.[168] IFRIC concluded that the issue of equity instruments was consideration paid to extinguish, either in whole or in part, a financial liability and fell within IAS 39.43. The issue of equity instruments could be seen as constituting two transactions: first, the issue of equity instruments by the debtor for cash; and, second, the payment of that cash by the debtor to the creditor to extinguish the liability. The difference between the carrying value of the liability extinguished and the fair value of the equity instruments issued is to be recognized through the profit and loss account.

9.96 In the UK the Urgent Issues Task Force issued information sheet 87 on 23 April 2010 asking for comments on the draft so as to maintain convergence of FRS 26 in the UK with IAS 39. Consequently this treatment will govern the loan relationship rules subject to specific statutory overrides.

9.97 Because the release of a debt gives rise to an accounting profit, without more the UK rules would mean that there was a taxable profit on the release.[169] In order to

[166] Although the debt-for-equity exchange is often stated to be structured in this way, in the author's opinion from a legal perspective it is difficult to see how this works; if the debt is waived or released in its entirety there is in theory nothing to issue the shares out of as the liability has ceased to exist.

[167] A credit to the P&L account on the basis that the liability has been extinguished.

[168] This International Accounting Standard is to be adopted for accounting periods after 1 July 2010, although earlier adoption is recommended.

[169] This assumes the parties are not connected.

prevent this, section 322, CTA 2009 provides that the company is not required to bring into account a credit in respect of the release, if the release is in consideration of shares forming part of the ordinary share capital of the debtor company or in consideration of any entitlement to such shares. This section therefore deals with debt-for-equity swaps. There are a number of points to note.

9.98 First, the shares issued in exchange for the debt must be ordinary shares. Ordinary shares are all the company's issued share capital (however described) other than capital the holders of which have a right to a dividend at a fixed rate but have no other right to share in the company's profits.[170] The creditor receiving the new shares may wish to structure the equity so as to preserve some sort of priority over existing equity holders; the rights attaching to the new shares need to be carefully structured so as not to make them something other than ordinary shares. Furthermore, notwithstanding the clear definition of ordinary share capital in the legislation, HMRC have indicated that they expect the shares to grant 'meaningful economic upside' to the creditor, thus implying that the shares ought to be retained (or the value associated with those shares ought to be retained) for a period of time, ie it is not enough that the shares will be worth something in the future; the former creditor, now equity holder, has to have some prospect of accessing that value—so an immediate sale of the shares at their current market value is unacceptable. From a theoretical point of view, this is understandable because the substance of the transaction is that the debt has been released but without the fiscal consequences of a debt release because some worthless shares were acquired and immediately disposed of; however, there is no authority for this gloss on what is otherwise clear legislation.

9.99 Secondly, where the debt is not in the parent company, but is in company further down the group because, for example, of previous structural subordination, it may be necessary to move the debt up to the ultimate parent company. The reason for this is that the debt must be exchanged for ordinary shares. It would therefore be possible for the creditor to own more than 25 per cent of the ordinary share capital in a subsidiary company of the group and, thus, for this company and its subsidiaries to no longer be members of the parent company's group. This would mean that group relief would no longer be available between the company in which the creditor becomes a shareholder and its subsidiaries and those companies above the company in which the creditor becomes a shareholder. The debt therefore should be moved up the group by way of novation so as to ensure that company is not 'degrouped'.[171]

---

[170] CTA 2010, s 1119.

[171] For group relief purposes, a company is a member of a group if it is a 75 per cent subsidiary. Such a grouping allows losses to be surrendered to a profitable company. Consequently, if a debt-for-equity swap gives the creditor 30 per cent of a subsidiary company, that company and any of its

The exchange of debt for equity in a subsidiary company could also degroup the company and its subsidiaries from the group above for capital gains tax purposes which might give rise to charges under section 179, Taxation of Chargeable Gains Act ('TCGA') 1992 on any asset which has been transferred between the two halves of the group in the previous six years before the degrouping event. **9.100**

Thirdly, the section refers to the right to entitlement to ordinary shares and this would encompass the situation where the creditor is given warrants in consideration for the release. **9.101**

As far as the creditor is concerned the release will result in an impairment loss or release debit. A debt-for-equity swap will be a 'conversion' for the purposes of section 132, TCGA 1992. Consequently it will be a reorganization within section 126, TCGA 1992. Loan relationships are qualifying corporate bonds and as such are not within the charge to corporation tax on chargeable gains. Where a loan relationship is exchanged for shares it is deemed to have been disposed of at its market value at the date of the reorganization and the replacement shares are deemed to have been acquired at that value.[172] Consequently, if the debt is converted into worthless shares or shares that are worth less than the nominal value of the debt, the creditor will obtain relief for the loss. **9.102**

Where the debt was held on trading account, provided the debt had not already been treated as impaired and a loss already taken to profit and loss account, the shares received in exchange for the debt will be fair valued on acquisition by the creditor and any loss or further loss accounted for at that time. **9.103**

9.3.3.3.1 Debt-for-equity swap creditor becoming connected The dichotomy between connected companies debt, where special rules apply, and unconnected companies debt, where the tax treatment follows the accounts, is brought into sharp focus where, as the result of a debt-for-equity swap, the creditor becomes connected with the debtor as a consequence of coming to control the debtor by acquiring more than 50 per cent of the debtor company's ordinary share capital. Because the rules state that where a company is connected at any point in the accounting period it will be treated as connected throughout the accounting period,[173] for the creditor the consequence of becoming connected would be that no relief would be available for the debt written off. In order to deal with this, section 356, CTA 2009 provides an exception to the normal rule,[174] by providing **9.104**

subsidiaries will not be able to surrender, or have surrendered to them, losses to any part of the group above the now 70 per cent shareholding.

[172] TCGA 1992, s 116(10)(a).

[173] CTA 2009, s 348(6).

[174] Ibid., s 354.

that an impairment loss or release debit[175] in relation to a liability to pay an amount to a company (the 'creditor company') under its creditor relationship is not prevented from being brought into account by section 354 if three conditions are satisfied: first, the creditor company treats the liability as being discharged; second, that it does so in consideration of (a) any shares forming part of the ordinary share capital of the company on which the liability would otherwise have fallen, or (b) any entitlement to such shares; and third, there would be no connection between the two companies for the accounting period in which the consideration is given if the question (whether there is such a connection) were determined by reference only to times before the creditor company (a) acquired possession of the shares or (b) acquired any entitlement to them.

9.105 It should be noted that this is a 'one-off' relief. It applies on the occasion of the creditor becoming connected with the debtor. If there is a further debt-for-equity swap after the companies have become connected, the creditor will get no relief for any impairment loss or release debit. As far as the debtor is concerned, once it is connected to the creditor it will not require the exemption under section 322, CTA 2009 whereby no loan relationship credit needs to be brought into account because it will now be connected to the creditor and the accounting rules will be overridden by section 353, CTA 2009.

9.106 The relief under section 356, CTA 2009 only applies to the debt that is treated as discharged in consideration for the issue of ordinary shares or any entitlement to such shares. If the creditor has different debts evidenced by different loan agreements and only one of them is subject to the debt-for-equity swap, the others will become connected party loan relationships on the happening of the debt-for-equity swap. The consequence of this is that they will now have to be accounted for on an amortized cost basis. Furthermore, the debtor will be required to bring into account for tax purposes a credit of an amount equal to the difference between the nominal value of the loan and 'the pre-connection carrying value', which is the amount that would be the carrying value of the asset representing the loan relationship in the creditor's accounts if a period of account had ended immediately before the companies became connected.[176]

9.107 The rationale behind this provision appears to be that the creditor will get a deduction for the write down when the companies are not connected (albeit that the debt still exists), but any subsequent release when the companies are connected will not be taxable because the companies will have become connected and the connected parties rules mean that the creditor cannot take a deduction (but already has when the parties were unconnected) and the debtor will not be taxable

---

175 Ibid., s 476(1).
176 Ibid., s 362.

on the profit on release. There is therefore asymmetry of treatment. The charge is therefore intended to tax the credit on the release for which relief has been given to the creditor but which would fall out of charge once the parties are connected.

Although a tax charge in such circumstances may give rise to an unexpected expense in the restructuring, it is likely, given the need for the restructuring, that the company will have losses that it may be able to use to reduce the tax charge. The impact of the tax charge will then be in the future when the company becomes profitable again and the losses that would otherwise be available to be carried forward and used against these profits will have been used on the profit arising on the release. **9.108**

9.3.4 Debt repurchases

Where debt is repurchased, the tax consequences will depend on whether the parties are connected or not. Where the parties are not connected the tax treatment will follow the accounts. Consequently, where the debt is trading in the market at a discount, a purchase by the debtor will give rise to a taxable credit equal to the difference between the liability extinguished and the price paid. **9.109**

Where the parties are connected, the creditor will not get an impairment loss but conversely the debtor will not be taxed on any discount. **9.110**

Again, the dichotomy between the connected companies provisions and those applying when there is no connection has led to the introduction of specific rules to cover perceived abuse. The most recent amendments were made by the FA 2010. In order to understand the changes it is necessary to look at the law as it was. **9.111**

Prior to the amendments, section 361, CTA 2009 applied if a company was a party to a loan relationship as a debtor and another company became a party to the loan relationship as a creditor and immediately afterwards the debtor and creditor were connected. If the acquisition was not at arm's length or there had been a connection between the companies in the three years beginning four years before the acquisition, the creditor was treated as having released its rights under the loan relationship when it acquired them. The purpose of the section was to prevent a company taking a deduction for an impairment loss and then, after becoming connected, releasing the debt with no tax consequence. However, the section would prejudice rescue situations where a third party bought a company's shares and at the same time bought the company's debt at a discount. Therefore, the condition as to not being connected within the three years beginning four years before the acquisition was included. In a genuine rescue situation there would have been no prior connection. However, as economic conditions worsened and companies' debt started to trade at a discount it became the practice for a company wishing to buy in its debt to set up a subsidiary to do it. The subsidiary **9.112** was connected and had not been connected in the three years commencing four years before the acquisition for the simple reason that the subsidiary did not then exist. Once the subsidiary had bought in the debt at a discount and satisfied the conditions of section 361, CTA 2009, it then simply released the parent from the liability to pay; however, being connected party debt, the parent did not need to recognize the credit for tax purposes when taken to the profit and loss account. By this means, the purpose of the section was defeated.

9.113 Section 361, CTA 2009 was amended by Schedule 15 to FA 2010 so as to remove the timing condition and in its place was substituted three 'relevant exceptions'. These are: first, the corporate rescue exception;[177] second, the debt-for-debt exception;[178] and third, the equity-for-debt exception.[179] Where one of these exceptions applies there is no deemed release on acquisition; however, if, subsequent to the acquisition, there is a release of those rights, if the corporate rescue exception or the debt-for-debt exception applied, the debtor is required to bring into account the credit that would have otherwise have to have been brought into account. There is no requirement to bring in any credit if the equity-for-debt exception applied. However, if one of the first two exceptions has applied, it will not be possible to avoid the tax charge on a subsequent release of the original debt, by swapping that debt for equity.[180]

9.114 Consequently, where a subsidiary now purchases in the debt a charge will arise unless one of the three exceptions applies, and if they do a charge will arise if the debt is subsequently released unless it was the equity-for-debt exception that applied.

9.3.5 Tax consequences of a change in control

9.115 Where there is a change in ownership or change of control of a company because of the debt restructuring, and particularly where there is a debt-for-equity swap, there may be a number of adverse consequences.

9.116 Trading losses carried forward may be lost if the change in ownership occurs three years either side of a major change in the nature or conduct of the company's trade or at any time after the scale of the company's activities have become small or negligible and before any considerable revival of the trade.[181] There are similar rules for other types of losses.[182]

---

177 Ibid., s 361A.
178 Ibid., s 361B.
179 Ibid., s 361C.
180 Ibid., s 322(4), CTA 2009.
181 CTA 2010, s 673O.
182 Ibid., s 677.

Changes in control can also trigger degrouping charges for corporation tax on chargeable gains[183] and also for stamp duty land tax purposes.[184] **9.117**

9.3.6 Conclusion

The UK rules for restructuring debt are quite narrow in scope. Provided the restructuring follows the tax legislation, most adverse consequences can be avoided. However, the narrow scope often means that much preparatory work can be required to fit the actual circumstances into ones which will not suffer adverse tax consequences. Similarly, a failure to appreciate some of the subtleties of the restructuring rules can result in unexpected tax consequences and increased tax costs. **9.118**

183 TCGA 1992, s 179.
184 FA 2003. Sch 7.

10

RESTRUCTURING OF STRUCTURED FINANCE TRANSACTIONS

10.1 Introduction

10.1.1 Upheaval in the global capital markets

The structured finance and securitization markets, which had their origins with the residential mortgage-backed securities first issued in the US in the late 1970s, had developed by the end of 2006 into a multi-trillion dollar global market. In addition to the traditional categories of mortgage loans, consumer credit, corporate trade receivables and corporate bank loans, a broad variety of financial assets had been securitized, and a number of complex investment products based upon securitization techniques, often combined with credit derivatives, had been developed and issued in large volume. Structured finance had come to account for a significant proportion of the world's source of financing, its growth catalyzed by, among other things, a quantum shift by banks from the 'originate and hold' model to one of 'originate and distribute,' in large part to transfer and spread risk. Growth was also driven by investor demand for yield in a market awash with liquidity. **10.01**

The structured finance market appeared to be booming, but there was growing unease over the decline of residential real estate values that had begun in certain **10.02** regions of the US by mid-2006, coupled with the volume and increasingly lax credit standards of US subprime mortgage lending. By late 2006, some observers, including academics and regulators, were expressing concern over the US subprime market developments, but were hopeful that the broad distribution of credit risk through securitization would mitigate the potential adverse effects.[1] It would not be long before the world learned otherwise.

10.03 In mid-2007, an upheaval in the global capital markets began that has not yet run its course. The underlying causes may be debated for years to come, but the immediate cause was the implosion of a mountain of leverage built upon subprime mortgage lending in the US, the effects of which were exacerbated by the further multiples of leverage and systemic risk created by credit derivatives. The subprime mortgages had been bundled into residential mortgage-backed securities ('RMBS'), which were then repackaged into, and often synthetically multiplied by, complex securities known as collateralized debt obligations, or 'CDOs' (CDOs with significant exposure to subprime RMBS are sometimes referred to in this chapter as 'subprime CDOs'). The CDOs in turn had been sold in enormous quantities to institutional investors around the world and the related risks were hedged (or risk positions taken) through a complex web of credit derivatives, the extent of which has not yet been fully quantified or unraveled.

10.04 In early July 2007, Moody's and Standard & Poor's announced downgrades of numerous tranches of subprime RMBS, placed hundreds of additional tranches on negative credit watch, and within days (joined by Fitch) placed hundreds of investment-grade tranches of subprime CDOs on watch for downgrade. These actions, and the waves of downgrades that soon followed, triggered a liquidity crisis, first in the asset-backed commercial paper ('ABCP') markets, then more broadly in the interbank funding and repo markets.[2] By the fall of 2007, the downgrades and illiquidity of subprime RMBS and CDO tranches had led to substantial mark-to-market losses by a number of major financial institutions. Among other revelations in the late spring of 2007 and the months that followed was that, despite the billions of dollars of CDO securities sold by the originating banks, a staggering amount of exposure to subprime mortgage risk had remained concentrated in the hands of relatively few financial institutions; among them, the

---

[1] Monetary and Capital Markets Department, Global Markets Monitoring and Analysis Division, of the International Monetary Fund, 'Financial Market Update' (December 2006) 1.

[2] The turmoil in the ABCP markets is believed to have been due primarily to concern over the degree to which the many structured investment vehicles and commercial paper conduit entities that depended on the commercial paper market for their funding were directly or indirectly exposed to subprime mortgage assets. See, on this issue, and generally on the causes and timeline of the liquidity crisis, G.B. Gorton, *Slapped by the Invisible Hand: The Panic of 2007* (Oxford University Press, Inc., 2010) 123–7, 148–52.

originating banks.[3] This occurred for a variety of reasons, including that, in the drive during 2006 and early 2007 to meet investor demand for high-yielding mezzanine tranches of CDOs, many banks had retained the 'super senior' tranches (the most difficult to shed, being the largest in size and lowest-yielding), having underestimated the risk of such securities, or having found it more difficult than expected to buy credit protection. In other cases, banks initially did transfer super senior tranches to off-balance sheet vehicles they had created but reacquired much of that exposure when they funded or purchased assets from those vehicles due to the difficulties in the ABCP markets.[4]

By the fall of 2008, further deterioration in the value of asset-backed securities, the shock to the global capital markets caused by the failure of Lehman Brothers and the near-failure of AIG, and the interconnections of the world's major financial institutions through a web of credit derivatives and other financial arrangements, came close to causing a meltdown of the global financial banking systems and securities markets.[5] Although government intervention averted that catastrophe, the economies of the US and many other countries remain fragile, growing slowly, if at all, and are vulnerable to new shocks. In this environment, major financial institutions and corporations have failed, and there is consideration of 'restructuring' everything from corporations to financial markets and regulatory systems. What, then, of the financial products that, although not the cause of the underlying dislocations in the global economies, precipitated and fuelled a crisis in spectacular fashion? Can they be restructured? The answer is a highly qualified . . . sometimes. **10.05**

10.1.2 Structured finance restructurings are opportunistic

The importance of structured finance products to the global capital markets and the sheer volume of these securities and associated derivatives contracts leads to a tendency to analogize the special purpose entities ('SPEs') that engage in these transactions to operating companies and to consider how they might be restructured. However, SPEs are nothing like operating companies; they share (when not **10.06**

[3] Losses on mezzanine tranches of CDOs apparently had been broadly dispersed globally, but losses on senior and super senior tranches were concentrated in a relatively small number of large financial institutions and monoline insurers. Bank for International Settlements (Basel Committee on Banking Supervision, The Joint Forum), 'Credit Risk Transfer Developments from 2005 to 2007' (July 2008) 10-11.

[4] Ibid. 14, 16.

[5] Among other things, major originators of subprime CDOs and others who had acquired exposure to those assets had attempted to shed risk (or were intermediating between buyers and sellers of that risk) through credit derivatives only to find that their counterparties did not have (or absent the government bailouts, would not have had) the financial strength to make the expected payments, or were contesting the contract terms.

organized as trusts) only the formalities of corporate organization, and even that with important modifications to achieve bankruptcy remoteness. SPEs are not designed to live indefinitely or to generate development and business opportunities internally. They have limited corporate purposes, do not have employees, are set up to run on automatic pilot with limited decision-making assigned to an administrator or investment advisor, do not produce anything (though some structures play a key role in financing manufacturing companies) and engage in transactions that are engineered constructs based on specific modelling assumptions. SPEs are designed to protect the debt securities they issue with over-collateralization and subordination, and sometimes other credit enhancement techniques, and, when multiple classes of debt securities are issued, to provide the greatest protection to the most senior class outstanding. The transaction documents governing structured finance securities generally have built-in mechanisms to redirect cash flows if the SPE experiences deterioration in the quality or performance of its assets, and in many structures control of remedies following a default is given to the most senior class. The existence of these types of provisions is a core reason restructurings are rare in the structured finance markets. Restructuring would involve overriding the mechanisms specifically provided for in the transaction documents and, accordingly, while potentially improving the outcome for some classes of investors, would undermine the expectations and contractual entitlements of others.

10.07 The ability to succeed in restructuring a structured finance transaction is opportunistic; in addition to the key structural issue mentioned above, multiple factors make restructuring impracticable in most instances of troubled or defaulted structured financings.[6] Because a structured finance vehicle is not an operating company but an engineered construct, its inability to repay the investment-grade securities issued typically implies one or more fundamental structural flaws (such as materially inaccurate data or assumptions relating to the credit quality of the underlying assets, or insufficient liquidity), a market dislocation that causes difficulty in valuing assets, or a combination of such factors. Most restructurings would involve substantive amendments to transaction documents, but structured financings often involve investors too numerous and/or of varying levels of sophistication to make a consent process feasible, even where investor interests may appear to be generally aligned. In addition, many structures involve multiple

[6] One exception is certain traditional structures, such as trade receivables, credit card securitizations or bank commercial paper conduits, where it may be possible for the sponsor of the programme (the manufacturing company or bank that originates the assets in question) to inject additional equity or other enhancement into an existing structure without the consent of other parties. However, providing that type of support can raise legal and other issues—including the integrity of the 'true sale' analysis as well as tax and accounting issues—that require consideration and in some circumstances may preclude the action from being taken.

classes of securities with strongly competing interests. Legal issues, including securities laws, often overlaid with cross-border complications, may present an obstacle to restructuring. Tax and accounting considerations also often present significant challenges. Moreover, opportunities for judicially-aided restructurings are limited by the 'bankruptcy remoteness' features that typically restrict the ability of a special purpose entity to voluntarily file a bankruptcy petition and prohibit its investors from putting it into involuntary bankruptcy. Thus, for many transaction types, achieving a successful restructuring could require flouting the bankruptcy remoteness principles that underlie structured finance.

10.1.3 Factors that enable a restructuring to occur

Notwithstanding the many reasons for which restructuring is atypical in the structured finance markets, in some cases a confluence of factors may make it feasible. **10.08** This may occur, for example, if the problem with the transaction is primarily a liquidity issue, with assets retaining substantial intrinsic value, coupled with there being investors that are relatively few in number and consist substantially of sophisticated institutions, and/or a court process that can provide legal certainty to the negotiated outcome and protection from third party claims. Occasionally, more subtle factors may come into play, such as political considerations, the existence of business relationships between parties, or the avoidance of reputational risk.

Discussed immediately below are certain practical and legal issues commonly **10.09** faced in the context of distressed or defaulted structured finance transactions, followed by a discussion of transaction types that were particularly significant in the period leading up to and during the financial crisis, the characteristics that make them more or less susceptible to being restructured, and examples of some notable restructurings. Because of the cross-border nature of many structured financings and the similarity of the structures discussed, whether documented under New York law or English law, the material is organized primarily by transaction type and structural considerations rather than by legal jurisdiction.

10.2 Issues in restructuring

10.2.1 Practical issues

10.2.1.1 Identifying the creditor constituency

Among the challenging issues following the failure of a structured finance transac- **10.10** tion is to identify and then coordinate discussions between the various creditor constituencies. Although generally required to be sophisticated institutional investors (at least for the transaction types discussed in this chapter), the creditors can vary widely in financial sophistication, from large financial institutions, pension funds and hedge funds to other commercial entities that may be less familiar with the intricacies of structured finance products and, sometimes, middle-market companies, small municipalities and even natural persons. The interests of such creditor groups can vary widely, making it difficult and time intensive to reach a consensus.

10.11 Although not uniquely a structured finance problem, the form in which securities are issued by SPEs also can pose practical difficulties. Securities usually are issued in the form of global notes held by a depository on behalf of a clearing system for the benefit of the participants of that clearing system. The SPEs communicate with the participants (normally financial institutions) only indirectly, through the clearing system. In addition, there usually are a number of intermediaries, such as brokers, between the participant and the end investor. This indirect path adds time and complexity to the process of communicating with investors.

10.12 While some structured finance transactions are held by a relatively small number of investors, there usually is a large number of ultimate investors who must act through noteholder meetings whereby they instruct a trustee to take action. The trustee is appointed by the SPE under an indenture, trust deed, or similar instrument, to protect the interests of and serve as the interface with the noteholders.

10.13 It is not the business of the trustee to make commercial decisions or take risk. Although the transaction documents sometimes permit, or require, that the trustee exercise its discretion following a default, the trustee ordinarily will act only in accordance with the instructions of the noteholders and, even then, only if it has received a satisfactory form of indemnity. Meetings are expensive and time-consuming to coordinate and agreeing on the form of indemnity can be a challenge.

10.2.1.2 Advising creditors

10.14 While holders of subordinated securities generally will be treated separately in any restructuring discussions involving senior creditors, it is important for the trustee and senior creditors (and, in England, the receiver, if appointed) to meet and discuss the various options with a view to developing a consensual approach to a possible restructuring. Such discussions also can address intercreditor issues of the type that ordinarily require resolution before the restructuring itself is embarked upon, such as payment waterfall priorities, or actual or threatened litigation. Resolving such issues can take a significant period of time.

10.15 Typically, an ad hoc committee of senior creditors will be formed and will appoint counsel and a financial adviser to advise the committee. Because committee counsel advises the group as a whole, it must take care not to become embroiled in intercreditor or other issues where it may not be able to act impartially. It is therefore common for each creditor (or sub-groups of creditors) to appoint its own counsel to advise independently but, at the same time, liaise and co-ordinate with committee counsel. The fees of committee counsel, together with those of any financial adviser appointed, typically can be paid by the trustee as an administrative expense under the governing documents, provided that the trustee first receives a direction to do so by the requisite percentage of creditors under the governing documents, together with an indemnity in acceptable form. Otherwise, creditors generally are expected to cover the cost of their own counsel.

10.2.1.3 Maintaining confidentiality

It is important that price-sensitive information provided to the senior creditors be treated confidentially and that recipients of such information agree not to trade in securities issued by the SPE or any affiliate to avoid any breaches of applicable securities law (for example rules relating to market abuse or insider trading) by not only those creditors but the SPE as well. A confidentiality agreement is usually entered into between members of a senior creditors' committee and the trustee, and potentially other key transaction parties, and best practice would suggest this should be done. The committee then becomes a restricted creditors committee whose main function will be to liaise with the various interested parties and, where appropriate, their advisers, and often to liaise with unrestricted creditors as well, provided that the unrestricted creditors have accepted the appointment of the restricted creditor committee and have agreed to be bound by other terms deemed appropriate. **10.16**

10.2.1.4 Tax and accounting considerations

Any attempt to restructure a structured finance transaction is virtually certain to raise tax and accounting issues. For example, SPEs generally are structured so as to avoid being subject to entity-level income taxes and any tampering with the structure may affect that treatment or the income tax treatment of the holders of the securities the SPE has issued. Among potential issues under the US income tax rules, a restructuring that causes one or more classes of the SPE's interests that had been treated as debt for income tax purposes to be treated as equity for those purposes could, potentially, change an SPE's tax classification from that of a 'branch' (or 'disregarded entity') to a partnership or, even more dramatically, a 'publicly-traded partnership taxable as a corporation'. Moreover, because the income tax treatment of an SPE often is based upon its being formed and conducting its corporate affairs in a jurisdiction that does not impose a corporate income tax, even the manner and jurisdiction in which restructuring negotiations are conducted and decisions are made potentially can affect the characterization for tax purposes of where the SPE is deemed to be resident (eg where it is managed and controlled under UK income tax principles), or doing business, and therefore potentially **10.17** subject to taxation. Accounting issues also are likely to arise, both of a type that can be encountered in any restructuring of debt (such as recognition of gain or loss) or issues specific to SPEs, such as whether off-balance sheet vehicles maintain that status or become consolidated with an affiliated operating company.

10.18 The specific issues raised will vary substantially depending on the type of structure involved, the manner in which the proposed restructuring is to be effected, the relevant jurisdictions, often the type of assets involved, and other facts and circumstances pertinent to a particular transaction. In addition, certain issues may be of great concern to one set of transaction parties and not others. For example, a particular tax or accounting issue may be material to the holder of an equity tranche or residual interest, but not to senior noteholders, or vice versa, such that different interest groups within a transaction may have to retain separate advisors. Discussion of tax and accounting issues is beyond the scope of this chapter, except to note that experts in those areas should be retained as early as possible in a potential restructuring to advise the relevant party or parties (eg trustee, receiver, transaction sponsor, noteholder group, equity holder, etc.) so that the parties can assess the tax or accounting consequences and factor them in appropriately before taking any actions that might have, potentially irreversible, adverse effects.

10.2.2 Legal issues

10.2.2.1 Securities laws

10.19 Participants in any restructuring must comply with applicable securities laws in any trading of securities and any solicitation to purchase securities from other securityholders. To the extent securityholders are working with the issuer to effect a restructuring, they may become privy to confidential information and under US and UK securities laws, as applicable, will be restricted from trading with counterparties who do not have access to such information. In some situations a securityholder may seek to acquire a percentage of securities of the same class or another class to have a bigger influence in actions to be taken or, in some restructurings, a financial institution may seek to acquire securities to effect a 'vertical slice' transaction, as occurred in the case of certain distressed SIVs. In certain circumstances the US tender offer rules[7] could apply to such solicitations if not conducted as individual negotiations and compliance with those rules generally would be commercially unfeasible.

[7] The Williams Act of 1968 amended the Securities and Exchange Act of 1934 (15 USCA, s 78a et seq.) to regulate the conduct of cash tender offers; see ss 13(d) and (e) and 14(d)-(f) of the Securities Exchange Act of 1934.

10.2.2.2 Bankruptcy remoteness

10.20 SPEs are structured as 'bankruptcy remote' entities. While there are some differences in SPE bankruptcy remoteness requirements depending on whether New York or English law governs the transaction documents, as well as variations for particular structures or due to the law of the jurisdiction in which the SPE is formed, certain key features are typical of most SPEs that are structured to be bankruptcy remote.[8] These common features include: (a) the SPE is restricted to engaging in the business and activities necessary to carry out its role in the transaction, (b) the SPE grants a security interest in its assets to a trustee or collateral agent for the benefit of its noteholders and certain other transaction parties, (c) the SPE may incur only permitted debt,[9] and (d) noteholders and other transaction parties agree not to initiate bankruptcy or insolvency proceedings against the SPE, typically until the expiration of a stated period (determined by reference to preference periods under applicable bankruptcy law) following the payment in full of the SPE's debt obligations. These requirements are intended to make it less likely that the SPE would become subject to bankruptcy or analogous proceedings, and consequently to the potential delays in distributions, loss of rights to collateral or other potential changes to contract terms that may occur in such proceedings.

10.21 In addition, for financing structures that involve an operating company parent and a securitization subsidiary, and either entity is potentially subject to US bankruptcy law, a key goal of structuring the subsidiary as a bankruptcy remote SPE is to isolate it, to the extent possible, from the effects of a bankruptcy of its parent or other operating company affiliates.[10] In such transactions, another key bankruptcy remoteness requirement, designed to lessen the likelihood that the parent entity could put its SPE subsidiary into bankruptcy, is that such SPEs have one or more directors (or managers, in the case of LLCs) independent of the parent or other operating company affiliates. The independence requirement is coupled with a requirement that the unanimous consent of all directors be obtained before

[8] Over time, bankruptcy remoteness and related 'SPE criteria' have developed as an amalgam of rating agency requirements and the factors deemed necessary by transaction counsel in order to give the legal opinions, such as 'non-consolidation' opinions, that are required as a condition to closing of many types of structured finance transactions.

[9] For many structures, permitted debt will be only the debt issued upon a single closing date, while other types of structures may involve continuous offerings of securities (such as commercial paper or medium term notes), or separate series of debt issued on multiple occasions. But any incurrence of debt will be subject to the satisfaction of specific conditions and requirements.

[10] A related, but distinct, goal in such structures is to reduce the likelihood that the assets and liabilities of the SPE could be substantively consolidated with those of the parent, should the parent become subject to bankruptcy proceedings. To mitigate the risk of substantive consolidation, SPEs in such structures generally are subject to a litany of corporate separateness requirements, such as being adequately capitalized for the business to be conducted, not commingling assets, and observing corporate formalities.

the filing by the SPE of a voluntary bankruptcy proceeding, and the organizational documents for this type of SPE usually require that the independent director(s) consider the interests of the SPE and its creditors (rather than those of the parent entity, its shareholder) in determining whether to consent to a voluntary filing by the SPE. However, recent developments in the context of the market for commercial mortgage-backed securities, or 'CMBS' have raised concern about the degree to which bankruptcy remoteness techniques can be relied upon; these developments are discussed below under 'Commercial mortgage-backed securities'.

10.2.2.3 Receivership as a restructuring tool

10.22 Under English law, receivership is an enforcement procedure available to secured creditors arising out of the relevant charge document. This is the case for both receivers and managers under a fixed charge and also administrative receivers under either a floating charge or a qualifying floating charge,[11] as further discussed below. Application can also be made to the court for the appointment of a receiver and manager in circumstances where, for example, there is an urgent need to protect and preserve secured assets.

10.23 The principal definition of an administrative receiver is set out in section 29(2) of the Insolvency Act 1986:

(a) a receiver or manager of the whole (or substantially the whole) of a company's property appointed by or behalf of the holders of any debentures of the company secured by a charge which, as created, was a floating charge, or by such a charge and one or more other securities; or
(b) a person who would be such a receiver or manager but for the appointment of some other person as the receiver of part of the company's property.

10.24 By contrast, a fixed charge receiver is normally appointed under a security instrument over specific assets and usually has powers more limited than those of an administrative receiver. A fixed charge receiver does not benefit automatically from the many statutory advantages of an administrative receiver.[12] Rather, a fixed

---

[11] Prior to 15 September 2003 a creditor who had a floating charge over the whole (or substantially the whole) of the property of a company could appoint an administrative receiver. From 15 September 2003 the Enterprise Act 2002 amended the Insolvency Act 1986 with the effect that the ability to appoint administrative receivers became much more limited. Now, only the holder of a qualifying floating charge may appoint administrative receivers. A qualifying floating charge is a floating charge created on or after 15 September 2003 where one of the statutory exceptions applies—a capital market arrangement, a public-private partnership, a utility project, an urban regeneration project, a project financing, a financial markets arrangement, an arrangement with a registered social landlord or an arrangement with a protected railway or other special companies.

[12] An administrative receiver automatically enjoys wide statutory powers conferred by Sch 1, Insolvency Act 1986, which include the powers to raise or borrow money and grant security over the company's property, to bring or defend any action or other legal proceedings in the name and

charge receiver derives his powers from the Law of Property Act 1925, usually as those statutory powers are amended and extended by the terms of the mortgage deed, given that the powers within that Act are generally considered to be too limited to be of much practical use.

In an attempted restructuring, English law receivership may provide a relative advantage to SPEs that have documents governed by English law, compared to those that have documents governed by New York law. Receivership has been shown to be a useful tool in dealing with defaulted or distressed structured finance transactions, although issues may arise concerning the type of receiver that can be appointed. **10.25**

When an SPE is formed under the law of a country other than England, which often is the case even where the transaction documents are governed by English law, formal English insolvency proceedings such as administration or liquidation are of little or no relevance or use, because the SPE generally will have its centre of main interests ('COMI') in a jurisdiction other than England. In addition, as discussed above, SPEs typically are structured to be bankruptcy remote (albeit, not bankruptcy proof) and their transaction documents are intended to discourage bankruptcy or insolvency proceedings. Any case for the assertion of jurisdiction is made even more difficult by the fact that it is normal for SPEs to be structured so as to have no connection to England. **10.26**

English law receivership is a contractually based enforcement technique for secured creditors. The very fact that it is not recognized as a collective insolvency proceeding for the purposes of the EU Regulation on Insolvency Proceedings (1346/2000) means that it has the potential to be a useful restructuring tool in dealing with distressed foreign SPEs (as, for example, proved to be the case with SIVs, a structure discussed below). Even though a security trust deed will normally make provision for a floating charge (which, if created pre 15 September 2003 or if a qualifying floating charge with the application of the capital market arrangement exception,[13] would enable an administrative receiver to be appointed), for foreign SPEs difficult issues are raised whether the security trustee can appoint an administrative receiver or whether the better view is that he should appoint a fixed charge receiver to deal with the secured assets. This is because a foreign SPE **10.27**

on behalf of the company, and to present or defend a petition for the winding up of the company. These powers can be, and usually are, incorporated in security documents by express reference to Sch 1, Insolvency Act 1986, thereby giving to a fixed charge receiver the same powers albeit, by the nature of the fixed charge receiver's appointment, applicable to less extensive assets.

[13] An administrative receiver can be appointed in pursuance of an agreement that is or forms part of a capital market arrangement if a party incurs (or is expected to incur) a debt of at least £50 m during the life of the arrangement and the arrangement involves the issue of a capital market investment (s 72B, Insolvency Act 1986).

will not fall within the definition of 'company' under section 1 of the Companies Act 2006 (formerly section 735(1) of the Companies Act 1985) thereby appearing to create difficulty for an administrative receiver (as defined by section 29 of the Insolvency Act 1986) to be appointed. The decision whether to appoint a fixed charge receiver is not burdened by such jurisdictional issues. However, to try to benefit from the more extensive appointment provided by an administrative receivership, or to ensure that all interested parties, in particular the security trustee and the receivers themselves, understand the full nature and extent of the appointment, consideration has been given in appropriate situations to the *Bulk Commodities* case.[14] In that case, the court noted that the definition of 'company' used in the Companies Act 1985 applies 'unless a contrary intention appears'. The court then applied the contrary intention proviso, stating that the provisions relating to administrative receivers apply both to companies registered under the Companies Acts and to unregistered (or foreign) companies. Even though an entity was an unregistered company (under the Companies Act), it may nevertheless have become subject to an administrative receivership appointment if the facts supported its being an appointment over the whole or substantially the whole of a company's property. That ruling proved important in dealing with SIVs that had suffered enforcement events, but will not be available for future restructurings of foreign SPEs, because the Companies Act 2006 (Consequential Amendments, Transitional Provisions and Savings) Order 2009 effectively overruled the judgment in the *Bulk Commodities* case by the introduction of a new section 28 into the Insolvency Act 1986. With effect from 1 October 2009, the ability to appoint administrative receivers of foreign companies has been removed.

10.28 When an SPE suffers an enforcement event or event of default, the security constituted by the deed of charge will normally become enforceable, whereupon the security trustee typically will become exclusively entitled to exercise any and all rights in relation to the secured assets or collateral[15] or, if it so elects, to appoint a receiver. Prior to the appointment of a receiver, issues concerning the SPE and its assets must be dealt with by the security trustee on behalf of the various secured creditor constituencies and other transaction parties with an interest in the collateral. The views held on a broad range of issues can be extremely diverse and, though the formation of an informal and restricted steering committee can assist, the process can be slow and burdensome, leading some parties to become frustrated. This can be exacerbated by the acutely risk-averse approach taken by the

[14] *Re International Bulk Commodities Ltd* [1993] Ch 77.

[15] The floating charge over the SPE's assets generally will be converted immediately and without notice into a fixed charge on the occurrence of a specified and related event, such as the delivery of an acceleration notice.

majority of trustees. No criticism is intended; it is well understood that the trustee role is circumscribed and that they are not paid to assume risk. The practical result, however, can be that few important decisions concerning the operation of a distressed SPE are effected in short order.

Against this backdrop, there are a number of advantages to the trustee's appointing a receiver. In England, receivers of SPEs have been partners in large and well-respected international firms of accountants. They are used to dealing with large and complex cases with multi-layered, and often fragmented, creditor groups and can quickly bring stability to a difficult and challenging situation. **10.29**

A receiver of an SPE will act as its agent resulting in a useful practical separation from the security trustee. There is no principal/agency relationship between the security trustee and the receiver unless the former intermeddles in the decisions of the receiver in carrying out his duties and obligations to his appointor (generally, the security trustee on behalf of the secured creditors). **10.30**

In theory, the actions of a receiver can effectively override requirements in the security trust deed for consents and majority approvals of secured creditors when important decisions need to be taken. For example, receivers have the authority to settle actual or threatened litigation and to dispose of the entirety of the asset portfolio. That said, receivers normally seek such formal confirmations before taking any important steps and indeed, there may be an insistence by the security trustee for them to do so. Taking into account the diverse interests of the secured creditors and other transaction parties that generally will be involved in the restructuring of an SPE, the building of a consensus is critically important and receivers are well placed to do so. **10.31**

10.3 Transaction types

10.3.1 The rise and fall of structured investment vehicles

For banks and other financial institutions, an important financial engineering tool was the use of off-balance sheet structures. One such structure was the structured investment vehicle ('SIV'). **10.32**

10.3.1.1 The SIV structure

An SIV is a special purpose investment company, usually incorporated in a jurisdiction such as the Cayman Islands, the Channel Islands, the Republic of Ireland or the Netherlands Antilles, that provides the benefit of a low or zero corporate tax regime. An SIV generally funds itself by a mixture of, in order of seniority: (a) senior debt in the form of ABCP, with short maturity periods, commonly a maximum of 175 days; (b) medium-term notes; and (c) capital notes representing **10.33** equity-like funding. The ABCP typically would be A-1/P-1 rated and the medium-term notes typically were triple-A rated. Although SIVs in the aggregate obtained most of their funding though US medium-term notes (particularly after the initial asset-acquisition period),[16] they also relied substantially on the issuance of ABCP in the US and European markets. The so-called 'SIV-Lite' variant of the structure was more highly leveraged, typically held relatively riskier assets and relied even more heavily on ABCP funding.[17] Before the onset of the financial crisis, SIVs made healthy returns for investors in their capital notes from the net spread between their cost of funding (short and medium term, with the highest ratings for those categories, and therefore relatively inexpensive) and the yield on the SIV's asset portfolio (longer term, generally less highly rated, and therefore relatively high return). The investment manager would generate fees from its management of the asset portfolio and would also share in the profits. These portfolios generally comprised investment-grade debt securities including RMBS (based on prime, sub-prime and 'Alternative-A' mortgage loans)[18] and CDOs. At the height of SIV investment, these vehicles held in the order of $400 bn in assets.[19]

10.3.1.2 Impact of the financial crisis

10.34 The SIV structure, now virtually extinct, was among the most high profile of the failed structured finance products following the onset of the financial crisis, due to the fundamental mismatch between short-term liabilities and long-term assets when liquidity for rolling over short-term liabilities and for selling assets both disappeared. As discussed above, by mid-2007 defaults in the US subprime market had caused the rating agencies to begin downgrading subprime RMBS securities and CDOs based on those securities, and a crisis of confidence in the credit markets began. For SIVs, the lack of market liquidity adversely affected both their ability to fund themselves and their ability to sell portfolio holdings. The dramatic effect on SIVs resulted from the almost immediate withdrawal of liquidity in the ABCP market due to investor concern about SIVs' exposure to mortgage-backed assets. Because SIVs were so dependent on the ABCP market for funding, urgent action had to be taken to prevent a series of collapses.[20] However, SIVs found it

[16] This was the case at least through the end of 2005. See, C. Polizu, 'An Overview of Structured Investment Vehicles and Other Special Purpose Companies' in A. De Servigny and N. Jobst (eds), *The Handbook of Structured Finance* (The McGraw-Hill Companies, 2007) 627-32.

[17] The Cairn and Golden Key vehicles discussed below were SIV-Lites.

[18] Alternative-A, or 'Alt-A', mortgages are US residential mortgages that are not considered subprime but do not conform to 'prime' criteria in one or more respects, such as limited documentation of income, highly leveraged borrowers or higher loan-to-value ratios.

[19] J. Hughes, 'Completion of SIV asset disposal near' *Financial Times*, 7 July 2009.

[20] Unlike ABCP conduits, which generally were required to have bank liquidity lines equal to 100 per cent of their outstanding ABCP, SIVs typically had coverage of only around 20 per cent.

difficult to sell their portfolio holdings, particularly any mortgage-backed or other asset-backed securities. The SIV structure had been undermined by market conditions in which (a) the market values of investment grade securities no longer reflected their high ratings, (b) over-collateralization of liabilities was a formula that no longer functioned when assets were illiquid, and (c) the ABCP market, long considered to be stable and liquid, had frozen.

The impact on SIVs varied depending on whether liquidity support from the sponsor or another source was readily available. Unsurprisingly, a fire-sale of portfolio assets was considered to be an option of last resort because of a lack of willing buyers and resulting depressed market prices. Also, with a number of SIVs facing potential insolvency, there was the risk of a widespread offloading of assets onto the market, thereby exerting further downward pressure on bids. Some SIVs with bank or financial institution sponsors were taken back on balance sheet or were provided with backstop facilities to safeguard the market reputation of the sponsor. This happened in the case of Citigroup's SIVs (Beta, Centauri, Dorada, Five, Sedna, Vetra and Zela)[21] and HSBC's SIVs (Cullinan and Asscher) among others. Cairn Capital, a hedge fund based in London, was able to successfully refinance the commercial paper funding for its HGF SIV with a term loan from Barclays Capital. However, those unable to obtain sponsor or third-party support were forced to take steps to meet immediate payment obligations, the most pressing of which was maturing ABCP that could no longer be rolled. Actions taken included the use of breakable deposits, drawing down fully on liquidity facilities, arranging repo agreements with creditors and auctioning asset portfolios. Unfortunately, with underlying asset values depreciating rapidly, these steps proved insufficient and many SIVs breached their net asset value and/or liquidity tests, precipitating a series of restructurings, note payment defaults and significant deleveraging. **10.35**

10.3.1.3 Restructuring options

One major challenge in any SIV restructuring is to meet the expectations of a **10.36**
diverse and generally sophisticated secured creditor constituency. Optionality and flexibility are therefore key. Some secured creditors are only interested in retaining the possibility of receiving par at some point in the future and will

This reduced level of liquidity support was thought to be adequate due to structural features such as limits on the amount of debt that could mature in a given period and tests (including market value overcollateralization tests, which if not satisfied required the sale of assets) that SIVs were required to run frequently. But in the extreme market dislocations of 2007 and 2008, those protections proved insufficient.

[21] Citigroup consolidated its SIVs in mid-December 2007 only after months of work among Citigroup, Bank of America and JPMorgan Chase, at the behest of the US Treasury Department, to design a SIV bail-out fund (the Master Liquidity Enhancement Conduit, or 'M-LEC'). In late December 2007 it was announced that the M-LEC structure would be abandoned.

oppose any proposed write-down. Others may want a quick cash exit, even if at a level substantially below par value. Some may want or need to hold only A-1 or P-1 rated paper.

10.37 Although each case is different, there have tended to be three overarching options:

- maintain the status quo (hold the portfolio and wait for asset appreciation or cashflow repayment);
- sell the portfolio to a third party;
- sell the portfolio to a Newco (cash/par notes/notes in Newco/'vertical slice' of portfolio). Mezzanine and capital noteholders may realize an immediate loss on sale.

10.38 Another major challenge is timing. Senior creditors often desire that the SIV's problems be dealt with as soon as possible. If the proposals involve a restructuring, there may be a myriad of issues that require resolution before this can be commenced. Factors vary from case to case, but can include disputes over priority under payment waterfalls, actual or threatened litigation, indemnity and costs issues involving the trustee, the receivers and the relevant clearing systems and how interest is to be dealt with where ABCP has been issued with different terms as to interest entitlement.

10.39 *Cheyne Finance* was the first of the distressed SIVs to adopt a restructuring proposal that had the attraction for secured creditors of optionality and flexibility. The major elements of the Cheyne Finance restructuring have been used in one form or another in subsequent transactions, some of which are currently being negotiated, although it is important to stress again, that because SIV structures vary so widely, each case must turn upon its own facts and documentation.

10.40 In *Cheyne Finance*, the receivers sought proposals from a number of investment banks and selected one submitted by Goldman Sachs for a restructuring transaction that provided four options for creditors:

- cash exit (this would also apply to creditors who failed to make an election);
- pass through notes issued by Gryphon, a Goldman Sachs vehicle;
- zero coupon notes issued by Goldman Sachs that would benefit from its credit rating;
- for creditors electing for Gryphon pass through notes only, the ability to surrender the notes to Gryphon in return for a strip of the old portfolio on a pro rata basis which they could then manage themselves.

10.41 The restructuring was based upon an auction of a vertical strip of the asset portfolio. The percentage of the portfolio that was to become the strip to be put up for auction depended upon the proportion of creditors electing the cash or zero coupon note options. On this basis of calculation, 20 per cent of the portfolio was auctioned. A total of 11 investment banks were invited by the receivers to bid for the assets.

The balance of the portfolio was sold to Goldman Sachs based upon the price paid at the auction but pro rated. The proceeds from the auction and the sale of the balance of the portfolio to Goldman Sachs were paid to the receivers in order that they could distribute cash to creditors in accordance with Cheyne Finance's documentation and, in particular, in accordance with the priorities set out in the payment waterfall provisions. **10.42**

10.3.1.4 Legal developments in the SIV context

The market crisis that befell the SIVs, as well as certain drafting issues common in SIV documentation, have generated a significant amount of case law by English courts in a short period of time. While much of the analysis is specific to the SIV model, some of these rulings may prove to have relevance for issues arising in other types of structured finance transactions that are distressed or in default. **10.43**

10.3.1.4.1 Insolvency The English courts have had the opportunity to analyse, in the case of SIVs, the impact of extreme market volatility, upon the solvency or, conversely, the insolvency of the vehicle. **10.44**

Section 123(1)(e) of the Insolvency Act 1986 provides that: 'A company is deemed unable to pay its debts if it is proved to the satisfaction of the court that the company is unable to pay its debts as they fall due.' This is the 'commercial' or 'cashflow' test under which the court will determine if, on the evidence, the company is paying its debts as they fall due. **10.45**

Section 123(2) of the Insolvency Act 1986 provides that: 'A company is also deemed unable to pay its debts if it is proved to the satisfaction of the court that the value of the company's assets is less than the amount of its liabilities, taking into account its contingent and prospective liabilities.' This is the 'balance sheet' test under which a company is deemed to be unable to pay its debts if there is a shortfall of assets to liabilities, including contingent and prospective liabilities. **10.46**

It is possible for a company to be insolvent under the cashflow test but not under the balance sheet test or vice versa. These tests are determined by a court as a matter of fact after evidence has been adduced. **10.47**

In the *Cheyne Finance* case[22] the English Companies Court decided that the commercial or cashflow test of insolvency under section 123(1)(e) of the Insolvency Act 1986 does not exclude the consideration of prospective or contingent debts **10.48**

---

22 *Cheyne Finance plc (in receivership)* [2007] EWHC 2402 (Ch) *(Cheyne No. 2)*.

and that the standard of proof to be used in proving the inability to pay debts was on a balance of probabilities.

10.49 The judge considered that there were two issues to be decided:

- first, whether it is permissible to consider senior debts falling due in the future when making a determination under the commercial or cashflow test (the so-called 'futurity' question); and
- second, what standard of proof is required whether a company is, or is about to become, unable to pay its relevant debts as they fall due, in order for a receiver to properly make a determination with regard to whether an 'insolvency event' has occurred.

10.50 As to the futurity question, senior creditors with short maturity dates had argued that the parties had agreed to a deliberate omission of section 123(2) of the Insolvency Act 1986 from the relevant documentation, and that, accordingly, the receivers had to apply the commercial or cash flow test in section 123(1)(e) of the Insolvency Act 1986, which omits all contingent and prospective liabilities. The court rejected that argument for the following reasons:

- first, that before the forerunner to the Insolvency Act 1986 (the Insolvency Act 1985) the courts had considered the question of inability to pay debts without any distinction between a balance sheet insolvency and a commercial insolvency and a submission that commercial insolvency could not be established by reference to future debts before 1985 would have been unsuccessful (*Byblos Bank Sal v Al-Khudhairy*[23] considered);
- second, that there was no English authority to support the view that because only section 123(2) of the Insolvency Act 1986 expressly referred to contingent and prospective liabilities, there could be no consideration of future debts under section 123(1)(e) (the court made reference to a considerable volume of Australian authority indicating that a commercial insolvency test allowed references to debts that would fall due in the future); the addition of the words 'as they fall due' in section 123(1)(e) was synonymous with 'become due' and amounted to a futurity requirement; and
- third, that the parties chose to define 'insolvency event' by reference to section 123(1) and not section 123(2) because they wanted the company's solvency or insolvency to be adjudicated on the basis of a commercial test as opposed to a balance sheet test.

10.51 As a result, the court held that the definition of 'insolvency event' allowed the receivers to consider the company's ability to pay senior debts falling due in the future.

[23] *Byblos Bank Sal v Al-Khudhairy* [1987] BCLC 232.

On the standard of proof issue, the court held that in considering whether or not the company is or is about to become unable to pay its senior debts as they fall due on a balance of probabilities, the receivers must be satisfied (after inquiry) that inability to pay is more likely than not. 10.52

In *Invertec Ltd v De Mol Holding BV*[24] Arnold J., in discussing the futurity concept raised in *Cheyne Finance,* stated: 10.53

> In deciding whether V was able to pay its debts as they fell due on 6 October 2005 one must consider not merely those debts which were actually due that date, but also those debts falling due in the future, and in particular those falling due soon. This, of course, also entails consideration of the resources which will be, or are reasonably expected to be, available to the company to pay those future debts when they fall due.

It is clear from the *Cheyne Finance* example that each case will turn upon its specific facts and the evidence that can be adduced. In *Cheyne Finance,* the court gave no indication of how far into the future a creditor is entitled to look when asserting that a company fails or will fail the commercial test. For companies that have ceased trading, as was the case with Cheyne Finance, it is arguable that coming to a conclusion of insolvency that is supported by the evidence would be far easier than for a company that is continuing to trade. Furthermore, although there appears to be no limit to the futurity element, logic would seem to dictate that the further into the future a creditor looks, even if it can show that there is a point in time where the company will not be able to pay its debts, the greater may be the influence of external factors or variables that might affect the outcome to a material degree, whether positively or negatively from the creditor's perspective. 10.54

10.3.1.4.2 Pari passu or 'pay as you go'? A number of failed SIVs (Cheyne Finance,[25] Whistlejacket,[26] Sigma,[27] and Golden Key[28]) have been the subject of scrutiny by the English courts, for the first time throwing a spotlight on the interpretation of clauses in security trust deeds and related documentation that previously had received little attention. Until the financial crisis, there had been no need to consider the order of payment as between creditors upon the distress or insolvency of an SIV, as no such distress situations or insolvencies had occurred. 10.55

The arguments put before the courts in these cases concerned whether or not, even given contractual terms to the contrary, the *pari passu* principle of distribution should be applied to payments under the relevant structure in a situation of distress or insolvency or whether, on a close and strict interpretation of the 10.56

[24] *Invertec Ltd v De Mol Holding BV & Another* (2009) EWHC 2471 (Ch).
[25] *Cheyne Finance plc (in receivership)* [2007] EWHC 2402 (Ch) (*Cheyne No. 2*).
[26] *Re Whistlejacket Capital Ltd (in receivership)* [2008] EWCA Civ 575.
[27] *Re Sigma Finance Corporation (in administrative receivership)* [2009] UKSC 2.
[28] *Re Golden Key Ltd (in receivership)* [2009] EWCA Civ 636.

particular documents, there should be payment of obligations in the order in which they mature, the so-called 'pay-as-you-go' approach. In *Cheyne No. 1*, receivers had been appointed in respect of the distressed Cheyne SIV pursuant to the terms of its documents. However, rather than Cheyne's debts being accelerated, they were to be redeemed through an orderly wind-down by the receivers involving payments to creditors on their specified due dates. This resulted in 'time-subordination' in respect of Cheyne's senior debts; ie the obligations that fell due later in time were effectively subordinated to those that fell due earlier, notwithstanding their *pari passu* ranking, due to the risk of funds being exhausted before the later due dates. Despite the significant disadvantage for the holders of later-maturing debt, the High Court agreed with the pay-as-you-go construction of the documents and directed the receivers to distribute on that basis.

10.57 A similar approach was taken in *Golden Key*. In that case, notice of a mandatory acceleration event had been given by Golden Key's security trustee on 24 August 2007, and the receivers were seeking direction as to the construction of the transaction documents with respect to the payment of obligations falling due before the mandatory acceleration. Representative creditors A and B held commercial paper that matured on 23 and 24 August respectively. Representative creditors C and D held commercial paper that matured later and argued that the date for payment of all outstanding commercial paper should be postponed to 24 September (the accelerated redemption date), and then paid *pari passu*. The Court of Appeal held that, on the correct construction of the documents, commercial paper scheduled to mature after the mandatory acceleration event fell due for payment on 24 September and should be paid *pari passu*, but commercial paper maturing on or before the mandatory acceleration did not have its maturity date postponed, and so representative creditors A and B were entitled to be paid in priority to other holders of commercial paper—therefore on a pay-as-you-go basis.

10.58 In contrast to *Cheyne No. 1* and *Golden Key*, in *Whistlejacket* the courts ruled in favour of the *pari passu* principle on the basis that it could not have been the commercial intention for creditors within the same class whose payments fell first in time to be given priority over those with payments falling due later if the available funds had been exhausted before payment to the latter. It was argued that provisions specifying when payments were to be made were merely an expression of how the trustee's discretion would be exercised if it chose to exercise its discretion, rather than imposing an obligation on the trustee to make such payments. Therefore, following the onset of insolvency, the receivers were required to treat the creditors within each relevant class on a *pari passu* basis. The receivers could make payments to creditors as and when their debts fell due for payment, but would have to withhold such sums as were necessary to ensure that *pari passu* treatment was achieved. In this way they would be able to ensure the creditors of the same class were not time subordinated.

In *Sigma*, the pay-as-you-go analysis was followed by the lower court and court of appeal; however, the Supreme Court reversed those judgments. The Supreme Court's approach emphasized the commercial context in which the SIV was structured, as well as a preference for construing the documentation as a whole, and (as in *Whistlejacket*) the importance of clauses granting discretion to the trustee. By a majority of 4-1, the Supreme Court ruled that the payment provisions in question appeared in the context of an assumption that the SIV would retain sufficient assets to cover debts due to its secured creditors and cautioned against over-literal interpretation of contractual clauses. For those reasons it held that the clear intent underlying the provisions in question was to treat short-term liabilities on the same basis—as part of the short-term pool, and therefore *pari passu*—whether they came due before or during the realization period. **10.59**

Each case turned upon the particular transaction documents and facts involved, and it would therefore be imprudent to use a particular decision as a template for any future application unless there is sufficient similarity of the relevant facts and documents. However, the cases, in particular *Sigma*, evidence the preference of English courts for treating members of the same creditor class equally, and their willingness to depart from the ordinary meaning of the words used to achieve that outcome, even if *pari passu* treatment is only remotely suggested by the relevant contractual provisions. **10.60**

10.3.2 Collateralized debt obligations

The acronym 'CDO' once little-known outside banking and institutional investor circles, is now linked in the public mind with the financial crisis of the late 2000s. In particular, CDOs with portfolios consisting substantially of subprime RMBS[29] not only experienced heavy losses during the credit crisis, but are widely perceived as having exacerbated the effects of the housing bubble and the losses generated when it finally burst. **10.61**

10.3.2.1 The CDO structure

The CDO structure had been developed in the late 1980s as a means to repackage financial assets in a managed pool using a tranched capital structure, but experienced tremendous growth in the half dozen years preceding the inception of the credit crisis in mid-2007. Early CDOs used managed pools of high yield bonds to back a senior tranche of debt securities, typically triple-A rated, supported by **10.62**

---

[29] ABS CDO is the term commonly used in the industry for CDOs with heavy exposure to subprime RMBS, but is somewhat of a misnomer because the term 'ABS' suggests a portfolio of any of several types of asset-backed securities. For this reason, we refer to the CDOs in question as 'subprime CDOs'.

tranches of lower-rated debt and an unrated equity tranche. Use of the CDO structure quickly spread to other asset classes such as investment grade bonds and corporate loans; in the latter case, the structures were referred to as collateralized loan obligation ('CLO') transactions. In an effort to obtain higher yields in a low interest rate environment with an ever-increasing tolerance for risk, CDOs began to be structured with portfolios consisting of other complex structured products, most notably RMBS,[30] CMBS, and tranches of other CDOs (when the portfolio consisted primarily of tranches of other CDOs, the resulting structure was called a 'CDO-squared').[31]

10.63 CDOs aggregate assets that may individually carry significant credit risk and 'transform' these pooled assets into triple-A rated obligations primarily by the following structuring techniques: (a) subordination of one or more other classes of securities; (b) collateral quality criteria relating to diversification, credit quality and limitations on certain types of assets; (c) principal and interest cashflow over-collateralization tests that, if failed, restrict reinvestment unless the tests are satisfied or maintained, and divert cash flows to pay down senior classes until over-collateralization is restored; (d) limitations on trading and (e) the grant of various control rights to the most senior CDO class. These structural features, some of which are discussed further below, were designed to enable the CDO to obtain less expensive financing and to produce investment product of higher credit quality (and a necessarily smaller principal balance) than that of the CDO's portfolio of assets. However, during the course of the economic upheaval that began in 2007, these same features contributed to the early default and liquidation of CDOs in adverse market conditions. Most significantly, the structural subordination features endowed the different classes of securities issued by a CDO with conflicting interests that made it highly unlikely that a restructuring plan beneficial to all classes of securities could be designed or that the noteholders would have any incentive to attempt to renegotiate the CDO transaction (ie even for portfolios of higher credit quality than subprime RMBS).[32]

---

[30] Although CDOs are subject to rating agency 'diversity' requirements, many ABS CDO portfolios consisted entirely of RMBS (often predominantly subprime RMBS) and subprime CDOs. Such concentrations in one industry sector, subprime residential mortgages, introduced significant correlation risk into the ABS CDO structure. Moreover, the layering of structured products compounded exponentially the degree of leverage and correlation risk, and the analytical complexity of these structures relative to the (complex in their own right) CDOs with portfolios of corporate bonds or bank loans.

[31] Other applications of CDO technology are the 'synthetic CDO' in which the CDO issuer acquires exposure to a portfolio of assets by entering into credit default swaps referencing specified corporate credits or ABS rather than acquiring those debt obligations directly, and the 'hybrid CDO' in which the portfolio consists of assets acquired both in the cash market and synthetically. See below under 'The significance and impact of credit derivatives'.

[32] Generally, a restructuring would require the consent of all noteholders of each class.

The relative sizes of the note classes or 'tranches' of a CDO were determined by the investment bank and the asset manager based upon their modelling of expected collateral performance to achieve specified rating levels based on rating agency criteria. Such modelling is highly dependent upon assumptions about the rate of defaults and correlation risk (the factors that may make multiple credits default simultaneously), general economic conditions and expected recoveries on defaulted assets. The most senior class in a CDO typically represents 60 per cent or more of the balance of all securities issued in that CDO. Each subordinated class usually is smaller in size than each of the classes senior to it. The most subordinated note or (preference share) tranche can represent as much as 15 per cent or as little as a few percentage points of the full capital structure. In some cases, in particular the CDOs with exposure to subprime mortgages originated after 2004, the transaction modelling proved to be based upon flawed data and assumptions.[33] **10.64**

Subordination in CDOs creates a priority of loss allocation. The first class to bear losses on the underlying CDO assets is the most subordinated tranche, and, thereafter, each other class in reverse order of seniority. Once net realized losses on the CDO collateral exceed the stated balance of a class (and all classes that are subordinated to that class, if any), it is unlikely that class would receive further distributions of any significance. Once a class of CDO securities loses the expectation of future cash flows, even in respect of interest (for the reasons discussed below), there is no incentive for the noteholders of that class to participate in any restructuring of the CDO transaction or to invest any additional funds into the CDO. **10.65**

The mechanics that cut off payment to the subordinated classes in a CDO with an asset pool that is deteriorating in credit quality are the 'cashflow coverage tests' which mandate minimum interest and principal over-collateralization levels for each class of rated debt. In general, failure to meet these coverage tests results in restrictions on the asset manager's ability to trade the asset pool and in the diversion of both interest and principal proceeds collected on the CDO assets (and, in the case of proceeds of asset sales, not immediately reinvested in assets that improve the failed tests) to pay down the principal of the most senior class of notes until the coverage tests for that class are satisfied and then to pay down the principal of any other class whose coverage test is not satisfied. The effect of this waterfall diversion **10.66**

[33] Some market participants believe that the problem with ABS CDOs is deeper than the flawed data and market dislocations that undermined so many of the transactions done in the mid-2000s and is inherent in the extreme complexity and compounded model risk of the two-layer structure (ie where the issuing entity's portfolio consists of assets each of which is itself a complex structured security, dependent on modeled assumptions), as opposed to one-layer CDO structures, such as CLOs or CDOs based on corporate bonds, where the underlying credits can be more readily analyzed. Bank for International Settlements, 'Credit Risk Transfer Developments from 2005 to 2007' (July 2008) 8.

is to withhold interest payments from subordinated classes and to amortize the CDO transaction earlier.[34]

10.67 Failure to satisfy the cashflow coverage tests described above is not an event of default. However, failure to maintain a specified over-collateralization level (set at a lower level than the cashflow coverage tests) for the most senior class is an event of default in most CDOs. The cashflow coverage tests and the over-collateralization default are based upon the par value of the CDO assets. The par value of each CDO asset is reduced by certain mandatory 'haircuts' if the asset's rating has been downgraded beyond certain levels or if certain adverse events have occurred with respect to the asset.[35] As a result of these haircuts, coverage test failure and the over-collateralization default are likely to be triggered much earlier than the occurrence of actual losses on the CDO asset portfolio. The over-collateralization default typically has been the first event of default to occur and therefore the immediate cause of default and liquidation for many of the subprime CDOs that have liquidated to date. Consequently, while protecting the controlling class, the coverage tests and the over-collateralization default can exacerbate the consequences of deteriorating credit quality in a CDO portfolio for other classes by resulting in the liquidation of the asset portfolio at a time when the prices that the CDO will obtain may be lower than could be obtained at a later time or ultimately recovered on the deteriorated assets, and often before an actual payment default on the most senior class.[36]

10.68 The effect of subordinating one or more CDO classes to one senior class and the operation of the coverage tests both cause the respective interests of the different CDO classes to diverge. This divergence is compounded by another structural feature of CDOs—the control rights granted to the most senior class of notes outstanding (often referred to as the controlling class). The controlling class ordinarily is the only class entitled to accelerate the notes following an event of default (the trustee also has the right to do so, but typically would not, absent direction by the controlling class). Moreover, for most ABS CDOs done in the 2005–2007 period, if the event of default is a failure to pay interest on or maintain a minimum

[34] Beginning in mid-2006, there were some ABS CDOs (known as 'triggerless' CDOs) that did not have these features or had them only to a limited extent. Triggerless CDOs were a minority of the ABS CDOs outstanding in the market, but were a growing proportion of the transactions done in 2007, before new issuances substantially ceased.

[35] Defaulted assets typically were required to be held at the lesser of a rating agency specified recovery rate and market value, introducing market and illiquidity risk to the haircut determinations.

[36] However, when all the default and recovery statistics are in for the relevant vintages of subprime CDOs, it may prove that these features did not have that great an effect on other classes (other than that interest on senior notes may have been paid for a somewhat longer period); ie, that due to the poor credit quality of the underlying assets, in most cases classes below the super senior level may not have received distributions of principal even without the accelerated timing of events of default and liquidations that occurred.

level of over-collateralization for the controlling class, that class typically has the right to direct the trustee to liquidate the collateral and distribute the proceeds even if the expected liquidation proceeds would be insufficient to pay the outstanding balance of all (or any) classes of notes. The controlling class also may elect to accelerate the notes following an event of default but direct the trustee to maintain the pool of assets and allow each asset to amortize in accordance with its terms. For most CDOs, if interest payments have been missed on the senior class or if the default over-collateralization level is not satisfied, the CDO also would be out of compliance with its coverage tests, meaning that all collections on the CDO assets would be redirected to the most senior class as described above.[37] Thus, once a CDO asset pool deteriorates to the extent that triggers the cashflow par over-collateralization test, the most senior, controlling CDO class has the right to exercise extensive control rights, while at the same time becoming entitled under the CDO payment waterfall to receive all collections generated by the CDO assets for so long as the tests are breached, whether or not any losses are actually realized on the asset pool. These structural features were implemented to support the triple-A rating of the most senior CDO class and minimize its credit risk. However, they also result in the controlling class having little, if any, incentive to renegotiate the CDO transaction or relinquish any rights to potentially salvage value for the CDO as a whole or improve the position of the subordinated classes. In short, the fundamental structural features of a cash CDO make it effectively impossible to restructure. The same is true of hybrid CDOs, and generally of synthetic CDOs, discussed below.[38]

10.3.2.2 The significance and impact of credit derivatives

Credit derivatives came into being in the early 1990s as isolated transactions referencing a single corporate credit but in the mid-1990s began to be used more broadly, often embedded in complex structured transactions. In those early days credit derivatives were used mainly in structures by which large banks removed high yield corporate loans from their balance sheets and repackaged them into **10.69**

[37] In addition to the coverage tests, many CDOs have a 'default waterfall' that alters the regular waterfall such that all interest and all principal of the most senior class have to be paid in full before any amounts, including accrued interest, can be paid on subordinated classes.

[38] Synthetic CDOs often are issued in single tranches, which do not raise the cashflow diversion or the 'tranche warfare' impediments to restructuring applicable to other types of CDOs. However, any CDO that has all or a substantial portion of its assets in the form of CDSs will face an equally significant obstacle to restructuring, namely that the interests of parties to a CDS are naturally diametrically opposed. And even where an institutional swap counterparty may be willing to consider a restructuring, it may not be feasible to do so because of related hedging transactions to which it is a party.

rated securities.[39] These transactions (an early form of synthetic CLO) freed up capital for the banks and created investment product for institutional investors, such as insurance companies, that wanted exposure to such loans but would have faced capital charges or other regulatory constraints if holding the unrated underlying loans directly. From those origins, which demonstrated the flexibility of credit derivatives as a structuring tool, the product rapidly developed into a number of forms, and, in its many varieties, grew exponentially in the period from approximately 1996 through 2007.[40] What is more, the credit derivatives market grew essentially free from regulation and meaningful reporting requirements.

10.70 10.3.2.2.1 **Credit default swaps** The most common form of credit derivative—the credit default swap, or 'CDS'—is a bilateral financial contract between two institutions (or between a financial institution and a special purpose entity) under which one party (the 'buyer') pays a premium to purchase credit protection and the other party (the 'seller') pays losses if a default or other credit event occurs with respect to a specified reference entity, or if a specified level of defaults occurs within a portfolio of reference entities.[41] The buyer also may be referred to as the party 'shorting' the reference credit, while the seller is referred to as 'going long' on the reference credit. In any CDS each party is exposed not only to the long or short risk it has taken on the reference credit, or reference portfolio, but also to the credit risk of the other party, or 'counterparty risk'

10.71 10.3.2.2.2 **Synthetic and hybrid CDOs** A number of complex structured products were developed based upon the bilateral CDS, notably synthetic CDOs and (cash/synthetic) hybrid CDOs. Synthetic CDOs are securities issued by SPEs and linked to the performance of a portfolio CDS between the SPE, as protection seller, and an institutional swap counterparty, as protection buyer. Synthetic CDOs sometimes were structured as the issuance of a full capital structure of senior and subordinated debt securities and an equity tranche. They also were structured as a single tranche issuance representing a band of credit risk within a hypothetical capital structure—from the so-called 'attachment point' to the 'detachment point'—tailored to the specifications of a corporate investor or a portfolio manager for placement into another CDO, and known as 'bespoke synthetic CDOs'. In the typical structure, the proceeds of the securities issued by the

[39] On the development of credit derivatives and the early structures, see G. Tett, *Fool's Gold: How the Bold Dream of a Small Tribe at J.P. Morgan was Corrupted by Wall Street Greed and Unleashed a Catastrophe* (Simon & Schuster, Inc., 2009).

[40] Even after the massive deleveraging that began in 2007, the volume of outstanding CDS remains gargantuan; statistics published by the Bank for International Settlements show $30.26 tn in notional amount outstanding of CDS at the end of June 2010, the most current numbers available: <http://www.bis.org/statistics/otcder/dt21.pdf>.

[41] There can be many complex variations, including based upon leverage, tranching, the method by which loss is determined and otherwise.

SPE were used to purchase highly rated, liquid investments that are pledged to a trustee as collateral for the obligations of the SPE to both the noteholders and the swap counterparty. The investor was therefore exposed to, among other risks, the performance of the reference portfolio and the collateral, and counterparty risk. As with cash CDOs, the portfolios of synthetic CDOs could consist of corporate debt, bank loans or structured securities. However, synthetic CDOs also could readily be structured to introduce desired levels of leverage, ie where investment returns, or losses, are determined on the basis of a notional amount many times greater than the amount invested.

By 2005, credit derivatives and synthetic CDOs based on corporate credits were being created in large volume. However, the lack of standardized documentation for CDSs on RMBS, CMBS and CDO securities (the assets most desired for ABS CDOs at the time) was holding back the development of a liquid market for CDSs on those assets, and therefore the volume of synthetic CDOs based on those assets. In June 2005 this obstacle was eliminated when the International Swaps and Derivatives Association ('ISDA') published the first standardized confirmation for CDSs on mortgage-backed securities—the Pay-As-You-Go (or 'PAUG') confirmation[42]—and CDO issuance based on RMBS increased dramatically.[43] **10.72**

The standardized Credit Derivatives Definitions published by ISDA in 2003 defined credit events for corporate borrowers, of which the most commonly specified are the 'failure to pay', 'bankruptcy' and 'restructuring' events. However, the principal on asset-backed securities is rarely due before stated maturity and, other than for the most senior tranches, a failure to pay interest usually is not an event of default. Structured finance securities are issued from bankruptcy remote structures, such that bankruptcy is not a meaningful event of default, and, as discussed in this chapter, asset-backed securities are rarely restructured. The PAUG form modified the failure to pay event so that it applied only to a failure to pay principal at maturity (or earlier liquidation), dropped the bankruptcy and restructuring events, and added 'floating amount' events that tracked the cash flows and mechanics of RMBS and CMBS. These floating amount events introduced payments that could occur on multiple occasions when there was a shortfall in an **10.73**

---

[42] The first PAUG form was designed to cover mortgage-backed securities. Although that form was used with some amendments to write CDS on CDOs, a form specifically tailored for use with CDO securities was published by ISDA in June 2006.

[43] Data published by the Securities Industry and Financial Markets Association ('SIFMA'), although not separately breaking out CDOs with primarily RMBS portfolios or including unfunded synthetic tranches, indicates that CDOs with primarily 'structured finance' portfolios (which they define as including RMBS and CDOs) went from a global issuance volume of $83.3 bn in 2004 to $157.6 bn in 2005, $307.7 bn in 2006 and $259.2 bn in 2007 (with the preponderance of the 2007 issuance, $200.7 bn occurring in the first half of the year). There was then a sharp decline, to $18.4 bn in 2008 and $331 m in 2009. See under 'Structured Finance, Global CDO Issuance' at <http://www.sifma.org/research/statistics.aspx>.

interest coupon, a writedown of principal or, for securities that do not expressly provide for writedowns, an 'implied writedown' based on undercollateralization.[44] The PAUG form also provided for reimbursement payments to be made by the buyer of protection to the extent any shortfall or writedown were reversed.

10.74 The introduction of floating amount payments not only permitted a seller of protection to approximate investment in structured securities, but also eliminated the need for a buyer of protection to physically deliver the reference obligation or be exposed to the valuation uncertainties of cash settlement via market quotes to benefit from its contract.[45] This was particularly important, because the market demand for investment product based on exposure to the high-yielding mezzanine tranches of subprime RMBS could not be met by the amount of such tranches actually issued and available for purchase in cash form. The PAUG confirmation was, therefore, a tremendously significant market development, because it freed CDS traders and CDO structurers from settlement risk and made it possible to create investment product that exceeded the amount of mezzanine mortgage-backed securities actually issued and outstanding by many multiples. The standardized document enabled the major financial institutions that act as swap dealers to intermediate trades in which hedge funds and other investors went short on the housing market, while high yielding investment product was created for institutional investors who went long, all without having to source a cash asset. In hindsight, however, it can be seen that the PAUG confirmation catalyzed the explosive growth of subprime CDO issuance and related CDS activity from mid-2005 to mid-2007 that introduced into the global capital markets an enormous degree of leverage and systemic exposure to subprime mortgage risk which in turn precipitated the liquidity and credit shocks of 2007 and 2008.

10.75 The PAUG not only led to increased volume of synthetic CDOs with material exposure to subprime RMBS, it also made possible a new structure—the cash/synthetic hybrid CDO based on mortgage-backed securities—which was issued in high volume between mid-2005 and mid-2007. The typical hybrid CDO was based primarily on mezzanine tranches of subprime RMBS, often with a significant bucket of subprime CDOs, and had an unfunded super senior tranche comprising 65–80 per cent of the capital structure. On the asset side, the SPE would sell protection under the CDSs to a major financial institution as the buyer of protection, often the same institution that acted as the underwriter and/or

[44] These features of the PAUG could cause a synthetic or hybrid CDO to be required to make payments or realize losses with respect to a reference obligation at times when no payments were required or losses realized by the reference obligation.

[45] Unlike credit default swaps written on corporate credits, those on asset-backed securities reference a particular security rather than a corporate name and permit physical settlement only upon delivery of the reference obligation.

liquidity provider. The unfunded liabilities of the CDO were represented by a liquidity facility (in the form of a traditional bank facility or a swap) that would fund losses on the CDSs as and to the extent necessary. If the facility were drawn upon, the amounts drawn would be repaid senior to all other debt obligations of the CDO, and junior only to amounts owing to the CDS counterparty (and any interest rate or currency hedge counterparty) and to administrative expenses and the fees of the trustee and other service providers.

CDOs of all types usually generated related credit derivatives outside the CDO structure. The financial institution that acted as buyer of protection under the CDSs used in the CDO structure typically hedged that exposure in various ways, including by entering into offsetting CDSs with hedge funds and other institutional investors who desired to short the reference assets. Similarly, the holder of the most senior tranche in the structure—the super senior counterparty in a synthetic CDO, the provider of the super senior tranche in a hybrid CDO or the holder of the most senior class in a cash CDO—typically would hedge its exposure, often by purchasing protection from a monoline insurance company or other institution. It is primarily through this type of trade that the monoline insurers and AIG financial products became so heavily exposed to subprime CDOs. **10.76**

10.3.2.2.3 The 'Montreal Accord' and the Canadian ABCP restructuring Another type of hedge used by the financial institutions that structured and acted as counterparties to CDOs was the 'leveraged super senior' credit default swap ('LSS CDS') entered into between the financial institution and an SPE. For the financial institution the structure was a hedge, from the perspective of the investors in the SPEs that sold protection under LSS CDSs, it was a highly leveraged synthetic CDO. In a structure widely used in Canada, an institutional swap dealer would enter into an LSS CDS with a Canadian commercial paper conduit structured as a trust. By June 2007, the volume of Canadian ABCP backed by credit derivatives and other non-traditional asset categories was approximately CDN $35 bn, the preponderance of which was backed by LSS CDSs and most of which was issued not from trusts sponsored by the large Canadian banks but from trusts structured by one of several boutique finance companies and referred to as 'third party' ABCP.[46] **10.77**

The Canadian LSS CDS structures often were levered 10:1, meaning that the conduit only would be required to raise funds sufficient to purchase collateral equal to 10 per cent of the portion of the reference portfolio determined to be the 'super senior' tranche (ie the portion senior to a significant first loss position), but **10.78**

[46] B. Erman, J. McNish, T. Perkins, H. Scoffield, 'Anatomy of a Panic' *Globe and Mail*, 17 November 2007.

would receive an effective spread based on the full 'super senior' tranche.[47] Attractive as that leveraged yield might appear, the use of leverage magnifies losses as well as gains, and instruments like the LSS CDS can be highly volatile. Moreover, although the conduit was not required to incur a loss greater than the relevant fraction (10 per cent in this example) of the 'super senior' tranche, the LSS CDS counterparties had the right to make margin calls if certain triggers were hit, based upon (depending on the particular deal) specified credit spreads, mark-to-market determinations or losses experienced in the reference portfolio. If the conduit could not meet the collateral call, the swap counterparty would be entitled to terminate the deal on a basis that in all likelihood would produce a substantial loss to the conduit and accordingly to its investors. The resulting ABCP was highly rated by DBRS and broadly distributed in Canada, including to retail investors.

10.79 As described above in this chapter, turmoil erupted throughout the global ABCP markets in the summer of 2007. In Canada, the third-party ABCP market froze on 13 August 2007; the conduits could not roll their maturing paper. ABCP issuers are required to maintain liquidity facilities against such contingencies. But in what became known as 'the Canadian wrinkle' the third party ABCP issuers had facilities that would fund only in the event of a 'general market disruption' a term that was not clearly defined.[48] Most of the banks providing liquidity lines to the third-party ABCP conduits did not fund the requested draws and those conduits faced a three-day grace period after which they would be in default under the indentures governing the ABCP. In most or all cases, that default would have given the swap counterparties the right to terminate the swap transactions and realize on the collateral, and would have given the commercial paper investors the right to cause the liquidation of the conduits' assets.[49] Under the market conditions then prevailing, ABCP investors and other deal parties could have suffered potentially devastating losses. Within that grace period, however, the largest ABCP investors and the LSS CDS counterparties worked around the clock to reach a standstill agreement, dubbed the Montreal Accord, that set the stage for a complex and protracted restructuring process.

---

[47] DBRS, 'Fundamentals of Leveraged Super Senior CDOs' (June 2005) available at <www.dbrs.com/research/149269>.

[48] The third party ABCP with this limited liquidity was rated only by DBRS. In September 2007, DBRS announced that it would require any new ABCP issuers to have 'global style' liquidity; ie that would provide the broader coverage customary in rated ABCP issued in other jurisdictions, including the US. DBRS Press Release, dated 12 September 2007, available at <http://www.dbrs.com/research/214413>/.

[49] Information for Noteholders prepared by the Pan-Canadian Investors Committee for Third Party Structured Asset-Backed Commercial Paper, dated 20 March 2008, xi, available at <www.ey.com/ca/commercialpaper> (cited below as the 'CCAA Information Statement').

In September 2007, a committee of the larger institutional and corporate investors (the 'Investors Committee') was formed,[50] and in late December the Investors Committee announced an agreement in principle (the 'Framework Agreement'),[51] on the basis of which the ABCP and its underlying assets would be restructured. In broad outline, as further refined over the next several months, the Framework Agreement contemplated the division of the assets among three to-be-formed trusts, the Master Asset Vehicles (or, MAVs 1, 2 and 3).[52] The preponderance of the assets, and all the CDSs, would be allocated to MAVs 1 and 2. The critical features of the contemplated restructuring were that it would provide for (a) the LSS CDS margin triggers to be changed from a mark-to-market to more remote 'spread/loss' matrix triggers based upon public CDS indices, (b) a pool of additional collateral to be available to the LSS CDS dealers (the 'traditional' securitized assets that in addition to the LSS CDS and their originally pledged collateral were to be conveyed to the MAVs 1 and 2), (c) a potential reallocation of collateral, on the basis of the swap dealers' relative needs, in the event certain triggers were hit, (d) substantial margin facilities (initially expected to be a total of CDN $14 bn to be allocated between MAV 1 and MAV 2), to be provided by the investors in MAV1, and to be provided by a group of Canadian banks in MAV2, and (e) the exchange of the short-term ABCP notes for term notes that would more closely match the expected maturities or amortization of the underlying assets and would be issued in senior/subordinate tranches. Another key provision of the Framework Agreement was the condition to closing that full releases from potential liability be granted to the sponsors, trustees, investors, liquidity lenders, swap counterparties, commercial paper dealer and other parties involved with the ABCP conduits. This would prove controversial. **10.80**

To implement these proposed terms, a process was needed that would give legal certainty to the restructuring and the releases and provide a framework for seeking investor consents. The parties to the Framework Agreement determined to file a plan of compromise and arrangement (the 'Plan') under the Companies' Creditors Arrangement Act (Canada) (the 'CCAA') with the Ontario Superior Court of Justice (the 'Superior Court'). This presented new legal challenges, notably (a) that the CCAA had not been used to restructure common law trusts and **10.81**

---

[50] The unwieldy official title was the 'Pan-Canadian Investors Committee for Third Party Structured Asset-Backed Commercial Paper'. It consisted of approximately 15 financial institutions and institutional investors, which collectively held roughly two-thirds of the outstanding third party ABCP. CCAA Information Statement, 22-3.

[51] Available at <www.ey.com/ca/commercialpaper>.

[52] The allocation of assets depended in the first instance on the manner in which they had been initially funded—if funded by ABCP backed by both CDSs and traditional assets, they were allocated to MAV1 or 2; if funded by ABCP backed solely by traditional assets, they were allocated to MAV3. In turn, the split between MAV 1 and MAV 2 depended upon the form of the margin funding that would be provided.

(b) claims by opponents of the Plan that the third-party releases were an impermissible confiscation of property rights and also outside the jurisdiction of a CCAA proceeding. The first issue was solved by replacing the institutional trustees of the conduits with new shell companies that were declared insolvent. The release was more problematic; it was initially sanctioned by the Superior Court but, following investor challenges, the court required that the release be revised as a condition of the Plan's approval, and an amendment to the Plan was filed that excluded from the release certain claims based upon fraud.

10.82 As so amended, the Plan was approved by note holders at a meeting held on 25 April 2008, and on 5 June 2008, Justice Campbell of the Superior Court issued a sanction order approving the Plan and stating his 'reasons for decision'.[53] Among other things, Justice Campbell found the third party releases to be permissible under the CCAA because they were (a) rationally related to the purpose of the Plan and necessary for it, and (b) the parties being released had contributed in a 'tangible and realistic' way to the Plan.[54]

10.83 The sanction order was appealed by objecting investors, principally on the basis that the third-party releases were confiscatory, with some investors also arguing inequitable treatment because they were not eligible for the ABCP buyback extended to certain retail investors by their selling brokers.[55] On 18 August 2008, the Ontario Court of Appeal issued a decision upholding the decision of lower court. The decisions of both the lower court and the Court of Appeal were marked by a pragmatic approach and a keen awareness not only of the need to balance the interests of the affected noteholders but also the potential broader economic significance of the proceedings. For example, in concluding that the Plan was 'fair and reasonable' (as the CCAA requires and the Superior Court had held), the Court of Appeal noted that CCAA proceedings necessarily involve a 'balancing of prejudices' in that all interested parties are adversely affected to some degree, and further indicated that it was proper to consider the market and economic context,

---

[53] *Re Metcalfe & Mansfield Alternative Investments II Corp.* O. J. No. 2265 (2008).

[54] Ibid. at paras 143, 144.

[55] The ABCP had been sold to a wide variety of investors, including retail investors, and the plight of the individuals whose savings were trapped in the frozen ABCP was extensively chronicled in the Canadian press. However, the 1,800 or so retail investors ended up having more leverage than was at first evident. Although holding only approximately CDN $350 m of the more than CDN $30 bn of ABCP being restructured, they constituted a majority by number of investors. And the Plan required approval by both $66^2/_3$ per cent of the aggregate amount of ABCP outstanding and by a majority of investors. Ultimately, a buyback plan was developed by which retail investors who had invested less than CDN $1 m would have their ABCP purchased at par by the selling brokers upon the closing of the restructuring. See J. McFarland, B. Erman, K. Howlett and T. Perkins, 'How ordinary investors got sold on ABC', *Saturday's Globe and Mail*, 8 August 2008 (last updated 31 March 2009), available at <http://www.theglobeandmail.com/report-on-business/article701775.ece>.

stating that the lower court 'was correct in adverting to the importance of the restructuring to the resolution of the ABCP liquidity crisis and to the need to restore confidence in the financial system in Canada'.[56]

When, on 19 September 2008, the Supreme Court of Canada denied an appeal from the Court of Appeal decision, it seemed that all obstacles had been removed and a closing would soon follow. However, that expectation and the often-stated goal of the Investors Committee (and, not incidentally, the Canadian government)[57] to achieve a completely private solution were undermined by the turbulence of the global capital markets that followed the bankruptcy of Lehman Brothers, the AIG bailout and other events occurring earlier that week. As credit spreads in the CDS market continued to widen through that fall, the Investors Committee determined that it was necessary for the spread/loss triggers to be revised to be more remote, but the swap dealers would accommodate only if billions of dollars of additional margin funding could be provided. As a last resort, the Investors Committee approached the Canadian federal government to seek the further margin funding.[58] On 24 December 2008, the federal government, together with the governments of the provinces of Alberta, Ontario and Quebec, announced that they, together with one of the MAV1 investors, would provide additional margin funding of CDN $3.45 bn to be allocated between MAVs 1 and 2, and the MAV1 investors agreed to increase their aggregate margin funding commitment for MAV 1 by CDN $1 bn. With the additional funding in place, the restructuring closed on 21 January 2009. **10.84**

The Canadian ABCP restructuring was a remarkable achievement, due to its size, the number and disparate nature of the investors, the differing interests of the swap dealers, new margin lenders and other participants, and the staggering complexity of the restructured liabilities and underlying assets. These included not only the LSS CDS, but also the many other structured products in the asset pool, each of which was complex in itself and in many cases involved multiple parties whose consents to amendments were required. Moreover, having been arranged by several different finance companies, originally funded through 20 separate conduit issuers, and involving numerous asset classes, there was no uniformity to the documents for those underlying securitization programmes. The Canadian **10.85**

---

56 *Re Metcalfe & Mansfield Alternative Investments II Corp.* [2008] ONCA 587.

57 For example, speaking in February 2008, Bank of Canada Governor Mark Carney stated, 'It was absolutely clear from moment one that there was not going to be any public money put behind any of this because these are decisions of financial market participants.' *Reuters UK*, 18 February 2008, available at <http://uk.reuters.com/article/idUKN1820571220080218> (the 'Carney Remarks').

58 J. Greenwood, P. Viera, E. Callon, 'ABCP Committee goes begging to Ottawa' *Financial Post*, 10 December 2008, available at <http://www.canada.com/story_print.html?id=1058893&sponsor=>.

ABCP restructuring occurred in a possibly unique combination of circumstances, including a relatively small and very sophisticated core group of investors, swap dealers and lenders, a court system that addressed the process relatively quickly and in a pragmatic manner, and, due to the size and political sensitivity of the exposures, the support of Canadian financial regulators, which at critical times, even before the ultimate provision of the additional margin funding, may have influenced various financial institutions to stay in the process.[59] To that extent, the Canadian ABCP restructuring is largely *sui generis*, rather than a model for future restructurings of structured products. However, the CCAA processes employed, including the use of court-sanctioned releases to facilitate the consent of parties that otherwise may not have participated in a restructuring, are now legal precedent in Canada, and possibly may influence future restructurings in other jurisdictions.

10.3.3 Commercial mortgage-backed securities

10.3.3.1 The CMBS structure

10.86 Commercial mortgage-backed securities ('CMBS') are securities issued by bankruptcy remote SPEs, backed by mortgages on commercial real estate such as multifamily residential buildings, office buildings, shopping malls, other retail establishments, hotels and resorts. The securities are normally issued in series, sold through the capital markets and rated by one or more rating agencies.

10.87 A typical CMBS deal starts with a lender/originator originating one or more commercial loans to one or more SPE owners of real property. These borrowers provide collateral to the lenders, usually comprising a mortgage over the real estate, an assignment of the rents from the properties and the various bank accounts of the borrower.

10.88 A pool of loans is then packaged as security for a CMBS issuance. The originating bank or a different arranging bank (in the US, typically one or more investment banks) selects the relevant commercial loans, or senior participation interests in loans, and structures the transaction as a tranched issuance with layers of investment-grade, non-investment-grade and unrated securities. The proceeds of the issuance are used to pay the originator for the purchase of the underlying loans.

10.89 Principal is paid sequentially, first to the investment grade notes until they are paid in full, then the next lower class, and so on, though in many transactions most principal on the underlying loans and, thus, on the CMBS securities, is paid only

[59] Mark Carney, Governor of the Bank of Canada, indicated that the Bank of Canada had 'acted as a "light-touch" facilitator for talks between various market participants'. Carney Remarks, above.

at maturity from the refinancing of the loans. Interest-only classes are also sometimes issued. Losses are borne in the opposite direction, with the most junior tranches written off first. The size and number of tranches in any individual deal are different and cater to investors' varying degrees of appetite for risk.

In Europe, approximately $200 bn of CMBS loans are outstanding and over half of that amount will need to be refinanced between 2011 and 2013.[60] The comparable figures for the US are approximately $709 bn of CMBS loans outstanding as of January 2010,[61] with approximately $150 bn maturing from 2010 through 2013.[62] Moreover, that $150 bn in CMBS only accounts for a portion of the approximately $1.3 tn of US commercial real estate loans maturing from 2010 through 2013 and requiring refinancing.[63] Refinancing is likely to be very difficult for the majority of CMBS loans[64] and many loans will be in default even before maturity, often due to missed interest payments, or, with respect to European loans, breaches of the loan-to-value covenants in the loan agreements. A continuing decline in property values, already down substantially from the height of the market, is expected to exacerbate the refinancing problem. Significant losses are expected to be incurred on CMBS and, as occurred in the case of RMBS, the losses are expected to be magnified by the considerable amount of CDSs that have been written on CMBS.[65] **10.90**

In CMBS structures, a covenant breach or payment default on an underlying loan does not in itself lead to a default at the CMBS notes level. In European CMBS, however, failure to pay the coupon on the CMBS notes may cause a default; thus, as commercial leases come up for renewal and rents are negotiated downward, the CMBS notes themselves may be in default in some European deals. There generally is no default concept at the CMBS notes level in US CMBS; the typical US structure employs pass through payments, and shortfalls accrue. **10.91**

---

[60] A. Sakoui and D. Thomas, 'European property groups face debt time-bomb' *Financial Times*, 20 September 2009.

[61] Congressional Oversight Panel, February Oversight Report, 'Commercial Real Estate Losses and the Risk to Financial Stability' ('COP February Report') (10 February 2010) 54, data provided by the Commercial Real Estate Securities Association.

[62] Ibid. at 73, fig. 31, data provided by Foresight Analytics LLP.

[63] Ibid. at 73, data provided by the Real Estate Roundtable.

[64] By July 2009, US CMBS loans were already suffering a delinquency rate of 3.14 per cent (a greater than six-fold increase over the preceding year), and one major real estate lender was estimating that refinancing would be difficult for nearly two-thirds of the CMBS loans due to mature through 2012. L. Wei and P. Grant, 'Commercial Real Estate Lurks as Next Potential Mortgage Crisis' *Wall Street Journal*, 31 August 2009 (citing data from Realpoint LLC and Deutsche Bank, respectively) available at <http://online.wsj.com/article_email/SB125167422962070925-lMyQjAxMTIwNTAxNjYwNzY0Wj.html>.

[65] COP February Report at 59.

10.3.3.2 Particular issues for potential CMBS restructurings

10.92 Due to the expected refinancing problem, many CMBS transactions or the underlying mortgage loans will need restructuring. For US transactions, to the extent restructuring occurs, it invariably will occur on the mortgage loans (as opposed to a restructuring of the CMBS securities). In US CMBS, a 'REMIC' (real estate mortgage investment conduit) structure is typically used; a REMIC is a tax vehicle that is established pursuant to and must meet certain qualifications under the US Internal Revenue Code, which makes it difficult to restructure at the CMBS notes level. However, subject to certain tax-related limitations, the underlying mortgage loans potentially can be restructured.[66]

10.93 Certain other structural features of both the US and European structures, relating to the servicing of the mortgage loans, raise particular issues that make restructurings difficult to achieve. CMBS structures use a servicer who is responsible for collecting and distributing payments and reporting on the transaction generally, and is paid a fee for these services. If an underlying loan is in default or there are other problems, the loan is moved to 'special servicing' and a special servicer takes over the role of enforcement and coordinating any restructuring effort. The special servicer usually is paid a monthly fee plus a success fee (typically 1 per cent of the liquidation proceeds or proceeds from a workout). A special servicer may also own interests in the more subordinated classes of a CMBS deal and may be the controlling class (as described below).

10.94 Special servicers are required, pursuant to the servicing agreement, to comply with the 'servicing standard'. This standard requires them to service the loan on behalf of all the securities holders with the goal of maximizing recoveries on the loans but always taking into account the net present value of such recoveries. Consequently, liquidation and enforcement on the underlying collateral is not a given; the special servicer must consider whether restructuring options would lead to a better result. Moreover, the special servicer must act at the direction of

[66] The REMIC rules significantly restrict the ability of transaction parties to modify loans in a CMBS structure. In view of the difficulties for CMBS structures caused by conditions in the commercial real estate market, the US Internal Revenue Service issued a revenue procedure and tax regulations in September 2009 that were intended to facilitate modification of underlying mortgage loans. Generally, under the revenue procedure, the servicer may modify a loan if, based on all the facts and circumstances, the holder or servicer reasonably believes that there is a significant risk of default of the loan upon maturity of the loan or at an earlier date. This reasonable belief must be based on a diligent contemporaneous determination of that risk, which may take into account credible written factual representations made by the issuer of the loan if the holder or servicer does not know or have reason to know that such representations are false. There is no time frame as to how far in the future the default may be. Other federal tax regulations now generally permit releases, substitutions and addition of collateral and changes in guarantees, other credit enhancements and certain other changes, even if they are 'significant modifications,' as long as the mortgage loan remains 'principally secured' by real property.

the majority holder of the 'controlling class' which usually is the most junior class of securities whose total outstanding certificate balance is not less than 25 per cent of the initial principal amount of such class. Or, in certain cases, especially in US structures, actions with respect to particular loans are subject to the consent or direction of the 'directing holder' which typically is the majority holder of a subordinate interest in a loan (which subordinate interest may be held within or outside the CMBS trust) of which the total outstanding balance is not less than 25 per cent of the initial principal amount.[67] Pursuant to the transaction documents, the majority controlling class holder or directing holder, as applicable, can direct the special servicer and influence the restructuring strategy, provided that the special servicer does not have to follow any such directions if the special servicer determines that such direction would violate the servicing standard. The majority controlling class holder or directing holder, as applicable, typically has the right to remove and replace the special servicer, with or without cause.

These structural features are not problematic when the interests of the senior creditors and the junior creditors are aligned, as they typically are in a rising real estate market. However, under market conditions where values are stagnant or falling, and refinancing is difficult or impossible to obtain, senior noteholders (who do not benefit from default interest or any other increase in rate that may be negotiated in connection with an extension), generally would prefer to enforce on the underlying collateral (given that any recovery is likely to be enough to pay the most senior notes) while the junior holders, who are totally or partially out of the money, would prefer to work out the loan and wait and hope that a recovery in the property market will increase the return available to them. This tension creates a conflict of interest for the special servicer, which must make decisions on behalf of all the holders, yet is appointed by a junior holder and indeed may be an affiliate of the junior holder. **10.95**

When faced with a defaulted loan, the special servicer has two broad choices—enforce on the security and sell the underlying property or extend the term of the loan (in some cases, with modification of other terms as well). As a result of the inherent conflicts created by the servicing standard and the influence of the controlling class, or directing holder, and the fact that CMBS trusts typically cannot provide 'seller financing' when there are few other financing options for real estate buyers, most special servicers have been extending loan maturities and not taking enforcement action, often to the frustration of the senior noteholders. In the US structures, however, such extensions often are limited by the terms of the governing pooling agreements (ie above and beyond the REMIC-related requirements **10.96**

[67] The rights granted to the junior holder in CMBS structures contrasts with the treatment of intercreditor rights in CDOs and most other structured products that employ senior/subordinated tranching, where the most senior class outstanding is the controlling class.

described above), and in the case of floating rate CMBS transactions, are strictly limited.

10.97 As defaults on the underlying loans continue and issuers begin to default on payments on the CMBS notes (or, in the US case, such payments are deferred), transaction parties may become more highly motivated to negotiate and compromise. Conversely, an improving market with more financing available also may make restructurings more feasible. What is clear, however, is that in most cases a successful restructuring—except to the extent it can be achieved through restructurings of underlying loans in compliance with the existing CMBS documents—will require the consent of a wide group of creditors, often with conflicting interests. Much will depend on the rights of those creditors under the applicable documentation and the law.

10.3.3.3 The General Growth Properties proceedings

10.98 Another approach was taken, however, when in April 2009 General Growth Properties ('GGP') and its main operating subsidiary, GGP Limited Partnership, and over 170 of their affiliated, bankruptcy remote SPEs, commenced voluntary cases under chapter 11 of the US Bankruptcy Code.[68] Prior to those proceedings, the prevailing view among securitization practitioners in the US was that the independent directors of bankruptcy remote SPE subsidiaries would not consent to a voluntary filing by the SPE so long as its assets were performing. However, in the GGP proceedings, the independent managers (the entities in question were LLCs) consented to the filings by the company's SPEs, notwithstanding that the SPEs were structured to be bankruptcy remote and, in most cases, had performing assets and were not in imminent danger of defaulting.

10.99 Along with its more than 750 subsidiaries and affiliates, GGP operates a nationwide network of shopping malls. The shopping malls, owned by individual GGP subsidiaries organized as bankruptcy remote SPEs, are pledged to secure mortgage loans, most of which are in pools backing CMBS. Prior to commencing bankruptcy proceedings, GGP had attempted to restructure voluntarily out of court.[69] Thus the filing of GGP and its operating company affiliates was not a surprise, but the concurrent voluntary bankruptcy filings of a large number of GGP's affiliated

[68] *Re General Growth Properties, Inc., et al.* Chapter 11 Case No. 09-11977 (ALG) (Bankr. SDNY).

[69] At the time of the filing of the chapter 11 petitions, GGP entities had approximately $11.8 bn outstanding in mortgage debt that had matured or was due to mature between the petition date and the end of 2012. Of this amount, 68 loans, aggregating approximately $10 bn in outstanding principal, were CMBS loans. GGP had cited the inability to work within the CMBS structures to refinance or extend that debt as the primary reason for the commencement of bankruptcy proceedings. Findings of Facts, Conclusions of Law, and Order Confirming the Plan Debtors Joint Plan of Reorganization under Chapter 11 of the Bankruptcy Code, filed 15 December 2009, at 16.

SPEs had not been anticipated and raised broad concerns not only in the CMBS market but in the securitization industry generally about the continuing ability to rely on bankruptcy remote structures.

Motions to dismiss the voluntary filings were filed by creditors of certain of the GGP SPEs, mainly on the basis that they were bad-faith filings because they were premature, given that the SPEs in question were solvent. The bankruptcy court rejected the creditors' objections and allowed the SPEs to continue their bankruptcy cases.[70] The court based its decision on a number of factors, primarily that, (a) under the Bankruptcy Code, a debtor need not be insolvent to voluntarily file for bankruptcy, (b) the moving creditors did not establish that the SPEs were unreasonable in concluding that the condition of the CMBS market created uncertainty about whether they would be able to refinance their debt when it came due (although that was years in the future), and (c) the SPEs were entitled, in determining whether to voluntarily file, to consider the interests of GGP; that, in fact, under Delaware corporate law the directors of a solvent company are required to consider the interest of the company's shareholders when exercising their fiduciary duties.[71] **10.100**

Despite the particular aspect of the GGP proceedings that raised concern for the securitization market—the fact that the filing SPEs evidently were not insolvent or, in most cases, in imminent danger of financial distress—on another level the court's decision can be seen as a reminder of the truism, perhaps forgotten during benign economic periods, that the provisions designed to make an SPE bankruptcy remote do not make it bankruptcy proof, nor do they entirely isolate such SPEs in the event of the parent's bankruptcy. Moreover, it has long been recognized that under US bankruptcy law securitization transactions involving the 'core assets' of an operating company (or of complex, integrated entities such as GGP and its multitude of operating company and SPE affiliates) involve heightened risk of substantive consolidation—or, as in the GGP case, a lesser but nevertheless significant impingement on the affairs and assets of the SPEs—on the basis that the core assets are necessary to the successful reorganization of the operating company.[72] Although the court in the GGP proceedings emphasized that the entities were not being substantively consolidated, the core assets concern is implicit in its statement that 'Movants do not explain how the billions of dollars **10.101**

[70] *Re General Growth Properties, Inc.* 409 BR 43, 57 (Bankr. SDNY 2009).

[71] Ibid. 61-5. That is a principle of Delaware corporate law, however it is not the case for limited liability companies if their formation documents otherwise provide. That was not done, however, in the formation documents for the GGP SPEs.

[72] See discussion of the 1991 Days Inns bankruptcy, in which substantive consolidation was ordered, in the Committee on Bankruptcy and Corporate Reorganization of The Association of the Bar of the City of New York, 'Structured Finance Techniques' (1995) 50 The Business Lawyer 527, 561-3.

of unsecured debt at the parent levels could be restructured responsibly if the cash flow of the parent companies continued to be based on the earnings of subsidiaries that had debt coming due in a period of years without any known means of providing for repayment or refinance.'[73]

10.102 In any event, restructurings were achieved in the GGP proceedings. In December 2009, the bankruptcy court confirmed plans of reorganization involving over 200 GGP debtors and approximately $11.5 bn of secured mortgage loans; by late March 2010, the aggregate amount of restructured mortgage loans approved by the bankruptcy court had reached $14 bn. GGP filed a plan of reorganization in July 2010, which included splitting itself into two separate companies, and, as so reorganized, emerged from bankruptcy in November 2010. Given the enormous amount of commercial mortgage debt that will be coming due over the next several years, the difficulties foreseen with refinancing and the obstacles to effecting restructurings within a CMBS structure, it seems likely that others may attempt to follow the GGP example.

10.4 Conclusions

10.103 The cataclysmic events of the last three years have demonstrated how quickly the dogma of embedded modelling assumptions and belief in the continued expansion of structured finance as the optimal method of spreading financial risk on a global scale could be blown away by the winds of economic change—albeit in this case, those winds were of hurricane force and may have effected permanent changes in the economic world order.

10.104 However it might be wished for, especially in the face of trillions of dollars of defaulted transactions and a looming refinancing crisis in the commercial real estate market, there simply is no overall template for the restructuring of structured finance transactions. To some market participants, restructuring a structured finance transaction may seem to be an oxymoron. Even those who have had experience dealing with distressed situations in this sector, while perhaps not taking such an extreme view, would nonetheless agree that such restructurings have been and probably will continue to be highly opportunistic, difficult to achieve, and relatively rare.

[73] *Re General Growth*, 62-3. Although the GGP court did not view substantive consolidation as necessary or appropriate, in another large bankruptcy proceeding, involving a hotel chain financed by a CMBS transaction, a court-appointed examiner delivered a report recommending substantive consolidation on the basis that the operating companies and SPEs were being operated as a single economic unit. *Re Extended Stay, Inc., et al.* Chapter 11 Case No. 09-13764, (JMP) (Bankr. SDNY), Report of Ralph R. Mabey, as Examiner, filed 8 April 2010, at 255.

11

COMPROMISING SHAREHOLDER CLAIMS GENERALLY AND IN LISTED COMPANIES

11.1 Introduction

In both UK and US bankruptcy proceedings, shareholders rank lowest in terms of recovery. In consensual restructurings, however, shareholders in both jurisdictions may be able to position themselves to retain some potential upside in exchange for their cooperation in the restructuring process. Likewise, in the context of non-consensual arrangements, shareholders in both the US and UK may also seek to leverage their position, especially in cases where they have an influence in the restructured business, whether this is by virtue of their involvement as management or key employees, or in providing further funds to the distressed business. As a matter of UK law, various restructuring techniques exist which facilitate the compromise of shareholder rights, or allow them in certain circumstances to be left out of the restructuring entirely; we consider these techniques in this chapter. In summary however, both in the US and as a matter of UK law, a consensual solution is often the preferred route so shareholder cooperation is often sought, and to this extent the shareholders may continue to influence the restructuring process. **11.01**

11.2 US

11.02 Under the US Bankruptcy Code,[1] shareholders are generally last in line to receive any recovery in a case under chapter 11 of the Bankruptcy Code, regardless of whether the case is a liquidation or a reorganization. The bedrock of chapter 11 is the 'absolute priority rule'. Stated simply, the 'absolute priority rule' provides that, with certain exceptions, a junior class of claims or equity interests cannot receive any distribution from the bankrupt estate unless all senior classes have been paid in full. As such, shareholders do not receive any recovery on account of their claims or equity interests under a chapter 11 plan unless all creditors are paid in full[2] and, as a result, shareholders typically find their equity interests extinguished in a chapter 11 plan as a result pursuant to the 'cram down' provisions of the Bankruptcy Code.[3] Because the Bankruptcy Code does not distinguish between publicly and privately traded securities, whether an equity interest is publicly traded is irrelevant in determining the priority or amount of recovery to shareholders.

11.03 A debtor need not be insolvent to file for chapter 11. Therefore, it is possible for shareholders to retain some of their equity interests under a chapter 11 plan if there is enough value in the reorganized enterprise to pay creditors in full. Moreover, even when prospects for equity recovery look slim at the beginning of a chapter 11 case, a turnaround in the economy or improvements in the debtor's operations during the chapter 11 case may result in significant recoveries for shareholders.[4]

11.04 Unlike a committee of general unsecured creditors, which is established as of right under the Bankruptcy Code to represent the interests of all unsecured creditors in the chapter 11 case,[5] a committee of equity holders is not established automatically. Instead, in chapter 11 cases where there may be even some prospect for recovery to shareholders, shareholders typically form ad hoc committees to represent their interests in a chapter 11 case or can petition the appropriate office of the US Trustee, which oversees the bankruptcy process on behalf of creditors and shareholders, to appoint an official committee of equity holders to represent the interests of all shareholders in a chapter 11 case (the 'equity committees'). Unlike ad hoc committees,

---

[1] 11 USCss 101-1532 (the 'Bankruptcy Code').

[2] Claims of shareholders that relate to the purchase and sale of securities of a debtor or an affiliate of a debtor can be subordinated under the Bankruptcy Code: 11 USCs 510(b). If the security sold is common stock, for example, shareholders' claims relating to the purchase or sale of such stock would have the same priority as the common stock—ie last in line. Ibid.

[3] 11 USCs 1129(b).

[4] See, eg, *Re USG Corp.* Case No. 01-2094 (JKF) (Bankr. D. Del. 2001)(chapter 11 plan confirmed that provided for shareholders to retain all of their equity interests); *Re Pilgrim's Pride Corp.* Case No. 08-45664 (DML) (Bankr. ND Tex. 2008) (chapter 11 plan confirmed that provided for shareholders to retain 36 per cent of their equity interests).

[5] See 11 USCs 1102.

equity committees' expenses (including legal fees) are reimbursed by debtors' estates. Equity committees are becoming increasingly common in large chapter 11 cases and their focus is negotiations over a chapter 11 plan and salvaging some value for shareholders. Typically their goal is achieved through either (a) securing value for shareholders through a consensual chapter 11 plan whereby a settlement is reached among most or all stakeholders that provides a distribution to shareholders even though creditors are not getting paid in full and the chapter 11 plan would not otherwise satisfy the absolute priority rule, or (b) by arguing for a greater valuation of the reorganized enterprise that would result in a surplus for shareholders after payment in full to all creditors. In the latter case, valuation of the reorganized enterprise usually becomes the critical issue in confirming the chapter 11 plan.

As mentioned above, the absolute priority rule generally prevents shareholders **11.05** from receiving any recovery on account of their claims or equity interests if not all creditors are paid in full. In the case of a consensual chapter 11 plan, where the chapter 11 plan is accepted by all classes of claims and equity interests, the distribution scheme may be altered, however, to provide a recovery to shareholders even where not all creditors are paid in full. Multiparty negotiations among a debtor, an equity committee, the official committee of unsecured creditors, and the secured lenders can lead to consensual chapter 11 plans where shareholders receive some recovery notwithstanding the absolute priority rule.

Even in non-consensual chapter 11 plans, shareholders may receive a distribution **11.06** under a chapter 11 plan if not all creditors are paid in full under two scenarios: (a) upon contribution of new value to the debtor as part of the chapter 11 plan (the 'new value exception'), or (b) as a gift from a class of creditors having priority of distribution (the 'gifting exception'). Both these exceptions are controversial and courts have tried to narrow the scope of their applicability. Notably, neither exception is mentioned in the Bankruptcy Code but are judicially created concepts that have evolved over time.

The new value exception is premised on the notion that shareholders of the debtor **11.07** should be permitted to buy back into the reorganized company. Proponents of the new value exception argue that the new value exception is appropriate because any stake shareholders receive in the reorganized debtor is on account of the new value they provided to the reorganization and not on account of their preexisting equity interests and, therefore, is not a violation of the absolute priority rule. Courts, however, including the US Supreme Court, have recently held that even if the new value exception exists, the 'new value' that would have to be provided to the reorganization and the debtor must be something other than 'sweat equity'.[6]

---

[6] See, eg, *Norwest Bank Worthington v Ahlers* 485 US 197 (1988) (promise of future labour does not warrant exception to the absolute priority rule).

These courts have even suggested that shareholders cannot just contribute 'new value' without the debtor permitting other parties to compete (eg through an auction) for an opportunity to provide such 'new value' as well.[7]

11.08 The gifting exception also is not without controversy. The gifting exception is premised on the notion that creditors are free to 'gift' a portion of their distributions under a chapter 11 plan to whomever they choose—even if that means that shareholders may receive a recovery while intermediate creditors do not get paid in full (or at all). Under the gifting exception, for example, senior lenders who may otherwise be entitled to all the equity in the reorganized debtor may agree to allow existing shareholders to retain or receive some portion of the equity in the reorganized entity in exchange for the shareholders' support for the chapter 11 plan, even though unsecured creditors may not be getting paid in full. Courts in the US continue to debate the appropriateness of the gifting exception and its scope, especially where creditors other than secured lenders attempt to 'gift' some of their distributions to junior classes of creditors or shareholders.[8]

11.09 In conclusion, notwithstanding the fairly simple principle that shareholders are last in line on the priority scale, chapter 11 provides some opportunities for shareholders to influence the reorganization and have an opportunity to recover on their equity interests.

11.3 UK

11.10 The starting point in any UK restructuring is to determine from an early stage who has an economic interest in the distressed business, as this factor will normally determine the restructuring strategy, in particular, whether it is to take place on a consensual or non-consensual basis. However, the broader interests of the stakeholders should not be entirely overlooked. In particular from the UK perspective, certain stakeholders may have a significant part to play in a restructuring in terms of facilitating the deal structure and satisfying certain legal requirements. These broader interests may, absent any economic interest, result in certain parties being able to extract some nuisance or 'hold out' value in exchange for their cooperation.

---

[7] See, eg, *Bank of Am. v 203 N. LaSalle St. P'ship* 526 US 434, 454 (1999).

[8] *CompareOfficial, Unsecured Creditors' Comm. v Stern (Re SPM Mfg. Corp.)* 984 F2d 1305 (1st Cir. 1993) (finding that secured lender may gift some of its recovery under the plan to unsecured creditors); *Re Protocol Servs., Inc.* 2005 Bankr. LEXIS 3191 (Bankr. SD Cal. 2005) (allowing senior lenders to gift some of their equity interests to unsecured class of noteholders), with *Re Armstrong World Indus.* 432 F.3d 507 (3rd Cir. 2005) (holding that asbestos claimants' waiver of warrants under the plan so that they may be distributed to shareholders violated the absolute priority rule); *Re OCA, Inc.* 357 BR 72 (Bankr. ED La. 2006) (finding that grant of participation rights by secured creditors to shareholders violated the absolute priority rule).

In this section we are going to consider one such group of stakeholders—the shareholders.

From the UK law perspective, the existence of such ancillary factorsmay result in shareholders cooperation being sought to achieve a consensual restructuring. Shareholder cooperation is not, necessarily, a necessity, since there are restructuring techniques that may be used to override such rights. The position of shareholders in relation to entities incorporated in the US or many European jurisdictions differs. The division appears to be determined by whether a jurisdiction is debtor or creditor friendly. In many of the European jurisdictions, there have been recent and significant legislative developments to promote rescue procedures and, in particular, the adoption of the US debtor in possession style reorganization mechanisms. These processes, which may be invoked at an early stage when a debtor is distressed but not technically insolvent, remain protective towards the insolvent debtor and inclusive of shareholder interests where there is some prospect of recovery to shareholders. For example, 'equity committees' are becoming increasingly common in US chapter 11 proceedings. English insolvency law, however, while undergoing significant changes in the promotion of a rescue culture by simplifying and making more accessible the administration procedure (which can also be employed in the pre-insolvency stage) still provides a forum that is more creditor friendly and does not impose any obligation on the administrator to consult with shareholders (although he may voluntarily seek to do so). We will discuss later in this chapter how this allows certain creditors, in particular circumstances, to take control of the business and/or the restructuring process. **11.11**

We are going to focus on the different kinds of restructuring taking place in the UK market and the role that shareholders have to play in a restructuring, first by looking at the situations that arise which require a compromise of their rights; second by considering the various restructuring techniques employed to circumvent these rights; and finally by looking at the specific issues that arise in the context of listed companies (by which, unless the context otherwise indicates, we mean premium listing of shares that are admitted to trading on the market of the London Stock Exchange). **11.12**

11.3.1 Who are the shareholders?

The type of investors in a business is in part driven by the nature of the business itself. There are different types of legal entity that are suited to different business models. From the UK law perspective the three most common forms of legal entity are: (1) private companies limited by shares ('private companies'); (2) public limited companies ('public companies'); and (3) partnerships. For the purposes of this section we are concerned only with private and public companies. It should also be noted that financial institutions have a bespoke resolution regime in the **11.13**

UK and shareholders in those companies are afforded certain rights in a restructuring. A consideration of the restructuring of financial institutions and also insurance companies (where special rules also apply) is beyond the scope of this chapter.

11.14 Private companies are restricted as to who they can seek as investors in their business and are not allowed to offer their shares for sale to the public. Public companies are not limited in the same way, and have access to a broader spectrum of investors to enable them to raise equity funds from the public. This means that shareholders come in all different shapes and sizes. In the context of private companies, they range from individual investors with small stakes to private equity houses who may have provided funding for a management buyout, with a view to realizing their investment by way of a sale or flotation at a later date. In the context of public companies, individual shareholders with small shareholdings may co-exist with sophisticated institutional or strategic investors.

11.15 For both private and public companies, while the company is solvent, the directors of a company must act in a way that promotes the success of the company for the benefit of the shareholders as a whole. The shareholders will therefore have control and influence over the company when it is in good financial health. When a company is nearing insolvency, however, the directors still owe their duty to the company but must act in the interests of the company's creditors, not the shareholders. This, together with the shareholders' appetite and ability to provide further investment, their attitude to risk and whether their approval is needed to achieve the desired restructuring will dictate how they participate in a restructuring. The starting expectation of creditors (senior and mezzanine lenders) will invariably be that if value breaks in the debt, and shareholders are not willing to inject new monies, they should not continue to control or have a say in the restructuring of the relevant entity or indeed receive any benefit. We analyse below the extent to which that expectation may be realized.

11.3.2 Economic interest

11.16 The priority ranking in an insolvency will serve as an important backdrop to any proposals for a restructuring, especially in circumstances where, absent a restructuring, a formal insolvency process is the only alternative. In the event of a formal insolvency, a defined order of priority of claims comes into play, where-shareholders will rank last in terms of priority after all creditors have been paid. (In the US, the absolute priority rule contains similar provisions, which means that shareholders are not entitled to recover anything unless all senior classes of creditors have been paid in full.) Notwithstanding the absence of an economic interest (or offers to inject new monies) there are often situations in the context of a restructuring that require shareholder cooperation. That requirement gives a form of value to shareholders' entitlements and the requirement for cooperation from the lenders' perspective needs to be minimized wherever possible. Some of the English restructuring techniques used to achieve this are discussed below.

11.3.3 Valuation

In order to determine who has an economic stake in the business concerned there needs to be a valuation of the business. This is a key factor in the negotiation of any restructuring. **11.17**

There is no statutorily-imposed method of valuation in the context of a restructuring. Much will depend on the nature of the business, the particular circumstances of the debtor and the timing of any realizations. Different methodologies may be appropriate, which will normally be determined by an expert valuer. Even then, the values will not be certain or exact and may fall within a wide range. **11.18**

In a recent English case, *Re Bluebrook*,[9] the issue of how a distressed business was valued was fundamental to the success of the restructuring. The case highlights the importance of companies undertaking a rigorous valuation exercise when pursuing a restructuring which excludes stakeholders on the basis that they lack any economic interest. It also confirms that English law has a mechanism for dealing with out-of-the-money hold outs. While the focus of the case was in relation to creditors who were excluded from the restructuring, it has equal resonance for shareholders, who essentially rank lowest in the priority order.[10] **11.19**

11.3.4 Situations requiring a compromise of shareholder rights

As a starting point, it is generally accepted that a restructuring that takes place on a consensual basis preserves the value in a distressed business, whereas a restructuring that takes place on a non-consensual basis and often in conjunction with a formal insolvency process may be value destructive. One of the reasons for this is that goodwill is preserved, in addition to keeping restructuring costs to a minimum. So while it may, as a matter of English law, be possible to effect a restructuring on a non-consensual basis and in particular without shareholder cooperation, in practice this is often the least favoured option, although it may be used to significant advantage in negotiations. From this perspective, the entrenched rights of shareholders that arise as a result of their rights in the articles of association or a shareholders' agreement, in addition to their statutory rights, may be key to achieving a consensual restructuring. Shareholder approvals and authorities may also have **11.20**

---

9 [2009] EWHC 2,114 (Ch) ('IMO Car wash case').

10 See Chapter 7 for more details on binding the minority or out of the money classes of creditors.

an impact on the restructuring timetable, as notice periods for shareholder meetings have to be adhered to. Lack of time is often a key driver in the restructuring process. In this way, shareholders' rights may have great significance although, as we have seen, economically they do not enjoy a priority position. In exceptional circumstances (some would say very exceptional), it should also be noted that the court may intervene in the exercise of shareholder rights. For example, in the well-known case of *Standard Chartered Bank v Walker*,[11] the court granted an injunction against shareholders who were to vote down a restructuring. Vinelott J. recognized that 'it is no doubt only in an extreme case that the Court will interfere by injunction with the exercise by a shareholder who is also a debtor with his own property—the voting rights attached to his own shares'. In that case, such boundaries had been crossed. The court recognized that, absent the restructuring (which had taken many months to put together) being effective, the likely alternative was a liquidation. In addition, the injunction served to protect the lender's security over the other shares that it held.

11.21 In a restructuring taking place on a non-consensual basis (and in the absence of exceptional court intervention) we consider in this chapter the different techniques that may be available to facilitate a restructuring in the absence of shareholder approval. In particular, we consider the ability to effect disposals, the use of prepackaged administration sales, and formal compromise arrangements, specifically schemes of arrangement pursuant to Part 26 of the Companies Act 2006 ('CA 2006'), which may offer a solution in circumstances where shareholder cooperation is not forthcoming.

11.22 Depending upon the nature of the problem that requires a fix, different solutions may be required. Distressed companies may experience liquidity issues, due to the lack of finance available in the markets, or they may require a 'right sizing' of the balance sheet where the level of debt means that the company is over geared and the company cannot service the debt. There may also be business or commercial reasons why an entity needs to restructure. This may involve a rationalization of the costs or a new focus on core aspects of the business.

11.23 There may also be restructuring situations that require the cooperation of shareholders because their participation is necessary in a different capacity. For example, whether a shareholder is a key supplier, part of the existing management team or, a key employee, and therefore forms an essential part in the planned restructuring, there are definite advantages in ensuring their cooperation. For those who do maintain an economic interest, it may be in their interest to offer shareholders a small equity stake in exchange for their cooperation.(This is analogous to the 'gifting exception' to the absolute priority rule, a concept which is being developed as

[11] [1992] BCLC 535, CA.

a matter of practice in the US.) Equally if a shareholder is providing new monies in the context of a UK restructuring, then maintaining relations and securing cooperation will be essential. (This is analogous to the 'new valuation' exception from the absolute priority rule which arises under chapter 11 proceedings in the US.)

11.3.5 Funding issues

If liquidity is the main source of difficulty, then access to funding will be paramount **11.24** in the context of a restructuring. Funds may be required to provide for an increase in the demand for working capital or reduce borrowings. Access to funds for distressed businesses may derive from a number of sources, namely any free cash available from the company's own resources, the provision of new facilities from existing or new lenders, proceeds raised from the disposal of non-core assets and cash generated from further equity investment, for example by way of a cash injection or, in the case of a public company, a rights issue. This is frequently why secured creditors have the upper hand in the context of a restructuring. Not only do they have the most significant economic interest in a distressed company and priority over other stakeholders, they are also often the source of additional funding. The ability to provide new monies in a restructuring can significantly enhance a stakeholder's bargaining position. Where further equity investment forms part of the restructuring, the negotiating position of the shareholder is undoubtedly improved and becomes the focus, rather than the value of its shareholding at the time of the restructuring. Equally, if a shareholder is in a position to provide a forgiveness of debt, this will usually mean that they have greater control. Perhaps less obvious is where funds are to be generated by a disposal, which may, in certain circumstances require shareholder approval. This may represent a 'hold out' or nuisance value which may result in shareholders being offered a continued stake in the restructured business—even though in economic terms they may not at the time of the restructuring have an interest. Hold out or nuisance value for shareholders is also generated by the shareholders' control of the membership of the board of directors, which is a power that continues irrespective of their economic interest and which they have freedom to exercise as they will. In listed public companies there are often borrowing restrictions in the articles of association restricting the power of the directors to borrow money to a multiple of share capital and reserves. Waiver of the limit is necessary to continue trading and this requires a shareholder vote. The problem usually arises at the early stage of restructuring discussions and the shareholder vote is usually easily obtained because of the dire nature of the alternative that would involve an elimination of all shareholder value.

11.3.6 Balance sheet restructuring

Whilst shareholders may not retain any economic interest or be able to provide **11.25** further funding, they may well be required to participate because of the nature of the restructuring or their dual role as management, key employee or supplier to the business. In particular, where the restructuring requires the 'right-sizing' of the balance sheet, for example where lenders may be prepared to write off some of their debt in exchange for an equity stake, shareholder cooperation will be key. This may require, for example, the shareholders to take a more prominent role than their economic stake reflects if their approval is required, such as in relation to the issue of new capital or the disapplication of pre-emption rights. Equally shareholder approval may be required for certain disposals which may form part of the capital reorganization. In these ways shareholders may be an essential part of the restructuring process.

11.3.7 Implementation techniques

11.26 We have set out above some of the bargaining chips that may be employed by a shareholder in the context of a restructuring. We are now going to consider some of the techniques that can be employed to circumvent the need for shareholder cooperation, or at a minimum be used as leverage to arrive at a consensual solution. The restructuring techniques that have been prevalent in the most recent round of restructurings are disposals, in particular pre packs, debt for equity swaps, and schemes of arrangement. In many cases restructurings have been achieved using a combination of these methods. When analysing the implementation a distinction needs to be drawn between shareholder hold-up rights and board hold-up rights even where the board and the shareholders are the same or the board comprises directors who represent the shareholders. The board ought to be acting for the creditors, and the shareholders act for themselves.

11.3.7.1 Sales

11.27 **11.3.7.1.1 Consensual sales** Disposals that form part of the restructuring strategy are usually carried out on a consensual basis with the cooperation of shareholders. From a practical perspective (especially for owner-managed businesses), allowing prospective purchasers access to and providing information on the relevant business or assets being sold will be key. From a legal perspective, there may also be a requirement for shareholder approval to the disposal. We consider the specific approvals in this regard below, which may arise as a result of shareholder rights as set out in the articles of association or incorporated into a shareholders' agreement. At the end of the chapter we also highlight these issues in the context of listed companies (see below).

11.28 **11.3.7.1.2 Non-consensual sales** Absent the cooperation of the shareholders, the lenders may also seek directly to enforce their security. It is usual for the secured lenders to have taken a full security package over the shares and assets of a company and/or its group. The enforcement process will normally involve a disposal of the assets or shares at a holding company level to a third party purchaser or to a lender-owned vehicle. This can be achieved in a number of ways, including via a formal insolvency process. In the case of a sale to third party purchasers, the value derived is likely to be less than would be achieved in a consensual/going concern basis, particularly if this is executed by the appointment of a receiver or administrator who will conduct the sale on an 'as seen basis' and provide no representations or warranties.

11.3.7.1.3 Prepackaged administrations In addition to a sale by way of enforcement, for non-consensual disposals, where shareholder consent and/or cooperation is not forthcoming because no deal can be done with the shareholders, a prepackaged sale ('pre pack') may offer a viable alternative.[12] **11.29**

For listed public companies, in the context of a prepackaged sale of the business or significant assets of the business by an administrator, the administrator will technically be bound by the Listing Rules as agent of the company (unless the shares have been delisted).Therefore, the approval of shareholders for certain disposals may technically be required. In practice, however, an administrator may be willing to proceed without the formal consent or seek a formal waiver to shareholder approval. (See Listed Companies section below for formal requirements imposed by the Listing Rules and the ability to circumvent them.) **11.30**

11.3.7.1.4 Intercreditor agreement mechanics In a non-consensual restructuring, a creditor's rights to enforce will be key. Creditor priority is often documented at the outset by an intercreditor agreement. The intercreditor agreement normally prohibits junior creditors from taking enforcement action until the senior creditors' liabilities have been discharged. Junior creditors will also be unable to make a demand, accelerate, sue for payment, or enforce any security or guarantees before the senior creditors have been satisfied. More importantly, where cooperation from shareholders is not forthcoming, the intercreditor agreement will usually contain provisions and set out the circumstances in which the security agent will be able to effect a disposal of shares and assets upon majority consent of the senior lenders. This will allow a sale of assets and/or a transfer of liabilities or release of liabilities, including intergroup liabilities. This is particularly useful where security has been taken at a sub-holding company level (as is the norm in leveraged transactions), which enables the lenders to take control of the operating business by either effecting sale or transferring the business to a new-company owned by the lenders. Structurally, this enables the senior lenders to exercise their enforcement rights without interference from junior creditors and the ultimate shareholders. **11.31**

---

[12] See chapter 8.

11.32 11.3.7.1.5 **Debt for equity swaps** A debt for equity swap involves the creditors of a company exchanging their debt for some form of equity. In its simplest form and in the context of a consensual swap this will take place at the holding company level. In circumstances where the indebtedness is at the subsidiary level of the company issuing shares, there are two main ways of structuring the debt for equity conversion. Firstly, by transferring the debt due to the lender from the subsidiary to parent by way of a novation, or alternatively by the lender effectively enforcing its rights under a parent guarantee, although in this regard care needs to be taken to avoid triggering any cross-defaults and precipitating action by other creditors at the operational level.

11.33 In many cases it will be the key financial creditors, such as the company's banks and bondholders, that participate in the debt for equity swaps but there is no restriction on who may be included. In practice, however, ordinary trade creditors are usually kept whole. In a consensual restructuring, it may also be necessary to provide the existing shareholders with an incentive to cooperate, by allocating some of the new shares to them.

11.34 Converting part of the debt for equity therefore may provide a solution to the company's gearing while, at the same time, not requiring any additional financing (although it may also be in conjunction with the provision of new monies). How it is implemented will depend on various factors, including the nature of the existing debt, equity and security structure, and balancing the complex issues arising from the interests of competing creditors, shareholders, and the board. If the company is listed then there are additional factors that will be applicable (see our section on Listed Companies).

11.35 The main objectives of a debt for equity swap are clear: a strengthened balance sheet; improved liquidity; and an improved position with creditors. From the company's and board's viewpoint, a debt for equity swap reduces gearing, improves cash flow and strengthens its balance sheet, which in turn relieves pressure from creditors, and addresses any concerns that the directors may have about their duties and potential personal liability issues. From the lenders' perspective, the retained debt will become performing debt and they will have the upside if the enterprise value improves. For key customers and suppliers it puts contractual relationships on a sounder footing, encouraging suppliers to provide or restore essential credit terms and credit insurers to keep lines in place, while reassuring customers that long-term or further orders will be fulfilled. Existing shareholders' interests in the company will be diluted or eliminated. A consensual debt for equity swap may be the only viable option for preserving at least some potential for a return on their equity investment.

11.36 There are no hard-and-fast rules on the form that the equity may take, it may be ordinary, preference, or convertible shares. It may also involve equity-based instruments, such as warrants or options. Whatever form the equity stake takes, it will often seek to achieve a priority of return in favour of the converting creditors and impose restrictions to preserve that priority, for example by limiting the issue of new shares and payment of dividends to ordinary shareholders.

As a matter of English law, a debt for equity swap can be implemented either within or outside of a formal insolvency process. For the swap to take place consensually the agreement of the relevant stakeholders, which will normally include the existing shareholders, is required. This usually arises as a result of shareholders being requested to waive pre-emption rights and allow new equity to be issued. (See further explanation of these in our section on Companies Act requirements as set out below.) If a debt equity swap is done without shareholder approval it will have to be done at a sub-holding company level, with the top holding company board resolving to implement the value issue in the sub-holding company. **11.37**

Within a formal process a swap may be facilitated by (a) an enforcement of security to transfer shares to a newco; or (b) an administration (which we have already considered in the context of disposals and pre-packs); or (c) a scheme of arrangement pursuant to the CA 2006. The use of schemes of arrangement may be particularly useful where unanimity among secured lenders would otherwise be required by virtue of provisions contained within the security documents, but is not achievable in practice, as it permits the 'binding' of a dissenting minority, as long as the requisite majority votes in favour. In practice, and by way of example, this has arisen in cases such as the restructuring of the McCarthy& Stone Group (2009) and IMO Car Wash (2009). **11.38**

11.3.7.1.6 Schemes of arrangement A scheme of arrangement is a statutory contract or arrangement between a company and its shareholders and/or its creditors (or any class of them) made pursuant to the CA 2006, sections 895–901.[13] **11.39**

Schemes are most prevalent in the context of compromising claims of creditors in a restructuring and the voting thresholds are often used effectively to disenfranchise junior or non-consenting senior creditors (who are holding out, in circumstances where unanimous consent is required). Schemes, when used in conjunction with disposals in an enforcement scenario and in reliance upon the ability of the security agent to effect that disposal and release security and liabilities under the provisions contained within an intercreditor agreement, can also have the effect of disenfranchising shareholders. In fact, schemes are often used to exclude stakeholders from participating in a restructuring. **11.40**

In the context of an English restructuring it is established practice that where a stakeholder no longer holds an economic interest, it is acceptable to ignore such **11.41**

[13] See chapter 7 for further detail on schemes of arrangement.

stakeholders.[14] In this respect, schemes are a legitimate mechanism for excluding shareholders where the value of the business breaks in the debt. It will not, however, overcome instances where the restructuring also necessitates cooperation of the shareholders (for example a simple debt for equity swap at the holding company level), unless this takes place in conjunction with an enforcement mechanism where the business is transferred to a lender-owned newco. It should also be noted that schemes generally require the cooperation of management to promote the scheme (although technically a creditor can propose a scheme).

11.42 In the context of the restructuring of the British Energy Group in 2004, the ability to circumvent shareholders' rights was fully explored, not least because in that case two groups of shareholders, together holding 10.22 per cent of the shares, threatened to stop the restructuring. The British Energy restructuring is a good example of how shareholders' rights may be compromised using each of the mechanisms we have considered above. In that case, a scheme of arrangement was used to compromise claims with creditors that, among other things, involved a debt for equity swap. As part of the restructuring it was also envisaged that the principal holding company would become a wholly owned subsidiary of a new company. The new company was ultimately to provide the equity required for the debt for equity swap. In order to achieve this, the shareholders were invited to approve a members' scheme of arrangement.

11.43 In the diagram below we set out how British Energy was to be restructured by way of a members' scheme of arrangement.

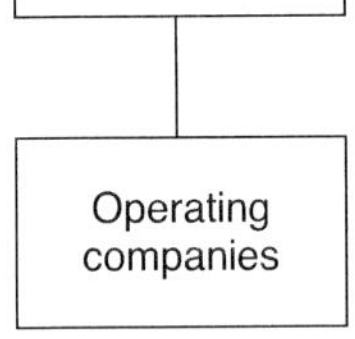

Group structure immediately before restructuring

[14] See *Re Tea Corporation* [1904] 1 Ch 12 referred to below.

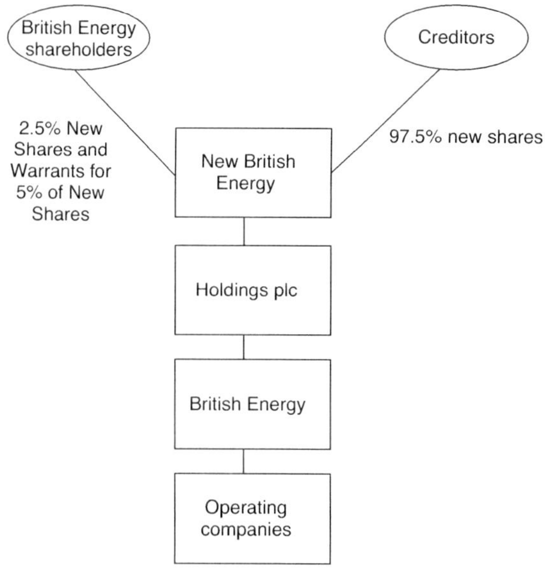

Group structure after the implementation of a members' scheme of arrangement

The advantages in proceeding with a members' scheme were largely based on tax benefits to the group and in addition avoided the need to transfer the business to a holding company. The members' scheme involved a reduction in capital by the cancellation of its shares, which was the mechanism to be used to reduce the deficit in the company's profit and loss account. The members' approval was therefore required in the context of the cancellation of the shares.[15]As can be seen from the diagram above, the shareholders were to receive new shares in the new company representing 2.5 per cent of the issued share capital and warrants entitling them to subscribe for further new shares equal to 5 per cent. If the members' scheme was not approved, the equity sweetener would of course not be available to existing shareholders. **11.44**

As an alternative, however, it was also recognized that if the members' scheme of arrangement was not approved, the company could pursue the restructuring by way of disposal of the business to a new company and in consideration for the business, the holding company would perform all the company's outstanding liabilities. In the context of the sale, had British Energy's shares been listed, shareholder approval would have been required as the disposal constituted a Class 1 transaction for the purpose of the Listing Rules (see further below). If shareholder approval was obtained for the disposal but the scheme was not approved shareholders would receive no new shares, but would receive warrants entitling them to subscribe for new shares equivalent to 5 per cent of the share capital. **11.45**

15 See Listed Companies section below regarding the cancellation of shares.

11.46 The Group structure following the disposal, without a members' scheme, but with shareholders' approval would be:

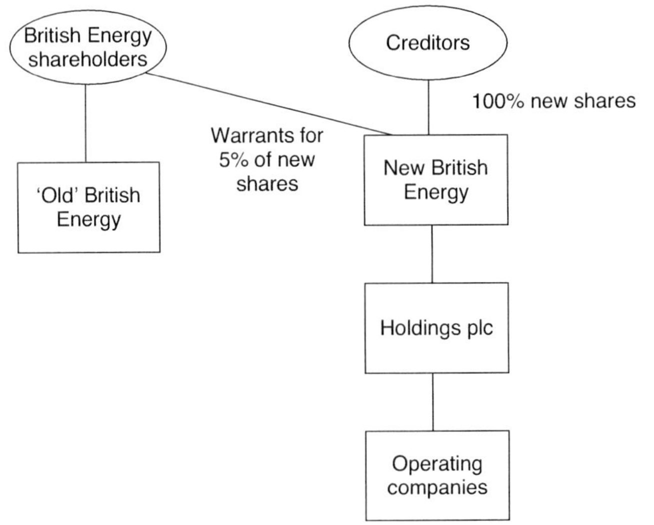

11.47 As a further alternative in the absence of shareholder approval under the Listing Rules for the disposal, British Energy would delist and effect the disposal that shareholders had voted down and the shareholders would then remain holders of shares in an unlisted company without any assets, following which 'old' British Energy would be eventually wound up with no return to shareholders (see diagram below).

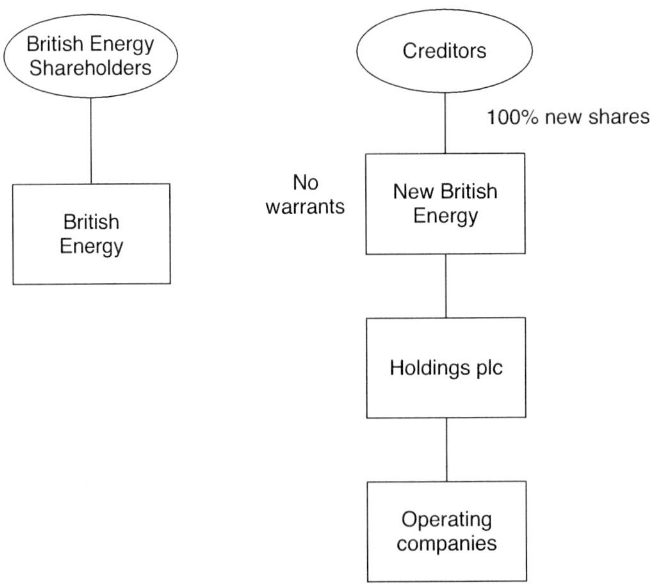

Group structure following the disposal without a members' scheme or shareholder approval

As can be seen from the diagrams above, there were a number of different options and incentives made available to the shareholders. A key factor, however, in this analysis is that the British Energy Group could have achieved the restructuring without any involvement of its shareholders, but their cooperation would, it was hoped, be obtained because they preferred to have a small interest rather than receive nothing, which would have been the result had the transaction proceeded without their support. **11.48**

The technique of having a plan (in the jargon know as 'Plan B') which is a plan as to how the restructuring would be implemented without the cooperation of an out of the money stakeholder group is one used in significant restructurings. The expectation is that the existence of the Plan B will force the out of the money constituency to cooperate and accept the relatively small stake offered to them. We refer below to what actually happened in the British Energy case (see paragraphs 11.87–11.88 below). **11.49**

11.3.8 Shareholder rights

11.3.8.1 Serious loss of capital

A further issue that needs to be taken into account in the context of a restructuring is whether the directors of a company are obliged to take action under the CA 2006, section 656. Section 656 provides that the directors of a public limited company are compelled to convene a general meeting in the event of a 'serious loss of capital'. The position is regarded as 'serious' where the company's net assets fall to half or less of the amount of its called up share capital. In the current climate, asset values have sometimes plummeted overnight and so this has been an additional factor in the context of many restructurings. The issue can be addressed by the shareholders at a meeting. The purpose of the meeting is to consider whether any, and what, measures should be taken to deal with the situation. In the context of a restructuring, the effect of the section 656 is not great, but it does require an explanation of what is going on to be made to shareholders at what might be an early and inconvenient time from the point of view of a proposed restructuring. The resolution proposed is normally a holding resolution not an implementing resolution. In the case of a listed company the resolution may be an increase in directors' borrowing powers to enable the company to continue trading. **11.50**

11.3.8.2 Borrowing restrictions

We referred above to the impact of borrowing restrictions. Clearly any that exist may need to be changed on implementation of a restructuring as well as to enable trading to continue in the period when the restructuring is under discussion. **11.51**

11.3.8.3 General company law requirements

11.52 In relation to a debt for equity swap, whether it takes effect in conjunction with a pre pack or a scheme of arrangement, there are certain Companies Act requirements that need to be adhered to.

11.53 We explain some of the key aspects of the Companies Act requirements in a little more detail below.

11.3.8.4 Disapplication of statutory pre-emption rights

11.54 Although shareholders' consent is not required for the conversion of debt for equity, the allotment of shares in satisfaction of debt will be treated as an allotment for cash and therefore in accordance with the CA 2006, sections 561–577, there must be a disapplication of existing shareholders' pre-emption rights.

11.3.8.5 Authority to allot shares and create new classes of shares

11.55 Pursuant to the CA 2006, sections 549 and 551, the directors of a company must be authorized by the company's articles or by way of shareholder approval to allot new shares. In addition, shareholders' consent may be required if a new class or type of equity is to be created, for example if convertible shares are to be issued then the articles of association will need to be amended.

11.3.8.6 Reduction in capital

11.56 It should also be borne in mind that often, where a company has effected a restructuring, especially in the case of a debt for equity swap, there will often be significant accumulated losses on its balance sheet. These losses can be eliminated by way of a reduction in capital. For private companies, the reduction in capital requires the consent of shareholders and either the court's approval or a statement of solvency from the directors in accordance with the CA 2006, section 642. For public companies, the court's consent is a requirement pursuant to the CA 2006, section 641. In the context of the Marconi Group restructuring (2003), the provisions of section 135 CA 1985 applied, which contained a similar requirement for the court's approval to the capital reduction. In that case, the court required an undertaking designed to protect creditors to the effect that the company would maintain special reserves and not make any distributions to shareholders until creditors had been paid out in full.

11.3.8.7 Listed companies

11.57 Understandably, there are additional protections for shareholders in relation to listed companies. In particular, the fact that the shares have been made available to the public means that there is a greater emphasis on information being made available to all shareholders and obligations to seek shareholder approval in relation to significant developments in the company's financial position. Timing in a restructuring is usually critical and the additional disclosure requirements and consents and the attendant costs in complying with these factors should not be underestimated and need to be factored into the restructuring timetable when dealing with a listed company.

11.3.8.8 General disclosure obligations

In a restructuring context there is often a tension between being able to protect the value of the business while at the same time maintaining a dialogue with investors. Other stakeholders, such as the management and lenders, for example, may prefer to achieve a restructuring out of the glare of any public scrutiny, whereas shareholders will often require as much information as possible about their investments. The Disclosure and Transparency Rules ('DTRs'), which form part of the FSA Handbook, contain a continuing obligation on companies with securities admitted to trading on the London Stock Exchange to notify a relevant regulatory information service as soon as possible of any 'inside information' which directly concerns the company. 'Inside information' is information that is precise, not generally available to the public, that relates directly or indirectly to the company and that, if made public, would be likely to have a 'significant effect'on the price of the company's shares. **11.58**

Notifiable developments may relate to a change in a company's financial condition, performance of its business or performance expectations and major new developments in the business. This would include an expected downturn in profits, an anticipated breach of financial covenants or another indication of financial distress, which may arise in the context of a restructuring and if it is sufficiently significant, will fall within'inside information'as defined above. In the context of the difficulties encountered by the Marconi Group, the FSA issued a public statement in April 2003 that the Group had breached the Listing Rules by failing to notify its change of financial condition, although no fines or further action was taken in respect of its failure. The lack of consequence was because the FSA did not have any power to impose any such sanctions. This is no longer the case (and under the current more aggressive regulatory climate fines would be likely). **11.59**

There is no set percentage or other figure that determines whether or not there is a 'significant effect'on the share price, and this will vary from company to company. The FSA has recently rejected a suggestion that a share price fall of 10 per cent or more attributable to a particular piece of information is necessary for it to have had a significant effect on price. The relevant legislation provides that information would be likely to have a significant effect on price if, and only if, it is information of a kind that a reasonable investor would be likely to use as part of the basis of his investment decisions. **11.60**

11.61 If the financial viability of a company is 'in grave and imminent danger', the DTRs specifically permit a delay in public disclosure of information for a limited period where such disclosure would seriously jeopardize the interest of existing and potential shareholders by undermining the conclusion of specific negotiations designed to ensure the long-term financial recovery of the company. However, the DTRs do not currently permit a company to delay public disclosure of the fact that it is in financial difficulty or that its financial condition is worsening.[16] The 'grave and imminent danger' exception is therefore effectively limited to creditor and related negotiations.

11.3.8.9 Suspension of listing

11.62 In certain circumstances, the London Stock Exchange will suspend trading of a company's shares including: when the listing of securities is itself suspended; where the ability of the Exchange to ensure the orderly operation of its market is, or may be, temporarily jeopardized; or on request by a company.

11.63 As mentioned above, it is possible for a company to approach the FSA for a suspension of its listing if, for example, there has been a material development that it is not yet in a position to announce (eg it is in financial difficulties but close to finalizing a rescue package) and there is a sudden material movement in its share price or a leak of information. In those circumstances, the suspension would be framed in terms that the shares were being suspended for a short period pending an announcement by the company. A typical period of suspension is not more than 48 hours; the FSA generally discourages extensions beyond this and will put pressure on the company to clarify the position and resume the listing as soon as possible. A suspension of listing will also result in the suspension of trading of the company's shares on the London Stock Exchange.

11.64 If trading has been suspended, as in the context of a restructuring, the Exchange may impose conditions to the resumption of trading. In any event, the company must still comply with the Exchange's admission and disclosure standards during a suspension. The Exchange may also cancel the right of a company to have its securities traded.

11.65 Subject to the appropriate procedures being followed, where a company has contravened any of the admission and disclosure standards, the London Stock Exchange may either censure the company privately or publicly, impose a fine, or make an order that the company make restitution to any person or cancel the right of the company to have its shares traded on the Exchange.

---

[16] See DTR 2.5.4G.

11.3.8.10 Cancellation of the listing

Once listed, a company that wishes the FSA to cancel its listing must first issue a circular to shareholders and obtain approval in a general meeting of no less than 75 per cent of its shareholders voting in person or proxy. **11.66**

The requirement for shareholder approval referred to above will not apply where the company notifies a regulatory information service that the financial position of the company or group is so precarious that, but for its proposal for reconstruction that is necessary to ensure its survival and which proposal would be jeopardized by the company's continued listing, there is no reasonable prospect that the company will avoid going into formal insolvency proceedings. The company will also be required to explain in its announcement why the cancellation is in the best interests of those to whom the company or its directors have responsibilities (including both shareholders and creditors) and why the approval of shareholders will not be sought before the cancellation of the listing.[17] **11.67**

11.3.8.11 AIM

A company admitted to AIM will not face the same level of ongoing disclosure requirements and restrictions as a company with its securities admitted to trading on the Exchange's main market. **11.68**

Admission to AIM is ideally suited to mid-sized companies looking to raise capital without incurring the regulatory burden and restrictions imposed by a listing on the main market. AIM has separate disclosure regime in rules 10 and 11 of AIM Rules for Companies. Most pertinent for restructuring is the requirement to disclose any changes in its financial condition that, if made public, would be likely to lead to a substantial movement in the price of the company's shares. **11.69**

11.3.8.12 Cancellation of listing on AIM

To cancel a listing on AIM, a company is required to obtain a special resolution from its shareholders and announce its intention to delist at least 20 clear business days before such date. **11.70**

In addition to the increased disclosure obligations referred to above, shareholder approval will also be required to facilitate significant disposals, or the allocation and issue of new equity. **11.71**

We now consider some of the specific issues that arise in the context of disposals and debt for equity swaps in the context of restructuring a listed company. **11.72**

[17] Listing Rule 5.2.7.

11.3.8.13 Listing issues on disposals

11.73 Chapter 10 of the Listing Rules governs the acquisition and disposal of shares and assets by listed companies. It classifies these transactions according to the size of the transaction in relation to the company itself, using a number of 'percentage ratio tests'. These tests are based on the gross assets, profit, consideration and gross capital of the company. Depending on the ratio the company may have to send a circular to shareholders to convene a meeting to obtain shareholder approval for the transaction. For example, where a disposal involves more than 25 per cent in value of the company's gross assets, this will be a class 1 transaction and require shareholders' approval. A working capital statement would also be required to be made in the circular sent to shareholders, which essentially has to confirm that there will be sufficient working capital for at least the next 12 months—essentially the lenders would need to underwrite this.

11.74 In the context of a restructuring, shareholder approval for a disposal may be waived in accordance with paragraph 10.8 of the Listing Rules for companies in financial difficulty. This was the case in the Marconi restructuring. Waiver of the requirement for shareholder consent and producing a circular to effect a significant transaction in regard to a listed company if it is in serious financial difficulties may be sought, but there is no definition of what constitutes serious financial difficulties. Listing Rule 10.8.1G recognizes that companies may find themselves in a position where they have no alternative other than to dispose of a substantial part of their business within a short space of time to facilitate their requirement for working capital or to reduce its liabilities. The company must however be able to demonstrate that (a) they could not reasonably have entered into negotiations earlier to enable shareholder approval to be sought; (b) all alternative methods of finance have been exhausted and the only option remaining is to dispose of a substantial part of the business; and (c) in taking such a decision, the directors are acting in the best interests of the company and shareholders as a whole and that unless the disposal is completed, a formal insolvency process is likely (with confirmation from the financiers that no further funds are available unless the disposal is effected). A full announcement must be released to the market no later than the date the disposal is agreed.

11.3.8.14 Listing issues in relation to debt for equity swaps

11.75 In addition to the Companies Act requirements set out above (eg for the disapplication of pre-emption rights and the authority to allot shares) there are some specific considerations that arise in the context of listed companies when effecting a debt for equity swap. Particular issues that arise include:

- whether the company is still suitable for listing post its restructuring pursuant to Listing Rule 6.1.19, in particular whether 25 per cent of the company's shares remain in public hands; and

- if a lender becomes a 10 per cent substantial shareholder (and therefore a related party) under the Listing Rules, the company will, post restructuring, need to comply with the rules relating to related party transactions where there are dealings between the lender and the company going forward. Chapter 11 of the Listing Rules governs transactions with related parties.

Those taking an equity stake will also need to be cognisant of whether acquiring an interest in shares triggers the Takeover Code requirement to make a mandatory cash offer to all other shareholders. **11.76**

11.3.8.15 Takeovers

Rule 9 of the City Code on Takeovers and Mergers (the 'Code') requires that, except with the consent of the Panel, an offer must be made to all other shareholders (and to holders of certain other target securities) by any person who acquires, whether by a series of transactions over a period of time or otherwise, interests in shares carrying 30 per cent or more of the voting rights of a company. Such offers are referred to as 'Rule 9' or 'mandatory' offers. **11.77**

In the context of a restructuring on a debt for equity swap, shares are issued as consideration for a release or cancellation of debt. Where such an arrangement would lead to a person (or a number of persons acting in concert) holding over 30 per cent of the voting shares of the company, this would normally trigger a mandatory bid obligation under Rule 9. However, there is a procedure under the Code whereby such an obligation can be waived if there is an independent vote at a shareholders' meeting and a majority (voting on a poll) approve the acquisition of the relevant stake by the incoming controlling shareholder. This dispensation is known as 'whitewash' and the detailed requirements are set out in appendix 1 to the Code. Full information and independent advice must be provided to shareholders so they can vote on a fully informed basis. **11.78**

11.3.8.16 Prospectus Rules

Where a listed company proposes to issue any further shares in the context of a restructuring, whether it is in the context of a debt for equity swap or a rescue rights issue (see further below), it will need to consider whether a prospectus will be required under the Financial Services and Markets Act 2000 ('FSMA') and the Prospectus Rules. Under section 85 of FSMA, a prospectus will be required where there: **11.79**

- an offer of listed or unlisted transferable securities to the public in the UK; and/or
- an application for admission of transferable securities to trading on a regulated market in the UK (eg the London Stock Exchange—but not AIM, as it is not a 'regulated market').

It is a criminal offence to breach section 85 FSMA and it could result in a fine and/or imprisonment.

11.80 If a transaction involves both an offer to the public and an application for admission to trading, then to avoid the requirement to publish a prospectus, an exemption must be available in relation to both triggers.

11.81 In respect of the public offer limb, the following are generally the most useful exemptions available, but particularly in the context of a restructuring:[18]

- offers to 'qualified investors' only. These include banks, investment institutions, national and regional governments, and certain natural persons and small and medium sized entities (SMEs) that meet certain criteria;
- offers to fewer than 100 persons (other than qualified investors) per EEA member state;
- where the minimum consideration that may be paid by any person is at least €50,000 (or the equivalent); and
- where the transferable securities being offered are denominated in amounts of at least €50,000 (or the equivalent).

11.82 Different exemptions are available in respect of the application for admission to trading limb. These include:

- offers of shares comprising, over a 12-month period, less than 10 per cent of the number of shares of the same class already admitted to trading on the same regulated market;
- where shares are issued as a result of the exercise of a conversion or exchange right, provided the shares are of the same class as shares already admitted to trading on the same regulated market; and
- where the securities being issued are already admitted to another regulated market (provided certain conditions are met).

If no exemption is available in either case, then a prospectus will be required.

11.83 The time required to draft the prospectus will depend largely on how recently the company has published a prospectus, as it will be much less onerous to update a fairly recent document than to prepare a draft from scratch, and the extent to which the company has centralized records of matters such as material contracts,

[18] A Directive to amend the Prospectus Directive was published in the Official Journal of the European Union on 11 December 2010. The amending Directive makes a number of changes to the provisions of the Prospectus Directive which will need to be implemented by Member States into the provisions of their domestic laws. Member States have until 1 July 2012 to do so. In particular, the definition of 'qualified investors' is amended to align with that of 'professional clients' for the purposes of Directive 2004/39/EC on markets in financial instruments (MiFID) and a number of the thresholds in the exemptions described here are to change: the '100 person' exemption is increased to 150 persons; and the €50,000 thresholds referred to are each increased to €100,000.

key properties, material litigation and so on. In any case, it is likely to take at least a week and in many cases two or three.

The draft prospectus must then be submitted to the UKLA for review at least 10 working days before the intended publication date (or, if the company does not already have securities admitted to trading in the UK, 20 working days in advance). **11.84**

It is also likely to take at least a couple of weeks to complete the work required for the directors to give the working capital statement (where the directors confirm that the working capital available to the company will meet its needs for the next 12–18 months), although this can be done in parallel with the UKLA review period. **11.85**

In the context of any restructuring, time will be of the essence, and the additional time required to draft a prospectus will need to be factored into the restructuring timetable for a listed company. **11.86**

11.3.8.17 Delisting and transfer to AIM

To ease disclosure and dispense with its continuing obligations under the Listing Regime, a company in need of restructuring may elect to cancel its listing or consider a transfer to AIM. In particular for disposals this will minimize the need for shareholder approvals. An AIM company will not have to obtain shareholder approval for Class 1 transactions and will not have to obtain shareholder approval for related party transactions. In the restructurings of Queens Moat Plc and British Energy, delisting was sought to avoid the need for shareholder approval to the fall-back business sale that would be used to effect the restructuring if shareholder approval was not obtained. It is important to understand that these cases proceeded under a regime where delisting was driven by the board alone who would apply to delist pursuant to the rules and legislation. The rules now require shareholder approval to delist. However, as referred to above, shareholder approval may be dispensed with[19] if, but for the delisting/restructuring, 'the company' would be forced to pursue a formal insolvency process. An announcement has to be made that, but for the delisting, there would be a formal insolvency, and that there is a proposal necessary to ensure the survival of the company or its group and the continued listing jeopardizes completion of that proposal. The announcement must explain why the cancellation is in the best interests of those to whom the company or its directors have responsibilities (including the bodies of securities holders and creditors taken as a whole) and why the approval of shareholders will not be sought before the cancellation. Finally the announcement must give **11.87**

---

[19] Listing Rule 5.2.7.

20 days' notice of the proposed cancellation. There is no recent experience of this exemption being relied upon in a restructuring context. The interesting question is whether the listing authority would delist in circumstances where the given reason for not seeking the approval of shareholders is that they would vote against the proposal to exploit 'hold out value'; it is an interesting question because that is the circumstance where the exception will be used.

11.88 In the case of British Energy, certain shareholders sought to oppose the implementation of the restructuring without shareholder approval by passing resolutions that would prevent the board of British Energy implementing the sale, which was the method by which the restructuring would be implemented, absent shareholder approval. The board of British Energy was placed in the situation where its articles might have required it to breach the restructuring agreement with creditors that British Energy had entered into. The board responded by accelerating the delisting process so that it could, if necessary, implement the restructuring even if the proposed resolutions were passed. To some extent the matter turned on the precise drafting of the proposed special resolutions. This all occurred before the requirement for shareholder approval for delisting described above.

11.4 Conclusion

11.89 Every restructuring will be different, and while in most cases shareholders of a distressed business will have no economic leverage in a restructuring (unless they are providing new monies), their cooperation will have a significant part to play in whether the stakeholders are able to restructure the business on a consensual basis or not. In the event that a consensual approach is not possible, as demonstrated above, the English law has effective and recognized practices to effectively compromise the rights of shareholders.

12

EMPLOYEES AND TRADE UNIONS

12.1 Introduction

At first blush, the UK and US case law and statutory regimes that are applicable in insolvency to employees and the unions that represent them appear to be quite different. However, a more thorough review reveals that the goal in both jurisdictions is the same: to reduce the harsh impact of insolvency on those who are usually the least at fault for the subject company's predicament—its employees. Indeed, among other similarities, both systems provide for priority in right of payment for a portion of the compensation due employees, have stringent notice requirements in the event of termination or rejection, impose penalties and require information sharing and good faith negotiations. The underlying objective of each system is to level the playing field and to incentivize the employer and the union to reach a consensual solution to avoid the risks and burdens mandated by each regime. Whether the legislators, administrators and jurists in either jurisdiction have gone too far or not far enough in developing tools for one side or the other will depend on the reader's perspective (as is almost always the case). The purpose of the two sections in this chapter is to objectively describe the law in each jurisdiction and the various challenges facing practitioners in trying to reorganize a company under such mandates. **12.01**

12.2 Employees and trade unions in the US

12.02 In many instances, the principal terms of the employer/employee relationship are memorialized in a collective bargaining agreement ('CBA'). The terms of a CBA—compensation, bonuses, severance, retention and lay-offs, to name a few—go to the very essence of the employer/employee relationship. Financial terms and work-rule provisions to which an employer agrees in better days can prove ruinous during times of economic hardship, pushing a troubled company increasingly close to insolvency. For an employer seeking to 'right-size' its workforce or to reduce employee obligations that have become excessively onerous, modification of one or more CBAs is frequently an important objective should a distressed company seek chapter 11 protection. This chapter seeks to provide an understanding of the changing landscape at the intersection of bankruptcy and labour laws in the US and to illustrate some of the challenges that debtors and employees face in modifying a CBA.

12.03 Part I of this chapter describes the development of section 1113 of title 11 of the United States Code (the 'Bankruptcy Code'), which provides authority in limited circumstances for a debtor to terminate its contractual obligations under a CBA. In Part II, the standards for rejection of a CBA under section 1113 of the Bankruptcy Code are discussed. Finally, Part III discusses the effects of rejection and the monetary damages to which rejection may give rise.

12.2.1 Bildisco and section 1113

12.04 Bankruptcy relief offers a troubled company a variety of tools by which a debtor can modify or eliminate burdensome obligations and emerge reorganized as a healthy company. Section 365 of the Bankruptcy Code, dealing with assumption and rejection of executory contracts and unexpired leases, is one of the most important of these tools. Section 365 provides debtors with broad powers to reject contracts and leases no longer necessary to current operations or containing unfavourable economic terms before emerging from bankruptcy.[1] Courts typically approve contract and lease rejections under the lenient 'business judgment' standard—the debtor need only demonstrate that, in the reasonable exercise of its discretion, it has determined that rejection may benefit the estate and

[1] Section 365(a) provides that a debtor may 'assume or reject any executory contract or unexpired lease. . . .' 11 USC s 365(a) (2005). An executory contract is 'a contract under which the obligation of both the bankrupt and the other party to the contract are so far unperformed that the failure of either to complete performance would constitute a material breach excusing the performance of the other'. See Vern Countryman, 'Executory Contracts in Bankruptcy: Part 1' (1973) 57 Minn. L. Rev. 439, 460. This definition has been widely accepted by bankruptcy courts.

its creditors.[2] In most circumstances, rejection of an executory contract or lease under section 365 constitutes a pre-petition breach, excuses the debtor from further performance, and gives rise to a general unsecured claim that may be discharged for less than full value under a plan of reorganization.

For many troubled companies, their CBAs are often the source of great burden and offer the possibility for tremendous upside if modifications are possible. Outside of bankruptcy, the modification or termination of CBAs has long been governed by the National Labor Relations Act (the 'NLRA').[3] Under the NLRA, it is an unfair labour practice for an employer to unilaterally modify or terminate a CBA and any attempt to do so will be ineffective.[4] Nothing in the NLRA indicates that Congress intended that it apply only to solvent employers. Nonetheless, the version of section 365 included in the Bankruptcy Code when it became law in 1979 appeared to apply to all executory contracts, including CBAs. This tension between the debtor's broad powers to reject burdensome contracts and the restrictions on unilateral modification or termination contained in the NLRA came to a head in 1984 in *NLRB v Bildisco and Bildisco*.[5] **12.05**

Prior to 1984, many courts had held that debtors could reject CBAs under section 365 (or its predecessor under the Bankruptcy Act)[6] under certain circumstances.[7] The standard courts applied in determining whether a debtor could use section 365 to reject a CBA, however, varied significantly.[8] Some courts, including the Second Circuit in *Rea Express, Inc.*, authorized rejection of CBAs only where **12.06**

---

[2] See *NLRB v Bildisco and Bildisco* 465 US 513, 523 (1984); *Control Data Corp. v Zelman (In re Minges)* 602 F2d 38, 42–3 (2nd Cir. 1979). See also *In re HQ Global Holdings, Inc.* 290 BR 507, 511 (Bankr. D. Del. 2003) (stating that a debtor's decision to reject an executory contract is governed by the business judgment standard and can only be overturned if the decision was the product of bad faith, whim, or caprice).

[3] 29 USC ss 151–169 (2006).

[4] Ibid. at s 158(d). Upon finding that the employer has engaged in an unfair labour practice, the National Labor Relations Board (the 'NLRB') is empowered to order that the employer 'cease and desist from such unfair labor practice, and to take such affirmative action including reinstatement of employees with or without backpay, as will effectuate the policies of this Act'. Ibid. at s 160(c). As a result, attempts to unilaterally modify or terminate a CBA will be ineffective.

[5] *NLRB v Bildisco and Bildisco* 465 US 513 (1984).

[6] Section 313(1) of the Bankruptcy Act provided that: 'Upon the filing of a petition, the court may, in addition to the jurisdiction, powers, and duties conferred and imposed upon it by this chapter—(1) permit the rejection of executory contracts of the debtor, upon notice to the parties to such contracts and to such other parties in interest as the court may designate.' See *Shopmen's Local Union No. 455 v Kevin Steel Prods.* 519 F2d 698, 701 (2nd Cir. 1975) (holding that s 313(1) of the Bankruptcy Act permitted rejection of CBAs).

[7] Ibid. at 701 (collecting cases).

[8] *Bildisco* 465 US at 526–7. Prior to the Supreme Court's decision in *Bildisco*, every court of appeals that had considered the matter had determined that a more rigourous standard than merely determining whether rejection was an appropriate exercise of the debtors' business judgment. Ibid. at 523–4.

failure to do so would cause the debtor to liquidate.[9] Other courts were more permissive, allowing a debtor to reject a CBA 'after thorough scrutiny, and a careful balancing of the equities on both sides'.[10] The *Bildisco* case presented the Supreme Court with the opportunity to determine whether CBAs could be rejected pursuant to section 365 of the Bankruptcy Code or whether the attempted rejection of a CBA under section 365 violated the NLRA.

12.07 Bildisco and Bildisco ('Bildisco') filed a petition under chapter 11 of the Bankruptcy Code in 1980.[11] Approximately seven months after filing for bankruptcy, Bildisco sought to reject its CBA with the International Brotherhood of Teamsters, Chauffeurs, Warehousemen and Helpers of America (the 'Teamsters').[12] The bankruptcy court approved the rejection over the Teamsters' objection, basing its decision solely upon testimony from one of Bildisco's general partners that rejection would save the debtor approximately $100,000 in the following calendar year.[13] The Teamsters thereafter initiated proceedings before the National Labor Relations Board (the 'NLRB'), alleging that Bildisco had committed an unfair labour practice under the NLRA.[14] The NLRB found that Bildisco had violated the NLRA.[15] Further proceedings stemming from the bankruptcy court and NLRB decisions were consolidated and heard by the Third Circuit Court of Appeals.[16] The Third Circuit refused to enforce the NLRB's order and held that the NLRA did not apply and that section 365 permitted rejection of a CBA.[17] The case was remanded to the bankruptcy court for reconsideration of whether 'continuation of the collective bargaining agreement would be burdensome to the estate' and whether the equities balance in favour of rejection.[18]

12.08 The Teamsters and the NLRB appealed and the Supreme Court granted certiorari to settle the issue of which statutory scheme prevailed—bankruptcy or labour law. The Supreme Court in *Bildisco* concluded that (a) a debtor does not commit an unfair labour practice when it unilaterally alters or terminates a CBA and (b) a CBA is an executory contract that can be rejected pursuant to section 365.[19]

---

[9] *Bhd. of Ry., Etc. v REA Express, Inc.* 523 F2d 164, 172 (2nd Cir. 1975) ('[I]n view of the serious effects which rejection has on the carrier's employees it should be authorized only where it clearly appears to be the lesser of two evils and that, unless the agreement is rejected, the carrier will collapse and the employees will no longer have their jobs.').

[10] *Shopmen's Local Union No. 455 v Kevin Steel Prods.* 519 F2d 698, 701, 707 (2nd Cir. 1975).

[11] *NLRB v Bildisco and Bildisco* 465 US 513, 517 (1984).

[12] *Bildisco,* 465 US at 518.

[13] Ibid.

[14] Ibid. at 518–9.

[15] Ibid. at 519.

[16] See *Nat'l Labor Relations Bd. v Bildisco and Bildisco (In re Bildisco)* 682 F2d 72 (3rd Cir. 1982).

[17] Ibid. at 84–5.

[18] Ibid. at 81.

[19] *NLRB v Bildisco and Bildisco* 465 US 513, 530–4 (1984).

In doing so, the Court reasoned that the standard articulated in *REA Express, Inc.*, which permitted rejection only where the debtor would otherwise be forced to liquidate, was 'fundamentally at odds with the policies of flexibility and equity built into chapter 11 of the Bankruptcy Code'.[20] The Court went on to articulate a standard for rejection more stringent than the 'business judgment' standard typically applied under section 365 but less stringent than the *REA Express, Inc.* standard.[21] Under the *Bildisco* standard as articulated by the Supreme Court, a CBA could be rejected if the debtor demonstrated 'that the collective-bargaining agreement burdens the estate, and that after careful scrutiny, the equities balance in favour of rejecting the labour contract'.[22] The careful scrutiny applied by the bankruptcy court would not begin until the 'parties' inability to reach an agreement threaten[ed] to impede the success of the debtor's reorganization'.[23]

Congress, dissatisfied with the outcome of *NLRB v Bildisco and Bildisco*, enacted section 1113 and thereby removed CBAs from the purview of section 365—at least in the context of cases pending pursuant to chapter 11 of the Bankruptcy Code.[24] Section 1113 substantially restricts a debtor's ability to unilaterally alter or terminate a CBA.[25] Perhaps owing to the rapidity with which section 1113 was passed by Congress in response to *Bildisco*,[26] however, section 1113 is by no means a 'masterpiece of draftsmanship'.[27] The language of section 1113 left many issues for the courts to resolve. Without clear guidance from Congress or a definitive interpretation by the Supreme Court, the results have been inconsistent.[28] **12.09**

[20] Ibid. at 525.

[21] Ibid. at 526.

[22] Ibid.

[23] Ibid.

[24] Bankruptcy Amendments and Federal Judgeships Act of 1984, Pub. L. No. 98-353, s 541, 98 Stat. 333 (1984). Although s 1113 generally removed CBAs from the purview of s 365, it remains applicable to municipal debtors. See 11 USC s 901 (2005). See also *In re City of Vallejo* 403 BR 72, 78 (Bankr. ED Cal. 2009) (holding that municipality was entitled to reject CBA if it satisfied standard articulated by Supreme Court in *Bildisco*).

[25] See, eg, *Peters v Pikes Peak Musicians Ass'n* 462 F3d 1265, 1269 (10th Cir. 2006) (noting that s 1113 restricts a debtor's ability to unilaterally reject a collective bargaining agreement during bankruptcy); *United Food & Commercial Workers Union, Local 211 v Family Snacks, Inc. (In re Family Snacks, Inc.)* 257 BR 884, 891–2 (BAP 8th Cir. 2001) (noting that '[s]ection 1113 contains detailed substantive and procedural requirements with which a debtor must comply to modify or reject a CBA').

[26] Congress' response to *Bildisco* was swift; s 1113 was hastily enacted only five months after the *Bildisco* decision. See *United Food and Commercial Workers Union, Local 770 v Official Unsecured Creditors Comm. (In re Hoffman Bros. Packing Co., Inc.)* 173 BR 177, 182 (BAP 9th Cir. 1994) (noting that the hasty enactment of s 1113 was 'not a tidy process' and that passage of s 1113 was not 'accompanied by a committee report, and there is no dependable legislative history' on which to rely).

[27] *In re Am. Provision* 44 BR 907, 909 (Bankr. D. Minn. 1984).

[28] See *Birmingham Musicians' Protective Ass'n, Local 256–733, of the Am. Federation of Musicians v Alabama Symphony Ass'n* 211 BR 65, 69 (ND Ala. 1996). See also *In re Moline Corp.* 144 BR 75,

12.2.2 Standards for rejection of collective bargaining agreements

12.10 While some aspects of section 1113 continue to be disputed, courts are in agreement that a debtor seeking to reject a CBA pursuant to section 1113 must satisfy the following nine factors:

- Prior to filing a motion to reject a CBA, the debtor must make a proposal to the union to modify the CBA.
- The debtor's proposal must be based on the most complete and reliable information available at the time.
- The modifications must be necessary to permit reorganization.
- The proposed modifications must assure that all creditors, the debtor, and other affected parties are treated fairly.
- After submitting the proposal to the union, the debtor must provide the union with information to evaluate the proposal.
- Between the time of the proposal and the time of the hearing on the motion to reject, the debtor and the union must meet at reasonable times.
- The debtor must confer with the union in good faith in an attempt to reach mutually satisfactory modifications of the CBA.
- The union must refuse to accept the debtor's proposal without good cause.
- The balance of equities must clearly favour the rejection of the CBA.[29]

The more important of these requirements are discussed in greater detail below.[30]

12.2.2.1 The necessity requirement

12.11 Section 1113(b)(1)(A) of the Bankruptcy Code requires that, before rejecting a CBA, a debtor first make a proposal to the union that provides for 'those necessary modifications in the employees benefits and protections that are necessary

78 (Bankr. ND Ill. 1991) (noting that Congress failed to make clear section 1113's relationship to other provisions of the Bankruptcy Code).

[29] See, eg, *In re Am. Provision Co.* 44 BR at 909 (finding that 'nine requirements can be gleaned from s 1113'); *Truck Drivers Local 807, Int'l Bhd. of Teamsters, Chauffeurs, Warehousemen & Helpers of Am. v Carey Transp., Inc.* 816 F2d 82, 86 (2nd Cir. 1987) (noting that the bankruptcy court had adopted the nine-step analysis of s 1113 set out by the *American Provision* court).

[30] Although this chapter discusses only the most commonly contested issues related to the rejection of a CBA under s 1113, each of the *American Provision* requirements is a potential stumbling block for debtors. For example, in *Frontier Airlines*, the debtor had made its initial proposal to the union and subsequently sought authority to reject the CBA. *Teamsters Airline Div. v Frontier Airlines, Inc.* No. 09 Civ. 343, 2009 WL 2168851, at *2 (SDNY 2009). During and after the rejection hearing, but before the bankruptcy court issued its ruling, the debtor made subsequent proposals. Ibid. at *2–3. Based partially on these later proposals, the bankruptcy court granted the debtor's motion to reject the CBA. Ibid. at *4. On appeal, the district court vacated the bankruptcy court's order authorizing rejection because s 1113(c)(1) requires a debtor to make a proposal satisfying the requirements of s 1113 'prior to the [termination] hearing.' Ibid. at *8.

to permit the reorganization of the debtor. . .'.[31] The necessity requirement was the subject of lengthy Congressional debate before enactment of section 1113.[32] Neither the text of section 1113 nor the legislative history surrounding its enactment yield a definitive answer as to which modifications are 'necessary'. As a result, the necessity requirement has produced substantially diverging lines of authority in various courts.

Under the minority view, applied primarily in the Third Circuit, modifications satisfying the necessity requirement of section 1113 must be 'essential' to the continuation of the debtor's business.[33] In *Wheeling-Pittsburgh Steel Corp. v United Steelworkers of America*, the Third Circuit examined whether the concessions sought by the debtor from its unionized employees were necessary.[34] The disputed language of section 1113(b) required the debtor to propose modifications that were 'necessary to permit... reorganization'.[35] On the other hand, the language of section 1113(e), dealing with temporary relief during the pendency of a case, allowed for interim modification of the terms of a CBA if the modifications were 'essential to the continuation of the debtor's business'.[36] At issue was whether 'necessary' in section 1113(b) carried a meaning different from 'essential' in section 1113(e). Finding no answer in the statute itself, the court looked to the legislative history of section 1113 for guidance. In light of the fact that section 1113 was enacted in response to the Supreme Court's rejection of a strict standard for rejection of a CBA in *Bildisco*,[37] the Third Circuit rejected the 'hypertechnical argument that "necessary" and "essential" have different meanings. ... The words are synonymous'.[38] Consequently, courts applying the minority view hold that modifications under section 1113 must be limited to only those which will prevent the liquidation of the debtor.[39] **12.12**

The majority view, applied by the Second and Tenth Circuits and numerous lower courts,[40] holds that the necessity requirement does not require that proposed modifications be essential to the survival of the debtor. Instead, courts adopting the majority view require that the debtor's proposal include modifications designed **12.13**

[31] 11 USC s 1113(b)(1)(A).

[32] See *Wheeling-Pittsburgh Steel Corp. v United Steelworkers of Am.* 791 F2d 1074, 1082–4 (3rd Cir. 1986). See also Bruce H. Charnov, 'The Uses and Misused of the Legislative History of Section 1113 of the Bankruptcy Code' (1989) 40 Syracuse L. Rev. 925, 946–58.

[33] *Wheeling-Pittsburgh Steel Corp.*, 791 F2d at 1088.

[34] Ibid. at 1088–9.

[35] Ibid. at 1086.

[36] Ibid. at 1085.

[37] See above n. 33 and accompanying text.

[38] *Wheeling-Pittsburgh Steel Corp.* 791 F2d at 1088.

[39] Ibid. at 1089.

[40] See *Carey* 816 F2d at 89–90; *Sheet Metal Workers' Int'l Ass'n, Local 9 v Mile Hi Metal Sys., Inc. (In re Mile Hi Metal Sys., Inc.)* 899 F2d 887, 892–3 (10th Cir. 1990).

to improve the debtor's financial health.[41] In *Truck Drivers Local 807 v Carey Transportation, Inc.*, before the petition date, the debtor had unsuccessfully negotiated for a proposed CBA modification providing for approximately $750,000 in annual cost savings.[42] The union rejected the proposal and Carey Transportation filed for chapter 11 protection.[43] Immediately thereafter, the debtor sought modifications to the CBA that would have provided it approximately $1.8 m of annual savings.[44] At issue, among other things, was whether the cost reductions contained in the proposed post-petition modification sought by the debtor met the necessity requirement because they substantially exceeded the cost reductions of the pre-petition request.[45] The bankruptcy court approved the modifications proposed by the debtor and the district court agreed.[46]

12.14 On further appeal, the Second Circuit examined the legislative history of section 1113 and affirmed, holding that although the proposed modifications were not the bare minimum required to successfully reorganize, what is 'necessary' for purposes of section 1113 is not just those modifications essential to the debtor's immediate survival.[47] Under *Carey*, bankruptcy courts considering a debtor's proposal should look not to whether the modifications will prevent liquidation, but rather whether the modifications are critical to the debtor's long-term financial health after emergence from bankruptcy protection.[48] The court reasoned that the Third Circuit's holding in *Wheeling-Pittsburgh* left debtors with a conundrum: 'an employer who initially proposed truly minimal changes would have no room for good faith negotiating, while one who agreed to any substantive changes would be unable to prove that its initial proposals were minimal'.[49]

[41] See *Carey* 816 F2d at 89–90 (stating that any proposal must contain 'necessary, but not absolutely minimal, changes that will enable the debtor to complete the reorganization process successfully').

[42] Ibid. at 85–6.

[43] Ibid. at 86.

[44] Ibid.

[45] *Truck Drivers Local 807, Int'l Bhd. of Teamsters, Chauffeurs, Warehousemen & Helpers of Am. v Carey Transp., Inc.* 816 F2d 82, 89–91 (2nd Cir. 1987).

[46] *Re Carey Transp. Corp.* 50 BR 203, 213 (Bankr. SDNY 1985).

[47] *Carey* 816 F2d at 92–3.

[48] Ibid. at 89–90. See also *N.Y. Typographical Union No. 6 v Royal Composing Room, Inc. (In re Royal Composing Room, Inc.)* 848 F2d 345, 350 (2nd Cir. 1988) (approving modifications beyond 'bare bones relief' and noting debtor's 'need for long-term flexibility in order to have a truly successful reorganization'); *In re Appletree Markets, Inc.* 155 BR 431, 441 (SD Tex. 1993) (stating 'creditors are not likely to extend additional funds to a reorganized debtor unless there is a reasonable basis to conclude that the reorganization will be successful and not merely a prelude to another reorganization or liquidation').

[49] *Truck Drivers Local 807, Int'l Bhd. of Teamsters, Chauffeurs, Warehousemen & Helpers of Am. v Carey Transp., Inc.* 816 F2d 82, 89 (2nd Cir. 1987).

12.2.2.2 *The fair and equitable requirement*

Section 1113(b)(1)(A) further requires that modifications proposed by a debtor must assure that all 'creditors, the debtor and all of the affected parties are treated fairly and equitably'.[50] The 'fair treatment' requirement does not require identical or equal treatment of all parties, but instead seeks to ensure that the burden of reorganization will be borne by all groups.[51] Some courts have looked unfavourably on proposals under which other constituencies, such as managerial employees, would not bear their share of concessions.[52] To ensure that represented workers share in the debtor's recovery, some courts have considered essential the existence of a 'snap-back' provision, under which the modified CBA would revert to its original terms if the debtor's performance exceeded expectations.[53] **12.15**

12.2.2.3 *The good faith requirement*

Section 1113(b)(2) requires that, between the making of the proposal and the hearing on the debtor's motion seeking to reject a CBA under section 1113, the debtor must 'meet, at reasonable times with the authorized representative to confer in good faith in attempting to reach mutually satisfactory modifications' of the CBA.[54] This duty has been interpreted broadly: **12.16**

> The union should be supplied with detailed projections and recommendations, perhaps made by a management consultant, preferably one who is independent of the interested parties. The debtor should present full and detailed disclosure of its difficulties and its proposed short-run and long-run solutions.[55]

---

[50] 11 USC s 1113(b)(1)(A).

[51] See, eg, *Bowen Enters., Inc. v United Food and Commercial Workers Int'l Union, Local 23, AFL-CIO-CLC (In re Bowen Enters.)* 196 BR 734, 743 (Bankr. WD Pa. 1996) (holding that fair and equitable does not require identical treatment of all parties, but a proposed modification may not 'place a disproportionate share of the financial burden of avoiding liquidation on bargaining unit employees').

[52] See *In re The Lady H. Coal Co., Inc.* 193 BR 233, 242 (Bankr. SD W. Va. 1996). In *Lady H. Coal Co.*, the debtor sought authority to reject its CBA and to sell substantially all of its assets to a third party. Ibid. at 236. The sale agreement would not have assumed employee obligations but would have provided the debtor's two remaining officers with one-year consulting agreements providing for compensation far greater than court-authorized post-petition salaries. Ibid. at 242. The court denied the debtor's motion to reject its CBA on the grounds that the disparity between the treatment of represented workers and managerial employees did not satisfy the fair and equitable requirement of s 1113. Ibid. at 242–3. See also *In re Sol-Sieff Produce Co.* 82 BR 787, 794 (Bankr. WD Pa. 1988) (finding proposed modifications fair and equitable where (i) all employees of the debtor had suffered a wage reduction, (ii) the debtor had sought grace periods and extensions from suppliers, and (iii) the union failed to provide counterproposals or explanation for rejections of proposals). Although fair and equitable frequently requires burden-sharing between management and labour, it 'does not mean equal in all respects.' Ibid. at 794.

[53] See *Wheeling-Pittsburgh Steel Corp. v United Steelworkers of Am., AFL-CIO-CLC* 791 F2d 1074, 1093 (3rd Cir. 1986) (holding that bankruptcy court's conclusion that modification based upon worst-case scenario was fair and equitable without considering need for mechanism by which employees would share in a better-than-expected future could not be affirmed).

[54] 11 USC s 1113(b)(2).

[55] *In re K&B Mounting, Inc.* 50 BR 460, 467 (Bankr. ND Ind. 1985). But see *In re Salt Creek Freightways* 47 BR 835, 839 (Bankr. D. Wyo. 1985) (holding that union's request to include duty to disclose company information relevant to evaluating union's counterproposals).

12.17 Good faith therefore requires a showing that the debtor 'has seriously attempted to negotiate reasonable modifications'.[56] Although the debtor is typically the subject of accusations of bad faith, unions cannot simply adopt a 'take it or leave it' approach to negotiations and hope to avoid rejection.[57]

12.18 The good faith requirement is substantially intertwined with the other requirements of section 1113. For example, as noted above, one line of cases interpreting the necessity requirement requires that the debtor's proposal include only those modifications essential to the debtor's survival.[58] This approach has been criticized because a debtor submitting a proposal that would truly effect only those changes that are essential to the debtor's survival cannot afford to give any more without causing its own collapse. It is unclear how such a debtor, which would have no choice but to adopt a 'take it or leave it' approach, can satisfy its obligation to negotiate in good faith.[59]

12.2.2.4 Rejection without good cause

12.19 Section 1113(c)(2) requires that a court shall only approve the rejection of a CBA after 'the authorized representative of the employees has refused to accept [a proposal that meets the other requirements of section 1113] without good cause'.[60] Determining what constitutes 'good cause' is made on a case-by-case basis, but has been interpreted by courts to mean that a union must articulate and discuss in detail with the debtor before the hearing its reasons for declining to accept a proposal.[61] Refusal to participate meaningfully in the negotiation process will damage a union's claim to good cause for its rejection of a debtor's proposal.[62]

---

[56] *Re Kentucky Truck Sales, Inc.* 52 BR 797, 801–2 (Bankr. WD Ky. 1985) (finding good faith requirement satisfied where testimony at rejection hearing 'indicated the willingness of both parties to discuss various contract concessions').

[57] *N. Y. Typographical Union No. 6 v Royal Compsing Room, Inc. (In re Royal Composing Room, Inc.)* 848 F2d 345, 349 (2nd Cir. 1988) (stating 'where a union refuses to negotiate in order to obtain a different combination of benefits, it may not challenge the particular combination, or any vital element, contained in the debtor's proposal').

[58] See above nn. 33–39 and accompanying text.

[59] See above n. 49 and accompanying text.

[60] 11 USC s 1113(c)(2).

[61] See *In re Royal Composing Room, Inc.* 62 BR 403, 408 (Bankr. SDNY 1986), affd 78 BR 671 (SDNY 1987), affd 848 F2d 345 (2nd Cir. 1988). Although the debtor is said to bear the ultimate burden of showing a lack of good cause, the union must come forward with reasons for declining to accept the debtor's proposal. See *Carey* 816 F2d at 92. If the debtor provides evidence that the CBA is not economically feasible and the union fails to produce countervailing evidence, the union may be found to have rejected the proposal without 'good cause'. See *Re Valley Steel Prods. Co., Inc.* 142 BR 337, 341–2 (Bankr. ED Mo. 1992).

[62] See *Truck Drivers Local 807 v Carey Transportation* 816 F2d 82 (2nd Cir. 1987). But see *In re Bruno's Supermarket, LLC* 2009 WL 1148369 (Bankr. ND Ala. 2009). In *Bruno's Supermarket*, the union insisted upon the inclusion of a provision requiring any asset purchaser to negotiate in good faith as a successor with the union. The debtor asserted that the demand for a successorship clause 'will . . . absolutely prevent a sale, lead to liquidation, and ultimately result in nearly 4000 lost jobs'.

12.2.2.5 Balance of equities must clearly favour rejection

Section 1113(c)(3) states that a court will approve a proposed CBA rejection only if 'the balance of equities clearly favours rejection of such agreement'.[63] This requirement, which derives from the core of the Supreme Court's holding in *Bildisco*,[64] is generally subsumed within the other requirements for CBA rejection under section 1113. The Second Circuit, in *Truck Drivers Local 807 v Carey Transportation, Inc.*, set out six permissible equitable considerations under section 1113(c)(3): **12.20**

- the likelihood and consequences of liquidation if rejection is not permitted;
- the likely reduction in the value of creditors' claims if the bargaining agreement remains in force;
- the likelihood and consequences of a strike if the bargaining agreement is voided;
- the possibility and likely effect of any employee claims for breach of contract if rejection is approved;
- the cost-spreading abilities of the various parties, taking into account the number of employees covered by the bargaining agreement and how various employees' wages and benefits compare to those of others in the industry; and
- the good or bad faith of the parties in dealing with the debtor's financial dilemma.[65]

As the *Bildisco* Court noted, '[t]he Bankruptcy Code does not authorize free-wheeling consideration of every conceivable equity, but rather only how the equities relate to the success of the reorganization'.[66] **12.21**

Congress enacted section 1113 of the Bankruptcy Code and left the requirements to the interpretation of the courts, resulting in significant disparities in application. Also left open to interpretation were the effects of rejecting a CBA under section 1113. **12.22**

Ibid. at *17. Certain bidders, however, had indicated that they would be willing to discuss a renegotiated CBA with the union. The court concluded that this was precisely the result that the union had demanded and their rejection of the debtor's proposals, none of which contained successorship clauses, was not without good cause. Ibid. at *18.

[63] 11 USC s 1113(c)(3).

[64] 'The Bankruptcy Court must consider the likelihood and consequences of liquidation for the debtor absent rejection, the reduced value of creditors' claims that would follow from affirmance and the hardship that would impose on them, and the impact of rejection on the employees.' *Nat'l Labor Relations Bd. v Bildisco and Bildisco* 465 US 513, 527 (1984). See above nn. 5–22 and accompanying text.

[65] *Truck Drivers Local 807 v Carey Transportation, Inc.* 816 F2d 82, 93 (2nd Cir. 1987).

[66] *Nat'l Labor Relations Bd. v Bildisco and Bildisco* 465 US 513, 527 (1984); see also *In re Maxwell Newspapers, Inc.* 146 BR 920, 933 (Bankr. SDNY 1992) (adopting similar language).

12.2.3 Effects of rejection

12.23 Section 365, embodying a concept long part of US bankruptcy law,[67] clearly states that rejection of a contract effects a pre-petition breach of that contract.[68] As a result, after a debtor rejects a contract under section 365, the contractual relationship between the debtor and the contract counterparty is terminated and the counterparty is entitled to file a claim for damages resulting from the breach. Section 1113, by contrast, provides mechanics for rejection of a CBA, but contains no guidance as to the effects thereof. Although a debtor that satisfies the nine substantive and procedural requirements set out above is permitted to 'assume or reject a collective bargaining agreement',[69] courts have struggled to determine the precise implications of rejection. This section discusses the nature of the ongoing relationship between an employer and a union after rejection as well as the damages, if any, that employees subject to a rejected CBA may recover from a debtor.

12.2.3.1 Post-rejection labour relations

12.24 The plain language of section 1113 provides the debtor with authority to reject a collective bargaining agreement.[70] It does not provide authority to modify or impose terms in an existing collective bargaining agreement.[71] In this sense, relief under section 1113 is an all-or-nothing endeavour.[72] Even if the debtor is authorized to reject a CBA, however, its relationship with its union does

---

[67] The contract-rejection power of a debtor predates the enactment of s 365 of the Bankruptcy Code in 1979. For example, s 313(1) of the Bankruptcy Act provided that: 'Upon the filing of a petition, the court may, in addition to the jurisdiction, powers, and duties conferred and imposed upon it by this chapter—(1) permit the rejection of executory contracts of the debtor, upon notice to the parties to such contracts and to such other parties in interest as the court may designate.' See *Shopmen's Local Union No. 455, Int'l Ass'n of Bridge, Structural and Ornamental Iron Workers, A.F.L.-C.I.O. v Kevin Steel Prods., Inc.* 519 F2d 698, 701 (2nd Cir. 1975).

[68] 11 USC s 365(g)(1).

[69] 11 USC s 1113(b).

[70] 11 USC s 1113(b)(1).

[71] Although s 1113 empowers a bankruptcy court to authorize rejection, not modification, of a CBA, some courts may condition entry of the rejection order upon the debtor's implementation of a prior offer. See *N.Y. Typographical Union No. 6. v Maxwell Newspapers, Inc. (In re Maxwell Newspapers, Inc.)* 981 F2d 85, 91–2 (2nd Cir. 1992) (conditioning its order permitting rejection on agreement by debtor-in-possession to keep its last offer open).

[72] Section 1114 authorizes the modification or termination of retiree benefits under a standard that is largely identical to the standard for rejection of a CBA under s 1113. See 11 USC s 1114. In contrast to the all-or-nothing relief granted under s 1113, however, s 1114 empowers bankruptcy courts to directly effect modifications of retiree benefits. Ibid. at s 1114(g). The power to directly implement modifications may be a trap for the unwary. For example, as the s 1114 hearing approaches, a debtor may seek fewer concessions to obtain a consensual result than it would if the issue were litigated. But if the paired down concession offer/request constitutes a 'proposal' for purposes of s 1114, it could be implemented by the court. Section 1114 therefore demands that a debtor be careful in negotiations to avoid inadvertently limiting its potential litigation result.

not end. Instead, the debtor remains subject to the requirements of applicable labour law.[73]

Applicable labour law, particularly the NLRA, prohibits an employer from implementing unilateral changes to the status quo until the employer and the employee representative have reached an impasse in bargaining.[74] Even after entry of an order under section 1113, the debtor and its union must therefore return to the negotiating table.[75] Although rejection of a CBA does not free the parties from the duty to collectively bargain, their respective bargaining positions are substantially altered by the entry of an order under section 1113. A union whose CBA has been rejected is under pressure to concede to a debtor's proposed concessions because failure to do so may permit the debtor, after exhausting the dispute resolution process of the NLRA, to impose its own terms. **12.25**

The debtor's newfound leverage after CBA rejection may be countered, at least in part, if termination of a CBA also terminates a union's no-strike obligation.[76] The union's freedom to strike or take other economic action, such as a work slowdown, is qualified by practical concerns. If the union believes that economic action, such as a strike, would compel the permanent shut-down of the relevant business unit and the resulting loss of the union members' jobs, the union will have to balance its interest in resisting the debtor's proposals against the union's obligations to fairly represent its members who will most frequently be focused upon retaining their employment.[77] For many debtors, already suffering from financial instability and operational upheaval, the trauma inflicted by a prolonged or widespread strike could be a death blow. **12.26**

Although some semblance of the pre-rejection balance of power remains under the NLRA, the application of industry-specific labour laws may significantly alter the rights of the parties. For example, in *Northwest Airlines Corporation v Association of Flight Attendants*, the Second Circuit enjoined a labour union of flight attendants **12.27**

---

[73] See *Nat'l Labor Relations Bd. v Bildisco and Bildisco* 465 US 513, 553–4 (1984). But see *In re Salt Creek Freightways* 47 BR 835, 842 (Bankr. D. Wyo. 1985) (implying employer was free to impose terms and conditions of employment after rejection); *In re Allied Delivery Syst.* 49 BR 700, 704 (Bankr. ND Ohio 1985) (same).

[74] *Louisiana Dock Co., Inc. v Nat'l Labor Relations Bd.* 909 F2d 281, 288 (7th Cir. 1990).

[75] If the parties bargained to impasse prior to rejection, the debtor may be permitted to immediately implement the changes contained in its last proposal. *In re Allied Delivery Syst. Co.* 49 BR 700, 704 (Bankr. ND Ohio 1985).

[76] Whether a union is entitled to take economic action after rejection of a CBA depends in large part on whether industry-specific labour laws apply. See below nn. 78–86 and accompanying text.

[77] For much the same reason, purchasers frequently have very high leverage in seeking purchaser-friendly CBAs for newly acquired operations. A purchaser may submit a bid conditioned upon the union's acceptance of the purchaser's proposed CBA. Because the debtor may close the business if it cannot achieve its proposed modifications, the union, which is charged with protecting the interests of its members, is under tremendous pressure to accept an economical and efficient CBA offer from a purchaser.

from striking after rejection of a CBA.[78] The debtor, an airline carrier, was subject to the Railway Labor Act (the 'RLA').[79] The RLA, designed to protect interstate commerce by avoiding disruption in air and rail travel,[80] contains 'status quo' provisions that require a carrier and a union to engage in an 'almost interminable' renegotiation process after a CBA becomes amendable.[81] In addition, the RLA imposes a second duty to 'exert every reasonable effort to make [agreements]... and to settle all disputes', even when the status quo provisions of the RLA are not in effect.[82] The union had argued that the debtor's rejection of the CBA constituted a unilateral change in the status quo under the RLA and that, as a result, the union became free to exercise its right to strike.[83] The Second Circuit agreed with this contention, but held that the 'status quo' provisions of the RLA operated independently of the duty to exert all reasonable efforts to settle disputes.[84] While rejection of the CBA under section 1113 caused an abrogation of the former, it did not eliminate the latter.[85] Because further negotiations between the parties had not been determined to be futile, the union was not entitled to strike.[86]

12.2.3.2 Claims arising from rejection of collective bargaining agreements

12.28 In addition to leaving post-rejection labour relations to the courts in enacting section 1113, Congress also did not include provisions relating to the monetary effect of rejecting a CBA in the statute.[87] Under section 365, the rejection of an executory contract effects a pre-petition breach of that contract and gives rise to a general unsecured claim for damages. Some courts have concluded that section 1113 governs only the mechanism for rejection of a CBA and that section 365 continues to govern the effects of rejection.[88] In such courts, unions subject to a

---

78 *Northwest Airlines Corp. v Ass'n of Flight Attendants* 483 F3d 160 (2nd Cir. 2007).

79 See 45 USC s 181.

80 See 45 USC s 151a (stating that one purpose of the RLA is '[t]o avoid any interruption to commerce or to the operation of any carrier engaged therein').

81 *Northwest Airlines Corp. v Ass'n of Flight Attendants* 483 F3d at 167 (citations omitted).

82 Ibid. at 168. See also 45 USC s 152.

83 *Re Northwest Airlines Corp.* 346 BR 307, 344 (Bankr. SDNY 2006).

84 *Northwest Airlines Corp. v Ass'n of Flight Attendants* 483 F3d 160, 169–70 (2nd Cir. 2007).

85 Ibid.

86 Ibid. at 175–7.

87 Legislation proposed in February 2010, if enacted, would resolve the question of whether rejection of a CBA gives rise to a claim. See H.R. 4677, 111th Cong. s 201 (2010); S. 3033, 111th Cong. S 201 (2010). Under these bills, s 1113 would be amended to explicitly provide that rejection of a CBA gives rise to a rejection damages claim pursuant to s 365(g).

88 See, eg, *United Food and Commercial Workers Union, Local 328, AFL-CIO v Almac's Inc.* 90 F3d 1, 5 n.4 (1st Cir. 1996) (recognizing circuit divide over whether a claim for damages is permitted after the rejection of a collective bargaining agreement under s 1113 and stating in dicta that 'because the relevant language of section 365(g) has not changed since *Bildisco*, collective bargaining agreements would appear still to be subject to the section's general provisions'); *Adventure Resources, Inc. v Holland* 137 F3d 786, 798 (4th Cir. 1998) (stating that s 1113 governs only the conditions under which a debtor may modify or reject a collective bargaining agreement, and concluding that

rejected CBA would be entitled to file a claim for all amounts that would have been paid by the debtor under the CBA until its expiration. Other courts, recognizing that allowing potentially enormous CBA-rejection damage claims may assure the failure of the reorganization, have concluded that section 1113 entirely removes CBAs from the purview of section 365. As a result, such courts have held that rejection of a CBA does not give rise to a rejection damages claim.[89] In a variation on the latter approach, the Second Circuit has held that termination of a CBA pursuant to section 1113 abrogates the agreement without causing a breach.[90] In the absence of a breach, the union would not be entitled to a claim for damages.[91]

Equally complex is the law relating to pre-petition obligations arising under a collective bargaining agreement. As noted above, the bankruptcy process is, in many respects, about breaking promises. Not all promises are created equal, however, and Congress has sought to favour the payment of employee claims above most other unsecured claims.[92] Employee claims, like all others, must generally be paid under a plan of reorganization.[93] A minority of courts has interpreted section 1113 to override otherwise applicable provisions governing the payment of pre-petition claims. Such courts have held that the failure to pay pre-petition obligations arising under a CBA would constitute a unilateral modification in violation of section 1113(f). As a result, such courts hold that claims arising under a CBA before rejection are entitled to superpriority or first priority status.[94] The majority **12.29**

s 365 continues to apply to collective bargaining agreements, except where such an application would create an irreconcilable conflict with s 1113).

[89] *Re Blue Diamond Coal Co.* 147 BR 720, 729–30 (Bankr. ED Tenn. 1992); *In re Armstrong Store Fixtures Corp.* 139 BR 347, 350 (Bankr. WD Pa. 1992).

[90] *Northwest Airlines Corp. v Ass'n of Flight Attendants* 483 F3d 160, 160 n.3 (2nd Cir. 2007) ('a debtor who rejects a contract pursuant to that statutory authority [s 1113] abrogates rather than breaches the CBA at issue'). The *Northwest* court did not explicitly rule on whether abrogation of a CBA gives rise to a claim for damages, but instead remanded to the bankruptcy court. See below n. 91.

[91] *Re Northwest Airlines Corp.* 366 BR 270, 276–7 (Bankr. SDNY 2007). The Bankruptcy Court also held that the union was not entitled to any damages for interim modifications to the collective bargaining agreement made pursuant to s 1113(e). Ibid. at 276.

[92] Claims for post-petition wages and contributions to employee benefit programmes generally are afforded administrative priority. See 11 USC s 503. Claims for prepetition employee wages and contributions to employee benefit plans are priority claims under s 507(a)(4) and (a)(5). See 11 USC s 507(a)(4), (5).

[93] Section 1129(b)(9) prohibits a court from confirming a plan of reorganization unless the plan pays all administrative claims and most other priority claims of the debtor in full in cash or deferred cash. See 11 USC s 1129(b)(9). Administrative claims consist of, among other things, claims arising from post-petition transactions with the debtor. 11 USC s 507(a).

[94] See, eg, *United Steelworkers of Am. v Unimet Corp. (In re Unimet Corp.)* 842 F2d 879, 884 (6th Cir. 1988) (holding that benefits under an unrejected collective bargaining agreement must be paid as they come due regardless of whether they would be entitled to administrative priority under s 507(a)(2) or 503(b)); *In re Typocraft Co.* 229 BR 685, 690–1 (Bankr. ED Mich. 1999); *In re Manor Oak Skilled Nursing Facilities, Inc.* 201 BR 348, 350 (Bankr. WDN.Y. 1996).

view, in contrast, provides pre-petition claims arising under a CBA the same priority as any other claim arising under an unrejected executory contract.

12.2.4 Conclusion

12.30 The law dealing with modification of contractual relationships between a company and its unionized workforce in a chapter 11 context is unsettled and its application varies depending on which jurisdiction is applying it. At first blush, the resulting confusion could lead to a conclusion that the system is unworkable. Ironically, however, the uncertainty associated with both the statutory scheme and its application provide the basis for a dynamic negotiation between the parties that often times results in agreements that permit the company to survive and its employees to remain employed.

12.3 Employees and trade unions in the UK

12.3.1 Advantages of a strategic approach

12.3.1.1 Survival planning

12.31 The remainder of this chapter explores the employment issues that arise when a UK employer is facing financial crisis. It considers not just the pure legal rights of employees, but also the practical, commercial and employment relations issues that may arise.[95] One scenario is an employer's sudden and catastrophic financial collapse into insolvency, brought about by extreme market conditions or the loss of a major customer. A more challenging scenario, in employment relations and legal terms, is that of gradual or long-term decline. This presents an opportunity to restructure and trade out of difficulty, hopefully avoiding the uncertainty of administration.

12.32 When the survival of the company is at issue, time is of the essence and a company risks limiting its options by not addressing employee options at an early stage. If the stage is reached where an administrator is appointed, he may be dealing with a confused and possibly poorly motivated workforce, who may not have been paid, together with militant union representatives. The administrator will have to decide whether employees are an asset or liability and, crucially, whether he has the time and cash to be able to consult or negotiate with the union or employee representatives; often he will not. The administrator may simply lack the necessary imagination and determination, despite the difficult circumstances. Much depends,

[95] Law and commentary excludes Northern Ireland. Note issues of interpretation can arise under Scottish law and procedure.

therefore, on whether the company's management at least put the company on the right path to restructure before entering into administration.

A well-timed and thorough restructuring of a workforce can be vital in avoiding a formal insolvency process. Indeed, it may be seen as a gross failure on the part of management for employees to suddenly find themselves in administration without having first had an opportunity to find ways of avoiding it. Insolvency is not an attractive option for employees in the UK and the risk of it is often influential in the collective bargaining process. **12.33**

12.3.1.2 Constraints to rapid change

Typical legal and employment relations constraints to rapid change include: **12.34**

- ineffective work practices that substantially favour employees but that may have contractual status;
- difficult employee/ trade union relations and collective bargaining agreements that may contain unhelpful or bureaucratic dispute resolution procedures;
- an absence of employee representatives, an employee representative body or a recognized union with whom to negotiate and consult;
- one or more class of employees who have significantly greater bargaining power than the others;
- lack of certainty as to the contractual status of terms and conditions of employment, possibly derived from a multiplicity of union collective agreements inherited from business acquisitions. Prohibitively expensive inherited enhanced redundancy terms can be a particular problem with ex public sector employees;
- compliance with legal obligations to inform and consult for up to 90 days with employee/union representatives on collective redundancies and upon business transfers;
- lack of a proper understanding of the composition of the workforce and its respective rights; and
- the 'acquired rights' of employees that are preserved upon business sales. Such protection can be complex when disposing of assets and businesses.

The above may all contribute to a weak bargaining position vis-a-vis a potential buyer of the business, the latter being deterred not just by the company's trading position, but also by employee liabilities, poor employment relations and the costs of restructuring. The above issues are, however, all capable of being addressed to avoid the worst case scenario of insolvency. **12.35**

12.3.2 Insolvency

The UK ranks joint eighth out of 155 countries for the speed with which it deals with troubled businesses; and ninth for the percentage of claims recovered **12.36** by creditors. This compares with joint twenty-third and fifteenth respectively for the US.[96]

12.37 The UK insolvency regime is considered to be a benign one for business owners, giving employees little voice or protection once a company enters formal insolvency.[97] Employees complain that they are a soft target for redundancy compared with employees in other EC states and that US-based multinational companies seek to incorporate US-style chapter 11 insolvency practices into the UK.

12.38 There are three key forms of corporate insolvency in the UK: liquidation, administration, and receivership. This chapter focuses on administration. This is because administrative receivership has now become, as a result of changes to the administration procedure, almost completely redundant and because, upon liquidation, all employment contracts terminate automatically. In administration, the employment of the workforce is not automatically terminated and may be maintained for a period of time where the aim of the administration is the rescue of the business as a going concern.

12.39 Although the primary aim of administration is rescue of the business as a going concern, the outcome in 56 per cent of administrations post Enterprise Act 2002 is liquidation, with 38 per cent ending in business rescue and only 3 per cent in corporate rescue.[98]

12.3.2.1 Employee protection in insolvency

12.40 In general, as a result of the Employment Rights Act 1996[99] and the Trade Union and Labour Relations (Consolidation) Act 1992,[100] employees in the UK have the same rights when their employer is put into an insolvency process as they would ordinarily have. So, for example, as against an insolvent employer, employees retain the right to claim for arrears of pay, unfair dismissal, redundancy pay and, where there is a collective redundancy, the right to a protected period of employment of up to 90 days.

12.41 Employees of an insolvent business sold as a going concern have the right to be employed by the new owner of the business on their pre-existing terms and conditions, so that all their 'acquired rights' remain intact. This takes place under the

---

96 World Bank, 'Doing Business Report 2009' (referred to in a memorandum from the Insolvency Service to the House of Commons Business and Enterprise Committee, p 18, 6 May 2009).

97 See <http:shameonyounortel.co.uk>.

98 Dr Sandra Frisby, 'Insolvency Outcomes: Research Findings' (July 2006) <www.insolvency.gov.uk>.

99 Referred to as ERA 1996.

100 Referred to as TULRA 1992.

Transfer of Undertakings (Protection of Employment) Regulations 2006 ('TUPE'),[101] which implements the EC Acquired Rights Directives[102] and employees transfer with the special protection against dismissal that would normally apply on a business transfer.

Nevertheless, the fact of the insolvency of an employer vastly reduces the effect and value of such statutory rights. Employees will almost inevitably rank with the company's other unsecured creditors for dividend purposes. Further, TUPE has introduced an important (if rare) exception whereby certain employee protections on business transfer may be disapplied in the case of a business rescue out of administration (see paragraph 12.89 below). **12.42**

12.3.2.2 Moratorium on employee claims

The moratorium on legal proceedings that applies in administration applies equally to employee claims, including those in an employment tribunal.[103] Hence the leave of the court is required to pursue claims arising from dismissals carried out by administrators, including under protective awards. However, in *Carr v British International Helicopters Ltd*,[104] referring to the guidance in *In re Atlantic Computer Systems plc*,[105] the EAT commented that, in the case of claims for unfair dismissal and redundancy, leave should only rarely be refused. As claims for protective awards arising from dismissals by administrators are likely to be good claims on their merits, and to result in substantial awards, leave to file such claims will normally be granted. There is a greater likelihood of such claims being brought where there is a trade union representing the dismissed employees, as unions will be conscious of the extent to which a claim is financially viable. **12.43**

12.3.2.3 Preferential debts and guaranteed debts

Only very limited classes of employee pre-petition claims are given protected status under English law. The protection afforded to employees is provided in two ways: **12.44**

(a) giving preferential status to certain limited classes of employee debts over and above other creditors; and
(b) providing a state guarantee in respect of certain debts.[106]

[101] SI 2006/246 replacing the TUPE Regulations 1981 (SI 1981/1794).
[102] Directive 2001/23/EC and Directive 77/187/EEC.
[103] IA 1986, Sch B1, para 43(6).
[104] [1994] IRLR 212.
[105] [1991] All ER 476.
[106] ERA 1996, s 184.

12.45 Even preferential employee debts will only rank third behind administration expenses and debts secured by fixed charges. They will, however, rank in priority to unsecured debts and debts secured by floating charges, including the 'prescribed part' reserved for unsecured creditors. Employee debts without preferential status or state guarantee are unsecured debts which may be irrecoverable on an insolvency (see table below).

Preferential debts[107]	**Guaranteed debts**	**Unprotected and unsecured debts**
4 months' arrears of gross remuneration • £800 cap (unchanged since 1976) • Includes overtime and contractual commission and bonuses • includes protective award (only in respect of dismissals *before* insolvency)	8 weeks' arrears of pay • £400 p/w cap (in total maximum £3,200) • includes protective award (only in respect of dismissals before insolvency)	Arrears of pay more than the £800 cap for preferential debt or the 8 weeks' guaranteed capped pay.
	Statutory notice pay • £400 p/w cap	Compensatory award for unfair dismissal • as much as £68,400 per employee[108]
	Statutory redundancy pay	Notice pay more than statutory notice
Holiday pay—no limit	6 weeks' holiday pay • £400 p/w cap Basic award for unfair dismissal Statutory sick pay Statutory maternity pay	Protective award in respect of dismissals arising *after* entering insolvency • up to 90 days' uncapped pay per employee
Employer pension contributions arrears[109] • 12 months' maximum	Employer pension contribution arrears[110] • 12 months' maximum	

12.46 Under ERA 1996 and the Pensions Schemes Act 1993, the Secretary of State may become subrogated to the rights of the employee where the Secretary of State has made a payment out of the National Insurance Fund. Such payments do not reduce the total amount payable by the insolvent company. The Secretary of State takes over the claim, which may have preferential status.

107 IA 1986, Sch 6.
108 As at 1 February 2010.
109 IA 1986, Sch 6, Pensions Schemes Act 1993, Sch 4.
110 Pensions Schemes Act 1993, s 124.

12.3.2.4 Risks of terminating employment

While there can be financial consequences, there is normally no legal right to restrain a company, including when in administration, from giving short notice of termination of employment even when this may result in breach of: **12.47**

- the notice provisions of individual contracts of employment—giving rise to damages claims;
- collective consultation obligations, giving rise to protective award claims; and/or
- unfair dismissal legislation, giving rise to compensation claims.

Administrators, concerned at the prospect of imposing further liabilities on an insolvent company, must decide whether such claims will adversely impact on the claims of existing creditors, in which case they need to be avoided at all costs. This will depend on whether: **12.48**

(a) any such claims will be preserved by TUPE as claims against a purchaser of all or part of the business. In time, the existence of these claims is likely to affect materially the value of the business and could thus deter potential purchasers;
(b) the financial burden of incurring any such liabilities could outweigh the financial burden of ongoing payroll costs;
(c) the company has sufficient assets for realization and distribution among unsecured creditors, once secured creditors and administration expenses are paid out; or whether the claims will then be against effectively an insolvent estate.

12.3.2.5 The 14-day period—the dilemma of adoption of contracts

If an administrator continues the employment of any employees beyond 14 days after their appointment, they are deemed to have adopted their contracts of employment.[111] The consequence of this is that liabilities under those contracts are paid in priority even to the administrator's fees and expenses. As a consequence, where there is to be a sale of the business in administration as a going concern, the administrators will try very hard to do so during these 14 days. If a sale cannot be achieved in that period, then in practice in many instances the company will cease to trade and the employees will be dismissed. **12.49**

Adoption of employment contracts does not, however, entail the administrator becoming the employer or assuming liabilities in respect of employees other than liabilities under their contracts that arise after the date of adoption. **12.50**

[111] IA 1986, Sch B1, para 99.

12.3.2.6 Prepack sales of businesses

12.51 A prepack administration is 'an arrangement under which the whole or part of a company's business or assets is negotiated with a purchaser before the appointment of an administrator, and the administrator effects the sale on, or shortly after, his appointment'[112]

12.52 The benefits and drawbacks of pre packs remain a matter of fierce debate. The Insolvency Service has stated that that a 'pre-pack may offer the best chance for a business rescue, preserve goodwill and employment, maximize realizations and generally speed up the insolvency process'.[113] R3, the trade body for insolvency practitioners, has stated that, 'pre-packs are a frequently misunderstood tool' and their potential benefits must not be 'lost in the debate over the perceived impact on creditors'.[114]

12.53 Employees fare relatively well out of prepack administrations and are seen as key stakeholders in making them work. The House of Commons Business and Enterprise Committee Report of May 2009 reported that early signs indicated that higher numbers of staff are transferred to the new company under a prepack administration than would otherwise transfer.[115] This may, however, be more to do with the application of TUPE.

12.54 Where a purchaser takes on some or all of an insolvent company's employees in a prepack administration, the issue of whether or not TUPE applies is likely to be a key issue. The fact that the sale of a company's business or assets comes about by way of a pre pack does not, in itself, make any difference to the application of TUPE. The application of TUPE is a matter of employment law and it is, perhaps, not surprising that Statement of Insolvency Practice 16[116] makes no mention of TUPE. However, there are two factors that are particularly relevant to TUPE in a prepack scenario: firstly, whether the administrator in question was appointed 'with a view to the liquidation of the assets of the transferor' within the meaning of regulation 8(7) of TUPE. This is relevant to whether TUPE applies at all and is discussed at paragraphs 12.61–12.73 below; secondly, whether any dismissals carried out by the administrator were connected with the transfer of employees to the purchaser. This is relevant to whether liability for the dismissals transfers under TUPE to the purchaser and is discussed at paragraphs 12.74–12.80 below.

---

[112] Statement of Insolvency Practice 16.

[113] Enterprise Act 2002—Corporate Insolvency Provisions: Evaluation Report (January 2008) 147, referred to in House of Commons Report of Business and Enterprise Committee (May 2009).

[114] Association of Business Recovery Professionals, 'Pre-packaged business sales', briefing notes referred to in HC report ibid.

[115] House of Commons Report of Business and Enterprise Committee (May 2009) ibid.

[116] Statement of Insolvency Practice 16 on pre-packs.

An administrator has greater legal flexibility to transfer employees, carry out mass redundancies and effect changes to terms and conditions than is normally the case. However, that is often more relevant in theory than in practice. A carefully planned business sale, without the intervention of an administrator, perhaps in conjunction with collective redundancies and/or collectively agreed changes to terms and conditions of employment, is generally preferable to a sale effected through an administrator. **12.55**

However, where administration becomes the most or only viable option, a planned prepack sale of the business out of administration is preferred. Leaving aside the *Oakland* case (see paragraph 12.69 below), it is best to take, from the outset, a strategic approach based on TUPE applying, with all its limitations and uncertainties, than to proceed under the mistaken belief that TUPE can somehow be avoided in an insolvency process. The normal expectation is that TUPE will apply to a sale of a business as a going concern by an administrator. **12.56**

12.3.3 TUPE Regulations 2006

12.3.3.1 TUPE—its consequences

The main consequences of TUPE applying to a business sale are: **12.57**

(a) The employment of employees who are 'assigned' to the relevant business or part of the business is automatically transferred to the new 'owner' of the business or part (the 'transferee') under regulation 4(1) of TUPE, unless the employees object to the transfer. Continuity of employment is preserved.
(b) All rights and liabilities relating to transferring employees' contracts of employment transfer with them to the transferee (including liability for any arrears of pay, pre-transfer breaches of contract, or any form of unlawful discrimination on the part of the transferor).
(c) Transferring employees are entitled to be employed by the transferee on the same terms and conditions of employment as they were before the transfer (subject to some key exemptions relating to continued membership of occupational pension schemes). Any variation of terms and conditions, even with employee consent, will be void if the change is for a reason connected to the transfer, unless it is for an economic, technical or organizational reason (an 'ETO reason') entailing changes to the workforce.
(d) The dismissal of any employee by either the transferor or the transferee will be automatically unfair (for the purposes of Part X ERA 1996) if the dismissal is because of the transfer, or for a reason connected with the transfer that is not an ETO reason entailing changes to the workforce.
(e) The transferor and transferee have obligations to consult with and provide certain information to representatives of affected employees.

12.3.3.2 When does TUPE apply?

12.58 There are two scenarios where TUPE applies:

- on a transfer of an 'undertaking, business or part of an undertaking or business', which immediately before the transfer is situated in the UK;
- where there is an organized grouping of employees whose principal purpose is carrying out activities for a party and those activities are then taken over by another party (ie a change of service provider).

12.59 TUPE will apply in the first scenario to the sale of a business by an administrator, if it constitutes a transfer of an 'economic entity which retains its identity';[117] TUPE would not be expected to apply to a sale of shares, as this should not result in a transfer of the business. An 'economic entity' is defined as 'an organized grouping of resources which has the objective of pursuing an economic activity, whether or not that activity is central or ancillary'.[118] A mere collection of assets will not be sufficient to constitute an 'economic entity'. Importantly, 'resources' means not only tangible and intangible assets, but also employees. The economic entity must be stable: not necessarily commercially viable, but at least an on-going economic enterprise.

12.60 In the first scenario of a business transfer, when considering whether the entity retains its identity post-transfer, a large range of factual matters are taken into account, including:

- whether tangible assets, such as buildings/machinery, are transferred;
- the value of intangible assets at the time of transfer, for example goodwill, and whether they have transferred;
- whether the majority of employees assigned to the business have transferred; and
- the degree of similarity between the business activities carried on before and after the transfer.

12.3.3.3 TUPE and insolvency

12.61 As outlined in at paragraphs 12.44–12.46, the legal position of employees in a terminal insolvency process is, fundamentally, a weak and vulnerable one. However, noting the considerable protections afforded to employees under TUPE, an administrator must assess the extent to which its employees would benefit from those protections on a business sale out of a company in administration.

---

117 TUPE, reg 3(1).
118 Ibid., reg 3(2).

The 2006 TUPE Regulations introduced a key distinction between two categories of insolvency proceedings: 'relevant insolvency proceedings' and 'bankruptcy or analogous proceedings'. If the normal TUPE tests are satisfied, and the transfer takes place when a company is in 'relevant insolvency proceedings', then there will be an automatic transfer of employee under regulations 4 and 7 to the purchaser of the business, albeit not all employee liabilities will transfer with them. In this scenario, liabilities for redundancy pay and debts guaranteed by the state remain with the insolvent company. Otherwise, if the transfer takes place when a company is in 'bankruptcy or analogous proceedings', there will be no automatic transfer of employees or related liabilities to the purchaser. In other words, the key employee protections normally afforded by TUPE do not apply. **12.62**

The above distinction is not explained in the TUPE Regulations and is not one made by the Insolvency Act 1986. As a result, it is not clear into which category administration falls, which is important because of the totally different consequences under the Regulations depending on the type of proceedings which apply. **12.63**

Relevant insolvency proceedings (where the automatic transfer principle applies) are intended to cover non-terminal insolvency proceedings aimed at rescue, and are defined by Regulation 8(6) of TUPE as: **12.64**

> insolvency proceedings which have been opened in relation to the transferor not with a view to the liquidation of the assets of the transferor and which are under the supervision of an insolvency practitioner.

Bankruptcy or analogous proceedings (where TUPE is all but disapplied completely) are broadly intended to cover insolvency proceedings leading to liquidation, and are defined by regulation 8(7) as: **12.65**

> bankruptcy proceedings or analogous insolvency proceedings which have been instituted with a view to the liquidation of the assets of the transferor and are under the supervision of an insolvency practitioner.

Guidance issued by the UK Department for Business, Innovation and Skills (BIS) provides that 'relevant insolvency proceedings' include any collective insolvency proceedings during which the whole or part of the business or undertaking is transferred to another entity as a going concern (ie to which TUPE applies), covering: **12.66**

- administration (which is the most common type of insolvency proceeding); and
- administrative receivership (although the process is now largely defunct, as a result of the Enterprise Act 2002).[119]

[119] BIS Guidance, a Guide to the 2006 TUPE Regulations, June 2009.

12.67 The BIS guidance goes on to state that 'bankruptcy and analogous proceedings' (where TUPE is largely disapplied), include:

- bankruptcy;
- compulsory liquidation; and
- creditors' voluntary liquidation

12.68 Both TUPE and BIS guidance fail to deal comprehensively with the situation where, as is usually the case, the administrator knows from the outset of the process that the company cannot be rescued as a going concern, but believes that administration will result in return for unsecured creditors, rather than taking it straight into liquidation. In such a situation, the end result will be liquidation, but parts of the business may first be sold as a going concern.

12.69 This kind of scenario was at the heart of the *Oakland* case,[120] where the EAT upheld an employment tribunal's decision that administration *can* constitute 'bankruptcy or analogous proceedings' within the meaning of regulation 8(7) of TUPE. It also criticized the BIS Guidance for being unhelpful. Unfortunately, on appeal, the Court of Appeal[121] did not consider it necessary to deal with the issue, but did comment, obiter, that it is 'strongly arguable' that administration *cannot* fall under regulation 8(7).

12.70 Since the facts of *Oakland* are quite typical of an insolvency situation, this EAT decision remains of interest, albeit in the light of the Court of Appeal's comments and the EAT's more recent decision in *OTG Ltd v Barke* [2011] UKEAT 0320_09_1602, pending any further appeal, *Oakland* is unlikely to be followed in future.

12.71 In the OTG case, the EAT held that administration cannot fall under regulation 8(7).

12.72 That being so, evidence as to the purpose of the administration, in accordance with IA 1986 Schedule B1, paragraph 3(1), should not be relevant to whether a business sale by an administrator is subject to TUPE.

12.73 Being subject to regulation 8(6) rather than regulation 8(7) TUPE does have the advantage at least that regulation 9 of TUPE, which facilitates changes to terms and conditions of employment where a transferor is subject to 'relevant insolvency proceedings' (see paragraphs 12.90–12.91 below).

120 *Oakland v Wellswood (Yorkshire) Ltd* [2008] UKEAT 0395 08.
121 *Oakland v Wellswood* [2010] IRLR 82, CA.

12.3.3.4 Is the dismissal connected with the transfer?

Regulation 7 protects employees against dismissal in a way that can frustrate a reduction in staff overheads. In particular, an administrator may wish to seek to agree in advance with a potential buyer of the business which employees could be retained and which the administration should make redundant. Such a collusive approach with a buyer would, however, fall foul of regulation 7(1) of TUPE. Trips deals with dismissals in two situations: 12.74

- Where the sole or principal reason for the dismissal is the transfer itself or a reason connected with the transfer that is not an economic, technical or organizational reason ('ETO reason') entailing changes in the workforce. Such dismissals are automatically unfair [122] and liability for dismissals carried out by the transferor will transfer to the transferee.
- Where the sole or principal reason for the dismissal is not the transfer itself but is a reason connected with the transfer which is an ETO reason entailing changes in the workforce.[123] In this situation, liability for the dismissals will remain with the transferor. In an insolvency situation, the Redundancy Payments Office would be liable for the statutory notice and redundancy pay.

Redundancy will normally be an ETO reason. The words, 'entailing changes in the workforce' are critical to deciding whether the ETO reason exists, referring to either a reduced need in the number of employees required or a change in the functions required of the employees. Dismissals are potentially fair, and typically will be fair, if the employer, whether transferor or transferee, carries out a proper redundancy process. 12.75

Redundancies carried out as a cost-cutting measure in relation to a business that cannot pay its debts as they fall due and cannot, therefore, afford to retain its employees would have an ETO reason. 12.76

A cost-cutting measure to facilitate a sale of the business, carried out at the request of the buyers of the business, would not be an ETO reason and all dismissals as a result would be automatically unfair and liability would transfer to the buyer. 12.77

Case law has established the following general principles: 12.78

- If dismissals are carried out in close proximity to a TUPE transfer, then it is possible to infer that the dismissals are connected to the transfer.
- If it is argued that the principal reason for these dismissals is economic, an administrator should have a reasonable explanation as to why redundancies carried out by him were not carried out before administration.

---

[122] TUPE, reg 7(1).
[123] Ibid., reg 7(2).

- If there is collusion about dismissals between the buyer and the administrator, or between the buyer and seller before administration, then those dismissals will be treated as connected with the transfer. Although there may be a good underlying business or 'economic' reason for any such dismissals, if the collusion produces evidence that the sole or principal reason for the carrying out of the dismissals is to facilitate a TUPE transfer, then there is no economic reason for them.
- The dismissals may still be held to be connected with the transfer in the absence of any collusion, even where a buyer of the business has not been identified at the time of the dismissals.
- Following the appointment of an administrator, a crucial factor will be the extent to which he can demonstrate that he was compelled to carry out the dismissals by the particular financial circumstances applying at the time to protect the continued operation of the business and for no other reason.

12.79 In *Thompson v SCS Consulting Ltd*,[124] although dismissals were carried out by the receiver at the request of the buyer, the EAT upheld the employment tribunal's decision that, in the particular circumstances, there was no collusion to effect a transfer. The tribunal was entitled to take into account the fact that there would have been no viable business if the employees had been retained and that they would have been dismissed by the receiver in any event.

12.80 In *Dynamex Friction Ltd v AMICUS*,[125] an administrator made approximately a third of the workforce redundant and transferred the remainder to a new company, in which the sole director of the insolvent company had a financial interest and later acquired a controlling shareholding. The Court of Appeal held that the tribunal had been entitled to find that there had been no collusion between the administrators and the new company or the ex director of the insolvent company, that the administrators had had no assets with which to pay wages, and that they had dismissed the employees in spite of any potential sale, not with a view to effecting one.

12.3.3.5 Strategic dilemmas for administrators

12.81 There are a number of strategic issues surrounding employment that an administrator will need to consider, these are:

- Which employees an administrator can afford to retain during the initial 14-day post-appointment period and for how long. If substantially all employees are dismissed immediately following the appointment, with no cash available to

[124] [2001] IRLR 801.
[125] [2008] IRLR 515.

pay them and no prospect of a sale and, therefore, no prospect of any employees being transferred under TUPE, it is unlikely that any claim for unfair dismissal or for a protective award would be entertained by an employment tribunal. The claims would be dealt with by the Redundancy Payments Office.

- Reasonable consultation is required in deciding which employees to retain, to avoid undermining credibility and losing employees essential to continued operation and trading; for example staff critical for health and safety reasons.
- Where there is scope to retain employees for a period of time and where dismissals on appointment would risk undermining a sale of the business as a going concern, there is still the need to assess whether redundancies are required on 'economic' grounds within the meaning of regulation 7 of TUPE. Ideally, redundancies may have already been carried out or proposed by the company before entering administration, and collective consultation may be under way.
- There is then the dilemma of whether the appointment of the administrator was made 'with a view to the liquidation of assets or not', within the meaning of regulation 8 of TUPE and whether or not the *Oakland* case would apply to the situation. It may be that regulations 4 and 7 of TUPE do not apply at all.
- Where there has been a delay in carrying out dismissals, there is then the risk of undermining any 'economic' reason, particularly where a TUPE transfer follows shortly thereafter. The reasons for carrying out the dismissals need to be transparent and well documented.
- There can be an over emphasis of unfair dismissal claims and protective awards being unsecured or valueless. This can lead to an underestimation of the need for and value of effective communication. Proper consultation with employees can often achieve acceptance, or even agreement to dismissals or changes to terms and conditions. There may be compelling reasons for consultation in commercial and employment relations terms, if not in strict legal terms.
- Where many dismissed employees are suddenly left empty handed as unsecured creditors but others, including perhaps 'failed' senior managers, are transferred under TUPE with their bonus arrangements intact, there may be employment relations issues for the new company, as well as reputational issues for the administrators.
- There may simply not be the time to go through a fair process of redundancy consultation in administration. Thus, the more steps a company takes before administration to comply with its obligations under section 188 TULRA and under regulations 13 and 14 of TUPE, the stronger its business case for redundancy will be, with reduced prospects of claims being transferred to a buyer of the business.
- An administrator cannot cure defects in a prepack sale of the business where regulation 8(6) of TUPE applies if there has been collusion before administration between the seller and the buyer such that dismissals are TUPE connected.

- Changes to terms and conditions of employment may, in theory, be easier to carry out in administration as far as TUPE is concerned, but, in practice, the preparatory work should be done at an earlier stage.

12.3.4 Employment relations and consultation

12.3.4.1 Changes to terms and conditions of employment

12.82 Reducing payroll costs in times of recession to improve liquidity or to stave off redundancies or even insolvency, for example by implementing pay cuts, short time working or lay offs, can be achieved quickly by agreement with a recognized union. However, if a package of long-term changes is required to enable substantial reductions in a company's cost base (for example changes to working hours and shift patterns, enhanced redundancy terms, job functions and work practices) seeking agreement with employees may be a difficult, slow and ultimately uncertain process. Continuation as a viable business may be dependent on achieving a consensual restructuring and a carefully managed survival strategy will factor in a realistic timescale.

(a) *Consensual change.* Changes to terms and conditions can be agreed under a collective agreement where there is a recognized union for the employees concerned or agreed on an individual basis where there is not.

(b) *Enforced change.* If consensual change cannot be achieved, enforced change takes place by giving notice of termination of existing contracts of employment with back-to-back offers of employment, preserving continuity of employment, but on new terms and conditions. Any such terminations are dismissals and hence there has to be a fair reason for dismissal and a reasonable process of prior consultation. Depending on the scale of the changes involved and the prospects for survival of the company, claims for compensation and protective awards could be substantial and potentially result in insolvency.

12.83 Accordingly, where a company is struggling to survive, time and effort invested in securing contractual changes by agreement can be a sound investment.

12.84 Proposals to serve notices of termination to bring about enforced changes to terms and conditions of employment constitute proposals to dismiss by reason of redundancy for the purposes of collective redundancy consultation under section 188 TULRA, because the dismissals are unconnected to the circumstances of the individual employee.[126] Hence, a minimum consultation period of up to 90 days (30 days if under 100 employees are affected) is triggered and consideration should be given to serving section 188 notices and HR1 forms at the same time or soon after commencing consensual negotiations with union or employee representatives.

[126] TULRA, s 195.

A failure to consult over these proposals would incur a protective award in the same way as a failure to consult over proposed job losses.

12.3.4.2 Changes where collective agreements apply

In the UK, contractual obligations derived from collective agreements can often lack clarity. Not all matters concerned by an agreement are necessarily reduced to writing and tend to be drafted without legal input. Collective bargaining arrangements can themselves be unclear or be found to contain unhelpful or bureaucratic dispute resolution procedures. Hence, where notices are being served under section 188 TULRA in relation to changes to terms and conditions of employment, consideration should also be given to serving notice of termination of the collective agreements from which the individual terms are derived. Although collective agreements are binding between employer and union in honour only,[127] reasonable notice of termination should be given (which could be six months or even more). **12.85**

The incorporation of collectively agreed terms in individual contracts of employment is beyond the scope of this chapter. A key issue to note, however, is whether a provision in a collective agreement is 'apt for incorporation' into individual contracts. This test was considered by the Court of Appeal in *Malone v British Airways plc*,[128] where it was found that the provisions of a staffing level agreement for cabin crews on BA flights were not appropriate for incorporation into individual contracts. **12.86**

The Court of Appeal decision in *Parkwood Leisure Ltd v Alemo-Herron*[129] considered the effect of TUPE on the terms and conditions of transferring employees where collective pay bargaining arrangements continue to operate for non transferring employees after the transfer. It was held, upholding the approach of the European Court of Justice, that where employees have transferred under TUPE, the transferee is not bound by *subsequent* collective agreements made by the transferor, in the absence of a clear agreement to the contrary. This upholds the approach of the European Court of Justice.[130] This decision is of particular relevance to employees who have transferred from the public sector and who were previously subject to public sector pay bargaining machinery. **12.87**

Note also that collective bargaining arrangements cannot be circumvented by offering new terms and conditions on an individual basis while these arrangements remain in place, without falling foul of section 145A TULRA. This prohibits **12.88**

[127] Ibid., s 179.
[128] [2010] EWCA Civ 1225.
[129] [2010] EWCA Civ 24.
[130] *Werhof v Freeway Traffic Systems GmbH* [2006] IRLR 400.

offering inducements that would result in an employee's terms of employment no longer being determined by collective agreement.

12.3.4.3Restrictions under TUPE

12.89 Care is required where changes to terms and conditions are taking place in the context of a TUPE transfer, as such changes will be void under regulation 4(4) TUPE if the sole or principal reason for them is:

- the transfer itself; or
- a reason connected with the transfer that is not an 'ETO reason' entailing changes in the workforce. As in relation to regulation 7 of TUPE, there is no statutory definition of an ETO reason, but the same principles and case law apply.

12.90 Following the appointment of an administrator, regulation 9 of TUPE results in an important relaxation if this restriction applies, which permits changes to terms and conditions, before or after transfer, where:

- at the time of transfer, the company is subject to 'relevant insolvency proceedings';
- the sole or principal reason for the changes *is* the transfer or a reason connected with the transfer that is *not* an ETO reason entailing changes in the workforce;
- the changes are designed to safeguard employment opportunities by ensuring the survival of the business; and
- the seller, buyer or insolvency practitioner agrees to the changes with appropriate representatives of the employees.

12.91 It is therefore possible to agree, for example, pay cuts or reductions in benefits to facilitate a transfer where there are 'relevant insolvency proceedings'. Of course, in practice, effecting pay cuts or benefit reductions may not be easy in the context of administration and it is advisable that much of the hard negotiation takes place before entering administration.

12.3.4.4 Collective consultation

12.92 **12.3.4.4.1 General consultation obligations** In a restructure involving job losses and/or business transfers, specific information and consultation obligations may apply under TULRA or TUPE. The company may also have a general obligation to consult with employee or union representatives or with employee representatives under the terms of an information and consultation agreement. This is likely to have arisen voluntarily, although the Information and Consultation of Employees Regulations 2004 (ICE Regulations) now require employers to put in place information and consultation agreements where as few as 10 per cent of employees make a formal request for one.[131]

There may also be obligations under an information and consultation agreement at European level, to a European Works Council, established under the Transnational Information and Consultation Regulations 1999 (TICE Regulations).[132] As with agreements reached under the ICE Regulations, such procedural agreements are only mandatory if a formal request for such an agreement has been made by a sufficient percentage of employees. **12.93**

Typically, effective information and consultation structures, often referred to as 'works councils', can take many months to implement, even at national level. Where there is no recognized union and a fundamental restructuring is required, consideration should be given to electing representatives well in advance of making proposals. **12.94**

12.3.4.4.2 Collective redundancy consultation Where an employer is proposing to 'dismiss as redundant' 20 or more employees at one establishment within a 90-day period specific consultation obligations apply under section 188 of TULRA. For these purposes, redundancy includes dismissals relating to changes to terms and conditions of employment. In these circumstances, the employer must consult all appropriate representatives of the employees who may be dismissed or affected by the dismissals or measures to be taken in connection with them 'in good time'. **12.95**

If it is proposed that: **12.96**

- 20 or more but fewer than 100 employees are to be dismissed, consultation must take place for at least 30 days before the first dismissal; or
- if 100 or more employees may be dismissed, consultation must take place is for a minimum of 90 days before the first dismissal.

Circumstances may require longer periods to satisfy the requirement of consultation beginning 'in good time'. For example, if 95 dismissals are proposed, a 90- or 60-day consultation period could be more appropriate than 30 days. The number of employees to be dismissed includes volunteers for redundancy. So, for example, if there were three volunteers for redundancy and 17 compulsory redundancies, this would still trigger collective consultation. **12.97**

Importantly, there is no exception to the duty to inform and consult when the dismissals are proposed or carried out by an administrator. **12.98**

---

[131] Implementing Directive 2002/14/C.

[132] Implementing Directive 97/74/EC.

12.99 Consultation in a redundancy situation must include ways of:

- avoiding the dismissals;
- reducing the numbers to be dismissed; and
- reducing the impact of the dismissals on employees.

12.100 Consultation must be meaningful 'with a view to reaching agreement with the appropriate representatives'. Ignoring representatives' objections on key matters, such as choice of redundancy selection criteria, weakens any argument that consultation was undertaken with a view to reaching agreement. An employer cannot argue that consultation would, in the circumstances, be futile or useless, even when the company is insolvent.

12.101 *Notification requirement* The employer must confirm to employee representatives in writing the reasons for the proposed dismissals and certain information about how the redundancies are to be effected, including the numbers and descriptions of employees proposed to be dismissed as redundant and the proposed selection method to be used ('the section 188 notice').

12.102 Notice of the proposed redundancies must be served on the Secretary of State at the Redundancy Payments Office (using 'form HR1') at the same time as serving the section 188 notice.[133] Failure to serve a HR1 is a criminal offence and attracts a maximum fine of £5,000.[134] This was made very clear in March and November 2009 in letters from the Minister of State at BIS to insolvency practitioners. Clearly, there are reputational issues, aside from the threat of sanction, and pressure has also been brought to bear on R3, the Association of Business Recovery Professionals, by the Government to take disciplinary action against members where appropriate. On 22 October 2009, a memorandum of understanding was signed between R3, the Insolvency Service and Jobcentre Plus.

12.103 *Trigger event* An employer's duty to consult arises only once the employer has formulated its proposals in respect of dismissals. A proposal is a state of mind more certain and further along the decision making process than when dismissals are merely contemplated.

12.104 In *Akavan Erityisalojen Keskusliitto AEK ry and Others v Fujitsu Siemens Computers Oy*,[135] the ECJ held that:

- An employer's consultation obligations are triggered once a strategic or commercial decision has actually been taken, requiring consideration of plans for redundancies.

---

[133] TULRA, s 193.
[134] Ibid., s 194.
[135] C-44/08 [2009] ECR I-8163.

- In a corporate group:
  - Whether the strategic decision is taken by the subsidiary or by the parent company, it is always the subsidiary employer who is obliged to inform and consult (even if not properly and immediately informed of the decision by the parent).
  - The obligation to consult only arises when the parent company has identified the subsidiary which will be affected.
  - The consultation procedure must be concluded by the subsidiary employer before the decision to terminate employment contracts is taken by the parent company.

Affected employees 'Employee' means an individual who works under a contract of employment,[136] which excludes agency workers. When identifying 'affected employees', the employment status of consultants, contractors or temporary workers should be considered carefully to determine whether they are, in fact, employees. **12.105**

The business reasons for redundancies The established principle is that the business reason for proposals to reduce the number of employees is not a matter for consultation under section 188 TULRA. However, in the case of a total site closure, where the decision to shut down is inseparable from the decision to make the employees redundant, the reasons for closure become a matter for consultation. In *UK Coal Mining Ltd v NUM*,[137] the EAT found that 'the obligation to consult over avoiding the proposed redundancies inevitably involves engaging with the reasons for the dismissals, and that in turn requires consultation over the reasons for the closure'. The reasoning behind that decision is now open to question in the light of *United States of America v Nolan*,[138] in which the Court of Appeal decided that the issue of the scope of employers' obligations in the case of a workplace closure had to be referred to the ECJ, whose decision is now awaited. **12.106**

Appropriate representatives for redundancy and TUPE consultation The rules concerning the appropriate representatives for collective consultation are very similar in redundancy and TUPE situations. **12.107**

Where there is a recognized independent trade union representing employees who may be affected by proposed redundancies, a transfer of an undertaking or any measures connected to either, the employer must inform and consult with that union. If there is no such recognized trade union, the employer may inform and consult with any existing representatives (provided that their remit and method of election or appointment gives them suitable authority) or else employee representatives specifically elected or appointed for that purpose. **12.108**

136 TULRA, s 295.
137 [2008] IRLR 4.
138 [2011] IRLR 14.

12.109 *Consultation on business transfer—TUPE Regulations 2006* The following information must be disclosed to the appropriate representatives 'long enough before a relevant transfer' to enable consultation to take place:[139]

- the fact of the relevant transfer, the proposed date of transfer and the reasons for it;
- the legal, economic and social implications of the transfer for the affected employees, including any implications for pay and benefits post-transfer and any requirement to relocate;
- the measures (including redundancies) that the transferor/transferee envisages taking in relation to its affected employees and, if none are envisaged, that fact; and
- the measures the transferor envisages that the transferee will take in relation to the transferring employees and, if none are envisaged, that fact. The transferee must provide this information in sufficient time to enable the transferor to comply with its notification obligations.

12.110 The obligation to consult arises if the transferor/transferee envisages taking measures in connection with the transfer in relation to any affected employee, and must take place with a view to reaching agreement on those intended measures. The transferor/transferee must have some degree of certainty as to the measures it envisages; there is no obligation to consult on mere hopes or possibilities.

12.111 **12.3.4.4.3 Pension changes** Employers are required to carry out consultation where they are proposing to make 'listed' changes to active or prospective members' pension arrangements. At least 60 days' notice of the changes and background information must be provided to enable consultation with the union or other elected representatives.[140]

12.3.4.5 Protective awards

12.112 **12.3.4.5.1 Protective awards in redundancy cases** A protective award is made to affected employees with whose appropriate representatives the employer failed to consult properly.[141] The main purpose of the protective award is to penalize the employer. Regard is had to the seriousness of the employer's default and the degree of prejudice suffered by affected employees; for example whether the consultation could have made a difference to the employer's decision.

12.113 The award may be up to 90 days' actual pay, even where the numbers being dismissed are fewer than 100 and the required consultation period is 30 days.

---

[139] TUPE, reg 13

[140] Occupational and Personal Pension Schemes (Consultation by Employers and Miscellaneous Amendment) Regulations 2006 (SI 2006/349).

[141] TULRA, ss 188–190.

There is no statutory cap on a week's pay and the protected period shall be such length as the tribunal determines just and equitable in all the circumstances. **12.114**

The Court of Appeal gave some useful guidance in the case of *Susie Radin Ltd v GMB*[142] on factors to be considered when deciding on the period the protective award should cover: **12.115**

- The award is a sanction against the employer rather than compensation for the employee; it is not necessary to consider the loss suffered by the affected employee(s) as a result of the failure to consult.
- The tribunal has a wide discretion, but it should focus on the extent of the employer's fault.
- The seriousness of the fault can range from being merely technical to a complete failure to provide any of the required information and to consult.
- Whether the employer's failure was deliberate and whether it had access to legal advice.
- Where there has been no consultation, the tribunal should start by imposing the maximum 90-day period and only reduce it to take into account of any mitigating factors.

Arguments that consultation would have been futile are irrelevant. **12.116**

12.3.4.5.2 **Protective awards in a TUPE scenario** In a TUPE scenario, the maximum protective award is 13 weeks' actual pay per affected employee. This is payable in addition to any sums owing under the contract of employment or any damages for breach of contract in respect of the protected period. The protective awards for redundancy and TUPE are also cumulative. **12.117**

If the transferor gave proper notice but did not receive from the transferee the 'measures' information to give to the appropriate representatives, the transferee is liable to pay the protective award. **12.118**

12.3.4.5.3 **Special circumstances defence** TULRA provides a 'special circumstances' defence to a protective award where it was not 'reasonably practicable' for the employer to comply with its obligations under section 188, provided it takes 'all such steps toward compliance with that requirement as are reasonably practicable in those circumstances'.[143] **12.119**

There is also a similar 'special circumstances' defence under TUPE.[144] **12.120**

---

[142] [2004] IRLR 400.
[143] TULRA, s 188(7).
[144] TUPE, reg 15(2).

12.121 Special circumstances are not defined in the legislation. However, the following principles can be extracted from case law:

- The fact of insolvency or the appointment of an administrator will not, in itself, amount to special circumstances; the circumstances must be 'exceptional and out of the ordinary'[145] and it is often the case that the possibility of entering into an insolvency process is known for some time.
- The need to carry out redundancies by an administrator will not be a special circumstance in the absence of any element of sudden disaster or unexpected insolvency.[146]
- Commercial pressures and deadlines are unlikely, in themselves, to be special circumstances, but a rapid and unforeseen sequence of events shortly before a deadline may just get over the threshold if, importantly, there has otherwise been a thorough attempt to take all reasonable steps 'toward compliance'.[147]
- The decision of the employer's US parent company to withdraw financial support has been held not constitute a 'special circumstances' defence.[148]
- Even if there are special circumstances that mean a 30- or 90-day consultation period is not reasonably practicable, the employer is still obligated to comply with its consultation obligations in what time is available. Even when there may be as few as two to three days available for consultation, effective use of those days can make a major difference to the level of any protective award made.[149]

12.3.4.6 Industrial action

12.122 Any restructuring process in a unionized environment invites the risk of industrial action. It is beyond the scope of this work to address detailed industrial action management or planning. It is, however, vital that employers are aware of the different legal protections that apply under the different types of industrial action:

- Unofficial industrial action—industrial action that has not been authorized or endorsed by the union. It is possible for a single union representative to authorize or endorse industrial action. An employer is able to dismiss selectively those participating and dismissed employees have no right to complain of unfair dismissal.
- 'Unprotected' official action—industrial action authorized or endorsed by a union that does not comply with statutory requirements concerning balloting of union members and service of notices. There is no right to claim unfair

---

145 *Bakers Union v Clarks of Hove Ltd* [1978] 1 WLR 1207.

146 *GMB v Rankin and Harrison* [1992] IRLR 514, EAT.

147 *Unison v Somerset County Council(1) Taunton Deane Borough Council (2) and South West One Ltd (3)* UKEAT/0043/09.

148 *GMB and Amicus v Beloit Walmsley Ltd (in administration)* [2004] IRLR 18.

149 *Shanahan Engineering v UNITE* [2010] UKEAT/0411/09/DM.

dismissal if all participating employees are dismissed and such employees have not been selectively re-engaged within a three-month period from their dismissal.[150]

- If any participating employee has not been dismissed, or there is selective reengagement of those dismissed, then all dismissed employees have the right to claim unfair dismissal.
- Industrial action that starts off as unprotected official action can be repudiated by the union at national level, so making the action unofficial at the end of the next working day after the date of repudiation.[151]
- 'Protected' official action—industrial action called by a union that complies with all statutory requirements concerning balloting of union members and service of notices. An employee has absolute protection against dismissal for taking part in industrial action for a period of at least 12 weeks from when he first participated.

[150] TULRA, s 238(3).
[151] Ibid., s 238(4).

13

PENSION SCHEME TRUSTEES AND REGULATORS

13.1 Introduction

Superficially, the UK and the US pensions regime when companies are restructuring look similar. Both countries have a significant number of defined benefit pension plans, both have a regulatory safety net for those plans and both have active regulatory bodies to patrol that safety net that can play a substantial role in the restructuring of the sponsoring employer. Under both regimes, substantial debts can be triggered on the employers. **13.01**

But the differences are as important as the similarities. The US system has a single regulator, the PBGC, which has direct powers of enforcement and real bite. Meanwhile, the UK system (nominally based on the US system) has the trustees of the plan, who normally must be involved, and two regulators—the Pensions **13.02**

Regulator and the PPF—both of whom have a role to play. The regulatory enforcement powers are cumbersome and of uncertain effect in critical aspects. In the US, the system and practice are well-established. In the UK, the system remains relatively new, the scope of the powers are not fully understood, the regulators are still exploring their options, and the various parties are still prone to tread on each other's toes.

13.03 The potential size of the pensions liabilities are such that they may well play a very substantial part in any proposed restructuring where the group has substantial defined benefit pension plans. Many restructuring practitioners feel uncomfortable with the detail of pensions and employee benefits law, but they should take heart from the fact that many pensions practitioners feel uncomfortable with the concepts underlying restructuring.

13.2 UK

13.2.1 Introduction

13.04 Where a distressed employer has UK operations and a UK final salary pension plan, pensions will probably be important if not central to any restructuring. The potential debt owed to the pension plan may well be large (often it is the largest creditor of the UK company) and many of the players will have no overwhelming concern for the company's survival. The trustees of the pension plan are legally separate from the employer, but will usually include past and present employees among their number, some of whom may well stand to lose personally, depending on what is proposed in relation to the pension plan. Emotions may well be running high and it is likely that most of the trustees will have no prior experience of restructuring. The regulatory structure is not particularly intuitive. There are two UK regulatory bodies that are stoutly independent, including from each other. These are not promising conditions for quickly coming to a solution. Negotiations may be protracted.

13.05 Employers in the UK offer a variety of different workplace pension arrangements. In a restructuring, the most complex issues arise in connection with defined benefit (usually final salary) pension schemes. These are usually established under a trust, and provide members with a specified level of benefits at retirement. Employees usually make a fixed contribution; the employer is responsible for funding the balance and will bear the risks associated with fluctuating investment returns and the cost of buying a pension from an insurer at retirement. In recent years, many of these schemes have closed or wound up because they are costly for employers. However, unless they have been completely secured with the insurer the employer may still have substantial costs in relation to this.

In many cases, defined benefit arrangements have been replaced with defined contribution (or money purchase) pension schemes (whether under trust or through personal pension plans). The benefits provided are not fixed: they will be determined by the level of contributions made to the scheme, the investment return on the contributions and (usually) the cost of buying a pension from an insurer at retirement. **13.06**

An employer's financial liability for defined contribution schemes and personal pensions is essentially fixed, and these schemes do not raise difficult issues on a corporate restructuring (though some arrangements that are apparently money purchase may have defined benefits elements). This chapter deals with matters that arise in respect of defined benefit schemes. **13.07**

13.2.2 Pensions legislation affecting insolvency and restructuring

UK pension plans are highly regulated. Defined benefit plans are usually trust-based and are also subject to a vast body of legislation. The Government, alarmed by the suggestion that some solvent employers might wind up their defined benefit pension plans without funding benefits in full, introduced a new set of requirements to counteract this. **13.08**

The Pensions Act 2004, which introduced these reforms, established the following arrangements: **13.09**

- Increasing the employer's obligations to the pension plans. Any underfunding at the point at which the plan went into winding-up would be owed by the employer to the trustees as a debt (commonly known as a section 75 debt). The debt is now to be calculated by reference to the cost of securing all benefits with an insurer.
- A new Pensions Regulator, with a proactive stance toward educating trustees and sweeping new powers to intervene in scheme affairs.
- A scheme specific funding requirement,[1] which requires (for most schemes) all funding to be negotiated and agreed between employers and trustees. Trustees will need to be fully aware of the importance of dealing with conflicts of interest and the need to investigate the strength of the employer's covenant when settling the funding regime. There is a statutory requirement for trustees to have adequate knowledge and understanding of their role, and the Pensions Regulator produces guidance on these matters.
- The Pensions Regulator has taken on the role of appointing an independent trustee on the insolvency of an employer participating in a defined benefit

[1] Pensions Act 2004, ss 221-233; Occupational Pension Schemes (Scheme Funding) Regulations 2005 (SI 2005/3377).

pension scheme.[2] (Previously, the insolvency practitioner would be responsible for appointing an independent trustee.)

- A new Pension Protection Fund (the PPF), providing compensation (up to a specified level) to members of occupational defined benefit schemes whose employers become insolvent at a time when the scheme has insufficient assets to provide those benefits on winding-up.
- Provisions intended to prevent scheme employers from avoiding liability to their pension schemes. They are also intended to ensure that group companies are responsible for pension scheme liabilities within the group, even if they do not actually participate in the scheme. These provisions are known as moral hazard or anti-avoidance legislation.

13.2.3 Apportionment arrangements and withdrawal arrangements

13.10 Where a scheme has more than one employer, and one of the employers stops participating in the scheme, the law intervenes to stop that employer walking away from its obligations. If the scheme has a funding deficit, the trustees will need to satisfy themselves that the proportion of the deficit or debt attributable to the employer leaving the scheme is made good.

13.11 A withdrawal event can arise if an employer becomes insolvent, or the scheme winds up, or the employer gives notice to stop participating. It can also occur if, for example, a participating employer stops employing active scheme members—perhaps because the few remaining active members leave the scheme. (If a participating employer stops employing active members but intends to recruit new employees who will join the scheme within a year, the employer may be able to ensure that a debt does not arise. It will need to serve notice on the trustees within one month of ceasing to employ active members.)

13.12 When a withdrawal event occurs, the employer can make an immediate payment of the debt (calculated on the buy-out basis). Alternatively, a withdrawal arrangement or apportionment arrangement can be made to defer the debt payment.[3]

13.2.3.1 Withdrawal arrangements

13.13 A withdrawal arrangement is an agreement between the withdrawing employer, a guarantor and the trustees. The employer must agree to make a payment at least equal to the debt calculated on the scheme specific funding basis (rather than the buy-out basis). The guarantor agrees to pay the difference when the scheme winds up or if the Pensions Regulator orders payment. The trustees may agree to a

[2] Pensions Act 1995, s 23.

[3] Ibid., s 75; the Occupational Pension Schemes (Employer Debt) Regulations 2005 (as amended).

withdrawal arrangement only if the funding test (described below) is met and the guarantor has sufficient financial resources to pay the difference when it falls due.

If the withdrawing employer wishes to pay less than the debt calculated on the scheme specific funding basis, the withdrawal arrangement would require the approval of the Pensions Regulator. **13.14**

13.2.3.2 Apportionment arrangements

A scheme apportionment arrangement is an arrangement made by the employers and the trustees under the scheme rules. The scheme rules will need to set out how the employer debt is to be apportioned among the employers remaining in the scheme. The rules may need to be amended for this purpose, and the trustees have a statutory power to modify the scheme by resolution. An apportionment arrangement is more flexible than a withdrawal arrangement because no guarantor is required and the withdrawing employer may not need to make a payment at all. The trustees may only agree to an apportionment arrangement if the funding test (described below) is met, and if the arrangement will not adversely affect the security of members' benefits. **13.15**

It is also possible to make a regulated apportionment arrangement, which requires the approval of the Pensions Regulator (and does not require the funding test to be met). However, these are rare in practice. They only apply where a scheme is already being assessed for entry to the Pensions Protection Fund or is expected to enter an assessment period. The Regulator applies stringent criteria before agreeing to such an arrangement. **13.16**

13.2.3.3 Funding test

The funding test is met if the trustees are satisfied that the remaining employers are reasonably likely to be able to fund the scheme so that it can afford to meet the scheme funding requirement. The trustees can assume this is the case if the remaining employers are able to meet the payments due under the schedule of contributions. **13.17**

13.2.4 The Pension Protection Fund

13.2.4.1 Funding the PPF

When the PPF accepts responsibility for paying compensation to members of a scheme, the scheme's assets will be transferred to the PPF. These will be insufficient to pay for the compensation, so the PPF is also funded through a levy on all occupational defined benefit schemes.[4] There is a risk-based element to the levy **13.18**

4 Pensions Act 2004, ss 174–181A.

calculation, which takes account of factors such as the scheme's funding position and the likelihood of an insolvency event occurring in relation to the scheme. This aspect of the levy was designed to protect well-funded, secure schemes from having to pay substantial contributions. However, the risk-based levy has proved controversial in practice, as the most vulnerable schemes, with weak employers and large deficits, have been faced with significant levy payments.

13.2.4.2 Schemes eligible for PPF compensation

13.19 The PPF covers occupational defined benefit pension schemes and hybrid schemes (ie schemes that provide more than one type of benefit) that have started to wind up on or after 6 April 2005. Schemes that began winding up before that date do not qualify for the PPF, but may qualify for another government scheme, the Financial Assistance Scheme.[5] (That scheme pays compensation to members of underfunded defined benefit schemes which started to wind up between 1 January 1997 and 5 April 2005, where the employer is insolvent or no longer exists, or where a compromise agreement has been reached with the employer.)

13.2.4.3 Qualifying for entry to the PPF

13.20 There are essentially three ways in which a scheme can be accepted by the PPF:

- An insolvency event occurs in relation to a scheme's employer, and the insolvency practitioner confirms that a scheme rescue is not possible (ie that no-one else will assume responsibility for the scheme). Details of the relevant insolvency events are set out in section 121(2) of the Pensions Act 2004.
- The trustees of a scheme apply for it to be accepted by the PPF. This is known as a section 129 application.[6] Trustees may do this if they think that the employer is unlikely to continue as a going concern. The employer must be a public body, a charity or a trade union (and meet criteria set down in legislation).
- The Regulator informs the Board of the PPF that it believes the employer is unlikely to continue as a going concern. The Board must then notify the scheme trustees.

13.21 Once one of these events has occurred, the scheme will enter an assessment period during which the Board of the PPF must determine whether it has a duty to assume responsibility for the scheme.

[5] Ibid., s 286; Financial Assistance Scheme Regulations 2005 (SI 2005/1986).

[6] Pensions Act 2004, ss 128-129; Pension Protection Fund (Entry Rules) Regulations 2005, regs 7-8.

13.2.4.4 Level of PPF compensation

The level of PPF compensation varies between different categories of members,[7] and is summarized below. The benefits in respect of which compensation is paid are known as 'protected liabilities': 13.22

- Pensioners who have reached the scheme's normal retirement date at the assessment date (ie the date of the employer insolvency) receive 100 per cent of the annual rate of the pension being paid before the assessment date. The same is normally true for ill-health retirees.
- Members and pensioners who have not reached the scheme's normal retirement date at the assessment date will receive 90 per cent of the annual rate of their pension entitlement before the assessment date, subject to a cap (currently approximately £28,000 a year). Pensions not yet in payment will be revalued until they are put into payment.
- In all cases, pension earned on or after 6 April 1997 will increase annually in line with the Retail Prices Index (to a maximum 2.5 per cent).[8] No increases are payable on pension earned before 6 April 1997.
- A spouse's pension will be paid on the death of a member, equal to 50 per cent of the member's pension. This can be paid to an unmarried partner if there is no spouse, but only if the scheme rules provide for this.

13.2.4.5 Multi-employer schemes

The way in which the PPF legislation applies to schemes with more than one participating employer is extremely complicated. This is largely because multi-employer schemes are structured in many different ways and the regulations attempt to set out what will happen in the case of each particular structure.[9] 13.23

A segregated scheme is divided into different sections for different employers. Any contributions are allocated to a specific section, and the assets of that section can only be used to meet the liabilities in respect of that section. If there is any element of cross-subsidy between different sections, or if the employers have a mutual obligation to fund the whole scheme as well as their individual section, the scheme is a non-segregated scheme. Effectively each section is then treated as a separate scheme for the purposes of PPF eligibility. 13.24

Different provisions apply for employers in non-segregated schemes (or in a section of a segregated scheme which has more than one employer). For these schemes, 13.25

[7] Pensions Act 2004, Sch 7.

[8] This may change to an increase in line with the Consumer Prices Index under proposals set to take effect from 31 March 2011.

[9] Pension Protection Fund (Multi-employer Schemes) (Modification) Regulations 2005 (SI 2005/441).

what happens on an employer insolvency will depend on whether there is a partial winding-up rule in the scheme's trust deed and rules.

13.26 A partial winding-up rule is a requirement or an option for the trustees to wind up the part of the scheme attributable to a particular employer when that employer ceases to participate in the scheme. It makes little difference in practice whether the scheme's partial winding-up rule is expressed as an obligation on the trustees or as an option for them to wind up a section of the scheme. Where the partial winding-up is optional, regulations provide that the option will be deemed to have been exercised unless the trustees actively decide they will not do so.

13.27 When a scheme has a partial winding-up rule and one of the employers becomes insolvent, the scheme will be assessed to see if it is eligible to enter the PPF in respect of the members attributable to that employer. If the scheme has no rule relating to partial winding-up, it will not be eligible for the PPF (a debt, however, will normally be owed by the employer to the plan trustees) until *all* the employers in the scheme have become insolvent. At this point, the entire scheme will be assessed to see if it is eligible to join the PPF.

13.2.4.6 Assessment period

13.28 Where a scheme employer suffers an insolvency event, the scheme (or part of the scheme in the case of some multi-employer schemes) enters a period of assessment to ascertain whether it is eligible to enter the PPF.

13.29 Assessment periods must by law last a minimum of 12 months,[10] although in practice they tend to last between 18 and 24 months. During this time, the board of the PPF determines whether or not a scheme satisfies the statutory requirements to enter the PPF. This will include a full assessment of its funding position and an assessment of the benefits provided by the scheme.

13.30 If, at the end of the assessment period, the board decides that no scheme rescue is possible and the value of the scheme's assets is less than the value of its protected liabilities (ie the PPF compensation payable), the board must assume responsibility for the scheme. If this happens, the PPF will take on all its assets and liabilities. The scheme will be left as a shell for the trustees to wind up.

13.2.4.7 Benefits

13.31 Benefits payable during an assessment period must be reduced to the level of compensation that the PPF would pay if the board assumed responsibility for the scheme (as described above).

---

[10] Pensions Act 2004, s 172.

During an assessment period, the scheme (or part of the scheme) is effectively frozen. No new members can be admitted and no further contributions paid, other than those owing at the date of the employer's insolvency.[11] Transfers from the scheme are restricted and no benefits may accrue to members (except statutory increases and money purchase benefits attributable to the investment of member contributions in respect of pensionable service before the assessment period). The trustees remain primarily responsible for running the scheme and protecting its assets during the assessment period, but the board may take control of the running of the scheme if it wishes to do so. For instance, it may direct the trustees in relation to the investment of the scheme's assets, the incurring of expenditure and the instigation or conduct of legal proceedings.[12] **13.32**

13.2.4.8 Winding-up

The scheme cannot begin to wind up during the assessment period, unless directed to do so by the Regulator, which has a power to trigger winding-up to protect the PPF.[13] If winding-up does occur, no steps may be taken to discharge any liability, and any attempt to do so is void (unless the PPF subsequently validates it).[14] **13.33**

13.2.4.9 Employer debts

During an assessment period, the rights and powers of trustees in relation to any debt owed to them by the employer (including contingent debts such as the winding-up debt) are exercisable by the board of the PPF and not the trustees. The board will also be responsible for collecting any debts payable from the employers. **13.34**

The board is not bound by any insolvency arrangement that relates to a debt that, at the time of the arrangement, was a contingent debt from the employer. The Board could, in theory, ignore any settlements of employer debts and even company voluntary arrangements if they were concluded at a time when the debt they were compromising had not yet arisen. **13.35**

13.2.4.10 The PPF and the role of the insolvency practitioner

The PPF has produced a helpful note on the role of insolvency practitioners. A copy can be found on the PPF's website at <www.pensionprotectionfund.org.uk>. **13.36**

---

11 Ibid., s 133.

12 Ibid., s 135; Pension Protection Fund (Entry Rules) Regulations 2005 (SI 2005/590); Pensions Act 2004, s 133; Pensions Act 2004, s 134.

13 Pensions Act 2004, s 135(2), (3).

14 Ibid., s 135(4); Pension Protection Fund (Entry Rules) Regulations 2005 (SI 2005/590).

13.37 Insolvency practitioners need to understand:

- their duty to notify the PPF, the Pensions Regulator and the trustees within 14 days of the occurrence of each insolvency event of an employer in an occupational defined benefit scheme (or a former employer that still has a liability for a section 75 debt), or within 14 days of the insolvency practitioner becoming aware of the pension scheme. There is a standard form notification (known as a section 120 notice) on the PPF's website for this purpose;
- that the PPF assumes the pension scheme's role of creditor of the insolvent employer during the assessment period;
- that they have a duty to confirm whether or not the pension scheme can be rescued, ie whether another company or person is prepared to take responsibility for it. This has provided rare in practice. The insolvency practitioner must issue either a scheme failure notice stating that the scheme cannot be rescued, or a withdrawal notice stating that the scheme has been rescued. Again, there is a standard form notification (known as a section 122 notice) on the PPF's website for this purpose; and
- that the PPF assigns an assessment team member to each pension scheme to liaise with the insolvency practitioner.

13.2.5 The Pensions Regulator

13.2.5.1 Anti-avoidance provisions

13.38 With effect from 6 April 2005, the Pensions Regulator was given a range of new powers aimed at preventing employers from dumping liabilities on the PPF and increasing the security of members of pension schemes. These are known as the moral hazard provisions.

13.2.5.2 Contribution notices

13.39 The Regulator may issue a contribution notice to an employer in a final salary pension scheme, or to a person connected with the employer or an associate of the employer within the meaning of the Insolvency Act 1986. These include directors, employees, those who control more than a third of the employer's shares and all companies in the group: careful consideration will need to be given as to who exactly is connected with or an associate of the employer. The Regulator can do so where it believes that the employer or person was a party to an act, or deliberate failure to act, and the main purpose, or one of the main purposes, of the act or failure was:

- to prevent the recovery of the whole or any part of the debt on the employer; or
- otherwise than in good faith, to prevent such a debt becoming due, to compromise or otherwise settle the debt, or to reduce the amount of the debt.[15]

[15] Pensions Act 2004, s 38 (as amended).

The contribution notice will require the person to pay a specified sum into the scheme. This contribution could be as much as the total shortfall in the employer debt (or, where there is no debt yet due, the total shortfall assessed as if the debt were due). This would be legally enforceable as a debt. 13.40

The Regulator can only impose a contribution notice if it is reasonable to do so—although it is the Regulator which decides what is reasonable. Relevant factors can include, for example, the degree of involvement of the person in the act or failure to act, the relationship that the person has with the employer, the involvement that the person has with the scheme, and the person's financial circumstances. 13.41

13.2.5.3 Bonas

It is worth noting that, while the Regulator has had the power to issue a contribution notice since April 2005, it has only just exercised this power for the first time. It has done so in relation to the Bonas Group Pension Scheme. The Regulator decided that the company's owners had placed Bonas into a prepack insolvency to avoid the pension liability while retaining the business and employees. Also, the owners had not engaged openly with the plan trustees or the Regulator. These were acts to prevent the recovery of the whole or any part of a debt which was, or might become, due from the employer in relation to the scheme. 13.42

The owners argued that as any section 75 debt could only have been recovered from Bonas, and Bonas never had the means to pay the debt, it could not be correct that the owners intended to prevent recovery of that debt. The Regulator rejected this argument and found that section 38 of the Pensions Act 2004 did cover attempts to prevent payment by any party of a debt on the employer. 13.43

13.2.5.4 Financial support directions

The purpose of a financial support direction is to ensure that groups of companies stand behind their pension liabilities. The Regulator may issue a financial support direction if it is of the opinion that an employer to the scheme is a 'service company' or is 'insufficiently resourced'.[16] 13.44

A company will be a service company if its turnover is 'solely or principally derived from amounts charged for the provision of the services of the employees of [the company] to other members of the group'. 13.45

A company is insufficiently resourced if it has insufficient net assets to enable it to cover 50 per cent of the estimated employer debt in relation to the scheme and there is a person who qualifies under the legislation and whose resources are not 13.46

[16] Ibid., ss 43-51.

less in value than the amount that is the difference between the value of the resources of the employer and the amount that is the prescribed percentage (probably 50 per cent) of the estimated employer debt.

13.47 A financial support direction requires the recipient to ensure that financial support for the scheme is in place within a specified period. Financial support arrangements can mean making all the members of a group jointly and severally liable for the whole or part of an employer's pension liabilities, or making a holding company liable for the whole or part of the employer's pension liabilities. It is not itself legally binding, but if not complied with, the Regulator can take further steps as described below.

13.48 Again, the Regulator can only issue a financial support direction if it is reasonable to do so. The factors it will consider include the value of any benefits received directly or indirectly by the proposed recipient from the employer.

13.49 Until recently, the Regulator had issued only one set of financial support directions, against Sea Containers. This was a surprising choice of precedent, since Sea Containers was in chapter 11 bankruptcy in the US—although it is possible that the financial support direction was part of a larger deal. It has now issued financial support directions in relation to Nortel and has declared an intention to do so in relation to Reader's Digest.

13.50 In January 2010, the Pensions Regulator issued a warning notice against certain entities within the Nortel group including a number of US entities. At the end of February 2010, in response to a motion by the US debtors, the US Bankruptcy Court of the District of Delaware made an order against the trustees of the Nortel Networks UK Pension Plan and PPF declaring that their participation in the Pensions Regulator's proceedings (in respect of Nortel US entities involved in the chapter 11 process) would breach the chapter 11 stay. The trustees and PPF have appealed Gross J.'s order though the matter has yet to reach the hearing stage.

13.51 As noted above, financial support directions are not legally binding. However, if one is not complied with, the Regulator can then issue a legally enforceable contribution notice. This notice is enforceable in the UK as a debt claim by the pension scheme trustees. Elsewhere in the EEA, it is thought to be enforceable under the principles of the Lugano Convention, though this is still to be fully explored. In all jurisdictions, the question of whether this is enforcement of a debt or seeking to give effect to a regulatory direction (and the differing rules on enforcement that may flow from that distinction) will need to be explored.

13.52 The question of how the Regulator's powers should be regarded by the US bankruptcy courts has been the matter of debate in each of these cases. In both *Sea Containers* and *Nortel*, those courts have been asked what status should be afforded to a claim by trustees based on those powers in the context of the US bankruptcy proceedings and how such a claim sits within the chapter 11's automatic stay.

Interestingly, the two cases have resulted in different decisions made at first instance by the US bankruptcy court (on both occasions, in Delaware). *Sea Containers* effectively set the precedent by finding in support of the trustees' claim. In *Nortel* the judge decided that the trustees' claim was in breach of the stay, but with the *Nortel* case subject to appeal this remains an area of developing law. **13.53**

13.2.5.5 Clearance

A clearance procedure is available under the Pensions Act 2004, under which the Regulator can provide confirmation that a particular set of circumstances will not lead to a contribution notice or a financial support direction. This is optional, not compulsory, though the Regulator likes to be involved. In practice, this is an option that is usually taken up on restructurings, given the obvious scope for the Regulator to consider use of its powers. **13.54**

13.2.5.6 Power to appoint independent trustee

Since 6 April 2005, the Regulator has had the power to appoint an independent trustee when the insolvency practitioner notifies the Regulator of an insolvency event in respect of a scheme employer. However, in practice, the Regulator generally decides not to do so where an independent trustee is already in place. As a result, many schemes try to ensure that the independent trustee is appointed before the insolvency event occurs, especially where the insolvency event is part of an agreed restructuring of pension scheme liabilities. **13.55**

13.2.6 Pension scheme restructuring

Before the PPF was established, there were a number of cases where a company was in financial difficulties and its section 75 debt was compromised by the trustees of the pension scheme. These were generally known as 'Bradstock' compromises, because of the court case on which they were based.[17] **13.56**

Trustees could compromise the section 75 debt if they honestly and reasonably believed that insistence upon repayment of the full amount owed would result in the employer becoming insolvent and the scheme recovering significantly less than was being offered in compromise. It was in scheme members' interests for the trustees to compromise the debt if the employer was prepared to pay a sum more **13.57**

---

17 *Bradstock Group Pension Scheme Trustees Ltd v Bradstock Group plc* [2002] EWHC 651.

than the amount that would be recovered if the employer was forced into insolvency.

13.58 It is worth noting that Bradstock compromises could only be made after the section 75 debt had been triggered, and not in anticipation of it arising. Bradstock agreements usually resulted in a write-off of a significant part of the company's section 75 debt, in return for a much smaller payment by the employer to the scheme.

13.59 There were concerns that employers could be using Bradstock agreements to walk away from their obligations to their pension schemes—effectively using the compromise to fund the turnaround, while other creditors were not being required to share the pain.

13.60 The Pensions Act 2004 put greater controls on the use of Bradstock agreements. A pension plan now ceases to be eligible for PPF protection where the trustees enter into a legally enforceable agreement the effect of which is to reduce the section 75 debt, unless the arrangement has been signed off by the Pensions Regulator and the PPF. There are certain exceptions to this general principle, such as where the level of benefits that can be provided from the scheme following the compromise exceeds the level of PPF compensation. However, unless it is absolutely certain that the relevant exceptions apply or the arrangement has received regulatory sign-off, it is unlikely that trustees will voluntarily enter into such agreements in the future.

13.61 Nevertheless, the financial considerations driving employers to restructure their pension liabilities are undiminished. If anything, they have been made more pressing by the introduction of the new scheme specific funding requirement, the impact of continuous mortality improvements, the increase of the risk-based PPF levy and the more aggressive approach required of trustees in safeguarding the position of their pension scheme.

13.2.6.1 The pension stakeholders

13.62 Pensions restructurings involve a number of stakeholders with very different agendas to the other parties to the deal.

13.63 **13.2.6.1.1 The trustees** Trustees have a primary duty to protect the scheme to which they are appointed. Legislative changes implemented by the Pensions Act 2004 have forced trustees, with the support of the Regulator, to take a proactive stance in policing the employer covenant and devising means of reducing deficits.

13.64 Some commentators have raised concerns that the availability of PPF protection may incline trustees to trigger an insolvency rather than to support a restructuring. Certainly, this may operate as leverage in commercial negotiations. However, trustees will usually be supportive of a solution that benefits the scheme and often results in a far more certain path to PPF protection while still allowing the employer's business (and members' jobs) to be saved.

The circumstances surrounding a pensions restructuring may be complex and beyond the experience of lay trustees. They often entail significant issues of confidentiality, commercial sensitivity and conflicts of interest that may be exacerbated by the involvement of member trustees in negotiations concerning the future of a business in which they may have a vested interest (often as employees, directors or shareholders). **13.65**

Independent trustees can play a vital role in such cases, promoting the interests of the scheme with due regard to such issues and bringing with them experience of similar restructurings and current market practice. **13.66**

13.2.6.1.2 The Regulator For all practical purposes, clearance from the Regulator is an essential part of any pensions restructuring. That is not to say that many deals are not struck without seeking Regulator clearance. However, without it, the parties cannot be confident that the deal they have struck will not be attacked at some future point or that the Regulator might not seek further funding for the pension liabilities from the employer's shareholders, directors or those associated with them. This was seen most publicly in the *Reader's Digest* case, where the Regulator declined to endorse a deal that had been contingently agreed by both the trustees and the PPF—a deal that the Regulator had been closely involved with negotiating from the outset. **13.67**

At its crudest, a pensions restructuring is a device that is designed to allow employers to walk away from their pension obligations and to oblige the PPF to pick up the tab. Realistically, the Regulator will only clear such structures where they offer the best outcome for the scheme—one which is appreciably better than a traditional insolvency—and the PPF's agreement with the proposal is a necessary but not sufficient condition (see below). **13.68**

There is no objective test for when or how to make an approach to the Regulator. However, the Regulator encourages parties attempting to restructure their business in a way that will limit the pension debt to make a timely approach for clearance. The cases described in this chapter indicate that an early, collaborative approach and regular updates are more likely to elicit a supportive response from the Regulator. Presenting the matter to the Regulator as a fait accompli at the end of a process when there is no time or opportunity to pursue alternatives is a high risk strategy and the Regulator is quite capable of acting unpredictably in such circumstances. **13.69**

As a practical matter, the Regulator's deliberations can be opaque. It is a deliberative body with formal reporting lines and those with whom the other parties communicate will probably not be able to commit the Regulator to a course of action. **13.70**

It is entirely possible that other decision-makers within the organization may see things quite differently from the case handler.

13.71 13.2.6.1.3 **The PPF** It may be tempting to think of the PPF as peripheral to the restructuring negotiations—perhaps because the trustees have primary responsibility for the scheme or because the PPF is *obliged* to accept eligible, underfunded schemes whose employers have suffered an insolvency event. Nothing could be further from the truth.

13.72 In cases where PPF protection is the end-game of the restructuring, the PPF's support will be required as it is the party exercising the creditor rights following an insolvency event. The PPF therefore plays a central role in negotiations, frequently displacing the trustees as the lead party actively defending the interests of the scheme as if they had already assumed the scheme's creditor rights.

13.73 The PPF is able to effect a compromise of the scheme debt without jeopardizing PPF eligibility where the trustees cannot do so. Clearance from the Regulator may well hinge on an expression of support for the proposals from the PPF. Trustees as well as other stakeholders tend to defer to the view of the PPF on all significant commercial issues to ensure that what is agreed is deliverable.

13.74 Frustratingly perhaps, this does not mean that other stakeholders can expect the PPF to commit unconditionally to accepting the schemes into the PPF. The PPF must undertake a formal assessment period to determine whether it is obliged to accept schemes and it cannot contract out of this or to treat it as a mere formality. This often means that the effectiveness of some or all the restructuring is subject to some conditionality. Nevertheless, the existence of some form of written assurance from the PPF that it will support the restructuring, for example by agreeing to exercise the scheme's vote in favour of a company voluntary arrangement, is vitally important and may be the key that unlocks the process. The PPF is also prepared to look at some areas that may affect eligibility before the assessment period starts (for example, the position of former employers—see below), as a form of due diligence.

13.75 Considerable importance is attached by parties to the timing and manner of the approach to the PPF. Unlike the Regulator, it will have a commercial interest in the outcome of negotiations if it is to accept responsibility for the scheme. Details of what is on offer to the scheme, and why it is worth having, need to be factored in to the approach. However, much like the Regulator, the PPF has an eye on the bigger picture and will not react well to a last-minute gambit with only a marginal upside to the scheme against insolvency.

13.76 The PPF has a very different negotiating style from the Regulator. You will get a very clear idea from the PPF of its expectations and its reporting lines are much clearer to the outsider.

13.2.6.2 Pensions Act 2004 negotiations in practice

The Regulator and the PPF have now developed a practice for dealing with such applications. As will be seen from the cases, where the employer's covenant is being improved the prospects for a successful application are much greater. **13.77**

In *Heath Lambert*, the Regulator gave clearance for an arrangement under which the assets of the employer company were sold to a newco special purpose vehicle in which the scheme would take a 10 per cent shareholding. The deal was a part of a wider debt restructuring in which other lenders capitalized some of their debt and new finance was introduced to the business. **13.78**

The trustees and the PPF were unable to secure cash payments but could expect to see a return if the business performed well. It appears to have been critical to the thinking of both the Regulator and the PPF that the only alternative to the deal struck was an insolvency of the profitable business in which little or nothing would have been recovered by the scheme as an unsecured creditor and that around 1,800 jobs would have been put at risk. The PPF will expect the plan (or the PPF itself) to participate substantially in the profits made by the business after offloading its pension plan. Employers should not see the PPF as a dumping ground, but a last resort. **13.79**

In *Sheffield Forgemasters*, a similar approach was taken. The surviving group announced in August 2007 that it had reached an agreement with the pension plan trustees to repurchase their 30 per cent shareholding, and offer the shares to its employees at half their then value and with preferential lending terms. The company's intention was to offer a basic number of shares to any employee buying in, but to offer further shares as a means of recognizing any pension deficit felt by certain parts of the workforce. **13.80**

In *Marconi*, the Regulator cleared a deal struck with the trustees under which the business would be sold and a large chunk of the £1.2 bn purchase price of the business would be used to secure the scheme benefits. It was agreed that £185 m would be paid to the scheme immediately, with an additional £490 m being paid into an escrow account. The money held in escrow was retained on trust for Telent, the residual employer, but with security in favour of the trustees. Entitlement to the funds would be determined by the outcome of an actuarial valuation of scheme assets against liabilities on a buy-out basis. The trustees would get the funds to the extent of any deficit on that basis; Telent would get the funds to the extent of any surplus. The remainder of the sale proceeds were paid to the existing Marconi shareholders. **13.81**

It appears that the Regulator's decision to grant clearance for the deal was influenced by the trustees' intention to demand immediate payment of significant sums due to the scheme (which would have put Marconi into insolvency) if clearance was not granted. **13.82**

13.83 In November 2007, Telent's shareholders agreed a £398 m sale to The Pension Corporation. The Pension Corporation's plan appears to be to seek to sell the Telent business but to retain responsibility for the scheme assets and liabilities with a view to making a return on, among other things, an improved investment strategy.

13.84 In the *Swissport* case, Candover (its owners) and the trustees reached an agreement with the Regulator's support under which Candover would put £6 m in to the Swissport scheme so as to clear the scheme's FRS17 deficit (that is to say, the deficit calculated on the basis required for the audited accounts). The members were then given the choice of:

- transferring their benefits to a new Swissport final salary scheme;
- transferring their benefits to a personal pension scheme; or
- going into the PPF.

Candover and Swissport also agreed to pay for members to take financial advice on which option was best for them. This arrangement allowed the PPF to mitigate significantly its exposure to the scheme debt—potentially by as much as £13 m.

13.85 Court sanction for a restructuring was obtained in *L & Others v M Ltd.*[18] This case concerned a component manufacturer that was in financial difficulties and that could no longer rely on parent company support for ongoing trading. In order to survive, it needed (as part of a wider restructuring) to be released from its obligations to its final salary scheme. The scheme was £38 m in deficit on a buy-out basis and was potentially reliant on the PPF's compensation if substantial further funding was not found. Without this solution, M would have been forced into insolvency, and then the scheme stood to recover little or nothing.

13.86 The company, the trustees, the PPF and the Regulator agreed in principle to a proposal under which the scheme would enter a PPF assessment period following an insolvency event and, conditional upon its entry into the PPF, the scheme would receive an equity stake in M. The problem in *L v M* was that the value of M's business was deemed particularly sensitive to any association with a formal insolvency process and, therefore, the success of the restructuring as a whole depended upon achieving a solution to the pension deficit problem that took the deficit off M's balance sheet and avoided a formal insolvency of M.

13.87 The solution proposed was for the scheme to be reopened to allow a new employer, Newco, to participate in the scheme for a short period. A few employees who were active members of the scheme were to be transferred to Newco, to ensure that it was a proper 'employer' for these purposes. The scheme rules were also to be

[18] [2006] EWHC 3395 (Ch),

amended so that, when an employer ceased to participate, the trustees had the power (permitted by legislation) to allocate any debt on the employer on a basis other than the statutory formula. M was then to cease to participate in the scheme, triggering its section 75 debt. This debt would be set at £1 under the trustees' power in the rules, with the balance of the debt being assumed by Newco. M would exit the scheme, pay its £1 debt, and cease to be liable for any further debt to the scheme. Once M had left the scheme, the scheme would then go into winding-up, triggering the full section 75 debt for Newco. Newco would be unable to pay its debt and would suffer a qualifying insolvency event, triggering a period of assessment for entry of the scheme into the PPF.

The concern, however, was that this arrangement might amount to a compromise that would prevent the scheme from being eligible under the PPF entry regulations. The regulations provide that a scheme is not eligible for the PPF where the trustees have, before the commencement of a PPF assessment period, entered a 'legally enforceable agreement the effect of which is to reduce the amount of any [employer debt]'. All parties (and in particular the trustees) therefore wanted comfort that amending the scheme rules and apportioning M's section 75 debt in the manner proposed would not preclude PPF eligibility. **13.88**

The court decided that PPF protection was still available. The rationale for the court's decision was that the agreement would be made before any debt became due, even though it would have the effect of reducing a debt in the future. It is also evident that the judge recognized that the proposal would only be put into effect through the collaborative efforts of the company, the trustees, the PPF and the Regulator and that, as a result of the proposal being effected, M's restructuring could be achieved, which itself would result in a preservation of M's business and the continued employment of its workforce (including many members). **13.89**

This decision has opened up the possibility of a solvent restructuring solution for employers of final salary pension schemes in deficit, while maintaining their PPF eligibility. It is particularly helpful in circumstances involving multiple employer schemes where a formal insolvency of each employer would be impractical, expensive and even more damaging to stakeholder value. A similar approach was subsequently undertaken in *Dana*. **13.90**

13.2.6.3 Ilford

With the existence of the PPF, the possibility for trustees of pension plans to game the system arose. There were concerns that trustees might be obliged to do so, to maximize the benefits for beneficiaries. The point was argued before the court in *ITS v Hope* (more usually referred to as the *Ilford* case). In that case, the trustee of a pension scheme sought court directions whether it could properly implement a proposal to purchase annuities for members, in exercise of a power to buy out **13.91** benefits, in circumstances where the sponsoring employer was insolvent, the scheme was significantly underfunded, and the trustee intended in due course to take steps to cause the scheme to enter the PPF.

13.92 The proposal had been specifically designed to take advantage of the PPF compensation, and sought to apply in the purchase of annuities a disproportionately large share of the scheme assets in a way that could not possibly be justified if the PPF did not exist.

13.93 The judge concluded that a proposal of this nature was obviously not consistent with the policy of the legislation establishing the PPF. He held that the prospective availability of compensation under the PPF, if and when the scheme entered the PPF, was not a relevant factor for the trustee to take into account in the exercise of a power to buy out benefits because to take it into account would be contrary to the clear legislative policy of the Pensions Act 2004, and would thus be contrary to public policy.

13.94 This case has unfortunately been much overinterpreted. The judge went out of his way to stress that this was very much based on the specific question put to him. In his own words:

> Further than that I would not, at present, go, bearing in mind that the existence of the PPF is in certain contexts a legitimate matter for trustees to take into account, and the dangers of invoking public policy in relation to a situation which is not before the court. I would, however, say that if my conclusion in the present case is soundly based, I would expect a similar approach to be adopted in any instance where trustees seek to take advantage of the existence of the PPF as a justification for acting in a way which would otherwise be improper.

13.95 In other words, it is not that the existence of the PPF is something that trustees must inevitably ignore when exercising their powers, but that they must not manipulate affairs to maximize the value of the PPF's safety net to the plan in a way not intended by the legislative framework. The precise way in which trustees must consider the PPF when making its decisions remains to be explored.

13.2.6.4 Common themes

13.96 Those considering such restructurings should look at the following common elements to all these cases:

- *a viable business*—one which is capable of being rescued and returned to solvent trading;
- *the prospect of a better outcome for stakeholders on restructuring than in a traditional insolvency*. This was a central consideration for trustees entering into Bradstock agreements and it is just as true for the PPF and trustees in the post-Pensions Act 2004 environment;

- *time*—although time was undoubtedly a precious commodity to those involved in these cases, the problem, the cause and the solution were identified early enough to allow something to be done;
- *money*—the sums at stake were sufficient to warrant the resources required to investigate and implement the most appropriate restructuring solution;
- *stakeholder support*—the will (and often the need) was there on the part of the key stakeholders to support the business through a restructuring as opposed to all other alternatives. This often involved managing the process over a considerable period of time while maintaining a high degree of confidentiality;
- *professional advice*—the delivery of proper professional advice throughout the process is critical to the success of these restructurings. This is particularly the case as regards advice on valuations and outcomes in insolvency and on the legality of the proposed changes to be effected by the restructuring.

13.2.6.5 Reaching agreement

In cases where PPF protection is sought, it is the PPF that sets the price for agreeing to support the compromise. The PPF looks at each case individually. The PPF has confirmed its intention to take equity in the surviving business as a matter of course as an anti-embarrassment measure. This may be as little as 10 per cent where significant outside investment is a part of the deal or as much as 33 per cent where the surviving business is backed by the same parties. This might operate as an incentive to existing management or shareholders to look for external finance to fund the restructuring, although experience suggests that new funders are hard to find at the eleventh hour. The PPF will not take more than 33 per cent equity, as it does not want a controlling interest in the company. **13.97**

The components of the price that the PPF will normally be looking for are (in declining order of value): cash up front; cash in instalments; securities or collateralized assets; senior secured debt; debt with fixed and/or floating charges; subordinated debt; preference shares and convertible bonds; and ordinary share capital. This is not an exhaustive list and these components are not necessarily available. The PPF is prepared to look at a wide variety of means of recovering value for the scheme above that which would be available to it as an unsecured creditor in an insolvency. **13.98**

The PPF is as flexible as the situation will allow to negotiate the best commercial outcome available for the scheme, provided that it is demonstrably better than the alternatives (usually traditional insolvency). However, the PPF will not feel pressure to do deals for nominal amounts above the insolvency outcomes. The PPF cannot afford to be seen to be supporting employers offering only marginal benefits to the scheme. Indeed, it regards some failures to reach agreement as having the silver lining of encouraging generosity from employers and their owners. **13.99**

13.2.6.6 Technical considerations

13.100 Without an insolvency trigger, a final salary pension scheme cannot enter the assessment period that is the prerequisite to PPF admission. The implementation of one of the formal UK insolvency processes is therefore a vital part of any pensions restructuring that seeks to pass responsibility for the pension scheme to the PPF.

13.101 Evidently, this can create a tension with the underlying objective of the restructuring process, which aims to preserve value in the business for all stakeholders (including the pensions creditor) as against outcomes in insolvency. The UK insolvency regime has nevertheless proved itself remarkably flexible and the pensions and restructuring professions equally creative in delivering solutions to get around the damaging effects of insolvency.

13.102 Taking steps to put the employer company through a formal process was perhaps less damaging in cases such as *Heath Lambert* and *Sheffield Forgemasters*, where the insolvency of the group was already in the public domain. However, the use of a prepack process and the preference for the company voluntary arrangement over other alternatives in cases such as *Perplas* and *Pittards* shows the importance of ensuring that the insolvency impacts as little as possible on the underlying business and its day-to-day dealings with the outside world.

13.103 Even more sophisticated use of insolvency techniques was deployed in *L v M* and *Dana*, where the risk to value was deemed so serious that a newco was used to divorce completely the 'taint' of insolvency from the surviving business while all unconnected, unsecured creditors other than the pension creditor were paid in full. The ability to reapportion debt from the employers to a newco in the manner approved in *L v M* offers real advantages in cases involving multi-employer schemes where an insolvency process of each employer would be too cumbersome and damaging to value. Nevertheless, the mechanism can succeed only because the PPF, the trustees and the Regulator are prepared to allow it to happen. Clearance is a crucial part of any such sophisticated restructuring, given the obvious pension scheme debt avoidance and the Regulator's powers to impose contribution notices and financial support directions (see above).

13.2.6.7 The problem of former employers

13.104 Whilst it may sound an obvious point, it is critically important to identify the employers participating in the pension scheme. This is often easier said than done. The PPF works in a complex manner for multi-employer schemes. It is important to ensure that all the former employers are dealt with so as to enable the whole scheme to enter the PPF assessment period at once. In very broad terms, an employer that ceased to participate in the scheme on or after 6 April 1997 will continue to be liable to it unless:

- no section 75 debt was due when it ceased to participate;

- a debt became due and was paid;
- a debt became due and has not been paid solely because the employer has not been notified of it in sufficient time to pay it; or
- a debt became due, but it is unlikely to be recovered without disproportionate cost or within a reasonable time.

It is important to ascertain, before the qualifying insolvency event, whether there are any former employers who have not been discharged from liability—and it is amazing how often this happens in practice. Steps should be taken to ensure that the companies in question are discharged before the PPF assessment period, for example by the trustees investigating the financial position of the employer and concluding that any debt due from it falls under the fourth bullet point above. Otherwise, the risk is that the qualifying insolvency event puts only the employees attributable to the insolvent company into the PPF, and not the whole scheme. This would be a deal-breaker for the trustees and this should be a priority for the employers and those connected with them to resolve. 13.105

13.3 US

The protection of employees' pension benefits is a fundamental concern in the UK and US, and both countries heavily regulate the establishment, design and operation of pension plans, particularly defined benefit pension plans. Most defined benefit pension plans primarily covering US employees are comprehensively regulated under the Employee Retirement Income Security Act of 1974, as amended ('ERISA'),[19] which includes a mandatory pension termination insurance programme administered by the Pension Benefit Guaranty Corporation ('PBGC'), a US federal corporation.[20] Unlike the cluttered situation in the UK in which pension trustees, a Pension Regulator and a Pension Protection Fund are all involved, the PBGC is solely responsible for representing the interests of the pension plan and its participants,[21] as well as the PBGC's own interests, in addressing the possible termination of the pension plan and the concomitant assumption by the 13.106

[19] 29 USC s 1001, et seq.

[20] 29 USC ss 1301–1371. This chapter examines defined benefit pension plans which are subject to the PBGC's plan termination insurance programme and generally does not address other types of pension plans. Also, the examination is further limited to 'single-employer plans' and not 'multi-employer plans'. See nn. 9 and 10. Accordingly, all references to any pension plan herein is intended to be a reference to single-employer plans subject to the PBGC's plan termination insurance programme, unless the context indicates otherwise.

[21] Notwithstanding that the PBGC's obligation to pay unfunded pension benefits under a plan is capped at a maximum amount, the PBGC has the sole and exclusive right to recover the full amount of the plan's unfunded pension liability from the employer (and plan participants do not have any claim against the employer for such liability in excess of the PBGC's maximum amount). 29 USC s 1362.

PBGC of the obligation to pay pension benefits. Any employer seeking to avoid or minimize its unfunded pension liability during any business restructuring must comply with the applicable requirements of ERISA, including its provisions relating to the pension termination insurance programme, and generally cannot resort to the rights of a debtor under the US Bankruptcy Code to evade such compliance.[22] Accordingly, the opportunity for an employer to achieve a meaningful reduction in its obligation to satisfy its unfunded pension liability depends on the rights of the PBGC and the role it plays in any business restructuring. This section of the chapter briefly examines the interplay between the rights of a debtor undertaking a business restructuring under the US Bankruptcy Code and the rights of the PBGC under ERISA in administering the pension termination insurance programme.

13.3.1 Pensions legislation affecting insolvency and restructuring

13.107 Employers in the US are not required to provide any level of pension benefits to their employees, though both employers and employees contribute to a federal social security programme that is intended to provide a modest level of retirement income. If employers opt to provide pension benefits, the design, administration, and operation of the pension plans through which such benefits are provided are subject to the requirements of ERISA.[23] There are many similarities in the manner in which employees' pension benefits are protected in the UK and the US in the event of an employer's insolvency. In particular, pension plans covering rank-and-file employees are legally separate from the employer sponsoring them and are required to be funded by contributions from the employer, employees or both.[24] In the case of most defined benefit pension plans, there are statutory minimum funding requirements and mandatory participation in a plan termination insurance programme.[25] However, the establishment of a single federal corporation

---

[22] A pension plan may not be rejected as an executory contract by an employer in lieu of complying with ERISA's plan termination provisions. See, eg, *LTV v Pension Benefit Guaranty Corporation.*

[23] ERISA was enacted to curb employer practices believed to be abusive, and the protection of employees' rights to their pensions is a principal purpose of ERISA. Accordingly, in the case of pension plans covering employees generally, ERISA includes requirements as to minimum participation, vesting and funding, as well as establishing fiduciary and other standards of conduct.

[24] Pursuant to s 502(d) of ERISA, 29 USC s 1132, an employee benefit plan is treated as a separate entity from the employer sponsoring the plan, and any money judgment against the plan is enforceable solely against the plan as an entity. Moreover, in the case of a pension plan, all assets of the pension plan generally must be set aside in a separate trust and not inure to the employer's benefit. 29 USC s 1103. A pension plan's assets do not constitute the employer's own assets, and hence are not directly involved in the employer's reorganization proceeding under the US Bankruptcy Code. Note: an employer's unfunded pension plans (eg supplemental retirement, excess benefits and deferred compensation plans) do not have assets and the foregoing does not apply to such plans.

[25] ERISA s 4021(b), 29 USC s 1321(b).

(PBGC), with the sole function of administering the pension termination insurance programme in the US, simplifies the difficult task of determining when and under what circumstances an employer should be permitted to terminate a pension plan and have the plan termination insurance programme assume responsibility for administering and paying pensions to retirees up to statutory limits. Moreover, the PBGC appears more apt and, under the applicable regulatory structure, is permitted to enforce its statutory rights more promptly and aggressively than its counterparts in the UK.

13.3.2 Pension termination insurance program 13.108

(a) *Covered plans.* Most defined benefit pension plans primarily covering employees in the US are required to participate in the PBGC's pension termination insurance programme,[26] including most single-employer plans and multi-employer plans.[27] As is the case in the UK, the treatment of single-employer plans under the plan termination insurance programme differs markedly from the treatment of multi-employer plans, although the reasons for such disparate treatment may be different in each country.[28] In the US, multi-employer plans appear to be treated differently due to the greater number of employers participating in multi-employer plans and the lowered expectation that such plans will terminate. As a result, the board of trustees of a multi-employer plan (and not the PBGC) enforces the plan's rights in any employer's restructuring or insolvency (and termination of theplan rarely arises as an issue). This chapter generally addresses single-employer plans and not other pension plans.

[26] The exceptions from mandatory participation are governmental plans, certain church plans and unfunded pension plans covering only a select group of management or highly compensated employees or providing benefits in excess of statutory limits. 29 USC s 1003. Pension plans established and primarily covering employees outside the US are also excluded from the application of ERISA.

[27] A single-employer plan is defined in ERISA as any employee benefit plan other than a multi-employer plan, which generally is a plan maintained pursuant to more than one collective bargaining agreement and to which more than one unrelated employer contributes. ERISA s 3(41), 29 USC s 1002(41). A single-employer plan is somewhat of a misnomer because such term includes a plan to which more than one unrelated employer contributes (but not pursuant to any collective bargaining agreement), which is commonly referred to as a multiple employer plan.

[28] Limited protection applies to multi-employer plans, which are pension plans covering employees who are represented by a union or similar employee representative and whose participation in the pension plan is required by a collective bargaining or other similar agreement. The rules governing multi-employer plans differ markedly from the rules applicable to single employer plans due to the ongoing nature of such plans and their rights against each participating employer. This chapter focuses on single employer plans, and generally does not address any employer's participation in or withdrawal from any multi-employer plan, or the insolvency or reorganization of a multi-employer plan.

(b) Premiums are payable to the PBGC for plan termination insurance coverage as to each single-employer plan on a risk-adjusted basis and based on the number of participants.[29] The unfunded pension liability assumed by the PBGC upon plan termination is funded by such premiums and the recoveries by the PBGC on its claims against the employer. No financial support is provided directly by the US federal government.

(c) *Plan termination insurance.* In the event of a termination of a pension plan with insufficient assets to pay all of its pension benefit obligations, the PBGC will assume responsibility to pay unfunded pension benefits up to statutory limits.[30] The assets of a pension plan are allocated to cover payment of accrued, vested benefits under the pension plan sequentially to different categories of benefits in accordance with a priority schedule set out in ERISA until such assets are exhausted, and funded pension benefits following such allocation will be paid in the ordinary course without regard to any statutory limits otherwise applicable on a plan termination.[31] The unfunded pension benefits, after such allocation, are subject to a maximum limit on the individual pension amount guaranteed by the PBGC, as well as limits on early retirement benefits, plant shutdown and other contingent benefits, recently added benefits and non-pension benefits.[32] The determination of what pension benefits are guaranteed by the PBGC can be a complicated task, and the PBGC itself may take years after a plan termination to finish its guarantee obligations. However, in the case of a plan termination during 2010, the maximum pension benefit guaranteed by the PBGC, commencing at age 65 as a single life annuity is $4,500 per month.[33] Such maximum is adjusted annually to reflect increases in the federal cost-of-living index.

13.109 13.3.3 Termination of single employer plans—involuntary or distress termination

(a) *ERISA requirements for a plan termination.* ERISA sets out specific standards and procedures to be followed to terminate a single-employer plan.

---

29 29 USC s 1306. See also the discussion below regarding a reorganized employer's continuing obligation to pay PBGC premiums for three years after a business reorganization under chapter 11 of the Bankruptcy Code.

30 ERISA s 4022, 29 USC s 1322.

31 ERISA s 4044, 29 USC s 1344.

32 29 USC s 1322 (single-employer plans) and 29 USC s 1322a (multi-employer plans). There is a five-year, pro rata phase-in of new benefits added to a pension plan, limitations on the calculation of early retirement benefits, exclusion of certain contingent or ancillary benefits, and the elimination of lump sum payments (other than a de minimis amount). A good description of the statutory limits may be at the PBGC's website at <http://pbgc.gov/>.

33 ERISA s 4007, 29 USC s 1307. The payor for a single-employer plan includes the contributing sponsor of such plan.

An underfunded single-employer plan may be terminated pursuant to ERISA either at the initiation of the PBGC by commencing a federal court case seeking an involuntary termination[34] or at the initiation of the employer by submitting an application to the PBGC for its approval of a distress termination.[35] The standards and procedures applicable to an involuntary termination are much different from those applicable to a distress termination. In both cases, however, there is a substantive requirement whether the employer's financial condition and surrounding circumstances are such that the applicable standard for a plan termination has been satisfied.[36]

(b) *Coordination between ERISA and the Bankruptcy Code.* An employer undergoing a restructuring or insolvency proceeding under the US Bankruptcy Code and seeking to reduce or avoid its unfunded pension liability might prefer to exercise its statutory rights as a debtor to accomplish that reduction or avoidance. However, a single-employer plan covered by the PBGC's plan termination insurance programme may only be terminated in accordance with the requirements of ERISA, and not by circumventing such requirements by exercising the authority provided to a debtor undergoing a reorganization in a case commenced under the US Bankruptcy Code.[37] In particular, a single-employer plan may not be terminated by a debtor attempting to reject the plan as an executory contract.

(c) *PBGC's right to exercise discretion.* The inability of a debtor to reject a pension plan as an executory contract in lieu of complying with the plan-termination provisions under ERISA is important because it eliminates the debtor's opportunity to act without any approval of the PBGC. As a debtor cannot initiate an involuntary plan termination, it is required to comply with the ERISA requirements for a distress termination in seeking to reduce or avoid its unfunded pension liability, including the submission of an application to the PBGC for its approval of the distress termination, the provision of 60 days' prior notice of the proposed plan termination to plan participants and other interested persons, and the provision of information to the PBGC in support of its eligibility for a distress termination.[38] The PBGC generally has

[34] 29 USC s 1342.

[35] 29 USC s 1341(c). A single-employer plan may also be terminated in a 'standard' termination in which all pension benefit liabilities are satisfied in connection with such termination, but a standard termination is not typically relevant to a financially distressed employer. 29. USC s 1341(b).

[36] In the case of an involuntary termination, the substantive standard to be satisfied is set out in s 4042(a) of ERISA, and in the case of a distress termination, the substantive standard is set out in s 4041(c)(2)(B) of ERISA. 29 USC ss 1342(a) and 1341(c)(2)(B), respectively.

[37] Note: The reference to 'Bankruptcy Code' is to the Bankruptcy Code of 1978, as amended, USC Title 11, and presumably a common defined term will be used consistently through the treatise. *LTV v Pension Benefit Guaranty Corporation.*

[38] As set out in s 4041(c)(2)(B)(ii) of ERISA, the necessary distress criteria is met: 'if such person has filed, or has had filed against such person, as of the proposed termination date, a petition seeking

the right, in its discretion, to decide whether the requirements for a distress termination of an underfunded pension plan have been satisfied (although an exception applies to a debtor in a reorganization case under the US Bankruptcy Code). As the PBGC assumes liability for unfunded pension benefits upon a plan's termination, it is not a disinterested decision-maker and, in practice, refrains from approving plan terminations to the greatest extent practicable. In fact, the PBGC can and often does strongly advocate for the continuing sponsorship of single-employer plans by debtors reorganizing under the US Bankruptcy Code or by purchasers of a debtor's business.

(d) *Bankruptcy court's discretion to approve a distress termination.* Although the PBGC generally has discretion to approve any distress termination, in the case of a debtor in a reorganization proceeding under the US Bankruptcy Code, the bankruptcy court or other appropriate federal court (and not the PBGC) appears to have the right to determine the most critical, substantive requirement for approval of the distress termination—whether the debtor 'will be unable to pay all of its debts pursuant to a plan of reorganization and will be unable to continue in business outside a chapter 11 reorganization process and [such court] approves the termination'.[39] The bankruptcy court is likely to be far more impartial than the PBGC in construing and applying such distress termination standard.

(i) The 'reorganization standard' for a distress termination has been difficult for bankruptcy courts to interpret and apply, and the few judicial decisions to date that have applied such standard have struggled, largely because the plain meaning of the statutory provision appears to establish an overly lenient or permissive standard for any distress terminations of pension plans. The plain and literal meaning of the statute establishes an easy threshold that many reorganizing debtors could readily meet,[40] ie they cannot pay all their existing debts and require the

---

reorganization in a case under title 11, United States Code, or under any similar Federal law or law of a State or political subdivision of a State (or a case described in clause (i) [liquidation case] filed by or against such person has been converted, as of such date, to a case in which reorganization is sought, such case has not, as of the proposed termination date, been dismissed, such person timely submits to the [PBGC] any request for the approval of the bankruptcy court (or other appropriate court in a case under such similar law of a State or political subdivision) of the plan termination, and (IV) the bankruptcy court (or such other appropriate court) determines that, unless the plan is terminated, such person will be unable to pay all its debts pursuant to a plan of reorganization and will be unable to continue in business outside a chapter 11 reorganization process and approves the termination.'

[39] 29 USC s 1341. *Re Wire Rope Corp. of America, Inc.* 287 BR 771, 777 (Bankr. WD Mo. 2002) (PBGC will be bound by a final and non-appealable order of the bankruptcy court with respect to a debtor as to criterion (IV) of s 1341(d)(1)). See also 29 CFR s 4041.41(d)(1)(iv).

[40] See, eg, *Falcon Products* 2005 WL 3416130 at *9-11 (authorizing distress termination); *Philip Service* 310 BR at 805-9 (refusing to authorize distress termination); *U.S. Airways* 296 BR at 743-7 (authorizing distress termination); *Wire Rope* 287 BR at 776-82 (same); *Sewell Manufacturing* 195 BR at 183-6 (same).

protection of the US Bankruptcy Code to avoid an interruption in operating their businesses.[41] Instead of torturing the statutory language to establish a higher threshold, in the author's view courts should embrace a simple and direct approach by adopting the permissive standard and construe their right to approve the distress termination as a discretionary power to be exercised in a manner consistent with the US Bankruptcy Code. The few judicial decisions to date regarding distress terminations by reorganizing debtors can be readily reconciled to establish guidelines for when a bankruptcy court should approve a distress termination of a single employer plan, recognizing that each court's judgment may differ when exercising prudent discretion. While the particular circumstances of prior cases involving distress terminations appear to differ markedly, a common factor for approval of any distress termination appears to be *necessity*, with different courts struggling with the degree of *necessity* to be required. PBGC naturally seeks to limit the discretion exercised by bankruptcy courts by advocating a narrower interpretation of the distress criteria, but courts do not appear to have accepted PBGC's narrow perspective.[42]

(ii) Courts have considered whether a debtor must make a showing as to *a particular* plan of reorganization or as to *any* hypothetical plan of reorganization that could be brought before the court (ie a debtor need only show an inability to obtain confirmation of *any* plan of reorganization without termination of the pension plan, not just the particular plan

[41] The standard for the distress termination of a single employer pension plan is articulated in s 4041(c)(2)(B) of ERISA. See 29 USC s 1341(c)(2)(B), which was enacted as part of the Single Employer Pension Plan Amendments Act of 1986, Pub. L. No. 99-272, 100 Stat. 237, and was amended by the Pension Protection Act of 1987, Pub. L. No. 100-203, 101 Stat. 1330. The purpose of the legislation was to provide debtors facing 'cases of severe business hardship' the ability to terminate their pension plans and thereby shift liability for guaranteed pension benefits onto the Pension Benefit Guaranty Corporation. See H.R. Rep. No. 300, 99th Cong., 1st Sess. 279 (1985), reprinted in 1986 USCCAN 930.

[42] As the bankruptcy court in *Wire Rope* explained: '[T]he PBGC suggested that, before it could allow the distress termination of the [pension] [p]lans, the Court would have to find that, *but for* the termination of the [pension] [p]lans, the [d]ebtor would be forced into liquidation. The import of this statutory standard, the PBGC argues, "is that creditors sometimes will have to accept lower recoveries in order to allow a pension plan to continue as long as *some* plan of reorganization is feasible without termination of the pension plan." The PBGC further argues that the Court should not find that the reorganization test for a distress termination has been met 'unless the [d]ebtor introduces sufficient factual information to enable the Court to evaluate the [d]ebtor's other options and to conclude that a distress termination is the only feasible alternative to liquidation.' *Wire Rope* 287 BR at 780 (emphasis in original) (internal citations omitted). The *Wire Rope* court refused to apply such a strict application of the Reorganization Test and authorized a distress termination upon finding that the debtor could not confirm a plan of reorganization and would 'most likely go out of business' absent termination of the pension plan. Ibid. at 781.

of reorganization).[43] Further, the bankruptcy court's determination appears to be made in the aggregate for all single-employer plans rather than on a plan-by-plan basis.[44]

(iii) 60-day notice of intent to terminate. Concurrent with or before applying for and providing notice of a distress termination of a single employer plan to the PBGC, a written notice of an intent to terminate ('NOIT') the plan in a distress termination must be sent at least 60 days and not more than 90 days before the proposed termination date to all participants (including non-vested participants, alternate payees and beneficiaries of deceased participants receiving benefits) in the plan, as well as any unions whose members are participants in the plan. No particular form of NOIT is required, but certain information is required to be included in the NOIT.[45] Failure to issue a NOIT complying with the notice requirements may cause the distress termination application to be null and void.[46]

(iv) Information provided to the PBGC. An application (Form 600) for a distress termination must be filed with PBGC at least 60 days before the proposed termination date, and such application constitutes notice to the PBGC of such proposed distress termination.[47] In addition, the same information that is provided to the PBGC must be provided to affected parties upon such party's request, although a reasonable fee may be charged for information provided (other than in electronic form).

(v) A single-employer plan may be terminated in a distress termination if, among other requirements, each contributing sponsor of the plan and each member of any sponsor's controlled group meets any of the necessary distress criteria (and the same criteria need not apply to all such sponsors and members): (a) liquidation in bankruptcy or insolvency proceedings, (b) reorganization in bankruptcy or insolvency proceedings, or (c) termination required to enable payment of debts while staying in business or to avoid unreasonably burdensome pension costs caused by a declining workforce. Non-US entities are not specifically excluded from having to meet the distress termination criteria, and the applicability of ERISA to such entities remains unsettled. However,

---

[43] See *Wire Rope* 287 BR at 777-8; *U.S. Airways*, 296 BR at 743-4; *Re Philip Services Corp., et al.* 310 BR 802, 808 (Bankr. SD Tex. 2004). But see *Re Falcon Products, Inc.*, 2005 WL 3416130, *5-6 (Bankr. ED Mo. 26 October 2005) (considering the debtor's efforts to confirm any other plan of reorganization as a factor in determining whether the reorganization requirement has been satisfied).

[44] See *Re Kaiser Aluminum Corp.* 456 F3d 328 (3rd Cir. 2006).

[45] 29 CFR s 4041.43(b).

[46] 29 CFR s 4041.44(c).

[47] 29 CFR 4041.43(a)(4).

single employer plans have been terminated notwithstanding the existence of non-US entities as members of the contributing sponsor's controlled group.

(e) *PBGC's approval of any distress termination.* Notwithstanding that section 4041(c) of ERISA appears to explicitly provide that the bankruptcy court determines if the statutory standard is satisfied and that it approves the plan termination, the PBGC appears to take the position that the bankruptcy court's approval is not exclusive and the PBGC's approval is also required, including its right to make its own independent and separate decision on the same matter decided by the bankruptcy court. The PBGC's position is supported by the lack of any specific wording that the court's decision is exclusive, but the PBGC's interpretation effectively renders the court's impartial judgment null and void. The right of the PBGC under ERISA to effectively second-guess the bankruptcy court's decision ultimately will be resolved by the courts. Until then, the PBGC's position may be an example of how a self-interested PBGC seeks to vigorously and aggressively protect its interests under the plan termination insurance programme and ERISA. Nevertheless, a debtor must comply with all the requirements under ERISA for a distress termination, and the PBGC can use fastidious compliance with such requirements as leverage to delay or frustrate a debtor's proposed plan termination depending on the circumstances.

(f) *Involuntary termination by the PBGC.* In addition to an employer's right to initiate a plan termination pursuant to an application for a distress termination, the PBGC may and, in some cases, must initiate an involuntary plan termination by commencing a case in a US federal court seeking such termination. The PBGC may seek an involuntary termination if it determines, among other reasons,[48] that the plan will be unable to pay benefits when due or the possible long-run loss to PBGC with respect to the plan 'may reasonably be expected to increase unreasonably if the plan is not terminated'.[49]

(i) An insolvent plan is unable to pay benefits when due, and such insolvency typically occurs due to the availability of a lump sum distribution of an employee's pension benefits under the pension plan. However, ERISA has been amended to restrict the payment of lump sum distributions by significantly underfunded pension plans to substantially reduce the likelihood of pension plans becoming insolvent.

---

[48] There are several additional statutory reasons for an involuntary termination by PBGC of a covered plan: (a) the plan has not met the statutory funding requirements under s 412 of the US federal tax code, (b) a notice of deficiency with respect to the tax under s 4971(a) of the US federal tax code has been mailed, or (c) a distribution of $10,000 or more has been made to a substantial owner (other than by reason of such individual's death) and immediately after such distribution there are unfunded, vested benefits under the plan. ERISA s 4042(a), 29 USC s 1342.

[49] ERISA s 4042(a)(4), 29 USC s 1342(a)(4).

(ii) The PBGC generally refrains from involuntarily terminating single-employer plans and what likely constitutes a 'reasonable expectation of an unreasonable increase in the possible long-run loss to PBGC' remains unsettled. However, there are a few circumstances in which a PBGC-initiated involuntary termination of an underfunded single-employer plan is likely: (a) an insolvent employer that is in liquidation, (b) the members of the employer's controlled group that is jointly liable for unfunded pension benefits is being reduced by sales or other transfers of such members; or (c) the pension plan's assets are being dissipated to provide benefits that would not be guaranteed if the pension plan were terminated. In each of these situations, the PBGC may likely incur a greater burden if the pension plan is terminated at a later date, either as a result of the amount of unfunded guaranteed benefits being larger or a diminution of the PBGC's rights to recover the amount of unfunded benefit liabilities against the employer and members of its controlled group.

(iii) Any employer sponsoring an underfunded single-employer plan and undergoing a liquidation will inevitably result in a plan termination unless there is an expectation that a purchaser or other transferee of any portion of the employer's assets may assume continued sponsorship of such plan. An underfunded pension plan practicably cannot exist without any plan sponsor. The PBGC may be patient to await the possible succession in plan sponsorship so long as its prospects for recovery on its claim for unfunded benefit liabilities against the employer controlled group is not materially affected.

(iv) At first blush, an involuntary termination of an underfunded pension plan by the PBGC might appear desirable from the employer's perspective, but that is not always the case. The plan termination results in (a) recognition of the PBGC's otherwise inchoate claim as a general, unsecured creditor for the full amount of the unfunded benefit liability against the employer and thereby reduces the expected recovery by other unsecured creditors under the employer's plan of reorganization, and (b) the imposition of the reorganized employer's obligation to pay, following its emergence, premiums to the PBGC (in addition to the amount recovered by the PBGC on its claim for the unfunded pension liability). Also, the plan termination could impede the sale or other transfer of a member of the employer's controlled group as such member, as of the plan termination date, is jointly and severally liable to the PBGC.

(v) Reduction in the size of the employer's controlled group. The PBGC has a separate claim for the full amount of the unfunded pension liability of a single-employer plan against the employer sponsoring such plan and each member of the employer's controlled group of businesses as of the date of termination of such plan. If one or more members of the employer's controlled group are permitted to exit the group before the date of an underfunded plan's termination, such member or members avoid liability to the PBGC. The PBGC is well aware of its separate right against each member of the employer's controlled group and the potential impact on the PBGC's aggregate recovery against such group,[50] and actively monitors actual or proposed changes to such group. If the PBGC's potential aggregate recovery might be materially diminished as members of the employer's controlled group exit the group, the PBGC is motivated to take action to terminate a pension plan and thereby fix the composition of the employer's controlled group as of the plan termination date.[51] The PBGC has similar concerns if the assets of a member of the controlled group are sold rather than equity interests in the member because the member whose assets were sold could be liquidated or could transfer the sale proceeds to another member of the employer's controlled group in a manner that effectively has the same impact on the PBGC's aggregate recovery as in the case of the selling member exiting the employer's controlled group.[52]

(vi) These same concerns led to the PBGC initiating an involuntary termination of a single-employer plan sponsored by Lehman Brothers Holding Inc. ('LBHI') which, at the time of such proposed termination, was a debtor in a chapter 11 case and in the process of selling most of its subsidiaries or their assets, notwithstanding that the plan was only modestly underfunded after its surplus had been eroded by a substantial stock market decline. The PBGC was unwilling to gamble on a stock market recovery or the likelihood that plan sponsorship would be continued by a purchaser or a reorganized member of the employer's

[50] The PBGC is not permitted, by exercising its rights against members of an employer's controlled group, to recover more than the full amount of the unfunded pension liability.

[51] The liability to PBGC of each contributing sponsor of a covered plan and each member of its controlled group creates a structural priority in favour of PBGC, which favours PBGC if other debts are not similarly structured, such as all members of a controlled group agreeing to be borrowers under a loan or all borrowers agreeing to pledge their assets under a secured loan. A borrower's pledge of its equity interests in any subsidiary does not defease the structural priority of PBGC's claim against the subsidiary (if it is a member of the contributing sponsor's controlled group).

[52] The statutory liability of a contributing sponsor of a covered plan or a member of the sponsor's controlled group to PBGC is inchoate until the covered plan is terminated. Thus, PBGC is exposed to greater risks in seeking to collect against such contributing sponsor and such members if they were to pay a dividend or otherwise distribute substantial assets up the chain of ownership and thereby reduce the amount available to pay by each member. The PBGC's concerns may be alleviated by a debtor's covenant to provide prior notice to the PBGC of or to restrict the employer's controlled group from effecting actions that could adversely affect the PBGC's aggregate recovery against the employer's controlled group.

controlled group, and sought an involuntary plan termination before a significant member of the employer's controlled group could be sold and thereby exit the group. Although PBGC recovered less than the full amount of its aggregate claims against LBHI, as a result of PBGC's claims against each member of LBHI's controlled group of businesses on the date of the plan termination, PBGC did recover an amount exceeding the plan's total unfunded benefit liability.[53]

(g) In the case of an overfunded single employer plan (ie the value of the plan's assets exceeds its accrued benefit liabilities), the plan's surplus could readily disappear due to changing interest rates, investment losses or other reasons such that the PBGC may be legitimately concerned about the continuation of the plan without a financially viable plan sponsor. In such cases, the single employer plan could be terminated by the debtor in a standard termination pursuant to which the plan's obligations to pay benefits are fully discharged by distributing annuities or lump sum cash payments to participants in the plan. Any surplus assets may be recovered by the plan sponsor if permitted by the terms of the plan and subject to applicable income and additional taxes on such surplus.[54]

13.110 13.3.4 Rights of the PBGC following any plan termination

(a) Notwithstanding that ERISA governs pension plan terminations by a debtor during a reorganization proceeding under the US Bankruptcy Code, the operations of the debtor and the claims against it to be resolved in such reorganization proceeding are governed by the provisions of the Bankruptcy Code. In particular, the 'automatic stay' under section 362 of the Bankruptcy Code applies to relieve the debtor of its statutory obligation to make minimum funding contributions to its single-employer plans (but notably does not relieve a debtor from making contributions to any multi-employer plan in accordance with the applicable collective bargaining agreement by reason of section 1113 of the Bankruptcy Code). A debtor typically obtains the approval of the bankruptcy court of authority (but not an obligation) to pay

[53] PBGC is not entitled to recover, by reason of the joint and several liability of each member of a controlled group, an aggregate amount exceeding the unfunded benefit liability of a terminated plan. However, PBGC had additional claims for other amounts, including premiums payable to PBGC, which were taken into account in reaching a settlement with PBGC.

[54] In addition to applicable US federal, state and local income taxes on the reversion of any surplus pension assets, s 4980 of the US federal tax code imposes an additional tax up to 20 per cent of the reversion amount or, in the case of any employer who, as of the plan termination date, is not in bankruptcy liquidation under chapter 7 of the Bankruptcy Code, up to 50 per cent of the reversion amount. IRC s 4980. There are circumstances described in such section permitting the tax rate applicable to the reversion to be reduced or eliminated depending on the use of all or a portion of the potential reversion.

the wages and provide the benefits to employees performing services to the debtor during its proceeding under the Bankruptcy Code, and the debtor arguably could pay the 'normal cost' of pension benefits accruing with respect to such services.[55]

(b) Claim for unfunded pension liability. The PBGC has a claim against the employer for the full amount of the unfunded pension liability, and such claim generally constitutes a general, unsecured liability contingent upon plan termination. Section 502 of the Bankruptcy Code generally allows for claims in an amount as of the date of filing a petition for commencement of a case under the Bankruptcy Code ('petition date'), and such amount generally constitutes a general unsecured claim against a debtor that is a contributing sponsor or a member of the sponsor's controlled group. A relatively small amount of such unfunded pension liability (up to $10,950 multiplied by the number of plan participants) may be entitled to an unsecured claim with a higher priority status; ie the amount arising from services rendered by employees during the 180-day period before the petition date or, if earlier, the date of cessation of the debtor's business.[56] However, the applicable amount may be exhausted by reason of wages and other benefits accruing during the same period, and there is an aggregate cap of $10,950 for each employee for all wages, salaries, commissions and employee benefit contributions during the relevant 180-day period.[57]

(c) In a typical chapter 11 case, a debtor obtains authority on or shortly after the petition date to pay wages, salaries and commissions earned during 180-day period immediately before the petition date, as well as unpaid employee benefits earned during such period by employees, such that the aggregate amount

---

[55] Although a debtor arguably could make contributions equal to the normal cost of pension benefit accruals, in the event the applicable pension plan is terminated and the plan's assets are insufficient to cover such accruals, the employees most probably will not be entitled to payment from the PBGC for such benefits. As a result, it is arguable that the debtor is not permitted to fund such accruals because any such contributions will be used by the PBGC to satisfy unfunded pension benefits that accrued before the employed filed for bankruptcy (an apparent violation of the automatic stay).

[56] There are different levels of priority of payment of expenses and claims against a debtor. Allowed unsecured claims for contributions to any employee benefit plan arising from employee services rendered during the relevant 180-day period are entitled to the status of a fifth priority claim up to the amount of $10,950 multiplied by the number of employees covered by such plan; but such product is reduced by the aggregate amount of allowed unsecured claims for wages, salaries and commissions earned during the same 180-day period paid as fourth priority claims, as well as the aggregate amount paid on behalf of employees to any other employee benefit plan. Bankruptcy Code s 507(a)(5).

[57] The $10,950 fourth class priority for wages, salaries and commissions applies separately for each employee, and any unused amount for one employee cannot be applied to a different employee. However, the $10,950 fifth class priority class applies on an aggregate basis as to each employee benefit plan, and not separately as to each employee. Thus, each plan may pay benefits to an employee in excess of $10,950 subject to the aggregate limit.

allowed for fifth priority claims may be substantially reduced or exhausted by the time any single employer plan is terminated.

(d) Controlled group liability is joint and several. In the event of a termination of a single-employer plan, whether initiated by PBGC as an involuntary termination or by a plan administrator as a distress termination, each contributing sponsor of the plan and each member of such sponsor's 'controlled group'[58] is jointly and severally liable for the total amount of the plan's unfunded benefit liabilities as of the plan termination date, plus interest at a reasonable rate from the plan termination date.[59]

13.3.5 363 Sale of assets by debtor

13.111 The PBGC aggressively protects its interests by seeking to have employers retain active sponsorship of their underfunded pension plans, which the PBGC accomplishes by not exercising its authority to involuntarily terminate pension plans and by strictly applying the requirements for and vigorously contesting distress terminations by employers, regardless of its status largely as an unsecured creditor of the employer. An employer's pursuit of a distress termination to substantially reduce its obligation to fund its unfunded pension liabilities can be a tedious, time-consuming and disruptive effort, even if its prospects for successfully effecting a distress termination are bright. In addition, the imposition of additional premiums payable to the PBGC by any reorganized employer for three years following its emergence from its reorganization can be a substantial expenditure. An employer can effectively avoid the misery of a distress termination proceeding and the post-emergence PBGC premiums by effecting its restructuring pursuant to a sale of its business operations under section 363 of the Bankruptcy Code. A sale of selected business assets and specified liabilities (specifically excluding ownership of any member of the employer's controlled group) can be accomplished without the purchaser being concurrently obligated to assume sponsorship of any pension plan. Thus, the pension plan is left behind with the original employer that typically will be liquidated following the sale. Since a liquidating employer

---

58 A contributing sponsor's 'controlled group' generally includes each person that is under 'common control' with the contributing sponsor, as determined in a manner consistent with the rules under s 414(b) and (c) of the US federal tax code. A full explanation of the 'common control' rules is beyond the scope of this chapter, but as a general principle 'common control' is based on substantial ownership of a person and not on rights to influence the management or conduct of the person. For example, in the case of a partnership, a limited partner owning 80 per cent of more of the total capital interests or total profits interests in the partnership generally will be treated as under common control with the partnership, notwithstanding that the limited partner does not have a right to manage the partnership. Conversely, a sole general partner owning less than 80 per cent of the capital or profits of a partnership will not be treated as under common control with the partnership, notwithstanding that the general partner exclusively manages the partnership.

59 ERISA ss 4062 and 4064. The interest rate charged by PBGC is the same annual rate as is prescribed under s 6601(a) of the US federal tax code.

cannot effectively continue its sponsorship of a pension plan, the PBGC eventually will be required to assume sponsorship of the pension plan by means of an involuntary termination.[60] The restructuring of General Motors Corporation was effected through a 363 Sale, although the avoidance of unfunded pension liabilities does not appear to have been a substantial reason for the use of section 363.

Due to the statutory criteria for an involuntary termination by PBGC or a distress termination by a plan administrator, a debtor seeking to terminate a single employer plan or to completely withdraw from a multi-employer plan might consider a sale of its operating businesses and related assets to a purchaser pursuant to section 363 of the Bankruptcy Code ('363 Sale'). PBGC could object to the 363 Sale to avoid the single employer plans being abandoned, but the bankruptcy court will evaluate the merits of the 363 Sale and not the eligibility of the debtor to effectuate a distress termination of its single employer plans. Thus, a 363 Sale leads to greater probability that a debtor's single employer plans will be terminated, even in circumstances in which the distress termination criteria might not have been met.

13.3.6 Termination in violation of a collective bargaining agreement is not allowed

A distress termination of a single-employer plan which is required to be maintained pursuant to a collective bargaining agreement is not permitted unless the collective bargaining agreement is modified to eliminate such requirement or is rejected, in each case in compliance with section 1113 of the US Bankruptcy Code.[61] Section 1113 sets out standards and procedures for the modification of collective bargaining agreements by a debtor in a reorganization proceeding under the US Bankruptcy Code. A debtor is constrained by section 1113 in seeking to modify or reject a collective bargaining agreement to terminate a single-employer plan or withdraw from a multi-employer plan. As a result of the standards applicable under section 1113 and the practical difficulties of 'taking away' a defined benefit plan from organized workers, debtors are not always able to terminate single-employer plans or withdraw from and replace multi-employer plans covering union-represented employees, notwithstanding that such plan termination or complete withdrawal may have compelling financial advantages to the debtor and neutral or beneficial advantages to such employees as well. The prohibition applies only to distress terminations and does not apply to an involuntary termination by PBGC pursuant to section 4042 of ERISA. 13.112

[60] An employer could, after concluding the 363 Sale, apply for a distress termination and, if the employer is liquidating, will automatically qualify for a distress termination.

[61] ERISA s 4041(a)(3), 29 USC s 1341(a)(3).

13.3.7 PBGC premiums payable by reorganized debtors

13.113 To discourage terminations of single-employer plans by reorganized debtors and to increase the recovery by PBGC as a result of such terminations, in the event of a termination of a single-employer plan by reason of an involuntary termination by PBGC or a distress termination by a reorganizing debtor, three annual premiums will be payable to PBGC with respect to such terminated plan. Each post-termination annual premium generally is equal to $1,250 multiplied by the number of participants in the terminated plan as of the day before its termination date.[62] Such premiums are payable starting with the first calendar month beginning after all the debtors' chapter 11 cases have been discharged or dismissed.[63] The premium does not appear to be dischargeable pursuant to the Bankruptcy Code and thus appears enforceable against a reorganized debtor.[64]

13.3.8 Restoration of terminated plans

13.114 PBGC has the ability to restore a terminated single-employer plan to its plan sponsor.[65] In *Pension Benefit Guaranty Corp. v The LTV Corp.*,[66] PBGC successfully restored a previously terminated single-employer plan to its original plan sponsor as a result of the sponsor's adoption of a new single-employer plan. PBGC has an anti-follow-on policy that generally prohibits a sponsor, having terminated a single-employer plan at a cost to PBGC, from promptly establishing another single-employer plan eligible for termination insurance coverage by PBGC. As a consequence of a termination of a single-employer plan, it is common for plan sponsors to consider make-whole arrangements pursuant to which participants in the terminated plan are provided the difference, if any, between their accrued benefit under the terminated plan and the PBGC-guaranteed benefit. Such make-whole arrangements are practicably difficult to implement with precision outside of a single-employer plan because of the restrictions against the use of unfunded plans for other than a select group of management or highly compensated employees.

---

[62] 29 CFR s 4006.7(b). The premium rate is $2,500 (aggregate $7,500) for certain plans of commercial passenger airlines and airline catering services.

[63] ERISA s 4006(b)(7)(C)((ii), 29 USC s 1306(b)(7)(C)(ii).

[64] An employer that terminated a defined benefit plan while undergoing a chapter 11 bankruptcy reorganization could not avoid paying a termination premium to PBGC by calling the termination premium an unsecured, pre-petition claim that was dischargeable under the Bankruptcy Code. *Pension Benefit Guaranty Corporation v Oneida Ltd.* 562 F3d 154 (2nd Cir. 2009), revg *Oneida Ltd. v Pension Benefit Guar. Corp.* 383 BR 29 (Bankr. SDNY 2008).

[65] ERISA s 4047, 29 USC s 1347.

[66] 496 US 633 (1990).

13.4 Conclusion

The comprehensive regulatory schemes applicable to pension plans in the UK and the US primarily focus on protecting employees' rights to their pension benefits, and the underlying principles by which both countries implement such protection under their respective laws are basically the same. The concerns and rights of the applicable pension regulators appear broadly similar. However, the establishment in the US of the PBGC with the sole and exclusive purpose of administering the pension termination insurance programme, including approval of plan terminations, and enforcing its rights against employers, together with its practice of aggressively enforcing such rights and continually seeking legislative changes to the regulatory scheme to enhance its financial position, results in material differences in the specific manner in which pension plans are dealt with in any employer's restructuring in the US. **13.115**

14

CROSS-BORDER ISSUES

14.1 Introduction

> One thing which the credit-crunch and its after effects have highlighted is that, as we all really knew, the world we live in today is truly borderless, at least where business is concerned. Banks span continents. Their counter-parties, and the counter-parties of their counter-parties, criss-cross the globe. Business conglomerates operate on as wide a global scale, with parent companies in one jurisdiction, subsidiaries, special purpose vehicles, project companies, joint venture partners, spanning many more jurisdictions. In many ways we live in a world of capitalism sans frontières. Living in such a world opens out the possibility, as the credit-crunch has rather painfully shown, of bankruptcy sans frontiéres.
>
> Lord Neuberger, a member of the Supreme Court of England and Wales[1]

14.01 The practical concern in any insolvency is how to collect and manage the assets of the estate and co-ordinate the proceedings so as to maximize the return to creditors. This process can be particularly complicated in an international or cross-border

[1] Extract from a speech given by Lord Neuberger at the Insolvency Law Dinner in London on 11 November 2009.

insolvency where, for example, the debtor conducts its business in different countries, the debtor's assets and/or creditors are situated in different countries or parallel proceedings are being conducted in respect of the same debtor in one or more countries. The legal issues that arise from these practical complications include, for example, what country has jurisdiction over the debtor and its assets, what law is applicable to the insolvency procedure, whether the opening of proceedings in one country precludes the opening of proceedings in another and, if not, what the effect of the foreign proceedings is on the local proceedings, whether the courts of one country will recognize and/or provide assistance to a foreign officeholder or in respect of a foreign proceeding and whether local and foreign creditors should be treated alike.[2] Notwithstanding certain common principles in approach to these issues between jurisdictions,[3] the approach of different countries differs in respect of these legal issues.

14.02 Two sets of opposing approaches have been identified and advocated regarding the fundamental principles underpinning international insolvency—unity versus plurality and universality versus territoriality. The unity versus plurality debate focuses on whether a single state, the state that the company has its closest juridical connection to, should assume insolvency jurisdiction with all other states deferring to that state. The alternative approach provides for concurrent insolvency proceedings in different jurisdictions where certain connecting factors such as assets, place of business or creditors exist. The universality versus territoriality debate focuses on whether all assets of the debtor regardless of location or only those assets situated in the jurisdiction in question should be the subject of an insolvency proceeding opened in a single state.[4] The international insolvency laws of different states and the various international arrangements in relation to multi-jurisdictional insolvencies reflect the different approaches to differing degrees.

14.03 The main sources of cross-border insolvency law in the UK are (a) the Council Regulation (EC) No. 1346/2000 on Insolvency Proceedings (the 'EC Regulation');

[2] For further general discussion refer to R. Goode, *Principles of Corporate Insolvency Law* (3rd edn, Sweet & Maxwell, 2005).

[3] Such as, for example, the collective nature of insolvency proceedings, the preferential treatment of certain unsecured creditors, the principles of *pari passu* distribution, the focus on achieving the best results for creditors by way of rescue or agreement with creditors rather than liquidation, and the avoidance of certain transactions that are detrimental to the general body of creditors which were entered into by the debtor in the period preceding the insolvency. For further general discussion refer to R. Goode, ibid. above n. 2.

[4] The debates are closely related in that where jurisdiction is limited to local assets and a territoriality approach is asserted, the position in relation to the unity/plurality debate is determined to be, by necessity, plurality of proceedings. However, where jurisdictions assert a universalist approach, the approach to the unity/plurality debate remains open. For further discussion on these approaches and principles refer to Atkin's Court Forms/Companies—Insolvency (Volumes 9(2), (3), (4))/ Practice/Q: International Insolvency/1: In General/150. Theory, R. Goode, ibid. above n. 2; and I. Fletcher, *The Law of Insolvency* (Sweet & Maxwell, 2002).

(b) the Model Law on Cross-border Insolvency (the 'Model Law') developed by the United Nations Commission on International Trade Law ('UNCITRAL') and adopted by at least 20 countries in an effort to harmonize cross-border insolvency proceedings; (c) section 426 of the Insolvency Act 1986; and (d) the underlying common law.

Traditionally the English approach reflected the principle of universality[5] as regards its own insolvency proceedings while demonstrating a reluctance to do so in respect of foreign insolvency proceedings. In appropriate cases, however, the English courts have recognized and assisted in foreign proceedings and, in some instances, acted on the basis that those foreign proceedings should take precedence and the English proceedings should be ancillary only.[6] The prominence of the principles of universality and comity has become more obvious in English law since the implementation of the EC Regulation and the adoption of the Model Law and has complicated the traditional English approach somewhat.[7] Also of significance are the recent endorsements of the universalism approach by the Privy Council in *Cambridge Gas Transport Corp v Official Committee of Unsecured Creditors of Navigator Holdings plc*,[8] and the House of Lords in *Re HIH Casualty and General Insurance Ltd; McMahon v McGrath*.[9] **14.04**

In contrast to the overlapping and sometimes contradictory scheme of cross-border insolvency laws in the UK, cross-border insolvencies in the US are governed only by chapter 15 of the Bankruptcy Code ('chapter 15'), which is based on the Model Law. Prior to the enactment of chapter 15 in 2005 by the US Congress ('Congress') cross-border insolvency was governed by only one provision of the Bankruptcy Code, section 304, and a patchwork of US common law developed over the past two centuries. **14.05**

The US corporate bankruptcy system is based on the principles of rehabilitation of a debtor enterprise and the equal treatment of similarly-situated creditors. In furtherance of this later principle, US courts and legislators have long recognized that the settlement of creditor claims should be conducted in a single proceeding, **14.06**

---

5 See discussion in *Cambridge Gas Transport Corp v Official Committee of Unsecured Creditors of Navigator Holdings plc* [2007] 1 AC 508, PC.

6 For further discussion refer to R. Goode, ibid. above n. 2.

7 For further discussion on this refer to M. Stocks and B. Griffiths, 'Trends in co-operation in cross-border corporate insolvencies' (2009) available at <http://www.practicallaw.com/5-500-2082> (accessed on 18 May 2010).

8 [2007] 1 AC 508, PC.

9 [2008] 1 WLR 852, HL. See also *Re HIH Casualty and General Insurance Ltd; McMahon v McGrath* [2008] 1 WLR 852, HL at paras 6–10 and 30 per Lord Hoffmann and *Cambridge Gas Transport Corp v Official Committee of Unsecured Creditors of Navigator Holdings plc* [2007] 1 AC 508, PC at paras 16–17 per Lord Hoffmann. Note also the comments of Lord Neuberger in his speech given at the Insolvency Law Dinner in London on 11 November 2009 above n. 1.

and generally at a single place, which is better for both the creditors and the debtor, because all creditors would thus *share alike* and be equally bound by the debtor's discharge.[10] Since the introduction of bankruptcy laws in the US, however, courts have struggled with the application of this principle to cases involving debtors with assets and/or creditors in both the US and abroad ('cross-border insolvencies'). Although the enactment of chapter 15 did not resolve every cross-border issue, it is a vast improvement over the bankruptcy laws in the US of the past two centuries and is the current structure in the US for dealing with cross-border insolvencies

14.07 Common cross-border issues include, for example, (a) whether a US or UK court has jurisdiction over a debtor's creditors that are located outside their territorial jurisdiction, (b) whether to help enforce insolvency laws of foreign countries that may be contrary to domestic insolvency law principles, and (c) how to coordinate insolvency proceedings in two or more countries. As enterprises have become more global, insolvency laws in both the UK and the US have evolved to try to address problems arising from cross-border insolvencies.

14.08 This chapter discusses the statutory framework in both the UK and the US regarding cross-border insolvencies and the issues that remain outstanding. Section 14.2 of this chapter discusses international insolvency in the UK and section 14.3 international insolvency in the US.

14.2 Cross-border insolvency in the UK

14.2.1 EC Regulation on insolvency proceedings

14.09 The EC Regulation was adopted by the Council on 29 May 2000 and came into force on 31 May 2002 across the European Union (with the exception of Denmark).[11] The aim of the EC Regulation is 'improving the efficiency and effectiveness of insolvency proceedings having cross-border effects' within Europe.[12] The EC Regulation governs the exercise of jurisdiction to open insolvency proceedings, the law applicable to those insolvency proceedings and their effects. Although the EC Regulation introduces certain conflicts of laws rules, it does not seek to harmonize the substantive insolvency laws of the EU member states but rather to provide a framework within which those differing systems can operate.

[10] See John Lowell, 'Conflict of Laws as Applied to Assignments for Creditors' (1888) 1 Harv. L. Rev. 259, 264.

[11] The EC Regulation does not bind Denmark—please refer to para 33 of the preamble to the EC Regulation.

[12] Recital 8 EC Regulation.

The EC Regulation became part of the national law of each EU member state without any need for implementing legislation on the part of the member state.[13] Accordingly, the EC Regulation applies equally to all member states and, to the extent the national law of a EU member state conflicts with the provisions of the EC Regulation, the EC Regulation takes precedence.[14] Guidance on the interpretation, intention and scope of the provisions of the EC Regulation has been derived by the courts in the EU from the preamble to the EC Regulation[15] and from the Virgos-Schmidt Report.[16] **14.10**

By way of summary, the EC Regulation provides for:[17] **14.11**

(a) determination of the jurisdiction in which insolvency proceedings may be opened and recognition in other member states of that proceeding and the office holder in respect of that proceeding;
(b) determination of the law applicable to those insolvency proceedings and matters that might be affected by those proceedings; and
(c) co-ordination of concurrent insolvency proceedings and the sharing of information.

14.2.1.1 Determination of the jurisdiction in which insolvency proceedings may be opened and recognition in other member states of that proceeding and the officeholder in respect of that proceeding

The ability to commence certain insolvency proceedings in an EU member state is governed by the EC Regulation. The EC Regulation applies to collective insolvency proceedings that entail the partial or total divestment of the debtor and the appointment of an insolvency office holder where the centre of the debtor's main interests is located in a member state.[18] The EC Regulation contemplates three **14.12**

---

[13] See Treaty establishing the European Community (Rome, 25 March 1957; TS 1 (1973); Cmnd 5179), art 249 and s 2(1) European Communities Act 1972; see also commentary in Sealy and Milman, *Annotated Guide to Insolvency Legislation 2010,* vol. 2, (13th edn, Sweet & Maxwell, 2010).

[14] *Case C-184/89 Nimz v Freie und Hansestadt Hamburg* [1991] ECR I-297. 'Any national court must, in a case within its jurisdiction, apply Community law in its entirety and protect rights which the latter confers on individuals and must accordingly set aside any provision of national law which may conflict with it, whether prior to or subsequent to the Community rule.' Case 106/77 *Amministrazione delle Finanze dello Stato v Simmenthal SpA* [1978] ECR 629; see also *Marshall v Southampton and South-West Hampshire Area Health Authority (No. 2)* [1990] 3 CMLR 425, CA.

[15] In *Schweizerische Lactina Panchaud AG (Bundesamt für Ernährung und Forstwirtschaft) v Germany (No. 346/88)* [1989] ECR 4579 the European Court of Justice accepted that the preamble may be referred to where the text of the EC Regulation was unclear or imprecise.

[16] A report dated 3 May 1996 prepared by Professor Virgos and Mr Schmit in relation to the European Convention on Insolvency Proceedings (a convention first proposed in 1963 and on which the EC Regulation was largely based).

[17] See J. Marshall, *European Cross Border Insolvency* (Sweet & Maxwell, 2008).

[18] Articles 1(1) and 14 EC Regulation.

categories of proceedings—main proceedings, secondary proceedings and territorial proceedings—and specifies the types of proceedings that constitute insolvency proceedings falling within the remit of the EC Regulation in each member state.

14.2.1.2 Main proceedings

14.13 The EC Regulation grants jurisdiction to the courts[19] of a member state to open main proceedings where the debtor's centre of main interests is situated in that member state.[20] The EC Regulation does not contain a definition of the term 'centre of main interests' ('COMI'); however there is a rebuttable presumption that a debtor's COMI is in the jurisdiction of the debtor's registered office.[21] Some guidance as to what was intended by the term can be found in Recital 13 to the EC Regulation, which states that a debtor's 'centre of main interests' should correspond to the place where the debtor conducts administration of his interests on a regular basis and is therefore ascertainable by third parties. In addition, the Virgos-Schmidt Report contains some useful commentary on the concept and the underlying rationale for it.[22]

14.14 A body of case law has developed as to the location of a debtor's COMI since the EC Regulation was adopted. The recent decision in *Re Stanford International Bank Ltd (in liquidation)*[23] (a case in relation to the Cross Border Insolvency Regulations 2006 (SI 2006/1030) (the 'Cross-Border Regulations')) provides a useful summary of a number of authorities in this regard. The leading authority remains the ruling of the European Court of Justice in *Re Eurofood IFSC*[24] where the rebuttable presumption that a company's COMI is in the place of its registered office was considered. The ECJ held that the presumption can only be rebutted if there are factors, objective and ascertainable by third parties, that enable it to be established to the contrary.

14.15 In the recent decision of *Pillar Securitization S.a.r.l and others v Spicer and another*[25] the court considered whether the COMI of a Guernsey limited partnership was

[19] Article 2(d) EC Regulation provides that for the purposes of the EC Regulation the term 'court' means the judicial body or other competent body of a member state empowered to open insolvency proceedings or take decisions in the course of such proceedings. Recital 10 EC Regulation sets out that the expression 'court' is to be given a broad meaning, reflecting the fact that insolvency proceedings do not necessarily involve the intervention of a judicial authority, and is to include 'a person or body empowered by national law to open insolvency proceedings'.
[20] Article 3(1) EC Regulation.
[21] Article 3(1) EC Regulation.
[22] See paras 73–75 of the Virgos-Schmidt Report.
[23] [2010] EWCA Civ 137.
[24] Case C-341/04.
[25] [2010] EWHC 836 (Ch).

in England. The court, citing *Eurofood* and *Stanford International*, set out the following principles to be applied in determining the location of COMI:

(i) There is a presumption that the body's COMI is in the state where its registered office is located.
(ii) The presumption can be rebutted only by factors which are both objective and ascertainable by third parties. Thus the court is to have regard to factors already in the public domain, or which would be apparent to a typical third party doing business with the body, excluding such matters as might only be ascertained on inquiry.
(iii) Accordingly, the place where the body's head office functions are carried out is only relevant if so ascertainable by third parties. [26]
(iv) Each body or individual has its own COMI, there is no COMI constituted by an aggregation of bodies or individuals.

The relevant time for assessing COMI was considered in *Re Susanne Staubitz-Schreiber.*[27] In that case the ECJ ruled that the COMI of a debtor should be assessed on the date of the filing of the application to open insolvency proceedings. In this respect, the recent case of *Hellas Telecommunications (Luxembourg) II SCA*[28] held that a company's COMI had changed from Luxembourg to England three months before the date to which COMI was to be assessed and this was so despite the company's registered office remaining in Luxembourg.[29] **14.16**

Where main proceedings are commenced, the legal effects of those proceedings must be recognized in all other member states except in any member state in which territorial or secondary proceedings have been commenced or where the EC Regulation provides otherwise.[30] In addition, where the office holder appointed in respect of the main proceedings has complied with certain formalities, the office holder must also be recognized and is able to exercise his powers in other member states.[31] **14.17**

[26] Earlier authorities had suggested that the COMI of an entity was located where its head office functions were carried out—see, for example, *Re Daisytek-Isa Limited and others* [2004] BPIR 30, *Re BRAC Rent-a-Car International* [2003] 1 WLR 1421 and *Re Collins & Aikman* [2006] BCC 606.

[27] [2006] ECR I-701.

[28] [2010] BCC 295.

[29] In reaching this conclusion the judge had regard to certain factors including that its head office and principal operating address were now both in London; notice of the change of address was provided to its creditors; a press release announcing that its activities were shifting to England had been made; a bank account had been opened in London; it had registered under the Companies Act 2006 in England; and all negotiations between the company and its creditors had taken place in London. The judge in that case noted that '[t]he purpose of COMI is to enable creditors in particular to know where the company is and where it may deal with the Company'. He therefore took the view that one of the most important features in determining COMI is the location of the negotiations between the company and its creditors.

[30] Article 17(1) EC Regulation.

[31] Articles 18 and 19 EC Regulation.

14.2.1.3 Secondary proceedings

14.18 Where the COMI of the debtor is located in one EU member state, another EU member state shall have jurisdiction to open proceedings only where the debtor has an establishment in that other member state.[32] Accordingly, secondary proceedings can be opened in one or more EU member states and run in parallel with the main proceedings.

14.19 An establishment is any place of operations where the debtor carries out a non-transitory economic activity with human means and goods.[33] Unlike in respect of COMI, there is very limited English case law on the meaning of establishment.[34] Commentators consider that the presence of an establishment would likely include activities of a commercial, industrial or professional nature conducted through an organization (such as a branch, an office, a factory, a workshop) with a degree of permanence and repetition.[35] The Virgos-Schmidt Report also contains some useful commentary on the concept of establishment and, in particular, notes that the mere presence of assets in a member state shall not be sufficient to constitute an establishment and would therefore not give rise to an ability on the part of the relevant member state to open proceedings. [36]

14.20 The proceedings will constitute secondary proceedings and will be limited to winding-up procedures where main proceedings have already been commenced.[37] The effects of such proceedings are restricted to the assets situated in the territory of that member state.[38]

14.2.1.4 Territorial proceedings

14.21 Where main proceedings have not been commenced in the EU member state where the debtor's COMI is located, it may be possible to open territorial proceedings in another EU member state on the basis of the existence of an establishment. Unlike secondary proceedings, territorial proceedings are not limited to winding-up proceedings but, upon the commencement of main proceedings, the office holder of the main proceedings may request that the territorial proceedings be converted into winding-up proceedings.[39] The effects of territorial proceedings

[32] Article 3 EC Regulation.

[33] Article 2(h) EC Regulation.

[34] See eg *Telia AB v Hilcourt (Docklands) Ltd* [2003] BCC 856, *Shierson Vlieland-Boddy* [2005] 1 WLR 3966, CA.

[35] R. Goode, ibid. above n. 2, 593. See also J. Marshall, ibid. above n. 17, and *Tolley's Insolvency Law Service*, Div. E 'European Insolvency Issues/Distinction between main proceedings and territorial proceedings/Territorial proceedings': art 3(2).

[36] See paras 70–1 of the Virgos-Schmidt Report.

[37] Article 3(2) and (3) EC Regulation.

[38] Articles 3(2) and 27 EC Regulation.

[39] Articles 3(2) and 37 EC Regulation.

are restricted to the assets situated in the territory of the member state that opened the proceedings.

14.2.1.5 Types of proceedings

Annex A lists the types of proceedings that will constitute 'main proceedings' in each jurisdiction and Annex B lists the proceedings that will constitute 'secondary proceedings'. Broadly, the types of proceedings that constitute 'main proceedings' include winding-up proceedings and reorganization proceedings, while 'secondary proceedings' are limited to winding-up proceedings. **14.22**

The corporate insolvency procedures of the UK that constitute main proceedings and are listed in Annex A include winding up by or subject to the supervision of the court, creditors' voluntary winding up with the confirmation of the court, administration including appointments made by an out of court appointment and voluntary arrangements under insolvency legislation.[40] The UK corporate insolvency procedures that constitute secondary proceedings include winding up by or subject to the supervision of the court, winding up through administration, including appointments made by filing prescribed documents with the court, and creditors' voluntary winding up with the confirmation of the court.[41] Receivership and administrative receivership procedures are not available as main or secondary proceedings as these procedures are not collective insolvency procedures and neither is a scheme of arrangement under section 895 of the Companies Act 2006 as it is a proceeding under corporate rather than insolvency law.[42] **14.23**

14.2.1.6 Determination of the law applicable to insolvency proceedings and matters which might be affected by the proceedings

The EC Regulation provides for a uniform choice of law in relation to insolvency proceedings to which the EC Regulation applies. Generally, the law applicable to insolvency proceedings and their effects (including the conditions for the opening of the proceedings, their conduct and their closure) shall be the law of the member state within which the proceedings are opened.[43] Article 4(2) contains a list of matters to be determined by that law; however, the list is not exhaustive. **14.24**

[40] Annex A EC Regulation.

[41] Annex B EC Regulation.

[42] Insolvency proceedings in respect of insurance undertakings, credit institutions and investment undertakings are not governed by the EC Regulation as they are covered by separate European legislation.

[43] Article 4 EC Regulation.

14.25 The general rule is, however, subject to a number of important exceptions set out in articles 5–15 including in relation to third parties' rights in rem;[44] set-off;[45] reservation of title;[46] contracts relating to immovable property;[47] payment systems and financial markets;[48] contracts of employment;[49] effects on rights subject to registration;[50] community patents and trade marks;[51] the validity of acts that have detrimental consequences for the creditors;[52] protection of third-party purchasers;[53] and the effects of insolvency proceedings on law suits pending.[54]

14.2.1.7 Co-ordination of concurrent insolvency proceedings and the sharing of information

14.26 Subject to certain exceptions, the EC Regulation contains duties on the office-holders in main and secondary proceedings to co-operate with each other[55] and to communicate information that may be relevant to the other proceedings, in particular the progress made in lodging and verifying claims and measures aimed at terminating the proceedings.[56] Further, the office holder in secondary proceedings must provide the office holder in main proceedings with an early opportunity to submit proposals on the liquidation or use of the assets in the secondary proceedings.[57]

14.27 In the recent decision of *Re Nortel Networks SA*[58] the court considered an application by the English administrators of the Nortel group of companies requesting the High Court to send letters to courts in a number of European jurisdictions asking those courts to notify the administrators of any application to open secondary insolvency proceedings in respect of any of the group companies. This was to enable the administrators to be heard in such applications and to explain why such proceedings would not be in the interests of the creditors. The High Court in that case accepted that the duty imposed on officeholders to co-operate under article 31 extended to the courts that exercised control of secondary insolvency proceedings. Accordingly, the court authorized the letters to be sent, noting that

44 Article 5 EC Regulation.
45 Article 6 EC Regulation.
46 Article 7 EC Regulation.
47 Article 8 EC Regulation.
48 Article 9 EC Regulation.
49 Article 10 EC Regulation.
50 Article 11 EC Regulation.
51 Article 12 EC Regulation.
52 Article 13 EC Regulation.
53 Article 14 EC Regulation.
54 Article 15 EC Regulation.
55 Article 31(2) EC Regulation.
56 Article 31(1) EC Regulation.
57 Article 31(3) EC Regulation.
58 [2009] BPIR 316.

it was 'highly desirable' that the requested assistance be sought from the foreign courts.

14.2.2 Implementation of the UNCITRAL Model Law on Cross Border Insolvency Proceedings (the 'Model Law') in Great Britain

14.2.2.1 The Model Law

The United Nations Commission on International Trade Law ('UNCITRAL') adopted the Model Law in May 1997. The aim of the Model Law is to provide a framework for recognition, assistance and co-operation in cross-border insolvencies. The Model Law is intended to enable foreign courts and office holders to seek and obtain recognition from overseas jurisdictions of their insolvency proceedings and to facilitate co-operation between courts and office holders in different jurisdictions. The Model Law does not attempt to unify local substantive insolvency laws or impose a single global insolvency law nor does it contain conflicts of laws rules. **14.28**

In contrast to the EC Regulation, the Model Law is a voluntary framework that does not have the force of law. Accordingly, to give effect to the Model Law, countries must elect to implement it and, in so doing, may determine when and to what extent they wish to implement it. At the time of writing it has been implemented by at least 20 countries.[59] However, as countries have the flexibility to depart from the standard text of the Model Law, there are national differences in the way it has been implemented by each such country. **14.29**

14.2.2.2 Implementation in Great Britain

The Model Law (with certain modifications) was implemented in Great Britain by the Cross-Border Regulations on 4 April 2006[60] and Schedule 1 contains the text as enacted in Great Britain. In construing the Cross-Border Regulations, regard is to be had to the international origin of the regulations and the need to promote uniformity in its application and the observance of good faith.[61] **14.30**

---

[59] Australia (2008), British Virgin Islands; overseas territory of the United Kingdom of Great Britain and Northern Ireland (2003), Canada (2009), Colombia (2006), Eritrea (1998), Great Britain (2006), Japan (2000), Mauritius (2009), Mexico (2000), Montenegro (2002), New Zealand (2006), Poland (2003), Republic of Korea (2006), Romania (2003), Serbia (2004), Slovenia (2007), South Africa (2000), and the US (2005). For current list of states that have implemented the Model Law refer to <http://www.uncitral.org/uncitral/en/uncitral_texts/insolvency/1997Model_status.html>.

[60] Application of these regulations are confined to England, Wales and Scotland and for this reason the Cross-Border Regulations refer to 'British Insolvency Law' and 'British Officeholders'. Additional regulations (the Cross Border Insolvency Regulations (Northern Ireland) 2007 (SRNI 2007/115) were enacted in 2007 to extend the Model Law to Northern Ireland).

[61] Schedule 1, art 8 Cross-Border Regulations.

Assistance in interpretation may be derived from the Model Law itself, documents produced by UNCITRAL and its working group in relation to its preparation and a supplemental guide, the 'Guide to the Enactment of the Model Law on Cross Border Insolvency' produced by UNCITRAL to aid interpretation.[62]

14.31 By way of summary, the Cross-Border Regulations provide for:

(a) recognition in Great Britain of, and relief and assistance from Great Britain in relation to, certain foreign insolvency proceedings and foreign office holders;
(b) direct access for foreign office holders to the courts in Great Britain and the ability to commence British insolvency proceedings;
(c) co-operation and communication between British courts and foreign courts and office holders;
(d) certain rights for foreign creditors; and
(e) regulation of concurrent insolvency proceedings in a foreign state and Britain.

14.32 Accordingly, the Cross-Border Regulations apply where, for example, a foreign court or foreign representative seeks assistance in relation to a foreign proceeding from Great Britain; concurrent insolvency proceedings are taking place in a foreign state and Britain, and where a foreign creditor requests commencement of, or wishes to participate in, a British insolvency proceeding.

14.2.2.3 Recognition of foreign proceedings

14.33 Availability of relief and assistance from the courts of Great Britain turns on recognition of the foreign proceeding pursuant to the Cross-Border Regulations. A foreign representative may seek recognition by application to a court in Great Britain.[63] The High Court heard its first reported case for recognition and relief under the Cross-Border Regulations in November 2006 in the case of *Re Rajapakse.*[64] In granting a recognition order, the Registrar also produced a note containing some practical observations for practitioners when making such applications including what documents must be filed, the process for filing such documents and how to effect service.

---

[62] Regulation 2(2) Cross-Border Regulations. Also refer to 'Practice Guide on Cross-Border Insolvency Cooperation' which was adopted by UNCITRAL on 1 July 2009 and which considers the practical aspects of co-operation and communication in cross-border insolvencies including, in particular, how agreements between the courts or companies in different states can promote efficient administration of such insolvencies <http://www.uncitral.org/pdf/english/texts/insolven/Practice_Guide_english.pdf>.

[63] For information concerning the documents which need to be filed on application, see eg Sch 1, arts 15, 16 Cross-Border Regulations.

[64] [2007] BPIR 99.

Assuming the relevant supporting information is submitted with the application to court and all formalities are complied with, the foreign proceeding will be recognized where it meets the following requirements:[65] **14.34**

(a) *the debtor is not a company or other entity of the type that the Cross-Border Regulations do not apply to*: The Cross-Border Regulations do not apply to insolvency proceedings in respect of insurance companies, credit institutions and certain other regulated companies.[66] In *Rubin and Lan v Eurofinance SA and other*,[67] the High Court held that a foreign proceeding (in that instance, a US liquidation) of an entity lacking legal personality in England (in that instance, a trust fund) could be recognized by the English courts;
(b) *the debtor company has a place of business or assets in Great Britain or the courts of Great Britain are otherwise an appropriate forum*;[68]
(c) *a foreign representative*[69] *has been appointed to foreign proceedings*[70] *that have been commenced*;
(d) *the foreign proceedings are collective proceedings that are subject to the supervision and control of the court*: As with the EC Regulation, the Cross-Border Regulations apply to collective insolvency proceedings. The Cross-Border Regulations therefore apply to foreign proceedings including reorganization and rescue procedures as well as bankruptcies and liquidations but not to receiverships or similar types of non-collective proceedings;[71] and
(e) *the debtor has its COMI or otherwise has an establishment in the state in which proceedings have been commenced*:[72] Recognition of two categories of insolvency proceedings are provided for in the Cross-Border Regulations—foreign main proceedings and foreign non-main proceedings. Foreign main proceedings are proceedings that are taking place in the country of the debtor's COMI. Foreign non-main proceedings are foreign proceedings that take place in a state where the debtor has an 'establishment'. Where proceedings are commenced in a country that is neither the COMI of the debtor nor where it has an establishment, those proceedings will not be eligible for recognition.

As with the EC Regulation, the term 'centre of main interests' is not defined in the Cross-Border Regulations but is subject to a rebuttable presumption that it is **14.35**

[65] For further discussion refer to J. Marshall, ibid. above n. 17.
[66] Schedule 1, art 1(2) Cross-Border Regulations.
[67] [2010] 1 All ER (Comm) 81.
[68] Schedule 1, art 4(2) Cross-Border Regulations.
[69] Schedule 1, art 2 (j) Cross-Border Regulations.
[70] Schedule 1, art 2 (i) Cross-Border Regulations.
[71] For discussion in relation to whether a proceeding is a proceeding to which the Cross-Border Regulations relate, see *Re Stanford International Bank Ltd (in liquidation)* [2010] EWCA Civ 137.
[72] Schedule 1, art 17(2) Cross-Border Regulations.

located in the country of the debtor's registered office.[73] The meaning of 'centre of main interests' under the Cross-Border Regulations was recently considered in *Re Stanford International Bank Ltd (in liquidation)*.[74] The decision of the Court of Appeal in that case confirmed that the term 'centre of main interests' under the Cross-Border Regulations has the same meaning as under the EC Regulation[75] and further confirmed that the presumption of COMI being located in the country of the debtor's registered office can only be rebutted by factors objective and ascertainable to third parties.[76]

14.36 Unlike the concept of COMI which, as described above, has a common meaning in the EC Regulation and in the Cross-Border Regulations, the definition of 'establishment' differs between the two.[77] An establishment is defined in the Cross-Border Regulations as any place of operations where the debtor carries out a non-transitory economic activity with human means and assets or services.[78] By contrast, the EC Regulation refers to 'goods' rather than 'assets or services'. Commentators suggest that it is probably not necessary to give too literal a meaning to the word 'goods', as it is frequently used in EC documents in the more general sense of 'assets'.[79] Other commentators have suggested that, notwithstanding the choice of wording in the EC Regulation, the intention is to cover not only goods but intangible property, services and facilities.[80]

14.2.2.4 Effects of recognition

14.37 Upon recognition of proceedings as foreign main proceedings, an automatic stay of certain types of creditor action comes into effect. These include a stay on commencement or continuation of certain proceedings in respect of the debtor's assets, rights, obligations or liabilities,[81] execution against the debtor's assets,[82] and the transfer or disposal of the debtor's assets.[83] The stay does not extend to any creditor's right to enforce security over the debtor's property,[84] to repossess goods in the

---

[73] Schedule 1, art 16(3) Cross-Border Regulations.
[74] [2010] EWCA Civ 137.
[75] [2010] EWCA Civ 137 at para. 31.
[76] Ibid.
[77] See para. 14.36 above in relation to the definition of 'establishment' under the EC Regulation.
[78] Schedule 1, art 2(e) Cross-Border Regulations.
[79] Sealy & Milman, ibid. above n. 13, 137.
[80] See, for example, R. Goode, ibid. above n. 2, 593
[81] Schedule 1, art 20(1)(a).
[82] Ibid., Sch 1, art 20(1)(b).
[83] Ibid., Sch 1, art 20(1)(c).
[84] Ibid., Sch 1, art 20(3)(a).

possession of the debtor pursuant to a hire purchase agreement,[85] in relation to certain arrangements governed by statute,[86] or to set off against a claim of the debtor (provided these rights were available in a British winding-up procedure).[87] The stay will also not affect the right to request or initiate the commencement of, or file a claim in, British insolvency proceedings (provided they are restricted to assets located in Britain).[88]

In addition, discretionary relief may be granted in respect of foreign main proceedings. Unlike main proceedings, no automatic stay applies on recognition of foreign non-main proceedings. Discretionary relief may, however, be granted. Discretionary relief available includes protections in respect of the debtor's assets and estate;[89] the examination of witnesses, taking of evidence and delivery of information regarding the debtor's assets, affairs, rights, obligations or liabilities;[90] allowing the foreign representative or another person designated by the court to administer or realize all or part of the assets of the debtor that are located in Great Britain;[91] and any further relief that is available to British insolvency office holders under the laws of Great Britain.[92] In addition, where a court is satisfied that the interests of creditors in Great Britain are adequately protected, it may entrust the distribution of all or part of the assets of the debtor that are located in Great Britain to the foreign representative or another person designated by the court.[93] **14.38**

Upon recognition of either foreign main or foreign non-main proceedings, discretionary relief may be granted where it is necessary for the protection of the assets of the debtor or the interests of the creditors,[94] the court is satisfied that the interests of the creditors and other interested parties are adequately protected[95] and, in relation to foreign non-main proceedings, the court is satisfied that the relief relates to assets that, under the law of Great Britain, should be administered in those proceedings or concerns information required in those proceedings.[96] **14.39**

---

85 Schedule 1, art 20(3)(b) Cross-Border Regulations.
86 Ibid., Sch 1, arts 20(3)(c) and 1(4).
87 Ibid., Sch 1, art 20(3).
88 Ibid., Sch 1, art 20(5).
89 Ibid., Sch 1, art 21(1)(a)–(c).
90 Ibid., Sch 1, art 21(1)(d).
91 Ibid., Sch 1, art 21(1)(e).
92 Ibid., Sch 1, art 21(1)(f).
93 Ibid., Sch 1, art 21(2).
94 Ibid., Sch 1, art 21(1).
95 Ibid., Sch 1, art 22.
96 Ibid., Sch 1, art 21(3).

14.40 The following recent cases considered applications for assistance pursuant to the Cross-Border Regulations:[97]

(a) In *Swissair Schweizerische Luftverkehraktiengesellschaft*[98] the court considered an application by a Swiss liquidator for the remittal of assets realized in the UK by English liquidators (net of their expenses and a small amount for a claim with preferential status under English law) to the Swiss liquidator. The court allowed the remittal of the assets in that case for distribution in the Swiss liquidation (which was the main proceeding). In so doing, the court held that the interests of creditors in Great Britain were adequately protected as the distribution under Swiss law would be on a *pari passu* basis and the protocol entered into by the Swiss liquidator and English liquidator protected the interests of the creditors who had submitted proofs in the English liquidation.

(b) In *Rubin and Lan v Eurofinance SA and others*[99] the court was asked by US joint receivers and managers to allow them to enforce a summary judgment that they had obtained in New York proceedings against the trustees of a trust fund as if that judgment was a judgment of the English court. The High Court refused to allow the US joint receivers and managers to enforce the judgment under the Cross-Border Regulations as enforcement of foreign judgments was a matter to which common law applied and one that fell outside the scope of the Cross-Border Regulations.

(c) In *Perpetual Trustee Co, Ltd v BNY Corporate Trustee Services Ltd and Lehman Brothers Special Financing Inc.*[100] the court considered a request from the claimant, Perpetual Trustee Company Limited, that the High Court send a detailed letter of request to the US Bankruptcy Court for the Southern District of New York proposing an allocation of functions between the two courts in relation to parallel proceedings in those courts and requesting the US court not to make any order requiring the first defendant to act in a manner contrary to English law or to orders of the English courts. The High Court refused to send the letter, noting that to do so before any ruling in the US proceedings had been handed down would be 'judicial bad manners' and potentially counterproductive. The court was, however, willing to send a limited letter of request.[101]

[97] See also *HIH Casualty and General Insurance Limited, Re v McGrath* [2006] 2 All ER (D) 209 (Mar) at paras 143–6 as, although proceedings begun before the implementation of the Cross-Border Insolvency Regulations, the position under the Cross-Border Regulations was discussed.

[98] [2009] BPIR 1, 505.

[99] [2010] 1 All ER (Comm) 81.

[100] [2010] BPIR 228.

[101] Note the conflicting judgments in the parallel US and UK proceedings relating to these matters. For further commentary on this refer to Public Law Company, 'US decision in Perpetual

(d) In *Logix Corp Between: D/s Norden A/s v Samsun Logix Corp & Ors,*[102] the High Court considered a request for permission to enforce a contractual lien arising under an English law governed contract against a debtor in insolvency proceedings in Korea where that lien was the subject of litigation in Korea. In that case, the English court had recognized the Korean insolvency proceedings and had granted a stay preventing creditors from issuing proceedings against the debtor and its property. The court refused the application as to allow it would pre-empt the outcome of the Korean litigation. The court recognized, however, that by refusing to allow enforcement of the lien, the applicant was effectively forced to submit to the jurisdiction of the Korean court and, where the Korean court found that the lien was invalid, that would preclude the applicant from enforcing the lien in England. The court therefore held that, where subsequent English proceedings were initiated to challenge a Korean court order, no challenge could be brought against the applicant on the basis that the lien was invalid by virtue of the applicant having participated in the Korean proceedings.

14.2.2.5 Direct access to the courts

A foreign representative may make applications directly to the British courts[103] and may apply, subject to meeting certain criteria, to commence proceedings under British insolvency law.[104] In addition, where a foreign proceeding is recognized, the foreign representative is entitled to participate or intervene in a proceeding regarding the debtor under British insolvency law.[105] **14.41**

Where a foreign proceeding has been recognized in Great Britain, a foreign representative is also granted certain rights of access to British courts in respect of transactions (such as preferences and transactions at an undervalue) entered into by the debtor before insolvency and may, in certain circumstances, apply to have such transactions reviewed or for relief to be granted in respect of them.[106] **14.42**

case creates a cross-border conflict' (1 February 2010), available from <http://uk.practicallaw.com/1-501-3756>, accessed 18 May 2010.

[102] [2010] BPIR 1367.

[103] Schedule 1, art 9 Cross-Border Regulations.

[104] Ibid., Sch 1, art 11.

[105] Ibid., Sch 1, arts 12 and 24.

[106] Sections 236, 239, 244, 245 and 423 of the Insolvency Act 1986 applying in a modified form and provided transactions occurred after the Model Law came into force. See Sch 1, art 23 Cross-Border Regulations.

14.2.2.6 Co-operation and communication

14.43 Co-operation is a core element in the Cross-Border Regulations.[107] Where a foreign court or representative seeks assistance in respect of a foreign proceeding from a court of Great Britain, the court may co-operate to the maximum extent possible with the foreign court or representative and may co-operate and communicate with the foreign court or representative either directly or through a British insolvency office holder.[108] By contrast, a British insolvency office holder is required (subject to certain provisos) to co-operate in such circumstances.[109]

14.44 In addition, the Cross-Border Regulations do not limit the power of a court of Great Britain or a British insolvency office holder to provide additional assistance or co-operation (for example, pursuant to section 426 of the Insolvency Act 1986) to that available under the Cross-Border Regulations.[110]

14.2.2.7 Foreign creditors

14.45 Prevention of discrimination against foreign creditors in insolvency proceedings is specifically covered in the Cross-Border Regulations which provide that foreign creditors have the same rights in relation to the commencement of, and participation in, proceedings under the law of Great Britain as creditors in Great Britain.[111] The Cross-Border Regulations further provide that a foreign creditor's claim is not to be given a lower priority solely because the holder of the claim is foreign.[112] The Cross-Border Regulations also provide that foreign creditors must be notified whenever notification is required to be given to creditors in Great Britain in accordance with British insolvency law.[113]

14.2.2.8 Concurrent proceedings

14.46 In respect of concurrent proceedings in Great Britain and in a foreign jurisdiction, the Cross-Border Regulations provide for cooperation and coordination. The form of the co-ordination depends on which proceeding was commenced first and whether the foreign proceeding is a foreign main proceeding or foreign non-main proceeding.[114] Where the British courts have recognized foreign main proceedings, proceedings in Great Britain are restricted to any assets of the debtor located in Great Britain and such other assets which, under the law of

---

[107] Paragraph 173 of *Guide to the Enactment of the Model Law on Cross Border Insolvency*.
[108] Schedule 1, arts 25 and 26 Cross-Border Regulations.
[109] Ibid., Sch 1, arts 26 and 27.
[110] Ibid., Sch 1, art 7.
[111] Ibid., Sch 1, art 13(1).
[112] Ibid., Sch 1, art 13(2).
[113] Ibid., Sch 1, art 14.
[114] Ibid., Sch 1, arts 29 and 30.

Great Britain, should be administered in that proceeding to the extent necessary to implement co-operation and co-ordination.[115]

14.2.2.9 Application of the Cross-Border Regulations

The Cross-Border Regulations are subject to certain laws of Great Britain[116] and to the EC Regulation.[117] As with the EC Regulation the British courts are also entitled to refuse to grant relief sought where to do so would be manifestly contrary to public policy.[118] **14.47**

14.2.3 Cross-border jurisdiction under the Insolvency Act 1986

Section 220 and 221 of the Insolvency Act 1986 and their predecessors would not, on the face of it, appear to have any obvious connection to cross-border insolvency. The title of Part V of the Act is 'Winding Up of Unregistered Companies'. Nevertheless, these sections have been central to the development by the English courts of the jurisdiction to wind up foreign companies in England and Wales. Clearly a foreign company would not be capable of being registered as a matter of English law in its entirety; appropriate that they be wound up as registered companies. The test applied by the courts is to ask whether it can be demonstrated that the company has a sufficient connection with England and Wales to enable the court to accept it has jurisdiction. **14.48**

With the introduction of EC Regulation on insolvency and the incorporation of the Model Law with the English legislative framework, the need for the courts to use creatively the provisions of the Act dealing with unregistered companies has diminished. Nonetheless, the principles remain extremely important, particularly in the context of reorganizations of companies through schemes of arrangement. Schemes are dealt with extensively elsewhere in the book and therefore I do not propose to deal further with the topic here. **14.49**

Section 426 Insolvency Act 1986 provides that the UK courts shall provide relief and assistance in insolvency proceedings upon the request of the courts of certain designated jurisdictions, which mainly includes Commonwealth countries and former British Colonies. Section 426, where it applies, therefore provides an alternative means of relief and assistance to that provided in the EC Regulation and the Cross-Border Regulations. **14.50**

---

[115] Schedule 1, art 28 Cross-Border Regulations.
[116] Ibid., Sch 1, art 1(4)–(7) (particularly in relation to financial markets legislation).
[117] Ibid., Sch 1, arts 3.
[118] Ibid., Sch 1, art 6.

14.51 As at the date of writing, the countries and territories designated by the Secretary of State and therefore able to request assistance in matters of insolvency from the courts of the UK include Anguilla, Australia, the Bahamas, Bermuda, Botswana, Brunei, Canada, Cayman Islands, Falkland Islands, Gilbaltrar, Hong Kong, the Republic of Ireland, Malaysia, Montserrat, New Zealand, South Africa, St Helena, Turks and Caicos Islands, Tuvalu and the Virgin Islands.[119] In addition, the courts of the Channel Islands and the Isle of Man are able to apply for assistance under section 426.[120]

14.52 The types of assistance capable of being provided by the UK courts include any comparable relief that could be given under the inherent jurisdiction of the courts, substantive English insolvency law or substantive insolvency law of the foreign jurisdiction.[121] Assistance will normally be provided upon request except where there are strong reasons for not providing such assistance.[122]

14.53 An application pursuant to section 426 was considered by the House of Lords in *Re HIH Casualty and General Insurance Ltd; McGrath & Another & Others v Riddell & Others.*[123] In that case, the House of Lords authorized English provisional liquidators of Australian insurance companies to repatriate assets collected in English ancillary winding-up proceedings to the Australian liquidators notwithstanding that differences existed between Australian and English law in relation to the *pari passu* distribution of assets that could have adversely affected certain creditors in England.[124]

14.54 Other forms of assistance that have been provided pursuant to section 426 have included[125] the granting of an administration order,[126] the appointment of a receiver,[127] the granting of orders pursuant to section 236 of the Insolvency Act 1986 allowing the examination of an officer of a company[128] and access to

---

[119] Co-operation of Insolvency Courts (Designation of Relevant Countries and Territories) Order 1986 (SI 1986/2123); Co-operation of Insolvency Courts (Designation of Relevant Countries) Order 1996 (SI 1996/253); Co-operation of Insolvency Courts (Designation of Relevant Country) Order 1998 (SI 1998/2766).

[120] Section 426(11) Insolvency Act 1986.

[121] Section 426(5) Insolvency Act 1986 and *Hughes v Hannover-Rückversicherungs AG* [1997] 1 BCLC 497.

[122] *England v Smith (Re Southern Equities Corp)* [2001] Ch 419; *Re HIH Casualty and General Insurance Limited; McGrath & Another & Others v Riddell & Others* [2008] 1 WLR 852, HL.

[123] [2008] 1 WLR 852, HL.

[124] Note, however, the difference in opinion between their Lordships as to the basis of the jurisdiction for doing so

[125] See R. Goode, ibid. above n. 2.

[126] *Re Dallhold Estates (UK) Pty Ltd* [1992] BCLC 621.

[127] *Re a Debtor, ex p. Viscount of the Royal Court of Jersey* [1981] Ch 384; *Re Osborn, ex P. Trustee* [1931-2] B & CR 189.

[128] *England v Smith (Re Southern Equities Corp)* [2001] Ch 419, CA.

documents in the possession of administrative receivers,[129] the making of orders under sections 212, 213, 214 and 238 of the Insolvency Act 1986[130] and a declaration recognizing the rights and title of a foreign insolvency office holder.[131]

14.2.4 English common law

The English common law position has been recently described by Lord Hoffmann (reading the judgment of the Privy Council) in *Cambridge Gas Transport v Official Committee of Unsecured Creditors of Navigator Holdings plc and* others, which decision also reaffirmed that cross-border relief was available pursuant to common law in addition to relief under statutory and international cross-border provisions.[132] Lord Hoffmann stated in that case:[133] **14.55**

> The English common law has traditionally taken the view that fairness between creditors requires that, ideally, bankruptcy proceedings should have universal application. There should be a single bankruptcy in which all creditors are entitled and required to prove. No one should have an advantage because he happens to live in a jurisdiction where more of the assets or fewer of the creditors are situated. . . As Professor Fletcher points out (Insolvency in Private International Law (1999 OUP) at p 93) the common law on cross-border insolvency has for some time been 'in a state of arrested development', partly no doubt because in England a good deal of the ground has been occupied by statutory provisions such as s 426 of the 1986 Act, the European Council Regulation on Insolvency Proceedings (1346/2000/EC) and the Cross-Border Insolvency Regulations 2006 SI 2006/103, giving effect to the UNCITRAL Model law. . .

This universal approach was expressly endorsed by the majority of their Lordships in the recent House of Lords decision of *Re HIH Casualty and General Insurance Ltd and other companies; McMahon and others v McGrath and another.*[134] Lord Hoffmann stated in that decision that there 'should be a unitary bankruptcy proceeding in the court of the bankrupt's domicile which receives worldwide recognition and that it should apply universally to all the bankrupt's assets'[135] and, on the basis of the court's inherent jurisdiction, considered that the requested assistance in that case should be granted.[136] **14.56**

In the recent decision of *Swissair Schweizerische Luftverkehraktiengesellschaft*,[137] the High Court ordered an English liquidator to pay assets realized in England **14.57**

[129] *Re Trading Partners Ltd* [2002] BPIR 606.
[130] *Re Bank of Credit and Commerce International S.A. (No. 9)* [1994] 3 All ER 764.
[131] *Hughes v Hannover Ruckversicherungs-Aktiengesellschaft* [1997] 1 BCLC 497.
[132] [2007] 1 AC 508, PC.
[133] Ibid. at paras 16–18.
[134] [2008] 1 WLR 852, HL.
[135] [2008] 1 WLR 852, HL at para. 6
[136] See Part 4 (s 426 Insolvency Act 1986) of this chapter.
[137] [2009] EWHC 2099 (Ch).

and Wales to the Swiss liquidators. The court held that it had the power to do so at common law where the foreign insolvency regime provided for a *pari passu* distribution of any such realizations to creditors.

14.58 Other examples of the exercise of common law powers by English courts in relation to cross-border or foreign insolvency matters include *Lazard Brothers and Co. v Midland Bank Ltd*,[138] *Felixstowe Dock and Railway Co. v US Line Inc.*[139] and *Harms Offshore Aht 'Taurus' GmbH & Co Kg v Bloom & Ors.*[140]

14.3 Cross-border insolvency in the US

14.59 In sharp contrast to the long history of international insolvency in the UK, before 1978 the US did not have any statutory framework for dealing with cross-border insolvencies.[141] In fact, before the twentieth century, the US only had uniform bankruptcy laws from 1800 to 1803, 1841 to 1843, and 1867 to 1878;[142] during all other periods, individual US states were allowed to enact their own bankruptcy laws. Moreover, when the Model Law was enacted as chapter 15 of the Bankruptcy Code, it completely replaced the existing statutory framework. However, much of the common law that was developed before the enactment of chapter 15, still guides the courts analysis of issues that arise in chapter 15 cases.

14.3.1 Cross-border insolvencies prior to the Bankruptcy Reform Act of 1978

14.60 The patchwork of intermittent federal and state bankruptcy laws presented many of the same problems that cross-border insolvencies do today, including jurisdictional issues and harmonization of conflicting bankruptcy laws. Yet, neither the state nor federal bankruptcy laws before 1978 addressed how to deal with cross-border issues.[143] Instead, US courts had to decide what effect, if any, to afford bankruptcies adjudicated in other states and in other countries.

---

[138] [1933] AC 289.

[139] [1989] QB 360.

[140] [2009] EWCA Civ 632.

[141] For an in-depth discussion of the historical development of cross-border bankruptcy law, see Charles D. Booth, 'A History of the Transnational Aspects of United States Bankruptcy Law Prior to the Bankruptcy Reform Act of 1978' (1991) 9 B.U. Int'l L.J. 1.

[142] Act of 4 April 1800, ch. 19, § 1, 2 Stat. 19 (repealed 1803); Act of 9 August 1841, ch. 9, § 1, 5 Stat. 440 (repealed 1843); Act of 2 March 1867, ch. 176, §§ 11, 39, 14 Stat. 517, 521, 536 (repealed 1878).

[143] Because states were initially allowed to enact their own bankruptcy laws, the term 'cross-border' applied to both cases in other states as well as cases in other countries. Booth, above n. 141 at 6.

In early cases, US courts applied the 'territoriality approach' to cross-border issues. Under the 'territoriality approach', courts focused on the rights of citizens in its jurisdiction with respect to the assets located within its borders, preferring those rights to the rights of foreign creditors.[144] Subsequent cases modified the territoriality approach by adopting ever more broad principles of equality and the universal treatment of creditors, known as the 'universality approach'.[145] The first case to adopt the universality approach in any meaningful way was *Canada Southern Railway Co v Gebhard* in 1883.[146] *Canada Southern* involved a law suit in the US brought by Canadian debtors that sold bonds to US creditors, among others, to build and maintain a railway in Canada. The Canadian debtors commenced the law suit in the US to enforce the Canadian 'Arrangement Act' against the US creditors, thus, subjecting them to the Canadian insolvency proceeding. In that case, the US Supreme Court rejected a US creditor's argument that it should not be subjected to a Canadian insolvency proceeding finding that: **14.61**

> every person who deals with a foreign corporation impliedly subjects himself to such laws of the foreign government, affecting the powers and obligations of the corporation with which he voluntarily contracts, as the known and established policy of that government. . . .[147]

While it appeared that the Supreme Court was moving away from territoriality, however, the universality approach was not broadly applied. Two years later, in *Hilton v Guyot*, the Supreme Court declined to recognize a French proceeding because the courts of France did not give full faith and effect in the judgments of the US, stating:

> 'Comity,' in the legal sense, is neither a matter of absolute obligation, on the one hand, nor of mere courtesy and good will, upon the other. But it is the recognition which one nation allows within its territory to the legislative, executive or judicial acts of another nation, having due regard both to international duty and convenience, and to the rights of its own citizens or of other persons who are under the protection of its laws.[148]

Moreover, even though the Supreme Court espoused the principles of universality, at the same time it upheld the states' ability to adopt the territoriality approach when adjudicating issues of international comity.[149] Thus, the application of comity varied from circuit to circuit.

---

[144] See, eg, *Ogden v Saunders* 25 US 213 (12 Wheat 213) 213, 269-70 (1827) (holding that a discharge under a state law cannot discharge a debt due a citizen of another state); *Harrison v Sterry* 9 US 289 (5 Cranch 289) (1809) (preferring domestic creditors to foreign creditors).

[145] See Booth, above n. 141 at 5.

[146] 109 US 527 (1883).

[147] Ibid. at 537.

[148] *Hilton v Guyot* 159 US 113, 164 (1895) (denying comity for want of reciprocity).

[149] See *Clark v Williard* 294 US 211 (1935) (upholding a states' right to apply the territoriality approach even if a race of the swiftest could prevail over equal distribution of assets); *Disconto*

14.62 Although the application of comity differed, the universality approach continued to develop and gain favour. In *Re Stoddard (Norske Lloyd Insurance Co.)*, for example, the Court of Appeals of New York ('Court of Appeals') adopted an approach that allowed it to protect the citizens located within its jurisdiction while pursuing equality of creditor distribution.[150] In that case, the Court of Appeals rejected the argument that US assets of a foreign corporation, which had creditors in the US and abroad, should be used to satisfy the US creditors in full and only the remaining assets to be sent to the foreign representative for distribution to other creditors.[151] The Court of Appeals instead held that amounts that are in the US that are not subject to any creditors' liens should be transmitted to the foreign representative for distribution to all creditors.[152] However, the court reserved the right of US creditors to prove and defend their claims against the foreign debtor in the US.[153]

14.63 Ten years later, in *Re Aktiebolaget Kreuger & Toll*, the Second Circuit Court of Appeals (the 'Second Circuit') pursued a more pure universality approach and assured the parties that the administration of assets 'would be without any thought of preferential treatment of American creditors unless indeed preferential treatment were given in Sweden as against American creditors'.[154] Cases from the late 1960s leading up to the enactment of the Bankruptcy Reform Act of 1978 continued to limit the application of territoriality.[155]

14.64 The catalyst for the adoption of section 304 of the Bankruptcy Code was found during the financial crisis of the late 1970s in the cases of three failed non-US financial institutions pending in the Bankruptcy Court for the Southern District of New York (the 'SDNY Bankruptcy Court')—*Bankhaus I.D. Herstatt K.G.a.A. (Herstatt), Israel-British Bank (London) Ltd. (IBB), and Banque de Financement, S.A. (Finabank).*[156] The cases pending before the SDNY Bankruptcy Court were

Gesellschaft v Unbreit 208 US 570 (1908) (same). Not all state courts were applying the territoriality approach. See, eg, *Martyne v Am. Union Fire Ins. Co.* 110 NE 502, 505 (NY 1915) (applying a universality approach).

150 151 NE 159 (NY 1926).

151 Ibid. at 166

152 Ibid. at 165.

153 Ibid.

154 20 F Supp 964, 965 (SDNY 1937), affd 96 F2d 768 (2nd Cir. 1938).

155 *Waxman v Kealoha* 296 F Supp 1190 (D. Haw. 1969) (extending comity because the defendant 'failed to show that any local creditors would be prejudiced', even though the action was to recover amounts owed by Hawaiian citizens to foreign creditors); *Clarkson Co. v Shaheen* 544 F2d 624, 629-30 (2nd Cir. 1976) (construing exceptions to comity narrowly); *Re Colorado Corp.* 531 F2d 463, 468 (10th Cir. 1976) (holding the Bankruptcy Court could not deny comity to a Netherlands Antilles order because of a lack of reciprocity in Canada).

156 *Banque de Financement, S.A. v First Nat. Bank of Boston* 568 F2d 911 (2nd Cir. 1977) ('*Finabank*'); *Israel-British Bank (London) Ltd. v Federal Deposit Ins. Corp.(Re Israel-British Bank (London) Ltd.)* 536 F2d 509 (2nd Cir. 1976), *cert. denied,* 429 US 978 (29 November 1976);

considered 'ancillary cases' because each of the three financial institutions were also subject to insolvency proceedings in their respective nations. Notably, while all these financial institutions had assets located in the US, none of them conducted banking operations in the US.[157] The foreign representatives filed cases in the US to stop creditors from racing to the US courts to attach property that these institutions had in the US. In *Herstatt* and *IBB*, creditors sought dismissal of the ancillary cases pending in the SDNY Bankruptcy Court based on section 4(b) of the US Bankruptcy Act (the predecessor to the Bankruptcy Code) that excluded banking corporations from involuntary bankruptcy and section 2(a)(22) of the US Bankruptcy Act, which allowed a court to suspend or dismiss proceedings after considering 'the rights or convenience of local creditors and all other circumstances'.[158] Domestic creditors were hoping that the SDNY Bankruptcy Court would consider their rights to attach property in the US and favour domestic creditors over foreign. While *Herstatt* resulted in a settlement dismissing the case in the SDNY Bankruptcy Court, a decision was reached in *IBB*, which held that the 'banking corporation' restriction under section 4(b) of the US Bankruptcy Act did not apply to foreign corporations and found no reason *IBB* should not be afforded the protections of the US Bankruptcy Act.[159] Interestingly, had either financial institution had operations in the US they would have been excepted under the banking corporation restriction and would not have qualified for bankruptcy protection.[160] In the *IBB* decision, the court espoused the universality approach by aiding the foreign representatives in administering the foreign banking proceedings of its own countries and stressed that the 'theme of the Bankruptcy Act is equality of distribution of assets among creditors. . . . The road to equality is not a race course for the swiftest'.[161]

The *Finabank* court went even further and explicitly rejected the territoriality approach.[162] Hours before the expiration of the four-month limitation period for avoiding preferences under the US Bankruptcy Act, Finabank filed for chapter XI protection (the predecessor to the chapter 11 of the Bankruptcy Code) seeking to **14.65**

Joseph D. Becker, 'International Insolvency: The Case of Herstatt' (1976) 62 A.B.A. J. 1290 (discussing the case of *Herstatt Bank* that sparked an international race of creditors, which resulted in a settlement and consensual dismissal of the case).

[157] *Finabank* 568 F2d at 911; *Re Israel-British Bank* 536 F2d at 509; Becker above n. 156.

[158] Bankruptcy Act § 22(a) (1970), repealed by the Bankruptcy Act of 1978, 92 Stat. 2549.

[159] *Re Israel-British Bank* 536 F2d at 513.

[160] See *Re Israel-British Bank (London) Ltd* 401 F Supp 1159, 1164 (SDNY 1975) ('There is a law now in force for the control and regulation of national banks, and it was thought best not to interfere with that law. In certain contingencies the government is responsible for the assets of such banks, and it is but reasonable that it should have entire control of them and of their liquidation in cases of dishonesty or insolvency') (quoting 30 Cong. Rec. 602, 55th Cong., 1st Sess. (1897)).

[161] *Re Israel-British Bank* at 513.

[162] *Finabank* 568 F2d at 921.

avoid attachments made by US creditors pursuant to US bankruptcy law.[163] These creditors contended that the SDNY Bankruptcy Court should protect the rights of US creditors that have attachments on US property of the foreign debtor and dismiss the case pending before the SDNY Bankruptcy Court, so that those creditors could foreclose on their rights (the pendency of the ancillary case had stayed enforcement of creditors' rights against Finabank in the US).[164] The SDNY Bankruptcy Court dismissed the case and the District Court for the Southern District of New York affirmed.[165] On appeal, the Second Circuit disagreed, stating that the rights that should be protected were the rights of creditors being forced 'to participate in foreign proceedings in which their claims will be treated in some manner inimical to [the US'] policy of equality'.[166] The Second Circuit upheld the foreign representatives rights to file a main proceeding under chapter XI and suggested two possible ways to coordinate the bankruptcy proceedings in both the US and Switzerland: (a) there could be a full chapter XI proceeding in the US coordinated with the Swiss proceeding where US creditors could elect to appear in the US proceeding and the assets of the debtor would be distributed on a pro rata basis to all creditors including those that appeared in the chapter XI proceeding, from assets in Switzerland and the US, or (b) it could exercise jurisdiction to set aside the attachments on US property and then suspend the proceeding to allow the assets to be distributed through the Swiss proceeding.[167] This suggestion of allowing the court to act in either a primary or an ancillary role was adopted in sections 303 (which allowed a foreign representative to file involuntary cases) and 304 (which governed ancillary cases) of the US Bankruptcy Code and was a substantial step in the direction of universality.

14.3.2 Section 304 of the Bankruptcy Code

14.66 Section 304 of the Bankruptcy Code,[168] was designed to 'give maximum flexibility in handling ancillary cases' and to enter appropriate orders to apply the 'principles of international comity and respect for the judgments and laws of other nations. . .'.[169] Specifically, section 304 of the Bankruptcy Code allowed a foreign representative to file an ancillary proceeding giving the US court the ability to enjoin the commencement or continuation of any action against a debtor or enforce any judgment against the debtor or any act to create or enforce a lien with

[163] Ibid. at 914.
[164] Ibid.
[165] Ibid.
[166] Ibid. at 921.
[167] Ibid.
[168] 11 USC § 304, repealed by BAPCPA, Pub. L. No. 109-8, § 802, 119 Stat. 23, 146.
[169] H.R. Rep. No. 95-595 p. 325 (1977), reprinted in 1978 USCCAN 5963, 6281; S. Rep. No. 95-989 p. 35 (1978), reprinted in 1978 USCCAN 5787, 5821.

respect to property in a foreign proceeding or to provide other appropriate relief.[170]

14.67 Section 304 ancillary proceedings were narrower in scope than bankruptcy proceedings under chapter 7 and 11 of the Bankruptcy Code (which are the provision pursuant to which corporations generally file for bankruptcy in the US) and aided foreign bankruptcy representatives by providing for discovery and a structured distribution of assets.[171] Importantly, unlike chapters 7 and 11, they did not create a bankruptcy estate, result in the appointment of a trustee, or culminate in the conventional plan of reorganization or liquidation.[172] However, the expansive interpretation of section 304 allowed bankruptcy judges to apply the laws creatively to assist a foreign representative in the collection and distribution of assets and balance the rights of US creditors.[173] For example, because section 304 did not empower the foreign representatives to commence actions to avoid fraudulent or preferential transfers under the Bankruptcy Code, US courts permitted the representatives to seek such relief under their own foreign avoidance law.[174] Thus, the court was able to create a remedy to prevent preferential distributions without expanding a foreign creditor's rights under the foreign bankruptcy law.

14.68 In determining whether to recognize foreign proceedings, US courts weighed the factors set out in section 304(c) of the Bankruptcy Code, which sought to balance the need to protect US creditors with just treatment of all creditors.[175] Early cases focused on whether application of the foreign laws sought to be enforced in an ancillary proceeding adhered to fundamental notions of fairness and due process or violated US public policy.[176] Courts afforded different weights to the various

---

[170] 11 USC § 304, repealed by BAPCPA, Pub. L. No. 109-8, § 802, 119 Stat. 23, 146.

[171] H. Evelyn, Jason Biery, L. Boland, and John D. Cornwell, 'A Look at Transnational Insolvencies and Chapter 15 of the Bankruptcy Abuse Prevention and Consumer Protection Act of 2005' (2005) 47 BCL Rev. 23, 33.

[172] Lawrence P. King, *Collier on Bankruptcy* ¶ 304.01[1] (15th edn, rev. 2004).

[173] *Re Culmer* 25 BR 621, 624 (Bankr. SDNY 1982) ('Pursuant to Section 304(b), the Court is free to broadly mold appropriate relief in near blank check fashion without the necessity of trial when a party in interest does not controvert the petition, or after trial if there is controversion.').

[174] *Re Maxwell Commc'n Corp.* 93 F3d 1036, 1054-5 (2nd Cir. 1996); *Metzeler v Bouchard Transp. Co. (Re Metzeler)* 78 BR 674, 677 (Bankr. SDNY 1987) (holding that 'a foreign representative may assert, under § 304, only those avoiding powers vested in him by the law applicable to the foreign estate'.). See also 11 USC ss 542, 543, 544, 545, 547, 548, 549, 550, 553.

[175] 11 USC s 304, repealed by BAPCPA, Pub. L. No. 109-8, s 802, 119 Stat. 23, 146 (listing the following factors: '(1) just treatment of all holders of claims against or interests in such estate; (2) protection of claim holders in the United States against prejudice and inconvenience in the processing of claims in such foreign proceeding; (3) prevention of preferential or fraudulent dispositions of property of such estate; (4) distribution of proceeds of such estate substantially in accordance with the order prescribed by this title; (5) comity; and (6) if appropriate, the provision of an opportunity for a fresh start for the individual that such foreign proceeding concerns.').

[176] See, eg, *Cunard S.S. Co. Ltd. v Salen Reefer Services AB* 773 F2d 452, 459-60 (2nd Cir. 1985); *Re Culmer* 25 BR at 629-30.

304(c) factors, some relying almost exclusively on comity, while others placed equal emphasis on all factors.[177] While section 304 gave US courts great flexibility, the result was a case-by-case application of the law, which was not much different from the prior law. Thus, because of its great flexibility, the application of section 304 was relatively unpredictable and relief based on the same fact pattern could vary depending on the jurisdiction.[178] Interested parties were left with nothing more than an educated guess whether they would be afforded recognition and the aid of a US bankruptcy court.

14.69 In addition, while the case-by-case approach gave the court ample flexibility, it appeared that section 304's unpredictability and limited relief drove a growing number of foreign corporations to try to commence cases under chapter 7 or 11 of the Bankruptcy Code, which offered a broader array of protections and certainty than section 304. For example, both *Re Axona* and *Re Maxwell* involved foreign debtors that filed two main bankruptcy proceedings in separate countries.[179] These cases tested the ability of courts to coordinate two main cases in parallel insolvency proceedings where the insolvency laws of each country differed.[180] In *Re Axona,* foreign representatives of a Hong Kong winding-up proceeding were not satisfied with only Hong Kong avoidance powers that would be afforded in an ancillary proceeding under section 304 of the Bankruptcy Code. To take advantage of the more expansive avoidance powers under chapter 5 of the Bankruptcy Code, including avoidance of fraudulent and preferential transfers, the foreign representative filed an involuntary chapter 7 petition under section 303(b)(4) of the Bankruptcy Code and filed chapter 5 avoidance actions against third parties.[181] After recovering property utilizing the chapter 5 avoidance powers, the foreign representative moved to suspend the chapter 7 case and transfer the assets to the Hong Kong estate for distribution.[182] A domestic creditor that was the subject of an avoidance action moved to dismiss the chapter 7 case and void all proceedings that were taken in the chapter 7 case, arguing that allowing the foreign representative to take advantage of chapter 7 permitted it to unilaterally avoid transactions that would have not been available under

---

[177] Compare *Re Culmer* 25 BR at 629 (focusing on comity) with *Re Papeleras Reunidas, S.A.* 92 BR 584 (Bankr. EDNY 1988) (weighing all factors equally).

[178] See, eg, *Re Treco,* 240 F3d 148, 158-60 (2nd Cir. 2001) (weighing all factors equally); *Re Toga Mfg. Ltd.* 28 BR 165, 168 (Bankr. ED Mich. 1983) (focusing on comity). See generally Elizabeth J. Gerber, Note, 'Not all Politics is Local: The New Chapter 15 to Govern Cross-Border Insolvencies' (2003) 71 Fordham L. Rev. 2051.

[179] *Re Maxwell Commc'n Corp. v Barclays Bank (Re Maxwell Commc'n Corp.)* 170 BR 800, 802 (Bankr. SDNY 1994) (parallel proceedings of a US chapter 11 case and UK administration); *Re Axona Int'l Credit & Commerce Ltd.* 88 BR 597 (Bankr. SDNY 1988) (parallel proceedings of a US chapter 7 case and a Hong Kong winding-up proceedings).

[180] *Re Maxwell Commc'n Corp.* 170 BR at 802; *Re Axona Int'l Credit & Commerce* 88 BR at 598.

[181] *Re Axona Int'l Credit & Commerce,* 88 BR at 603.

[182] Ibid.

Hong Kong law.[183] The bankruptcy court found there was nothing improper about the foreign representative using section 303 of the Bankruptcy Code to afford itself the powers of avoidance under US law rather than conduct an ancillary proceeding under section 304, where only Hong Kong avoidance powers were available.[184] The court denied the motion to dismiss, allowed the funds to be transferred to Hong Kong for distribution to all creditors and suspended the US proceeding.[185]

Re Maxwell also involved a conflict of law relating to US avoidance powers. *Re Maxwell* was unique in that there were parallel restructuring proceedings occurring in both the UK and the US that involved a joint plan of reorganization and scheme of arrangement under each nation's respective laws.[186] *Re Maxwell* dealt with the ability of a foreign representative to extraterritorially apply US avoidance powers where the 'center gravity of the transaction' was outside the US.[187] The transfers sought to be avoided using US avoidance powers were payments of debt incurred by a foreign debtor outside the US that were also paid outside the US.[188] In *Re Maxwell,* the bankruptcy court held that 'where a foreign debtor makes a preferential transfer to a foreign transferee and the center of gravity of that transfer is overseas, the presumption against extraterritoriality prevents utilization of section 547 to avoid the transfer'.[189] Thus, while the foreign representative could avail itself of US avoidance laws, the transaction must have some connection to the US. Therefore, the court held that the foreign representative could not cherry-pick provisions of different bankruptcy schemes to create a super bankruptcy scheme combined with the powers of each country in which it had proceedings.[190] **14.70**

14.3.3 Chapter 15 of the US Bankruptcy Code

Since the enactment of the Bankruptcy Code, there have been a growing number of multinational corporations, a growing number of bankruptcy cases and a growing desire to have a single global statutory framework for resolving cross-border insolvencies.[191] The difficulties of a case-by-case approach and an effort to reconcile **14.71**

---

183 Ibid. at 604.
184 Ibid.
185 Ibid. at 619.
186 *Re Maxwell Commc'n Corp.* 170 BR at 801.
187 Ibid. at 812.
188 Ibid. at 808.
189 Ibid. at 814.
190 Ibid.
191 John H. Dunning and Sarianna M. Lundan, *Multinational Enterprises and the Global Economy* (2nd edn, Edward Elgar Publishing, 2008) 19-23 (discussing general trends in multinational enterprises); Alan Deaton, 'Large and Small Companies Exhibit Diverging Bankruptcy Trends' *FDIC Bank trends*, January 2002, <http://www.fdic.gov/bank/analytical/bank/bt0201.html> ('A record 257 publicly traded companies filed for bankruptcy in 2001, representing a 46 percent increase over

international insolvency law in a global sense led to the enactment of chapter 15 of the Bankruptcy Code. Although section 304 of the Bankruptcy Code allowed a flexible approach in applying different laws within the US bankruptcy framework, it was not always clear how these laws would be applied. In a world where there was a growing number of international businesses with assets in various countries, a more predictable treatment of those assets in the case of insolvency was greatly desired.

14.72 As part of the Bankruptcy Abuse Prevention and Consumer Protection Act of 2005 ('BAPCPA'), chapter 15, titled 'Ancillary and Other Cross-border Cases', was enacted as part of the Bankruptcy Code to incorporate the Model Law.[192] The objectives of chapter 15 are:

- cooperation between courts of the US, US trustees, trustees, examiners, debtors, and debtors in possession; and the courts and other competent authorities of foreign countries involved in cross-border insolvency cases;
- great legal certainty for trade and investment;
- fair and efficient administration of cross-border insolvencies that protects the interests of all creditors, and other interested entities, including the debtor;
- protection and maximization of the value of the debtor's assets; and
- facilitation of the rescue of financially troubled businesses, thereby protecting and preserving employment.[193]

14.73 Chapter 15 is a much more comprehensive statutory scheme than the pre-BAPCPA section 304. First, it provides a more reliable framework for seeking relief from the US bankruptcy courts, grants automatic relief upon recognition of a foreign main proceeding, treats all creditors, whether foreign or domestic equally,[194] and restricts suspension or dismissal under section 305 of the Bankruptcy Code once recognition has been granted to cases where 'the purposes

the prior years' record of 176 filings.... These companies brought some $258.5 billion in assets into bankruptcy, more than double the assets of public company bankruptcy filings in 2000.'); see, eg, *Re Maxwell Commc'n Corp.* 93 F3d at 1036 (involving one proceeding in the US and one proceeding in the UK); see also *United States v BCCI Holdings (Lux.) S.A.* 48 F3d 551 (DDC 1995) (involving subsidiary banks operating in 75 countries with proceedings in both the US and UK); *Re Axona Int'l Credit & Commerce Ltd.* 88 BR at 598 (involving proceedings in Hong Kong and the US).

[192] See BAPCPA, Pub. L. No. 109-8, s 801, 119 Stat. 23, 134-45 (codified at 11 USC s 1501-32).

[193] 11 USC s 1501.

[194] 11 USC s 1513. But see *Re Dow Corning Corp.* 280 F3d 648 (6th Cir. 2002), cert. denied, 537 US 816 (2002) (allowing foreign creditors to receive smaller distributions under the plan in a case prior to the enactment of chapter 15 of the US Bankruptcy Code). In addition to equal treatment, foreign creditors are afforded special notice under s 1514 of the Bankruptcy Code. 11 USC s 1514.

of [chapter 15] would be best served by dismissal or suspension'.[195] Second, chapter 15 retains the flexibility of section 304 in that a US bankruptcy court has the ability under section 1507 of the Bankruptcy Code to mould relief to meet specific circumstances if US citizens are being unjustly injured.[196] Third, chapter 15 provides entirely new and broader set of rights to a foreign representative that depends on various factors, such as whether the foreign proceeding is recognized and whether the foreign proceeding is a main or non-main proceeding.[197] Finally, chapter 15 has been successful in fixing some, but not all, of the problems presented by section 304 of the Bankruptcy Code. This section discusses procedures and rights under chapter 15 and current issues that have arisen since its enactment that have yet to be resolved.

14.3.3.1 Recognition of foreign proceedings

The availability of the new broad set of rights granted by chapter 15 is dependent upon recognition of the foreign representative. The US bankruptcy court will grant recognition to a foreign proceeding if: **14.74**

- such foreign proceeding for which recognition is sought is a foreign main proceeding or foreign non-main proceeding within the meaning of section 1502;
- the foreign representative applying for recognition is a person or body; and
- the petition meets the requirements of section 1515.[198]

Not all foreign proceedings qualify for recognition; only a 'foreign proceeding' that is 'a collective judicial or administrative proceeding . . . under a law relating to insolvency or adjustment of debt in which proceeding the assets and affairs of the debtor are subject to . . . supervision by a foreign court, for the purpose of reorganization or liquidation' will suffice.[199] For example, in *Re Gold & Honey*, the court denied recognition because the foreign proceeding was an Israeli receivership **14.75**

---

[195] 11 USC s 305(a) ('The court, after notice and a hearing, may dismiss a case under this title, or may suspend all proceedings in a case under this title, at any time if . . . a petition under section 1515 for recognition of a foreign proceeding has been granted; and the purposes of chapter 15 of this title would best be served by such dismissal or suspension.'); *Re Tradex Swiss AG* 384 BR 34, 44 (Bankr. D. Mass. 2008)) ('Although the Petitioning Creditors argue that the Chapter 7 petition should not be dismissed under s 305(a)(1) because dismissal is not in the best interest of the creditors, it is s 305(a)(2) that applies.'). However, if a foreign proceeding has not been recognized under chapter 15 of the Bankruptcy Code a party-in-interest must show that suspension or dismissal is in the best interests of creditors and the debtors. *Re Monitor Single Lift I, Ltd.* 381 BR 455, 462-3 (Bankr. SDNY 2008) (discussing s 305(a)(1) dismissal); *Re Compania de Alimentos Fargo, S.A.* 376 BR 427, 434 (Bankr. SDNY 2007) (same).

[196] 11 USC s 1507; see also H.R. Rep. No. 109-31, Pt. 1 at 3 (2005), reprinted in 2005 USCCAN 88, 91 (discussing the need for bankruptcy reform).

[197] See Biery et al., above n. 171 at 49.

[198] 11 USC s 1517.

[199] 11 USC s 1502(3). For purposes of chapter 15, foreign court is defined as 'judicial or other authority to control or supervise a foreign proceeding'. 11 USC s 101(23).

proceeding initiated by and administered for the benefit of a secured creditor and was not a 'collective proceeding'.[200]

14.76 Moreover, the foreign proceeding must be 'pending' at the time of recognition.[201] However, what it means for a foreign proceeding to be 'pending' is not always obvious. In *Re Oversight and Control Commission of Avánzit,* for example, the court recognized a Spanish insolvency proceeding known as a *Convenio* even though the *Convenio* Plan had been approved and the former management was allowed to regain control of the company. The court reasoned that because the debtor was required to make payments under the Convenio for the following two years, and if it failed, it would face liquidation in the Spanish Insolvency Court, the proceeding was still 'pending' in the foreign court.[202] The court noted that the goals of chapter 15 would be 'frustrated if 'foreign proceeding' was interpreted in a manner that cut off assistance at a time when cooperation, certainty, fairness, asset values and financial relief [was] most needed, simply because the debtor successfully prosecuted its reorganization case'.[203]

14.77 Recognition under chapter 15 is also subject to a public policy exception under section 1506 of the Bankruptcy Code, which states that '[n]othing in [chapter 15] prevents the court from refusing to take an action governed by [chapter 15] if the action would be manifestly contrary to the public policy of the US'.[204] However, courts have interpreted this as a very high burden to meet and have held that the term 'manifestly' limits this relief 'only to the most fundamental policies of the US'.[205]

14.78 Refusal to recognize a foreign proceeding has severe repercussions. Not only is chapter 15 relief unavailable to the foreign representative, but it appears that the foreign representative would be unable to avail itself of other chapters of the Bankruptcy Code.[206] Section 1511 states '*[u]pon recognition of a foreign proceeding,* the foreign representative may commence (1) an involuntary case under section 303; or (2) a voluntary case under section 301 or 302 if the foreign proceeding

[200] *Re Gold & Honey, Ltd.* 410 BR 357 (Bankr. EDNY 2009); see also *Re Betcorp Ltd.* 400 BR 266 (Bankr. D. Nev. 2009) (holding that an Australian voluntary 'winding-up' of a gaming corporation was a foreign main proceeding because it was a collective proceeding subject to ultimate 'court involvement' if the company was found to be insolvent).

[201] *Re Oversight & Control Comm'n of Avánzit, S.A.* 385 BR 525 (Bankr. SDNY 2008).

[202] Ibid.

[203] Ibid. at 535.

[204] 11 USC s 1506.

[205] *Re Iida* 377 BR 243, 259 (BAP 9th Cir. 2007); *Re Gold & Honey, Ltd.* 410 BR at 371-3 (holding that the pubic policy exception was one of several reasons for denial of recognition).

[206] 11 USC s 1511. But see *Re Bear Stearns High-Grade Structured Credit Strategies Master Fund Ltd.* 374 BR 122, 132 n. 15 (Bankr. SDNY 2007), affd 389 BR 325 (SDNY 2008) (noting the inconsistencies in the statute between ss 301, 302, 303(b)(4) and 1511(b) of the Bankruptcy Code).

is a foreign main proceeding'.[207] Thus, failure to be recognized appears to leave the foreign representative remediless and without the ability to protect assets of the foreign debtors in the US, satisfaction of creditors will turn into a race of the swiftest.

14.3.3.2 Foreign main proceeding v Foreign non-main proceeding

A foreign proceeding will only be recognized if it qualifies as a foreign main or foreign non-main proceeding.[208] Because it is possible that there could be multiple proceedings in foreign jurisdictions, chapter 15 distinguishes between whether a proceeding is main or non-main proceeding.[209] This was designed to foster cooperation among the various proceedings.[210] As an example, assume a foreign debtor with its COMI in the UK, ancillary operations in France and assets in the US commences insolvency proceedings in both the UK and France and both foreign representatives seek recognition under chapter 15 of their respective foreign proceedings with the aim of selling the US assets in those proceedings. To prevent a fight between the foreign representatives for control of the US assets, chapter 15 distinguishes between the proceeding in the UK, which would be a foreign main proceeding, and the proceeding in France, which would be a foreign non-main proceeding. Chapter 15 would then allow only the foreign representative of the UK proceeding certain automatic rights such as the right to sell the US assets. As discussed below, there are significant differences regarding the rights afforded to foreign main proceedings and foreign non-main proceedings.[211] **14.79**

A foreign proceeding will be recognized as 'a foreign main proceeding if it is pending in the country where the debtor has the center of its main interests . . . '.[212] A foreign non-main proceeding is any other proceeding 'pending in a country where the debtor has an establishment', with 'establishment' defined as 'any place of operations where the debtor carries out nontransitory economic activity'.[213] Section 1516 provides that 'in the absence of evidence to the contrary, the debtor's **14.80**

[207] Ibid. (emphasis added); *Lavie v Ran* 384 BR 469 (SD Tex 2008), affd 406 BR 277 (SD Tex. 2009); *Re Bear Stearns* 389 BR at 339. But see *Re Compania de Alimentos Fargo* 376 BR 427 (Bankr. SDNY 2007).

[208] 11 USC s 1517.

[209] See UNCITRAL, Model Law on Cross-Border Insolvency with Guide to Enactment at pt. 2 ¶¶ 44-6, U.N. Sales No. E.99.V.3 (1999); see eg, *Re British Am. Ins. Co. Ltd.* 425 BR 884 (Bankr. SD Fla. 2010) (recognizing a St Vincent and the Grenadines proceeding as a foreign non-main proceeding, but denying recognition to a Bahamian proceeding).

[210] UNCITRAL above n. 209 at 44-6.

[211] 15 USC s 1517.

[212] Ibid.

[213] 11 USC ss 1502 and1517.

registered office, or habitual residence in the case of an individual, is presumed to be the center of the debtor's main interests'.[214]

14.81 Only those proceedings recognized as foreign main proceedings are entitled to the specified relief under section 1520 of the Bankruptcy Code, which, unless the court orders otherwise, upon recognition automatically extend the adequate protection provisions of section 361, the automatic stay provisions of section 362 (which stay collection and certain other actions of creditors), the sale or use of property provisions of section 363 (which, among other things, provide for sale or use of property in the ordinary course of business without court approval), the post-petition transactions provisions of section 549 (which enable the foreign representative to avoid unauthorized post-petition transfers), and the post-petition security interest provision of section 552 of the Bankruptcy Code to the foreign proceeding with respect to assets within the territorial jurisdiction of the US.[215] In addition to this relief, the representative of a foreign main proceeding can request additional relief under section 1521.[216] The only relief unavailable to the foreign representative is avoidance power under certain sections of the Bankruptcy Code.[217] Thus, recognition as a foreign main proceeding vests the foreign representative with the tools they need to facilitate the cooperation of the various jurisdictions automatically without the need to justify each request to a US bankruptcy judge.[218]

14.82 In contrast, if the proceeding is recognized as a foreign non-main proceeding, no automatic relief stems from recognition. The foreign representative must request the desired relief under section 1521 and must meet a higher standard than that

[214] 11 USC s 1516(c).
[215] 11 USC s 1520.
[216] 11 USC s 1521.
[217] Ibid.
[218] It is important to note that, unlike the protections granted automatically upon the filing of a petition under other chapters of the Bankruptcy Code, such as the stay of collection and other actions under s 362 or the creation of a bankruptcy estate under s 541, the filing of a chapter 15 petition does not afford a debtor any automatic protection until after the proceeding is recognized by the US court as a foreign main proceeding. If the foreign representative requires provisional relief before the court considers whether to grant recognition either as a foreign main or foreign non-main proceeding, they must request such relief under s 1519, which states: 'From the time of filing a petition for recognition until the court rules on the petition, the court may, at the request of the foreign representative, where relief is urgently needed to protect the assets of the debtor or the interest of the creditors, grant relief of a provisional nature, including—(1) staying execution against the debtor's assets; (2) entrusting the administration or realization of all or part of the debtor's assets located in the United States to the foreign representative or another person authorized by the court including an examiner, in order to protect and preserve the value of assets that by their nature or because of other circumstances, are perishable, susceptible to devaluation or otherwise in jeopardy; and (3) any relief referred to in paragraph (3), (4), or (7) of section 1521(a).' 11 USC s 1519(a). Thus, while there is no automatic protection, the foreign representative can request such protection at the outset of the chapter 15 case. See, eg *Innua Can. Ltd.*, No. 09-16362, 2009 Bankr. LEXIS 994 at *12 (Bankr. DNJ 25 March 2009) (granting provisional relief).

required by a foreign main proceeding in that, 'the court must be satisfied that the relief relates to assets that, under the law of the US, should be administered in the foreign non-main proceeding or concerns information required in that proceeding'.[219] For example, if a foreign representative wanted to sell property of the foreign debtor that was located in the US pursuant to section 363 of the Bankruptcy Code in the foreign non-main proceeding, the foreign representative would have to petition the court and show that the particular asset should be administered in the foreign non-main proceeding that is recognized by the US bankruptcy court rather than pursuant to another (perhaps main) foreign proceeding as well as meeting the statutory burden for a sale of assets under section 363 of the Bankruptcy Code.[220] The court must be satisfied that the foreign representative of a non-main proceeding has the authority to administer the assets before it can make a determination whether a sale is appropriate.[221] This creates a much higher burden for the foreign representative to act in the non-main proceeding that is not present in a case that is recognized as a foreign main proceeding.

The difference between recognition as a foreign main proceeding and a foreign non-main proceeding largely rests on the determination of the debtor's centre of main interests or 'COMI' and has been the subject of several decisions.[222] In *Re Tri-Continental Exchange*, for example, a case involving a Caribbean 'tax haven,' the court carefully considered the derivation of the term 'center of main interests' as it was originally used in the European Union Convention on Insolvency Proceedings (the 'EU Convention') as well as the more common term used in the US, 'principal place of business'.[223] The court noted that under the EU Convention, 'the key question is the situs of the conduct of the administration of the debtor's business on a regular basis that is known to third parties'.[224] The court held that although the only operations of the *Tri-Continental Exchange* debtor involved a fraudulent scheme, that scheme was conducted in the nation of St Vincent and the Grenadines.[225] The court concluded that St Vincent's was the debtor's COMI **14.83**

[219] 11 USC s 1521.

[220] Ibid. It is possible for there to be no foreign main proceeding and the only foreign proceeding be recognized as a foreign non-main proceeding. See *Re SPhinX, Ltd.* 351 BR 103, 122 (Bankr. SDNY 2006).

[221] 11 USC s 1521.

[222] See, eg, *Re SPhinX Ltd.* 371 BR 10 (SDNY 2006), affg 351 BR 103 (Bankr. SDNY 2007); *Re Bear Stearns High-Grade Structured Credit Strategies Master Fund Ltd.* 374 BR 122 (Bankr. SDNY 2007), affd 389 BR 325 (SDNY 2008); *Re Basis Yield Alpha Fund (Master)* 381 BR 37 (Bankr. SDNY 2008); *Re Tri-Continental Exchange* 349 BR 627, 633-4 (Bankr. E.D. Cal. 2006).

[223] 349 BR 627, 633-4 (Bankr. ED Cal. 2006).

[224] Ibid. at 634-5 (citing EU Council Reg. (EC) No. 1346/2000 ¶ 13).

[225] Ibid. at 629.

and recognized the St Vincent's proceeding as a foreign main proceeding.[226] Thus, the fact that the business was not legitimate did not preclude recognition.

14.3.3.3 Relief available to a foreign representative

14.84 Regardless of whether the proceeding is recognized as a foreign main or foreign non-main proceeding, the court may grant the following relief upon the request of the representative including:

- staying the commencement or continuation of an individual action or proceeding concerning the debtor's assets, rights, obligations, or liabilities to the extent they have not been stayed under section 1520(a);
- staying execution against the debtor's assets to the extent it has not been stayed under section 1520(a);
- suspending the right to transfer, encumber or otherwise dispose of any assets of the debtor to the extent this right has not been suspended under section 1520(a);
- providing for the examination of witnesses, the taking of evidence or the deliver of information concerning the debtor's assets, affairs, rights, obligations or liabilities;
- entrusting the administration or realization of all or part of the debtor's assets within the territorial jurisdiction of the US to the foreign representative or another person, including an examiner, authorized by the court;
- extending relief granted under section 1519(a); and
- granting any additional relief that may be available to a trustee, except for relief available under sections 522, 544, 545, 547, 548 550, and 724.[227]

14.85 This relief will be granted 'only if the interests of creditors and other interested entities, including the debtor, are protected' and certain conditions may be imposed by the court for granting such relief, including the giving of security or the filing of a bond.[228] In addition, a court may grant any 'additional assistance' under section 1507(a) of the Bankruptcy Code, '[s]ubject to the specific limitations stated elsewhere [in chapter 15] . . . '.[229] Finally, if the foreign representative is requesting injunctive relief pursuant to chapter 15, the foreign representative must comply with the standards, procedures, and limitations applicable to an

[226] Ibid. See also *Re Ernst & Young, Inc.* 383 BR 773, 782 (Bankr. D. Colo. 2008) (holding the operations of the fraudulent corporation were directed from Canada and recognized the Canadian proceeding as a foreign main proceeding).

[227] 11 USC s 1521.

[228] 11 USC ss 1521 and 1522.

[229] 11 USC s 1507.

injunction (other than the requirement of filing an adversary proceeding).[230] While additional relief may be granted, as an ancillary proceeding under chapter 15, a foreign representative cannot exert all the powers that would be available under the US Bankruptcy Code to cases filed under other chapters of the Bankruptcy Code.[231] For example, it is clearly enumerated in the statute that the power to avoid prepetition transfers using chapter 5 of the Bankruptcy Code is not available to the foreign representative.[232] Interestingly, however, a foreign creditor is still able to avoid prepetition transfers in US proceedings using its own laws.[233] Moreover, releases of claims and causes of actions against the debtor (and in certain cases, third parties) and substantive consolidation of the assets and liabilities of one or more affiliated debtors are generally not available under chapter 15, even though they are available for cases under other chapters of the Bankruptcy Code, but courts generally do enforce releases and substantive consolidation if it was granted in the foreign main or foreign non-main proceeding under the laws of that jurisdiction.[234] While this may initially seem counterintuitive, these rules are designed to give the foreign representative the protections and benefits needed to facilitate actions in the foreign proceeding, but not to create new powers and causes of action that would not generally be available under the foreign proceeding.

14.3.3.4 Co-operation and communication

In the US, cross-border protocols and court-to-court communications, while **14.86** encouraged, are not mandatory and may not be binding under chapter 15 of the Bankruptcy Code.[235] Foreign representatives in *Re Maxwell* and *Re Quebecor*

[230] 11 USC s 1519(e); *Re Pro-Fit Holdings, Ltd.* 391 BR 850, 862 (Bankr. CD Cal. 2008) (holding that provisional relief pursuant to s 362 requested by the foreign representative did not require and adversary proceeding); *Re Ho Seok Lee* 348 BR 799 (Bankr. WD Wa. 2006) (holding foreign representative was entitled to seek a permanent injunction without filing an adversary proceeding).

[231] See, eg, 11 USC s 1521(a)(7).

[232] Ibid.

[233] *Re CSL Austl. Pty. Ltd. v Britannia Bulkers PLC,* No. 08 Civ. 8290(PKL), 2009 WL 2876250 at *4 (SDNY 8 September 2009); *Re Atlas Shipping A/S* 404 BR 726, 745-6 (Bankr. SDNY 2009); *Condor Ins. Ltd. v Petroquest Res. Inc. (Re Condor Ins. Ltd.)* 601 F3d 319, 329 (5th Cir. 2010) (reversing the lower court decision and holding that avoidance actions may be brought in a chapter 15 ancillary proceeding).

[234] *Re Metcalfe & Mansfield Alternative Invs.* 421 BR 685, 700 (Bankr. SDNY 2010) (enforcing third party releases contained in a Canadian plan); *Re Ionica PLC,* 241 BR 829 (Bankr. SDNY 1999); First Amended Plan of Reorganization for Loews Cineplex Entertainment, *Re Loews Cineplex Entm't,* No. 01-B-40346(ALG) (Bankr. SDNY) (14 January 2002) (allowing for substantive consolidation in eliminating guarantees in a prepackaged reorganization where there were no objections to the plan).

[235] 11 USC s 1527 ('Cooperation [with foreign courts and foreign representatives] *may* be implemented by any appropriate means, including . . . approval or implementation of agreements concerning the coordination of proceedings . . . .') (emphasis added). Cf. *Stonington Partners, Inc. v*

World Inc. have demonstrated the benefits of protocols, court-to-court communications, and joint hearings in facilitating the coordination and reorganization of cross-border insolvencies. In both these cases, the debtors implemented and adhered to cross-border protocols and conducted joint hearings resulting in a coordination of the domestic and foreign proceedings.[236] Breakdowns can occur, however. In particular, because the protocols are not mandatory, not every party required to facilitate coordination between foreign estates feels obligated to participate.[237] Parties that are key to negotiations are not mandated to participate in the global resolution of issues regarding debtors across various jurisdictions. For example, in 2009, Lehman Brothers Holdings Inc., as debtor-in-possession, and a number of court-appointed foreign administrators in the *Lehman Brothers* bankruptcies, filed the first ever multilateral cross-border insolvency protocol to provide a framework for multinational cooperation among the separate proceedings.[238] The protocol is unprecedented in scope and its participants include Lehman Brothers Holdings Inc., KPMG Hong Kong, KPMG Singapore, PPB Australia, and trustees for affiliates in Germany, the Netherlands, the Netherlands Antilles, Switzerland and Luxembourg.[239] In addition to signatories, representatives from Bermuda and Japan have participated in meetings designed to advance the objectives of the Protocol. However, a notable missing party to the Lehman Protocol and meetings was Lehman Brothers International Europe, which holds significant intercompany claims against its parent, Lehman Brothers Holdings Inc., and may hold vital information regarding claims of its global affiliates.[240] The administrator of Lehman Brother International (Europe) cited the fact that the protocol

Lernout & Hauspie Speech Prods., N.V. (Re Lernout & Hauspie Speech Products, N.V.) 310 F3d 118, 132 (3rd Cir. 2002) (encouraging protocol similar to that used in *Maxwell* noting its success).

236 *Re Lernout & Hauspie Speech Products, N.V.* 310 F3d at 132 (recognizing the success of the *Maxwell* protocol); *Re Quebecor World Inc.* Case No. 08-10152 (Bankr. SDNY 9 April 2008) (emerging after only 18 months from restructurings in both the Canadian and US court confirmed their plan of reorganization in a joint hearing held on 30 June 2009); see also *Re Livent, Inc.* No. 98-48312 (AJG) (Bankr. SDNY) (holding joint hearings).

237 *Aino v Maruko, Inc. (Re Maruko, Inc.)* 200 BR 876 (Bankr. SD Cal. 1996) (failing to implement a multinational cross-border protocol, which led to difficult and contentious issues regarding the coordination of the proceedings and plan treatment).

238 Press Release, Alverez & Marsal, Lehman Group of Companies Signs Cross-Border Insolvency Protocol (26 May 2009) (on file with author).

239 See *Lehman Bros. Holdings Inc.* Official Representatives and Other Participating Affiliates Pursuant to the Cross-Border Insolvency Protocol for the Lehman Brothers Group of Companies, Report of Activities through 15 January 2010, Case No. 08-13555 (Bankr. SDNY 2 February 2010) (Docket No. 6914).

240 See *Lehman Bros. Holdings Inc.* Cross-border Insolvency Protocol, Case No. 08-13555 (Bankr. SDNY 26 May 2009) (Docket No. 4020); Letter from Hon. James M. Peck, Judge, US Bankruptcy Court Southern District of New York, to Mary K. Warren, Esq., counsel to the Joint Administrators of Lehman Brothers International (Europe) (13 April 2009), Case No. 08-13555 (Bankr. SDNY 2 February 2010) (Docket No. 3350) (inviting Ms Warren to participate in a conference call regarding the international protocol).

'is likely to unfairly raise affiliates' expectations of the level of access and information that it will provide'.[241]

14.3.3.5 Foreign creditors

As in the UK, chapter 15 seeks to prevents discrimination against foreign creditors in insolvency proceedings by providing that foreign creditors have the same rights in relation to the commencement of, and participation in, proceedings under the law of the US as domestic creditors.[242] Section 1513 of the Bankruptcy Code provides that a foreign creditor's claim is not to be given a lower priority solely because the holder of the claim is foreign.[243] In addition, section 1514 of the Bankruptcy Code is a special notice provision, that requires that foreign creditors be notified whenever notification is required to be given to domestic creditors in accordance with domestic insolvency law.[244] **14.87**

14.3.3.6 Current Issues in chapter 15

While fixing the problems inherent in section 304, however, US courts continue to struggle with new issues created by the promulgation of chapter 15.[245] First, the Model Law has not been universally adopted. Only 20 countries have adopted the Model Law since its inception.[246] Thus inconsistencies remain when dealing with foreign creditors and foreign debtors of those countries that have not adopted the Model Law whether a foreign jurisdiction that has not adopted the Model Law will recognize ancillary proceedings and what rights will be afforded to those debtors.[247] Because there can be many cases pending in various nations, issues arise regarding affiliates, such as treatment of intercompany claims and protection of debtor's affiliates that need to be resolved for more efficient administration of cross-border insolvencies.[248] One possible solution for handling **14.88**

[241] 'Lehman protocol divides administrators' *The Banker*, 27 May 2009, available at <http://www.thebanker.com/news/fullstory.php/aid/6625>.

[242] 11 USC s 1513.

[243] 11 USC s 1513(b)(1).

[244] 11 USC s 1514.

[245] See generally Hon. Allen L. Gropper, 'Current Developments in International Insolvency Law: A United States Perspective' in *Bankruptcy & Reorganizations: Current Developments 2010* (Practicing Law Institute, 2010), vol. II, 867.

[246] See above n. 55.

[247] Justin Luna, Note, 'Thinking Globally, Filing Locally: The Effects of the New Chapter 15 on Business Entity Cross-Border Insolvency Cases' (2007) 19 Fla. J. Int'l. L. 671, 674-5; see also Yaad Rotem, 'The Problem of Selective or Sporadic Recognition: A New Economic Rationale for the Law of Foreign Country Judgments' (2010) 10 Chi. J. Int'l L. 505 (discussing international cooperation and the problems inherent in selective or sporadic recognition of foreign judgments).

[248] *Eclaire Advisor Ltd. v Daewoo Eng'g & Constr. Co., Ltd.* 375 F Supp 2d 257 (SDNY 2005) (involving intercompany loans between the American subsidiary and the Korean parent); *Lyondell Chem. Co. v CenterPoint Engergy Gas Svcs. Inc. (Re Lyondell Chem. Co.)* 402 BR 571 (Bankr. SDNY

these issues is to establish cross-border protocols that facilitate court-to-court communications.[249]

14.89 Second, chapter 15 has not meaningfully addressed the coordination of cases where proceedings of affiliates are pending in separate jurisdictions. Conflicts of laws can and have arisen when courts interpret the same actions based on their own unique statutory schemes.[250] This very problem recently surfaced in the cases of *Lehman Brothers International (Europe)* and in *Lehman Brothers Holdings Inc.*[251] A creditor of Lehman Brothers Special Financing ('LBSF'), an affiliate of Lehman Brothers Holdings Inc., seeking to determine the relevant priority of the payments to parties of a swap contract first commenced litigation in England in the High Court of Justice, Chancery Division against BNY Corporate Trustee Services Limited ('BNY') seeking priority payment pursuant to 'Noteholder Priority' under the terms of the swap agreement.[252] LBSF intervened in the English litigation and, during the pendency of the English litigation, LBSF commenced an adversary proceeding in the US chapter 11 proceeding of Lehman Brothers Holdings Inc. and filed a complaint against BNY seeking declaratory judgment that the Noteholder Priority clause was an unenforceable ipso facto clause[253] and that any party modifying LBSF's right to the priority of payments would be in violation of the automatic stay.[254] Thus, at issue in both cases was a provision in the swap agreement that reversed the priority of the payments upon the filing of a bankruptcy petition.[255] An English court, applying English law held that: (a) the swap contracts were governed by English law; (b) the reversal of priorities was valid and enforceable; and (c) the swap contract counterparty had priority

2009) (granting preliminary injunctions for non-debtor entities to afford them time to file their own insolvency proceedings if they chose to do so); *Re ABC-NACO, Inc.* 294 BR 832 (Bankr. ND Ill. 2003) (involving intercompany claims between an American debtor and its wholly owned Canadian subsidiary in receivership).

[249] See, eg, *Lehman Bros. Holdings Inc.* Cross-border Insolvency Protocol, Case No. 08-B-13555 (Bankr. SDNY 26 May 2009) (Docket No. 4020); *Re Quebecor World Inc.* Case No. 08-10152 (Bankr. SDNY 9 April 2008) (Docket No. 4564) (cross-border protocol); *Solv-Ex corp.* Case No. 97-14361 (Bankr. DNM 4 February 1998) (Docket No. 146) (cross-border protocol).

[250] *Perpetual Tr. Co. Ltd. v BNY Corporate Tr. Servs. Ltd.* [2009] EWCA (Civ) 1160, available at 2009 WL 3643805; *Lehman Bros. Special Fin. Inc. v BNY Corp. Tr. Servs.Ltd. (Re Lehman Bros Holdings Inc.)* 422 BR 407 (Bankr. SDNY 2010); *Cambridge Gas Transp. Corp. v Official Comm. of Unsecured Creditors of Navigator Holdings plc* [2006] UKPC 26, [2007] 1 AC 508 (appeal taken from Isle of Man), available at 2006 WL 1546603; *Re Navigator Gas Transp. PLC* 358 BR 80, 89 (Bankr. SDNY 2006).

[251] *Perpetual Tr. Co. Ltd.* [2009] EWCA (Civ) at 1160; *Re Lehman Bros Holdings Inc.* 422 BR at 407.

[252] *Re Lehman Bros Holdings Inc.* 422 BR at 410.

[253] Clauses or provisions in contracts that are triggered by the filing of a bankruptcy proceeding are typically referred to as 'ipso facto clauses'.

[254] *Re Lehman Bros Holdings Inc.* 422 BR at 410.

[255] Ibid. at 410-1.

over LBSF.[256] However, the US bankruptcy court applied US law which states that ipso facto provisions are void as a matter of law and held to the contrary.[257] The US court recognized that the decision was contrary to the English decision, but was bound by the laws of the Bankruptcy Code and held that the reversal of rights constituted an ipso facto clause that is unenforceable under section 365 of the Bankruptcy Code.[258] The result was that that in England the swap counterparty had priority over LBSF, but in the US LBSF had priority. The US bankruptcy court noted the discrepancy and described the situation as one that 'calls for the parties, this Court and the English Courts to work in a coordinated and cooperative way to identify means to reconcile the conflicting judgments'.[259] This conflict has yet to be resolved.

Third, several issues remain regarding the recognition of a foreign main and foreign non-main proceedings. In the well-known trilogy of the Cayman Island fund cases—*Bear Stearns, SPhinX,* and *Basis Alpha*—the court again analysed COMI and recognition of a foreign main and non-main proceedings.[260] All three cases involved funds with registered offices in the Cayman Islands, where the funds were prohibited from conducting any business in the Cayman Islands.[261] Because the funds were not permitted and did not conduct any business in the Cayman Islands, all three decisions found that the entities' COMI were not the Cayman Islands.[262] Thus, none of these fund cases were recognized as foreign main proceedings. However, the similarities end there. **14.90**

Re SPhinX was the first of the fund cases to be heard.[263] In that case, the US court found that the debtor's COMI was not the Cayman Islands, but nonetheless recognized the foreign case as a non-main proceeding.[264] The court did not go into an in-depth analysis of whether the *SPhinX* debtor had an 'establishment' in the Cayman Islands, entitling it to foreign non-main recognition.[265] The court simply granted the *SPhinX* debtor foreign non-main recognition, subject to possible later modification pursuant to the provisions of section 1517(d) of the Bankruptcy Code, as there were no objections to recognition and the court saw no 'negative consequences'.[266] **14.91**

---

256 *Perpetual Tr. Co. Ltd.* [2009] EWCA (Civ) at 1160.
257 *Re Lehman Bros Holdings Inc.* 422 BR at 422.
258 Ibid.
259 Ibid. at 423.
260 *Re SPhinX Ltd.* 371 BR 10; *Re Bear Stearns* 374 BR 122; *Re Basis Yield Alpha Fund* 381 BR 37.
261 Ibid.
262 Ibid.
263 *Re SPhinX Ltd.* 371 BR 10.
264 Ibid. at 12.
265 Ibid. at 19.
266 Ibid.

14.92 In contrast, the bankruptcy judges hearing *Bear Stearns* and *Basis Yield Alpha Fund* each refused to grant foreign non-main proceeding recognition to the foreign proceeding, on the grounds that debtors had no operations in the Cayman Islands and, thus, did not have an 'establishment' there, a statutory prerequisite in the definition of a non-main proceeding.[267] Notably there were no objections to recognition of the foreign proceeding in either *Bear Stearns* or *Basis Yield Alpha Fund.*[268] The court found that it had an independent obligation to determine whether the foreign proceeding met the requirements of recognition and that the burden was on the foreign representative to establish the location of the entity's COMI or show that it has an establishment.[269] Ironically, the *Bear Stearns* and *SPhinX* decisions were both affirmed by Judge Sweet of the US District Court for the Southern District of New York, even though they seem to have contradictory outcomes.[270]

14.93 In addition, one more issue regarding COMI remains to be settled: the temporal framework that applies when determining COMI.[271] As noted above, COMI was borrowed from the EU, and US courts have struggled with its application. The plain language of sections 1502 and 1517 of the Bankruptcy Code and European precedent point to determining COMI as of the date of the commencement of the foreign proceeding.[272] However, US courts determine COMI as of the filing of the chapter 15 petition.[273] In *Re Betcorp,* the US court noted:

> If courts assess COMI with an eye to a debtor's operational history, there is an increased likelihood of conflicting COMI determinations, as courts may tend to attach greater importance to activities in their own countries, or may simply weigh the evidence differently. Given considerations to a debtor's operational history increases the possibility of competing main proceedings, thus defeating the purpose of using the COMI construct. Requiring the courts to give weight to the debtor's interests over the course of its operational history may destroy the uniformity and harmonization that is the goal of employing the COMI inquiry. . .. [A]n inquiry into the debtor's past interests could lead to a denial of recognition in a country where a debtor's interest are truly centered, merely because of past activities.[274]

---

267 *Re Bear Stearns* 374 BR at 122; *Re Basis Yield Alpha Fund* 381 BR at 51; see also 11 USC s 1502(5) ('foreign non-main proceeding' means a foreign proceeding, other than a foreign main proceeding, pending in a country where the debtor has an establishment'.).

268 *Re Bear Stearns* 374 BR at 122; *Re Basis Yield Alpha Fund,* 381 BR at 51.

269 *Re Bear Stearns* 374 BR at 126;

270 *Re Bear Stearns* 389 BR 325 (SDNY 2008) (J. Sweet); *Re SPhinX* 371 BR 10 (SDNY 2007) (J. Sweet).

271 See Mark Lightner, 'Determining the Center of Main Interests Under Chapter 15' (2009) 18 Norton J. of Bankr. L. & Prac. 519, 522.

272 See 11 USC ss 1502 and 1517.

273 *Re Betcorp* 400 BR at 291–91.

274 Ibid.

Thus, while the court noted the disagreement, it instead chose to interpret the statute to require a determination of COMI at the filing of the chapter 15 petition.[275]

Finally, a question remains whether US courts exercise personal jurisdiction over foreign creditors and foreign property. While the Bankruptcy Code appears to grant jurisdiction over all assets of the estate 'wherever located and by whomever held', the courts' actual jurisdiction is limited.[276] Several cases have held that the ability of US courts to exercise personal jurisdiction over a foreign creditor defendant depends on the same rules of personal jurisdiction applicable to other types of cases, including the creditor's level of contact with the debtor and the effect of its actions on the debtor's estate.[277] Thus, if the creditor does not have sufficient minimum contacts with the US, a US court may be unable to exercise personal jurisdiction over such creditor.[278] Furthermore, US courts have little control over property and actions outside their jurisdictional territory.[279] For example, US courts do not have jurisdiction over fraudulent transfers that occur outside the US and cannot stay foreign proceedings.[280] Thus, even if there is a foreign main proceeding, the US court's power is limited to territorial jurisdiction. This creates an imperative for foreign debtors to seek recognition in every jurisdiction in which the debtor owns property and complicates the cooperation of the foreign proceedings exponentially. **14.94**

---

275 Ligtner, above n. 271.

276 11 USC s 541(a) (emphasis added).

277 *French v Liebermann (Re French)* 440 F3d. 145, 149 (4th Cir. 2006), cert. denied 549 US 815 (2006) (discussing extraterritoriality); *Bernard L. Madoff Inv. Sec. LLC v Cohmad Sec. Corp. (Re Bernard L. Madoff Inv. Sec. LLC)* 418 BR 75 (Bankr. SDNY 2009) (finding sufficient minimum contract to exercise personal jurisdiction); *Probulk Inc. v N. of Eng. Protecting & Indem. Ass'n Ltd. (Re Probulk Inc.)* 407 BR 56, 63-4 (Bankr. SDNY 2009) (finding a trustee made out a prima facie case that personal jurisdiction existed over insurers where the action taken abroad would have a substantial, direct and foreseeable effect on the administration of the estate); *Re Chiles Power Supply Co.* 264 BR 533, 543 (Bankr. WD Mo. 2001) (finding minimum contacts were sufficient to exercise personal jurisdiction); *Williams v Law Soc'y of H.K. (Re Williams)* 264 BR 234, 242 (Bankr. D. Conn. 2001) (lacking personal jurisdiction over a US creditor that relocated from Hong Kong, because there was not sufficient minimum contacts); *Interbulk Ltd. v Louis Dreyfus Corp. (Re Interbulk, Ltd.)* 240 BR 195 (Bankr. SDNY 1999) (finding creditor submitted to jurisdiction of the Bankruptcy Court). But see *Midland Euro Exch. Inc. v Swiss Fin. Corp. Ltd. (Re Midland Euro Exch. Inc.)* 347 BR 708, 719 (Bankr. CD Cal. 2006) (noting that courts sometimes defer to the laws or interest of a foreign country and decline to exercise the jurisdiction they otherwise have); *Re Maxwell Commc'n Corp.* 170 BR 800, 809 (SDNY 1994) (discussing the presumption against extraterritoriality).

278 *Re Williams* 264 BR at 242.

279 See eg, *Re Peregrine Sys. Inc.* 2005 WL 2401955, at *2–3 (D. Del. 29 September 2005) (reversing the Bankruptcy Court's decision that the automatic stay applied to an action taken in Germany); *Re Midland Euro Exch.* 347 BR at 718 (holding trustee could not recover a fraudulent transfer that occurred abroad). But see *Re Gucci* 309 BR 679, 684 (SDNY 2004) (holding automatic stay applied to Gucci store located in Rome).

280 See, eg, *Re Midland Euro Exch.* 347 BR at 718–20.

14.95 Many of the thorny issues regarding the adoption of chapter 15 facing US courts today stem from the financial credit crisis that began in 2008. Ironically, it was a similar financial meltdown that stressed the prior system under section 304 and led to the creation of the Model Law. Although chapter 15 provides a comprehensive framework for addressing cross-border insolvencies, US bankruptcy law does not currently solve every cross-border issue facing US courts.

14.4 Conclusion

14.96 Those who drafted the EC Regulation and the Model Law and those who worked so hard to implement them did so in the hope and expectation that they would simplify and harmonize insolvency processes across-borders. The reality has not always matched those aspirations. We do now have courts and practitioners in different jurisdictions applying what look like the same general principles. We have had (sometimes in relation to the same company) stunning examples of successful cooperation (the Parmalat Dutch and Luxembourg companies reorganized through the Italian extraordinary administration proceedings), and seemingly irreconcilable clashes of insolvency law against insolvency law (as in *Re Eurofood IFSC*[281]).

14.97 It appears that the international community is headed toward a more global solution for international insolvencies, but is struggling with universal adoption and application of cross-border laws. Until countries become willing, however, to adopt the same priority scheme and the same principles underlying bankruptcy law, a truly global insolvency scheme would be impossible. Further, improving and expanding Cross-Border Regulations and chapter 15 may be the next best alternative to protect the rights of all creditors of multinational corporations and promoting harmony and compromise among cross-border insolvency proceedings.

14.98 Ultimately, however, whatever statutory regimes you have in place, if the process does not produce a result perceived as fair by the stakeholders involved, then it will be challenged, discredited and ultimately circumvented. Perhaps, at the end of the day, all we need is Lord Hoffmann's enunciation of the English common law position. Fairness between creditors is paramount.

[281] Case-341/04.

INDEX